THE AUSTEN CHAMBERLAIN DIARY LETTERS

THE CORRESPONDENCE OF SIR AUSTEN CHAMBERLAIN WITH HIS SISTERS HILDA AND IDA, 1916–1937

edited by

ROBERT C. SELF

CAMDEN FIFTH SERIES
Volume 5

CAMBRIDGE
UNIVERSITY PRESS

FOR THE ROYAL HISTORICAL SOCIETY
University College London, Gower Street, London WC1E 6BT

Published by the Press Syndicate of the University of Cambridge
The Pitt Building, Trumpington Street, Cambridge CB2 1RP
40 West 20th Street, New York, NY 10011–4211, USA
10 Stamford Road, Oakleigh, Melbourne 3166, Australia

First published 1995

A catalogue record for this book is available from the British Library

Library of Congress cataloguing in publication data applied for

ISBN 0 521 55157 9 hardback

SUBSCRIPTIONS. The serial publications of the Royal Historical Society, *Royal Historical Society Transactions* (ISSN 0080–4401), Camden Fifth Series (ISSN 0960–1163) volumes and volumes of the Guides and Handbooks (ISSN 0080–4398) may be purchased together on annual subscription. The 1995 subscription price (which includes postage but not VAT) is £35 (US$56 in the USA, Canada and Mexico) and includes Camden Fifth Series, volumes 5 and 6 (published in July and December) and Transactions Sixth Series, volume 5 (published in December). There is no volume in the Guides and Handbooks series in 1995. Japanese prices (including ASP delivery) are available from Kinokuniya Company Ltd, P.O. Box 55, Chitose, Tokyo 156, Japan. EU subscribers (outside the UK) who are not registered for VAT should add VAT at their country's rate. VAT registered subscribers should provide their VAT registration number.

Subscription orders, which must be accompanied by payment, may be sent to a bookseller, subscription agent or direct to the publisher: Cambridge University Press, The Edinburgh Building, Shaftesbury Road, Cambridge CB2 2RU, UK; or in the USA, Canada and Mexico: Cambridge University Press, 40 West 20th Street, New York, NY 10011–4211, USA. Copies of the publications for subscribers in the USA, Canada and Mexico are sent by air to New York to arrive with minimum delay.

SINGLE VOLUMES AND BACK VOLUMES. A list of Royal Historical Society volumes available from Cambridge University Press may be obtained from the Humanities Marketing Department at the address above.

Printed and bound in Great Britain by Butler & Tanner Ltd, Frome and London

Long Loan

This book is due for return on or before the last date shown below

1 4 DEC 2010		

St Martin's College

Long Loan

This book is due for return on or before the last date shown below

1 4 DEC 2018		

St Martin's College

THE AUSTEN CHAMBERLAIN
DIARY LETTERS

CONTENTS

PREFACE

A large number of debts of different kinds are incurred during the preparation of a study of this kind. First, and most obvious, I owe a deep debt of gratitude to the generosity of the University of Birmingham for granting its kind permission to reproduce so extensively the letters of Sir Austen Chamberlain to his sisters and to quote from the other Chamberlain family correspondence in their care. My thanks also to Dr B.S. Benedikz, the Keeper of Special Collections for sharing his encyclopaedic knowledge of the Chamberlain papers and family with me, and to his staff in the Heslop Room at the Birmingham University Library who provided so much assistance during this research. By the same token, the editor is also indebted to the owners, custodians and archivists of the other collections of private papers and diaries used in the preparation of the text. For access and permission to quote from copyright material in privately owned collections I am obliged to Earl Baldwin of Bewdley, the Earl of Balfour, the syndics of Cambridge University Library, the Master and Fellows of Churchill College, Cambridge, the Earl of Crawford and Balcarres, the Earl of Derby, Lord Elibank, Vice-Admiral Sir Ian Hogg, Lord Kennet, Professor K.S. Lambton, the Marquess of Salisbury, Mrs A. Stacey and the Trustees of the Bridgeman family archive, the Keeper of the Public Records and to the owners of the copyright of the Headlam and Scott Diaries. I have also quoted from collections held by a number of other libraries and institutions, namely the British Library, the Bodleian Library, Cambridge University Library, the Conservative Research Department, Durham Record Office, the House of Lords Record Office, the India Office Library, Liverpool City Central Library, the National Library of Scotland, the National Register of Archives (Scotland), the Public Record Office, the Scottish Record Office and Sheffield University Library. My thanks are due to the keepers, librarians and curators of these institutions and their staffs. Every effort has been made to trace the copyright holder of unpublished documents from which quotations have been made: I hope that those whom it was not possible to locate will accept my apologies.

Debts of a more personal kind also exist. I was fortunate to discuss Sir Austen's character and career with his son and daughter. I hope they feel their kindness and interest have borne some fruit. Mrs Renée Gerson also provided unwavering enthusiasm and encouragement and she can claim much of the credit for the work being undertaken at all. Thanks are also due to Mr John Barnes, who first proposed the value of such a project and to my friend and colleague Dr Iwan Morgan for his helpful comments on an earlier draft. In his role as Literary Director of the Camden Series, Dr John Ramsden provided not only useful technical guidance in the preparation of this work but also valuable comments and criticisms of the initial draft of the text before Dr David Eastwood took the manuscript under his wing and saw it through publication. Finally there is the vast debt of gratitude I owe to my wife, Katie, who not only contributed patient support, enthusiasm and countless hours of transcription and word-processing, but also served as a constructive and ever watchful critic who frequently saved me from myself. In the end she knew the subject of this work as well as I did myself. This volume is dedicated to her as a token of my heartfelt appreciation.

EDITOR'S NOTE

In order to produce a manuscript of a publishable length, the Austen Chamberlain letters in this volume have been abridged to exclude much material of an interesting, but essentially non-political nature. Where sentences and paragraphs have been removed these are marked by the use of suspension dots. As far as possible, however, the letters themselves have been reproduced in their original form. Although Sir Austen Chamberlain adopted idiocyncratic and often inconsistent spellings for many surnames, particularly of foreign politicians, his abbreviations and original spellings have been retained throughout. Editorial insertions have been made in some places for the sake of clarity, but these are always in square brackets. Only the style of the dating has been standardised from the authors own many and varied forms in the interests of consistency and clarity. Chamberlain almost always closed his letters with 'Your affecte. brother, Austen Chamberlain' or 'Your loving brother, Austen Chamberlain'. These have been omitted to avoid repetition.

AUSTEN CHAMBERLAIN (1863–1937)

The man and his diary letters

'Poor old Austen!' Leo Amery wrote three days before Chamberlain's death. 'He just missed greatness and the highest position, but his was a fine life of honourable public service. His real weakness was his over anxiety for good form which he was sometimes inclined to identity too much with loyalty'.[1] In many respects Amery's brief epitaph is typical of so many assessments of this ostensibly so simple but supremely enigmatic figure. There could be no denying Austen Chamberlain's distinguished career. He sat in the House of Commons for an unbroken period of forty-five years. It was a career that truly represented a 'link with time'.[2] Among the many tributes after his death, Lloyd George had reminded the Commons that Joseph Chamberlain had been congratulated on his son's maiden speech by Gladstone, a leader who himself had been first elected in the year of the Great Reform Act and first served under Peel.[3] As one MP recalled of the occasion, 'The younger Members felt that they had been carried back through Lloyd George to Gladstone away to the battles of the Reform Bill and the administration of the Duke of Wellington'.[4] Of his almost half a century in the Commons, Chamberlain spent over twenty-two years holding ministerial office. In 1895, at the age of only 32, he became Civil Lord to the Admiralty. Thirty-six years later in his last ministerial position he returned to his 'first love' as First Lord in the same department. In the interim, he held all the great offices of State except that of Prime Minister and Home Secretary. Rising from Postmaster-General, he served twice as Chancellor of the Exchequer and once as Foreign Secretary. He was also a member of Lloyd George's War Cabinet and held the India Office. Even at the age of 72 many still saw him as the obvious candidate for the Foreign Office after Hoare's forced resignation in December 1935. By any standard, this was a remarkable ministerial and parliamentary career.

---

[1] Amery Diary, 13 March 1937, J. Barnes and D. Nicholson, *The Empire at Bay: The Leo Amery Diaries 1929–1945* (1988), 437.

[2] Channon Diary, 17 March 1937, R.R. James (ed) *Chips: the Diaries of Sir Henry Channon* (1967), 117. Also Churchill to Lady Ivy Chamberlain, 18 March 1937, M. Gilbert, *Winston S. Churchill*, (8 vols, 1966–1988), V. Companion 3, 626.

[3] *House of Commons Debates*, 5 Series, 321 Col 2102, 17 March 1937.

[4] Nicolson Diary, 17 March 1937, N. Nicolson (ed) *Harold Nicolson: Diaries and Letters 1930–1939* (1966), 296.

Yet for all that was achieved, the inability of this pre-eminently professional politician to reach the top of the greasy pole and become Prime Minister cast a shadow of failure over his entire career. As Joseph Chamberlain's elder son, Austen was groomed for the highest office from birth.[5] His failure to achieve it, is one of the greatest enigmas of a long and varied career, and perhaps even of Conservative politics in the twentieth century. It was all the more remarkable because Chamberlain was fortunate enough to have two chances to obtain the ultimate prize. In 1911 he had the leadership within his grasp but let the fruit fall from his hand rather than split the party. Ten years later fortune smiled more favourably upon him when the beneficiary of his withdrawal in 1911 was forced to retire through ill health. This should have been Chamberlain's chance for the Premiership. During the next eighteen months, however, the Conservative leadership battled with mounting discontents over policy and leadership which culminated in his effective dismissal after the Carlton Club revolt in October 1922. As a result, Austen Chamberlain can claim the dubious distinction of being the only Conservative leader this century not to have risen to become Prime Minister.

Ultimately, it is this enigmatic failure rather than any of his successes which has defined Chamberlain's place in posterity. For most commentators, this failure is regarded as eloquent testimony to the character of the man and the politician. Above all, it is taken as proof of some more profound flaw in his nature which served fundamentally to debilitate his efforts to deliver against the early promise. As a colleague of forty years noted on hearing of his death, there was 'something lacking in his basic fibre which prevented him from reaching the highest place or attaining to the political stature of his father and younger brother'.[6] There is undoubtedly something in this view. Yet any assessment of Austen Chamberlain's career is rendered more complex by two factors which are often not accorded sufficient attention. First, by bearing the name and cultivating the appearance of his illustrious father, Austen Chamberlain invited an invidious and misleading comparison which has tended to obscure more balanced judgements of his real stature. Secondly, perhaps more than any other politician of the age, Austen Chamberlain's reputation has suffered from the tendency of contemporaries and subsequent historians to judge him on the basis of his superficial public persona. Singularly few, if any, politicians are genuinely one-dimensional political animals devoid of a deeper private personality. Yet this point is particularly pertinent when considering Austen Chamberlain. Beneath the stiff, cold, formal exterior of frock

[5] Sir Charles Petrie, *The Chamberlain Tradition* (1938), 21, 130.
[6] A. Clark (ed) *A Good Innings : The Private Papers of Viscount Lee of Fareham* (1974), 339.

coat, monocle and anachronistic manner there was a remarkable 'dual personality' at work.[7] Fascinated by the outward appearance, contemporaries and subsequent commentators have often failed to give sufficient attention to that other and very different private side of his nature.

The comparison with his father is an obvious but scarcely fortunate one. Far more than his half-brother, Austen Chamberlain was his father's son. Destined from the cradle to be his political heir, Austen enjoyed a relationship of extraordinary closeness with his revered father throughout his adult life. At Highbury, family life centred around Joseph Chamberlain for whom Austen, in particular, had 'the profoundest and most devoted admiration and affection'.[8] After the Home Rule split of 1886 he 'acted as a sort of A.D.C.' to his father.[9] With his election to the Commons in 1892 Austen became his father's assistant and young protege. Under the circumstances it was not perhaps surprising that in their twenty-three years in the Commons together Austen could only remember one occasion on which he had voted in the opposite lobby from his father.[10] For three years they even served in the same Cabinet until Joseph Chamberlain resigned to champion the cause of tariff reform in 1903. Thereafter Austen remained in office as 'the echo and exponent of his father',[11] forced to serve as an uncomfortable intermediary with a Prime Minister he never really understood. Yet for all his rising public fame, until the age of 41 he continued to live at home – 'an uncommon case even in those days'.[12] On the first evening spent under his own roof as Chancellor of the Exchequer, his main thought was to write to his father:[13]

I do not think there are many fathers who have been and are to their sons all that you have been to me; and my prayer tonight is

[7] B.J.C. McKercher, *The Second Baldwin Government and the United States, 1924–1929: Attitudes and Diplomacy* (Cambridge 1984), 7.

[8] Neville Chamberlain introduction to the German Edition of *Sir Austen Chamberlain*, reprinted in Petrie, *The Chamberlain Tradition*, 280. Also A. Chamberlain to Mary Chamberlain, 30 March 1913, A. Chamberlain , *Politics From Inside: An Epistolary Chronicle 1906–1914* (1936), 540–1.

[9] A. Chamberlain, *Politics from Inside*, 19.

[10] A. Chamberlain to Hilda, 12 April 1929, Austen Chamberlain MSS (Birmingham University Library) AC5/1/314.

[11] Churchill to T.J. Travis-Clegg, 9 October 1903, R.S. Churchill, *Winston S. Churchill: The Young Statesman, 1901–1914*, II. Companion 1, 230.

[12] 'Portrait of the three Chamberlains and my eldest sister Beatrice', July–November 1956 (hereafter Hilda Memoir) Beatrice Chamberlain MSS (Birmingham University Library) BC5/10/1, fol.1.

[13] A. Chamberlain to J. Chamberlain, 11 January 1904, *Politics from Inside*, 20.

that the perfect confidence which I have enjoyed for so long may continue unimpaired by our separation, and that I may do something to help you in the great work which you have undertaken. It is at once a great encouragement and a great responsibility to be heir to so fine a tradition of private honour and public duty and I will do my best not to be unworthy of the name.

During the remaining decade of Joseph Chamberlain's life that burden of responsibility was often to weigh extremely heavily upon the son – particularly after a paralysing stroke in 1906 compelled Austen to assume the role of principal lieutenant, spokesman and protagonist for his stricken father. Although he remained intensely loyal to the end, the experience cast a long shadow over his character and reputation. Yet the fact remained, as he wrote revealingly to his step-mother in 1911, 'I think more and more of what I owe to Father ... He has *made* me in every sense of the word and, if I accomplish anything in my career, it will be due to his teaching and his example ... Never did son owe more to his father and never did father more generously or more wisely help his son's career ... God grant that I may be to Joe something of what he has been to me for nearly fifty years'.[14]

Throughout the rest of Austen Chamberlain's life, the spectre of his father continued to be omnipresent. It was not cant when he confessed that his principal satisfaction in accepting the leadership in 1921 was the 'thought of the pleasure that it would have given to Father and Beatrice'.[15] During that unhappy period on the backbenches after the Carlton Club revolt, he took his Father's old seat of 1892–95 on the corner of the third bench below the gangway and rejoiced in the sentiment of it all.[16] Three years later when considering the Garter he was also sincere when he said that he 'did not think that I could bring myself to accept an honour which my much greater father had not worn.'[17] Throughout his later life his talk in unguarded moments was apt to turn to stories of his father[18] and in reading the long-awaited draft of Garvin's monumental *Life of Joseph Chamberlain*, Austen frequently confessed to finding his father 'almost like one of the forces of nature in his power'.[19] Against such a background there can be little reason to

[14] A. Chamberlain to Mary Chamberlain, 7 May 1911, *Politics from Inside*, 337. See also R. Jenkins, *Baldwin*, (1987), 170.

[15] A. Chamberlain to Ida, 25 March 1921, AC5/1/195.

[16] A. Chamberlain to Hilda, 26 November 1922, AC5/1/253.

[17] A. Chamberlain to Ida, 28 November 1925, AC5/1/370.

[18] Jones Diary, 1 June 1922, K. Middlemas (ed), *Thomas Jones; Whitehall Diary*, (2 vols, 1969), I, 200.

[19] A. Chamberlain to Hilda, 24 April 1933, AC5/1/614.

question Dangerfield's verdict that Austen Chamberlain had 'a father-haunted mind'.[20]

It was perhaps a measure of this near obsessive filial devotion that Austen Chamberlain should even have cultivated a similarity of appearance with his father. Throughout his life, he continued to display the characteristic frock coat, silk hat, orchid, monocle and Parliamentary manner long after the fashion for such attire and gestures had passed. Yet to those in a position to know, the comparison was barely skin deep. As his sister Hilda later recalled, 'Austen was a very different man from father, both in physique and temperament, and although there was a superficial likeness in certain gestures, accentuated by the eyeglass which his astigmatism necessitated his wearing, he could not escape the continual comparison with his father which often led to an under-estimation of his real independence of thought and action'.[21] Such comparisons inevitably harmed the elder son's reputation in the eyes of contemporaries and later historians. By consciously inviting comparison in external manner and appearance, Amery believed that Chamberlain 'naturally afforded a handle to the caricaturist and to the ignorant critic who, knowing little of his real qualities, were apt to dismiss him as a somewhat wooden and ineffective replica, owing his political advancement largely to parental influence'.[22] Lloyd George's mistress, Frances Stevenson, clearly applied such a frame of reference when she dismissed him as a 'pale imitation of his famous father ... totally lacking inspiration ... conscientious to the point of dullness'.[23] Attacking rumours of his impending return to office in 1918, the Northcliffe press had pursued a similar theme:[24]

Mr Austen Chamberlain, who entered public life with the inestimable advantage of being the son of his father, for which reason he was tolerated long after it became obvious that he had inherited none of his father's genius, has been pushed into one office after another without any serious reference to his qualifications for them. But he has never been anything more than an assiduous, honourable ineffective mediocrity ...

Even in the most fleeting references, historians have often been no

[20] G. Dangerfield, *The Damnable Question: A Study in Anglo-Irish Relations*, (Quartet ed, 1979), 73.

[21] Hilda Memoir, BC5/10/1 fol.6. Also H. Macmillan, *The Past Masters: Politics and Politicians, 1906–1936*, (1975), 128.

[22] L.S. Amery *My Political Life* (3 vols, 1953–1955) II, 303.

[23] Frances Lloyd George, *The Years that are Past* (1967), 184; A.G. Gardiner, 'Sir Austen Chamberlain', *Portraits and Portents* (1926), 106–113.

[24] *Daily Mail*, 17 April 1918, AC5/1/72.

more sympathetic in their assessment of this 'over-groomed offspring of an outstanding personality'.[25]

Closer analysis of the reasons for Chamberlain's failure to fulfil his early promise also appears to confirm the view that he was but a pale imitation of his father or half-brother. Ill-fortune and chance certainly played their part. In his study of uncrowned Prime Ministers, Thorpe outlines a number of factors in the inner workings of the Conservative Party which deprived Chamberlain (like Curzon and Butler) of the highest position in British public life. He was arguably the victim of 'negative choice' to the extent that he did not obtain the leadership in 1911, and lost it in 1922, because he was the wrong man representing the wrong values at the wrong time.[26] Thorpe would appear to be on surer ground in pointing to the importance of opportunism. Whatever else he was, Chamberlain was assuredly not Birkenhead's role model for the infamous Rectorial Address in which he declared that 'The World continues to offer glittering prizes to those who have stout hearts and sharp swords'.[27] In this respect, the failure to reach the top and then stay there, genuinely did reflect a difference in temperament from his father and half-brother, rather than simply one of the circumstances in which they found themselves.

According to his eldest child, Joseph Chamberlain 'chiefly admire[d] purpose and force of character'.[28] Indeed, in almost every respect Joseph Chamberlain was himself a classical example of what Lloyd George was later to describe as 'a man of push and go' – a man capable of the vast physical and mental exertion necessary to overcome the great test before them.[29] A self-made Victorian businessman, his entry into Birmingham municipal politics had ensured the town was 'parked, paved, assized, marketed, Gas-and-Watered and *improved* – all as the result of three years active work'.[30] After 1876 his intervention in national politics showed him to be a statesman of extraordinary energy and flair – some of it destructive, as he divided both great parties of the state within a period of less than twenty years. Frustrated in his own ambitions, he groomed his elder son to achieve the pinnacle of political power which eluded him. Austen's education at Cambridge

[25] P. Rowland, *The Last Liberal Governments: The Promised Land 1905–1910* (1968), 50. Also J. Grigg, *Lloyd George: The People's Champion, 1902–11*, (1978), 59; R. Blake, *The Unknown Prime Minister: The Life and Times of Andrew Bonar Law, 1858–1923*, (1955), 72.

[26] D.R. Thorpe, *The Uncrowned Prime Ministers* (1980), 5–12.

[27] 'Idealism in International Politics', Rectorial Address, Glasgow, November 1923, reprinted in *America Revisited* (1924).

[28] L.S. Amery, *My Political Life*, I, 361.

[29] A phrase first used on 9 March 1915 during Lloyd George's campaign for the third Defence of the Realm Act, R.J.Q. Adams, *Arms and the Wizard: Lloyd George and the Ministry of Munitions, 1915–16*, (1978), 39.

[30] J.L. Garvin, *Life of Joseph Chamberlain*, (later with J. Amery, 6 vols, 1932–1969), I, 202.

and his travels on the Continent were all preparations for the ascent towards that ultimate prize. Yet as Joseph Chamberlain came to recognise shortly before his death, this chosen heir was made from very different material from himself.

Whatever other virtues Austen Chamberlain possessed, contemporaries were virtually unanimous in the view that he lacked the drive, dynamism and sheer pugnacious capacity to fight of 'pushful Joe'. 'Naturally extremely sensitive Austen disliked having to fight' was his sister's view. He could certainly be resolute and unbending when circumstances demanded, as he proved during the battle over Indian cotton duties, over the future of the Coalition and during the evolution of the Locarno agreements. Yet there was little of that exultant joy of battle and the visceral thrill of political combat which had characterised his father's struggles.[31] On the two occasions when Chamberlain came close to reaching the top of Disraeli's greasy pole, he failed because ultimately he lacked the will to win without which leaders seldom achieve supreme political power. When all was said and done, he did not want to win enough to compromise either his public persona or his personal principles. Put simply, he lacked that ruthless determination, hardness and the sheer 'grit' his illustrious father had possessed in such abundance. In personal terms, this probably made him a better, kinder and more considerate man than his father. In politics, however, it also ensured that he would be incapable of achieving the ultimate goal for which his entire life had been a form of training. As Amery rather unflatteringly put it, in many ways Austen always appeared a 'damned faint-hearted ass if ever there was one'.[32]

There are a number of explanations for the absence of this necessary 'killer instinct'. His sister later contended that the 'very anxiety of that father to smooth his path by giving him all the advantages he himself had lacked, proved in the end a disservice in not forcing him early to grapple with the ordinary difficulties of life'.[33] His physical constitution also played a crucially damaging part in Chamberlain's political career. All the family agreed that Austen did not possess the 'eagerness of temperament and the inexhaustible vitality of Father'.[34] From early in life, he also suffered from serious attacks of sciatica and lumbago. Indeed, in many respects heredity had been doubly unkind to the elder son. Not only did he lack his father's vitality, untiring energy and zest for life, but what he did inherit from his mother's side was 'a certain

[31] Hilda Memoir, BC5/10/1 fol.7.

[32] Amery to Baldwin, 8 December 1923, Baldwin MSS 35/171 (Cambridge University Library).

[33] Hilda Memoir, BC5/10/1 fol.6.

[34] K. Feiling, *The Life of Neville Chamberlain* (1947), 287; N. Chamberlain to Hilda, 22 October 1916, NC18/1/85.

lack of drive, and distaste for exertion unless forced upon him'.[35] Even as a young man Austen acknowledged this influence. 'I have a good deal of the Kenricks in me by nature', he confessed to his step-mother in 1911, 'left to myself I don't think that I should have done much ill to anyone; but if I work and persist and fight with political beasts at Ephesus or elsewhere it is because I am his son and because "*Noblesse oblige!*" '.[36]

The impact of this joint inheritance is painfully obvious from Chamberlain's diary letters to his sisters during the last 20 years of his life. After periods of prolonged exertion and stress Chamberlain rapidly succumbed to a profound mental and physical exhaustion which often carried him to the point of breakdown and was only prevented by his legendary capacity to 'sleep the clock round'.[37] His temperamental disinclination to exertion also manifested itself in his candid confessions of profound ambivalence and lack of enthusiasm with every new office that he accepted. Even his rise to the Leadership of his Party and of the House of Commons was accepted as 'an obvious duty but without pleasure or any great expectation except of trouble and hard work'.[38] The effect of such a physical and mental inheritance deprived Chamberlain of the power to fight. More important, it also denied him the basic ambition for which to do battle. After an idle eighteen months working on his garden after the Carlton Club revolt, Chamberlain got to the heart of the matter when he confessed to his step-mother, 'My ambition was never very strong – perhaps I should have been a better man if it had been stronger – and now it is non-existent. I want nothing except to be let alone and left £10,000 a year!'[39] Lacking the necessary drive from within, Chamberlain found himself pushed along by others. Before the Great War Austen's only complaint about his father was the fact that he 'has been more ambitious for me than ever I have been for myself'.[40] After Joe's death, Austen's wife assumed the role. Even towards the end of his life Chamberlain confided in his sister, 'I need scarcely add that Ivy is more ambitious for me than I am or ever have been for myself ... and she does not like me to talk of being too old at 70, so I have to have regard for her feelings as well as my own'.[41]

Such ambition as Chamberlain did possess was further impeded by

[35] Hilda Memoir, BC5/10/1 fol.6.

[36] A. Chamberlain to Mary Chamberlain, 7 May 1911, *Politics from Inside*, 337.

[37] Hilda Memoir, BC5/10/1 fol.8; A. Chamberlain to Ida, 12 December 1920, AC5/1/183.

[38] A. Chamberlain to Hilda, 20 March 1921, AC5/1/194; to Mary Carnegie, 19 March 1921, AC4/1/1204.

[39] A. Chamberlain to Mary Carnegie, 26 April 1924, AC4/1/1243; to Ida, 4 November 1917, AC5/1/45.

[40] A. Chamberlain to Mary Chamberlain, 7 May 1911, *Politics from Inside*, 337–8.

[41] A. Chamberlain to Hilda, 28 October 1933, AC5/1/637.

a profound temperamental distaste for anything which suggested a lapse from 'good form' or political propriety. Looking back on the failure to obtain the leadership in 1911 Amery recalled 'the trouble with Austen was not undue humility or diffidence. He had quite a good opinion of himself. But he had an exaggerated fear of being regarded as pushful ... or other than scrupulously correct and loyal in all his personal dealings'.[42] This most honourable of defects was to obstruct his way to the top throughout his career. Precisely the same 'great horror of anything that savours of intrigue or pushfulness' had prevented him doing anything to secure the leadership in 1921.[43] It also inhibited him in actively intriguing to displace either Law or Baldwin, despite a supreme contempt for the leadership qualities of both. As even his friends lamented, Chamberlain was simply 'too genteel' in dealing with anything that 'savours of a breach of good form, personal loyalty, or political etiquette'.[44] Little wonder that often it was more the grand seigneur than the son of Birmingham that seemed to shine through.[45]

This lack of pushfulness and ambition did not go unnoticed within the family. In 1911 his failure to fight prompted 'criticism at home'.[46] After this the stricken father is alleged to have expressed greater faith in his younger son's political instincts and to have summed up Austen's limitations in the lament that he 'was born in a red box, brought up in one, and would die in one'.[47] His sister Hilda also later confessed that she felt he was guilty of failing to press his claim as far as he should and was 'too inclined to wait for people to come to [him]'.[48] The same self-effacing lack of pushfulness drove Neville nearly to despair. Austen's offer to accept a more junior office in June 1916 prompted the irritated complaint that 'his generosity is absolutely incorrigible'. Thereafter Neville's own correspondence to his sisters is regularly spiced with references to his brother's deficiencies in pressing his own claim to advancement.[49] The overall effect, as his sister Beatrice

---

[42] L.S. Amery, *My Political Life*, I, 386. Chamberlain banished himself from the Commons and the Clubs until the succession was settled, A. Chamberlain to Mary Chamberlain, 11 November 1911, *Politics from Inside*, 386.

[43] A. Chamberlain to J.C.C. Davidson, 20 March 1921, R.R. James, *Memoirs of a Conservative: J.C.C. Davidson's Memoirs and Papers 1910–37*, (1969), 103.

[44] Amery Diary, 4 March 1918, J.Barnes and D. Nicholson (ed), *The Leo Amery Diaries, vol I 1896–1929* (1980), 209.

[45] H. Macmillan, *The Past Masters*, 128. J. Wedgwood, *Memoirs of a Fighting Life*, (1940), 203.

[46] Hilda Memoir, BC5/10/1 fol.4, 7.

[47] Jones Diary, 26 February 1937 reporting S. Gwynn, T. Jones, *A Diary with Letters 1931–1950* (1954), 318.

[48] Hilda to A. Chamberlain 31 January 1918, AC5/2/85.

[49] N. Chamberlain to Ida, 2 July 1916, 24 November 1917, NC18/1/68, 139; see also Neville Chamberlain Diary, 1 June 1923.

put it, was that Chamberlain appeared 'a little too good for this world'.[50] With time this character trait became a legend. When Austen finally renounced his claim to ministerial office in 1931 in favour of younger men, his half-brother testily recorded that this 'latest action has greatly strengthened the "legend" that was already growing up of the "great gentleman" and model of chivalry'.[51] The career which began under the shadow of his father ended equally over-shadowed by that of his half-brother. After his promotion to ministerial office for the first time in November 1922, the younger brother was often perceived to be 'immeasurably superior to Sir Austen – in ability and in general attractiveness'.[52] Yet throughout his entire career Austen Chamberlain was painfully well aware that, although schooled for greatness like the Younger Pitt, his father was 'a bigger man than [he] should ever be'.[53] Reflecting on the family fame, he had acknowledged this privately in 1918: 'Here I sit in Father's chair at my Father's table and I think how much harder he would be working than I am and above all to how much more purpose! I wish that I had a more original and constructive mind. Neville is much nearer to Father in that than I am. But we must take ourselves as we are and do the best we can'.[54] Such a typically self-effacing assessment is an instructive starting point for historical evaluation of the man and his career.

When judged by his own lights and achievements, Austen Chamberlain was arguably no less great than Law or Baldwin under whom he served. Certainly his claim to greatness is far stronger than that of most of those contemporaries with whom he sat in Cabinet in these years; men like Amery whose much quoted, but scarcely disinterested, criticisms have done so much to colour the retrospective verdict. He was unquestionably far greater than Beaverbrook whose malign influence in promoting his friend Bonar Law did so much also to damn the historical reputation of his principal detractor. Yet the real tragedy for Austen Chamberlain is that, for all his weaknesses, his reputation has been blighted by comparison with his greater and very different father. Soon after Austen's death, Neville Chamberlain had recorded the hope that history would judge his half-brother alongside a Grey or a Salisbury rather than his own father.[55] It has not. Through his obsessive admiration for this dominant father, Austen must bear some of the

---

[50] D.R. Thorpe, *The Uncrowned Prime Ministers*, 51.

[51] N. Chamberlain to Hilda, 7 November 1931, NC18/1/760.

[52] Headlam Diary, 15 December 1925, Headlam MSS D/He/21(Durham Record Office). Also Jones Diary, 20 May 1923, *Whitehall Diaries*, I, 236; Major-General Sir Frederick Sykes, *From Many Angles: An Autobiography*, (1942), 311.

[53] A. Chamberlain to Ida, 28 November 1925, AC5/1/370.

[54] A. Chamberlain to Ida, 18 August 1918, AC5/1/96.

[55] N. Chamberlain to Ida, 21 March 1937, NC18/1/999.

blame for forcing the comparison upon observers. In such circumstances, it is tempting to echo Leo Maxse's lament before the Great War – 'If only Austen would wear spectacles and grow a beard!'[56]

Chamberlain's ostensible similarity to his father has undoubtedly served to mislead observers. The problem has been compounded, however, by the assumption that the public persona represented the entire picture. The Austen Chamberlain which emerges from contemporary and historical accounts often appears a narrowly one-dimensional figure: a cold, rigid, arrogantly aloof and pompous individual, curiously obsessed with a set of already anachronistic niceties about personal honour, loyalty and civic integrity in a world that had moved on. Typical of such assessments is Lord Salter's recollection of his Geneva days with the League of Nations:[57]

> Austen Chamberlain; formal; rigid; precise; correct in thought, in manner and in costume, with all the virtues of a good official, conscientious, industrious, meticulous; exact and competent within the limits of his habitual vision; with a sensitive personal honour, and perhaps a little too sensitively conscious of it. Without personal magnetism himself, he was very susceptible to it in others, in Lloyd George, in Briand, in Mussolini. Courageous withal, and loyal to his colleagues, his officials and his principles, he never shirked a responsibility or bent under pressure.

This projection of the public persona undoubtedly existed. It was impossible to miss. Yet at the same time, the external appearance has often served to obscure the existence of another, and very different, individual within that outwardly forbidding shell.

The familiar public persona of Austen Chamberlain during the years covered by these diary letters is that of 'the last of the Great Victorians':[58] a man firmly rooted in the traditions and customs of the Parliaments of his father and Gladstone rather than those of the inter-war years. Although never an easy or natural speaker, he retained 'all the old parliamentary phrases of the last century' and prided himself in the 1930s on being the 'last survivor of an older style of speaking'.[59] The impression was strikingly reinforced by the fact that he was one of the

[56] L.S. Amery, *My Political Life* II, 303.

[57] Lord Salter, *Memoirs of a Public Servant*, (1961), 203.

[58] J.R. Clynes, *Memoirs*, (1937) II, 254.

[59] Bridgeman Diary, November 1929, Bridgeman MSS S.R.O. 4629, II fol.189. (By kind permission of Mrs Stacey and the Trustees of the Bridgeman family archive); N. Chamberlain to Ida, 27 March 1926, NC18/1/520; A. Chamberlain to Ida, 14 May 1933, AC5/1/616; Lord Snell, *Men, Movements and Myself*, (1936), 248.

last Members to retain the tradition of wearing a silk top hat inside the Commons chamber, raising it whenever he was mentioned, whether in praise or criticism.[60] Worshipping the institution of Parliament with an 'intense adoration', he immersed himself in its practices, forms and traditions. 'Others have known its rules and conventions as well as he', Eustace Percy argued, 'but none in our day have so entered into its spirit. He did not approve it detachedly; it was his natural climate; he lived and rejoiced in it'.[61] Although Lloyd George's election for Carnarvon in 1890 denied Chamberlain the formal title of Father of the House after T.P. O'Connor's retirement in 1929, Chamberlain had the greater spiritual claim to the accolade. It was just one manifestation of his position as 'a natural insider'.[62]

The most obvious manifestation of this Victorian code of values could be detected in Chamberlain's 'old fashioned belief that it was necessary to conduct one's self in political life like a man of honour'.[63] It has often been argued that this represented ' some sort of latent anti-father complex' as the elder son 'specialised in loyalty (if only to atone for his father's activities in the opposite direction)'.[64] An obsession with personal honour certainly represented the *leitmotif* of his public and private life. In the Commons on the day after Chamberlain's death, Baldwin spoke for all present when he said that 'his chief characteristic may be summed up in the well-known line: "He reverenced his conscience as his King". Among the things most deeply-embedded in that conscience was a sense of loyalty ... In Austen Chamberlain I would say that it was the supreme and unshakeable loyalty to everything that he honestly believed to be right and believed to be best. It was a loyalty that was shown to his family, to his party, the House of Commons and to his country'.[65] Lloyd George was in a better position to know the truth than most when he declared that Chamberlain was 'a man who strained the point of honour always against himself ... No public man in our time ... sacrificed more to integrity, to honour and

[60] N. Waterhouse, *Private and Official*, (1942), 216; Sir Alexander Mackintosh, *Echoes of Big Ben: A Journalist's Parliamentary Diary 1881–1940* (1945), 122; A. Griffith-Boscawen, *Memories*, (1925), 260.

[61] Bridgeman Diary, November 1929, Bridgeman MSS II, fol.189; Lord Eustace Percy, 'Austen Chamberlain', *Public Administration*, XV. 2 (April 1937), 126.

[62] J. Grigg, *Lloyd George: The People's Champion*, 59.

[63] F. Williams, *A Pattern of Rulers* (1965), 20.

[64] L.S. Amery, *My Political Life* I, 368; A.J.P. Taylor, *The Origins of the Second World War* (1961), 53. For similar comments see D.R. Thorpe, *The Uncrowned Prime Ministers*, 9; D. Dutton, *Austen Chamberlain: Gentleman in Politics* (Bolton, 1985), 6; J. Ramsden, *The Age of Balfour and Baldwin, 1902–1940*, (1978), 164.

[65] *House of Commons Debates*, 5 Series, 321 col 2102, 17 March 1937, reprinted in S. Baldwin, *Service of Our Lives: Last Speeches as Prime Minister* (1937), 90.

to loyalty to friends, to his party and to his country'.[66]

Nor was this sense of honour contingent upon circumstance or personal friendship. Rather it sprang from a highly-tuned respect for public service as the finest career a man could pursue. For Chamberlain his principles were 'immutable and fixed laws' incapable of modification to suit political convenience.[67] 'The sort of integrity we demand of our statesmen ... is an integration of public and private honour', one of his colleagues later noted:[68]

> Austen Chamberlain was, above all, the embodiment of that integrity. He once said that his only conception of diplomatic negotiation was to lay his cards on the table. That is almost a description of his career, the explanation of his honourable successes and of his still more honourable failures. In public and in private life his cards were always on the table, and he would play only with one pack. His most obvious cards, the trumps he seemed most often to declare, were perhaps the old-fashioned ones of the gentleman's code: loyalty to his Prime Minister, insistence on resignation under public censure, mediation by straight dealing. He played these with the old sense of good form in action ...

Such a code prompted his resignation in 1917 over the Mesopotamia disaster and, again, in 1922 when public loyalty to Lloyd George demanded it at a time when he had privately made it clear that he was not committed indefinitely to his Prime Ministership.[69] The same values had motivated his attack upon the press lords in 1918 and his expression of distaste when he learned that a biscuit manufacturer had received a baronetcy soon after giving MacDonald a car. 'The cynic said: Every man has his price', he wrote disapprovingly to his sister, 'but not everyone has his McVitie & Price'.[70] As Amery summed it all up, he was one of those men 'born and bred in the tradition of public service who had given their lives to the faithful fulfilment of their duty as it came to them and to the maintenance of the standards which they set before themselves'.[71] It is easy to dismiss such qualities as 'boyish traits'.[72] It is even easier to understand how the unsympathetic could

---

[66] *House of Commons Debates*, 5 Series, 321 col 2174, 17 March 1937
[67] A. Chamberlain to Ivy, 2 August 1924, AC6/1/549.
[68] E. Percy, 'Austen Chamberlain', 125.
[69] A. Chamberlain to Pike Pease, 20 October 1922, AC32/2/114.
[70] A. Chamberlain to Ida, 14 September and 9 October 1924, AC5/1/330, 337.
[71] L.S. Amery, *My Political Life*, II, 304.
[72] J. Connell, *The 'Office' : A Study in British Foreign Policy and its Makers, 1919–1951* (1958), 70–71.

immortalise Chamberlain as the man who 'always played the game and he always lost it'.[73]

Yet despite warm tributes to his honour and integrity, there was something about this outwardly rather cold man which tended to preclude intimacy with colleagues and subordinates. His carefully planned preparation for high office had succeeded in instilling political knowledge, but without inculcating any real understanding of men or their management. As a result, Chamberlain simply lacked that vital quality of superficial bonhomie and easy familiarity with either back-benchers or supporters in the constituencies.[74] In consequence, there are probably as many stories about Chamberlain's aloof and wooden behaviour offending the sensibilities of loyal followers as there are concerning Edward Heath's very similar manner fifty years later.[75] When taking the leadership in 1921 he pondered privately whether he could 'cultivate pleasant habits to be hail fellow well met with all my "followers". I must try but I haven't shown much ability that way so far'.[76] During the next eighteen months he demonstrated no greater aptitude for the task than in the previous thirty years. As Birkenhead soon complained, 'I seldom see him and never get to know him any better'.[77]

There are a variety of explanations for this failure to mix well. Chamberlain's poor sight meant that he often failed to recognise people. This caused offence and gave rise to allegations of aloofness.[78] His family attributed the problem to a natural but excessive 'reserve' which was easily mistaken for a cold and austere temperament.[79] A loving but motherless childhood undoubtedly contributed to this reticence and private insecurity. There was also a substantial streak of vanity and conceit in Chamberlain's character which made him a poor listener and a reluctant synthesiser of opinion. 'Austen does not readily take suggestions either on gardens or politics' his half-brother complained in 1918. Moreover, when confronted with views contrary to his own, he tended to 'put on that air of patient and pained resignation that he

[73] This famous remark is attributed to Churchill by R. Blake, *The Unknown Prime Minister*, 73. Lord Beaverbrook, *Men and Power 1917–18* (1956), xiii attributes it to Birkenhead. Churchill to his wife, 26 December 1935 provides the only documented use with 'Poor man, he always plays the game and never wins it'. M. Gilbert, *Winston S. Churchill* (1981) V. Companion 2, 1363.

[74] Earl of Birkenhead, *Contemporary Personalities* (1924), 72–3.

[75] Channon Diary, 16, 17 March 1937, *Chips*, 117; H. Macmillan, *Winds of Change 1914–1939*, (1966), 174–5; J. Wedgwood, *Memoirs of a Fighting Life*, 203.

[76] A. Chamberlain to Hilda, 20 March 1921, AC5/1/194.

[77] Birkenhead to Law, 5 May 1921, R. Blake, *The Unknown Prime Minister*, 428.

[78] A.P. Nicholson, *The Real Men in Public Life: Forces and Factors in the State*, (1928), 63.

[79] N. Chamberlain introduction, Petrie, *The Chamberlain Tradition*, 282.

assumes when Bee talks about Women's Unionist Associations'.[80] Such defects were compounded by a rigid sense of hierarchy which helped to found another body of pompous tales at his expense; as for example, the rebuff to Cecil's proposals for government reorganisation in 1916 when he appeared 'profoundly shocked that an Under-Secretary should presume to enter on such topics!'.[81] When Chamberlain became leader, the dignity of his new position intensified all the worst aspects of this public persona. He soon showed himself a 'vain man' and 'pompous to the last degree'. With equals he appeared inaccessible, remote, 'aloof and reserved'.[82] To lesser mortals he remained 'irritable and unable to make friends easily of Members … impatient even to the point of rudeness when they sought interviews with him'.[83] This often staggering insensitivity towards party functionaries and juniors won him few friends and created many new enemies. For example, his high-handed treatment of Younger in 1921 was so remarkable that Younger eventually came to play a significant role in his leader's downfall, convinced that Chamberlain was 'quite stupid and obstinate with an impossible conceit which would smash anyone in public life'.[84] Even after 1922, this public tendency to flaunt his honour suggested to critics an excessive fondness for posing in 'his favourite role as Aristides – "the one just man" whom Athenians exiled because they were tired of hearing him called just'.[85]

An equally unfortunate consequence of Chamberlain's devotion to public honour and 'good form' was that it rendered him excessively sensitive to slights – whether real or imagined – throughout his career. This *amour propre* undoubtedly made him a prickly and difficult colleague, particularly for leaders whom he resented and believed were made of coarser clay. In May 1923 Baldwin's handling of the estranged former leader was little short of a disaster which left Chamberlain burning with indignation for weeks. It is not necessary to understand much about Chamberlain's personality to comprehend the extent to which Baldwin's suggestion that he could 'be bribed to good behaviour or bought off by a lucrative appointment [was] galling to a proud

[80] N. Chamberlain to Hilda, 7 July, 20 July 1918, NC18/1/175, 177. Also Neville Chamberlain Diary, 15, 21 July 1927. Bee was the family name for the eldest sister Beatrice.

[81] Viscount Cecil, *All the Way* (1949), 136.

[82] Frances Stevenson Diary, 12 May 1921, A.J.P. Taylor (ed) *Lloyd George: A Diary by Frances Stevenson* (1971), 216; Birkenhead to Law, 5 May 1921, *The Unknown Prime Minister*, 428. Also Sanders Diary, 2 July 1922 Bayford MSS (Conservative Research Department).

[83] Jones Diary, 20 May 1923, *Whitehall Diary*, I, 236.

[84] Younger to Lord Hugh Cecil, 11 December 1923, Quickswood MSS 31/145–6 (Hatfield House). For Younger's treatment see Jones Diary, 13–15 January 1940, *A Diary with Letters*, 447; Davidson draft memoir, R. R. James, *Memoirs of a Conservative*, 104.

[85] *Weekly Despatch*, mid-July? 1923, AC5/1/280.

man'.[86] Six months later Baldwin's frankness resulted in another bitter blow to Chamberlain's dignity.[87] Even at the age of 72, Chamberlain could still turn down a Cabinet seat and £5000 a year, at a time when he dearly needed both, because acceptance would be 'impossible for a man with any self-respect'.[88] The same sensitivity also ensured he was incapable of forgiving or forgetting a past offence. Moreover, on matters of honour his memory was long. Asquith's offer of the Ministry of Munitions in June 1916 provoked a characteristic diatribe: 'I am amazed that after the events of 1900 you should make such a proposal to me,' he told a no doubt startled Prime Minister. 'As long as I live I shall never forget that the whole of your party ... did their utmost to destroy my father's honour and to hound him out of public life'.[89] Similarly, eight years after the Carlton Club revolt, the mere mention of Leslie Wilson's name as a possible candidate for the Party Chairmanship was sufficient to provoke the threat to retire to the backbenches because 'he was absolutely and grossly disloyal at the time of the fall of the Coalition'.[90]

While political loyalty of this sort stemmed from an essentially noble quality, the supreme irony was that in bestowing such devotion Chamberlain appears to have been 'no judge at all of men or their motives'.[91] Indeed, among his most loyally supported friends were some of the most despised and mistrusted politicians of the age. Most conspicuous in this category were Birkenhead and Lloyd George. The former was renowned as a 'cad' and a 'loose liver'. The latter was infamous as the 'real corrupter of public life'.[92] Such associations cost him dearly. As one of the Carlton Club rebels encapsulated the problem in 1924, he had less fault to find with Chamberlain himself than with his 'perverted sense of loyalty to the two men in British public life – Lloyd George and Birkenhead – whom I dislike and distrust most'.[93] Moreover, not only did this dedication to his principles exact a high cost at the time, but in office together after 1924 none of that loyalty was repaid. Confronted by fierce opposition over his proposals for a

[86] A. Chamberlain to Birkenhead, 31 May 1923, AC35/2/18.

[87] R. Self, 'Conservative Reunion and the General Election of 1923: A Reassessment', *Twentieth Century British History*, 3.3 (1992), 266–7.

[88] A. Chamberlain to Hilda, 22 December 1935, AC5/1/718.

[89] D. Dilks, *Neville Chamberlain vol I 1869–1929* (Cambridge 1984), 172.

[90] A. Chamberlain to Hilda, 1 June 1930, AC5/1/503.

[91] Bridgeman Diary, November 1929, Bridgemann MSS II fol.189. Davidson draft memoir, R.R. James, *Memoirs of a Conservative*, 104.

[92] Curzon to his wife, 18 November 1923, Marchioness Curzon, *Reminiscences* (1955), 191; N. Chamberlain to Hilda, 17 November 1923, NC18/1/416; Dawson memo on conversation with Baldwin, 17 June 1923, J.E. Wrench, *Geoffrey Dawson and our Times* (1955), 219.

[93] W. Ormsby-Gore to Baldwin, 29 January 1924, Baldwin MSS 42/182–7. For a similar comment see Salisbury to Baldwin, 26 January 1924, Baldwin MSS 159/260.

Rhineland Pact – as later over Egypt, China and Russia – all Chamberlain could do was complain that 'the friend who owes most to me appears to be working against me and that his friends take the same line'.[94] Yet even at Birkenhead's death, Chamberlain could still genuinely feel the loss as a 'great blow'.[95]

Unfortunately this devotion to Birkenhead was not an aberration. In return for Horne's remarkable loyalty to Chamberlain in March, May and September 1923, Chamberlain fought hard on his behalf in November 1924 at a time when the Party generally rejoiced at Baldwin's revenge upon a disreputable 'Scotch cad'.[96] Even more extravagant efforts to assist Oliver Locker-Lampson (his PPS during the Coalition) in 1924, 1925, 1926 and 1929 were even less comprehensible to Austen's half-brother, who thought him 'the arch intriguer';[97] to Baldwin who believed there was truth in the rumours of financial impropriety;[98] or to the Parliamentary Party who believed Lampson 'a terrible fellow whom no one likes'.[99] Most remarkable of all, the 'infatuation' of both Austen and Ivy Chamberlain with Warden Chilcott was inexplicable to almost everyone.[100] Chilcott was an astonishingly flamboyant character with an ostentatious life-style, which included a Hampshire estate with its own private golf course, a yacht resembling a Trafalgar frigate and a Corsican estate where he hunted wild boar with a mounted entourage dressed in pink. The Chamberlains spent much time with Chilcott at his estate at Warsash, on the *Dolphin* and in Corsica where they holidayed every year until 1935 when the relationship was finally severed by their host's appalling behaviour towards the Queen of Spain.[101] Chamberlain shared Chilcott's admiration for Mussolini, but

[94] A. Chamberlain to Ivy, 15 March 1925, AC6/1/603. See also Davidson to Baldwin, n.d. (1926–7) Baldwin MSS 161/71.

[95] A. Chamberlain to Mary Carnegie, 9 October 1930, AC4/1/1302.

[96] See Victor Cazalet Journal, 6 November 1924, R. R. James, *Victor Cazalet : A Portrait* (1976), 99; Tyrrell to Baldwin, 1 November 1924, Baldwin MSS 42/226–7; N. Chamberlain to Hilda, 15 November 1924, NC18/1/462.

[97] Neville Chamberlain Diary, 19 March 1924. Also N. Chamberlain to A. Chamberlain, 21 April 1923, AC35/1/34.

[98] Churchill to Baldwin, 16 December 1926, Baldwin MSS; Sanders Diary, 17 November 1925.

[99] Headlam Diary, 25 June 1926, S. Ball (ed) *Parliament and Politics in the Age of Baldwin and MacDonald: The Headlam Diaries 1923–1935*, (1992), 93.

[100] Amery Diary, 20 March 1928, *Leo Amery Diaries*, 539. See also Davidson's disparaging remark in R.R. James, *Memoirs of a Conservative*, 104. For Chilcott's career and louche associations see P.J. Waller, *Democracy and Sectarianism: A Political and Social History of Liverpool, 1868–1939*, (Liverpool, 1981), 307, 481; T. Cullen, *Maundy Gregory: Purveyor of Honours*, (1974), Chapter IX.

[101] Information from Mrs T. Maxwell and Mr L. Chamberlain in interview with the editor, 12 October 1992; A. Chamberlain to Ida, 22 September 1935, 20 June 1936, AC5/1/708, 738.

presumably did not share his ominously anti-democratic views, although he did write an introduction to the book in which they appeared.[102] Chamberlain would certainly have been outraged had he known of Chilcott's scandalous efforts to obtain money from the Indian princes by claiming – not apparently, without some substance – the existence of an improper influence over Birkenhead while Secretary of State for India.[103] With friends such as Chilcott and colleagues like Birkenhead, Chamberlain scarcely needed to make enemies of his own. Rather he often appeared 'like a good man who got into bad company':[104] a leader too weak to realise that 'he was being used by certain clever people with first class brains'.[105] Yet despite repeated warnings, he proved remarkably incapable of recognising that 'less reputable people shelter behind [his] name to carry on intrigues'.[106]

The net result of the broader public persona was that Chamberlain was respected for his chivalry, but considered extremely difficult to love or even admire. Although certainly never a knave himself, for those who judged men by their friends he was also probably a fool. Indeed, underlying more general perceptions of pomposity, excessive sensitivity and an overwhelming *amour propre* there was often the view that such traits merely concealed a second-rate bore. Lloyd George believed that Chamberlain possessed 'an excellence of character rather than capacity'.[107] Law agreed that he 'could make a good speech but had not first-class political ability'.[108] As Prime Minister, Baldwin also swiftly came to the same conclusion that Chamberlain was 'the stupidest fellow he knew'.[109] Such doubts are echoed in the testimony of lesser figures. For example, in council Masterman considered Chamberlain a 'slow and commonplace mind'.[110] Together in Asquith's wartime coalition Cabinet, Runciman also found him 'insignificant and unsuggestive'.[111] In the same year Margot Asquith had declared with a typical flamboyance that 'Austen is more of a shopkeeper than a merchant – he

[102] W. Chilcott, *Political Salvation 1930–1932* (1932).

[103] For details see S. Roskill, *Hankey: Man of Secrets* (three vols, 1970–74) II, 420–4.

[104] 'The Eastern Crisis', n.d. Griffith-Boscawen MSS c.396/107, (Bodleian Library, Oxford).

[105] Sir Alexander Leith at Newcastle, *Morning Post*, 13 November 1922. Also Younger to Gwynne, 8 October 1922, Gwynne MSS 22, (Bodleian Library, Oxford).

[106] N. Chamberlain to A. Chamberlain, 23 April 1923, AC35/1/35.

[107] Lord Beaverbrook, *The Decline and Fall of Lloyd George and Great was the Fall Thereof* (1963), 233. For the source of this opinion see Frances Stevenson Diary, 17 March 1937, A.J.P. Taylor (ed), *Lloyd George: A Diary*, 326.

[108] Jones Diary, 20 May 1923, *Whitehall Diary* I, 236.

[109] Amery Diary, 19 June 1923, *Leo Amery Diaries*, 330.

[110] Masterman Diary, 12 October 1910, L. Masterman, *C.F.G. Masterman: A Biography*, (1939), 163.

[111] Hobhouse Diary, 22 June 1915, E. David (ed), *Inside Asquith's Cabinet: From the Diaries of Charles Hobhouse*, (1977), 249.

has no greatness and is a bore'.[112] When asked to explain Chamberlain's lack of greater success, Balfour also explained that it was because he was 'a bore'.[113] With equal candour Amery noted in 1931, 'I am afraid life has been full of disappointments for him: but then he has never really had sufficient confidence in himself, and, at bottom, there has not really been enough of himself to have confidence in. Nature intended him for a good lieutenant and eventually a elder statesman'.[114] Historians have not unnaturally followed where contemporaries led. As one such verdict has it, 'His looks did not belie his character: there was little here of shrewdness, nothing of pugnacity; none of his father's dynamism; rather a fear of being thought pushful'.[115]

Given the weight of testimony it is difficult to argue against such a portrait. Yet for all that, it can be reasonably objected that the tendency to focus too heavily on the superficial external appearance has tended to obscure another and different side of Chamberlain's personality. If Chamberlain appeared cold, aloof and conceited, this was only part of the picture. The reality of this complex figure is that throughout his career, Chamberlain consciously maintained what McKercher has called 'a dual personality: to his family he was a warm and devoted son, brother, husband and father; to the rest of the world including even his closest political colleagues, he embodied Victorian propriety – always correct and formal, loyal and adept at keeping his innermost thoughts private'.[116] Few observers outside the immediate family ever glimpsed or suspected the existence of this other side to his nature.[117] The vast majority tended to take Chamberlain at face value in much the same way as they had his rather less subtly complex father.

Anthony Eden, Chamberlain's PPS at the Foreign Office from 1926–9, recognised the fundamental truth of this proposition when he recalled that although in appearance and speech Chamberlain sometimes seemed stiff and forbidding, this had 'nothing to do with the real man who was warm-hearted, considerate and generous'.[118] It was this side of his nature which made him such a friend to younger men in the

---

[112] M. Asquith to Lloyd George, 17 May 1915, M. Gilbert, *Winston S. Churchill*, III. Companion 2, 898–899. Also to Strachey, 24 May 1915, C. Hazelhurst, *Politicians at War*, (1971), 285.

[113] Jones Diary, 13–15 January 1940, *Diary with Letters*, 447.

[114] Amery, *My Political Life*, III, 71. Amery Diary 8 July 1923 also notes 'the trouble with [Austen] is partly that he is rather stupid and also that he is too much worried about what people think of him'.

[115] C. Barnett, *The Collapse of British Power*, (Gloucester 1984), 329. Also, R. Blake, *The Unknown Prime Minister*, 72–3; R. Jenkins, *Baldwin*, 170.

[116] B.J.C. McKercher, *The Second Baldwin Government*, 7.

[117] A.P. Nicholson, *The Real Men in Public Life*, 62–3.

[118] Earl of Avon, *Facing the Dictators* (1962), 7. Also F.W. Pethick-Lawrence, *Fate Has Been Kind*, 145.

Commons and for which he was rightly famous. His note congratulating the Labour MP Willie Graham on his maiden speech in 1911 laid the foundations for a lifelong affection and respect.[119] Few who saw this desiccated old statesman in his later years as 'humourless and narrow-minded'[120] would have believed his propensity for private humour and self-mockery in the intimacy of the family circle, or occasionally when he let his guard down to officials, to show that other 'very delightful' side of his nature.[121] It is equally difficult to believe they would have recognised him as the same man who showed such an unaffected private delight in flowers, his garden or the frankly 'childish pleasure' he derived from wearing the Garter.[122]

This other, under-estimated, side of Chamberlain's character also at times greatly enhanced his political effectiveness. This was particularly so during his period as Foreign Secretary. Contrary to the sneers of Beaverbrook, or Amery's jibe that Chamberlain was a 'born bureaucrat', the fact remains that at the Foreign Office Chamberlain won the genuine respect and affection of his officials.[123] After 1924 the cornerstone of his diplomacy was built upon personal contact in order to discover the real qualities of those with whom he dealt and to establish cordial relations. In these dealings with Briand, Mussolini and even Stresemann, Chamberlain was in his element and largely because of this other side to his nature. As the foremost historian of Locarno has written, 'His correctness covered a boyish enthusiasm, sincerity and optimism, qualities which eased the negotiations of 1925 and did as much to promote the spirit of Locarno as did Briand's oratory'. He treated Briand and Stresemann honestly and they responded accordingly.[124] As he confided to his sister in 1927, 'Our diplomacy may not always have been the best possible but it has always been very simple, direct and honest'.[125] In some respects, his greatest weakness in these relationships stemmed from his strengths. Throughout his life, Chamberlain dem-

[119] T.N. Graham, *Willie Graham* (London n.d.), 181. Also C.R. Attlee, *As it Happened*, (1954), 78.

[120] Channon Diary, 16 March 1937, *Chips*, 117.

[121] Jones Diary, 20 May 1923, *Whitehall Diary*, I, 263; Sir Almeric Fitzroy Diary, 6 March 1920, *Memoirs* (London n.d.) II, 723; J. Connell, *The 'Office'*, 87–8.

[122] A. Chamberlain to Ivy, 13 February 1926, AC6/1/643; to Ida, 19 July and to Hilda, 9 November 1930, AC5/1/508, 520.

[123] Beaverbrook to Borden, 29 April 1925, Beaverbrook MSS C/51 (House of Lords Record Office); Amery Diary, 18 February 1927 *Leo Amery Diaries*, I, 447–8. For respect of officials see Lord Vansittart, *The Mist Procession* (1958), 334; McKercher, *The Second Baldwin Government*, 20, 22.

[124] J. Jacobson, *Locarno Diplomacy: Germany and the West 1925–1929*, (Princeton 1972), 74; D. Johnson, 'The Locarno Treaties' in N. Waites (ed) *Troubled Neighbours :Franco-British Relations in the Twentieth Century* (1971), 105; A. Chamberlain, *Down the Years* (1935), 151–172, 181.

[125] A. Chamberlain to Ida, 12 December 1927, AC5/1/440.

onstrated a susceptibility to the personal charm, flattery and magnetism of others. Despite himself, he quickly fell under Lloyd George's spell. He soon found himself captivated by Mussolini, although the influence was undoubtedly mutual.[126] Above all, his feelings for Briand swiftly 'ripened into a close and affectionate intimacy' which lasted unto death.[127] It is true that in each case such affection imposed costs upon both British policy and Chamberlain's reputation. On the other hand, however, a more cynical and duplicitous man would arguably not have succeeded at all. As even unsympathetic observers of the outward persona were forced to concede, 'he certainly seems to have succeeded where clever men might have failed – "his transparent honesty" has done the trick'.[128] Locarno was a triumph for precisely that 'plain good intent' which had characterised his entire career.[129]

Like his father and his half-brother, Austen Chamberlain was a prodigious letter writer in an epistolary age. Among the vast collection of private papers deposited in Birmingham University Library, the two longest sequences of letters from Austen Chamberlain are some 1158 written to his step-mother Mary between 1889 and 1936 and a further 1065 to his wife Ivy covering the years 1906–1935. Such correspondence undoubtedly involved a high level of commitment and dedication. Astonishingly, only when he made his first visit to the League at Geneva in December 1924 did he fail to write his daily letter to his wife when they were apart – the first time he had not found time to do so in eighteen years of married life![130] This volume contains an edited selection of the 762 letters written between November 1916 and his death in March 1937 to his maiden half-sisters Hilda and Ida, living together in Odiham, Hampshire.

Unlike his half-brother, Austen Chamberlain was never able to sustain a personal diary. In most respects, however, this family correspondence was perceived explicitly as an alternative form of diary. After his father's resignation from the Cabinet in 1903, and even more after his sudden stroke three years later, Austen Chamberlain had

---

[126] A. Chamberlain to Tyrrell, 18 October 1925, C. Petrie, *The Life and Letters of the Rt. Honourable Sir Austen Chamberlain* (2 vols, 1939–1940) II, 290, 295; A. Cassels, *Mussolini's Early Diplomacy* (Princeton 1970), 310–14; P. Edwards, 'The Austen Chamberlain – Mussolini Meetings', *Historical Journal*, XIV. I (1971), 153–164.

[127] A. Chamberlain, *Down the Years*, 178–188; Neville Chamberlain Diary, 22 October 1925.

[128] Headlam Diary, 19 October 1925, S. Ball (ed) *Parliament and Politics*, 71. For a very similar assessment see V. Massey *What's Past is Prologue*, (1963), 113.

[129] L.S. Amery, *My Political Life*, II, 303. Also Lord Salter, *Slave of the Lamp: A Public Servant's Notebook*, (1967), 56.

[130] A. Chamberlain to Hilda, 23 December 1924, AC5/1/342.

compiled detailed accounts of political events. With Balfour's agreement these were written to Joe's third wife Mary in order to keep his father informed. These letters covering the years 1904 to 1914 were subsequently published in 1936 as *Politics from Inside*. Although the correspondence to Mary continued until Austen's own death, the relationship cooled perceptibly after her re-marriage to Canon Carnegie in 1916. The letters to his sisters Hilda and Ida which commenced in the same year can rightly be described as the direct lineal descendants of those early diary letters to his stricken father at Highbury. Their primary value lies in the fact that they provide perhaps the most revealing and complete single account of the last twenty years of Austen Chamberlain's active political life during which he played a pivotal role in national and international politics. At the same time, however, they also offer a vivid insight into the complete man, where the public persona co-exists with that private side of his character so effectively concealed from all outside the family circle.

The origin of the diary letters can be traced not to any initiative of Austen's but rather to a family concern about his state of mind and physical health. Although never robust, by the spring of 1916 the elder Chamberlain brother gave his siblings cause for grave concern. In March Neville informed his sisters that 'A. seemed very stiff and rather depressed'. Two months later he was still '*Very* tired and in need of a rest'.[131] By October, the unremitting strain of work combined with depression about the progress of the war had taken their toll. A brief visit to Odiham had done him some good but Neville warned that he was 'evidently very much run down and one of these days he will have a nervous breakdown if he doesn't take better care of himself'.[132] Soon afterwards Austen Chamberlain suffered a partial collapse and was ordered to take two weeks rest. A month later, however, he still looked 'very white and wan and worn'.[133]

Concern about the health of their elder half-brother was undoubtedly one impulse which lay behind the initiation of the diary letters. The other was anxiety about the growing distance that had developed between the three younger children and their elder half-brother. By 1916 Neville was writing perhaps 80,000 words a year in unfailing weekly epistles of 8–10 pages to his sisters. They were writing a similar quantity back to him.[134] In contrast, the correspondence with Austen seems to have been extremely infrequent. Moreover, although Hilda and Ida were regular visitors to London they appear to have seen him

[131] N. Chamberlain to Ida, 19 March and to Hilda, 28 May 1916, NC18/1/52, 63.
[132] N. Chamberlain to Hilda, 22 October 1916, NC18/1/85.
[133] N. Chamberlain to Ida, 12 November 1916, NC18/1/88.
[134] D. Dilks, *Neville Chamberlain*, 165.

rarely. The result was that while the sisters were 'both quite certain that we shall never drift apart from [Neville] and Annie', Ida confessed in August 1916 that 'it would be easier to do so from Austen and Ivy'.[135] This was the motive that Hilda outlined in her opening letter four months later. This first approach set in progress an almost weekly correspondence for the next twenty years. 'I feel dreadfully that I am getting so cut off from your and Ivy's life and you from mine', she wrote on the day Lloyd George became Prime Minister, 'that I am proposing to write to you more or less regularly to give you news, hoping when you have the time & inclination you will answer, but not at all counting on getting an answer to every letter'. As she visited London less than she had anticipated when the sisters moved to Odiham, and much less than either Beatrice or Ida, Hilda added that such a correspondence would 'mean a great deal' to her.[136] Clearly the idea appealed to the older brother from the outset. Only three weeks earlier he had expressed a desire for closer contact with Neville to 'talk myself out to you and get your advice and help', as his father had with their Uncle Arthur.[137] He thus wrote back to Hilda on the same day as she had first proposed the idea assuring her 'how constantly I wish we could all be more together & how grateful I am for your offer to write to me'. At this stage he promised to write 'as and when I can'.[138] It was not until mid-February that Austen proposed something rather more formal:[139]

> I wonder whether I could write something like a diary letter to you. The trouble is that I cannot write to you as freely as I did to Father, tho' all my letters to Father were read to the Family circle. But then an oath is an oath even when sworn by a Cabinet Minister – which by the way I am not at this present time of writing – and whilst Balfour gave me leave to write everything to Father & tho' he knows my letters were family property at home[?], it isn't quite the same thing to sit down deliberately to write similar letters to anyone (or at least *for* anyone) but Father.

Within a month, however, the demands of his work had taken their toll and he was forced to concede that 'the "diary" letter like all diaries I have ever tried to keep has faded out of existence after a brief & ill-nourished life of a few days'.[140] Yet although the progress of the

---

[135] Ida to Neville Chamberlain, 25 August 1916, NC1/16/1/58.

[136] Hilda to A. Chamberlain, 7 December 1916, AC5/2/35.

[137] A. Chamberlain to N. Chamberlain, 17 November 1916, NC1/27/5.

[138] A. Chamberlain to Hilda, 7 December 1916, AC5/1/2 and reply 13 December 1916, AC5/2/36.

[139] A. Chamberlain to Hilda, 17 February 1917, AC5/1/11.

[140] A. Chamberlain to Hilda, 24 March 1917, AC5/1/18.

correspondence was somewhat erratic at first, the pattern of weekly diary letters soon became firmly established.

Austen Chamberlain did not take to the discipline of these weekly diary letters in the same way as his younger half-brother. That he found it difficult to lay aside his ministerial duties to devote time each Sunday to penning a personal account of the week was perhaps understandable. Yet it also reflected a more profound difference in the way the two brothers regarded the task. For Neville, the correspondence with Ida and Hilda was almost a necessity of life. For Austen the impulse to correspond was significantly less powerful.[141] As a result, more than once in the early years Austen had confessed to being a 'scurvy correspondent' who resorted to various subterfuges to conceal his laxness.[142] In the end, however, a variety of factors sustained the correspondence and conferred greater importance upon the diary letters for their author. First, almost immediately after the Armistice had been signed Austen's older sister Beatrice had fallen victim to the influenza epidemic which killed more people than the war itself. Her death gave an 'added value' to the regular correspondence now that he could not turn to Beatrice for news of those he loved but so seldom saw.[143] Second, there can be little doubt that with time Chamberlain simply acquired the habit of writing these letters in much the same way as he did before the War. As he confessed to Mary in 1914, 'letter-writing is like dram-drinking. The habit grows on you'.[144] Above all, perhaps, Chamberlain came to depend on the act of letter writing, in the strictest conditions of secrecy, as a cathartic personal release beyond the value of the correspondence as a source of news about the activities and thoughts of his sisters.[145]

There are a variety of reasons which explain why politicians dutifully keep diaries. Like all such diarists, Austen Chamberlain undoubtedly had at least one eye on posterity and desired to keep his own account of events – if only for the instruction and edification of his closest family. From early on in the correspondence, the sisters were thus instructed to retain all the letters.[146] A more immediate benefit was simply therapeutic. At one level, these letters provided an opportunity to 'gossip' – particularly when he was alone and without work to do:

[141] Dr. B.S. Benedikz to the editor, 19 December 1991.

[142] See A. Chamberlain to Hilda, 24 March 1919 and to Ida, 18 August 1921, AC5/1/122, 208.

[143] D. Dilks, *Neville Chamberlain*, 262; A. Chamberlain to Hilda, 24 March 1919, AC5/1/122.

[144] A. Chamberlain to Mary Chamberlain, 2 April 1914, *Politics from Inside*, 636.

[145] A. Chamberlain to Ida, 18 August 1921, AC5/1/208.

[146] A. Chamberlain to Ida, 20 October 1917, AC5/1/40. See also to Hilda, 1 March 1924, AC5/1/311.

'if I have no one to talk to', he explained in October 1917, 'I must babble in ink'.[147] The frequent absences of his wife either through illness or recuperating from it often left Chamberlain depressed and feeling like 'the domestic cat when the family has gone to the seaside'. One result was that it provided him with plenty of free moments for such diversion.[148] At a far deeper level, however, the absolute privacy of these diary letters to his sisters provided him with a vent for his frustrations and disappointments, a source of constant reassurance and support, and an opportunity to boast freely of his triumphs and successes. In this respect, the diary letters provided an outlet with all the sacred confidentiality of the confessional. In the intimacy of these letters he could relax and be himself, free to share secrets and private emotions, confident in the knowledge that none of it would be passed on, even to his half-brother.[149] As he noted after relaying one particularly feline story at Baldwin's expense, 'Oh Lord! I had to tell *somebody* and you are safe'.[150] In so doing, Chamberlain clearly felt that this correspondence enabled him to recapture at least some of the old intimacy of Highbury before the War when his political activities had been the focus of family interest.[151]

In such an environment, Chamberlain found expression for a spectrum of emotions which most of those who saw only the public persona would have been scarcely able to imagine. Certainly vanity played a part. Throughout his life Chamberlain was keenly aware of his own susceptibility to flattery. After receiving one such excessive compliment from Dollfuss, the Austrian Chancellor, he conceded 'I can swallow much flattery, but there are limits to my credulity even where my own merits are concerned'. Reading favourable reviews of *Down the Years*, however, he was more candid in admitting that 'under their influence I begin to think myself a devil of a good fellow, but I don't think a little flattery does me any harm. I have had my share of knocks in life'.[152] There is also much private humour, shared family sayings and jokes. One wonders if critics of that supposedly narrow-minded, pompous and humourless public persona like 'Chips' Channon would have guessed at Chamberlain's passion for 'shilling shockers' as reading material, or his delight in humorous mis-spellings, self-mockery or the frequent resort to phrases like 'I must fink, Auntie, I must fink'. Similarly, it is difficult to believe that the ever-punctilious Hankey who

[147] A. Chamberlain to Hilda, 17 February and 21 October 1917, AC5/1/11, 41.
[148] A. Chamberlain to Ida, 26 July 1924, AC5/1/327.
[149] A. Chamberlain to Hilda, 14 April 1923, AC5/1/270.
[150] A. Chamberlain to Ida, 7 December 1929, AC5/1/490.
[151] A. Chamberlain to Hilda, 23 December 1924 and Ida, 6 November 1927, AC5/1/342, 436.
[152] A. Chamberlain to Ida, 9 July 1933 and 22 September 1935, AC5/1/625, 708.

found Chamberlain so 'very meticulous and rather tiresome' about Cabinet minutes,[153] could believe him capable of demonstrating such a strong sense of fun when regularly reproving his sisters for the way they folded their letters.[154]

The diary letters also reveal the astonishing depth of Austen Chamberlain's family feeling. Although outwardly something of a 'cold fish', the closeness and intimacy of his family life was truly 'the ruling passion of his life'.[155] What he had valued so dearly in his first forty years under his father's roof at Highbury was later reproduced in 'the perfect and uninterrupted happiness' of his own married and family life.[156] With his sisters he also continued to feel a particular closeness, rejoicing in their 'unbroken and never clouded love and friendship'.[157] Within the confines of their epistolary relationship, Chamberlain was able to reveal this more emotional side of his nature. Perhaps the most striking feature to emerge from these letters about the private Chamberlain is his propensity for disarmingly candid effluxions of genuine affection and emotion. After one evidently over-wrought visit to Odiham following an operation upon his elder son, he wrote assuring them that there was 'no one that I would sooner be with when anxious & in sorrow than my sisters. I know you feel *with* me as well as for me & that you understand'.[158]

I thank God for giving me such sisters & I say with joy that I have been blessed more than most people – in my wife, in my home from childhood till now, in my brother & sisters – & in my own way I thank God & I thank & love you all.

That is the nearest that I can come to saying what I want to say to you & Hilda. Expression of our deepest & holiest thoughts is not very easy to any of us, but I want you both to know (& I think you *do* know) how deeply & tenderly I do love you, how much I owe to you & how glad I am to see you in your own home & in the place where you are doing so much & such good work. My dear sisters, I love you indeed, but I am also proud of you. God bless you both & guard you. Papa would be very pleased with his children.

Such freedom to express himself in these terms to his sisters was perhaps

---

[153] Hankey Diary, 11 June 1918, S. Roskill, *Man of Secrets* I, 573; T. Jones to Lady Grigg, 18 March 1937, *Diary with Letters*, 325.

[154] A. Chamberlain to Hilda, 11 August 1918; to Ida, 25 April 1924, AC5/1/95, 316.

[155] Petrie, *Life and Letters*, II, 66.

[156] A. Chamberlain to Ida, 23 July 1918, AC5/1/92; Neville Chamberlain introduction in Petrie, *The Chamberlain Tradition*, 281.

[157] A. Chamberlain to Ida, 11 May 1917 and 11 October 1931, AC5/1/24, 560.

[158] A. Chamberlain to Ida, 24 June 1917, AC5/1/30.

even more important because Chamberlain never enjoyed the same sort of relationship with his half-brother. Indeed, the diary letters are quite illuminating about the increasingly ambivalent relationship which existed between Joseph Chamberlain's two sons. On one hand, Austen was always anxious to advance his half-brother's career. 'I am like a hen with one chick & more anxious about him than I have ever been about myself, for I think I care more about his success than about any success or failure of my own' he wrote when Neville received his first national post in 1916.[159] By the time Austen's ministerial career had come to an end, he genuinely meant it when he told his half-brother that he felt 'something for your success of what Father thought of mine'.[160] Yet, for all this elder brotherly, even quasi-paternal interest, there was always a barrier between these two reserved figures which inhibited a frank exchange of views or real intimacy:[161] a barrier of temperament, undoubtedly reinforced by Neville's experiences during his dismal sojourn in the Bahamas while Austen was groomed for greatness.

Austen did occasionally consult his younger brother, as in the spring of 1917 over a possible trip to India and the offer of the Paris Embassy. Yet contrary to the impression given by Neville Chamberlain's biographer,[162] Austen did not share much political information with him. Indeed, at precisely the moment that these diary letters began, Neville often complained that, not only did his half-brother rarely talk about the substance of his work, but that he was actually 'curiously secretive about it'.[163] After the War there was also a political gulf between them. 'He thinks me wild', Neville told his sister in 1919, 'and I think him unprogressive and prejudiced'.[164] Although in Cabinet together after 1924, both were busy with ministerial duties and young families. Nor did any special bond of affection or even sympathy ever developed between their wives to bring them together.[165] Eden's much-quoted story in which Austen observed shortly before his death, 'Neville, you must remember you don't know anything about foreign affairs' may well have been a flippant remark subsequently accorded undue significance, as Carlton suggests.[166] It does highlight, however, an

[159] A. Chamberlain to Hilda, 21 December 1916, AC5/1/4.
[160] A. Chamberlain to N. Chamberlain, 5 November 1931, NC1/27/99.
[161] Mary Carnegie to N. Chamberlain, 31 October 1923, NC1/20/2/17. D. Dilks, *Neville Chamberlain*, 24–6, 72.
[162] D. Dilks, *Neville Chamberlain*, 187.
[163] N. Chamberlain to Ida, 22 April and to Hilda 1 July 1917, 1 February 1920, NC18/1/110, 118.
[164] N. Chamberlain to Hilda, 4 January 1919, NC18/1/196.
[165] For Ivy's less than flattering later views on Neville and his wife see Channon Diary, 2 May 1939, *Chips*, 196.
[166] Avon, *Facing the Dictators*, 445; D. Carlton, *Anthony Eden: A Biography* (1981), 100–101. See also J. Stuart, *Within the Fringe: An Autobiography*, (1967), 84.

underlying truth of the relationship. As Neville complained in 1936, Austen 'always finds it difficult to realise that I am no longer his little brother'.[167] From December 1916 onwards the sisters stood between the two brothers receiving complaints and anxieties from each about the other but not passing them on. As Austen shrewdly noted later in life, 'You sit between two brothers, one in and one out of office. I always think that ministers in office (self included) are apt to be too complacent and that men out of office are apt to think that nothing is being done or at least nothing done right – so between the two of us you ought to be near the truth'.[168]

From the political historian's perspective, perhaps the most striking emotion expressed by Chamberlain in the privacy of this closed epistolary relationship was that of unbridled contempt towards those who had seized the leadership which he felt rightly belonged to him. Indeed, it is one of the greatest paradoxes of this man famed, above all, for blind unfaltering loyalty to his leader in public, that he should have vented so much contemptuous spleen upon them in private. By his own admission, Balfour was the last man to whom he had looked up in politics.[169] After his departure in 1911, Chamberlain came bitterly to regret his own decision to stand aside for a man 'only a year or two older than [him]self and very much [his] junior in the House of Commons'. All that happened after 1911 confirmed Chamberlain's view that Bonar Law was a 'weak man' incapable of learning and likely to remain 'an amateur to the end of his days'.[170] Believing him thoroughly in the hands of born intriguers, he also came to see him as 'the most ambitious man whom I have ever known in politics'.[171] When Law re-emerged to cheat Chamberlain of the leadership for a second time in October 1922 it was the ultimate betrayal by a man whom he already heartily despised.[172]

If he had an abiding suspicion of Law, Chamberlain's frustration and outright contempt for Baldwin was even greater. It also remained undiminished throughout his entire leadership – with the brief possible

[167] N. Chamberlain Diary, 19 February 1936, K. Feiling, *The Life of Neville Chamberlain*, 293. See also Hilda Memoir, BC5/10/1 fol.11.

[168] A. Chamberlain to Hilda, 13 August 1933, AC5/1/629.

[169] A. Chamberlain to Hilda, 25 March 1930, AC5/1/495. See also the character sketch in *Down the Years*, Chapter XV.

[170] A. Chamberlain to Hilda, 20 March 1921, AC5/1/194. Also Amery Diary, 10 October 1917, *The Leo Amery Diaries*, 173.

[171] A. Chamberlain to Ida, 4 November 1917, AC5/1/45; *Down the Years*, 119–121, 125–6. Cf his sketch of Law, 224–5.

[172] Derby Diary, 23 November 1922; N. Chamberlain to Ida, 18 February 1923; Pollock memo, 'The Fall of the Coalition Government under Lloyd George in October 1922', n.d. (?1922) corrected 14 September 1931, Hanworth MSS d.432. fol. 163 (Bodleian Library, Oxford).

exception of his early years at the Foreign Office when Baldwin gave him much needed support. Ultimately, Chamberlain's attitude towards Baldwin, even more than towards Law, was prejudiced by the perception that his nominal leader was also his junior in rank, ability and experience. Graduates of the same Cambridge college missing each other by a term, Chamberlain had already been Chancellor of the Exchequer when he introduced Baldwin to the Commons in 1908. Returning as Chancellor again after the war, Baldwin had served as Chamberlain's junior minister – and 'under' him in the most literal sense of the word.[173] After he obtained .the leadership as an 'accident of an accident' in 1923,[174] Chamberlain was never able to regard Baldwin with anything other than a more extreme form of the same condescension he felt towards Bonar Law. Inevitably, this made public subordination difficult for a proud man to endure, as the frequent tirades against Baldwin's ineptitude and indolence in the privacy of his diary letters demonstrated.

Although this volume is concerned principally with the political content of these diary letters, it is important to emphasise that such material formed only a sometimes fairly small proportion of the regular weekly diet of news. At the time this correspondence with Austen began, the letters between Neville and his sisters had already taken on a familiar pattern which lasted until death: a combination of the garden, the children, the affairs of Birmingham and Odiham, alternate hopes and fears aroused by the war, spiced with tart comments upon the inadequacies of officials, Conservative leaders and the 'Squiffery' of the government.[175] Austen Chamberlain's letters tended swiftly to adopt precisely the same format and content.

Like all the family, gardening was Austen Chamberlain's great passion and principal pastime, at least until the sale of Twitt's Ghyll in 1929. Urged by his father to find a hobby to provide some form of necessary distraction from politics, Austen turned to gardening – although uncharacteristically he did not share the passion of his father or Neville for orchids.[176] Even when most burdened with official worries, the letters tended often to begin with references to gardening and the vagaries of the weather to which such an occupation made him particularly sensitive. 'You will think that I am foolish to garden so much but it rests the mind', he wrote during one personal crisis in preparation for the 1919 Budget.[177] Four months later he purchased

[173] H. Montgomery Hyde, *Baldwin: The Unexpected Prime Minister*, (1973), 47, 74; G.M. Young, *Stanley Baldwin*, (1952), 26–7.

[174] A. Chamberlain to Ida, 28 February 1931, AC5/1/532.

[175] D. Dilks, *Neville Chamberlain* , 165.

[176] Avon, *Facing the Dictators*, 130.

[177] A. Chamberlain to Ida, 18 April 1919, AC5/1/125.

Twitt's Ghyll; 'a pretty place and with a lovely view and just what Ivy has always dreamed of', but initially a source of grave anxiety that the cost would prove ruinous, requiring as it did the sale of his Worcester china and the glass.[178] At this house in Sussex, for the next decade Chamberlain enjoyed one of the happiest periods of his life and fulfilled his ambition of thirty years to build an alpine rock garden. Thereafter he remained an authority on the subject and was known to take time off from Geneva to embark on plant-finding trips.[179] In 1929 the need to sell Twitt's Ghyll for financial reasons was a heart-rending decision and the subject of gardening drops quite suddenly from the letters. Thereafter, although he apparently continued to have an alpine cold frame on the roof of Rutland Gate and retained his love of gardens and flowers, the subject does not really reappear until the last months of Chamberlain's life as he enthusiastically planned out a single small bed at his new house in Egerton Terrace.

A more consistent theme throughout the entire correspondence is Chamberlain's near obsessive concern with his own, and his family's, health. In part, this was understandable as the beginning of the diary letters coincided with the premature birth of his second son whose health and sight were to be a source of grave concern throughout the rest of his life. On the other hand, the morbid and usually alarmist diagnoses of often weird and wonderful ailments in these letters often takes on absurd proportions. While his wife's illnesses provide considerable material for anxious correspondence, his own state of health was always a good barometer of the political and official pressure upon a man who lacked the robust constitution of his father or half-brother.[180] Little wonder that he was to lament so often that 'we have more than our share of medical troubles' or to ask himself 'How is Ivy ever to have peace or I to make my income fit my expenditure?'[181] Yet as his rather more sceptical half-brother complained, 'altogether he and his family are so much in the doctor's hands that I feel inclined to prescribe the late Mrs Hall's gout remedy, "Just stamp the beggerin' thing out".'[182]

From the political content of the diary letters, Austen Chamberlain emerges as an increasingly conservative figure, mistrustful of the unpredictability of the new mass democracy and the rising spirit of class

---

[178] A. Chamberlain to Ida, 23 August and 6 December 1919, AC5/1/136, 144.

[179] 'My Cottage Garden', *Down the Years*, 292–306. Reprint of 1932 article in *The Countryman*. Petrie, *Life and Letters* II, 146–7. Also *The Garden: Journal of the Royal Horticultural Society*, 117.1 (January 1992), 37–9.

[180] A. Chamberlain to Hilda, 15 May 1924 and 12 March 1933, AC5/1/318, 611.

[181] A. Chamberlain to Ida, 7 October 1921; to Hilda, 25 April 1926, AC5/1/216, 380.

[182] N. Chamberlain to Hilda, 28 May 1916, NC18/1/63; Hilda to N. Chamberlain 26 January 1917, NC18/2/52.

consciousness. In many ways, his response to these new challenges is a dramatic proof of Cowling's proposition about the 'impact of Labour' after 1918.[183] Although 'by nature a born Conservative',[184] it is often on the basis of his desire to preserve the existing fabric of the old order against the threat of socialism that he is so unfavourably compared with the 'impetuous constructive radical' mind and vision of his father. When measured against such a benchmark he is seen as a more conservative, less dynamic and less innovative politician. By implication, he is also portrayed as a lesser man.[185] Yet what such a perspective often tends to ignore is that the parliamentary career of Joseph and Austen Chamberlain spanned a period of 60 years during which new challenges emerged to demand new policy responses. Chamberlain was all too keenly aware of this himself when he wrote that 'A man who enters politics young must be either extraordinarily gifted with foresight or singularly incapable of profiting by experience, if he does not find it necessary to modify and largely to recast his views in the course of his life'.[186] In such circumstances he believed that 'the only consistency which accords with political sagacity is consistency not of means & methods but of purpose'.[187]

For the naturally more conservative Austen, the seismic impact of the Great War upon British society and the electorate had transformed the entire political landscape – and largely for the worse. Like Lord Hugh Cecil he was remarkably swift in acknowledging that 'our old landmarks are submerged and it is not easy to find a resting place for the soles of one's feet'.[188] From 1917 onwards he recognised that just as the 'deluge' had swept away most of the great issues of Edwardian party controversy, the problem confronting politicians after the war would be the need to fill this unstable vacuum with new landmarks to impart meaning to electoral choice and passion to partisan devotion. 'What shall we inscribe on our standard?' he asked his half-brother in 1917, 'How and for what seek to rally Unionist and conservative ... forces after the war for the problems which then confront us?'[189] In particular, Chamberlain's focused on the need to combat 'what its exponents called a "class consciousness", but what [he] should call a

[183] M. Cowling, *The Impact of Labour 1920–1924 : The Beginning of Modern British Politics* (Cambridge 1971)

[184] Hilda Memoir, BC5/10/1 fol.6.

[185] L.S. Amery, *My Political Life*, II, 202; D. Dutton, *Austen Chamberlain*, 334; J. Grigg, *Lloyd George: The People's Champion*, 59; R. Jenkins, *Baldwin*, 170.

[186] A. Chamberlain to Lord Farrar, 9 November 1926, AC24/8/22.

[187] A. Chamberlain to Churchill, 20 October 1930, M. Gilbert, *Winston S. Churchill*, V. Companion 2, 201.

[188] A. Chamberlain to Ida, 20 March 1918, AC5/1/66.

[189] A. Chamberlain to N. Chamberlain, 24 September 1917, NC1/27/12.

class prejudice, which is something new in our political life'.[190] Two days before the Armistice, Chamberlain was anxiously anticipating a future 'full of difficulty and danger, strikes, discontents and much revolutionary feeling'.[191] Such logic led him ineluctably to the conclusion that these new circumstances demanded the perpetuation of the wartime coalition as the only sure bastion against the burgeoning forces of socialism. Upon such a foundation, he fervently believed in the necessity for a fundamental realignment of the constitutional right as the only effective means of containing the impact of Labour. It was to be a personally disastrous decision, but being the man he was he could do no other. These diary letters begin on the day that Lloyd George became head of the new wartime coalition. They end in the shadow of another and even greater war. As a result they embrace the two great themes of British politics in an age of profound domestic and international uncertainty. They provide a detailed and remarkable insight into a period that began with the impact of Labour and ended with the impact of Hitler.

[190] A. Chamberlain at the Coalitionist dinner, 30 November 1922, Petrie, *Life and Letters*, II, 210.
[191] A. Chamberlain to Ida, 9 November 1918, AC5/1/112.

I

'TIME'S STRANGE REVENGES'

Coalition and the India Office, November 1916 – July 1917

Like most Conservatives, by the spring of 1915 Chamberlain was gravely concerned by the Asquith government's conduct of the war. He was also convinced that the situation demanded a radical response. During the May 1915 crisis he played a significant role both in stiffening Law's resolve to join a coalition and in converting those like Carson and Cecil who doubted the wisdom of such a course: a position he defended with the argument that 'the responsibility of refusing is even greater than that of accepting, and in fact we have no choice'.[1] In the ministerial reshuffle which followed, he lobbied strenuously on behalf of Milner and was prepared to 'make any personal sacrifice ... to secure his inclusion'. Characteristically, however, Chamberlain took no part in the manoeuvring for office personally and declared himself content to 'go anywhere where I can be useful'.[2] In the event, Milner was excluded and Chamberlain received the India Office. Even with the benefit of a close relationship with the experienced Viceroy, Lord Hardinge, the burdens of this new department soon proved formidable. Chamberlain had no knowledge of India and its problems beyond his brief chairmanship of a Commission on Indian Finance two years before. Moreover, by 1915 India was deeply involved in the Imperial war effort and Chamberlain inherited a campaign in Mesopotamia with the realization that formal constitutional control from London would inevitably be much diluted during wartime. In his first letter to the Viceroy he had thus urged 'a rigorous concentration of effort on the essential points of the struggle' because there was 'always a danger that the General on the spot will see his own needs and opportunities so strongly that they will not take their proper place in the perspective of the whole scheme of the war'.[3] Unfortunately this proved to be an all too prescient apprehension.

When Chamberlain became Secretary of State the British force was on the point of capturing Amara. Under pressure from General Nixon and Hardinge Chamberlain reluctantly acquiesced in an advance upon Kut-el-Amara. Having seized this objective on 29 September, further pressure from the same quarter urged an advance on Baghdad: a strategy decisively reinforced by the Cabinet's desire to obtain 'a great success, such as we have not yet achieved in any quarter' at a crucial stage of the war in the Near East.[4] In early November 1915 the Prime Minister had spoken in moving terms of the need 'generally to maintain the authority of our flag in the East'. Three weeks later the British force suffered a crucial reverse at Ctesiphon only

[1] A. Chamberlain to Law, 17 May 1915, Law MSS 37/2/37.
[2] A. Chamberlain to Law, 21 May 1915, Law MSS 50/3/26.
[3] A. Chamberlain to Hardinge, 27 May 1915, AC 62/1.
[4] A. Chamberlain to Hardinge, 8 October 1915, AC 46/7/11.

20 miles from Baghdad and retreated to Kut by 3 December. On 29 April 1916 General Townshend's surrender of his starving garrison of 3000 British and 6000 Indian troops was nothing less than a disaster which severely damaged British prestige in India and the Near East and briefly appeared to threaten the government in Parliament.[5]

During this period Chamberlain was clearly under immense strain. From October 1915 onwards he despatched a flood of anxious telegrams and private letters to the unshakeably complacent Viceroy expressing his concern at reports of inadequate transport and medical arrangements for the wounded. Throughout he pleaded with Hardinge 'not to be content with easy assurances' and warned prophetically that 'we shall have no defence if all that is possible is not done'.[6] *Yet as criticism of the expedition gathered its political momentum, Chamberlain's worst forebodings were increasingly confirmed. It was perhaps a measure of this stress that Chamberlain did not leave London at all from his appointment in May 1915 until February 1916, when total exhaustion compelled him to take a four day holiday.*

These burdens and anxieties were exacerbated by his appointment as chairman of the newly established Man-Power Distribution Board on 22 August 1916. Chamberlain had been a supporter of conscription since May 1915. As a member of the inconclusive War Policy Cabinet Committee which examined the question in August 1915 he had also signed the more assertive supplementary report calling for compulsion.[7] *From his new position of direct responsibility, however, Chamberlain confronted insurmountable difficulties. Without executive power, the Board swiftly attracted the hostility of both the unions and major labour-employing departments which were rarely prepared to accept its decisions. Utterly powerless and isolated, the experiment soon fell victim to the chronic compartmentalisation of decision-making which so debilitated the war effort under Asquith.*[8] *Combined with his own departmental worries, the burden and the prolonged strain finally proved too much. In October, Chamberlain's health broke down altogether and he was ordered to take a fortnight's rest. As the government crisis developed during early December 1916, Chamberlain had returned to work but was still evidently exhausted and in the lowest of spirits.*[9]

Although Chamberlain's contribution to the outcome of the December 1916 crisis was by no means crucial, he did play a significant role in two respects. First, he was prominent in shaping the Unionist position at the meeting at Law's house on 3 December. As a result, it was agreed to stand aloof from an essentially Liberal

[5] A. Chamberlain to Ivy, 28 April 1916, AC 6/1/204.

[6] A. Chamberlain to Hardinge, 3 December 1915, cited D. Goold, 'Lord Hardinge and the Mesopotamia Expedition and Inquiry, 1914–1917', *Historical Journal*, 19.4 (1976), 940.

[7] Hankey Diary, 22 September 1915; Curzon to Churchill, 30 November 1915, M. Gilbert, *Winston S. Churchill*, III. Companion 2, 1183, 1297.

[8] K. Grieves, *The Politics of Manpower, 1914–18*, (Manchester, 1988), 41–60.

[9] See N. Chamberlain to Hilda, 22 October and to Ida 12 November 1916, NC 18/1/85,88.

quarrel in order to enable a stable government to emerge while avoiding the impracticable prospect of a Conservative administration. Secondly, along with Curzon and Cecil, he was one of the 'three C's' who met the Prime Minister two days later and so damagingly declined to serve under Asquith in the event of resignation by both Law and Lloyd George.[10] *Yet, as his letters to his sisters suggest, the creation of a Lloyd George Coalition was an outcome which aroused in him the most profound ambivalence: mixed feelings which reflected his very different perceptions of the two main protagonists. On one hand, he had a high personal regard for Asquith as 'a gentleman in the fullest sense of the word, very pleasant to work with, very loyal to his colleagues, and with a great equanimity in good and evil fortune which is in itself a considerable asset in times like these'. He also recognized that Asquith 'lacks the power to drive' and that in the conduct of policy he was far too inclined to wait upon events. In the starkest possible contrast, Lloyd George was undoubtedly a 'man of great energy and great resolution with quite extraordinary powers of gathering round him men of capacity'. For all that, however, Chamberlain disliked him personally and trusted neither his judgement nor his methods.*[11]

In this context, the charge that 'throughout the crisis he did not seem to know quite what he wanted'[12] *would appear to be unduly harsh and simplistic. Closer to the truth was that Chamberlain was all too clearly aware that all personal and party considerations needed to be subordinated to the ultimate goal of victory. His problem in December 1916 was quite simply that he loathed the self-evident means to achieve this end. Whatever Asquith's moral superiority, he had to go because Chamberlain shared the widespread conviction that Lloyd George could win the war and Asquith patently could not. The subordination of personal and party goals to this greater national need had guided him consistently through the crises of August 1914 and May 1915. In December 1916 his retention of the India Office without a seat in Cabinet was dictated by the same motivations – albeit a position he approached with little relish given a new leader for whom he felt little personal trust or respect. Indeed, the only real consolation Chamberlain derived from his own uncongenial position after December 1916 was the knowledge that Lloyd George had been compelled reluctantly to accept Curzon and Milner into the five man War Cabinet: a malicious satisfaction enhanced by his own role in the appointment of his half-brother Neville as Director-General of National Service. For the rest, however, he was engulfed by a physical and mental exhaustion so profound that his family were relieved that he had not obtained a more active post.*[13] *As he told the Viceroy, 'I should have been sorry to leave unfinished work in which I have been*

---

[10] For his contemporary account of the crisis and his role see A. Chamberlain to Lord Chelmsford, 8 December 1916, AC 15/3/8. Reprinted in A. Chamberlain, *Down the Years*, 115–128.

[11] *Ibid*, 109–10,116. Chamberlain gave vent to some of that suspicion when consulted by Asquith on Lloyd George's appointment to the War Office in June 1916. See C. Petrie, *The Life and Letters*, II, 50–53.

[12] D. Dutton, *Austen Chamberlain*, 134.

[13] N. Chamberlain to Ida, 9 December 1916, NC 18/1/92.

deeply interested. But I should have been a happier man if I could have regained my freedom'.[14] *To add to his anguish, on 12 January 1917 Chamberlain's son Lawrence was born prematurely. For the next two weeks, while his life hung in the balance, a distraught Chamberlain confessed 'there is only one subject of which I can think'. As he wrote in a diary he kept at the time, 'we have had a fortnight of great heart-rending anxiety. More than once it seemed that the end had come, but thank God! when the doctors had given him up, he took a turn for the better & has been mending. When first weighed he was only 3lbs 12ozs'.*[15]

AC5/1/1   11 November 1916
                                                    9 Egerton Place

My dear Hilda,

. . .

I am much better & refused to go to the office today, so as to have a little time to look after my own affairs. I have got a Man Power report off my chest & everyone disagrees with it – a few because they know something of the problem & the scope of our reference & most because they know nothing of either the one or the other. But I'd sell my job for 6d. to the first comer if he were fool enough to take it.

Well, well, sufficient to the day! I dare say we shall be out of office soon. Carson[16] will get us out if he can, & when the Ll.G.,[17] Carson, Churchill[18] ministry is formed I shall feel justified in going on long

---

[14] Postscript to A. Chamberlain to Lord Chelmsford, 8 December 1916, AC 15/3/8.

[15] A. Chamberlain to Hilda, 13 and 20 January 1917, AC5/1/7–8; notes copied from an old diary 28 January 1917, AC12/37.

[16] Edward Carson (1854–1935) Unionist MP for Dublin University 1892–1918 and Belfast (Duncairn) 1918–1921. Leader of Irish Unionist Party 1910–21. Irish Solicitor-General 1892; Solicitor-General 1900–1905; Attorney-General 1915; 1st Lord of Admiralty 1916–17; Minister without Portfolio 1917–18. Knighted 1900. Created judicial life peer 1921.

[17] David Lloyd George (1863–1945) Liberal MP Caernarvon Boroughs 1890–1945. President, Board of Trade 1906–1908; Chancellor of Exchequer 1908–15; Minister of Munitions 1915–16, Secretary for War 1916; Prime Minister 1916–22. Created Earl Lloyd-George of Dwfor 1945.

[18] Winston Leonard Spencer Churchill (1874–1965) Conservative MP for Oldham 1900–1904, as a Liberal 1904–1906. Liberal MP for Manchester NW 1906–1908, Dundee 1908–1922. Conservative MP for Epping 1924–45 and Woodford 1945–64. Under-Secretary for the Colonies 1905–1908; President, Board of Trade 1908–1910; Home Secretary 1910–11; 1st Lord of Admiralty 1911–15 and 1939–40; Chancellor Duchy of Lancaster May-November 1915; Minister of Munitions 1917–1919; Secretary for War and Air 1919–21; Colonial Secretary 1921–22; Chancellor of Exchequer 1924–29; Prime Minister 1940–45 and 1951–55. Minister of Defence 1940–45 and 1951–52. Created K.G. 1953.

leave & they may dismiss poor old Dr Ethe but I'm d—d if I will to please any of them.

AC5/1/3

14 December 1916
9 Egerton Place

My dear Hilda,

. . .

Well, you are happy and relieved & Neville[19] (to whom I sent the whole story) being as he says 'only the man in the street', is happy & relieved & Ida[20] & Beatrice[21] are happy and relieved, & I hope for the best! But I take no pleasure in a change which gives me a chief whom I profoundly distrust – no doubt a man of great energy but quite untrustworthy; who doesn't run crooked because he wants to but because he doesn't know how to run straight; who has tired out the patience of every man who has worked with him & most of those who haven't worked with him; who let his Unionist colleagues down about conscription at the critical moment & then took up the question again when he thought the audience were more favourable & the limelight more concentrated on himself: who allows references to appear in the papers to a note by himself on Roumania which *none* of his colleagues had seen, it having been shown only to the C.I.G.S. who would have none of it: who – but why continue?

I rejoice with you in the admission of Lord Milner.[22] Now as formerly I did my best to secure it – & Ll.G didn't mean it and didn't want it! Nor did he want anyone with an independent mind on his War Comtee but thank Heaven! he has had to do some things which he did not want.

[19] (Arthur) Neville Chamberlain (1869–1940) Conservative MP for Birmingham Lady-wood 1918–29, Edgbaston 1929–40. Director-General of National Service 1916–1917; Postmaster-General 1922–23; Minister of Health 1923, 1924–29, 1931; Chancellor of the Exchequer 1923, 1931–37; Prime Minster 1937–40; Lord President 1940.

[20] (Florence) Ida Chamberlain (1870–1942) Fourth child of Joseph Chamberlain and the second by his second wife Florence Kenrick. Active voluntary worker and District and County Councillor. Sister of Neville and half-sister to Austen.

[21] Beatrice Chamberlain (1862–1918) Eldest child of Joseph Chamberlain and his first wife Harriet Kenrick. Died during the influenza epidemic of 1918. Sister to Austen and half-sister to Neville.

[22] Alfred Milner (1854–1925) High Commissioner for South Africa 1897–1905; member of War Cabinet 1916–1918; Secretary for War 1918–19; Colonial Secretary 1919–21. Created K.C.B. 1895, K.G. 1921, Baron 1901, Viscount 1902. Distinguished Civil and public servant. Imperialist and focus of the Kindergarten of young admirers in South Africa.

You will see that I am sick of being told how beautiful the new world is and how pleased I must be to live in it. Still I hope it will be a better world and for the time at least I will twang my harp in my own little corner.

. . .

What a letter! all bad spirits and bad temper! But then my blessed servants (changed I know not how many times) have completely muddled my cellar & cellar book . . .

AC5/1/4   21 December 1916
                                                   9 Egerton Place

My dear Hilda,

'Well, what do you think of it all?' as Lord Rosebery[23] said on a famous occasion. Are you pleased or displeased, more full of regrets for the good work that is interrupted or of hope for the new & greater work undertaken? are you more proud that Neville was so unanimously chosen by the War Cabinet [as Director-General of National Service] & so urgently pressed to take this post in the very forefront of our struggle for national existence or more anxious lest the extraordinary difficulties of the task should prove too much even for him?

For myself all these feelings chase each other through my mind. I have had two bad nights caused by my anxiety for Neville – I am like a hen with one chick and more anxious about him than I have ever been about myself, for I think I care more about his success than about any success or failure of my own.

But if this gigantic task can be discharged by any one, I firmly believe that Neville is the man. The post was offered to Montagu,[24] who had one qualification which N. has not viz. previous experience and familiarity with at least a part of the problem and the methods of Govt administration & the organisation of Govt offices. It was declined by him – on reflection I think rightly, & so does the Prime Minister because he felt he was unequal to its discharge.

---

[23] Archibald Philip Primrose (1847–1929) Succeeded father as 5th Earl of Rosebery 1868. Under-Secretary, Home Office 1881–83; First Commissioner of Works 1884; Foreign Secretary 1886 and 1892–94; Prime Minister 1894–95. Resigned Liberal leadership 1896. Chairman L.C.C. 1889, 1892.
[24] Edwin Samuel Montagu (1879–1924) Liberal MP for Cambridgeshire 1906–1922. PUS for India 1910–1914; Financial Secretary to Treasury 1914–February 1915 and May 1915–July 1916; Chancellor of Duchy of Lancaster February-May 1915 and January-July 1916; Minister of Munitions 1916; Secretary for India 1917–22.

In prevision of this possibility I had written to Curzon[25] – 'If M. refuses, consider my brother'. When M refused, Curzon or Milner put forward N's name and everyone *jumped* at it. The Labour men[26] were warm in support & everyone who has spoken to me since has said the same thing: 'What a task! but if anyone can do it, it is your brother!'

What a tribute to the position which N has made for himself! He has had an excellent Press & starts with everyone's good will. God prosper him! But talk of a mother bringing out her eldest daughter at a first ball, talk of a father listening to the maiden speech of his son in the House of Commons, talk of – what you will! You won't find such an anxious fussy proud old soul as I am!

How I want to become Neville's Under Sec. I could really help him there but it would make him ridiculous & cannot be thought of. I will do what I can from outside.

. . .

I cannot help thinking that Germany's 'offer' tho' not the end is at last the beginning of the end.

AC5/1/5

24 December 1916
India Office

My dear Hilda,

. . .

No, the idea of the appointment did not originate with Lloyd George. That some such measure was necessary was a conclusion independently submitted to the old War Comtee by the Man Power Board first, & then in quick succession by Montagu & the military members of the Army Council.

The War Comtee accepted 'in principle' & appointed Montagu, Long[27] & myself with departmental officials to draw up a Bill and a

---

[25] George Nathaniel Curzon (1859–1925) Conservative MP for Southport 1886–98; Viceroy of India 1898–1905; Lord Privy Seal 1915–16; Lord President 1916–19 and 1924–25; Foreign Secretary 1919–24; Conservative Leader in Lords 1916–24. Created Baron 1898, Earl 1911, Marquess 1921.

[26] Arthur Henderson (1863–1935) and John Hodge (1855–1937) The latter Labour MP for SE Lancashire 1906–23. Minister of Labour 1916–1917; Minister of Pensions 1917–1919.

[27] Walter Hume Long (1854–1924) Conservative MP for Wilts (North) 1880–85, Wilts (Devizes) 1885–92, Liverpool (West Derby) 1893–1900, Bristol South 1900–1906, County Dublin South 1906–1910, Strand 1910–18, St George's Westminster 1918–21. Parliamentary Secretary to Local Government Board 1886–1892. President, Board of Agriculture 1895–1900; President, Local Government Board 1900–1905 and 1915–16; Chief Secretary for Ireland March–December 1905; Colonial Secretary 1916–1919; 1st Lord of Admiralty 1919–21. Created Viscount 1921.

scheme. We had two meetings that day & the next (Thursday & Friday) and I think my views as to the character of the organisation were generally accepted. Then we adjourned till Monday, leaving the officials to draft a bill & a scheme. Montagu whispering to me 'There is only one man who can do this job – yourself".

By Monday the Cabinet crisis was upon us & Long & I could go no further.

The War Cabinet took the question up at an early sitting while the P.M. was ill. Montagu was then suggested for the post & I urged that he should at least be called into consultation the next time we discussed the question, with which we could not make great progress whilst the P.M. was absent.

Having thereafter to write to both Curzon & Milner, I said: If Montagu refuses, consider Neville etc.

So when Montagu attended the next meeting & said (I think rightly) that is was not a job which he *could* do, Curzon suggested Neville, everyone jumped at it – the rest you know.

AC5/1/9   3 February 1917
                                          9 Egerton Place

My dear Hilda,

. . .

Yes, I agree with you: Germany's desperate measures are the outcome & sign of her desperate state, but has President Wilson any 'guts'? Hum! Wait & see!

AC5/1/12   17 February 1917
                                         9 Egerton Place

My dear Hilda,

. . .

. . . We shall all have to tighten our belts, I expect, still further, but I do feel convinced that this new submarine campaign[28] is the result and measure of Germany's suffering & brings us nearer – if still not very near – to the end. I am pretty well satisfied by what I hear of

[28] From February 1917 the Germans hoped to force Britain to sue for peace within six months through the use of unrestricted submarine warfare. In January 1917, the last month of the restricted campaign, Britain lost 49 ships (35 to submarines). In February this rose to 105 British ships (86 to U-Boats) soaring to 169 British vessels (all but 14 to submarines) in April, the worst single month.

President Wilson now and by the effect of Germany's new measures on our interests in the USA but he is not & never will be an heroic figure.

AC5/1/13   23 February 1917
                                                                9 Egerton Place

My dear Ida,

    . . .

Sunday . . .

    . . . What does Odiham think of Lloyd George's last speech?[29] That is real business I think.

    The situation is grave enough to warrant extreme steps & indeed to require them. I am convinced that we are nearing the end – still I fix no date for it. The Loan has been an amazing success.

AC5/1/14   25 February 1917
                                                                9 Egerton Place

My dear Ida,

    . . .

Monday. The [first War] Loan is an even more marvellous success than I thought. You will see the figures in the papers. They exceed Bonar Law's[30] wildest dreams. And meanwhile the Germans are retreating under Gough's[31] pressure on the Ancre and Maude[32] has retaken

[29] On 23 February Lloyd George told the Commons that it was essential to reduce imports and increase domestic food production as food stocks were 'alarmingly low'. This was intended to terrify Parliament and the country in order to pave the way for the contentious Corn Production Bill.

[30] Andrew Bonar Law (1858–1923) Conservative MP for Glasgow Blackfriars 1900–1906; Camberwell 1906–10, Bootle 1911–18, Glasgow Central 1918–23. Parliamentary Secretary to Board of Trade 1902–1905; Colonial Secretary 1915–16; Chancellor of Exchequer 1916–19; member of War Cabinet 1916–19; Lord Privy Seal 1919–21; Prime Minister October 1922–May 1923. Leader of Conservative Party 1911–21 and 1922–23.

[31] Lt-General Sir Hubert de la Poer Gough (1870–1963) Served South Africa 1899–1902. Commanded 1st Army Corps 1916 and 5th Army 1916–18. Chief figure in the Curragh incident 1914 when some officers threatened resignation rather than impose Home Rule on Ulster. The War subsequently changed his opinions so much that he declined to stand as a Carsonite in an Ulster constituency in 1918 but ran as an Asquithian in a 1921 by-election.

[32] Lt-General Sir (Frederick) Stanley Maude (1864–1917) Military career from 1884. Served Sudan and South Africa 1899–1901. Private Secretary to Secretary of State for War 1905. Chief of General Staff 5th Division, 1912–14. Commander 33rd Division 1915, 13th Division; Tigris Army Corp 1916. C-in-C Mesopotamia 1916.

Kut! But I wish they sank rather fewer vessels (always excepting Dutch vessels which rely on *their* guarantees) and that they would not bombard Broadstairs. A shell fell unpleasantly close to [Joe's] school this time and wrecked a cottage.

Confronted by an Indian budgetary crisis created by the increasing demands of war expenditure, in March 1917 the Government of India were authorized to increase the tariff on imported cotton goods from 3.5 per cent to 7.5 per cent without also raising the countervailing excise on Indian textiles. While this eased India's fiscal problems, assisted Bombay's cotton mills and mollified nationalist feeling, the damagingly protectionist effects of this measure created a political storm in Manchester, the supplier of 90 per cent of India's cotton imports in 1913–14. The Manchester Guardian *thus busied itself 'sending the Fiery Cross around Lancashire'.[33] A Lancashire trade deputation also lobbied the minister to change his mind. Chamberlain, however, was determined to stand firm and dismissed them with a lecture on their apparent ignorance of the changing conditions in India. Indeed, as he told the Viceroy, he felt the attitude of Lancashire 'both selfish and shortsighted, and I am moved to disgust when they profess that they are actuated by concern for the poor Indian peasant'.[34] Despite such ministerial confidence and determination there appeared to be some danger that the issue would actually undermine government stability. In the event, however, the government was never in real danger during the debate on 14 March and the vote was carried with a large majority.[35]*

By this stage, Chamberlain's confidence and understanding of Indian affairs had developed considerably. Confidence also engendered a desire to demonstrate to moderate Indian opinion that he sympathized with their legitimate aspirations: a goal reflected in his approach towards the issue of India's place in the councils of Empire and the growth of her self-governing institutions. The demand for direct Indian representation at Imperial Conferences on terms similar to those of the Dominions first emerged in July 1915 and was repeated by the new Viceroy, Lord Chelmsford, the following year. Although cautiously supportive of the idea given the Indian war effort, Chamberlain recognized that Dominion opposition would be intimately related to the even more vexed issue of Indian immigration and treatment in the Dominions. Despite Canadian and Australian opposition and the non-committal response from South Africa and New Zealand, Chamberlain's view prevailed. Indian delegates were thus invited to the Imperial War Conference and, on 13 April 1917, the Conference formally resolved that India should in future become a regular member.

[33] Lord Bryce to C.P. Scott, 11 March 1917, cited J. Turner, *British Politics and the Great War: Coalition and Conflict 1915–1918* (New Haven and London 1992), 189.

[34] C. Petrie, *Life and Letters*, II, 77–78.

[35] J. Turner, *British Politics and the Great War*, 188–90. For these events generally see C. Dewey 'The End of the Imperialism of Free Trade: The Eclipse of the Lancashire Lobby and the concession of Fiscal Autonomy to India', in C. Dewey & A.G. Hopkins (eds), *The Imperial Impact: Studies in the Economic History of India and Africa*, (1978).

Other questions concerning the treatment of Indians in the Dominions, however, remained unresolved and India's constitutional advance had to wait until Montagu succeeded Chamberlain at the India Office.[36]

AC5/1/16

6 March 1917
9 Egerton Place

My dear Hilda,

. . .

You will have seen today's excellent article in the Times about the Indian cotton duties. I have a rare hornets nest about my ears from Lancashire, the M. Guardian and I suspect all the other Liberal papers of that kidney desiring to make all the trouble they *dare*. I should like to tell the Manchester crowd exactly what I think of them, but this is a luxury of free speech which in these days of general restrictions I fear I must not permit myself.

. . .

Thursday night ... My hornets are buzzing and will sting if they can. But I will resign sooner than give way.

AC5/1/17

17 March 1917
9 Egerton Place

My dear Hilda,

. . . I was in the thick of the row about the cotton duties. All is well that ends well, & after talk of the Govt being defeated & long & grave faces from all the whips we got a very satisfactory majority & are naturally all the better thought of for having stuck to our guns. Indeed to have run away would have been fatal & I am happy to say the Govt was as happy on that point as I was myself ...

But what are the cotton duties to the capture of Bagdad or the revolution in Russia.

[36] See J. Turner, *Lloyd George's Secretariat*, (Cambridge, 1980), 128–136.

AC5/1/18   24 March 1917
                                                    9 Egerton Place

My dear Hilda,

... I begin to feel that I know something of India, but the more I know the more I see there is to learn and the more impressed I am by the immense difficulties of our task. You hear of the unchanging East, but what strikes me is the rate at which India is moving – at least on the surface where the current for the last ten or fifteen years has gone with ever increasing velocity. No doubt that below are deep still waters of ignorance, custom, prejudice & conservatism, but this only makes the problem more difficult, for how is one to meet the legitimate (as far as they are legitimate) aspirations & ambitions of the small but increasingly united & increasingly influential educated class who look to the institutions of Western democracy for their model ... when in fact the materials for a democracy do not exist.

...

Our Imperial War Cabinet sittings have been extraordinarily interesting. I am very much impressed by General Smuts[37] – a man of great ability & with a knowledge of Europe that I have never known in any other overseas statesman. Incidentally my colleagues from India have been delighted by their reception ... & I make bold to hope that henceforth India will be represented at all Imperial Conferences. So whenever I leave office I shall have to my credit two forward steps in Indian Imperial development; but if you suppose that young India will be grateful you are quite wrong. They would feel themselves traitors to their cause if they stopped to say thank you! They will merely observe that even a Tory couldn't altogether stop their progress.

Lloyd George dined in my house last night! Such are Time's strange revenges.

AC5/1/21   1 April 1917
                                                    9 Egerton Place

My dear Ida,

...

Yes, I am getting a little gratitude for the Cotton Duties ... It will

[37] Jan Christian Smuts (1870–1950) Fought against British in South African War 1899–1902. Commanded British forces against Lettow Vorbeck in German East Africa; represented South Africa at Imperial War Conference; appointed to War Cabinet 1917–1919. Prime Minister of South Africa 1919–24 and 1939–48.

be something gained if I can show 'moderate' Indians that I can & do sympathise with their legitimate aspirations.

AC5/1/22

6 April 1917
Rowfant
Crawley

My dear Hilda,

. . .

As for myself I am dog-tired & don't mean to touch work for three days unless where absolutely necessary. After that I hope to bring a rested mind to bear on the problem of Indian Reforms & on the discordant views of the Viceroy, Hardinge[38] & my Council, & perhaps when I have done that I shall have a mind of my own. Right or wrong I am not usually without an opinion of my own; but with these daily Cabinets & Conferences & with the masses of papers given us to read I have no time to study anything but the most immediately urgent questions since I received the Report of the Committee of Council on Chelmsford's[39] despatch.

I have not admired Pres. Wilson's policy utterances in the past but I must say I thought his last address to Congress admirable ... *Then* there was a very good simple statement of what the US were fighting for ... meanwhile the German retreat has gone faster than was intended by the German High command & both the French & ourselves have had considerable successes.

AC5/1/23

21 April 1917
Rowfant

My dear Ida,

. . .

We have secured India's place at future Conferences but on the subject of the treatment of Indians in the Dominions I now fear that we shall make no progress ... Perhaps we may still accomplish something, but I am not very hopeful. As to the general Indian problem

[38] Sir Charles, Baron Hardinge of Penshurst (1858–1944) Ambassador to Russia 1904–1906; Permanent Under-Secretary, Foreign Affairs 1906–11 and 1916–20; Viceroy of India 1910–16; Ambassador to France 1920–23.

[39] Fredric John Napier Thesiger (1868–1933) Viceroy of India 1916–21; 1st Lord of Admiralty, 1924. Succeeded father as 3rd Baron Chelmsford 1905, created K.C.M.G. 1906, G.S.C.I. 1916 and Viscount Chelmsford 1921.

of government, the more I discuss it with Meston[40] & Sinha[41] the more difficult I find it. "I am groping – we are all groping for a way" said Sinha to me ... and that is the truth – we are all groping. We have put the wine of Western democratic ideas into the old bottles of the East and there is a terrible ferment going on. Things were moving fast before the war, they are moving & will move faster now that all the world is hailing Revolution in Russia, hoping for it in Germany & proclaiming the freedom & independence of peoples.

AC5/1/26   20 May 1917
                                                              9 Egerton Place

My dear Hilda,

. . .

I have had an easier week & at last got off a long letter to the Viceroy explanatory of my views. But yesterday alas! I had a long and it seems to me, rather scared telegram from him asking permission to make a statement as to the 'goal' of Govt in India & as to coming reforms. I am disturbed by the rather panicky feeling betrayed in it & I & all my people think his statement of the goal bad & useless for the purpose of calming agitation for which he wishes to use it, whilst ... I don't think that he has really got to the heart of the problem or found the solution of it. So there's a peckful of worry for me. I am puzzling how to deal with him.

AC5/1/28   30 May 1917
                                                                     Rowfant

My dear Ida,

. . . The Cabinet are unable to deal with my business [on India][42] this week though urgently pressed by me to do so, so it must stand

[40] Sir James, Baron Meston (1865–1943) Indian Civil Servant. Financial Secretary, Government of India 1906–1912. Lt-Governor United Provinces of Agra and Oudh 1912–18, Member of Indian delegation to 1917 Imperial Conference and Imperial War Cabinet with Austen Chamberlain, the Maharajah of Bikanes and Sir S.P. Sinha.

[41] Sir Satyndra Passano Sinha (1864–1928) Barrister London and Calcutta. Advocate-General Bengal 1907–9, 1915–17; first Indian member of Viceroy's Executive Council 1909–10; President of Indian National Congress 1915; member of Indian delegation to Imperial Conference 1917 and Imperial War Cabinet 1917; member of Indian War Cabinet 1918; Under Secretary of State for India January 1919–September 1920. Governor of Bihar and Orissa 1920–21. Created Baron of Raipur 1919.

[42] On 22 May 1917 Chamberlain had circulated papers to the War Cabinet about Indian constitutional reform.

over to next week ... I am doing as little work as possible, not reading over-much, sleeping well & feeding up. Very immoral you may say but my doctor's views for once coincide with my own feelings. 'Anaemic and tired; pulse 10 below your normal which is very low at the best of times & your weight?' 'Ten stones 4' I say proudly. 'Well it isn't enough. You need meat twice a day. Fish lunches aren't good for you!' And so as I was feeling very tired and rather hollow, I am following his advice. . . .

And so with health ... flowers, birds, fish – oh yes! & butterflies & moths ... the day passes into bedtime. Good night! What a blessed thing it is to be idle 23 hours out of the 24!

Although Asquith had appointed the Committees of Inquiry into the Dardanelles and Mesopotamia on 20 July 1916 as a sop to his critics to avert parliamentary defeat, they rapidly turned into a 'damning indictment of the muddle and timidity of his government'.[43] The 132 page Mesopotamia Report – with the Vincent-Bingley findings on medical deficiencies as an appendix – represented such a comprehensive catalogue of administrative and military incompetence, arrogance and miscalculation as inevitably to beg comparison with the Crimea War.[44] The former Viceroy denounced the document as 'unfair and narrow-minded ... a travesty of fact and justice'. Chamberlain not unnaturally considered it 'The saddest and most appalling document that I have ever read'.[45] For his own part, while Chamberlain had been criticized by the Commission, this was largely for 'the substitution of private for official telegrams' to notify the Viceroy of his concerns about the medical arrangements.[46] In unrepentant mood, therefore, he initially resolved to marshall the case for his defence and fight it out. 'I won't pretend I am not suffering under the attacks on me', he wrote to Pike Pease; 'but on my soul I do not reproach myself with my share in what is past, and I do not believe that when the first horror of these revelations is past I shall be condemned'.[47] In the event, however, he was finally induced to resign by the Cabinet's decision to establish a Court of Enquiry which would then itself decide against whom action should be taken: a lack of decisiveness and courage which, he believed, could only severely undermine his authority as a minister at a crucial time.[48] In the Commons debate on 12 July, his resignation and spirited

---

[43] J.M. Bourne, *Britain and the Great War, 1914–1918* (1989), 131.

[44] Cd. 8610 *Report of the Commission Appointed ... to Enquire into the Operations of War in Mesopotamia, Parliamentary Papers* 1917–18 XVI. For the conduct of the Mesopotamia campaign see A.J. Barker, *The Neglected War: Mesopotamia, 1914–1918* (1967); B. Porter 'Britain and the Middle East in the Great War' , in P. Liddle (ed), *Home Fires and Foreign Fields: British Social and Military Experience in the Great War* (1985), 166.

[45] Lord Hardinge, *Old Diplomacy: The Reminiscences of Lord Hardinge of Penshurst*, (1947), 215; A. Chamberlain to Hilda, 7 June 1917, AC5/1/29.

[46] Cd. 8610, *Report*, 101 para 26.

[47] A. Chamberlain to Pike Pease, 29 June 1917, Petrie, *Life and Letters*, II, 86.

[48] A. Chamberlain to Lloyd George, 11 July 1917, Lloyd George MSS F/7/2/6.

defence of his own actions won him widespread respect. As one observer noted, out of a discreditable situation Chamberlain was 'the one man generally considered to have come out of it well'.[49]

AC5/1/29   7 June 1917
                                                       House of Commons

My dear Hilda,

We had a perfect ten days at Rowfant & rejoiced in the fresh air & sunshine, the country, the flowers & the birds. It did me good to get such a holiday – the longest I have had since Oct 1913! There was only one thing to mar it – no two: the boom of the guns in France distinctly audible & seeming to reproach me for standing idle even for a moment & the Report of the Mesopotamia Commission which I received towards the close of my stay & which is the saddest & most appalling document that I have ever read. The worst features are that not only was the expedition ill-found from the first but that high placed & responsible officers deliberately concealed the truth & reported falsely in reply to my enquiries. Hardinge, Duff,[50] Nixon,[51] 2 Medical Directors General & the Principal Medical Officer of the Forces[52] all come in for severe censure & I do not altogether escape blame, nor the Government & other authorities at home, but except in the case of the orders for the advance on Bagdad when I share responsibility (for what is declared to be a bad blunder) with the War Comtee I am blamed only for saying in 'private' telegrams or letters what I ought to have said in public i.e. formal, official despatches. A more fearful breakdown than that of the military organisation in India which we owe to Kitchener[53] has, I should think, never occurred. The whole

[49] Sanders Diary, 20 July 1917, J. Ramsden (ed.) *Real Old Tory Politics: The Political Diaries of Robert Sanders, Lord Bayford, 1910–35*, (1984), 88. For his speech and reaction to it see Petrie, *Life and Letters*, II, 89–93: *House of Commons Debates*, 95 col 2210–2234, 12 July 1917.

[50] General Sir Beauchamp Duff (1855–1918) Military Secretary to C-in-C India 1895–1899, Assistant Military Secretary (India), War Office 1899; served South Africa 1899–1901; Adjutant-General, India 1903–1906; Chief of Staff, India 1906–1909; Military Secretary, India Office 1910. C-in-C of India 1913–1916. A "Kitchener man". Alleged suicide in 1918.

[51] General Sir John Eccles Nixon (1857–1921) Commander Southern Army, India 1912–15 and Northern Army 1915; GOC Mesopotamia Expedition, April 1915–January 1916.

[52] Inspector-General Hathaway (Principal Medical Officer) and Surgeon-General Mac-Neese.

[53] Horatio Herbert Kitchener (1850–1916) Commander Dongola Expeditionary Force 1896 and Khartoum Expedition 1989; Chief of Staff, South Africa 1899–1900; C-in-C, South Africa 1900–1902; India 1902–09; Agent and Consul-General, Egypt 1911–14; Secretary of State for War August 1914–June 1916. Created K.G.M.G. 1894; K.G. 1915; Baron 1898; Viscount 1902 and Earl Kitchener of Khartoum 1914.

story saddens me dreadfully. Beauchamp Duff carries the heaviest load of responsibility but hardly anyone comes well out of it.

AC5/1/31

25 July 1917
Rowfant

[To Ida]

. . .

My handwriting has not recovered from the writing of something over 100 letters in the last week to people of all sorts & conditions who felt moved to write to me on my resignation ... Altogether a remarkable tribute; & what has specially pleased me has been the inducement of feeling that 'you have an instinct for the right courses': 'we always knew you would do the right thing' & so forth, which are all testimonies to character. It is curious that most of the men of Cabinet would say there was no need & indicate some surprise; whilst to the others it is clear I was right. I ask curiously: Would they have known it was right if I had not done it? & I think Robbins[54] of the B[irmingham] D[aily] P[ost] gave the answer, 'No, they hadn't thought it out clearly for themselves, but the moment you did it, this vague unrest crystalised & they believed that this was what they had always seen to be necessary' – like Father's experience with Tariff Reform.

Well, there's an end to my ambition to do big work for India & the Empire in that sphere. I think I was on the right lines; I was beginning to see my way: ... It *was* a sacrifice to give it all up, but it was clearly right & I can swallow down my regrets & enjoy & profit by the holiday which falls to my lot. I have my moments of blue devils, but they pass, & after all they are more due to the effects of long strain than anything else.

I do no gardening here, but I wander about; pick wild flowers, sit in the canvass chair under the trees, read Gibbon, sleep, get very hot, bathe ... and eat. I have always said that I could enjoy an idle life & now is the time to show it. I will have a good rest, & besides, a Minister who has first resigned is always in the way unless he takes himself off for a time.

. . .

... And ... After all, as I said to Hilda, its rather chic to have the Paris Embassy,[55] a Peerage, a special mission to India, a Secretaryship of State & your resignation all in your pocket within a week or ten days!

---

[54] Sir Alfred Farthing Robbins (1856–1931) Journalist, dramatist, author, prominent Freemason. London correspondent of the *Birmingham Daily Post* 1888–1923.

[55] Chamberlain was tempted by the offer of the Paris Embassy in June but was probably persuaded by Neville's view that it would end his career in domestic politics, N. Chamberlain to A. Chamberlain, 28 June 1917, AC35/1/25.

2

'ONE OUGHT TO BE USEFUL WHERE ONE CAN'

Committees and Commissions, August 1917 – April 1918

If Chamberlain's decision to resign in 1917 was a quixotic gesture of 'slightly misdirected principle',[1] it was also wholly consistent with his past conduct and character. As a result, he was undoubtedly gratified by the warm response generated by his instinctive sense of public rectitude when resignation appeared the only honourable course to adopt. Although soon lamenting the loss of 'inside information' he also derived initial solace from the prospect of a much needed rest and a real holiday. After two years in office, the strains were clearly beginning to tell upon him. In this respect at least, resignation can rightly be seen as 'a blessing in disguise'.[2] His withdrawal to recuperate was further assisted by his firm conviction that recently resigned ministers should 'take themselves off for a time' or risk becoming either an encumbrance to their successors or a focus for parliamentary intrigue and discontent. The decision was made still easier by the constant air raids on London at this time. In the autumn of 1917, therefore, Chamberlain decided to move the family from Rowfant – Godfrey Locker-Lampson's Elizabethan home near Crawley – first to Barton St. Mary, and then on to Thornhill House near East Grinstead where, for the next three years, he indulged his passion for gardening to the full.

Although Chamberlain undoubtedly revelled in his new-found freedom, this period out of office was not an idle interlude devoted solely to horticultural delights and leisurely reflections upon the future of post-war politics as his biographers suggest. On the contrary, despite his resignation, he continued to advise the Viceroy and Edwin Montagu, his successor at the India Office and during the summer the Prime Minister discussed sending him to India to investigate conditions and consider post-war developments. In the event, his refusal to accept this commission was perhaps fortunate as Montagu appears to have been playing a double game. In their direct dealings, Montagu was eager to enlist Chamberlain's support for an announcement on Indian constitutional reform at a time when he feared the Cabinet was likely to 'shy at the word "self-government".' When Chamberlain replied that he had read Montagu's memorandum on the subject 'with great interest and practically ... complete agreement', Montagu used this letter to persuade the Cabinet to accept his proposed declaration in favour of the 'progressive realisation of responsible government in India as an integral part of the British Empire'. He then invited his predecessor

---

[1] J. Turner, *British Politics and the Great War*, 216. Petrie also notes many felt it appeared 'a trifle quixotic', *Life and Letters*, II, 93, as does A. Mackintosh, *Echoes of Big Ben*, 79; J. Wedgwood, *Memoirs of a Fighting Life*, 125.
[2] C. Petrie, *Life and Letters*, II, 95.

*to join him on an official visit to India in a 'spirit of confidence and friendship'.
Arguing that the proposals were really Chamberlain's work, Montagu also contended
that such a public display of unity would 'strike imagination' both in London and
India.[3] Yet unknown to Chamberlain, at the same time Montagu privately held his
predecessor particularly culpable for the Mesopotamia disaster and had vigorously
opposed his leadership of such a delegation. 'I do not believe the public would
tolerate for one moment Chamberlain's being allowed to consider the reform of the
system of which he has been a conspicuous exponent', Montagu informed the Prime
Minister in July 1917, 'But be that as it may it cannot be right to send a man
who has shown he is intent on mending the lavatory tap when the house is
on fire'.[4] A month after Chamberlain's resignation Montagu was still insistent
upon this issue.[5] Within two months, however Chamberlain had accepted places on
committees dealing with both the finance and coordination of supplies from the
United States and the potentially thorny question of House of Lords reform.*

*After American entry into the war in April 1917, the Anglo-American relationship
changed appreciably as the USA asserted its position as an 'Associate' belligerent
power: a change in status which ensured that it could no longer be as easily
disregarded as when only the most important of the neutral powers. One manifestation
of this changing relationship was evident in the transformation of the Allied missions
to the United States. During the period of US neutrality, these missions had acted
essentially as poorly-coordinated 'private organizations, with neither help nor
hindrance from the American government'.[6] With American involvement in the war,
however, the Allied missions were compelled to reform their purchasing procedures
and join together in inter-Allied organizations. The principal impetus for this
restructuring came from McAdoo, the ambitious US Treasury Secretary, for whom
such an arrangement offered a defence against the political difficulties in Congress
and elsewhere created by concerns at the scale of loans to the Allies – and particularly
to Britain. The proposed Inter-Allied Council (I-AC), with a suitably distinguished
membership, would thus provide credibility for requests for further assistance while
simultaneously demonstrating to critics that strict control was being maintained on
spending and that such loans were being used exclusively for military supplies. After
some US financial blackmail and minor concession, Britain accepted the proposal
for an Inter-Allied Council for War Purchases and Finance in late August 1917.
In order to coordinate British submissions to this Council, an inter-departmental
Priority Committee – or American Board – was established in Whitehall to
determine the priority for requests from various British departments. The I-AC then
decided upon an order of priority for the Allied requests as a whole. Having done*

[3] Montagu to A. Chamberlain, 7, 15 August and reply 8 August 1917, AC15/5/2, 3, 8.
[4] E. Montagu to Lloyd George, 5 July 1917, Lloyd George MSS F/39/3/21.
[5] E. Montagu to Lloyd George, 11 August 1917, Lloyd George MSS F/39/3/29. In
Liberal circles Montagu also dismissed Chamberlain as 'a rather hide-bound Conservative', C.P. Scott Diary, 9–11 August 1917, T. Wilson (ed.), *The Political Diaries of C.P.
Scott 1911–1928*, (New York, 1970), 298.
[6] K. Burk, *Britain, America and the Sinews of War, 1914–1918*, (1985), 137.

so, these were conveyed to the American government's own Allied Purchasing Commission in Washington for its decisions on the likely terms and execution of these orders. The Allied missions in the USA then negotiated and executed the actual contracts.

In some respects, Chamberlain was an obvious choice for this new machinery. Before Northcliffe's appointment, he had been considered as a candidate for the leadership of the unified Mission in May 1917. As a former Chancellor he possessed the financial experience Northcliffe so manifestly lacked. He also possessed political status and, above all else, since his resignation he was free of other entanglements. He was thus duly appointed to chair the American Committee. In deference to McAdoo's desire for a distinguished statesman and a military man as the two British representatives on the I-AC, Smuts and Buckmaster were appointed along with Chamberlain who, as the third representative, would handle most of the actual work through the inter-departmental American Board: a structure the British Cabinet accepted on 26 September 1917 and on which Chamberlain agreed to serve in mid-October.[7]

Within a week of this acceptance, Chamberlain had also consented to serve on the Conference on Second Chamber Reform; a body intended to report upon its legislative powers, means of resolving differences with the Commons and possible composition. For all its drastic constitutional and political significance, the Parliament Act of 1911 was intended – as it declared in its preamble – to be no more than a temporary adjustment rather than a permanent solution to the House of Lords problem which had developed since the late nineteenth century. Although relegated to the foot of the political agenda by the outbreak of war, the success of the Speaker's Conference on electoral reform suggested that this might also provide a vehicle for the resolution of other pre-war issues.[8] *Moreover, as before the war, the two issues were inextricably linked. Indeed, for many Unionists by 1917 second chamber reform had come to be seen as a potential bulwark against Labour's future legislative excesses. As such it rendered palatable the proposed extension of the franchise: a view encouraged by both Law and Lloyd George and reinforced by the prospect of early reform.*[9]

Although the Bryce Commission commenced its deliberations on 2 October, Chamberlain did not join the Committee of sixteen peers and sixteen MPs until after its sixth meeting on 19 October when he replaced Arthur Clavell Slater, a fellow Unionist who had been appointed to the High Court. Despite his own initial apprehensions about his 'Radical' views on the subject, in both Unionist councils

---

[7] *Ibid.* Chapter 7, 146–151 for a detailed description of these events and the resulting machinery. For Chamberlain's own account of this work see *Down the Years*, 133. For the respect of his officials see Sir Andrew McFadyean, *Recollected in Tranquillity*, (1964), 66.

[8] J.D. Fair, *British Interparty Conferences: A Study of the Procedure of Conciliation in British Politics, 1867–1921*, (Oxford 1980), 183. For the Speaker's Conference of Electoral Reform see Chapter VIII. Also M. Pugh, *Electoral Reform in War and Peace, 1906–18* (1978), 68–86.

[9] D.H. Close, 'The collapse of resistance to democracy: Conservatives, adult suffrage, and the Second Chamber Reform, 1911–1928', *Historical Journal* 20.4 (1977), 894, 909.

and the Committee's deliberations he played an important role. As a thinker, Chamberlain emerged as a conspicuous champion of the case for a more democratic House of Lords – but always within clearly defined parameters. As a result, his 'innate Conservatism' led him to resist vigorously those Conservatives who wished to introduce the referendum as a means of resolving conflicts between the two Chambers. Believing they confronted 'an open attack on Parliamentaryism' from exponents of direct action, Chamberlain confessed to being 'frightened' by an innovation which would undermine representative institutions and so 'play straight into the hands of the most dangerous forces in the country'.[10] Yet despite such strong views, Chamberlain also proved himself relatively open-minded and generally prepared to meet the Liberals halfway. As a result, he played an equally crucial role as a consistent force for moderation and a seeker of compromise[11] on a committee which Bryce commended for its scrupulous avoidance of petty partisanship and 'recriminations over past controversies'.[12] In the event, however, the Report attracted little attention either while the war continued or during the reconstruction after it. Thereafter, although Conservative Party conferences continued to pass resolutions for reform almost annually from 1920–36, they did so in an increasingly academic way without sufficient public interest or political will to overcome the obstacles.[13]

The combined demands of the American Board and the Second Chamber Conference were arduous and occupied a great deal of his time during the ensuing months. Typically, Chamberlain approached the task with a characteristic lack of enthusiasm. First and foremost, he regarded such work essentially as a question of duty during wartime. As such it inevitably involved sacrifice and self-abnegation. He was also tormented increasingly by the fear of being drawn prematurely back into a government led by a Prime Minister whose personality and morality he found deeply suspect. This anxiety was intensified in late October 1917 by the possible offer of the Home Office: a department whose routine administration and responsibility for corporal and capital punishment Chamberlain considered profoundly unattractive. For all his doubts and strictures about the Prime Minister's personality, however, from his letters to his sisters it is clear that Chamberlain also soon accepted that Lloyd George was the only leader capable of winning the war. By the autumn of 1917, he was keen to distance himself from growing Diehard discontent under Lord Salisbury and content to support the government from outside. While avoiding

[10] A. Chamberlain to Selborne, 18 April 1918, AC15/6/16.

[11] See Sanders Diary, 9 and 20 December 1917, *Real Old Tory Politics*, 94; A. Chamberlain to Selborne, 15 March 1918 and reply, 20 March 1918, AC15/6/13–14. See also M. Pugh, *Electoral Reform in War and Peace*, 156.

[12] Cd, 9038, *Conference on the Reform of the Second Chamber: Letter from Vt Bryce to the Prime Minister*, April 1918, *Parliamentary Papers* X 1918. Fair takes issue with Close's assertions about the 'extent of disagreement' and the 'illusory hope of agreement'. Also N.R. McCrillis, 'Taming Democracy? The Conservative Party and House of Lords Reform, 1916–1929', *Parliamentary History*, 12.3 (1993), 259–80.

[13] Close, 'The collapse of resistance to democracy', 910–11; Fair, *British Interparty Conferences*, 156.

premature entanglements, therefore, from an early stage Chamberlain nurtured the expectation that he may one day soon rejoin it.[14]

AC5/1/32   11 September 1917
                                                          Rowfant

My dear Ida,

         . . .
   . . . I think that Montagu is doing well. He invited me to go to India with him, but I declined.

AC5/1/37   n.d. (16 October 1917)
                                                     9 Egerton Place

My dear Hilda,

         . . .
   I wrote to the P.M. accepting his invitation to take the chairmanship of his British Committee & a seat on the International one subject to the condition or request that I should be assured of receiving sufficient information as to the policy of the Government, which I suggested should be done by allowing me to see the Cabinet minutes – my experience of man-power questions having shown me how necessary this was. My letter went by hand last Thursday or Friday. I have so far had no reply which is characteristic, & so I don't yet know how I stand.

AC5/1/40   20 October 1917
                                                     9 Egerton Place

My dear Ida,

         . . .
   . . . I have consented to serve on the Comtee which is considering reform of the House of Lords – a sort of 'Speakers' Conference but with Lord Bryce[15] presiding. I have also agreed at the request of the

---

[14] A. Chamberlain to Salisbury, 19 October 1917, cited Petrie, *Life and Letters*, II, 102–3.

[15] James Bryce (1838–1922) Liberal MP for Tower Hamlets 1880–85, Aberdeen South 1885–1906. Under-Sec Foreign Affairs 1886; Chancellor Duchy of Lancaster 1892–94; President Board of Trade 1894–95; Chief Secretary for Ireland 1905–1907. British Ambassador to USA 1907–1913. G.C.V.O. 1918. Created Viscount 1914.

Government to be one of three delegates (Smuts & Buckmaster[16] being the others) to an Inter-Ally Military Council ... and to be Chairman of a British 'American Board' which will do all the work as far as we are concerned. The duty of the Council will be (under American chairmanship) to examine & recommend or reject all requests to America for assistance in money or materials or food & to certify for the protection of Mr McAdoo (Mak'Ado about nothing I call him) the US Secretary of the Treasury, that the demands are genuine 'military' needs & not an attempt to snatch trade from simple minded Americans, while the 'American Board' (so-called because it will be composed of myself & representatives of ten or 12 British departments) will compile, coordinate, compare, review &, if need be, curtail the British demands. Does the work attract me? No, but it needs doing apparently, for at present we act strictly on the scriptural maxim – let not thy left hand know what the right doeth – and there is much confusion.

As to the House of Lords Conference, I take Clavell Salter's[17] place after it has already held six sittings. This is a disadvantage. Further I am not sure that I know my own mind, & I am afraid of being too Radical for my party or friends, but this Edmund Talbot[18] says is 'impossible – they all seem to have given up the hereditary principle', whilst I hear from another source that on condition that the Second Chamber is made elective, Whittaker[19] & some other Liberal members of the Conference would give it powers in finance which shock Hugh Cecil[20] who champions the Common's rights & privileges. What a world! I know *what* I want to secure. I wish I knew *how* it could be done ...

...

I enquired of a good source (B.L.) how the war had gone since I left

---

[16] Stanley Owen Buckmaster (1861–1934) Liberal MP for Cambridge 1906–10, Keighley 1911–15. Solicitor-General 1913–15, Lord Chancellor 1915–December 1916; member Inter-Allied Commission on Finance and Supplies. Knighted 1913, G.C.V.O. 1930. Created Baron 1915 and Viscount 1933.

[17] Arthur Clavell Salter (1859–1928) Unionist MP for Basingstoke 1906 until appointed High Court Judge in 1917. Knighted 1917.

[18] Edmund Bernard Talbot (1855–1947) Unionist MP for Chichester 1894–1921. Junior Lord of Treasury 1905; Unionist Whip from 1905 until Chief Whip in 1913. Joint Parliamentary Secretary to Treasury May 1915–April 1921; Lord Lieutenant of Ireland 1921–22. Created Viscount Fitzalan of Derwent 1921. K.G. 1925.

[19] Thomas Whittaker (1850–1919) Newspaper proprietor and editor. Liberal MP for Spen Valley 1892–1919. Chairman and member of numerous Parliamentary Select Committees; Chairman of the Royal Commission on Paper. A radical on the House of Lords Conference. Knighted 1906.

[20] Hugh Richard Heathcote Gascoyne-Cecil (1869–1956) Conservative MP for Greenwich 1895–1906, Oxford University 1910–37; Provost of Eton 1937–44. Called Lord Hugh Cecil 1869–1941 when created Baron Quickswood. Member of Mesopotamia Commission 1916.

office. No change. I was told ... It is all a question of grit. We have got the German's beat if we & our allies hold on – Govt less popular than it was? Yes but not so near defeat as it had looked just after Montagu's & Churchill's accession to office. – Some uneasiness in the Ministry itself? Yes, Long & Cecil[21] very uncomfortable. 'They don't like the small War Cabinet which you forced on us' – The PM's idiosyncrasies lessen confidence, make his colleagues uneasy & gradually the malaise filters through to the public? Quite true, but you must take the man as he is. You can't change his nature or his habits. Danger of a conflict between him & the military now probably over but of course he irritates them. On the whole the speaker thinks more highly of Lloyd George than ever because George has now shown not only that he can put great energy & decision into a job but also 'that he can stick to it, which I never thought he could'.

Finally, as regards myself, if a suitable vacancy occurred in the Govt. it would of course be offered to me & one must occur by Xmas – the Home Secretaryship.

'A disagreeable office', I observed & did not pursue the subject.

He was afraid of Montagu: they ought to have made Cecil Sec of State and put Montagu in Cecil's place. I mentioned that I had done what I could to smooth Montagu's path both in the India Office & in the House. I doubted the wisdom of Mrs Besant's[22] release but had defended Montagu's action privately. In other respects I approve his policy so far as known to me. He could not carry Anglo-Indian opinion with him as far as I could have done but he was in a very strong position for saying no to unreasonable demands from the Indians.

[21] (Edward Algernon) Robert Gascoyne-Cecil (1864–1958) Conservative MP for Marylebone E. 1906–10, Hitchin 1911–23. Under-Secretary Foreign Affairs 1915–18; Minister of Blockade 1916–18; Lord Privy Seal 1923–24; Chancellor Duchy of Lancaster (responsible for League of Nations) 1924–27. President of League of Nations Union 1923–45. Called Lord Robert Cecil 1868–1923 when created Viscount Cecil of Chelwood. Nobel Peace Prize 1937.

[22] Annie Besant (1847–1933) Active feminist, socialist and theosophist. Essentially moderate in the Indian Home Rule Campaign but during the war grew impatient with the Indian National Congress and associated with B.G. Tilak to launch the Home Rule League: an action which led to her arrest by the Madras Government in July 1917. Her 94 days internment made her a martyr. After release became President of Congress but soon out-manoeuvred by Gandhi. Though lost influence during 1920s, continued to produce draft constitutions for a self-governing India.

AC5/1/42

23 October 1917
9 Egerton Place

My dear Ida,

. . .

. . . I have joined the Conference on the House of Lords, rather reluctantly, but I found that they wanted me and, if I may say so without causing my sisters to think me conceited, I did not see anyone available in our party who was likely to do it better or – why not be frank & say boldly – likely to do it as well . . .

. . .

PM wished to see me in reference to the 'American Board'. He was very friendly. I had made a most opportune speech last night. I must rejoin the Govt soon, he still thought I had done wrong resigning but it had enormously strengthened my own position. They needed men like me in such critical times.

I had asked that the Cabinet Minutes should be communicated to me for my guidance as Chairman of the Board. Did I mean those which concerned the Board directly or all their minutes? I said I meant all & explained why. Prime Minister said he had consulted Cabinet & they were willing to agree but only because they regarded me as a colleague who would join them at the first opportunity, or as B.L. put it 'We are ready; the only question is whether it commits you too much & that is for you to decide'.

Hum! ha! Why yes, I thought it might be embarrassing. I wasn't out for mischief & had no quarrel with them. Indeed my present mind was that if in 3 or 6 months there were a suitable vacancy, & it were offered to me, I should accept, but my mind might change & I shouldn't like to come under any obligation now; so I would be content with instructions that all minutes *affecting my work* were to be communicated to me if a generously wide interpretation were to be given to that phrase. PM thought that I ought in any case to see the Foreign telegrams. (They are communicated to Asquith[23]). I said I should be glad to do so, & we parted, the P.M. again expressing his strong desire to get me back as soon as possible. The real pull was coming – it was now all a question of nerve, grit and persistency – and so able, experienced & level-headed a person as your brother ought to be in the Govt. Oh Lord! I think he meant what he said. I wish I could feel

[23] Henry Herbert Asquith (1852–1928) Liberal MP for Fife (East) 1886–1918, Paisley 1920–24. Home Secretary 1892–1895; Chancellor of Exchequer 1905–1908; Prime Minister 1908–16; Secretary for War March-August 1914. Leader of Liberal Party 1908–26. Created K.G. and Earl of Oxford and Asquith 1925.

rather more confidence in him than I do. I should then be happier in supporting his Government from the outside or rejoining it if opportunity offers.

Incidentally the P.M. said that a letter I wrote to Montagu & by him read to the Cabinet was the decisive factor in their decision on Indian policy & on the terms of the declaration which Montagu made in their name just before the House rose for the recess.[24]

AC5/1/43

29 October 1917
9 Egerton Place

My dear Hilda,

. . .

. . . I don't want to be Home Secretary & I would like to be in the War Cabinet. But I think that the first is a possibility and the last an impossibility without such a reorganisation of the basis of Govt & enlargement of the Cabinet as the P.M. could not wisely undertake. I don't therefore entirely reject the idea of the Home Secretaryship or at least I desire to be free to accept the offer of a post in the government if made to me & therefore I have refused to go back to City affairs or to undertake other work which would make such acceptance impossible. I think I could be useful in some positions in the Govt & that in these times one ought to be useful where one can without too much regard to one's personal proclivities, & though I won't claim to be quite as unselfish as you picture me I am not more ambitious for myself than a man ought to be.

. . . What it comes to is this: – that with all his faults, & they are such as to cause me grave misgivings, I think our present P.M. is still the best man for the place & our present Govt as good as & stronger than any by which it could be replaced. For the present I shall support it from outside & do not exclude from my mind the possibility of entering it again if asked.

---

[24] In August 1917 the Montagu Declaration stated the intent of government policy was to provide for the gradual development of 'responsible government in India as an integral part of the British Empire'.

AC5/1/45   4 November 1917
                                                      9 Egerton Place

My dear Ida,

. . .

My family are united in disliking the idea of my re-entering the
Govt. without a seat in the Cabinet and are in a conspiracy to preach
caution and ambition to me! ... Certainly the Home Office has no
attractions for me & it would be in many ways a great sacrifice of my
personal inclinations to go there, though by the way you are mistaken
in supposing that the present holder of the post is younger than I in
anything but parliamentary years or that the office itself is not considered
one of the big posts of the Cabinet in normal times. In mere point of
precedence the Home Secretary ranks first of the Secretaries of State &
he generally has charge of some big bill & is therefore before the public.
But that counts for little with me. My capacity is administrative &
political rather than inventive & legislative & Home Office administration with its police work, details of factory inspectorship & the like
does not attract me, & much of it (the police work) actively repells [sic]
me. But above all, tho' very important & in certain possible con-
tingencies vital to national security, it seems very remote from the
war & while the war lasts I should like to be engaged on war work, or
if not directly or mainly upon that, then as I was at the India Office,
on some great Imperial problem. So the Daily Chronicle is premature
to say the least in appointing me to succeed Cave.[25] I will not go further
than that for the present. For the rest we must 'wait & see'.

As to ambition I don't think that I ever had more of it than is
necessary to make a man stick to his work until in the year or two
before Balfour's[26] resignation of the leadership colleagues & the course
of events suggested the possibility – & indeed it seemed at the time the
probability – of my succeeding him. Then my ambition was fired, for
that seemed to open great possibilities & I dreamed like others of being
head of a ministry that should make some history, domestic & imperial.
But when that chance failed & I made way for Bonar Law, my

---

[25] George Cave (1856–1928) Conservative MP for Kingston (Surrey) 1906–18. Solicitor-
General 1915–16; Home Secretary 1916–19; Lord Chancellor 1922–24, 1924–28. Knighted
1915. Created Viscount 1919.
   [26] Arthur James Balfour (1848–1930) Conservative MP for Hertford 1874–85, Manchester (East) 1885–1906, City of London 1906–22. President Local Government Board
1885–86; Scottish Secretary 1886–87; Chief Secretary for Ireland 1887–91; 1st Lord of
Treasury 1891–92, 1895–1905; Prime Minister 1902–5; 1st Lord of Admiralty 1915–16;
Foreign Secretary 1916–19; Lord President 1919–22 and 1925–29. Created K.G. 1922 and
Earl of Balfour later in same year.

'ambition' perished from want of sustenance & I can't revive it. I dare say I should have done no better than B.L. but some things would have been done differently & some not at all. He is a weak man & I thought him strong. He has little experience, but I thought he would learn. He does not learn & he will remain an amateur to the end of his days. He is a curious mixture – at one and the same time over-confident & over-modest, over-daring & over-timid, ambitious & fearful, satisfied with his own judgement in theory & utterly dependent on his surroundings in practice. And with it all, his two or three intimates are men like Max Aitken[27] and Goulding,[28] the latter infinitely superior in character to the former but both born intriguers, utterly incompetent to advise him, without knowledge or sagacity & the former casting upon him an atmosphere of suspicion by his conduct in financial operations & his louche associations. Bah! I am working myself into a temper, but by Jove! if I had been made leader some things in our Party record & I think some things in our National history would have been different. We could not have been worse led as a Party than we were before the War nor more inadequately represented by any leader than we were by B.L. in Asquith's Coalition Government.

I am disgruntled altogether today ... I am shocked & almost dismayed by the tone of Chelmsford's speech[29] ... This & Mrs Besant's release make a bad atmosphere for Montagu's reform. We are heading straight for another 'Ilbert Bill'[30] agitation by Englishmen on one side with great risks of another Ireland of Indians on the other.

How much of this criticism is lumbago & how much sound sense & wise position? At any rate I am alarmed & alarmed this time by an act of Chelmsford's, not of Montagu's. He seems to me to have lost his head. Scold your officials if you want or will but in private. Don't

---

[27] (William) Maxwell Aitken (1879–1964) Conservative MP for Ashton-Under-Lyne 1910–16. Chancellor of Duchy of Lancaster and Minister of Propaganda/Information 1918–19; Minister of Aircraft Production 1940–41; Minister of State 1941; Minister of Supply 1941–42; Minister of War Production 1942; Lord Privy Seal 1943–45. Knighted 1911. Created Baronet 1916 and Baron Beaverbrook 1917. Acquired *Daily Express* 1918 and later *Evening Standard*.

[28] Edward Alfred Goulding (1862–1936) Conservative MP for Worcester 1908–22. PPS (unpaid) to Local Government Board 1895–98. Chairman, Tariff Reform League Organisation Department 1904–12. Created Baron Wargrave 1922.

[29] Lord Chelmsford publicly rebuked Sir Michael O'Dwyer, the Lt-Governor of the Punjab, for an intemperate speech. See 'The War Service of India', *The Times*, 2 November 1917.

[30] Sir Courtney Peregrine Ilbert (1841–1924) Legal member, Council of Viceroy of India 1882–6; Clerk of the House of Commons 1902–21. In 1883 he proposed to extend the criminal jurisdiction of Indian magistrates over Europeans to the entire country rather than just the Presidency towns. A massive anti-Indian outcry followed in India and Britain and a modified bill was enacted. The racial nature of the protest became a classical source of propaganda for the developing Indian nationalist movement.

lecture them & apologise for them in public & beg of their angry & fractious critics that they may be excused & let go like naughty children. That way danger lays everywhere and above all in India. For the first time, I think that Chelmsford has made a really serious mistake & it is one which frightens me for its effect both on officials & public may be far-reaching.

In mid-November 1917 Chamberlain spent 'a very full and very interesting week' touring the Western Front battlefields of Vimy Ridge, Bapaume, Arras, the Somme and Ypres. Witnessing the devastation at first hand, he found that 'everything was very much what I expected it to be, but a little more so'. During his absence, Lloyd George had delivered a speech in Paris on 12 November supporting a system of unity of command in a new Inter-Allied Supreme War Council: a body which would possess the authority to review and revise the strategic plans proposed by the general staffs of each of the Allies. In so doing, his remarks about the appalling casualty lists and his condemnation of patchwork planning, wasteful tactical methods and, by implication, the generals who used them, were part of his strategy to undermine the authority of Haig and Robertson and establish Sir Henry Wilson as an alternative source of military advice. The result was a political storm in London with Asquith emerging rather unexpectedly on the side of the generals. As Chamberlain had consistently supported the General Staff he also initially viewed the situation with grave concern. Nonetheless, although Turner is correct in noting that he was 'particularly active in working up Conservative opposition' until 18 November,[31] as his letter to his sister demonstrates, his conversations that evening with Law and Lloyd George convinced him to drop both his opposition to the Inter-Allied War Council and his threat of parliamentary rebellion. He also attempted to influence Asquith to withdraw from a vote of censure or even a speech of acrimonious reproach. Whatever the precise impact of this plea, Asquith's speech disappointed the critics and Lloyd George enjoyed an easy personal victory in the debate. While an ominous portent for the government and the Liberal Party, Chamberlain played a significant role not only in the creation of the crisis and but also – and more important – in defusing it. The tension between the General Staff and the Prime Minister continued unabated, however, particularly after the rapid reversal of the gains made during the first ten days of the Cambrai offensive launched on the 20 November by Haig in search of a success somewhere on the Western Front: tensions that culminated in the following year in the crises over Robertson's resignation and the Maurice Debate.

[31] J. Turner, *British Politics and the Great War*, 238. Petrie and Dutton do not mention the incident.

AC5/1/47

20 November 1917
9 Egerton Place

My dear Hilda,

I got back on Saturday after a very full and very interesting week
[at the Front].
...

... My time in France was so fully occupied that I had difficulty in
snatching a quarter of an hour to read Lloyd George's Paris speech.
The Commander-in-Chief's attitude towards it and the proposals was
as "correct" as anyone could desire; but other people showed themselves
both angry and alarmed. I thought it my duty to play the peacemaker;
and explain that I thought they misunderstood the speech and were
unduly alarmed by the proposals. But my real feeling was that the
proposals themselves were rather dangerous, and that the speech was
thoroughly bad and mischievous.

No sooner had I got home than I was rung up by a man on the
telephone who asked if he could come round and see me. He had
heard from a rather indiscreet, and perhaps not wholly trustworthy
supporter of Lloyd George, that the Prime Minister intended on
Monday to elaborate and to justify the speech, giving chapter and
verse, or, in other words, statistics of our losses and gains, for every
statement that he had made. Under the circumstances some people
were urging Asquith to make a serious effort to turn Lloyd George out,
on the ground that he had become a public danger; and it was clear
to me that my name was being referred to among them.

I told my visitor that I took a serious view of the situation and a still
more serious view of the prospect if his information as to Lloyd George's
intentions was correct, but that I would have nothing to do with any
combination against Lloyd George beforehand, that I must re-read the
Paris speech carefully, and read the other statements which I had not
yet had an opportunity of seeing, and should then watch the course of
events, and act as I thought best at the moment.

This interview was followed by an express letter from Strachey[32] enclosing me his "Spectator" article and a letter which he had sent to Asquith
on the same lines, and on Sunday he rang me up on the telephone to
know my views. He made it clear that he was in communication with
Bonham Carter[33] and was going to tell Bonham Carter what I said.

[32] John St Loe Strachey (1860–1927) A Liberal Unionist from 1886 and co-editor of
the party's paper. Contributor to *Spectator* from 1887 and Editor and proprietor 1898–
1925. Editor *Cornhill Magazine* 1896–7.
[33] Sir Maurice "Bongie" Bonham Carter (1880–1960) PPS to Asquith 1910–16. Married
Asquith's eldest daughter, Violet, 1915.

I accordingly told him, that whilst I took a serious view of the position & especially of the speech, I thought a really useful purpose might be served by an Inter-Allied Council if its functions were properly limited and defined, and that in any case I thought his advice to Asquith bad.

Having thought the matter over, I went first to see Bob Cecil and learn from him how the ground lay. I found him not less anxious than myself, and we had obviously come to very much the same conclusions.

I then tried to see Milner, but he was out of town, and accordingly fell back upon Curzon to whom I explained the situation as I saw it, and said that I had come to tell him that, though, as he knew, I was anxious to support the Government, I could not do so if Lloyd George persisted in the intention which I had heard attributed to him – that if he repeated on Monday, and not merely repeated but emphasised ... the faults of the Paris speech, I should be compelled to vote against him, and I should not give a silent vote. I added that I was quite certain that large numbers of our Party would feel deeply the attack which he appeared to have made upon our military authorities, and if it were persisted in and not explained away, I anticipated serious division among the supporters of the Government. In order, if possible, to avert this trouble, and to save the Government, I had come to tell him what my feelings were.

He gave me a very interesting account of the situation, and undertook to communicate with Lloyd George.

The result was that at 6 o'clock on Sunday evening Bonar Law asked me to go down and see him. I had a good deal of conversation with him which was far from reassuring, but whilst we were in the middle of it the Prime Minister himself came in. Without having heard Bonar Law's statement of the case, or my objections to it, he gave his own reasons for the creation of the Inter-Allied Council and his ideas of the work that it would undertake – and all this on lines and in a spirit which was perfectly satisfactory to me.

Accordingly leaving that side of the question, I took up with him very seriously his Paris speech. He repudiated eagerly, and I have no doubt, sincerely, the interpretation which I attached to it; but I impressed upon him that though over in France I had taken a different line, and had acted, as I felt bound to do, as peacemaker and advocate for the Government, I myself had been shocked and dismayed by the tone of the speech, & that I thought it vital that he should remove the unfortunate impression which it had created.

Incidentally there was rather an amusing episode. I made him some allusion to press comments on the subject, and he said, "Oh yes, but you must not judge my speech by what hostile critics say." I rejoined, "It is not your critics, Prime Minister, with whom I am concerned – I have not read what they say. What fills me with terror is the defence made by your supporters. Look, for instance, at the Observer of this morning".

This led him to observe with satisfaction that the whole of the Sunday press was favourable to him.

I replied, "Yes, they are today, but do not assume too readily that the Press represents the country, or that they will abide tomorrow by what they have said today. They support you as long as you are successful, but if the wind of popular favour veers tomorrow, they will veer with it."

He paused, and then said slowly, "Yes, that is true – they have no responsibility". And I thought that I had perhaps planted in his mind the seed of a useful thought!

On the whole the interview was satisfactory, and I came away rather more happy.

Meanwhile I had sent a letter to Asquith repudiating Strachey's advice to him, adjuring him to pass by Lloyd George's bad history as lightly as he could and concentrate upon the safe-guards which are necessary for the future. In this way, I said, he might render a real service to the nation. If on the other hand he moved a vote of censure, or, even without doing that, made a speech of acrimonious censure, the Prime Minister would harden his heart and would attempt to justify his bad history, and would emphasise all the worst points of the Paris speech. The result would be inevitably to split that body of public opinion on which *any* Government must rely for the successful pros-ecution of the war, and not improbably to create division between soldiers and civilians of the most dangerous kind.

I told him that I had sent a warning to the Government, but it seemed to me that everything depended upon two men – himself and the Prime Minister; and though he probably did not view the situation from the same standpoint as myself, I felt sure that he would continue the patriotic attitude which he had adopted ever since his resignation.

You will have seen the result, or perhaps I should say, the sequel, for I am still wondering whether I was only the fly on the wheel, or whether I did in fact do some good. In any case Asquith was very moderate, and has had, I think, hard measure from the press, because owing to his moderation his speech was not as effective as it might have been. The fact is that Lloyd George had given him an incomparable opportunity, and that regard for the public interest prevented Asquith from using it.

Lloyd George's own speech was a prodigious personal triumph – almost too great a triumph I am inclined to say for our safety. His frank avowal that fearing that his Inter-Allied Council might be still-born, he had gone "Limehousing" in support of it, really disarmed criticism. These are not the manners which one would wish the Prime Minister of the country to adopt, but they are eminently characteristic of Lloyd George. By the way, I gave him something else to think seriously of when I pointed out that it would not do for the Prime Minister to use arguments which would then become the text and staple of all Pacifist speeches at the street corners.

AC5/1/48   2 December 1917
                                                  9 Egerton Place

My dear Hilda,

. . .
   What a *gaffe* of Lansdowne's.[34] How he of all men came to write that mischievous letter I cannot think. You know how much I have grown to like him as well as to respect his judgement. But hitherto, if he erred, it was always on the side of caution. He was slow to move, liked plenty of time for consideration & was by nature averse from bold & decisive courses. He is the last man I should have expected to write so inopportune & so unwise a letter. How could he talk about the 'freedom of the seas' as an open question? and how came it that he failed to see what an encouragement his letter would be to the Germans & to our pacifists? Well, it is all a mystery of the human mind which I cannot fathom.

AC5/1/49   3 December 1917
                                                  9 Egerton Place

My dear Ida,

. . .
   Lansdowne's letter has obviously encouraged all our pacifists. I fear it has done & will yet do much mischief both here & in Germany – perhaps in the Dominions & elsewhere also. The more I think of it the less I can understand his publishing such a letter without consultation with others, but with whom? Rumour says with Asquith but Geoffrey Howard[35] told me that Asquith knew nothing of if beforehand. It makes

---

[34] Henry Charles Keith Petty-Fitzmaurice (1845–1927) Succeeded father as 5th Marquess of Lansdowne in 1866. Under-Secretary of War 1872–74; Under-Secretary for India 1880; Governor-General Canada 1883–88; Viceroy of India 1888–1894; Secretary of War 1895–1900; Foreign Secretary 1900–1905; Minister without Portfolio 1915–16.

[35] Geoffrey Howard (1877–1935) Liberal MP for Eskdale 1906–10, Wilts (Westbury) 1911–18; Luton 1923–24. PPS to Asquith 1908–10, Junior Lord of Treasury 1915–16 and a Liberal Whip 1911–18.

A's speech at Birmingham next Tuesday one of great importance. I trust he will be as clear and decisive as he has been hitherto.

Dec 7 ... Now there is bad news ... Norman[36] is reported missing on Nov 30th. He was in command of a French mortar Battery. There is no further news ... I think that 'missing' with all its horrible & agonising uncertainties is the worst news of all.

AC5/1/56

18 January 1918
9 Egerton Place

My dear Hilda,

...

... I have been fairly occupied with the House of Lords Conference where we have at last stopped talking – very necessary at first but tiresome when prolonged indefinitely. Now we are taking decisions on definite propositions & so far I find myself voting on each point with the majority of the Conference & securing a measure of agreement which at times has seemed very unlikely ever to be reached.

After Russia's collapse, increasing anxiety that France or Italy would also be forced out of the war had prompted Lloyd George to attempt to assist his Allies: a strategy which, by limiting available manpower, also imposed a further constraint upon Haig's ability to plunge the army into a pointless repetition of the Passchendale offensive of 1917. In September 1917 it had been agreed to extend the British line by a further 28 miles to relieve the French. In January 1918 this was followed by the decision to create a mobile inter-Allied reserve to reinforce the Western Front wherever the Germans chose to attack. Ultimately, these proposals led to Robertson's 'resignation' as C.I.G.S. on 16 February but not before Lloyd George confronted another political storm at home whipped up by Col. Repington. Recently dismissed from The Times *by Geoffrey Dawson, Repington had no love for Sir Henry Wilson, Lloyd George's military instrument in the undermining of Robertson and Haig. He also believed (wrongly in this case) that an attack on the General Staff by Lovat Fraser in Northcliffe's* Daily Mail *on 21 January had been inspired by the Prime Minister. Repington's first article for the* Morning Post *three days later was thus a mischievous attack on manpower policy. On 11 February he launched a direct attack on the General Reserve scheme also feeding Asquith with the political ammunition to use against Lloyd George in the Commons debate next day. Despite an ill-judged parliamentary performance on 12 February, Lloyd George eventually*

---

[36] Norman Gwynne Chamberlain (1884–1917) Subaltern in the Grenadier Guards. Killed with all his company on 1 December; confirmed dead on 10 February 1918. The cousin both Chamberlain brothers knew and cared for most.

weathered the storm.[37] One consequence of the crisis was that after one of Lord Derby's many threatened resignations from the War Office in mid-February, Law offered Chamberlain the post only to withdraw it almost immediately when it was discovered Derby had not resigned after all.[38]

AC5/1/57

25 January 1918
Barton St Mary

My dear Ida,

. . .

The political pot has been boiling up these last few days! As far as I have heard anything about the Irish Convention[39] it stands thus:- Midleton[40] agreed with Redmond[41] on a scheme of Home Rule – I presume for all Ireland – on condition that the Irish Parlt. had control of internal revenue but that Customs remained with the Imperial Parlt. & formed Ireland's contribution to imperial revenue. To this scheme the Ulstermen would not have agreed & it looked a little time ago as if the split would rest with them. But Redmond could not carry his own party with him. At least so many refused to follow him that he has felt obliged to withdraw from his arrangement with Midleton, & the break up of the Convention therefore now lies at his door. You will see that efforts at conciliation are still being made but that there seems little chance of their being successful.

Carson resigned, I believe, in order that the Govt. may not be prejudiced by the allegation that it is dominated by an Ulsterman, & that his influence with Ulster may not be lessened by the idea that he is sacrificing Ulster to the convenience of the Cabinet – these contradictory ideas both being in circulation in different quarters at the same time as is not unusual in political questions, & the former in

---

[37] See J. Turner, *British Politics and the Great War*, 271–278.

[38] See Chamberlain's notes 18 February 1918, AC18/2/1; D. Lloyd George, *War Memoirs of David Lloyd George*, (6 vols, 1933–36) V, 2822.

[39] A 'Convention' to discuss the future government of Ireland met from July 1917–April 1918.

[40] (William) St John Brodrick (1856–1942) Conservative MP for Surrey (West) 1880–1885, Surrey (Guildford) 1885–1906. Financial Secretary to War Office 1895–98, Under-Secretary Foreign Office 1898–1900, Secretary for War 1900–1903, Secretary for India 1903–5. Succeeded as 9th Viscount Midleton 1907 and Earl 1920. Offered the Irish Viceroyalty 1918.

[41] William Archer Redmond (1886–1932) Nationalist MP for E. Tyrone 1910–18. Resigned and elected for Waterford City 1918–22. Member of Dáil for Waterford City to 1921 and Co. Waterford 1923–32 as an independent to 1926 and then as a member of the National League until 1932 when joined Cumann na nGaedheal.

particular being very mischievously employed in the United States where, as I understand, President Wilson is much concerned by the effect of the Irish differences on his own war programme &, I suspect, on his own position. Hughes[42] is equally embarrassed by Irish opposition in Australia. Altogether a pretty kettle of fish!

Then come the Cambrai debates, the resignation of Repington[43] from the Times, the attacks of the $\frac{1}{2}$d. Northcliffe[44] & Rothermere[45] Press on the Generals, an uneasy feeling that the P.M. is at the bottom of them or at least sympathises with them & is not sorry to see them, & the rather unskilful handling of the whole subject by Bonar Law in the House.

As to all of this I don't see the Press in question & I don't know exactly what they allege and where the truth lies, but two things seem to me clear at this stage. 1st that the Govt. would have done better to say rather more about the Cambrai affair &, secondly, that they have not asserted early enough or clearly enough that the soldiers are responsible to *them* & *they* to Parlt., that Parlt. can always deal with *them* but that it cannot & shall not deal with Generals over their heads or behind their backs. I might add a third comment: that the P.M.'s not undeserved reputation for a habit of rather underhand intrigue, to which he sacrifices those who serve under him, is a great misfortune both for himself & his country. The fact is, as I told B.L., that the P.M. will never be safe till he has fought Northcliffe & smashed him, as he can smash him if he chooses. That would make him really popular! but tho' afraid neither of Parlt. nor of the country, he is in a curious way afraid of the Press. So I turn prophet & proclaim that if Kerensky does not smash Lenin, Lenin will smash Kerensky once again, or in other words that if Lloyd George can't find the courage to throw over Northcliffe, Northcliffe will before long over throw him.

...

[42] William Norris Hughes (1864–1952) Australian politician for Labour then Nationalist then United Australia parties. In Labour Governments 1904–15; Prime Minister 1915–23. Attended Imperial War Cabinet 1918 and member of UK War Cabinet. Served in United Australia and Liberal Governments 1934–41.

[43] Lt-Colonel Charles à Court Repington (1858–1925) Forced to leave army in 1904 by Henry Wilson because of adultery with fellow officer's wife. Military correspondent of *The Times* 1904–18. Retained close links with General Staff in London and France during the war. Dismissed by Geoffrey Dawson from *The Times* in January 1918. Later worked for *Morning Post* and *Daily Telegraph*.

[44] Alfred Charles William Harmsworth (1865–1922) Founder of Amalgamated Press 1881 and proprietor of *Answers, Daily Mail, Daily Mirror, Evening News*. Proprietor of *The Times* 1908–22. Chairman British War Mission to USA 1917; Director of Propaganda in Enemy Countries 1918. Created Viscount Northcliffe 1905.

[45] Harold Sidney Harmsworth (1868–1940) Northcliffe's brother. Proprietor of *Daily Mirror* 1914–31; *Daily Mail, Evening News* and Associated Newspapers Ltd, 1922–40; Secretary for Air 1917–18. Created Baron Rothermere 1914, Viscount 1919.

I think that there is no chance of my being asked to fill the vacancy caused by Carson's resignation. I guess from something let fall by a private secretary before that resignation was known to the world or me that Balfour may give up the Foreign Office & join the Cabinet without a portfolio. In this case Bob Cecil would seem the natural person to be appointed Sec. of State for Foreign Affairs, but I have no idea whether Lloyd George likes him or could work with him. I think that *he* finds G. very difficult. In any case I have not been approached as to my willingness to join in any capacity, & at present there is no 'come – hither' in my eyes. So, if the family are wanted, they must be asked whether for District Council or Govt. you & I are not going to thrust ourselves forward if we are not wanted. There is plenty for us to do without that, & they may be thankful if they get us when or if we are asked.

AC5/1/59   8 February 1918
                                                     9 Egerton Place

[Typescript]
My dear Ida,

  . . .

I don't like the posture of public affairs. I don't like Beaverbrook kites or Repington paragraphs in the Morning Post. I don't like the former because I feel more and more how much injury is done to Government by their neglect to bear in mind the old adage – "Judge a man by the company he keeps". I don't like the latter because the root of it is in a personal quarrel with Henry Wilson[46] who turned R. out of the War Office. And I am the more uneasy because I am sure that in this case Repington has something to go upon and the answer cannot be given without injury to the public interest. But my information, which does not come from Government but is trustworthy, leaves me in no doubt that in this case the Versailles Council (i.e. the Ministers) are right in principle though some part of their application of the principle *may* be wrong. All, or at any rate a great part of what I have heard lately, makes me feel sure that the creation of the Versailles Council was a necessity, but I am very much afraid lest it should be judged rather by the most doubtful of its decisions than by those which were certainly wise and necessary.

[46] Field-Marshal Sir Henry Hughes Wilson (1864–1922) Deputy, later Assistant, Adjutant-General, Army HQ 1903–06; Director of Military Operations 1910–14. Assistant Chief of General Staff 1914; British Military Representative at Supreme War Council 1917. Chief of Imperial General Staff 1918–22. Unionist MP for N. Down February 1922 until assassinated on the steps of his London home on 22 June 1922.

All which is very obscure but is all that I can write to you and more than I should write to anyone outside the family.

I have had a busy week fighting the deuce of a battle against P.R. and being knocked out in the last round by the putting on of the Government Whips. Uncle Walter whom I met at Mary's last night and, I suspect, Neville, do not feel as I and Bee do on the subject – and I mean not as warmly – but all *our* old Birmingham upbringing and memories of the late seventies and early eighties are stirred by this revival of fads and crotchets which Bright and Father loathed and denounced and I had thought finally killed by the Reform Bill of '85. So I fought with vigour and passion, and though my case was in the end "compromised", the papers will have shown you that even in defeat it was something of a personal triumph. Members came to me with the assurance that I had converted them and changed their votes, and I believe that I illustrated again the unhappy truth that a Minister never speaks so well as when he has resigned!

Feb 9th.

... To my great annoyance the [Inter-Allied] Council sits again to-day, morning and afternoon, and I shall only get down to Barton St. Mary just in time for dinner, and as I must return by the first train on Monday for further sittings of the Council, all the holiday that I shall have secured in the 5 days recess will be a 'Sunday off'. George Lloyd[47] spends Sunday with us, and as he is just back from work with the Arabs in the Hedjaz and is besides a very intelligent fellow ...

...

The air is full of rumours as to changes in the Government in connection with the filling of Carson's place. I have heard that Balfour would give up the Foreign Office and enter Cabinet without portfolio, and also that Lloyd George had determined to offer the vacant place in the Cabinet to me. But as both rumours come from equally good authority, and as both cannot be true, it is very likely that there is no truth in either. Another rumour suggests that Beaverbrook will be the new member of the War Cabinet; but about this I don't worry as I do not think that Lloyd George yet desires to commit political suicide. But it is not to the advantage of himself or his Government that it should be possible for such a rumour to circulate. Beaverbrook's appointment as Director of Publicity can scarcely be described as a popular one. It adds to the prevalent feeling of irritation and soreness.

---

[47] George Ambrose Lloyd (1879–1941) Conservative MP for Staffordshire (West) 1910–18 and Eastbourne 1924–25. Governor of Bombay 1918–23; High Commissioner for Egypt and The Sudan 1925–29; Colonial Secretary and Leader of the Lords May 1940–February 1941. Created G.C.I.E. 1918, G.C.S.I. 1924 and Baron Lloyd 1925.

AC5/1/60   15 February 1918
                                              Barton St Mary

My dear Ida,

. . .

It has been a restless uneasy week in London & in Parlt. I was very busy with the Inter-Ally Council all Monday & Tuesday & missed the very unexpected & passionate scene in the House on the latter day. But I have had the story from many who were eye witnesses of it & all agree in the main facts. The Times account was simply falsified, & reading its report & description you would get no idea of the scene or its meaning. The P.M. was ill & probably worried & strained by controversies (still unsettled this morning) with Robertson[48] & Derby,[49] as well as being irritated by the rumours in the Press & by the leakage of secrets, for neither of which was he responsible *this time*. Instead of answering Asquith's questions quietly or explaining equally quietly that they could not be answered, he lashed himself into a rhetorical rage over the Press & gave an uneasy House the impression that he was trying like the cuttle-fish to escape under an inky cloud of his own making. Then suddenly at the height of his box-thumping he turned – meaning no evil say most, of malice prepense say a few – on Asquith with a passionate adjuration not to ask questions which the Germans would give anything to have answered. Asquith – surprised & angry say most, with astute & calculated passion say one or two – rose & protested, & he was received with loud, vehement & long continued cheering from *all* parts of the House. 'The most significant thing was that lots of *our* men were cheering' said one of the Unionist Whips to me. 'I saw them myself', he added, as if, even then, he could hardly believe the evidence of his own eyes. Lloyd George apologised at once & without qualification or reserve, but the House was thoroughly angry, he had lost his hold on them & could not recover it ... Lloyd George laboured on amidst the rude & angry interjections of a few & the sulky or angry silence of the many & sat down having failed as he had never failed before.

[48] Field-Marshal Sir William Robert Robertson (1860–1933) Assistant Director Military Operations 1901–07; General Staff, Aldershot 1907–10; Director of Military Training 1913–14; Chief of General Staff, BEF 1915; Chief of Imperial General Staff 1915–18; G.O. C-in-C Eastern Command 1918; C-in-C British Army on the Rhine 1919–20.

[49] Edward George Villiers Stanley (1865–1948) Conservative MP for SE Lancashire 1892–1906. Financial Secretary to War Office 1900–03; Postmaster General (in Cabinet) 1903–05; Under-Secretary for War July-December 1916; Secretary for War 1916–18 and 1922–24; Ambassador to Paris 1918–20. Created K.C.V.O. and K.G. in 1919. Succeeded as 17th Earl of Derby in 1908.

George Lloyd ... who came fresh from the House about 7.30 to report to me what had passed, had flocked out with the rest into the Lobby, had talked with several men – mostly Unionists but some Liberals – & was like the rest of them not a little excited. You know what the Lobby is in such circumstances. 'It was the beginning of the end, Lloyd George was done for: all the House was cheering *against* Lloyd George; everyone is saying he will have to resign & that you are the only man for the place', & so forth. I have been longer in Parlt. & know my House of Commons better so I offered to bet him half-a-crown that the P.M. would make a brilliant recovery next day & everybody would be saying that there never was such a marvellous fellow, that we couldn't do without him & no one could hold a candle to him.

But there was no next day in this sense for on Wednesday neither the P.M. nor Asquith was present when Herbert Samuel[50] resumed the debate. Samuel's theme was the failure of the home policy of Govt. all along the line, but Bonar Law, in his quietest, most business-like & most effective manner, made a crushing reply (in which he incidentally referred to Neville's task under the conditions prevailing at the time as 'an absolutely impossible task') & the Govt's position was strengthened by the debate. The allusion to Neville was warmly cheered all over the House. There is general recognition of the fact that he never had a fair chance.

Meanwhile everyone is still talking & thinking of the Versailles embroglio & the air is full of rumours. I do not know the truth for certain. I was sounded on Wednesday morning by an emissary of the War Office as to whether I would intervene, but I replied that I did not know enough to act usefully & could not act on an ex-parte statement, that I felt strongly about the way the War Office had blabbed & encouraged a press agitation in Lloyd George's worst manner thro' Repington who had certainly got information from the entourage of the C.I.G.S. or Haig,[51] & that I was sickened by their personal bickerings & animosities. So you see I gave no encouragement to anyone to be unreasonable or to make trouble where harmony & united effort are so necessary. I am told that the P.M. is correct in saying that Robertson agreed at Versailles to what was there proposed

---

[50] Herbert Louis Samuel (1870–1963) Liberal MP for Cleveland 1902–18 and Darwen 1929–35. PUS at Home Office 1905–09; Chancellor Duchy of Lancaster 1909–10 and 1915–16; Postmaster General 1910–14 and 1915–16; President of Local Government Board 1914–15; Home Secretary 1916 and 1931–32. High Commissioner for Palestine 1920–25. Created G.B.E. 1920, G.C.B. in 1926 and Viscount Samuel 1937.

[51] Field-Marshal Sir Douglas Haig (1861–1928) Chief of Staff India 1909–12; GOC Aldershot 1912–14; commander 1st Army 1914–15; C-in-C Expeditionary Force in France and Flanders 1915–19 and Forces in Great Britain 1919–20.

in respect of the Versailles' Council's functions, that Derby repudiated the agreement when R. came home, that at first R. said he would have no part or lot in any resignation or remonstrance by the Army Council, that subsequently he changed his attitude, that many compromises have been offered & rejected – Derby with the obstinacy of a weak man turning down all the P.M.'s efforts to find a via media – & that as late as this morning no solution had been reached & Robertson's resignation had been given or would shortly be given. If this is the result I should greatly regret it & shall be not a little anxious as to its effects both on the army & the public, especially the former: but as far as my present information goes, Robertson has not a really good case & the trouble will be due partly to having as S/S for War a man who carries no weight with either camp & is unfitted for the part of mediator, partly to incompatibility of temper between Robertson & the P.M. & last but perhaps not least to the fatal distress which the P.M. inspires in all who come into close contact with him.

This was in truth the real causa causans of the scene in the House which on all sides & not least on ours resents Beaverbrook's appointment & dislikes the doubtful characters & inferior persons with whom he surrounds himself. If he falls, one can only say "in j'as voulus, Georges Dandin. You have asked for it!"

AC5/1/61   17 February 1918
                                            [No address]

My dear Ida,

... I see R[obertson]'s resignation in the Observer today.
...
What will happen now? I fear the effect on the Army, yet I *think* R. is in the wrong. I don't in the least know how the House will take it.

After a skilful parliamentary performance by Lloyd George on 19 February the crisis provoked by Robertson's removal was finally resolved. Ironically, however, during a debate on Army Estimates on the very same afternoon, the Prime Minister's position was immediately rendered more difficult by Chamberlain's attack upon the prominence and insidious influence of newspaper proprietors in a government which included Rothermere as Secretary of State for Air, Northcliffe as Director of Propaganda in Enemy Countries and Beaverbrook as Minister of Information:[52] an attack he renewed on 11 March after a Daily Mail *attack upon Robertson and Jellicoe. In launching this challenge it has been suggested that Chamberlain was at least partly*

---

[52] *House of Commons Debates*, vol 102 col. 656–657, 19 February 1918.

motivated by rumours that the Conservative benches favoured a change in party leadership and a reconstruction of the government.[53] *A far more convincing explanation for the attack, however, was Chamberlain's suspicion of Lloyd George's motives for these appointments combined with a profound detestation of both the press lords and what he perceived to be their corrupting influence upon parliament, government and the constitution.*[54] *As Amery noted scathingly after dinner with Chamberlain, although he was 'full of beans' over the speech 'I am afraid [he] exhibited all his worst defects, namely his incapacity to realize that we are no longer in the parliamentary world of the '80s, and his lack of proportion in dealing with anything that savours of breach of good form, personal loyalty, or political etiquette. He is too genteel. F.S. O[liver] said afterwards that he must have included someone at Madame Tussaud's among his maternal ancestors'.*[55] *Whatever the impulse behind the attack, Chamberlain received widespread support both in the Commons and the party generally. Perhaps this reinforced Lloyd George's view that he was now sufficiently dangerous to warrant a swift return to the government front bench.*

AC5/1/62

22 February 1918
9 Egerton Place

My dear Ida,

...

As you will have seen my speech on Economic Policy has not come to birth, but I found occasion to make quite a different one last Tuesday which has fluttered the dove cotes considerably & will probably ensure that whenever I am down on my luck – as must happen at times to public men – there will be no lack of powerful enemies to give one a kick. However I was well aware of this before I spoke & had counted the cost. If you can't take risks, you shouldn't enter politics. It was time that what I said should be said & I thought that I was the right person to say it. What one calls 'the whole House', i.e. not every member in it but its corporate feeling, was wholly with me & members were grateful to me for belling the cat. Bob Cecil openly cheered me from

[53] J. Turner, *British Politics and the Great War*, 278: a view based on the contents of a letter from F.S. Oliver, 19 February 1918 – the day of the speech – referring to 'our talk last night'.

[54] For a passionate exposition of these objections see A. Chamberlain to Milner, Curzon and Carson, 21–22 February 1918, AC5/7/5, 7. For earlier expressions of distaste at press influence see A. Chamberlain to Hilda, 20 November 1917; to Ida 25 January 1918, AC5/1/47, 57; Amery Diary, 10 October 1917, *The Leo Amery Diaries*, 173.

[55] Amery Diary, 4 March 1918, *The Leo Amery Diaries*, 209.

the Treasury Bench & many members of the Govt. have privately thanked me for what I said.

I have been very busy since, for Unionists are begging me to table a resolution on the subject & men of all parties are constantly button-holing me to talk about what can be done, & I am using every effort to bring private pressure to bear on Lloyd George & members of the Cabinet to get the thing settled without further debate. B.L. is useless & the P.M. is excited & not, I suspect, pleased; but he is no fool & unless he wishes to fall I think I shall succeed without upsetting the Govt. If I fail to settle it in this way, I shall have to consider most carefully what I ought to do. It will be a most difficult problem, for the P.M. would have to treat such a motion as a Vote of Censure. If I carried it, I should destroy his Govt. If he beat me, the House would have condoned his iniquities; & I do not wish to produce either of these results.

AC5/1/63   2 March 1918
                                                Barton St Mary

My dear Hilda,

          . . .
          As to the Press question it stands thus. Curzon 'entirely agrees' but doesn't help. Fisher[56] agrees in the main or at least so far as to say that the P.M.'s methods are indefensible in this connection – the P.M. 'whom I like but have no illusions about. Of course he would throw over me or any colleague if we stood in his way or ceased to be useful, & of course he tells taradiddles, & of course does the right thing in a wholly wrong way but – – ' & he proceeds to express a doubt whether the P.M. can or ought now to undo the evil he has wrought! B.L. is in the P.M.'s pocket & will back him right or wrong & the P.M. confides to George Lloyd about the second time he meets him that B.L. is useless & weeps all the time on his shoulder whenever any difficulty threatens! Bob Cecil & Walter Long are very dissatisfied, very uneasy & in doubt what they ought to do if the P.M. won't give way, & the P.M. himself is busy intriguing & talking over this man & that & seeking with B.L.'s help to form a Party & find a programme for it with which they can go to a General Election as soon as the new Register is completed.

          I saw Walter Long who would resign, I am confident, if I urged him to do so. 'But', said he, 'we oughtn't to destroy this Govt. with such

---

[56] Herbert Albert Laurens Fisher (1865–1940) Liberal MP for Sheffield (Hallam) 1916–18 and English Universities 1918–26. President Board of Education 1916–22. Wardenn New College, Oxford 1925–40

problems immediately in front of us without seeing our way to a successor to the Premiership. Only you, Austen, or the Speaker[57] are possible'. I did not take this up, for I don't want to destroy the Govt. or to over throw Lloyd George. With all his faults he has certain great qualities specially valuable at this time & I want not to destroy him but to save him from his own folly & crookedness. So I guess that the end will be that he will have his own way, but will not be forgiven hereafter for affronting the House & public opinion & for pursuing a course of action rightly condemned by the public conscience as corrupt in intention, mean & underhand in execution & destructive of public confidence & of official loyalty. If the Cabinet would take Lloyd George by the throat, he would have to yield but they won't. If by tabling a resolution I forced Walter & Bob Cecil to resign, others would go to [sic] & the Cabinet would probably fall to pieces as well as Govt.. If not, the Resolution would probably not now be carried by the House who would be unwilling to vote against the Govt. in sufficient numbers on what would be made a question of Confidence; & thus the majority, hating the Govt. for making them vote & hating the vote they gave, would nevertheless condone & become accessories to the actions of the P.M. A pretty kettle of fish! What would you do? I shall do all I can privately & shall not say that I will not go to extremes, but I don't think if my bluff is called that I hold the winning hand.

The P.M. would like to get rid of Derby & Rhondda[58] & will I expect do so before very long, but he may find some difficulty in filling their places.

AC5/1/64   9 March 1918
                                          Barton St. Mary

My dear Ida

You are far too experienced in the ways of men to be much surprised on learning that, having invited your advice & received it (you & Hilda are in truth veritable Pooh-Bahs), I am going to act in defiance of it. But it is a rather disgruntled brother who writes to you, first because I am disgusted by the weakness of the Cabinet; secondly because Ll.

---

[57] James William Lowther (1855–1949) Unionist MP for Rutland 1883–1885; Penrith 1886–1921. PUS at Foreign Office 1891–2. Deputy Speaker 1895–1905; Speaker 1905–21. Chairman Conference on Electoral Reform 1916–17; Boundary Commission 1917; Federal Devolution Committee 1919; Review Committee on Political Honours 1923–4; Agricultural Wages Board 1930–40. Created Viscount Ullswater 1921.

[58] David Alfred Thomas (1856–1918) Liberal MP for Merthyr Tydfil 1888–1910 and Cardiff 1910. President Local Government Board December 1916–June 1917 and Minister of Food Control 1917–July 1918. Created Baron Rhondda 1916 and Viscount 1918.

George bamboozles the House too easily & they don't make him sweat for his offences as they should; thirdly because Annie has just wired that Neville has chicken pox & cannot dine with me on Tuesday; fourthly because I have got a cough & sore throat & fifth & lastly & what looms largest before my eyes as I write, because I have got a painful & very swollen nose! ...

But to go back to Lloyd George. I had an hour's talk with him just before he saw the Unionist War Comtee on Tuesday. He told me pretty much what he told them & that may be summarized as follows: First, he had laid it down since my speech that any *Minister* (i.e. not Northcliffe) must absolutely dissociate himself from all control of his paper while he is a Minister; 2nd that he had satisfied himself that Sutherland[59] had had nothing to do with any of the Press attacks & that he had (in effect) told Sutherland not to do it again or, in other words, to be more careful in future; 3rd that he himself had had no part in any of the attacks. 4th that the soldiers, not Jellico[sic],[60] had intrigued with the papers against him & had revealed secret information; & that Sutherland had only countered this by 'stating the facts – to press-men who came to him'; 5th that Rothermere & Beaverbrook had been appointed on their merits; that R. had done much good work quietly before going to the Air-Board. As to B., well the work was not exactly nice work – it was very like spying – it required a man without too many scruples & B. would not let any scruples stand in his way. In short he said as plainly as he decently could that it was dirty work & that therefore Beaverbrook was peculiarly well fitted for it.

This & the statement about the soldiers appear to have greatly impressed the Comtee! Those who have spoken to me about the matter since convey the idea that the P.M. is a devil of a fellow & that they admire & are more than half convinced – till next time, when, on some new point arising, they will run through the same gamut of feeling – uneasiness, doubt, disgust or anger for the hot fit; thoughts of Asquith (their bug-bear) doubt again, fear, an anxiety to find an excuse, a determination to save Lloyd George somehow, an easy satisfaction with an inconclusive but persuasive speech, & a mild hope that he will somehow behave better in future.

---

[59] William Sutherland (1880–1949) Assisted with OAP and National Insurance Acts and Lloyd George's land policy before Great War. Private Secretary to Lloyd George 1915–18. Liberal MP for Argyll, 1918–24. PPS to Lloyd George 1919–20; Junior Lord of Treasury 1920–22; Chancellor of Duchy of Lancaster 1922. Created K.C.B. in 1919.

[60] Admiral Sir John Rushworth Jellicoe (1859–1935) Naval career from 1872. Director of Naval Ordnance 1905–7; Controller of the Navy 1908–10; Command Atlantic Fleet 1910–11; 2nd Division Home Fleet 1911–12; 2nd Sea Lord 1912–14; Commander Grand Fleet 1914–16; 1st Sea Lord 1916; chief of Naval Staff 1917. Governor-General, New Zealand 1920–24. Created Earl Jellicoe.

I said above in vulgar language that they did not make him sweat enough. That is true, but he has had a mauvais quart d'heure this time. I think I really frightened him or he would not have gone to the War Comtee who had not previously received, nor on this occasion invited or expected, the compliment of his attendance. And Carson's appearance on the scene very much increased his fears as you may imagine & again revived the uneasiness of members, so after being snubbed rather clumsily & rudely by Bonar Law on Wednesday (on which I lost my temper & overwhelmed Edward Talbot with angry messages to him) I succeeded on Thursday in getting a promise that the P.M. would on Monday make a statement to the House on the whole subject. This will be done at question time, & directly we get to the Vote of Credit I shall make some comments but not take a division – a very inconclusive proceeding, as you can see, but all that I can do as I am not prepared to force Cecil & Long out of the Ministry. They both sit very loose in their saddles & it would not take much to make either of them go. To use another vulgar phrase, both of them are pretty well 'fed up' with pretty Fanny's ways. My difficulty will be not to *say* more than is fitting when I *do* nothing.

I ought to add that whilst the P.M. said that Northcliffe was Beaverbrook's appointment, not his own, he incidentally admitted that the object was to keep him out of mischief. I had said: 'The public believes, & I don't think you will deny it, that you sought to secure the support of their papers'. To which he replied: 'Rather to keep them out of mischief – believe me, far more that'. And he added that N. at large was a danger. '*You* can smash him', I said. 'Yes, it may come to that. I think it will, I am pretty sure that it will. But in the middle of a great war —— ' & there he broke off & took up some other point.

It has been a lovely day. This morning Ivy & I walked over to Shovelstrode[?] woods & returned with a basket of primroses. Our room is gay with flowers, daffodils, crimson polyanthus, anemones & Iris stylosa from our garden; a couple of sprays of forsythia from Mr. Hanburys; primroses & a brilliant bunch of coltsfoot (or is it hawkweed?) from the woods & railway embankment.

I had a busy week in London. We have made some progress at the Second Chamber Conference & may yet be able to get a scheme which a satisfactory majority will be willing to accept. Then I have been colloguing with Selborne,[61] Fred Oliver[62] & some others about federalism

---

[61] William Waldegrave Palmer (1859–1942) Liberal MP for Hampshire (East) 1885–86. In 1886 became a Liberal Unionist and held same seat until 1892. Liberal Unionist MP for Edinburgh (West) 1892–95. Under-Secretary for Colonies 1895–1900; 1st Lord of Admiralty 1900–1905; High Commissioner for South Africa 1905–10; President, Board of Agriculture 1915–16. Succeeded as 2nd Earl of Selborne 1895. Created G.C.M.G. 1905 and K.G. 1909.

[62] Frederick Scott Oliver (1864–1934) Businessman and publicist. Author of *Federalism*

for the United Kingdom as the only possible solution of the Irish question, now that half this country has given up the idea of maintaining the Union as it stands, we cannot get 'resolute government' for the time necessary to let the Home Rule idea die out, even if it would ever die out after all the encouragement it has had. And federalism is the only thing which would make Home Rule safe & the only form of Home Rule which Ulster could be got to accept, whilst for us devolution would seem to have become necessary when you think of the vast mass of work which lies before Parlt in the near future. I put forward the idea tentatively in a speech at Bromsgrove in 1912 or 1913, I think, but then rather as an invitation to Liberals to bring their H.R. Bill into such a form that it could be applied mutatis mutandis to Scotland & England. It is rather curious to see how far the division of administration has already gone as witnessed by the separate estimates & differing legislation of the three countries. In some ways therefore it would be a smaller revolution than at first sight it appears, but it would still be a prodigious change, & we must test opinion before we go further. The [Irish]Convention has, I think definitely failed. Horace Plunkett[63] was a bad &, I am told, a muddle-headed chairman, & if any chance still remained for it, I should think that Redmond's death will have extinguished the last ray of hope.

AC5/1/65

17 March 1918
9 Egerton Place

My dear Hilda,

. . .

Rumours of reconstruction of the Govt are rife. I dare say that the P.M. is thinking about it & I know that some of the Cabinet have been desiring it. My name has been freely mentioned for Ch. of the Exchequer, & B.L. has suggested it as a possibility – just as earlier he half offered the Home Secretaryship. I think that if I had shown any eagerness for either I could have had it. But I have been very cold and have not responded to his suggestions. In some ways I should like to be back in office, but with all his qualities & not a little personal charm the P.M. fills me with growing distrust. It was perhaps inevitable that as a general election casts its shadow before, he should think more of

and *Home Rule* (1910) and *Ordeal by Battle* (1915). Close relationship with Chamberlain over Irish issue.

[63] Horace Curzon Plunkett (1854–1932) Land reformer and promoter of agricultural cooperation. Conservative MP for Dublin County 1892–1900; Vice-President Department of Agriculture for Ireland 1899–1907; Chairman, Irish Convention, 1917–18; Senator Irish Free State 1922–23. Created K.C.V.O. 1903.

his personal position & give more time & attention to intriguing for support; but the more his attention wanders from the war the less I like him & I am not disposed to give him a blank cheque. The company he keeps does not endear him to me & I cannot shout myself hoarse over the cry Great is our David or proclaim myself his prophet. So I think it looks as if I should remain out & the longer I remain out the more he will desire to rope me in, it being the little man's nature to think that the way to keep a Govt in office is by dropping colleagues who have become unpopular or useless & by bringing in anyone who looks as if he might be dangerous when left outside.

AC5/1/66

20 March 1918
9 Egerton Place

My dear Ida,

...

The P.M. is seeking to found a new party under his own leadership – not merely to carry through the war, but to endure afterwards. He has Bonar Law absolutely under his thumb and the knowledge that that is so destroys B.L.'s influence in his own party, which of course would be absorbed in and indeed be the main portion of the new party. But I gather that though B.L. may be content with this prospect, the rest of his Unionist colleagues are not and do not relish the prospect of saddling themselves with the weight of the Welsh Old Man of the Sea for all time.

I have been warned of the danger from inside and outside the Government, and now am invited to discuss the position and the future of our Party and its programme with Curzon, Long, Selborne, the Cecils and others. I shall do so. Perhaps I shall see my way more clearly thereafter. All I see at present is that they are all very dissatisfied with Bonar Law and very uneasy as to the future. But in truth, as Hugh Cecil wrote to me the other day, our old land-marks are submerged and it is not easy to find a resting place for the soles of one's feet.

You see that the offensive has begun ... I suppose it will go on for three months or so & I fully expect that we shall have to give ground largely before it ends but not such vital points as the Channel ports, Amien, or the like. But first, second, third line trenches may go & we may retire 5,10,20 miles but without breaking. That is my forecast. – Serious enough but checkmate to the Germans in the end.

3

'I FEEL BOUND TO SERVE'

The War Cabinet, April 1918 – January 1919

*By the early spring of 1918 Chamberlain's return to the government represented
an increasingly attractive proposition for the Prime Minister. Chamberlain's stock
had certainly risen substantially since his attacks upon the influence of the press
lords in February and March. In some quarters he was already perceived to be 'the
alternative Prime Minister, if by some mischance Lloyd George were to be killed by
a golf-ball'.[1] As the Irish problem forced itself back to the top of the political agenda
there were also obvious dangers in leaving him on the backbenches as a focus for
Unionist discontent – particularly as he was known to hold strong views on the
need to extend conscription to Ireland.[2] Thus, when the crisis over the proposal to
link Home Rule and conscription broke in early April, Lloyd George finally resolved
that he should be offered office. To this end, on 9 April Law was despatched to
invite Chamberlain to join the War Cabinet. Despite his own ambivalence towards
Lloyd George's character and a continued concern about the influence of the press
lords, Chamberlain was also predisposed to return to office: a position reinforced by
the military crisis created by Ludendorff's massive offensive on 21 March.[3]*

*Chamberlain's rehabilitation immediately provoked an outburst of virulent con-
demnation from the Northcliffe press, so recently the subject of his attacks. In
particular, the* Daily Mail *denounced the 'ridiculous appointment' of a man who
had 'never been anything more than an assiduous, honourable, ineffective mediocrity'.
His recall from his 'proper obscurity' at that juncture was thus depicted as nothing
more than 'cynical trifling' and an 'act of folly'. Other sections of the press, however,
equally swiftly came to his defence. Indeed, Chamberlain was particularly amused
to find the previously hostile* Star *praising him on the following day as 'a man of
honour, of ability, and of courage' and ascribing the venom of the* Mail's *attack to
Chamberlain's parliamentary criticism of Northcliffe on 11 March:*[4] *a charge the*

---

[1] Lord Esher to Sir Henry Wilson, 12 March 1918, P. Fraser, *Lord Esher: A Political
Biography*, (1973), 388. Five days after his first attack upon the press Lords Lloyd George
first spoke of Chamberlain's inclusion in the War Cabinet, Hankey Diary, 24 February
1918, S. Roskill, *Hankey: Man of Secrets*, (1970) I, 501.

[2] A. Chamberlain to Law, 5 April 1918, Petrie, *Life and Letters*, II, 113. According to
Amery, Lloyd George had previously offered Chamberlain the post of Chief Secretary
for Ireland, *The Leo Amery Diaries*, 216. Entry for 19 April 1918.

[3] A. Chamberlain to Lloyd George, 10 April 1918, AC18/2/6. For these events see J.
Turner, *British Politics and the Great War*, 286–291.

[4] *Daily Mail*, 17 April; *The Star*, 18 April 1918. During the Boer War, the Liberal evening
newspaper, *The Star*, had been at the centre of allegations against Joseph and Austen
Chamberlain concerning improper political pressure to obtain contracts to supply cordite
for Kynoch's, a company in which they had a family interest.

Mail *subsequently denied, angrily claiming that 'the Northcliffe press voices the feeling of every father, mother or relative of the boys whose names appear in the sad lists printed in the last page of this journal every morning'.*[5]   *Although the press attacks eventually abated, they were to make a negative impression upon Lloyd George's view of Chamberlain's value to his government after the next election.*[6]

Although as a member of the War Cabinet he was free from normal departmental duties, Chamberlain shouldered an onerous workload during this period – particularly after his appointment as Chairman of the Economic Defence and Development Committee in June 1918 in conjunction with an informal involvement in Indian affairs. Initially, however, the greatest single burden was represented by Ireland. As a condition of accepting office in April he had stipulated that nothing should be done which was inconsistent with the adoption of a federal solution involving devolution for the United Kingdom as a whole: an option which, he hoped, would render such a solution more acceptable to Ulster opinion. Secondly, he urged that nothing be done to coerce Ulster into acceptance until the plan had been extended to other parts of the British Isles.[7] *Although the Prime Minister agreed to the former condition, he informed Chamberlain that the latter would not be practicable. After a talk with Law, Chamberlain agreed to drop this demand after receiving the promise of a place on the committee drafting the Irish bill.*[8]

For some time Chamberlain had been more convinced than ever that his father's proposal for 'home rule all round' was now urgently necessary if the government was to confront the new problems likely to emerge from the war. He was thus influential in persuading the Home Rule Committee to adopt a federal solution. At his prompting, Lloyd George was also induced to support the federal option in Cabinet on 23 April. Yet, the outcome of this meeting was to sever finally the federal alternative from the home rule issue: a decision which raised the immediate problem of Ulster and in so doing undermined the whole purpose of the attempt to link conscription with home rule.[9] *Within weeks, therefore, it was clear that the Unionists would bring the government down rather than accept home rule – even with the exclusion of Ulster – and the Nationalists would resist conscription to the very end. Despite initially high hopes of producing a good bill, Chamberlain's doubts about the problems to be overcome and the prospects of resolving them were swiftly intensified during the summer. Moreover, as a former Chancellor, Chamberlain became increasingly alarmed as the financial implications of the federal scheme became apparent.*[10] *Against a background of rising violence in Ireland and intractable policy disagreement in London, the committee soon agreed that 'as a preliminary to*

---

[5] 'How to Lose' *Daily Mail*, 19 April 1918. For Northcliffe's opposition see R. Pound and G. Harmsworth, *Northcliffe*, (1959), 626–7; Lord Newton, *Retrospection* (1941), 253.

[6] See Hankey Diary, 16 December 1918, S. Roskill, *Hankey*, II, 35.

[7] A. Chamberlain to Lloyd George, 10 April 1918, AC18/2/6.

[8] Lloyd George to A. Chamberlain, 13 April 1918 and reply 14 April 1918, Lloyd George MSS F/7/2/9.

[9] See J.D. Fair, *British Interparty Conferences*, 226–227.

[10] K. Middlemas (ed), *Whitehall Diary: Ireland*, III, 7.

proceeding with the Government's policy either in respect of conscription or of the grant of self-Government to Ireland it was first necessary that the new Irish Administration should restore respect for the government, enforce the law and, above all, put down with a stern hand the Irish-German conspiracy which appears to be widespread in Ireland'.[11] With the simultaneous appointment of Edward Shortt as Chief Secretary for Ireland and Lord French's appointment as a military Lord-Lieutenant, the way was open for a policy of 'thorough' in Ireland for the next two years. Although such a strategy enabled the government to consign political initiatives conveniently to the side-lines, Chamberlain continued to champion the cause of federalism long after any prospect had realistically disappeared.

AC5/1/70

14 April 1918
9 Egerton Place

My dear Ida,

...

I can only say now that I have been asked and have consented to join the War Cabinet & to serve on the Comtee to frame the Irish Bill, the only conditions upon which I have insisted being that the Bill must contain nothing inconsistent with the adoption of a general system of federal government for the United Kingdom. This was agreed to without difficulty.

The position both at home and in France is so grave that I have felt I could not do otherwise. In such times Asquith's half way house is untenable. Either you must be prepared to turn the Govt out & accept the full responsibility of your action, or you must support the Govt ungrudgingly & serve where you can be of most use. It isn't a time for balancing between I dare not & I would, for half-hearted criticism & half-hearted support ... I believe I can be of use & I feel bound to serve. A change of Govt *now* is unthinkable as Asquith showed. So give me your sympathy and good wishes.

AC5/1/71

20 April 1918
Thornhill House
East Grinstead

My dear Ida,

...

... To be praised by the 'Star'! But that is the result of Northcliffe's

[11] Jones Diary, 9 May 1918, *Whitehall Diary*, III, 9.

outburst. I agree with Hilda that it was inartistic to begin so early &
on so violent a note, but then as Geoffrey Dawson[12] said to Fred
[Oliver] he is very angry because I said he was not a gentleman & is
besides suffering from megalomania & vanity to a degree which is
really a disease. The Yorkshire Post dots the i's and crosses the t's very
prettily ... The Evening News ... gave them away badly by announcing
that my appointment was abandoned in deference to 'public & private
protests'. It looks foolish now. I wish it were true that N[orthcliffe]
would resign his appointment as a protest against mine. I should then
feel as if I had at any rate done some good.

I have attended my first Cabinet & been very busy all the week on
the Committee for drafting the Irish Bill. So far as we have worked on
sound lines & I think that we shall produce a good Bill, but that is the
least part of the battle. Ireland is full of unreason, North & South
alike & what fate awaits us on our Bill I know not. I am sure that
Carson would like a settlement & would be reasonable if his people
would let him, but the Ulster M.P.'s are terrified of the Belfast working-
men & Carson himself is not a little afraid of them. He fears that they
will resist conscription, & if they are going to resist at all he would
sooner that they resisted Home Rule. If we could federalise the whole
U.K. at once, he would accept our proposals & tell the Ulstermen that
their case for forcible resistance was gone, but how can we do that *in
the time*? Well, I joined the Govt because of their difficulties, not in
ignorance of them & we will do our best. But I never felt less pleasure
or elation in taking office – indeed I feel none – but I believe I can be
of use & I know that I ought to try.

AC5/1/81   4 May 1918
                                                   Thornhill House

My dear Hilda,

     . . .
The P.M. is a funny man. At 5 o'clock [yesterday] afternoon I had
left him. He had been at his best. Faced with great, indeed immense
difficulties he showed courage, determination & indifference to the
consequences – parliamentary & personal, I mean – so long as what
he had now come to think necessary was done. He had sent for me &
after I arrived for Bonar. I backed him; Bonar havered & gloomed. I
told them they must get Walter Long. Walter stormed & raged, was

---

[12] (George) Geoffrey Dawson (1874–1944) Private secretary to Milner in South Africa
1901–5. Editor *Johannesburg Star* 1905–10; Editor of *The Times*, 1912–19, 1923–41. Known
as Robinson until 1917.

redder than 10 Turkey cocks & in a most difficult mood. I restated the
P.M.'s case, laid stress on parts of it which the P.M. had slurred, pointed
out to Walter that it was *his* case & his policy too, in short won him
over to consent to what really was his own policy & left ... at 5
o'clock – policy & men to carry it out settled & all four of us agreed.
I need not say our subject was Ireland. Into details of policy & men I
must not enter, but the policy was strong, wise & necessary; the men
were suitable.

Would you believe that at dinner the P.M. discussed the whole thing
again with Milner, Oliver, Philip Kerr[13] & for a time Geoffrey Dawson
(formerly Robinson) of the Times! The P.M. was loud in praise of me –
'the only one of the lot with any guts' if you will pardon his vulgar
expression; but he changed or was induced to change his mind as to
men, and sent Fred to ask me to offer the Viceroyalty to the man
whom Long said wouldn't do instead of offering it to the man whom
all four of us had agreed upon in the afternoon.

I flatly refused – not because I think the man was a bad choice but
because Walter would have resigned, as I should have done, if so
treated. So I rang up the P.M. – 'gone to bed' – rang up Bonar, gave
him a lesson in behaviour to colleagues & how not to do things – was
rung up by the P.M. from bed, repeated my lesson to him. Fred sat an
amused listener to my side of the conversation & having heard me
splutter & swear & d–n everyone's eyes – the P.M.'s & Bonar's in
particular – while he told his story, explained that I was the perfect
diplomat as he heard my gentle & persuasive remonstrances, & left me
to follow up my conversation by a letter to the P.M., telling him that
his policy was right & would win if *wisely* & *firmly* executed & then
explaining where in lay wisdom & wherein lay firmness. My first advice
was: You must tell Long. You can carry him with you if you consult
him but not otherwise, & it is essential that you should carry him. My
second piece of advice was: if you want ___ for Viceroy tell him
yourself. He is a very simple & direct man himself & likes simplicity &
directness in others. And my third was: Stick to your point: the moment
___ or ___ gets over, let him *govern*. When you have a government &
not a pasteboard sham & the Irish realise it, go ahead.

Then I went to bed with a good conscience, feeling that I had done
something to prevent Bonar throwing up the sponge, Long from kicking
over the traces, & the P.M. from once again getting into an unholy
mess by doing things in the wrong way. And this morning I came down

[13] Philip Henry Kerr (1882–1940) Co-founder and first editor, *Round Table* 1910–16;
private secretary to Lloyd George 1916–21; Chancellor of Duchy of Lancaster August–
November 1931; PUS for India 1931–September 32; Chairman Indian Franchise Committee 1932; Ambassador to Washington 1939–40. Succeeded cousin as 11th Marquess of
Lothian, 1930. Created K.T., 1940.

by the 9 o'clock train, dug land from 11 till 1.30, sowed seeds & dug again from 2.30 till 5.0 & dug still more from 5.30 till past 7. Now I think I must go to bed, & won't I sleep! I breakfast every morning at 8.0 & work till 12.30 or one at night.

Sunday morning & pouring wet. Every prospect of a continuously wet day. I have not had one fine week end yet! O-o-oh!!!

My Friday's activities were not wasted. Letter from Long – 'I quite agree & will do as you suggest.'

Letter from the P.M. – 'Long agrees. I am communicating with ___. Your firmness yesterday was to me a source of great comfort. Among the horrible perplexities & anxieties one has to cleave one's way through, there is no support equal to that of a colleague who does not run away from a policy the moment he encounters difficulties. My Liberal colleagues have accepted my proposal _ _ _ _'

AC5/1/82   8 May 1918
                                       Offices of the War Cabinet

My dear Hilda,

. . .

Well, our troubles do not grow less. You will have seen French's[14] appointment announced before you got my last letter. He was the 5 o'clock choice. There are many advantages in a soldier & he is a man of courage & does not lose his head or change his mind at the first difficulties. But his difficulties & ours are immense. The situation in Ireland is very bad. A country can't be left for 10 years without a Govt & be none the worse for it. Of all the misdemeanours of the Asquith Govt the worst & the most serious for us now is the levity with which they drew and forwarded with their Irish Bill & the way in which they utterly neglected the duty of governing in Ireland & allowed North & South each to go their own lawless way unchecked, the police to be disorganised, the Magistracy to be packed with incompetents & crooks, & the whole Administration to be brought into well-merited contempt.

Friday evening. And at that point I was obliged to hurry off to the Cabinet, & then I worked, hammer & tongs, till 1 o'clock in the morning, lunch-time included & with only an hour & a half or so for talk with Ivy at dinner about all that was going on.

[14] Field-Marshal Sir John Denton Pinkstone French (1852–1925) Served Sudan 1884–5; South Africa 1899–1902. Chief of Imperial General Staff, 1911–14; C-in-C, BEF 1914–15; Home Forces 1915–18. Lord-Lieutenant Ireland 1918–21. Created Viscount French 1916 and Earl of Ypres 1922.

Part of my work consisted in 2 hours spent with the P.M. & Milner in going through the P.M.'s draft or, to speak more accurately, in discussing with the P.M. what he could & what he must, & what he could not & must not, say next day [for the Maurice Debate].[15] The further we probed the case with that very remarkable & invaluable Hankey's[16] assistance, the stronger it appeared to be, but the P.M. wanted to 'spread' himself & it was difficult to persuade him that directness, simplicity & brevity were the first qualities to aim at. He took our advice & criticisms very well & was, I believe, genuinely grateful for them. At least he said to others that we had really helped him. But the Times is right in saying that when he has a strong case he does not know how to put it. Anyone else might have produced less immediate effect, but anyone else would have stated the case in a way that would have carried more solid & lasting conviction – partly because they would have dealt more simply, directly & shortly with the actual changes & dealt with them first, reserving all comment, elaboration, censure & argument for later & separate treatment, partly because Lloyd George's word carries less conviction than almost anyone's. But you will be interested to know that having read all Hankey's precis of the papers & turned up many of the originals, I believe that Maurice[17] had not the slightest justification in the grave impropriety (it is a very mild word to use) of publishing any such letter at all & above all of publishing it without having made any representation to the Ministers whose veracity he impugned & without giving them any opportunity of correcting their inaccuracy if inaccuracy there had been. Nothing could for the moment palliate so grave a breach of discipline & confidence but the absolute necessity of correcting vitally important misstatements & the refusal of the Ministers concerned to acknowledge & correct publicly an unquestionable & vital error. The errors, if proved, were not of this character. Maurice himself was the official source of some of them. He had made no attempt to bring them to the notice of Ministers tho' he was in almost daily personal communication with them, & he does not appear to have said a word to anyone in the War Office about them until he had been relieved of his

[15] General Sir Frederick Maurice alleged Lloyd George had misled Parliament when claiming British forces in France were numerically stronger on 1 January 1918 than a year earlier. An Asquithian motion for an inquiry was debated in the Commons on 9 May 1918 – the only occasion in which they divided the House against the Government.
[16] Sir Maurice Pascal Alers Hankey (1877–1963) Secretary Committee of Imperial Defence 1912–1938; War Cabinet 1916; Imperial War Cabinet 1917–18; Cabinet Secretary 1919–38. Minister without Portfolio 1939–40; Chancellor of Duchy of Lancaster 1940–41; Paymaster-General 1941–42. Created K.C.B. 1916; G.C.B. 1919; Baron Hankey 1939.
[17] Major-General Sir Frederick (Barton) Maurice (1871–1951) Soldier from 1892. Director of Military Operations, Imperial General Staff 1915–18. Principal, Working Men's College 1922–23; Queen Mary College, University of London 1933–44.

post! There is a world of bad intrigue behind his conduct – of distrust of Lloyd George & hatred of Henry Wilson.

AC5/1/83   18 May 1918
                                                          Thornhill House

My dear Ida,

I came down here yesterday with sister Bee about 6 o'clock. We took a cup of tea & then wandered about the garden, watered our seeds & did little jobs till dinner time. Today I have been hard at work – good honest toil, none of your Cabinets or Comtees or interviews & the like but hard digging & weeding.

. . .

Well, I have had a jolly day's holiday. I wish the guns in Flanders had not boomed so loudly all day long. I know it is right & a duty to get all the holiday & change of thought I can but the guns seem a reproach to any enjoyment.

AC5/1/86   10 June 1918
                                                          9 Egerton Place

My dear Ida,

. . .

Our anxieties about France are constant, but this time the line seems holding [sic] pretty well & it would seem that the German's are paying heavily for any advance which they do secure. But it is a long & weary struggle & the end is far off, I fear. I have been doing a little useful work in some minor but not unimportant matters, but I am mightily troubled about Ireland & cannot see any way through the difficulties that confront us. The Govt had not really reached the measure of agreement which I understood them to have attained when I entered the Cabinet; they had not got their measures ready as I supposed them to have done on the military side; & I fear I must add that as long as Duke[18] remained Chief Sec. we were not properly informed of what was passing. Add that without any malicious intention I think the new administration has 'queered the pitch' by ill-drawn proclamations & that I fear the Govt won't accept definitely & whole-heartedly the one

[18] Henry Edward Duke (1855–1939). Conservative MP for Plymouth 1900–1906 and Exeter 1910–1918. Chief Secretary for Ireland July 1916 – April 1918. Lord of Appeal April 1918–November 1919 and President of Probate, Divorce and Admiralty Division 1919–33. Knighted 1918; created Baron Merivale 1925.

possible course still open to us but will nibble off bits of it – & you will begin to realise that I am not happy.

And then there is India! Again I can't get my way or the clear lead within definite time limits which I think the true path of safety. Some people still seem to think that safety lies in answering no questions & waiting on opinion & events. That is not my experience – but then before you express an opinion you must have one & by right it should be an opinion by which you will stand. Now some people have no opinion & some people are not sure that they will stand by their opinion until 'public opinion' has spoken. And to all those the last word of wisdom is: Let us commit ourselves to nothing – & by so doing we shall inevitably be committed to a great deal more than is in any way necessary.

AC5/1/87

14 June 1918
Thornhill House

My dear Hilda,

The sittings of the Imperial War Cabinet have begun & promise to be full of interest.

. . .

I have delivered my soul on Ireland & the Federal Solution in a long memorandum dictated during the week which I shall shortly circulate to my colleagues. Shall I do any good? I don't know, but at least I have had my way in two matters of internal organisation this week & see my path to some useful work if I am not disturbed. But I wish B.L. was not so utterly done up & that Long, who has many good qualities, was less personal & pernickety over trifles.

AC5/1/92

23 July 1918
9 Egerton Place

My dear Ida,

. . .

And how does Master Bosch feel? Pretty sick, I hope. He has had a nasty knock when all allowances are made for exaggeration & I hope that before he gets all his troops out of that salient he will have suffered still heavier losses ... I have never been certain that this was *the* great blow.... But whatever the Germans intended has failed.... It will be interesting to watch the effect on the neutrals of this failure. They have all been waiting for the great attack which the Germans told them would in effect be conclusive, & their belief in German military efficiency & the terror of German brutality have made them fearful of resisting any German demand or increasing German displeasure by any concession to the Allies. If, as I begin to believe, this attack was or has become the Great German Effort its failure must profoundly affect the on-lookers.

AC5/1/93

29 July 1918
9 Egerton Place

My dear Hilda,

. . .
. . . As to Ireland I can see no light, but I do not think that Dillon[19] evokes any support in the House or country – unless it be among the Labour Party who under Henderson's[20] guidance would pick up support anywhere. But I think H. is spoiling his chances by taking over all the pacifist Liberals as Labour candidates.

AC5/1/95

11 August 1918
Thornhill House

My dear Hilda,

. . .
Montagu's report[21] has had a very favourable reception in our House & a better one than he or I expected in the Lords. The difficulties are immense & the questions which he has left to be solved by Committees are crucial. I expect that in the end his scheme will be a good deal modified but I believe that its main features are right or perhaps I should say its basic principles.

[19] John Dillon (1851–1927). Leader of Irish Nationalist Party in succession to Justin McCarthy 1896–1900. Nationalist MP for Tipperary 1880–83 and Mayo East November 1885–1918. Chairman of Irish Nationalist Party 1918.
[20] Arthur Henderson (1863–1935). Labour MP for Barnard Castle 1903–1918, Widnes 1919–22, Newcastle East 1923, Burnley 1924–31; Clay Cross 1933–35. Labour Party Treasurer, 1904–12, Chairman 1908–10, 1914–17. President Board of Education May 1915–August 1916, Paymaster-General August–December 1916, Member of War Cabinet December 1916 August 1917, Home Secretary January–November 1924, Foreign Secretary 1929–31. Labour leader 1931–32. Chaired World Disarmament Conference 1932–35. Nobel Peace Prize 1934.
[21] Cd. 9109, *Joint Report on Indian Constitutional Reforms*. The Montagu-Chelmsford Report's proposals for a 'dyarchy' in the provinces and an elected majority in the central legislature were embodied in the government of India Act of December 1919.

Ludendorff's massive attack on the British Fifth and Third Armies on 21 March and two further major attacks swiftly forced the Allies into a headlong retreat which took the Germans to within fifty miles of Paris by early June. Like many observers, Chamberlain remained uncertain as to what to make of these military developments. In July the Allied counter-offensive began and on 8 August the Battle of Amiens demonstrated to both sides the catastrophic decline in German fighting power. Thereafter, as Chamberlain's almost dazed reaction demonstrates, the end came with an astonishing and wholly unexpected suddenness. Only American high-handedness and the prospect that the Germans might accept President Wilson's 'Fourteen Points' as a basis for peace served to blight his burgeoning sense of satisfaction and relief.

AC5/1/98   5 September 1918
Thornhill House

My dear Ida,

What wonderful happenings are there on the Western Front! One keeps wondering exactly what it all portends & how far we can force the Germans back. The transformation is so sudden I still cannot understand it, but within the last few days I have seen the first official statements from the military authorities on German demoralisation. Heaven send that it may spread & spread & spread!

AC5/1/101   14 September 1918
Thornhill House

My dear Ida,

Let me begin, as Neville says that all our letters begin, continue & end – with the weather. It is very important to us gardening & country folk, is it not? Well, our weather has broken with a vengeance ...
...
The good news from the Western Front continues but this weather, one would think, must bring all movement to an end ... However, I think it clear that the German edifice is cracking at last. If only there were a decent government in Russia or any chance of getting one!

AC5/1/103   22 September 1918
Thornhill House

My dear Ida,

Oh ho! There is to be no Cabinet tomorrow, so I telephoned London that I should not come up until tomorrow afternoon & then I asked if there was any news, & lo & behold! the news is that by this morning's official [sic] Allenby[22] had taken 8000 prisoners, 100 guns &c. Now that must be best part of half the whole Turkish force confronting him. And the reply went on; "it's on the tape (not yet officially confirmed) that he has got 18000 prisoners." And that would be the whole force, I should think, Germans included. He has certainly done brilliantly … So Master Turk gets his " 'it on the 'ead" just after Master Bosch & Master Bulgar has an uncomfortable time too. Oh! my dear Eyetalians, why did you not strike when you were asked to? Then Master Austrian might have been battered also.

. . .

I heard today from Sir John Nixon that the Army Council officially informed him that after investigation they cannot agree with the Mesopotamia Commission & accept his explanations. I am delighted!

AC5/1/104   24 September 1918
                                                              9 Egerton Place

My dear Hilda,

. . .

September 26 I think we have broken the railway strike but accounts vary from day to day & almost from hour to hour. In any case our last word in concession has been said, & if the men don't go back to work quickly, they will be sent to the army. So too with the Shipwrights on the Clyde. Govt must, can & does endure a great deal, but there are limits to what it can stand & I am glad to see a growing impatience amongst the public of the interruption of war work by men who, disregarding the advice of their own leaders & refusing to submit to or abide by awards, go out without caring what injury they cause to national interests.

Nothing but Dominic Thompson's exclamation fits the situation in Palestine. Prodijeous! Allenby is making a clean sweep of the Turkish forces confronting him. And if you turn to the Balkans, it is pleasant to think of the Serbian territory rewon & that British troops are on Bulgarian soil. It is fortunate for the Bulgars that they are British & not Serbian troops. The Serbs have a fearful debt to repay upon the Bulgars & will, I should think, show little mercy when their day comes.

. . .

The horrors in Russia have been awful. Even Germans & Austrians

[22] Edmund Henry Allenby (1861–1936) Soldier and statesman. Western Front 1915–1917. Commander Egyptian Expeditionary Force 1917–1919. High Commissioner for Egypt 1919–1925.

joined with the Neutral & allied representatives in protest against indiscriminate murder & blind fury of terrorism. I trust that we are going to get our missions safely out, but I am very anxious & very doubtful whether we have taken the right course. Equally competent authorities – even upon the spot – give directly contradictory advice & we have to make a shot at the truth. In such a case I don't feel that I can resist the man at the helm if he takes the opposite view to me. The probabilities are nearly equal, his closer & more constant touch with all that is going on will give him a 'feel' – an instinct if you like – which it is best to follow. In any case he *is* the man at the helm, & I am not.

AC5/1/105

28 September 1918
Thornhill House

My dear Ida,

...

Does the German edifice begin to crack? I rather think it does, tho' it may yet be long in falling. Wilson burst into my room yesterday morning ... It was the Bulgarian request for an armistice – asked for by the *Govt* & that *old* fox Ferdinand. But he won't get it till he has given such military pledges that there is no going back for him any more. And by pledges I *don't* mean words. Our successes in Palestine are already favourably affecting the situation in the Middle East but Master Turk will smile to see Master Bulgar beaten. He has been very much afraid of him. And on the West? Ding-dong, ding-dong! Fosch[23] [sic] leaves his enemy no rest & the German is at his wits end for men. Very secretly I will tell you that 100 of them from a North Prussian regiment with 3 officers walked over into our lines by St. Quentin the other day & gave themselves up. An occasional straggler may have come before & there has been talk which never comes off; but this is the first time that such an episode has occurred. Aururus mirabilis! What a change from March & April.

[23] Marshal Ferdinand Foch (1851–1929) Commander 9th Army 1914 coordinating Allied left flank in France. Retired with Joffre 1916 but returned as Chief of Staff in 1917 after failure of Nivelle offensive and became Allied Generalissimo at head of unified command from March 1918.

AC5/1/107   6 October 1918
                                                  Thornhill House

My dear Hilda,

. . .

Monday. No news as yet save that which The Times has brought but I am reassured by Barnes[24] speech. I look upon him as the first spot where weakness in our ranks would appear, for he is not very well informed & he is a great sentimentalist though a very honest, straightforward loveable man.

AC5/1/108   9 October 1918
                                                  Thornhill House

My dear Ida,

What exactly were the speculations in which I indulged when I last wrote, I no longer remember. They were probably wrong & certainly they are out of date, but no speculations could be stranger than the events. I think I anticipated a peace offer from Austria covering Prest. Wilson's 14 points. I don't think that I foresaw that the next offer would come from Germany, & I suspect that Germany only made it to forestall separate offers from Austria & Turkey, to placate her own people & to raise if possible dissension in each of the Allied countries. I doubt whether she has gained her first point except for the moment – in other words I think it likely that both Austria & Turkey will seek to negotiate for themselves. What effect it may have in Germany itself, I don't feel able to measure, but I am glad to think that the Allied peoples have been as unanimous as the Allied Govt in saying, "Get out first & talk afterwards", & that meanwhile our armies are pressing forward everywhere except in Italy!

. . .

Sunday night So the Germans accept the President's 14 points. I feared that they would, but does even the President know what he means by them? And if he does & if the Germans "mean the same thing", what then? Does that fix the terms of an armistice? No. No. No! Thank goodness! I am quite well enough to go up to town tomorrow & thank goodness also that the three Prime Ministers appear to be pretty stiff!

[24] George Nicoll Barnes (1859–1940) Labour MP for Glasgow (Blackfriars and later Gorbals) 1906–22. Minister of Pensions December 1916–August 1917; Minister without Portfolio 1917–January 1920. Resigned from Labour party on its withdrawal from Coalition to participate in Versailles negotiations.

AC5/1/110

26 October 1918
Thornhill House

My dear Ida,

. . .

What shall I say of the public news? The President has at last consented to consult his allies none too soon – but characteristically he has made it very clear that he wishes the lime-light man to keep the bullseye full on him & he wishes his allies – I beg his pardon! "the associated Governments" – to give him a testimonial of their unbounded admiration & gratitude which he may use for electoral purposes! Meanwhile he has put us all in the cart & our first business is to get out & to get him out. 'Freedom of the seas' – go to Jericho! He lays down 14 points & *2 speeches* as the basis of the armistice. The Germans accept & 'assume' the Entente powers agree with him. How can we enter our negotiations without telling the Germans that they 'assume' too much & how can we say that without putting the President's nose out of joint? There were difficulties enough already without his needlessly creating this fresh one. And mind you! he was furious when he thought that we were settling peace terms with Turkey, against whom he has never sent a soldier, without first consulting him! "I do not like you, Dr Fell"

Shall we have peace with Germany now? I am inclined to think so, but I am not at all sure. I hope so, but I consider that the President's correspondence has lessened the chances of it. It must be a peace on most onerous conditions for Germany in any case, but I at least would not fight on for vengeance only or even to secure punishment beyond what is inherent in the circumstances of the case – loss of all colonies, loss of Alsace-Lorraine, some losses in the East of Europe, some surrender of battleships &c. a large indemnity. Vengeance is a luxury that few can afford in public or private life. If we fight on, Germany is ruined, but at what a cost to ourselves. Our armies must dwindle; the French are no longer fighting; a year hence we shall have lost how many thousands more men? & American power will be dominant. Today *we* are top dog. *Our* fleets, *our* armies have brought Germany to her knees & today (more than at any later time) the peace may be our peace. So I am for peace if we can get a *good* peace i.e. a decisive peace & one that is as secure as human foresight can make it.

AC5/1/111   2 November 1918
                                            Thornhill House

My dear Hilda,

...
What am I to say of the week's history? There is too much of it
...
Sunday. No further news of the proposed Austrian armistice has
yet reached me. The Italian Military Attaché told our people that
it had been signed by Diag on Friday but he was, to say the least,
premature. Still the only serious question there is the one I put
above – has anyone now authority to sign, still more to enforce
compliance with the terms of any armistice? And will the internecine
racial conflicts which, with military disaster & starvation superimposed,
have broken up the Empire degenerate into class-warfare? Brigandage
was already rife; the authority of government gone, desertions
numerous. I expect that society trembles on the brink of dissolution.
    Meanwhile what of Germany? ... I think we have them at our
mercy & that they must accept our terms. I should not be surprised
to hear some day that the Emperor has abdicated. The people are
turning upon him, rather basely I think, the Kings have no love
for or real loyalty to him & even the army (as you doubtless saw
by the captured order published about a fortnight ago) is ceasing
to show him ordinary respect. When the game is up, we set our
teeth, fight on & often muddle through. That is not the German
way. Trucculent in success, overbearing & brutal in victory, when
they find that the game is lost they collapse morally as a people, &
even Prussian discipline will, I believe, be powerless to put 'grit'
into them. Someone told me that they have discovered that word
grit & that it is a quality which we possess & they do not. Left to
themselves they would lie flat, cry forfeit & – set to work slowly
silently & with infinite patience to begin all over again. But this
time I think autocracy & militarism have had their death-blow,
unless there is a military coup d'état, & I don't believe that their
military resources make that possible. But what a smash it must be!
Surrender of Alsace Lorraine, surrender of arms of battle-ships &
merchant ships, of Prussian Poland including part at least of East
Prussia & the birthplace of the Hohenzollerens surrender of their
colonies & of all their dreams of the 'drang nach osten', a huge
indemnity, & then for what is left a crushing load of taxation, a
starving people & starved industries. If the guilt was immense, the
punishment will be overwhelming. So be it! But I should like to see
Berlin bombed & Essen systematically destroyed. However I think I

mentioned that if we can get a *good* peace, I am ready to fore-go vengeance.

For some time Chamberlain had engaged in anxious musings about the magnitude of the problems likely to confront a post-war government. He was equally concerned about the prospects of an election and the threat from a reorganized Labour Party in the uncertain political world created by a newly enfranchised mass democracy. In these circumstances Chamberlain was convinced that the war-time coalition should be perpetuated. As he told Law on Armistice Day, 'the immensely difficult problems of demobilization and reconstruction make it important to preserve the Administration as a broad bottom now as during the years of war'.[25] Although unopposed in West Birmingham, there was much about the campaign which confirmed many of his worst forebodings.

AC5/1/112

9 November 1918
Thornhill House

My dear Ida,

. . .

If an armistice is signed there will be an election before long – the coalition against the rest. I am sorry for it but Bonar Law tells me that by now the House thinks of nothing else & the P.M. also has the obsession. Let us hope that it will turn out well. It is like dipping in a 'lucky bag' which childhood's memories tell me are apt to be a disappointment. I am anxious about the future which seems to me full of difficulty & danger, strikes, discontent & much revolutionary feeling in the air when the strain and patriotic self-repression of the last four years are removed.

AC5/1/113

8 December 1918
Thornhill House

My dear Ida,

. . . Neville & Annie lunched with us on Friday, both looking very tired but in good spirits, I think. N. says that he hopes to "give Master Kneeshaw[26] a jolly good knock" & I sincerely trust that he will. Of the

---

[25] A. Chamberlain to Law, 11 November 1918, AC35/1/6.
[26] J.W. Kneeshaw: Neville Chamberlain's radical Labour opponent in Birmingham Ladywood during the 1918 election.

others B'ham seats I do not know very much. Everywhere as far as I can learn there is a want of workers, absence of organisation & great apathy. Hardly any women come to the meetings, not more certainly than before they had the vote, & whether they will use their votes &, if so, how they will use them are questions which I cannot answer. In my own division organisation is simply not existent. Of 40 women on our Committee rolls 4 responded; of 800 men, 40! I can almost find it in my heart to regret that the inefficient Edwinson lost the chance of a contest which might have disciplined us into at least the nucleous[sic] of an organisation. If *any* body settled down to work there & got a body of 2 or 300 workers, he would win the seat today – not because of his own strength but because of everyone else's weakness. I should think that West B'ham is the division which is worst off in this respect, but as far as I can judge all are badly off. There will be much to do before any of us can consider ourselves safe, & for this election it looks to me pretty much of a toss up. I think that most of our men will be returned, but Hallewell Rogers[27] is said to be doubtful & Austin[28] to be likely to be beaten on his personal unpopularity.

As to the election generally, I have never hated one so much. The voters are apathetic, the dividing line of parties obscure & uncertain, the issues ill-defined, cranks numerous & the worst elements very much in evidence.

AC5/1/114   1 January 1919
                                             9 Egerton Place

My dear Ida,

. . .

. . . I wish I could get a little more rest, for I am very tired mentally as well as physically & a fortnight's holiday if it were obtainable would do me a world of good, but I must be back in town for the Cabinet on Tuesday. I have no hint so far of the P.M.'s intentions & in many ways am so uncomfortable that I don't seem to care. Perhaps it is mainly weariness but I feel that I have no real friend & no one whom I really trust among the present leaders – & that is discouraging.

The Govt would do better if it had a stronger Opposition in front of it. I am really sorry for Asquith's defeat, but I can feel no regret for

[27] Sir Hallewell Rogers (1864–1931) Chairman of Birmingham Small Arms Co. Coalition Unionist MP for Moseley division, Birmingham December 1918 until resignation in February 1921.
[28] Sir Henry Austin (1866–1941) Assisted in founding Wolseley Tool & Motor Car Co. Founded Austin Motor Company 1905. Conservative MP for King's Norton (Birmingham) 1918–October 1924.

Runciman[29] or McKenna[30] or Simon[31] or the lesser fry. They all tried to fight on exactly the old party lines, raised the old cries, went just as far in opposition as they dared & showed no such magnanimity or patriotism as Asquith in his retirement. As for the downfall of the Macdonalds[32][sic] Snowdens,[33] Outhwaites[34] & Hendersons I unfeignedly rejoice in it. It was deserved & it will be useful.

B'ham is united & the majorities good, but I wish the polls had been bigger.

[29] Walter Runciman (1870–1949) Liberal MP Oldham 1899–1900, Dewsbury 1902–18, Swansea West 1924–29, St Ives 1929–31. Liberal National MP St Ives 1931–37. Parliamentary Secretary Local Government Board 1905–7, Financial Secretary, Treasury 1907–8, President Board of Education 1908–11, Board of Agriculture 1911–14, Board of Trade 1914–16 and 1931–37. Lord President of Council 1938–39. Special Envoy to Czechoslovakia 1938. Created Viscount Runciman of Doxford 1937.

[30] Reginald McKenna (1863–1943) Liberal MP Monmouthshire North 1895–1918. Financial Secretary, Treasury 1905–7, President Board of Education 1907–8, 1st Lord of Admiralty 1908–11, Home Secretary 1911–15, Chancellor of Exchequer 1915–December 1916.

[31] John Allsebrook Simon (1873–1954) Liberal MP Walthamstow 1906–18, Spen Valley 1922–40. A Liberal National from 1931. Solicitor-General 1910–13; Attorney-General 1913–15; Home Secretary 1915–January 1916 and 1935–1937; Foreign Secretary 1931–35; Chancellor of Exchequer 1937–40; Lord Chancellor 1940–45. Knighted 1910, created Viscount Simon 1940.

[32] James Ramsay MacDonald (1866–1937) Labour MP Leicester 1906–18, Aberavon 1922–29, Seaham 1929–31. National Labour MP for Seaham 1931–35 and Scottish Universities 1936–37. Labour Party Secretary 1900–12, Chairman 1912–14, Labour Leader 1922–31. Prime Minister and Foreign Secretary January–November 1924, Prime Minister 1929–35, Lord President of the Council 1935 – May 1937.

[33] Philip Snowden (1864–1937) Labour MP Blackburn 1906–18, Colne Valley 1922–31. Chancellor of Exchequer January–November 1924, 1929–31; Lord Privy Seal 1931–32. Created Viscount Snowden 1931.

[34] Robert Leonard Outhwaite (1869–1930) Journalist. Unsuccessfully contested West Birmingham 1906. Liberal MP, Hanley July 1912–18.

4

'THE TIMES MAKE EVERYTHING EXTREMELY DIFFICULT'

The Treasury, January 1919 – April 1921

Chamberlain emerged from the government reshuffle which followed the 'Coupon' election as Chancellor of the Exchequer. In many respects the appointment appears unremarkable given his past experience and reputation. His first tenure of the office had been in October 1903 in the immediate aftermath of his father's departure from the Balfour Cabinet. Although only a few days from his fortieth birthday and widely regarded as a 'hostage for Joe',[1] he soon proved himself to be a capable minister. During this period a future Permanent Secretary at the department 'thought highly' of him as a 'hard worker and good official'.[2] Walter Long went even further in contending that he was 'without exception the best Chancellor of the Exchequer he ha[d] ever worked with'.[3] After leading the opposition to Lloyd George's 1909 budget, even former detractors were obliged to concede that Chamberlain was 'in the first rank as a debater and as a leader'.[4] It was a measure of this stature that at the outbreak of war in 1914 Lloyd George had invited him to attend the Financial Conference assembled to tackle the initial emergency. On one occasion the Chancellor had even asked Chamberlain to preside while he attended a Cabinet meeting. Although Lloyd George later presented this unique occurrence as 'a foretaste of the Coalition',[5] others rejoiced that Chamberlain was 'practically acting as chancellor of the exchequer' because Lloyd George, 'who knows very little of finance, has completely lost his head':[6] a preference initially echoed within the Treasury itself.[7] Against such a background, Chamberlain's appointment as Chancellor in January 1919 appears scarcely a controversial or unorthodox choice, particularly as he was deemed by both the City and the Treasury to be far sounder on the interests of finance than other

[1] Sir Alexander Mackintosh, *Echoes of Big Ben*, 47.

[2] Masterman Diary, 12 October 1910 [?], reporting Sir Robert Chalmers, Chairman of the Board of Inland Revenue 1907–11 and Permanent Secretary to the Treasury 1911–13, L. Masterman, *C.F.G. Masterman: A Biography*, 177.

[3] Crawford Diary, 6 July 1905, John Vincent (ed) *The Crawford Papers. The Journal of David Lindsay twenty-seventh Earl of Crawford and tenth Earl of Balcarres 1871–1940 during the years 1892 to 1940*, (Manchester, 1984), 80. Also Earl Winterton, *Orders of the Day*, (1953), 8.

[4] Churchill to the King, 9 April 1910, R.S. Churchill, *Winston S. Churchill II, Young Statesman, 1901–1914*, Companion 2, 1005.

[5] D. Lloyd George, *The War Memoirs of David Lloyd George*, 106.

[6] Lord Crawford to Lady Wantage, 11 August 1914, J. Vincent (ed), *The Crawford Papers*, 342.

[7] Basil Blackett Diary, 1 and 2 August 1914, R.F. Harrod, *The Life of John Maynard Keynes*, (Pelican ed, Harmondsworth, 1972), 231.

possible candidates such as Churchill, Worthington-Evans or Sir Auckland Geddes.[8]

Yet despite these credentials, the irony of this appointment was that it was an outcome desired neither by the new Chancellor nor the Prime Minister. Indeed, Chamberlain's return to the Treasury in January 1919 appears to have been due almost entirely to the insistence of Bonar Law. In May 1917, and again in May 1918, it was rumoured that Law had been utterly determined that Chamberlain should succeed him at the Exchequer rather than Lloyd George's own choice of Edwin Montagu.[9] In December 1918 Law remained equally adamant in his insistence.[10] Initially 'absolutely refusing' to consider the possibility because of the press hostility accompanying Chamberlain's return to the War Cabinet earlier in the year, Lloyd George was again inclined to make Montagu Chancellor: a choice which would then permit Chamberlain to return to the India Office.[11] In the event, the Prime Minister's wishes were over-ruled although his apprehensions were well founded as the Northcliffe press predictably made 'a dead set at Austen' from the outset.[12] Although by March the virulence of these attacks had prompted Chamberlain to ponder 'whether with such malevolent enemies in the Press I shall be able to survive the difficulties in my path',[13] Lloyd George's own breach with Northcliffe in the following month resolved at least this difficulty.[14]

If Lloyd George was initially reluctant, Chamberlain was even less enthusiastic about the prospect of a return to the Treasury himself. When first approached about the Treasury by Law in early January 1919 an 'ugly row' had ensued when it emerged that the office carried with it neither an automatic seat in Cabinet nor the official residence at No. 11 Downing Street. In reality, however, Chamberlain's righteous indignation concealed a more profound set of reservations.[15] First, his period at the Treasury between 1903–05 had given him a clear insight into the heavy burdens of that particular office at any time. When the first coalition was formed in May 1915 Chamberlain had thus been swift to renounce any claim he might have upon the office, while urging Law to accept it as 'the second in the Government when in the right hands'.[16] Secondly, he also found the nature of the work politically and temperamentally uncongenial. 'It is an office which unhappily has of necessity

---

[8] C. Wrigley, *Lloyd George and the Challenge of Labour: The Post-War Coalition 1918–1922*, (1990), 82.

[9] *Lord Riddell's War Diary, 1914–1918* (1933) Entry for 13 May 1917, 250. A. Chamberlain to Hilda, 17 March 1918, AC5/1/65.

[10] Hankey Diary, 16 December 1918, Roskill, *Man of Secrets*, II, 35.

[11] *Ibid.* Also Churchill to Lloyd George, 26 December 1918, M. Gilbert, *Winston S. Churchill*, IV. Companion I, 445

[12] Sanders Diary, Sunday, 9 February 1919. See also Churchill to Lloyd George, 21 November 1918 for Rothermere's animus towards Chamberlain, M. Gilbert, *Winston S. Churchill*, IV. Companion I, 421.

[13] A. Chamberlain to Ida, 2 March 1919 AC5/1/121.

[14] A. Chamberlain to Ida, 18 April 1919 AC5/1/125.

[15] For Chamberlain's detailed account of these events see *Down the Years*, Chapter VIII. For account of his complaints to Lloyd George see A.J.P. Taylor, (ed) *Lloyd George: A Diary by Frances Stevenson*, entry for 5 March 1919, 170.

[16] A. Chamberlain to Law, 17 May 1915, Petrie, *Life and Letters*, II, 24.

much contentious business ... with other offices', he informed Lloyd George. 'The Chancellor of the Exchequer has all the odium of raising the money. His colleagues have all the pleasure and kudos of spending it. Each of their demands may be in itself reasonable, yet in the aggregate they are often impossible'.[17] This was to prove a peculiarly prophetic judgement upon the next two years. Moreover, while such concerns were true of even the best of times, Chamberlain's apprehensions were gravely exacerbated by the belief that the government would inevitably confront severe financial difficulties and industrial conflict as a direct result of the war and its demands. As he told the Commons in his first Budget, although the Treasury had never been a sinecure, the Chancellor now faced a Parliament and an electorate whose wartime spirit of sacrifice was evaporating rapidly and who were demanding from an impoverished Treasury reduced taxation and the means necessary to deliver a 'land fit for heroes'.[18]

In addition to departmental concerns of this sort, Chamberlain's reluctance was reinforced by his very real scepticism about the level of political support he would receive as Chancellor in such onerous and difficult circumstances. Feeling himself without any genuine friends in the government,[19] contemptuous of Law's reliability and extremely doubtful about the degree of support and confidence he could expect from the Prime Minister, Chamberlain was keenly aware of the political weakness and vulnerability inherent in the acceptance of such an office: concerns apparently substantiated by Law's acquiescence in Lloyd George's attempt to exclude the Chancellor from the Cabinet and to resolve conflicts between the Treasury and the spending departments in an alternative forum.[20] In the event Chamberlain won this battle against both Lloyd George and Law with the adoption of the latter's proposal that the old War Cabinet should be retained. The omens, however, were scarcely propitious. Thus, although it was characteristic of Chamberlain that he should accept all new offices with the same protestations of weary apprehension, in this instance the profound lack of enthusiasm conveyed to his sisters clearly possessed far more genuine substance than most such declarations.

Certainly there was little about the budgetary and financial position with which to dispel concern at the gravity of the task before him. The Budget had increased from less than £150M when Chamberlain had last been Chancellor to £842M in 1918. Financing the war largely by borrowing rather than taxation had resulted in an increase in the National Debt from £650M at the start of the war to £7435M by the end of the financial year 1918–19.[21] Moreover, the problem of servicing this debt had been aggravated by the fact that much of it had been contracted at relatively high rates of interest, thus taking debt service charges from 11 per cent of central government expenditure in 1913 to 24 per cent in 1920. Above all,

[17] A. Chamberlain to N. Chamberlain, 11 January 1919, NC 1/27/45.
[18] Sir Bernard Mallet and C.O. George, *British Budgets, Second Series 1913–14 to 1920–21*, (1929), 179.
[19] A. Chamberlain to Ida, 1 January 1919, AC5/1/114.
[20] Lloyd George to A. Chamberlain, 9 January 1919, Lloyd George MSS F/7/2/20.
[21] Mallet & George, *British Budgets*, 180–182.

*government expenditure was running ahead of revenue to the extent that the 1918–
19 deficit totalled no less than 65.5 per cent of total expenditure.*[22] *Against such a
background of grave economic uncertainty and a wave of major strikes, Chamberlain
soon discovered that he had inherited a financial situation worse even than he feared
and with departmental estimates in a state of constant flux. Moreover, he did so in
circumstances in which the Treasury was hopelessly disorganized and gravely understaffed while the whole system of Treasury control he had known before the War
had been fatally undermined by Lloyd George's peacetime Chancellorship and then
the demands of four years of total war.*

   *It was a measure of Chamberlain's long-standing exhaustion and the burdens of
his new office that the stress of preparing his Budget for 1919 very swiftly took a
heavy toll upon him. When he first arrived in office, the Financial Secretary to the
Treasury noted that 'he is in that sort of condition that he may crack up, so I shall
feel like an understudy at the pantomime (or in a tragedy according to one's mood!)'.*[23]
*As so often in times of stress, his weight fell dramatically and he succumbed to
morbid self-doubts without the strength or ability to shake off his worries. By April
his condition was such that Neville and his sisters again feared that his health was
drifting inexorably towards a breakdown.*[24] *In the event, however, Chamberlain was
generally satisfied with his Budget and particularly with the reception given to his
two and a half hour speech on 30 April 1919.*[25]

   *Although the cessation of hostilities had meant the position was 'much less
depressing than the prophets had feared', the central theme of this essentially
transitional budget was to warn of the magnitude of the task before the nation and
to emphasize the need for national and individual economy. To this end, the
Chancellor announced a reduction in planned public expenditure from £2972M in
1918–19 to £1435M in 1919–20. On the revenue side, beyond the customary
expedients, including increased duties on spirits, beer and death, the Budget was
notable for two features. First, although he conceded that the 80 per cent tax on
war profits was highly productive, the Chancellor also acknowledged that it encouraged
extravagance among firms liable to Excess Profits Duty, acted as a brake on enterprise
and business development and was decidedly inequitable in its operation between
firms. Yet despite its defects, it was to be retained at a rate of 40 per cent as a
temporary measure on the grounds that war expenditure had not yet finished and the
government had not had the time to consider alternatives. For Chamberlain personally,
however, the most important feature of his first post-war Budget was the introduction
of Imperial preference into British financial arrangements – a policy 'with which
my father's name and fame will ever be linked'. Thus, while conceding that only*

[22] D.H. Aldcroft, *The British Economy, Vol I, The Years of Turmoil, 1920–1951* (Brighton
1986), 24.
[23] Baldwin to his mother, January 1919, A.W Baldwin, *My Father: The True Story*, (1955),
82.
[24] N. Chamberlain to Hilda, 13 April 1919 and to Ida, 20 April 1919 NC 18/1/208–
209.
[25] For a discussion of its content see Mallet and George, *British Budgets*, 175–230.

cocoa, rum and sugar were imported from the Empire in such quantities as to benefit significantly at present, Chamberlain contended that the policy 'should be judged not by its immediate results but by its vast potentialities'.[26]

The first test of Chamberlain's administration in his handling of the Budget was accomplished successfully. Moreover, in July he was able to reinforce the message about the gravity of the financial situation during a debate on the Consolidated Fund Bill when he informed the Commons that the position was now worse than anticipated with revenue well down and expenditure higher than expected.[27] On 23 October he was again forced to revise the deficit in the estimates to £473M – practically double the always misleadingly optimistic initial estimate of £243M.[28] For all the small crises, however, by the end of the year Chamberlain's authority and stock had been fully restored – particularly after a debate on finance in late November in which the expected 'great blow turned out a great triumph' when Chamberlain 'came out very strong'.[29] Yet for all this early success, Tom Jones still urged Hankey to consider the case for strengthening the Treasury. 'Watching as I do the Cabinet discussions day by day, one grows to have a horrible feeling that no one master mind is gripping our financial position in its entirety' he wrote on 11 July. 'The Chancellor of the Exchequer, conscientious, industrious and with much common-sense, is overwhelmed. One feels he is fighting a losing battle'.[30] A month later a less sympathetic observer at the Bank of England found the Chancellor 'hot, tired, worried and peevish!'.[31] On a happier note, the purchase of Twitt's Ghyll, his country home for the next decade near Mayfield in Sussex, was completed in August 1919 and he embarked immediately upon the fulfilment of an ambition of thirty years to create of an outdoor Alpine garden. Only here did Chamberlain find real rest and an almost spiritual satisfaction away from the demands of office and an economic situation that was about to take a turn dramatically for the worse.

[26] *Ibid*, 191–5, 199. For Chamberlain's reaffirmation of his faith in food taxes on the second day of the debate while emphasizing this was not the intent of these measures see *Ibid*, 201.

[27] Petrie, *Life and Letters*, II, 144.

[28] See Mallet and George, *British Budgets*, 229–30.

[29] Sanders Diary, Sunday 30 November 1919, J. Ramsden (ed) *Real Old Tory Politics*, 130. For Chamberlain's reaction see A. Chamberlain to Hilda, n.d. AC5/1/142. See also Davidson to Stamfordham, 23 December 1919, R.R. James (ed), *Memoirs of a Conservative*, 96.

[30] T. Jones to Hankey, 11 July 1919, *Whitehall Diary*, I, 90. But see A. Chamberlain to S. Baldwin, 15 April 1920, Baldwin MSS 175/10.

[31] Montagu Norman Diary, 13 August 1919, A. Boyle, *Montagu Norman: A Biography* (1967), 127.

AC5/1/115   19 January 1919
                                                        Thornhill House

My dear Ida,

... I enter on an office which I dislike with no circumstance omitted
that could increase my distaste for it. I do not feel sure that I shall get
any help or backing from the P.M.; the financial situation is full of
difficulty & the normal working of the Treasury control of finance has
been utterly overthrown first by Lloyd George as Chancellor & afterwards by four years of war. So I have a heavy heart & not very much
pleasure in prospect!

AC5/1/118   9 February 1919
                                                        9 Egerton Place

My dear Hilda,

    ...
    We are kept up here by the anxious state of public affairs & the
possibility of a Cabinet being called at any moment. For the moment,
but I fear that it is for the moment only, there is some appaisement.
We had made all arrangements to work every electric light & power
station if the electricians were called out, to run the tubes if the strike
was prolonged & to put every available army lorry on the London
streets; but we might have had to face a general strike on all railways,
we may have one yet & it is not unlikely that there will be general or
partial strikes in the coal-fields. Certainly I have no expectation of
getting through the year without some very serious trouble of the kind.
Smillie[32] the Miner's leader, is a Bolshevik at least, pacifist abroad &
class-war revolutionary at home. In the railway negotiations, difficulties
were increased, as is now so often the case, by the rivalries of two
Unions, each of which wishes to show that is does better for its own
men than the other, as well as by some real misunderstanding. At the
beginning the Govt was insufficiently informed as to the necessary
conditions of the motor-service driver's work, & at one moment it
looked very ugly for us & everyone. There were hot-heads on both
sides, in the Unions & among Ministers, who might easily have made
trouble, but happily wiser counsels prevailed. We mended our hand
where we had been led astray & stood fair on the principle for
which we were fighting, but the whole story illustrates the difficult of

---

[32] Robert Smillie (1857–1942) President Scottish Miners Federation 1894–1918, 1922–
1928; President MFGB 1912–21. Labour MP Morpeth 1923–29; Chairman PLP 1924

government dealing with the intricate & very various conditions of service in great trades & industries by broad declarations & general rules.

My own particular work is very arduous & very difficult. The financial position as indicated to me by my advisers is far worse than I or B.L. had supposed. Taxation must go up largely when the mass of people suppose that with the signing of the armistice they may expect early relief. France & Italy are imploring assistance which I cannot give & the U.S. Treasury is calling off all help. A cheerful instruction, indeed, & you may imagine how popular your brother will soon be!

AC5/1/119   16 February 1919
                                                       Thornhill House

My dear Ida,

... I am kept very busy, working long hours at one difficult problem after another, interrupted constantly by people who "must see me for a moment" & take anything from half an hour upwards, confronted with endless demands that I should receive deputations & with desperate appeals for help from France & Italy, quite uncertain what America will do, unable to find out what our expenditure will be this year & only able to make wild guesses at our future position. If I survive, it will be a wonder; if I make a success of it, it will be little short of a miracle!

...

This morning I have tried to worry out the financial situation only to find it hopelessly involved in riddles which no one can answer, have read a memorandum on the Lloyd George land-taxes which the Inland Revenue explain are unworkable as they stand, have yielded very little & that little with the maximum of expenditure, friction, unpopularity & injustice, & must be either wholly recast or totally abandoned. If Ll.G. were in opposition instead of being P.M. I would publish the Report, but how can I do this with him for my chief? And what am I to make of the mess which he has left for me to clear off?[sic] At present I don't see my way, nor have I much leisure in which to think it out ...

...

If miners & transport workers carry out their threats, we shall have one of the worst – indeed the worst – industrial dispute that we have ever seen. They will cause great suffering & great loss & of course incidentally play straight into the hands of recalcitrant Germany. The one good feature is that there are some reasonable men among the leaders, tho' it may be doubtful whether these can hold their own. And happily public opinion is, I think, hardening against them. But these are anxious times in every country & in every sphere of public life. It will need all the strength & wisdom any of us possess to pull through safely. Shall we do it? I think so somehow!

AC5/1/120

23 February 1919
Thornhill House

My dear Hilda,

. . .

The financial problems which assail me grow more & more difficult. The French are very chauvinistic & will not cut their coat according to their cloth. They think they should clothe themselves at my expense & not getting all they want from my representatives in Paris or through their agent in London have now turned Monsieur Cambon[33] on to squeeze me. Signor Stringler, the new Italian Finance Minister, came from Rome with a like purpose & carried off the promise of some good millions of mine. Both France & Italy are in queer street & I live only just round the corner & if I am not careful I shall find that they have dragged me into it before long. And meanwhile, as far as one can see, America is now as much 'all out' for business as for a few short months she was all out for war. The President with his lofty ideals & all his high fallutin' is surrounded by what Keynes[34] calls "a lot of Wall Street toughs" & tough enough they are. The amusing thing is that though very hard & shrewd business men, they can't express themselves. "What they like", says Keynes, "is to get together with us before the Conferences & then leave us to argue the case. When, as in such & such an affair, they differ from us & have to present their own case they do it miserably".

AC5/1/122

24 March 1919
9 Egerton Place

Yes, my dear Hilda, I have indeed been a very scurvy correspondent of late, but there are excuses as you allow. Only believe that whether answered or not your letters are a great joy to me & a link in our

---

[33] Paul Cambon (1843–1924) French Ambassador in London 1898–1920.
[34] John Maynard Keynes (1883–1946) Economist. Fellow King's College, Cambridge. Civil Servant from 1906; Treasury 1915–19. Principal Treasury Representative, Paris Peace Conference. Member of MacMillan Committee on Finance and Industry, 1929–31. Economic Adviser to government during and immediately after World War II.

loving family life which has an added value now that I cannot turn to Beatrice for news of those I love & so seldom see.[35]

...

... [T]he times make everything extremely difficult, all departmental estimates are very uncertain, the Treasury is understaffed & horribly over-worked & I am beset with problems which might well tax the brains of more expert financiers than myself besides a host of minor worries such as always fall to the lot of the Chancellor & are increased today by the number of new questions & new untrained ministers & departments & by the utter relaxation of Treasury control & of the Chancellor's financial supervision which has prevailed in recent years.

AC5/1/124

13 April 1919
Thornhill House

My dear Ida,

...

To tell the truth I am very tired, anxious about the Budget because I scarcely feel fit for all the work which it will involve & little worries seem big & won't be shaken off, & finally very anxious about Paris & all that is being done & not being done there. I ought to have six weeks holiday & instead I fear I shall get little more than two week-ends. Such is life. It is no use kicking against the pricks, but there are times when I wish that I could chuck the whole business.

I am anxious about Paris & all that it stands for. Europe does not settle down – quite the contrary. The Middle East & East are full of unrest & I am very dissatisfied at the line taken in Egypt where the P.M. & Balfour (or the P.M. alone) have given away after the revolt what they had refused to yield before it.[36] They *may* have been wrong in the first instance but they *must* have been wrong in the second. Such conduct is bad everywhere but fatal in the East.

[35] Beatrice, Austen's elder sister, had died from influenza soon after the Armistice.
[36] The arrest and exile of the 'father of Egyptian Independence' and leader of the Wafd, Sa'ad Zaghlul Pasha (1860–1927), prompted nationalist demonstrations, riots, sabotage and assassinations of British officers after March 1919.

AC5/1/125   18 April 1919
                                                     Thornhill House

Well, my dear Ida, what do you think of the position now? When
the P.M. does at last decide to break, he does it decisively does he
not?[37] "You may break, you may shatter the vase as you will" – how
goes it? No, I think not *much* of the perfume of old still clings to those
shattered fragments. I see that the Morning Post observes that I enjoyed
the P.M.'s speech. Well, so I did! It is a quaint world.

I am not sure whether Neville was in the House – I did not see
him – but if not both Ivy & I agree that he missed a treat. Lloyd
George did his part admirably. He was grave, restrained & moderate
in expression voice & gesture throughout – only letting himself go a
little, & not too much, when dealing with Northcliffe. He marshalled
his speech admirably, showed good sense, reticence where reticence
was required, & courage. I never liked him better, & there was but one
verdict throughout the House at the moment as to his success & the
masterly way in which he carried it off. Whether all will be equally
pleased on reflection, I do not know, for all have not his courage when
roused, nor his real qualities to support them if the Northcliffe Press
turns upon his supporters. But for myself I need not say that I am heartily
glad that he has at last burst his "embarrassing entanglements,["] & I
thoroughly enjoyed the wit & sarcasm of his attack on that mischievous,
vain & unscrupulous man.

I have had a very hard week & have a busy & anxious time before
me ... But I will get what rest & change of thought I can, for I badly
need both.

Good Friday I see I have not said one thing which struck me about
the P.M. which is all to his credit. What had roused him was not the
criticism of himself, but the mischievous setting of France against
England & the U.S.A., the excitation of every French fear, prejudice
or jealousy. I don't think that the P.M. is easily moved by personal
animosity or to personal retaliation, but all that there is in him of
statesman was roused this time to fierce indignation. I believe that the
Paris Daily Mail has been even worse than its English prototype.

Sunday evening ...

[37] Unionist backbench unrest created by denunciations of the Prime Minister's 'pro-
German' stance at Paris in the Northcliffe press prompted Lloyd George to return to the
Commons to launch a vigorous attack upon Northcliffe's attempts to sow dissension as
the product of 'diseased vanity' (a phrase meaningfully reinforced by simultaneous taps
on his forehead) and in so doing to evade some of the substantive concerns of
backbenchers.

[Postscript] I *must* work tomorrow. You will think that I am foolish to garden so much but it rests the mind!

AC5/1/126
25 April 1919
Thornhill House

My dear Hilda,

. . .

I have had three very busy & rather agitated days in London over the Budget – millions suddenly disappearing here, then reappearing in whole or in part elsewhere. Sudden discovery of a snag here or a rock there, all the ordinary concomitants of a Budget but magnified to Brobdingnagion proportions. I think that I have now got everything straightened out – unless some *dear* colleague tangles it up again. (You will not fail to observe the *double entendre* in the word dear – they are dear & most of them expensive).

Paris gives us little information beyond what you see in the papers. They have made an awful mess of the Middle East & of some other questions, which greater knowledge & expedition might have spared us; but honestly of all the four I think Lloyd George has done most (I might almost say everything) to bring them together & to secure some sort of agreement. The Italians are quite unreasonable & Prest Wilson behaves at moments like a professor in a chinashop!

Sunday night. I played about most of yesterday, but today I have been hard at work without intermission. Budget, Budget, Budget in 17 sections with introductory observations & farewell remarks. What a task! and in many respects opening as many questions as it settles, for some could not be settled now & some my colleagues, perhaps quite rightly, would not allow me to settle, & some require more time & study than I have been able to give to them since I took office.

AC5/1/127
28 April 1919
Thornhill House

My dear Ida,

. . .

I did another hard morning's work at the Budget & now have only a few trimmings to put to it ... I trust that no unwelcome surprises await me. It is a dull Budget except for Preference but that will not prevent me from having an arduous & perhaps lively time before I have done with it.

. . .

This morning's Daily Mirror has a front page of pictures of the Ch. of Ex. at work & at play, with his Budget his wife, his children & his flowers. Oliver Locker-Lampson[38] insisted that this was good business & arranged it all. They are rather good pictures of their kind, but that kind of good business goes against the grain with me. Why is an idle & curious public to be fed on my domestic life?

AC5/1/129   4 May 1919
                                                          Thornhill House

My dear Hilda,

Many thanks for your congratulations. I am well over my first big fence & a House which knew me not & had begun to distrust my capacity under the influence of almost daily carping criticism seems to think that after all I may have something in me. But it is only my first big fence & there are some very ugly jumps ahead of me both in the near & farther distance.

It was a big physical effort – it took me 2+ hours to deliver it & in the middle I suddenly went dizzy, but it was only momentary & I think no one noticed it, tho' everyone laughed as the stiff brandy & soda for which I had sent was handed to me just as I passed from spirits to beer! What I pride myself upon is that in the two day debate no one asked a single question as to my meaning, so I had succeeded in my great effort which was to be clear. And it was a satisfaction to stand where Father had so often stood to propose a definite preferential policy!

In order to assist in funding the huge amount of floating (short-term) debt, in June 1919 a Victory Loan campaign was launched. Although the money was much needed to relieve the budgetary problem and actually produced more than Chamberlain anticipated, he clearly had little sympathy with the new style of popular politics that accompanied such an appeal in the new mass democracy.[39]

[38] Oliver Stillingfleet Locker-Lampson (1880–1954) Conservative MP Huntingdonshire 1910–22, Birmingham Handsworth 1922–45. PPS to Austen Chamberlain as Chancellor, Lord Privy Seal and Leader of the House 1919–22 and a close friend.

[39] In 1926, Central Office proposed to film ministers at work with officials in shirtsleeves. 'Bovril may do this', a shocked Chamberlain wrote, 'but should Baldwins?'. G.M. Young, *Stanley Baldwin*, 26.

AC5/1/131
13 June 1919
Thornhill House

My dear Ida,

...

And I! I am speechless, breathless, indignant & dissolved in laughter at my own helpless imbecility in the midst of a modern day Loan campaign. Oliver Locker Lampson is a brick, he is giving up his whole time & devoting all his enthusiasm & energy to running or helping to run what is called "Publicity". I sniffed but resigned myself to fate when he said I must be photographed preparing my Budget speech. I said that he must arrange with Ivy & that I took no responsibility when in the same great cause he demanded that Ivy & the family should also be photographed in "their country home." I submitted – but think of my feelings! – when I was ordered into Downing Street garden to be cinema'd making a speech to an imaginary audience amidst shouts from the operator of "Throw up your right arm, Sir. Clench your fist, Sir, *please. Keep it* clenched! That will do, thank you!" Said I "If I look as big a fool as I feel, that will be an interesting photograph."

All this I have suffered & endured. I might as well be a musical comedy favourite or a pet of the Daily Mail. But imagine the climax. One – two – three guesses! No, you can't! On getting down here tonight we learn from Mrs. Dundas that a Mr. M. arrived today with a note from Oliver on C. of E.'s paper. "This is to introduce to you Mr. M. who will take photographs of the C. of E.'s children for the Victory Loan Campaign. I beg that you will give him every assistance in your power."

Whereupon Mrs. D., Diane & Lawrence are whisked off in a motor to the Village Post Office & are cinema'd buying imaginary Victory Bonds &, since the village children came out of school at that moment – Oh happy stroke of genius! – distributing bonds to the said children. I don't know whether to laugh or cry, so I decide to laugh. But oh, my dear, fancy me the tool & victim of these new methods & my innocent children made the instruments of such blatant advertisement.

And consider the case of conscience. These photos are I am told filmed at the cinema theatres tonight. "Lawrence & Diane, children of the C. of E. distributing Victory bonds to the village children at Thornhill." I shall have to do it if they have really let me in, or the humbug will be too patent. Oh lordy, lordy, lord! What next I wonder?

Need I add that L. & Diane thoroughly enjoyed it & played up dramatically.

14/6/19. We have not waited long for "the next"! Ivy was rung up on the telephone today by Mr. Walton, "Director of Press Publicity" who read to her a message which she was to deliver to the Sunday papers for women – "Why I buy Ivy [sic] Bonds!" "Well, Mr. Walton, it's not exactly what I should have written myself" Ivy mildly remonstrated; but she was at once over-ruled. It was just what was wanted & c. &c.

Will posterity judge us by these vulgarities & are they really as effective & as necessary as they are thought?

. . .

You see I write no politics. I am too tired & too disgruntled in many ways. But the Loan begins well. Experts foretold to me 250–350 millions *new* money (*new* money includes Treasury Bills & early maturing Exchequer Bonds *but* not conversions of early longer dated issues) I said that nothing less than 500 millions was worth having. I believe that we shall get 600 to 700 millions certain. I wonder whether we *can* get more. In my bones I feel that we shall, but I have nothing to base myself upon & when I was Chancellor 15 years ago we were as much troubled to get £10,000,000.

AC5/1/132   29 June 1919
                                                Thornhill House

So Peace is signed at last my dear Hilda. Will the world have rest? I think the C.I.G.S. calculated a little time ago that there were still 23 little wars going on, & the whole east of Europe (not to mention Russia[)] is still a weltering chaos. As to Germany I wonder & wonder & wonder. I thought that Brockdorff Rantzau's[40] main note read like that of a man who wanted to sign & to keep what he signed but who would not sign the first terms put forward by the Allies. Even the old Germany would not, I think, rashly challenge a new war in the West, but the chaos on their Eastern frontier & their hatred of & contempt for the Poles must be a dangerous temptation. Smuts spoke their true feelings for the Poles one day when he suddenly exploded: "Kaffirs, that's what they are!' But if Germany remains or becomes really democratic, they cannot repeat the policy of Frederick the Great & Bismarck & his late followers. No democracy can or will make aggressive war its year long study & business though it may easily enough flare up in sudden passion. But think of Germany with its 60 or 70 millions of people & France with its dwindling 40!

I shudder!

. . .

40 Ulrich von Brockdorff-Rantzau (1869–1928) German diplomat and politician. Foreign Minister in Ebert's government, December 1918–June 1919; Ambassador to Moscow 1922.

AC5/1/134   19 July 1919
                                                         Thornhill House

My dear Ida,

   ...

Well, Heaven send up peace, a real peace. I have little heart for celebrations yet ...

I am for the moment pessimistic. It is partly sheer fatigue of body & still more of mind. I have got more money by the Loan than anyone, who knew anything about it, expected but less than I had hoped. But expenditure is exceeding all bounds & circumstances are falsifying all Budget estimates. How we shall finance next year I can't see, & I was sorely tempted by a pressing invitation by the P.M., Balfour & Curzon to take – the Washington Embassy! But it did not attract Ivy & Joe's age made it impossible. I could not reconcile myself to going so far from him at this time. This is of course very secret ... You will understand that for obvious reasons it was not 'offered' to me. I was only 'sounded' as to the answer I should make *if* it *were* offered!

AC5/1/135   Saturday 2 August 1919
                                                         Thornhill House

My dear Ida,

True I was tired last week & only got down here on the Saturday in time for a 3 o'clock luncheon ... Today we did not get here till 6 o'clock – indeed it was 6.30 – & I am not merely tired but dead beat, physically & mentally, with a head stuffed with wool but wool which aches – dully as such stuff must ache if it aches at all.

   ...

Sunday morning ... The Budget went through very well & my handling of the Bill brought praise from all quarters, but the position is desperate. France, Belgium, Italy & Australia – all begging at my door not to speak of Poles, Tcheko-Slovaks, Roumanians & the rest; our own expenditure exceeding all estimates & the course of events depriving me of expected receipts. Taxes must go up!

AC5/1/138   21 September 1919
                                                              Thornhill House

My dear Hilda,

...

Cabinets have begun again & I shall be as busy as possible, I suppose, from now onwards. Just now I am vexed with the P.M. because he will negotiate & discuss with Clemenceau[41] & Feisal[42] without first enquiring into the facts. He appears without knowing it to have abandoned a claim of ours for £1,250,000 & to have landed us in further obligation which should belong wholly to the French. Why are we to pay a share of their Syrian enterprises? Well he is a difficult person to serve.

AC5/1/139   26 September 1919
                                                               9 Egerton Place

My dear Ida,

I begin a letter but will it ever reach you? The railway strike is declared & probably by tomorrow no trains will be running anywhere ... There must in any case be immense loss, widespread stoppage of industry & distress. It will tax our resources to the uttermost to secure by lorry & motor & canal the distribution of food & the country, just beginning to settle down to industry after $4\frac{1}{2}$ years war, is thrown back into strife & confusion. And all for what? For wages? No, they have had the fairest & even the most generous offers. For want of time to discuss & negotiate? Again no. Nothing of which they complain could happen before Dec 31st & then only if there had been a marked decrease in the cost of living. Why then strike at all? Well, because Thomas[43] has been swept aside by his ambitions second – & for the time being the young Bolshevists have got command. In short this is not a quarrel between capital & labour or a question of wages or conditions of employment. It is a revolutionary attempt to subvert

[41] Georges Benjamin Clemenceau (1841–1929) Radical journalist and politician. Deputy 1876–1893; Senator 1902–20. Minister of Interior 1906; Premier 1906–09; Premier and Minister of War 1917–20. President, Paris Peace Conference 1919. After failure to become President in 1920 retired from public life.

[42] Ibn Hussein Feisal (1885–1933) A leader of Arab revolt against Turks, 1916–19. Proclaimed himself King of Syria but deposed by French, 1920; elected under British protection Emir and then King of Iraq, 1921.

[43] James Henry Thomas (1874–1949) President NUR 1910 and General Secretary 1918–24, 1925–31. Labour MP Derby January 1910–May 1936 (from 1931 as National Labour). Colonial Secretary 1924, 1935–36; Lord Privy Seal 1929–30; Dominion Secretary 1930–35.

government & establish class rule. And what will be the end? I am a poor prophet. I did not think that the strike was coming off – not now at any rate – & it seemed to me that as time passed without its coming off, the opportunity for such a strike against the community was growing less & less. I was wrong, but I will prophesy again. The full force of the strike will be felt within the first few days, say a week, & in another week it will not indeed be over but it will be beaten. It is a challenge to the Government & a challenge to the nation & I believe that both will take it up & fight it through. But meanwhile it is the biggest internal struggle that we have ever had & a new experience for all of us.

AC5/1/140   11 October 1919
                                                         Twitt's Ghyll

My dear Hilda,

    . . .
    Well, I proved a false prophet about the strike from first to last. At first I did not expect it & at the last I thought it would continue & extend. It would have been a fearful struggle if that had happened, but the leaders of the other Unions did not want to strike now & all the Unions found the Govt & the public better prepared & stronger than they had expected. As to the railwaymen, Hankey, who was at all the conferences, told me he never saw a greater change in men & that they knew that they were beaten. So far so good. But what next, I wonder?

AC5/1/141   26 October 1919
                                                         9 Egerton Place

My dear Ida,

    . . .
    The financial position is difficult enough but it is not at all what the Times et hoc genus omne represent it to be ... But in these days of "stunts" & hysterics it is very difficult to find the juste milieu of statement which does not lead to childish pessimism on the one hand or to foolish & reckless optimism on the other. One thing, however, gives me great pleasure. If I have badly disgruntled half a dozen men in the Treasury – & that was inevitable- I have put fresh heart into the Office as a whole. My new chief, Warren Fisher,[44] is working admirably,

---

[44] (Norman Fenwick) Warren Fisher (1879–1948) Chairman Board of Inland Revenue 1918–19. Permanent Secretary, Treasury and Head of Civil Service, 1919–39.

the reorganisation is justifying itself already & the team-work is admirable. En fur si muove! Give me three years more & short of unforeseen catastrophe in Europe or Asia we will have our finances in a thoroughly sound position.

AC5/1/142

n.d.
Twitt's Ghyll

My dear Hilda,

Yes, I did make a good speech or at least everyone joins in saying so. The Lobby was enthusiastic, & my colleagues most flattering, only complaining that I had knocked the bottom out of the debate before it had well begun & left them nothing to say & nothing to answer. So Lloyd George was uproarious & Bonar Law was merry & all the world was pleased except Northcliffe & the Wee Frees.[45] Poor Maclean's[46] "I am placed in a most unfortunate position" at the close of the debate when his amendment was ruled out of order, was so naive & so irresistibly funny that we all rocked with laughter. But I went home wishing that one could keep the ship on an even keel & not spring from an extreme of unreasoning pessimism & even panic to an equally thoughtless pitch of complacent optimism. National finance is not a proper field for "stunts" & spurts of feeling. Reconstruction is a work of long breath as our French friends say. It required a broad view, a steady judgement & continuous effort & the new Times methods are destructive of all that is needed most. I am ready to justify my speech line by line & word by word, but I wish I might have written the headlines for the reports. I never said that there would be no new taxes next year – quite the contrary – nor even that there would be no *additional* taxation, but because careless writers have so expressed it I shall be told that I am a liar.

However there has been one good point about the whole thing. It has been a smashing defeat for Northcliffe. He may perhaps by now be getting some clearer idea of the limitations of his power. It was very interesting to observe how his attempt to bully the House of Commons has set the corporate feeling of the House against him. As for me personally, my stock has risen for the moment. It will fall again soon enough, but just now I have made "*the* speech of my life" & so forth.

[45] The Independent or Free Liberal Party formed after a meeting on 3 February 1919 under Maclean's chairmanship.
[46] Donald Maclean (1864–1932) Liberal MP Bath 1906–10, Selkirk & Peebles 1910–18, Peebles & Midlothian S. 1918–22, Cornwall N 1929–32. Chairman Parliamentary Liberal Party 1919–22 and Acting Leader in Commons February 1919–February 1920. President, Board of Education 1931–32. Knighted 1917.

You know House of Commons' enthusiasms & how soon they wear off. I told Warren Fisher a week before the debate when he was very kindly & genuinely anxious about my position that Northcliffe was overdoing it, that there would be a reaction just as there was at the time of the Budget & that when the waves receded he would find that it took a deal of washing to wear away the rock.

We dined last night at the palace. The King was very violent against Northcliffe 'a low upstart fellow" &c. &c. & the Queen very gracious & to the point. She has certainly developed a great deal & is now much .more on the spot when meeting anyone & much more ready with a personal remark.

. . .

[Postscript] Curzon congratulated me on my triumph. "I am a little frightened of it," I said. "It was too complete" "Never mind, my dear fellow, you have only to make another!" And I am going to next week in the City!

AC5/1/144

6 December 1919
Twitt's Ghyll

My dear Ida,

. . .

I began the week with the Premium bonds debate & as you will have seen that suggestion was decisively rejected by the House. I think that many members as they thought more about what was involved in it, liked it less & they were just in the proper mood to be influenced by debate. Of course Bottomley[47] did them no credit & Kinloch Cook,[48] who seconded, is a fool, so they had a bad start & I am assured that my speech changed many votes.

You will be amused by the Daily News' comment on it. Do you remember how Father used to say 'Yes, I'm quite ready to kiss & be friends, but I have got to knock him down first!' Apparently a libel action is good for the D.N.

---

[47] Horatio William Bottomley (1860–1933). Journalist and proprietor. Liberal MP South Hackney 1906–11 when the local Liberal Association withdrew their support. Resigned due to bankruptcy 1912. Re-elected December 1918 as an Independent but expelled from Commons on 1 August 1922 having been charged with fraudulent conversion. Sentenced to 7 years and released from prison 1927.

[48] Clement Kinloch-Cooke (1854–1944) Barrister and for many years leader writer on *Morning Post*. Edited the *Observer, Pall Mall Gazette, Empire Review*. Conservative MP Devonport January 1910–23, Cardiff East 1924–29. Vice-President of Tariff Reform League.

AC5/1/146   21 December 1919
                                                    9 Egerton Place

My dear Ida,

...

As for myself, I am pretty well done up. The pressure of work & the burden of anxiety continue unabated. Saul has spent his millions & David his tens of millions. If an economy is small, it is not worth while. If it is large, it is impossible; & I fight an endless & ungrateful battle with colleagues who think only departmentally. It is all very hateful & wearing & curiously enough my only ally is the Prime Minister. He occasionally gets an inkling of financial disaster, but then on certain subjects he pours out money like water. Well, if I get a little holiday I may take a more sensible view of my difficulties, but I look forward with unmitigated horror to the first six or seven months of next year.

You must get Keynes' book – the Economic Consequences of the Peace. He ought not to have written it, for he held an official position & from an ex official it is very indiscreet, but it is ably & indeed brilliantly written & his picture of the Council of Four & portraits of Clemenceau & Wilson are masterpieces. I read the description of Wilson with malicious pleasure. What irreparable harm that man has done by his ignorance, self-sufficiency, party spirit & obstinacy! And alas! we & all Europe pay the price whilst his countrymen disown him & all his works. I wish that I could say that I differ seriously from Keynes examination of Germany's ability to pay or from his view of the utter hopelessness of the Austria created by the Treaty. There is only too much truth in Keynes' gloomy picture tho' his attack on "politicians" for fixing an impossible indemnity is unfair since they or at least the English ones followed the advice of an ex-Governor of the Bank, Lord Cunliffe[49] & of one of the ablest of our Judges, Lord Sumner.[50]

Clemenceau was amusing when he was over here. Discussing men & affairs in France, he said "Barthou![51] Barthou is the kind of man who

---

[49] Walter Cunliffe (1855–1919) Director Bank of England 1895–1918, Governor 1913–18. Chairman of Committee on Currency and Foreign Exchanges after the war. Created Baron Cunliffe.
    [50] John Andrew Hamilton (1859–1934) Judge of King's Bench 1909–12, Appeal Court 1912–13, Lord of Appeal in Ordinary 1913–30. Created Baron Sumner 1913 and Viscount 1927.
    [51] Louis Barthou (1862–1934) French lawyer and politician. Member of Clemenceau's Cabinet 1906–09 and Briand's 1909–10. Prime Minister 1913. War Minister under Briand 1920; Minister of Justice under Poincaré 1922 and 1926; Senator 1922; Foreign Minister under Doumergue 1934. Assassinated with Alexander I of Yugoslavia at Marseilles 9 October 1934.

would kill his own mother. Now Briand[52] would not do that – he'd kill someone else's." For himself he said he had become a fetish in France "like those little golden pigs that ladies place in their bosom." Of Italy he spoke with contemptuous gloom. There would be a revolution there shortly. From the King downwards no one had any influence with the people. As to the new foreign minister Schialogia,[53] [sic] of what use was it to talk to him. "He is like that lump of coal – no, that coal would burn. He won't even do that. He's like this poker."

AC5/1/147

29 December 1919
Twitt's Ghyll

My dear Ida,

...

I have had four days without any office papers & with only two important letters to answer! It is an age since I could say as much. But what a troubled & troubling world it is. Ireland, the Soudan, Egypt, Syria, the Indian Frontier – none of them know peace. These murders in Ireland are terrible.[54] It really looks as if a section of Sinn Fein wishes to ruin the new Home Rule Bill before it is fairly launched. And they seem bolder & more desperate that the Feinians of the past.

I wonder how General Dyer's[55] own account of his doings struck you. It has left me sad & very uneasy.

1920 began with even more worries for the Chancellor as the British economy experienced one of the most violent fluctuations in its history. Following the removal

[52] Astride Briand (1862–1932) Major figure of French Third Republic. Premier ten times after 1909 and stable element at Quai d'Orsay during governmental instability of late 1920s. After war a champion of reconciliation with Germany. Locarno Treaty (1925) and Briand-Kellogg Pact outlawing war (1928) were major achievements. Defeated in presidential election 1931.

[53] Vittorio Scialoja (1856–1933) Italian lawyer and politician. Senator 1904; Minister of Justice 1909–10; Foreign Minister November 1919–June 1920. Delegate to Peace Conference 1919 and League of Nations 1921–32.

[54] Churchill stated that there had been 1500 political offences including 18 murders and 77 armed attacks during the latter half of 1919. On 19 December, an unsuccessful attempt was made to ambush Lord French, the Lord Lieutenant, and his party on their way to the Vice-Regal Lodge.

[55] Following the murder of four Europeans by a mob, an unarmed crowd assembled in an enclosed garden at Amritsar on 13 April 1919. Failing to disperse when ordered, Brigadier-General R.E.H. Dyer (1864–1927) ordered his troops to fire. After ten minutes 379 Indians were dead and a further 1208 wounded. Dyer subsequently justified his action as a 'merciful severity' which prevented an even greater loss of life throughout the Punjab.

of artificial wartime support for the currency in March 1919, sterling fell sharply on the exchanges from its pegged level of $4.7½ to $4.02 in November 1919 and then to a low of $3.20 in February 1920. Given the fact that ministers had been prompted to unpeg the exchanges in the spring of 1919 because of the costs of support and the danger of unemployment, they were initially not prepared to countenance the severe monetary measures necessary to restore the situation for fear of the political implications at a time when demobilization and reconstruction were getting under way. Nonetheless, the Chancellor was finally compelled to act by increasing Bank of England and Treasury alarm that the speculative inflationary boom which had begun in April 1919 was running out of control. Public expenditure was curbed, the Treasury note issue was limited, growth in money supply was reduced and in November 1919 Bank rate was raised to 6 per cent. It was subsequently raised to a peak of 7 per cent on 15 April 1920. Almost immediately the boom collapsed, to be followed by a severe and prolonged slump characterised by industrial stagnation and mass unemployment without parallel.[56]

Chamberlain and the Treasury have been judged harshly for their apparent mismanagement of policy during 1919–20. Blame for the failure to respond to the rapidly developing boom is attributed to the Treasury because they, and not the Bank of England, were the real arbiters of market conditions and monetary policy for much of 1919.[57] Similarly, the imposition of 'dear money' in March 1920 has been the subject of even more vociferous condemnation; a decision castigated for being both too late and too severe, thereby intensifying the effects of the slump and making it far harder to reverse.[58] Yet as Howson demonstrates, political concerns about *unemployment and the needs of reconstruction were crucial constraints upon the sort of monetary policy desired by the Bank in 1919. Similarly, the decision to act in April 1920 'was not taken lightly, let alone in haste. The Chancellor was in the end forced into it by the state of Treasury bill sales ... [and] ultimately dictated by gold standard considerations'.[59] Moreover, in justice it needs to be noted that all expert opinion felt deflationary finance was an ineluctable corrective to the rapidly developing speculative boom. Indeed, even Keynes publicly demanded a 'swift and severe dose of dear money' involving a sustained commitment to an 8 or even 10 per cent Bank rate to check inflationary pressure and restore business realism.[60]*

[56] See S. Howson, *Domestic Monetary Management in Britain 1919–38*, (Cambridge 1975), 11–24.

[57] E.V. Morgan, *Studies in British Financial Policy, 1914–25* (1952), 143, 203; Howson, *Domestic Monetary Management*, 10–11. Following the opinions of his subject, Boyle is particularly scathing of Chamberlain's ignorance, indecision and implied lack of courage on this point, *Montagu Norman*, 125–6.

[58] See, for example, A.C. Pigou, *Aspects of British Economic History 1918–25* (1947), 196–7; Morgan, *Studies*.

[59] Howson, *Domestic Monetary Management*, 11–12, 23–25.

[60] K.O. Morgan, *Consensus and Disunity: The Lloyd George Coalition Government, 1918–22* (Oxford 1979), 258, 369. Keynes also advised Chamberlain privately along precisely the same lines in December 1919–February 1920 and in a note in 1942 still held this view. Howson, *Domestic Monetary Management*, 19–20, 184 n.68.

Chamberlain's increasingly restrictive budgetary stance with regard to public expenditure also deserves closer examination. It was undoubtedly true that by temperament Chamberlain was essentially orthodox in his view of finance and the Treasury. As Waldorf Astor lamented on learning of Chamberlain's appointment to the Exchequer in 1919, he was 'not the man for new finance'.[61] Whatever his personal inclinations or insight into finance, however, the legislative exertions of a government eager to fulfil the ambitious promises of 1918, the perceived profligacy of his colleagues and the sheer scale of the demands upon an almost empty public purse increasingly compelled Chamberlain to play the role of an orthodox and restrictive Chancellor. Within a month of his appointment he had warned that the government could 'hardly make both ends meet on a peace basis, even at the present crushing rate of taxation'.[62] Throughout the summer of 1919 Chamberlain had harangued Cabinet colleagues about their extravagant policies and the need for more effective restraint upon expenditure if the country was to avoid bankruptcy.[63] By mid-July the Prime Minister was equally alarmed about the financial situation. A month later the new Cabinet Committee on Finance agreed to restore some measure of Treasury control over ministers and their spending plans.[64] Clearly, however, this did not entirely resolve the problem for the Chancellor when dealing with spenders like Churchill and Addison. Little wonder he complained to his sisters of the unremitting burden of 'an endless & ungrateful battle with colleagues who think only departmentally. It is all very hateful and wearing'.[65]

No sooner had it been resolved to adopt a 'dear money' policy than Chamberlain was thrust again into the turmoil of the Budget on 19 April 1920.[66] This time, although he began by emphasizing that the actual deficit of £326M was almost £100M more than the estimate, he reviewed the still buoyant economic situation with some confidence. Income tax, duties on beer, spirits, champagne and cigars were all increased, as were postal charges. The super-tax limit was reduced to £2000 and Corporation Tax was introduced at a shilling in the pound. Even for their architect, the abolition of Lloyd George's 1909 land duties proved to be an

---

[61] W. Astor to J.L. Garvin, 10 January 1919, Morgan, *Consensus and Disunity*, 82. For similar views on Chamberlain's conservatism and orthodoxy at the Treasury see Steel-Maitland's comment in 1914 and Montagu's in 1917 cited in Dutton, *Austen Chamberlain*, 115,156; N. Chamberlain to Ida, 12 January 1919, NC 18/1/197.

[62] Lloyd George to Churchill (telegram), 16 February 1919. The warning was reiterated at the War Cabinet on 18 March. M. Gilbert, *Winston S. Churchill*, IV. Companion 1, 539, 590.

[63] T. Jones to Hankey, 8 July 1919 records that Chamberlain 'drew a most lurid picture of the country's financial position', *Whitehall Diary*, I, 89. Also J.E. Cronin, *The Politics of State Expansion: War, State and Society in Twentieth Century Britain*, (1991), 87.

[64] K. Burk, 'The Treasury: from Impotence to Power' in K. Burk (ed) *War and The State: The Transformation of British Government, 1914–1919* (1982), 100–101. See also Lloyd George's statement, *House of Commons Debates*, 5 Series, 119 col. 1979–2207, 18 August 1919.

[65] A. Chamberlain to Ida, 21 December 1919, AC5/1/146.

[66] For the details of the 1920 Budget see Mallet & George, *British Budgets*, 231–284.

uncontroversial measure as they had raised no revenue in ten years.[67] *Far more controversial, however, was the decision to raise Excess Profits Duty to 60 per cent: a decision which incensed the FBI, and Chambers of Commerce, left the City 'much annoyed' and prompted the Northcliffe press to agitate for Chamberlain's dismissal in favour of Worthington-Evans.*[68]

Even more inflammatory was the unresolved question of the government's attitude towards some form of special war profits levy to fund social reform and to silence the critics of profiteering. Although Chamberlain had urged the Commons to 'lend no countenance to so hazardous and ... so disastrous an experiment' as a capital levy in his 1919 Budget speech,[69] *the possibility had been in the air since February 1920 when Chamberlain had been persuaded to establish a Select Committee on War Wealth. In the event, the Cabinet finally resolved against such a proposal on 4 June.*[70] *Like the Prime Minister, Chamberlain's attitude was largely pragmatic.*[71] *Although he accepted the merits of such a scheme, he was anxious about its repercussions politically and even more upon business confidence*[72] *– an open-mindedness revealed to his sisters and one which refutes hasty allegations that he 'firmly rejected' the idea because he was a 'very narrow, unimaginative Chancellor'.*[73] *Despite protests at the increased EPD from the FBI and its supporters in the Commons, therefore, Chamberlain responded with his usual determination not to be bullied, defending the measure as the only fair and feasible alternative to a levy on wealth. Thereafter, despite 'strong opposition' from this quarter, the Budget passed safely through its various stages and it was again widely considered that 'Austen did very well'*[74] *receiving 'many congratulations from the Prime Minister downwards'.*[75]

Given his objectives when he entered office, Chamberlain entered his final year at the Treasury with an increasing sense of satisfaction at his own performance and the position it had created for him in the House. For the first time since Asquith, a Chancellor had budgeted for a surplus and obtained it. Moreover, a deficit of £1690M in the financial year 1918–19 had been transformed into a surplus of £237.9M in 1920–21.[76] *The future, however, looked decidedly less assured. With taxation revenues reaching a peak of nearly £1500M in 1920–21, Chamberlain*

---

[67] K.O. Morgan, *Consensus and Disunity*, 158; P. Rowland, *Lloyd George*, (1975), 522.

[68] Sanders Diary, 23 June and 10 July 1920, J. Ramsden (ed) *Real Old Tory Politics*, 139–140.

[69] Mallet & George, *British Budgets*, 197.

[70] For this discussion see Jones Diary, 4 June 1920, *Whitehall Diary*, I, 114–5.

[71] For Lloyd George's view see *Lord Riddell's Intimate Diary of the Peace Conference and After 1918–23*, (1933). Entry for 30 May 1920, 200.

[72] A. Chamberlain to Ida, 27 May 1920, AC5/1/164. The Bank of England and Treasury were also opposed to the levy, J.E. Cronin, *The Politics of State Expansion*, 85.

[73] For this charge see M. Pugh, *Lloyd George* (1993), 140; B.P. Lenman, *The Eclipse of Parliament: Appearance and Reality in British Politics since 1914*, (1992), 71.

[74] Sanders Diary, 18 July 1920, J. Ramsden (ed), *Real Old Tory Politics*, 140.

[75] A. Chamberlain to Ida, 1 August 1920, AC5/1/171.

[76] D. Moggridge, *British Monetary Policy, 1924–31: The Norman Conquest of $4.86*, (Cambridge 1972), 24.

was convinced the tax limit had been reached. He thus turned his attention increasingly towards greater economies in government programmes: a strategy which inevitably spelled doom for Addison and the Coalition's hopes of using social reform as a platform for political realignment.[77] More immediately menacing, during the summer of 1920 praise for the Budget turned to criticism as the economy swiftly began to show the unmistakable signs of faltering before plunging into the depths of an unprecedented slump.[78]

AC5/1/148

10 January 1920
Twitt's Ghyll

My dear Hilda,

I got here at 8 o'clock on Thursday night after a most harassing time in London & was rewarded by a lovely day yesterday, but last night a regular Southwest gale got up & has blown ever since bringing with it floods of rain. It is all very well for Neville to complain that the weather is to our letters what King Charles' head was to Mrs. Dick's memorial, but if King Charles had been as persistently provoking as the weather is this winter I think that even the Lunacy Commissioners would have seen nothing unnatural in Mrs. Dicks' constant allusions to him. In short if fine weather is always to coincide with imprisonment in a public office, what is the use of it & how shall a man keep this temper from rising & his pen from straying? You will perhaps realise what I mean by saying that my work was harassing when I explain that two days of serious & heavy conference, consideration & argument produced this result. The Bankers & I agreed that the proposal of the Governor of the Bank was preposterous. The Governor & I agreed that the proposal of the Bankers was inadmissible. And, to complete the triangle, the Governor & the Bankers agreed that my proposal was ridiculous! So I said: Very well, you are all unhelpful & your proposals are out of court. I shall go my own way. I have two alternatives & I will choose between them but I won't pay 6% to please the Governor & I won't reduce money rates to please you.

And the Bankers having left, I told the Governor what I had provisionally decided which made him so unhappy that he went home & passed a sleepless night & looked very ill when he came to see me again next morning.

---

[77] See K.O. Morgan, *Consensus and Disunity*, 89–105; K.O. and J. Morgan, *Portrait of a Progressive: The Political Career of Christopher, Viscount Addison*, (Oxford 1980), Chapter 4–5.
[78] A. Chamberlain to Ida, 2 July 1920. AC5/1/167; N. Chamberlain to Hilda, 11 July 1920 NC 18/1/264.

But meanwhile I also had reflected in the early hours of the morning in no very happy state of mind & had come to the conclusion that I was going to fall between the two stools – the stool of the small investor who is not mainly concerned with interest but who cannot give me much money & the stool of "the City" which has much money but is greedy for interest & other conditions which do not affect the little man, so that I was going to give the little man more than he asked & yet not get in the big man.

Thus chastened & with my mind clearer after the night I was prepared to consider a new proposal made by the Governor & accepted it with some slight modifications, & now the Governor & the principal Bankers are convinced that I shall do very well on this new proposal without swallowing the bolus either of them had prepared for me. We shall see, but at least the matter is now decided so there is no more need to worry about it. But take my advice, don't run for the position of C. of E. when you enter Parlt.

AC5/1/150   1 February 1920
                                                        9 Egerton Place

My dear Ida,

    . . .

Yes, the Exchanges are exercising me & the attitude of aloofness of the American Treasury will, I think , make it impossible to do anything effective for them. The American mind is so ignorant of European conditions, so suspicious of the English intentions & so afraid of losing votes that they complicate every problem & give no help in settling any of them. If we take a Mandate, we are grabbing territory. If we ask them to do so, we are seeking to involve them in our troubles. If we help the Anti-Bolshevists, we are militarist. If we blockade the Bolsheviks, they protest that it is illegal. They will send no more help & order the withdrawl of all their soldiers. If we withdraw our blockade, they accuse us of seeking to steal & trade advantage from them. If we withdraw our troops, they ask why we acted without first consulting them & why we & the French take decisions without their leave. If we consult them, their representatives have no instructions, can take no responsibility & record the fact. No, they really are an impossible people in their foreign relations & most impossible of all when they have elections in prospect which is of course every two years!

And home affairs are not very much more gay. Another big strike is always possible. If you see *any* chance of getting in coal, coke or wood, take it. There *may* be trouble this month or next, & if there is, it will be general & more serious than last time.

AC5/1/151   28 February 1920
                                                        Twitt's Ghyll

[To Ida]

. . .

What do I think of Asquith's return?[79] Well, I think that first &
foremost it is a great personal triumph for Asquith & a pleasant smack
in the face to the Labour Party who were certain of their victory. Next
I am glad of it on personal grounds, for I always felt that whatever his
faults as Prime Minister, Asquith did not deserve to be so treated by
Fife. Third & lastly I think that the P.M. must be pretty sick, for the
victory confirms Asquith in possession of the Party machine & will
probably lead to some Liberal secessions in the House. And a postscript:
I think it will be good for us to have someone of Asquith's calibre
opposite us in place of Maclean & Adamson.[80]

And Russia? I think that the opening up of trade[81] is right & indeed
necessary. Bad as the Bolsheviks are, it is clear that none of the other
leaders got any real hold of the districts they held or conquered.
Kolchak[82] & Denekin[83] were honest men, Judenitch[84][sic] was, I think,
a reactionary adventurer. But all three were surrounded by unde-
sirables & I don't think that the actions done in the name of any of
them would bear much scrutiny. And if fighting stops, it is always
possible that the Red Army may turn on Lenin & Co. & in any case
likely that the character of their rule will gradually change for the
better. But meanwhile Europe urgently needs Russian wheat & flax &
butter &c. &c. & to maintain the isolation of Russia if that were possible

[79] On 12 February 1920 Asquith was elected for Paisley. He held East Fife from 1886–
1918.
[80] William Adamson (1863–1936) Labour MP for Fife West 1910–31; Scottish Secretary
1924, 1929–31; Chairman PLP 1917–21.
[81] On 16 January 1920 the Allied Supreme Council ended the blockade of Soviet
Russia in the belief this would 'do more to oust or modify Bolshevism than armed
intervention ever accomplished'. Lloyd George, *House of Commons Debates* 125 col 43, 10
February 1920.
[82] Alexander Vasilievich Kolchak (1870–1920) Vice-Admiral Russian Imperial Navy
1916; C-in-C Black Sea Fleet 1916–17; Minister of War in Siberian White Russian
Government 1918. Declared himself "Supreme Ruler" with dictatorial powers, November
1918 but resigned in favour of Denikin in December 1919. Shot by Bolsheviks February
1920.
[83] Anton Ivanovich Denikin (1872–1947) Entered Tsarist Army 1887; Deputy Chief of
Staff and Commander of Western Front (later S.W. Front) 1917; C-in-C White Forces of
South 1918–19. Escaped to France 1920 and emigrated to USA 1945.
[84] Nikolai Nikolaevich Yudenich (1862–1933) Russian soldier. Lt-General 1913; Commander Tsarist in Caucasus 1914; C-in-C White Russian North West Army July 1919.
Retired to England and France.

would be to increase the distress of all who suffer from want, short supplies & high prices. Winston maintains that his policy was never given a fair chance. I maintain that it was based from the first on a series of hypotheses which never at any time could have been realized & a series of military appreciations every one of which proved to be a misapprehension. I tried early to get a different hand played but I failed then to secure sufficient support. Now events have taken charge & forced a different policy upon us.

AC5/1/153   13 March 1920
                                                          Twitt's Ghyll

My dear Ida,

Feeling absolutely done up after another hard week, mainly devoted to the Budget & "Dear Money" … Do you know what it is to feel physically exhausted, as well as mentally tired, when your only exertions have been of the mental kind? It is very disagreeable but not an unusual experience for me in these days. I struck at last against the constant meetings, always two & often three a day – Supreme Councils, Cabinets, Conferences & Committees – & announced that I must begin to consider my Budget & should not be available for other work, but of course I was not let alone. I had to confer with the Governor of the Bank & with the Banker's Comtee – of course the Governor & the Bankers take diametrically opposite views, & I cannot make up my mind which is right. The Governor is orthodox; the Professors agree with him & so do my Treasury experts. But not only would the course he urges be universally unpopular & cause a fearful howl, but I cannot be certain that in the peculiar circumstances of the time it would be effective & it would cost the Treasury at the rate of £10,000,000 a year in interest for the first step kum que ça: On the other hand the Bankers are biassed by their interests, timid & collectively selfish. But then again my colleagues or at least those who count in such matters agree with them. What would you do?

Besides this trouble, I had one Cabinet, one Comtee & two business dinners & a deputation. Such is a Minister's life in these days! I think that I have earned a little rest. I have already disposed of Stamps & I think that I know what I am going to do about Dear Money, namely disappoint the Governor & put the Bankers on their honour to behave better than they have been doing, for as fast as I have 'deflated' they have 'inflated' & with 11 millions of Treasury Bills out they have the whip hand of me.

Poincaré[85] seems vicious. He is of course ambitious to be Prime Minister & not unlikely to succeed. Meanwhile his game is to show that Clemenceau sacrificed France & that he is made of sterner stuff – a dangerous & reckless game.

AC5/1/154

19 March 1920
Twitt's Ghyll

My dear Ida,

...

... I don't wonder that housing bothers you. It is causing me more anxiety in its financial aspects than any other question. I have no faith in Addison's[86] capacity or power of drive. He loses himself in talk & seems to me singularly muddle-headed for a man who is not altogether a fool.

...

Neville will have told you of the offer made to him & his refusal.[87] On the whole I am not sorry that he did not accept, tho' I was sorry that his reason was what it was.

...

... I hear that Northcliffe has given the command Hands off Chamberlain for the present!

---

[85] Raymond Poincaré (1860–1934) French Premier 1911–13; President of Republic 1913–20; Premier and Foreign Minister 1922–24; Premier 1926–29. Obstinate defender of extreme French claims and detested by Chamberlain and many other British negotiators.

[86] Christopher Addison (1869–1951) Liberal MP for Shoreditch 1910–22 and Labour MP for Swindon 1929–31 and 1934–35. Parliamentary Secretary Board of Education 1914–1915; Parliamentary Secretary, Ministry of Munitions 1915–1916; Minister of Munitions 1916–1917; Minister of Reconstruction 1917–1919; President Local Government Board 1919; Minister of Health 1919–1921; Minister without Portfolio 1921; Parliamentary Secretary, Ministry of Agriculture 1929–1930; Minister of Agriculture 1930–1931; Dominion Secretary 1945–1947; Commonwealth Secretary 1947; Lord Privy Seal, 1947–1951; Paymaster-General 1948–1949; Lord President of Council 1951. Created K.G. 1947; Baron Addison 1937 and Viscount 1945.

[87] Law tentatively offered Neville Chamberlain a junior ministerial position with the hint that this may be his last chance. Memories of his earlier treatment by Lloyd George at National Service were too strong and he declined without consulting his brother.

AC5/1/156   3 April 1920
                                                           Twitt's Ghyll

[Not addressed]

...

It may amuse you to hear that B.L. told me ... that the P.M. now
appreciates my value. "He did underrate you when he thrust the
Chancellorship at you!" Well its a funny world.

AC5/1/158   11 April 1920
                                                           Twitt's Ghyll

My dear Ida,

...

You ask about France's action in the Ruhr Valley.[88] She went in
against the expressed sense of every Ally & America & used black
troops to occupy Frankfort & might easily have provoked serious
trouble. I think Millerand[89] & Poincaré with Fosch [sic] to egg them
on very dangerous, & it was time to let them know that if they provoked
or provoke a row by isolated action, they will be left to settle it by
themselves as best as they can. They live in a night-mare terror of
Germany, but unless they are careful they will plant such memories as
Germany will never forget & someday will avenge. Fear is a bad
counsellor & fear coupled with ambition the worst of all. They are very
difficult to work with & their financial situation is a parlous one from
which they seem to think & indeed proclaim that it is everyone else's
business to rescue them, whilst they spend money to no purpose in
Syria or Germany & abuse us for everything that we do or don't do.

...

I don't think the Budget will be popular in any quarter, but I hope
that opposition will be disseminated by the multitude of possible
objections. I dread the speech; it will be awfully long.

[88] On 6 April 1920 the French used Moroccan troops as their advance guard in
occupying Frankfurt. Although racial tension on the Rhine had been rising since the
deployment of black French troops on the Rhine in the spring 1919, this event set the
stage for the first massive coordinated response from the Germans turning the race issue
into an international cause célèbre. See K.L. Nelson, 'The "Black Horror on the Rhine":
Race as a Factor in Post-World War I Diplomacy', *Journal of Modern History*, 42.4
December 1970, 606–628.
[89] (Etienne) Alexandre Millerand (1859–1943) French lawyer and politician. Elected as
extreme left Deputy in 1885. After 1899 various ministerial offices including War Minister
in 1914, Foreign Minister 1920. President of the Republic 1920–24.

AC5/1/159   16 April 1920
                                                   Twitt's Ghyll

My dear Hilda,

   Did you believe the Times for once when it said that Ministers were
very pleased with the C/E? In this case you could safely have trusted
that not too accurate journal. Did I promise last October that if they
were good & spent no more money I should be able to pay my way
this year without additional taxation & have a substantial balance for
the reduction of debt? Did they then spend an extra 40 million or so &
have I nevertheless got 160 millions for debt reduction? Am I going to
lay on new taxes all the same & make that 160 into 230 this year &
300 next. All these things are true, & they are pleased as well they may
be. And what is worth recording is that on my presenting lesser
proposals with the expectation that the P.M. would exclaim "But what
on earth do you need all that money for?" he observed instead: "I
don't think that you are doing enough" & thereby delighted me &
strengthened my hand ... Well, I shall be glad when Monday is over.
It has been & will be tremendous labour, but it is a good budget tho'
I say it as shouldn't [sic] & justifies my statement to you that if I get
three years more I will leave the national finances in a sound position.

AC5/1/160   25 April 1920
                                                   Twitt's Ghyll

My dear Ida,

   The Budget has certainly provoked an interesting situation. It's first
reception was distinctly favourable. It was 'bold & courageous' & so
forth. But now the interests are beginning to make themselves heard &
my foes are of my own household. The Federation of British Industries
is very strong in the House & its clamours are being echoed by the
Daily Telegraph, Chronicle, Express & Pall Mall whilst the Daily
News & Manchester Guardian continue to support me. I shall have
my own way in the end with minor consessions − something especially
for new businesses − but I shall have a big fight with the Big Bugs &
meanwhile the lesser plagues of Stamps & Beer & Spirits & Wines will
buzz & bite. But I have a rod in pickle for the Federation when it gets
troublesome. I offered them an alternative which many of their supporters now say would be the right thing & they would not have it. I
invited them to find an alternative & after 14 months they came back
with what in effect was an additional income tax. They have some
reason to be vexed or at least surprised but they are a selfish, swollen

lot, & if they think that they can bully this Chancellor because there are so many of them in the House, they will find that they are mistaken. It is good for them to be told at once that I stand or fall by my proposals. If they won't take them from me, they will get them & a Capital Levy from someone else.

AC5/1/161   30 April 1920
                                                       Twitt's Ghyll

My dear Hilda,

There are some advantages in having a Budget on hand, for if I have to work hard when I am at it it gives me an excuse for coming down here on a Friday morning for rest after my exertions & – forgive the boasting – my triumph. Of course I shall have a lot of trouble with it before I have done with it, but so far in spite of the violent opposition of a section of the public & the Press it has gone extremely well. I am struck, & I admit pleased, by the repetition in several papers of such phrases as 'a speech which changed votes'; 'Mr C matured late but he has come into his own'; 'like his father he developed after fifty' & so forth. And the allusions to 'courage & character' are frequent. All of which shows that one need not be too troubled by passing brutalities & injustices & that if one goes along steadily without being intimidated or discouraged, one *will* get one's reward. Certainly in this House I have a position quite my own & the pleasant feeling that men of all parties like & respect me. And I have found honour even in my own country, for at last the B.D.P.'s correspondent notices that I made a speech & even declares it a good one!

AC5/1/164   27 May 1920
                                                       Twitt's Ghyll

My dear Ida,

I do not often forget your birthday & the fact that I did so will perhaps make clear to you as well as anything that I could say how utterly tired out I was. Indeed, I was so tired that I was ill both in body & mind & the eight days that are all that I shall have here are none too many to recuperate. However yesterday I felt better & in this air, with this lovely weather & with change of thought I don't despair of patching myself up sufficiently. But I should be happier if I had made up my mind & got a Cabinet decision on War Levy or no War Levy. Pro: It is fair, it will produce a good round sum in a 2 or 3 years: it will meet the widespread feeling that the Profiteers have not contributed their share & will (this is to me the strongest reason) thus avert from capital in general the prejudice aroused by the sight of such big fortunes made during the War. Con: it will be a devil of a Bill to pass & to administer. Further the City & business generally is not only opposed to it but almost in a panic about it. And if they really scare themselves, they may cause something like a crash.

Lastly the alternative is continued E[xcess] P[rofits] D[uty], but E.P.D. is a poor reed to lean upon. If bad times come, it will produce nothing.

Now what shall I do? If it were not for fear that the child would scream itself into fits, I would have the Levy & the child would be all the better for it. But it might die of fright before it found out that it was not hurt.

AC5/1/165

6 June 1920
Twitt's Ghyll

My dear Hilda,

There is to be no War Levy & to tell the truth I am greatly relieved, first because I believe the decision to be right & secondly because it takes an immense burden of work & a most anxious responsibility from my shoulders. I am not *sure* that financial & commercial opinion as to the dangers of the War Levy is right. Indeed, I am sure that their fears are greatly exaggerated & that they underrate the danger that another Govt or another Chancellor, will give them something worse against which this levy would have been an insurance. But as trade is slacking & the credit position none too secure & since they were so frightened, I am sure that it would have been most dangerous to proceed & I should have been afraid of a catastrophe. And all the colleagues whose opinion on financial questions I value – Milner, Bonar Law, Horne[90] of the Board of Trade for the business view – Worthington Evans[91] & the Prime Minister – were of the same opinion. The counter opinion was held only by those who have no knowledge of finance & talked as

[90] Robert Stevenson Horne (1871–1940) Conservative MP for Glasgow Hillhead 1918–37. Minister of Labour 1919–20; President Board of Trade 1920–21; Chancellor of Exchequer 1921–22. Created K.B.E. 1918; G.B.E. 1920; Viscount Horne of Slamannan 1937.

[91] Laming Worthington-Evans (1868–1931) Conservative MP for Colchester 1910–29, St George's 1929–31. Minister of Blockade 1918–19; Minister of Pensions 1919–20; Minister without Portfolio 1920–21; Secretary for War 1921–22, 1924–29; Postmaster-General 1923–24. Created baronet 1916 (when assumed the additional surname of Worthington) and G.B.E. 1922.

politicians only – Winston, Montagu, Shortt,[92] Macnamara[93] & Curzon! Is it not amusing to see Curzon in the camp of the extremists & Lloyd George on the side of moderation & prudence.

Had the Cabinet been divided the opposite way, I would have gone forward with the levy with some reluctance & a good deal of anxiety, but with all good opinion supporting my doubts & increasing my fears, I should have refused if I had been pressed – which I was not.

AC5/1/166   27 June 1920
                                               Twitt's Ghyll

My dear Hilda,

. . .

I don't write to you about housing, for though I have no faith in Addison or the Ministry of Health, housing finance in my night-mare – the worst I think of all my troubles. But it is rash to speak thus with a Committee on the Finance Bill still to come & opposition battening on the enforced delays.

. . .

Garvin[94] is hard at work reading for Father's life & very keen about it. He is to finish the book in two years. I am now reading Buckle's final volumes of Dizzy, & find them very interesting – the mind of a seer in the body of a mountebank. 'East is east' though all the generations & Dizzy, tho' an English patriot was not an Englishman.

I return for a moment to Lympne[95] & Boulogne.[96] Ll.G. led throughout, demanded German disarmament which pleased the French, made peace with Italians & Belgians when Millerand had tactlessly rubbed up both, & failed only to get French cooperation in Russian affairs, very obviously because they were afraid of their small investors in

---

[92] Edward Shortt (1862–1935) Liberal MP for Newcastle-upon-Tyne 1910–22. Chief Secretary for Ireland May 1918–January 1919; Home Secretary 1919–October 1922.

[93] Thomas James Macnamara (1861–1931) Liberal MP for Camberwell North 1900–18 and Coalition Liberal for renamed Camberwell NW 1918–24. Parliamentary Secretary Local Government Board January 1907–April 1908; Parliamentary and Financial Secretary to Admiralty, 1908–April 1920; Minister of Labour March 1920–October 1922.

[94] James Louis Garvin (1864–1947) Editor of *The Observer* 1908–42 and *Pall Mall Gazette* 1912–15. Official biographer of Joseph Chamberlain.

[95] At the first Hythe Conference on 15–16 May 1920 Lloyd George and Chamberlain met Millerand and Marsal, the French Finance Minister, to repair the alliance and concert strategy concerning German disarmament and reparation payments for the impending meeting with the Germans. This was the first of several conferences held near Lympne at the luxurious home of Lloyd George's PPS Sir Philip Sassoon.

[96] Following his success at San Remo in April, at a further conference at Boulogne on 21–22 June Lloyd George and Millerand agreed to a lump sum for Germany's indemnity of £4,500M spread over 35 years.

Russian bonds. But it was a good meeting throughout. I like Millerand. He is honest & courageous whereas Poincaré – but you know Clemenceau's mot "Poincarre – poing carré? No: It is Point, *not* Carré Square. *Not Square!*"

AC5/1/167

2 July 1920
9 Egerton Place

My dear Ida,

...

I shall have a very arduous & difficult time with the Budget. The long delay interposed between its stages by the necessity for making progress with other bills has permitted the opposition to grow & organise & agitate & without a doubt the general outlook in trade has altered for the worse in the interval. There is a general malaise which tends to spread & to produce the very evils which it fears so that the case for my very severe proposals – made as you know more severe than I had originally intended by the Finance Comtee of the Cabinet – is less clear than it was when I opened the Budget. And of course I have a bad Press now as always but today the Daily Express has come to the rescue!

I wish I did not feel so tired all the time & were not troubled with slight sciatic pain in the leg which has hitherto been free. It does not raise one's spirits or make work easier or seem to leave me with any reserve of strength on which to draw. But I suppose I shall pull through!

AC5/1/168

11 July 1920
Twitt's Ghyll

My dear Ida,

This will be but a brief note for I feel awfully tired or incorrigibly idle, if you will. I return to town tonight to be able to be ready for the real Budget fight [on increase in EPD] tomorrow, Tuesday & I expect Wednesday. I cannot say that I feel fit for it. I seem to have no reserves of strength, & the more I rest & sleep as in these last two days, the more I feel how very tired I am.

I hope that I shall not have such a House as confronted Montagu on Thursday[97] & that, if I do, I shall not handle it so maladroitly. With the House in that temper nothing could have been so infuriating to it as his opening remarks – no word of sympathy with Dyer, no sign that Montagu appreciated his difficulties but as it were a passionate peroration to a speech which had not been delivered, a grand finale to a debate which had not begun. I am really sorry for Montagu. He is able, ambitious, nervous, highly strung. He has a most difficult situation to hand in India with a Viceroy who is none too able & with Councils in India & in London which seem to me below the average. Our party has always disliked & distrusted him. On this occasion all their English & racial feeling was stirred to passionate display – I think I have never seen the House so fiercely angry – & he threw fuel on the flames. A Jew, a foreigner, rounding on an Englishman & throwing him to the wolves – that was the feeling, & the event illustrates once again what I said of Dizzy. A Jew may be a loyal Englishman & passionately patriotic, but he is intellectually apart from us & will never be purely & simply English.

It is hard, for in this case the decision was not Montagu's but that of the Cabinet, based on most careful examination by a strong Cabinet Comtee & making all allowances for Dyer's difficulties I cannot see that with any regard for the principles on which our Empire is & must be conducted we could have done less. But when "Clemency Canning" is represented by Edwin Montagu, violent opposition is certain.

I returned home very sad & much upset by the whole tone of the debate. The new scheme in India is launched under the worst possible auspices.

AC5/1/170   24 July 1920
                                                      Twitt's Ghyll

My dear Hilda,

    . . .
    I spent Friday morning & afternoon in Cabinet conference on Ireland. Most puzzling & most distressing. Can modern democracy handle such problems successfully? The country is in revolution & many features of the situation are worse than anything that we have known in the past. And one can no longer rely upon *both* parties in the State to follow out a policy that requires years for its success. Can one

[97] Although relieved of his command and put on half pay after the Amritsar massacre, Dyer received much support in the Parliamentary debate on 8 July 1920 when Montagu was the victim of vigorous attack upon his Jewish origin from the Conservative right-wing. Although Churchill's intervention saved the day for the government, Carson led 129 Unionists in the vote against the Government on a censure motion.

rely even on one party to see a difficult problem through? A sensational Press upsets their nerves & makes them impatient, first clamorous for stern measures & then screams itself into hysterics when it sees what stern measures mean in practice. There is nothing worse than selling out on a policy which you can't carry through for such a policy, whatever its intrinsic merits, must always be wrong. I don't see my way clear. The old Unionist policy is not possible, for our people won't give it the time necessary for it to achieve its end. "Home Rule" seems now equally impossible. Is it to be Dominion Govt?

AC5/1/171   1 August 1920
                                                        Twitt's Ghyll

My dear Ida,

. . .

The Budget is through & I have had my own way & beaten the organised opposition of Press & Chambers of Commerce &c. by knowing my own mind – my hesitations have been to you alone – & by standing firm on the big points whilst being as conciliatory as possible on the small ones. I have had many congratulations from the P.M. downwards, but I don't know that anything pleased me more than a Labour M.P.'s comment to Neville – "Well he's taught us one thing at any rate – that what the Daily Mail calls a Deadhead is a head & shoulders above us any way. We couldn't have done that!". It really was a great feat of courage, perseverance, tact & hard work & a great personal triumph. But all this brag is for you & Hilda alone.

AC5/1/173   17 August 1920
                                                        Twitt's Ghyll

My dear Ida,

My holiday began at luncheon time today & we came down here by the afternoon train. A holiday! It seems too good to be true. And how long will it last? Poland may interrupt it at any moment. A coal strike may put an end to it. Trouble in the City – a not too remote possibility – would force me to hurry back to town. Geneva may demand my presence earlier than I expect – & if none of these things happen, something else equally disturbing may occur.

Meanwhile, however, I have a holiday & I mean to enjoy it.

You will have seen from the papers what has been happening about Poland. The Poles have committed every conceivable mistake both military & political. The Soviet Govt speaks fair but may be lying &

the French Govt takes the opportunity of Millerand's return from Lympne to recognise Wrangel[98] as a de facto government in defiance of the Lympne agreement & without telling us what they were doing. There was no concealing the fact that we were pursuing different & even contradictory policies which can only leave Germany as the tertius gaudens. The French know by this time that they have been very foolish but it is easier to knock Humpty Dumpty down than to set him up again. Nothing could exceed the strength or the universality of the feeling here that we want no more war & that England is not to be involved because Poland has played the fool or France encourages her in her folly. It is a pretty kettle of fish, & if the Russians are really playing false the effect of the French action on British opinion will only be to make it more difficult for a British government to take any action whatever to protect the independence of Poland.

As to the coal strike, it certainly looks as if we should have one in September & it is only too likely that the Transport workers will join in. If so, it will be a most serious struggle & we are not as well equipped to cope with it as we were when the railway men struck last year.

Altogether a cheerful prospect with which to begin a holiday, not to speak of Ireland which is always with us!

AC5/1/175   16 October 1920
                                                        Twitt's Ghyll

My dear Hilda,

. . .

And a coal strike! I had made up my mind – & so I think had my colleagues – that we were not going to have that trouble. I don't believe that in the end Smillie & Co wanted it any more than we did, but they had helped to raise forces & expectations which they could not allay or satisfy & now I suppose that we are in for a two month's struggle with infinite loss & suffering to the whole community. Is it not characteristic of Northcliffe that the Times & Daily Mail at once suggest that there should be "a compromise" by the Government giving away all that was in dispute. The public & especially the arm-chair men are very apt to criticise the P.M. for giving way too much & compromising too often in such disputes but this shows how right he & Horne (who has done *admirably*) were to leave no excuse for public opinion to rally to the strikers. There are no signs of the Transport Workers joining

---

[98] Baron Peter Nikolayevitch Wrangel (1872–1928) Distinguished Russian soldier of Russo-Japanese and Great War, succeeding Denikin as commander of anti-Bolshevik forces in south Russia. Held Crimea until November 1920 when evacuated to the Balkans.

in & at present the railway men are all right tho' Cramp,[99] their secretary is a revolutionary of the type of Smillie.

AC5/1/176

22 October 1920
Treasury Chambers

My dear Ida,

... & if the railway men come out as now seems likely correspondence like all else may well be very uncertain for a time. What a tragedy it is that when our resources were likely in any case to have been severely tried by inevitable distress, that this distress should be needlessly & immensely magnified by strikes among the best paid of our workmen who themselves stood in no danger of lack of employment but whose refusal to work throws every other industry at once out of gear & in a short time brings them to an absolute standstill. I dare say that you will have seen Horne's admirable statement of the Government case last Wednesday. He has handled the business throughout with great tact, courage & skill, & his speech could not have been bettered. It set the tone for the whole debate which was on a high level & reflected credit both on the Govt & the House.

The Irish debate next day was equally successful for the government, Asquith in particular cutting a very poor figure & being subsequently flattened out by Bonar Law.

...

Did I tell you that I had some reason to think that my name was being considered for the Viceroyalty of India? Well the P.M. has since offered it to me & I have refused it. I am coming to think that my greatest distinction in life will be the number of high appointments that I have declined – two Embassies (Paris when Derby took it, Washington when Grey[100] went there) a Secretaryship of State & now the Viceroyalty of India! The P.M. was very flattering. He said that I was so obviously the best man for India that he had felt bound to offer it to me but that I should be so great a loss to the govt at home with the difficult problems in front of us that though he did not know where to turn for India he was after all "rather relieved" – & for the time at any rate he

[99] Concemore T. Cramp (1876–1933) General Secretary, NUR 1920; Chairman Labour Party 1925; President, International Transport Worker's Federation 1926. Served on many Committees of Inquiry and Royal Commissions in 1920s.

[100] Edward Grey (1862–1933) Liberal MP for Berwick 1885–1916. Parliamentary Under Secretary Foreign Office August 1892–June 1895; Foreign Secretary December 1905–December 16. Succeeded grandfather as 3rd baronet 1882, created K.G. 1912 and Viscount Grey of Falloden 1916. Temporary Ambassador to USA 1919. Liberal leader in House of Lords 1916 and 1921–24.

was certainly speaking his real thoughts. Twenty or more years ago I remember saying that the Viceroyalty had no attraction for me, but my short tenure of the India Office changed my feelings. Present conditions in India are extraordinarily interesting, the responsibilities & opportunities of the new Viceroy will be immense, & if I were a bachelor or childless I should have been sorely tempted. But the children settled the matter & never left a moment's doubt in Ivy's mind or mine. I could not have faced a five year's separation from Joe & I suppose from Diane also at their ages. This, of course, is for your information only & the offer must not be talked about.

AC5/1/177

31 October 1920
9 Egerton Place

My dear Hilda,

. . .

... The coal strike *is* difficult to understand or rather the terms of its settlement. One of the miners representatives who has throughout been strongest in favour of peace voted against it on the grounds which he frankly stated that he would never be able to explain the figures to his fellow miners & when I asked why the South Wales leaders were so much against it I was told that it was not because they were Welsh but because they happened to be the only two men on the Executive who were clever enough at figures to understand it. You may say that this does not open up a hopeful prospect but I think that it will nevertheless carry the day. There was no surrender on our part & no yielding when the 'hitch' arose at the last moment & the settlement is based on the automatic adjustment of wages to output measured however not by a "datum line" but by "export values" in short by Tweedledum instead of Tweedledee.

Ireland – yes, the Irish situation is disagreeable, but when law breaks down, civilisation & its conventions disappear & human nature asserts itself. And it is a fact that the reprisals have secured the safety of the police in places where previously they were shot down like vermin, has caused the people to warn them again & again of ambushes & the like, & together with the steps taken by Govt is getting the Murder gang on the run by degrees.

... By the way you say nothing about the Indian appointment. Whoever goes will have as difficult a problem as Ireland & the Egyptian one is little better.

AC5/1/183

12 December 1920
9 Egerton Place

My dear Ida,

...

I had a most hectic week or ten days – Comtee on this, Comtee on that, Cabinet, Mesopotamia, Palestine, Greece, Turkey, Ireland & again Ireland, housing, bread, sugar, bacon, Education, Continuation Schools, Millers, Refiners, Civil Servants, Women, Marriage & equal pay, United States debt, German coal, the Expenses of the League of Nations, Typhus, the bankruptcy of Austria, Twelve little Arab boys & their twelve little [?] subsidies, who said what to whom & how he didn't say it (an awful row this – H & B calling each other liars across my body, each in a white heat of passion which they poured out to me because they were too angry to speak to one another & all because poor unhappy tired frightened & incompetent Smith – it really was Smith & that somehow seems to put the last touch to my annoyance – was too stupid & muddled to know what message he had carried from one to the other or to carry or report any message correctly) & MacNamara AND Addison. "Cold feet", I exclaimed at last in an outburst of exasperation, "it's not the Express, which, thank God! I don't read, it's my colleagues who are faced with the most dangerous financial situation that has ever confronted us & can think of nothing better to do than to dance on the edge of the precipice".

Well, I must be recovering if I can pour out my soul like this, I spent all yesterday in bed & all the afternoon asleep. The delight of it! Alas! I have not got Father's immense energy & now I remind myself of nothing but Mr. Pickwick's cab-horse. As soon as I get into my stall, I drop.

The debate went off very well. Of course Northcliffe & Rothermere had made the House very angry & lightened my task, & the Opposition is divided & very weak in debating power & Asquith was glad enough I think of the excuse of a meeting at Paisley for not showing up in the House where he could be immediately answered – at any rate he never gave us any indication that he was going to be absent or asked us to fix the date for a day on which he could attend which we should have done at once. If you want my opinion of my speech, I think that it was long & dull but not without weight or skill, & I think & a good many others thought that it settled the debate & the division. But it's 'cursed spite' that I, who never like the Office, should be Chancellor in such times as these. But I am increasingly happy in one thing. My reorganised Office works splendidly. They never let me down. It is only when I take a figure or an argument from a colleague or his office that I find cause to regret it afterwards.

I have left myself no time to write of Ireland. I shocked some of my colleagues some time ago by saying that I thought the time was at hand for a new Kilmainham Treaty openly avowed this time as Father wished & meant the original one to be. But the P.M. said "Not yet; we must beat the murder gang first." He was right & we are beating it & the less violent or more moderate are beginning to take courage, to find their voices & to recover their independence. McCreedy,[101][sic] John Anderson[102] & Greenwood[103] are a very strong combination & they are winning.[104]

AC5/1/186   1 January 1921
                                                  Twitt's Ghyll

My dear Hilda,

. . .

What a troubled year the past one has been! But we have some things to be grateful for & some that we have not managed too badly. A railway strike & a coal strike both overcome without serious injury to property or person, the Irish situation mending, a serious rebellion in Mesopotamia met & ended without any small disaster, France – shall I say? still our friend & America not yet our enemy. Let us be thankful for these mercies. And let us pray that the New Year may bring us further on the road to peace. For you & Ida I hope that it will be a happy one. I know it will be full of activity & usefulness.

[101] General Sir (Cecil Frederick) Nevil MacCready (1862–1946) Served Egypt and South Africa; Adjutant-General BEF 1914–16; Adjutant-General to the Forces 1916–18; Commissioner of Metropolitan Police 1918–20. G.O. C-in-C Ireland 1920–22.

[102] John Anderson (1882–1958) Civil servant, Secretary Ministry of Shipping 1917–19; Chairman Board of Inland Revenue 1919–22. Joint Under-Secretary to Lord Lieutenant of Ireland 1920; Permanent Under-Secretary Home Office 1922–32; Governor of Bengal 1932–37. Independent National MP for Scottish Universities 1938–50; Lord Privy Seal 1938–39; Home Secretary 1939–40; Lord President of the Council 1940–43; Chancellor of Exchequer 1943–45. Created K.C.B. in 1919, G.C.B. 1923 and Viscount Waverly 1952. A consistent voice for sanity amidst the carnage of 'retaliation'.

[103] (Thomas) Hamar Greenwood (1870–1948) Liberal MP York 1906–10, Sunderland 1910–22 and Conservative MP for Walthamstow (East) 1924–29. Under-Secretary for Home Affairs 1919; Secretary for Overseas Trade 1919–1920; Chief Secretary for Ireland 1920–1922. Created Baronet 1915, Baron Greenwood 1929 and Viscount 1937.

[104] On the previous day (11 December 1920) martial law was formally proclaimed for the whole of Ireland with considerable latitude for interpretation.

AC5/1/190   29 January 1921
                                                         Twitt's Ghyll

My dear Ida,

      . . .
      I find an awful lot of heavy work to do on my return [from Algeciras].
This year's finances will not turn out very badly but next year's causes
me anxiety. I am very glad that I got home just too late to go to Paris.
I had sooner that the P.M. & Worthington-Evans continued their
labours on Reparation. It is a thankless job & it is not easy to reconcile
French opinion or our own for that matter with common sense.

AC5/1/191   6 February 1921
                                                         Westbourne
                                                         Egbaston

My dear Hilda,

      . . .
      I had two excellent meetings here, indicating I think a revival of
interest & an improvement of organisation but I made two very heavy &
(except for the importance of the pronouncement about E.P.D.) very
dull speeches. And we have honoured Lloyd George & made him a
Freeman & an L.L.D & entertained him at the Jewellers, & whatever
be his past or present faults, I do not regret it & would not have
absented myself if I could, for he has great qualities & has rendered
great services. No living Englishman can compare with him & when
the history of these times comes to be written can you doubt that he
will stand out like the younger Pitt if not with the effulgence of
Chatham!

AC5/1/192   12 February 1921
                                                         Twitt's Ghyll

My dear Ida,

      . . .
      I am glad that you approved my Reparations speech. I hear that it
gave satisfaction in Paris & London if not in Washington, & it is just
as well that Washington should be reminded that, if they talk critically
of our claims upon Germany, there is an obvious retort which Asquith's
speech gave me the opportunity of making since he was taking the
same line as the States. But they have no intention of helping anyone.

They are opposed by their own taxation & their own debt & they are looking to us to help to repay it. Auckland Geddes[105] has brought back a very disagreeable account of the frame of mind of both parties & their hostility to everything English. I can only hope that his vision is distorted by the fact that even his children cannot go out of the house without police protection.

The P.M. has got courage & that is a quality which is none too frequent in his colleagues. He is preparing to take on a big fight with the building Unions &, being in for it, is means [sic] to do it thoroughly which I like. As he justly says, you can't fight without an army & since the Unions have wasted (with Addison's help) a year in negotiations only to give a flat refusal at the end, he now means to enlist the whole-hearted support of the masters by allowing them to fight on the question of output if they will join him in fighting on dilution. There may be a pretty big strike, so it is just as well your second house is nearly finished. Still when they see we are in earnest, they may back down about dilution & in that case output would not be pressed, but they must surrender before a strike not after it.

---

[105] Auckland Campbell Geddes (1879–1954) Unionist MP for Basingstoke 1917–20. Minister of National Service 1917–1919; President Local Government Board 1918–1919; Minister of Reconstruction 1919; President Board of Trade 1919–March 1920; Ambassador to Washington 1920–24. Created K.C.B. 1917, G.C.M.G. 1922. Baron Geddes 1942.

5

'HOW STRANGE IS FATE'

The Leadership, March – December 1921

On 17 March 1921 Bonar Law unexpectedly announced his resignation on grounds of ill-health. Having abandoned all expectation of obtaining the leadership for himself a decade earlier, Chamberlain now found the prize equally suddenly and unexpectedly within his grasp. His conduct during this period illustrates much about Chamberlain's character. In particular, it revealed again that lack of steely ambition and 'pushfulness' so evident in his father: a weakness he cloaked beneath an acute sensitivity to the outward appearance of political propriety and personal delicacy. As he wrote to J.C.C. Davidson after his succession, with regard to such matters he had 'a great horror of anything that savours of intrigue or pushfulness on the part of a possible candidate, and felt then as I felt ten years ago ... that the only right thing to do was to keep quiet and leave members to make up their own minds without either courting their favour or shunning responsibility if their choice fell upon me'.[1] Having thus 'emerged' by acclamation as undisputed leader,[2] another feature of Chamberlain's character swiftly manifested itself in his initial sense of weary trepidation at entering upon an apparently unpalatable task with grave reluctance. Like every other office, therefore, he confessed to his family that he accepted the leadership as 'an obvious duty but without pleasure or any great expectation except of trouble and hard labour'.[3]

Despite such protestations, Chamberlain's enthusiasm for the task soon increased. At a personal level, he derived enormous pleasure from his new position as Leader of the Commons – a post for which he had a special affection as a 'House of Commons man'. He also savoured it for the satisfaction such a promotion would have given to the ever-present spectre of his father. Moreover, released from the burdens of the Treasury, Chamberlain took on a new countenance 'almost gay and debonair with leisure for a joke and a tale' in stark contrast to his 'over-wrought' condition as Chancellor: a demeanour he exchanged with Horne, his successor at the Treasury.[4] Thus, although Chamberlain introduced the Budget on 25 April 1921 in order to permit Horne to wrestle with the coal strike, his mood remained distinctly

---

[1] A. Chamberlain to J.C.C. Davidson, 20 March 1921, R.R. James, *Memoirs of a Conservative*, 103.

[2] In proposing Chamberlain as leader in the Commons on 21 March 1921 Captain Ernest Pretyman first articulated the notion that Conservative leaders 'emerge' when he declared, 'Great leaders of parties are not elected they are evolved ... I think it will be a bad day for this or any party to have solemnly to meet to elect a leader. The leader is there, and we all know it when he is there'. *Gleanings and Memoranda*, LIII, 301.

[3] A. Chamberlain to Hilda, 20 March 1921, AC5/1/194. See also to Mary Carnegie, 19 March 1921, AC 4/1/1204.

[4] T. Jones to Law, 24 April 1921, *Whitehall Diary*, I, 152.

buoyant: a satisfaction enhanced by the knowledge that the surplus of over £230M was built upon the foundations laid by his stewardship of national finance and the relief that he would not have to return to the office again.[5] *Finally, his relish for the leadership was enhanced substantially by his close working relationship and developing respect for Lloyd George. Despite his initial apprehensions in January 1919, at the Treasury his relationship with the Prime Minister had flourished to the extent that he came to regard him as his 'best friend' and most robust supporter in Cabinet.*[6] *Contrary to informed opinion that the Prime Minister 'would never work in harness with Chamberlain',*[7] *when he became leader he was heartened by Lloyd George's desire that he should 'step fully into Bonar's shoes' and the trust which soon developed between them.*[8] *Indeed, although Lloyd George initially found his new counterpart 'pompous to the last degree, & increasingly so since he took Bonar's place',*[9] *this soon gave way to a grudging respect. Thus within three months Frances Stevenson noted that Lloyd George 'certainly gets on with him much better than he expected to. Austen plays the game & he sees that he can trust the P.M. who conceals nothing from him'.*[10]

One factor in this developing relationship was Chamberlain's obvious acceptance of the constraints imposed by Coalition and the problems inherent in such a 'largely opportunist' arrangement'.[11] *Indeed, despite his early scepticism and mistrust, by the spring of 1921 Chamberlain had become a convinced believer in the need for coalition as a bastion against Labour and its brand of class politics. In his short speech accepting the leadership he had thus called for party unity and support in the belief that 'there are moments when insistence upon Party is as unforgivable as insistence upon personal things when the difficulties which the nation has to confront call for a wider outlook and a broader union than can be found even within the limits of a single party'.*[12] *Two months later, in his first speech to his own backbenchers (significantly at the New Members Coalition Group which included Liberals) Chamberlain declared that he could 'foresee no end to the necessity of Coalition'. Although aware of objections, he urged that these must be 'put behind us and wills and minds bent to cooperation for bringing the country through its time of peril'. In*

---

[5] A. Chamberlain to Ida, 3 and 23 April 1921, AC5/1/196, 198.

[6] See, for example, A. Chamberlain to Hilda, 16 April 1920, 6 February 1921. Also to Ida 21 December 1919, 23 April 1921 AC5/1/146, 159, 191, 198. See also A. Chamberlain to Lloyd George, 16 July and 2 August 1920, Lloyd George MSS F/7/3/15, 16; to Law, 6 January 1921, Law MSS 100/1/8. Lloyd George was less flattering about Chamberlain as Chancellor, Hankey Diary, January 1921, Roskill, *Man of Secrets*, II, 215–6.

[7] Philip Kerr comment in Hankey Diary, 16 March 1921, Roskill, *Man of Secrets*, II, 224.

[8] A. Chamberlain to Hilda, 20 March 1921, AC5/1/194.

[9] Frances Stevenson Diary, 12 May 1921, *Lloyd George: A Diary*, 216.

[10] Frances Stevenson Diary, 11 June 1921, *Ibid*, 221. Also Lloyd George to Law, 7 June 1921, Blake, *The Unknown Prime Minister*, 428; Beaverbrook to Law, 13 May 1921, Lord Beaverbrook, *The Decline and Fall of Lloyd George*, 262.

[11] A. Chamberlain to Hilda, 20 March 1921, AC5/1/194.

[12] Chamberlain at the Carlton Club, 21 March 1921, *Gleanings and Memoranda*, LIII, (April 1921), 301.

such circumstances he concluded, 'When the conscience of men is stirred and tremendous events have brought them to considering anew the basis of their political belief, are the ties of party to be so rigid and omnipotent that we cannot look beyond them to the national interest, by the service of which alone can party be justified.' Nonetheless, although he warned that 'the man who thinks he can take up his life again in 1921 where he left it on August 4 1914 is a man who might as well be dead and buried', he denied that he was anxious to hasten that process of evolution by establishing a new party from the Coalition because 'parties grow rather than are made'. As he told Churchill, 'We must glide rather than burst into new conditions'.[13]

During the early months of his leadership, political circumstances appeared to be scarcely conducive to a closer relationship between the parties in the Coalition. Within his own party he acknowledged 'a growing feeling that "Coalition" is hateful [and] that "Fusion" is impracticable'.[14] Such worries were aggravated by fundamental divisions over policy. Action to safeguard industries from 'dumping' inevitably aroused partisan passions – particularly as the Coalition Liberals had forced the government to drop such legislation in both 1919 and 1920 because its provisions relating to 'key industries' and 'collapsed exchanges' were anathema to their free trade sensibilities. Although the Safeguarding of Industries Act finally reached the statute book in 1921 the issue continued to create tensions. Thus, in February 1922 Wedgwood Benn's motion of protest prompted a major Coalition Liberal revolt and in June another crisis arose over the protection of fabric gloves and glove fabric.[15] Similarly, Chamberlain's efforts in February 1922 to persuade his supporters that it would be 'madness' to go on with the old tariff reform programme prompted a minor revolt against the leadership in the form of a resolution declaring that protection remained 'in the forefront of Conservative policy'.[16]

During the summer of 1921 Coalition unity was also shaken by the resignation of Addison, its most active and radical reformer. Addison had increasingly become a target of right-wing criticism from the press, the Anti-Waste League and the Unionists. Having effectively hounded him out of the Ministry of Health in April 1921, by early June a large number of Unionist backbenchers tabled what amounted to a confidence motion, critical of Addison's £5000 salary as a Minister without Portfolio: a motion which both Chamberlain and McCurdy, the Liberal Chief Whip, believed would be carried easily.[17] Although Lloyd George gave every appearance of being prepared to abandon Addison as a scapegoat,[18] Addison turned on his critics

---

[13] 'The Future of the Coalition', *Daily Telegraph*, 6 May 1921. A. Chamberlain to Churchill, 8 April 1921, M. Gilbert, *Winston S. Churchill*, IV. Companion 3, 1431.

[14] A. Chamberlain to Ida, 24 July 1921, AC5/1/204.

[15] A. Murray to Lord Reading, 2 August 1922, Murray MSS 8808/149–152 (National Library of Scotland). Also *Gleanings and Memoranda*, LVI (1922), 145–7, 152–3, 254–5, 257–264.

[16] A. Murray to Lord Reading, 25 February 1922, Reading MSS 118/98 (India Office Library). Also L.S. Amery, *My Political Life*, II, 226–7.

[17] A. Chamberlain to Lloyd George, 9 June 1921, Lloyd George MSS F/7/4/5.

[18] Lloyd George to A. Chamberlain, 9 June 1921, Lloyd George MSS F/7/4/6.

and mobilized support. In the event, Lloyd George's belief that whether successful or not, 'he was creating the impression of failure',[19] combined with the determined antipathy of Chamberlain and his followers, ensured that both Addison and his housing policy were doomed. On 14 July he angrily resigned from the government altogether. In addition, the government suffered anxious moments over the threat of a major coal strike in the spring; over the Imperial Conference in June-July where the Imperial solidarity of Billy Hughes, the Australian premier, briefly triumphed over the forces of disintegration led by Smuts; over the Washington Conference and the rising tide of unemployment as the economy crashed into the depths of slump. Overshadowing all of these other issues, however, was the problem of Ireland.

In the 1918 election 24 of the 32 counties of Ireland returned nothing but republican members. Refusing to take their seats in London, these members then commenced to establish their own Dáil Eireann in Dublin. At its first meeting on 21 January 1919 independence was declared and the Irish republic was ratified. In the belief that a political solution was impracticable when confronting irreconcilable republicans, the Coalition responded initially by meeting rising terrorist violence with an equally vigorous policy of draconian suppression. Thus, although a Home Rule Bill was passed in December 1920 (providing for separate legislatures for north and south with a single Federal Council for All-Ireland as a link between them) the British government increasingly resorted to 'a policy of drift and unthinking retaliation'.[20] In May 1919 Sinn Fein was proscribed and Dáil Eireann declared illegal. With the appointment of Sir Nevil Macready as commander of British forces in March 1920 and the recruitment of the notorious Black and Tans, the British fought a bitter and brutal guerrilla war of reprisal and counter-reprisal with the IRA throughout south and west Ireland: a policy reinforced by the appointment of Hamar Greenwood as Chief Secretary for Ireland in the following month. His Restoration of Order in Ireland Act imposed something close to martial law with imprisonment without trial and trial by court-martial before full martial law was proclaimed for all Ireland on 11 December 1920. By October 1920 Lloyd George was able to declare 'We have murder by the throat';[21] a hard-line policy of coercion and retaliation sustained well into the spring of the following year.

As Churchill later recalled, by the spring of 1921 there were two options open to the Coalition: 'war with the utmost violence or peace with the utmost patience'.[22] In mid-May 1921 the policy of repression still held sway as the government continued to urge the need to 'hunt down the murder gang'. In June the goal had become 'a lasting reconciliation with the Irish people'. On 22 June the King's Speech opening the Parliament in Belfast was liberal and conciliatory in its appeal 'to all Irishmen to pause, to stretch out the hand of forbearance and conciliation, to forgive and forget, and to join in making for the land they love a new era of peace, contentment

---

[19] Lloyd George to C.A. McCurdy, 14 June 1921, Lloyd George MSS F/34/4/12.

[20] K.O. Morgan, *Consensus and Disunity*, 127.

[21] Lloyd George used the phrase to his Caernarvon constituency in October and at the Guildhall Banquet in November 1920. K.O. Morgan, *Consensus and Disunity*, 130.

[22] W.S. Churchill, *The World Crisis: The Aftermath*, (New York 1929), 304.

and good will'.[23] *Two days later de Valera, as 'the chosen leader of the great majority in Southern Ireland', and the Ulster Prime Minister, Sir James Craig, were invited for negotiations. As Churchill noted, 'No British Government in modern times has ever appeared to make so sudden and complete reversal of policy'.*[24] *A truce came into effect on 11 July and in August a dialogue began with de Valera as a prelude to protracted negotiations with the Sinn Fein leadership that continued from early October until the signing of the Anglo-Irish Treaty on 6 December 1921.*

A variety of explanations have been offered for this dramatic reversal of British policy. The effect of repression upon overseas opinion was undoubtedly harmful to British foreign policy – particularly in its dealings with the USA over naval disarmament and policy in the Pacific.[25] *Secondly, contrary to the extraordinarily sanguine assessments from the Irish Chief Secretary, the Republican guerrilla campaign proved 'too determined, too resilient and too resourceful to be put down by the military force which was employed against it'.*[26] *A third explanation focuses upon 'the revolt of the British conscience' against the methods rather than the aims employed*[27] *and the fact that the strategy of counter-violence was 'wholly at variance with the mood of conciliation and unity that [the Coalition] sought to convey in its other domestic and external policies'.*[28] *Perhaps the existence of an already tried and tested model of Dominion status welcome to British public opinion and sufficiently flexible to avoid immediate rejection by the Sinn Fein leadership also beckoned the Cabinet towards the course of negotiation.*[29] *Others, however, have ascribed particular significance to the changes in the Unionist leadership which occurred during the early months of 1921: changes which involved Carson's resignation from the leadership of the Ulster Unionist Council on 4 February and, more important, Austen Chamberlain's emergence as Conservative leader.*[30]

Chamberlain's role in the Irish Treaty was important but curiously indirect. Certainly he did not directly play a major role in the negotiations themselves. Although he attended five of the seven plenary sessions of the conference, after its seventh meeting the work of negotiation was conducted by sub-conferences of which he attended only nine of twenty-four.[31] *Nor did he contribute much through personal leadership in the Cabinet. Indeed, when standing in for Lloyd George during the early stages in August 1921 he appeared to be completely out of his political depth and his 'own nervous manner conveyed a feeling of mild panic to his colleagues'.*[32]

[23] D. Macardle, *The Irish Republic* (1968), 427.

[24] W.S. Churchill, *The Aftermath*, 304.

[25] K.O. Morgan, *Consensus and Disunity*, 131.

[26] C. Townshend, *The British Campaign in Ireland, 1919–21*, (Oxford 1975), 202.

[27] D.G. Boyce, *Englishmen and the Irish Troubles, 1918–22*, (Cambridge, Mass 1972), 180.

[28] K.O. Morgan, *Consensus and Disunity*, 131.

[29] N. Mansergh, *The Commonwealth Experience, vol I The Durham Report to the Anglo-Irish Treaty*, (1982), 231–243. Also K. Middlemas (ed) *Whitehall Diary, III Ireland 1918–25*, 71.

[30] J.D. Fair, *British Interparty Conferences*, Chapter XII.

[31] Petrie, *Life and Letters*, II, 162.

[32] T. Jones to Lloyd George, 11 August 1921, Lloyd George MSS F/25/2/2 and *Whitehall Diary*, III, 96–7. For earlier evidence of Chamberlain's infectious 'panic' see Jones Diary, 5 April 1921, *Whitehall Diary*, I, 137.

Chamberlain's major contribution, however, was indirect and lay in his personal flexibility on the question. Any leader of the Unionists was crucial to the ability to conduct and conclude such negotiations. Lloyd George had been extremely sensitive of the need for Conservative support in pursuing a policy of repression.[33] *When the Cabinet reversed this policy, such support became even more crucial. Although Joseph Chamberlain had parted from Gladstone over Home Rule in 1886, his elder son was not doctrinaire on the question. Moreover, in stark contrast to Law, he was without strong ties with Ulster.*[34] *Thus, as Fair argues, more than any other Unionist figure, Chamberlain 'led his party from the untenable position it had reached before the war. His party's support of the Coalition Government's policy of conciliation in Ireland was absolutely essential to any hope of a settlement'.*[35]

In practice, Chamberlain's attitude towards Ireland was both complex and ambivalent by the time he assumed the leadership. On one hand, he was clearly not so much of a Unionist as to preclude the possibility of thinking the unthinkable. Indeed, during 1920 he had unsuccessfully urged the opening of negotiations with Sinn Fein.[36] *In the privacy of family correspondence he had also speculated pessimistically about whether 'modern democracy [could] handle such problems successfully' and presciently suggested that the only solution to a seemingly intractable problem may lie in the radical option of Dominion status for Ireland.*[37] *On the other hand, however, Chamberlain had consistently endorsed the policy of 'thorough' and shared the general belief that it was possible to get 'murder by the throat' and defeat it through a harsh policy of authorized reprisals.*[38] *As late as mid-May 1921 he thus stood with Balfour, Horne, Worthington-Evans and the Prime Minister against the pleas of Liberal ministers for a military truce in the approach to the All-Ireland elections.*[39] *Moreover, after Smuts lunched with an 'anxiously preoccupied' King on 13 June and proposed that there should be a reference to Dominion status in his speech opening the Northern Ireland Parliament, Chamberlain had been resolutely opposed. Indeed, neither Balfour nor Chamberlain liked 'what they called the "gush" of Smut's draft' in which they detected the 'innuendo of oppression' and Lloyd George declined to endorse the proposal.*[40] *The King's speech had, however, been*

---

[33] See Beaverbrook to Law, 13 May 1921, *The Decline and Fall of Lloyd George*, 262–3.

[34] Law much later told Chamberlain that 'before the War had stirred deeper emotions . . . he cared intensely for only two things: Tariff Reform and Ulster; all the rest was only part of the game', *Down the Years*, 224. See also R. Blake, *The Unknown Prime Minister*, 125–6.

[35] J.D. Fair, *British Interparty Conferences*, 246.

[36] M. Gilbert, *Winston S. Churchill*, IV, 453.

[37] A. Chamberlain to Hilda, 24 July 1920, AC5/1/170. See also to Ida, 9 March 1918, AC5/1/64.

[38] See, for example, A. Chamberlain to Hilda, 4 May 1918, 24 July, 31 October and 12 December 1920 AC5/1/81, 170,177, 183.

[39] Jones Diary, 12 May 1921, *Whitehall Diary*, I, 157–8.

[40] *Whitehall Diary*, III, 76. For an account of Smuts meeting see Nicolson, *King George V* (1952), 349–51. W. Hancock, *Smuts, II, The Fields of Force 1919–50*, (Cambridge 1968), 57–9.

drafted by Sir Edward Grigg at Lloyd George's request in deliberately conciliatory terms[41] and on the terrace behind their adjoining Downing Street residences on the day after the King's speech in Belfast, Chamberlain urged Lloyd George to make one last effort for peace before returning to repression.[42] On the following day the invitation to de Valera was issued. Thus, although 'at first he had been hard to convince, saying that all his tradition was against it', by mid-July Chamberlain appeared to be convinced there was no alternative and prepared 'to go far' to reach an agreement.[43] Thereafter, despite an unflagging contempt for de Valera, the Irish negotiators, their tactics and prevarications, Chamberlain held fast to this determination to support the Prime Minister in the search for a negotiated settlement. Moreover, he did so fully conscious of the threat this posed to the unity of both the Coalition and his own party at a time when Diehard opposition was mobilizing: a threat rendered the more menacing after Law returned to England with his health apparently restored and imbued with a brand of 'Orange fanaticism' that made him a likely leader of a Tory revolt over Ulster.[44] Indeed, even these difficulties with his own party contributed indirectly to the eventual outcome, as Lloyd George exploited the constant spectre of Diehard revolt and an intractable Law ministry in order to maintain his hold over the Irish delegates. Thus, to assist Chamberlain in handling a potentially hostile party conference in Liverpool – the very 'stronghold of Orange Toryism' at which he expected to be 'fighting for his political life',[45] – the Irish were persuaded to continue to support the boundary commission proposal: a manoeuvre which appears to be a classic example of Welsh Wizardry borne out of 'a genuine concern on both sides over an Ulsterite revolt at Liverpool'.[46]

A more positive factor in shaping Chamberlain's role in these negotiations was his growing mistrust of Law. He knew that 'Bonar [was] seeing red on the subject of Ulster' and rightly suspected that this was a means of attempting to regain the leadership and break the Coalition.[47] The effect was to rekindle all the old animosities and resentments against his former leader that had grown within him since 1911. In the event, the annual meeting of the National Union in Liverpool on 17–18 November was carried off successfully and the Diehards were able to obtain less than 70 votes from the 1800 delegates at the meeting. Later that night, roused with 'the fire I usually lack', Chamberlain went on to make one of the finest speeches of his career.[48]

Now and again in the affairs of men there comes a moment when courage is

[41] K.O. Morgan, *Consensus and Disunity*, 131, 263.

[42] *Whitehall Diary*, III, 76.

[43] C.P. Scott Diary, 28 July 1921, T. Wilson (ed) *The Political Diaries of C.P. Scott*, 396.

[44] C.P. Scott Diary, 28 October 1921, *Ibid*, 403.

[45] A. Chamberlain to Hilda, 13 November 1921, AC5/1/220.

[46] J.D. Fair, *British Interparty Conferences*, 255.

[47] A. Chamberlain to Ivy, 8 and 9 November 1921, AC 6/1/456–7. See also Law to J.P. Croal, 12 November 1921, Law MSS 107/1/83, saying he was trying to get the party to follow him.

[48] Petrie, *Life and Letters*, II, 167–8.

safer than prudence, when some great act of faith, touching the heart and stirring the emotions of men, achieves the miracle that no arts of statesmanship can compass. Such a moment may be passing before our eyes now as we meet here. I pray to God with all my heart and soul that to each of us to whom responsibility is brought there may be given vision to see, faith to act, and courage to persevere.

As he told his wife afterwards, 'Today for them and for all there I am the leader, instead of merely bearing the title'.[49] Two weeks later, after anxious negotiations and much Welsh wizardry, at 2.10 am on 6 December 1921 the delegates signed the Anglo-Irish Treaty.

AC5/1/194   20 March 1921
                                                                        9 Egerton Place

My dear Hilda,

How strange is fate. Ten years ago I thought I should be chosen leader of the Party & resigned my chances not without regret to a man only a year or two older than myself & very much my junior in the House of Commons. It never occurred to me then or since that the chance would come to me again, & though Bonar Law has often complained of being very tired I thought his at least as good a 'life' whether political or otherwise as my own. And now he falls out so suddenly & unexpectedly that it leaves us all sad & breathless & the wheel of fortune turning full circle brings to me again what ten years ago I should have liked & what I now accept as an obvious duty but without pleasure or any great expectations except of trouble & hard labour. For we are no longer an independent Party with a clearly defined & perfectly definite policy but part of a coalition bound necessarily to much compromise & as such coalitions must be, largely opportunist. And we are on the eve of far the most difficult piece of legislation that we have yet attempted the Anti-dumping Bill. It is both intrinsically very difficult & it is the subject that divides the Coalition most, whilst things have begun to go ill with us in the country & members have been growing increasingly restive in the House. I am inclined to cry Oh cursed spite! but it is useless to lament & I must first make up mind to face our troubles bravely & do the best I can. But as one after another of one's old colleagues drops out of the ranks I feel sad & lonely & do not experience as of old the joy & fire of battle. But if the Opposition grows stronger & more effective perhaps

[49] A. Chamberlain to Ivy, 19 November 1921, AC 6/1/466.

more of the old fighting spirit will come back to me & others. Anyway this time I am in for it & there it is!

There has as far as I can gather been no serious thought of any other name. A few talked of Horne, but I do not think that the issue was ever in any doubt, tho' some inexperienced people have joshed[?] themselves about electing a "leader of the Party" and pulled in the names of the Lord Chancellor[50] & Derby. Of course no leader of the Party is ever elected – only a leader for one or other House. The leader of the Party is made by events, by his forming a Government or by survival or by supremely outstanding merit.

The P.M. wishes me to step fully into Bonar's shoes. I shall give up the Chancellorship at once, go to live in Downing Street & lead the House. I wonder how many members there are now who have known it longer than I – not many & yet I have been so busy that I have still to learn this House. I wonder whether I can cultivate pleasant colloquial habits. To be hail fellow well met with all my 'followers'. I must try but I haven't shown much ability that way so far!

AC5/1/195

25 March 1921
Twitt's Ghyll

Well, my dear Ida, I am beginning to like it, & I hope that you will consider that a healthy sign. We go necessarily to live in Downing Street & that does not conduce to economy which is a bore, but I am beginning to feel a decent honest pride in being leader of my Party & above all Leader of the House. No one who is so old & so devoted a parliamentarian as I am can treat that as anything but one of the highest honours that could come to him. The Party meeting was very cordial & gave me a great reception. My Liberal colleagues have been as warm in their greetings & even my political opponents have showered congratulations & good wishes upon me. More wonderful than all I have a good Press – Scotsman, Glasgow Herald, Yorkshire Post & Manchester Guardian – the four great independent provincial papers to which I looked – were all most appreciative & have made me almost forget my soreness at the way the newspapers have treated me since I attacked Northcliffe. Well, it is a good send off. It confirms what indeed I knew that the gibes & sneers of the last few years are not the real

[50] Frederick Edwin Smith (1872–1930) Conservative MP for Liverpool Walton 1906–18 and Liverpool West Derby 1918–19. Solicitor-General 1915; Attorney-General 1915–1919; Lord Chancellor 1919–1922; Secretary for India 1924–28. Knighted 1915, created Baronet 1918, Baron Birkenhead 1919, Viscount 1921 and Earl of Birkenhead 1922.

judgement of my countrymen upon me, & it encourages me for the work & troubles that lie immediately ahead.

. . .

It is curious to think of Ivy in Downing Street. What a difference from last time! She is already busy with the Board of Works. I believe that, when all is said & done, what gives me most pleasure is the thought of the pleasure that it would have given to Father & Beatrice.

By the way will it amuse you as much it did me to hear that when told that the Party would certainly choose me the P.M. threw up in his hands & cried He's an awful Tory, & that the party appears to share the view that I am more of a Conservative than Bonar. And the odd thing is that it is true, for I have a tradition & he had none. He always seemed to me curiously without the historic sense. I don't think that I ever heard him use an historic illustration or appeal to history or tradition or custom. The fact that he had had no experience of government did not trouble him when he took the leadership. What he was afraid of then was his want of faith. He was confident that he could lead without experience but afraid that the party might follow unwillingly because he had not blue blood in his veins. It's an odd world. How Lady Londonderry would have thrown herself on my neck if she had been still living! I always used to say that the number of fingers she gave me − varying from 10 to 2 − was a sure sign of the state of my fortunes.

I expect a very stormy time, for we have to take the Anti-dumping Bill directly after Easter. It is a fearful Bill made more fearful by the rules of procedure governing Money Bills, & is the most disruptive measure in the government's programme. The Wee Frees hope to detach Georgian liberals over it & some of our own men will be troublesome, whilst we shall disappoint a good many of our supporters in the country by not going far enough. The fact is that Protection is simple, Preference a little more complicated & Anti-dumping, Retaliation, countervailing [?] Exchange by duties are all as difficult & as little satisfactory as possible.

Wish me well!

AC5/1/196

3 April 1921
Twitt's Ghyll

My dear Ida,

. . .

The result of my two days with the P.M. in London is seen in the list of new appointments. Lord E. Talbot's nomination to the Viceroyalty [of Ireland] is very interesting & may be of great importance. I am very unhappy about the situation there, for I do not think that we are now making progress, & the suspicion, distrust & dislike are so strong on both sides that I do not know how to take a new step. Hilton Young's[51] & Edward Wood's[52] appointments are both good. H.Y. stood against me in 1906[53], I think, & was then rather a prig; but the War in which he lost an arm & was most gallant was as he has said the making of him. He is attractive, very able & has made several short but very effective speeches on fin[ancia]l questions. For the rest there was no room for new blood to my great regret, for we had four men to cases from expiring ministries.

You will be feeling much as we do about the miners. I suppose they are in that restless & rather spoiled mood in which nothing would really stop these continuous strikes & threats of strikes except fighting to a finish: but it is a disaster for the country.

Ivy & I opened a pint of champagne – great luxury – on Thursday night to celebrate the outcome of the Budget – a surplus only 3 million short of my original estimate. It is a very remarkable result considering the summer coal strike, the trade slump & other adverse factors as well as the immense figures with which we were dealing & it is a great satisfaction to me to lay down my office with my policy realised up to date.

AC5/1/198

23 April 1921
Twitt's Ghyll

My dear Ida,

...

I think that is was about midnight on Monday that I was told that I must make the Budget speech & on Tuesday evening I set myself to find out what the Budget was. Wednesday evening was devoted to the

---

[51] Edward Hilton Young (1879–1960) Liberal MP for Norwich 1915–23, 1924–1926 thereafter continued as a Conservative until 1929. Conservative MP for Sevenoaks 1929–1935. Financial Secretary to Treasury 1921–22; Chief National Liberal Whip 1922–23; Secretary Overseas Trade Dept 1931; Minister of Health 1931–35. Created Baron Kennet 1935.

[52] Edward Frederick Lindley Wood (1881–1959) Conservative MP for West Riding (Ripon) 1910–25. PUS for Colonies 1921–October 1922; President of the Board of Education 1922–1924 and 1932–1935; Minister of Agriculture 1924–1925; Viceroy of India 1926–31; Secretary for War 1935; Lord Privy Seal 1935–1937; Lord President 1937–1938; Foreign Secretary 1938–1940; Ambassador to Washington 1941–1946. Created Baron Irwin 1925; succeeded father as 3rd Viscount Halifax 1934 and created Earl of Halifax 1944.

[53] Hilton Young unsuccessfully contested East Worcestershire against Chamberlain in January 1910.

same task. On Thursday at 10.30 I sought an interview with the C.E. to tell him that it would not do, & found that he was of the same opinion. We altered it & at 11.30 that morning I explained the altered plan to the Cabinet. The Cabinet desired considerable alteration – in form rather than substance. I got $\frac{3}{4}$ hour for a lunch, attended at the Chancellor's reception of a deputation to discuss the provisions necessary on the winding up of the Excess Profits Duty, went straight from that to another Cabinet on another question, then took the Chancellor & two Treasury officials home to dinner for further discussions of the Budget & got to bed for the third night running at 1 a.m. with the Budget still unhatched, at most layed.

I could do nothing more till the Treasury people had recast the brief, so I motored down here yesterday at 9 o'clock & idled gently through the day, feeling very tired & not a little uncomfortable about my job.

Today I had my private secretary & a Treasury man down & got the thing into shape ...

Altogether a disagreeable week & a poor week-end for me. But think of the unhappy Horne with his budget *and* the coal negotiations & the P.M. with the coal negotiations & Briand – & then decide which post you would wish to occupy. I can't tell you how great is the relief to me of being freed from the responsibilities of C/E. For two years I have rarely come into Cabinet or Committee where 4/5ths of the agenda did not raise the question of Ways & Means, & it has been my disagreeable duty continuously to oppose the pet plans of my colleagues & to bring home to the Cabinet what the financial position of the country is. Now it is Horne's business, thank goodness, tho' that I can give him better backing than B.L. gave me. The P.M. was far & away my best friend, tho' when he did want to spend, he spent royally.

AC5/1/199   8 May 1921
             17 Dean's Yard,
             Westminster SW1

My dear Hilda,

  ...

... I have had a busy week of nothings such as must henceforth occupy much of my time; & I have made a second speech on our policy in my capacity as leader which has been well received by both wings of the coalition.[54] On the whole I am pleased with myself, for I

---

[54] Speech to New Members Coalition Group, 5 May 1921. Next day the *Daily Telegraph* commented that it 'was like all his speeches – the clean-cut, straightforward utterance of an honest, sagacious and fearless mind'.

think that I have 'bucked' our people & shown them how to put what Winston & Lloyd George have tried to say & in my opinion said very badly & very indiscreetly. Incidentally I have please [sic] Lloyd George: he is giving me his confidence which is essential to successful coop-eration & I think that he recognises that I am a force & that if he runs straight with me he will have no reason to complain of my action. Did you notice The Daily Telegraph article of May 6th on my speech? Now that I am leader, I think that I may expect more support in that quarter which has hitherto been worse than cold to me.

. . .

We hope to go to Twitt's Ghyll next Saturday for a week or so, but one cannot make plans with any assurance in these days. The coal dispute shows no sign of ending & people like the Times begin to fuss & say do something – when the only true policy is to sit tight & do nothing. Men who suffer from the fidgets should not meddle with politics.

Derby wishes to proclaim me Leader of the Party & warns me of intrigues fomented by Winston & F.E. I tell him that the Leader of a Party grows & is not elected & that all will be well in time, & when F.E. says to me genially that 'of course you don't think that I had anything to do with that silly business' I reply with equal geniality 'Why, of course not. Whatever I might think, I've never thought you a fool!' & we smile lovingly at one another & I feel that I have put things on their proper footing. Winston has come back from Egypt as cross as a bear with a sore head & thinks that all the world is out of joint since he is not C/E & the limelight is for the moment turned on to other players. He has so many good & even charming qualities & so much ability that it is tragic that he should not have a little more stability & judgement & a little less consciousness of self.

AC5/1/201   [?19 June 1921]
                                              11 Downing Street,

My dear Ida,

. . .

Westminster was bad – anti-Jew largely & still more anti-waste & anti-increased postal charges! We have a very difficult time in front of us & may be brought down by impatience of high expenditure & of all & each of the measures necessary to reduce it.

I am going to move a Guillotine resolution on the Protection of Industries Bill tomorrow & expect a devil of a row; but the opposition know it is necessary & would do the same in our place.

AC5/1/202   26 June 1921
                                                    11 Downing Street

My dear Hilda,

What a blessed thing is a quiet Sunday morning! I had my breakfast at 9.0; lay in bed till 11.0 reading Gosses canseries on "Books on the Table", then consumed one of Sir George Lloyd's delicious mangos in my bath (the proper place to eat it) &, coming down-stairs, cleared my table of work. Now I have a quiet afternoon before me till Ivy takes me out this evening to see Ben Jonson's St Bartlemy (if that is how he names it) at the Phoenix, & I shall devote my leisure to you & Madame Duclaux's 'Victor Hugo'.

Where shall I begin? I am wondering whether Dr. Addison has now decided to resign, whether the coal strike will be called off on Monday, whether de Valera[55] will accept our invitation, whether any truth &, if so, what truth lurked behind the Express (Beaverbrook) statement that the Lord Chancellor & Winston were thinking of revolt but that Winston backed out on finding that he had no backing – a report publicly & privately denied by Birkenhead but passed in silence by Winston who is sulky ever since Horne was made Chancellor – what will be the outcome of the extraordinarily important Imperial conferences now being held & of the divergence of view & attitude on the part of Australia & New Zealand on the one hand & Canada & S. Africa on the other with Great Britain as always the moderator & to some extent the arbiter. I am wondering whether we can make a real & effective friendship with the U.S.A. & cooperate fully & cordially with her without offending Japan & setting her free to go her own selfish & militarist way without check or control; whether the Dominions will tolerate our continuous & active share in European affairs & what Europe would be & do without us; whether France will be wise enough to conciliate their good will or so restless & provocative as wholly to alienate them; whether — — but there is already matter enough for thought, is there not? & you see the stuff of which government dreams are made.

The miners are a mystery. Hodges[56] & Herbert Smith[57] thought that

---

[55] Eamon de Valera (1882–1975). Sinn Fein MP for Clare East, 1917–21; member of Dáil for Co. Clare 1921–59; President of Dáil 1919–22; President Sinn Fein 1917–26; President Fianna Fail 1926–59; Minister for External Affairs, 1932–48; Taoiseoch 1937–48, 1951–54, 1957–59; President of the Republic 1959–73.

[56] Frank Hodges (1887–1947) General Secretary, MFGB 1918–1924; Member Royal Commission on Coal Mines 1919; Labour MP for Lichfield 1923–1924. Civil Lord of Admiralty January-November 1924. Secretary International Miners' Federation 1925–1927; member Central Electricity Board 1927–47.

[57] Herbert Smith (1862–1938) President Yorkshire Miners' Association 1906–38; President MFGB 1922–29; President International Miners' Federation 1921–29.

they would vote to accept the last terms offered without any guidance from the leaders & agreed to give none. Now they say that they could have had another 100,000 votes for the asking but that they were kicked by the extremists. In short the struggle has gone on for weeks & months because there was no leader of force & ability.

Will it be the same in Ireland? Possibly, for de Valera is a child without any experience of the world, without courage & without judgement. *But* at any rate I thought that the King's speech ought to be followed up by a last attempt at peace before we go the full lengths of martial law & when I put that idea to the P.M. he agreed & his letter, published today, is the result.

By the way I hear that the K[ing] now says 'Was it not a good idea of mine to visit Ireland & didn't I make a good speech?' Be it so, or at least let it appear so. But you know something of the hectic time I had 10 days ago. And all Society & the Clubs & the entourage said how wrong we were to take such risks & the Asquith's said we were making the K. a partisan until the poor K. himself began to think that we must be wrong & that we never ought to have advised him to go.

The Imperial Conference is far the most interesting that I have attended & in its issues by far the most important (N.B. The Times Washington despatches are directly inspired by Harding[58]) but it is too soon to say what will come out of it.

I live in a whirl e.g. Tuesday after doing letters &c. at 11.0 Conference 2 lunch 2.45 – 4 Questions 4.0 Speech to the National Union 4.30 Conference till 6.20, then Cabinet till 8.0 House till 5 a.m. Wednesday was a repetition of Tuesday without the speech & with the House rising at midnight. Yesterday morning in my first leisure I had a tooth out & was x rayed to find out what is the cause of the pain in my leg – & everyone says that I look years younger since I became leader.

My garden, oh my garden. What is happening to my poor plants. Alas! I shall not see them for yet another fortnight.

AC5/1/2033

July 1921
11 Downing Street

My dear Ida,

...

Things are going better. Coal is settled. Silesia is being evacuated by Polish & German irregular forces. Germany is keeping her promises.

---

[58] Warren Gamaliel Harding (1865–1923) American journalist and politician. Republican Senator Ohio 1915–21; 29th President of the USA November 1920. Died in office August 1923.

The French Parlty session will presently end. Ireland – well, Ireland hangs in the balance. I *think* that de V. & Co. will come, but it is difficult to know what he is at. Probably he does not know himself. He has no gifts of leadership & no experience of politics. I think too that the danger in the Imperial Conference is past, but it is difficult & not made easier by Hughes nagging at Meighen[59] who is himself sufficiently difficult in the quiet way of a shy & obstinate man. But how does the country get governed at all, when we have so much to do & no time for thought?

AC5/1/204   24 July 1921
                                                   11 Downing Street

My dear Ida,

    Shall I ever feel rested? It is now 4 p.m. & I have spent 24 out of the last 40 hours asleep & more than 30 of them in bed; yet I feel tired, unfit to read a serious book or talk on a serious subject, & it is with difficulty that I have roused myself sufficiently to write to you. I have treated you scurvily this last three weeks & my conscience reproaches me; yet the flesh is weak & the spirit unwilling, & I doubt whether this letter will be worth having when it is finished. It is the more provoking because I certainly have a very hard month in front of me & because I ought to be feeling much better, for Goadby has cured the sciatica (which was not sciatica but arthritis or neuritis in the hip joint) which had pained me for six months or more & failed, not unnaturally, to yield to my usual sciatica treatment. And what do you suppose was the cure that he applied? Why, the extraction of a tooth which was nothing but a poison factory – though why it should have discharged its poison into the hip joint I am not wise enough to tell. So I have had my jaws x rayed & now two [or] three more are condemned & must out when I can find the time to be fitted with a plate. Apparently they drop down or grow up because there are not corresponding teeth in the opposite jaw; thus they leave a cavity at the roots & – well,

    Satan finds some mischief still
    For empty holes to do!
But enough of dentistry. Let us talk politics.
    Is there going to be peace with Ireland? I don't know & neither does anyone else. We have gone to the utmost limits of concession both in substance & in form. "They cannot reject this" said Smuts "unless they

[59] Arthur Meighen (1874–1960) Canadian teacher, barrister, businessman. MP Liberal-Conservative 1908–32. Solicitor-General 1913; Secretary of State 1915–17; Minister of Interior 1917–20; PM 1920–21, 1926. Senator 1932–41. Represented Canada at Imperial Conference, 1921.

are smitten with madness". Yet de Valera has rejected it! Is that his last word? No. But will his next word be any better? Nobody can say. When the P.M. refused to admit further discussion except on the basis that the principles of our offer were accepted, he said that he could not ever 'transmit' such an offer. Then said the P.M. "The only question that I can discuss with you is upon what day the truce shall end" & de V. went livid, said that he would return to Ireland, discuss the matter with his friends, see Craig[60] & give his answer in writing. I hope that it may still be peace, for a renewal of strife will be a hideously ugly business – murder on the one side & drum-head courts martial on the other – but I am anxious – anxious lest being engaged in negotiation, the P.M. should give away more (& I cannot see what more there is to give away) & anxious lest the Irish leaders should once more prove themselves bereft of all sense & statesmanship. What can you expect of a dreamer like de Valera, a poet like Griffiths[61], a small solicitor like B[62] & a crooked-faced solicitor's clerk & gunman like Austin Stack?[63]

But all this is very secret. Even the Cabinet knows hardly as much.

Then too the Pacific Conference is in jeopardy because Harding & Hughes[64] & all their entourage are so utterly without experience how

[60] James Craig (1871–1940) Unionist MP for East Down 1906–18 and mid-Down 1918 until resigned June 1921. Treasurer of the Household 1916–1918; Parliamentary Secretary to Ministry of Pensions 1919–1920; Parliamentary and Financial Secretary to Admiralty 1920–1921. Created Baronet 1918 and Viscount Craigavon 1927. Sat in Parliament of Northern Ireland for Co. Down 1921–29 and North Down 1929–40. Prime Minister of Northern Ireland June 1921 until death in November 1940.

[61] Arthur Griffith (1872–1922) Journalist and a leader of Sinn Fein. Interned three times up to 1920. Sinn Fein MP for Cavan East June-December 1918. In 1918 returned for both E. Cavan and N.W. Tyrone but did not take his seat for either. Member of Northern Ireland Parliament for Fermanagh and Tyrone 1921–22. Member of Dáil for E. Cavan to 1921 and Cavan 1921–22 as a pro-Treaty member. Secretary for Foreign Affairs 1921–22. President of Dáil Eireann January-August 1922.

[62] Robert Childers Barton (1881–1975) Educated Rugby and Christ Church Oxford. Escaped Mountjoy Gaol March 1919 and re-arrested February 1920. Sentenced to 3 years under Defence of Realm Act. Sinn Fein MP for W. Wicklow December 1918 but did not take seat. Member of Dáil for W. Wicklow to 1921, for Kildare & Wicklow 1921–23 as an Anti-Treaty Member. Minister for Economic Affairs 1921–22. Signatory of 1921 Treaty but later opposed it.

[63] Austin Stack (1880–1829) Imprisoned Belfast Gaol for his part in Sinn Fein movement 1918 and escaped Strangeways October 1919. Sinn Fein MP for W. Kerry in December 1918 but did not take seat. Member of Dáil for W Kerry to 1921, Kerry & W. Limerick 1921–23 and Kerry 1923–27. An Anti-Treaty Member remaining a member of Sinn Fein after formation of Fianna Fail. Minister of Home Affairs 1921–22.

[64] Charles Evans Hughes (1862–1948) Attorney and professor of Law. Governor of New York 1907–8, 1909–10. Associate Justice, US Supreme Court 1910–16. Republican Presidential candidate 1916; Secretary of State 1921–25; Chairman, Washington Arms Limitation Conference 1921; Member, Permanent Court of Arbitration at The Hague 1926–30; Judge, Permanent Court of International Justice 1928–30; US Chief Justice 1930–41.

to handle these matters, so little inclined to show any consideration to the feelings of the Dominions & so much at the mercy of national vanity & prejudice.

And meanwhile we have a deuce of a lot of work to do in a jaded House of Commons, a very much divided Party, a growing feeling that 'Coalition' is hateful, that 'Fusion' is impracticable & that 'Union' on some larger whole with a new name must somehow be brought about. But how is that to be done & what is to be the name & how large a secession will there be when it is attempted? And will there be any more 'accidents' in the division Lobby before the Session ends?[65] Plenty of food for thought, you will allow & none too digestible.

AC5/1/205   25 July 1921
                                                 11 Downing Street

My dear Hilda,

    . . .

Did I write to you about Addison yesterday? . . . Addison was provocative & hostile in tone as well as in substance & I am not surprised that the P.M. who suffered much from him was angry, but as I said to the P.M. when I made him cut out of his letter the equivalent of that dreadful phrase in his speech: "You are the big man. He is the little one. You are up: he is down; & after all he was your man" But in these matters you cannot cure an old dog of his old tricks.

AC5/1/207   9 August 1921
                                                 11 Downing Street

My dear Hilda,

    . . .

I *think* that Ireland means peace & that delay serves peace, but who shall fathom the Irishman's mind . . .?

Of the Supreme Council I have as yet no news, but I think that it must reach agreement somehow. As to the American Conference, I fear that the Am[erican]s are making a bad hash of it partly from inexperience & partly because Harvey[66] has treated us both very badly,

---

[65] On 19 July 1921 the Government lost a vote on the taxation of cooperatives but Chamberlain, as Leader of the House, decided it was not a 'real' defeat and did not adopt the customary practice of adjourning the House for one day. *House of Commons Debates*, 5 Series, 144 col 2127.

[66] Col. George Harvey (1864–1928) Editor and proprietor, *North American Review*, 1899–1926. US Ambassador in London 1921–24.

not transmitting messages &, to speak quite frankly, not telling the truth so that there was at first a complete misapprehension of our attitude. This, I hope & believe, has now been cleared away, but it existed long enough to prevent Washington from accepting some suggestions of ours which would, we believe, have made success for more probably than it is now. The pity of it!

AC5/1/208   [mis-dated] 18 August 1921[67]
                                                       11 Downing Street

My dear Ida,

... I sympathise silently with your irritation at the ways of the Ministry of Health. Indeed as a householder I have expressed my mind freely to Mond[68] on the number of impertinent & useless questions he asks on the Census paper & on his choosing that means of putting Bottomley's advertisement of his latest press venture into every household. Poor Mond smiles grimly & says that Addison had made the Ministry a happy home for every confirmed & notorious crank. He is really doing good work there & I wish to Heaven that A. had been removed a year ago.

Meanwhile I have told the P.M. that I can't carry A's salary,[69] that it would require all his personal influence to do it & that he ought not so to strain the loyalty of his supporters. I have told A. the same & added that A. ought not to ask it of the P.M. but should offer his resignation, & A. has replied to me that he will be "fried, frizzled & crucified" before he will take such a dishonourable course & has told the P.M. by letter that the P.M. will be dishonoured if he accepts my advice, adding that he wishes for a "very early interview" & — that he has gone out of town till Monday! Did you ever know such a man?

Yes, my dear Ida, I have had a hectic week with Addison, Member's memorials (*Did* I give Godfrey Locker Lampson[70] a piece of my mind?

[67] Although this letter clearly bears this date, all the internal evidence relating to Smuts and Addison suggests that it must have been written in mid-June.

[68] Alfred Moritz Mond (1868–1930) Liberal MP for Chester 1906–10, Swansea 1910–23, Carmarthen 1924–28. Joined Conservative Party 1926. First Commissioner of Works 1916–1921; Minister of Health 1921–1922. Created baronet 1910 and Baron Melchett 1928.

[69] In early June a large number of Unionists had put down a motion criticizing Addison's £5000 salary as Minister without Portfolio. Chamberlain warned Lloyd George the majority of Unionist MPs would support it: a view endorsed by McCurdy, the Liberal Chief Whip.

[70] Godfrey Lampson Tennyson Locker-Lampson (1875–1946) Conservative MP for Salisbury January 1910–1918 and Wood Green December 1918–1935. PPS to Home Secretary 1916–18 and to Assistant Foreign Secretary 1918. Represented First Com-

When I lose my temper, it goes altogether, & 14 of his cosignatories voted to add 15 millions to the normal old age pensions charge & between 80 & 90 abstained, & Godfrey himself refused to help me by moving an amendment & was "unavoidably prevented" from attending to give an unpopular vote & "what the devil do *you* mean by threatening me & what do you think of yourself now? Unfortunately engaged? Yes, it is damned unfortunate that you are never free from engagements except when your conscience forces you to vote against the Govt!" Well, a leader should not lose his temper right out; he should let it rise occasionally but always like a captive balloon on the end of a rope.)

And on the top of all this Stamfordham[71] rings me up on the telephone in fierce & almost incoherent agitation – King's visit to Ireland, most important occasion, utterance of world-wide significance, General Smuts, Lord Fitzalan, addresses, drafts, not approved, no advice, Craig no Prime Minister, no answer, heard nothing, devil of a mess, King must apply to me to help him &c. &c. &c.

So I take much on myself, summon him to London, collect a few colleagues, telegraph to Ireland to tell Craig very politely that this is our business & not his, reject in toto the drafts submitted by Craig & Fitzalan, & send Stamfordham away reassured & able to reassure the King that he shall have proper advice from his responsible Ministers. For all which I receive a very grateful letter last night from S. with the additional statement that he must not make comparisons but that the K. *now* reads the Leaders daily letters from the House with great interest & finds that they throw a new light on what he reads in the papers.

By the way, look in my speech of yesterday (today's Times) at my delicate hint to the Dominion Ministers not to meddle with our domestic affairs. Meigham is the gallery nudged his neighbour & his neighbour nudges him, & I have reported the incident to H.M. as an indirect comment on Smuts' meddling. "All which is most humbly submitted by Y.M.'s most dutiful servant" who trusts that the hint will not be lost on Y.M.

So the letters[72] have a use! ...

missioner of Works in Commons 1924–1925; Under-Secretary Home Office 1923–1924 and 1924–1925 and for Foreign Affairs 1925–1929. Older brother of Oliver Locker-Lampson who had also served as PPS to Austen Chamberlain, 1919–22.

[71] Arthur John Bigge (1849–1931) Soldier 1869–1880. Assistant private secretary to Queen Victoria 1880–1895; private secretary 1895–1901, private secretary to Prince (later King) George V, 1901–1931. Created Baron Stamfordham 1911.

[72] In the belief that the daily 'King's Letter' had become 'redundant and farcical', Chamberlain had proposed to discontinue the practice when he emerged as leader but he was prevailed upon to retain them as more personal reports, N. Waterhouse, *Private and Official*, 218–19.

AC5/1/209

25 August 1921
11 Downing Street

My dear Hilda,

Why am I writing to you from this address? Why because those beastly Irish couldn't, wouldn't or didn't send their answer while Parlt was sitting but allowed just the few days to pass which would give us a taste of the pleasures of a holiday & then dashed the cup ... of liberty from our lips. So they sent word yesterday that their emissaries were crossing last night & that their answer would be delivered today – an answer which like all their answers, is a flat refusal, with a paragraph at the end which by all those professing to know their mind is said to be the most important thing in their letter like the sting of the wasp or the postscript of a lady's – but I am forgetting to whom I am writing.

Anyway it is a damned unpleasant letter (I alter the vowel where there is a blot so as not to shock to you [sic] if the phrase becomes a quotation from Mr Micawber) & not an easy one to answer except by saying Ooh! If that is your game, at it again, my boy & damned be he who first gives in (Another quotation you will perceive. I never swear except in quotations)

...

I write *from* here because of this damned Irish spot that all the perfumes of Twitt's Ghyll will not cleanse ...

AC5/1/211

3 September 1921
Twitt's Ghyll

My dear Hilda,

News I have none except that de V. has written another letter exactly on the lines of his first two & that it is conveyed to us on the best authority that, as in all de V's letters, nothing matters but the last paragraph & that this means acceptance & negotiation & peace. When you see the letter you will not think so, but then you are not a Sinn Feiner or a baby, & when you mean business you say so plainly, Lord save me from every having to deal with such people again! And by Jove, Lord save me from a P.M. who summons the Cabinet to meet at Inverness! I am furious; but I shall get no satisfaction as half of the Cabinet are shooting or holiday making in the Highlands. I simply splutter with rage.

AC5/1/213   17 September 1921
                                                      Twitt's Ghyll

My dear Hilda,

Winter is upon us with a cold east wind – such a change from the fierce summer heat of two days ago ...

The change will, I should think, have one good result from my point of view, for it should bring the P.M. south again, & to my mind he ought to be near London in present circumstances. The Irish position looks black indeed. The folly & ignorance of those people is beyond belief. We tell them quite clearly from the first that there is some thing that we cannot tolerate, & that is repudiation of their allegiance to the Crown & association with & in the Empire. And there-upon in a letter which is meant to be an acceptance of our invitation & when they all desire a meeting & peace from Michael Collins[73] downwards (except some of the younger commandants) they repeat & emphasize this preposterous claim & assume that it will not affect our attitudes. I do not see how they or we can now get out of this impasse. The P.M. has acted very properly & sent a very good reply, but what next? War, I fear, with all its ugly incidents, & all because they have blundered into a position from which they have not the courage or the skill or the power to extricate themselves. And meanwhile the rest of the world seems as much at cross purposes as ever ...

9.0p.m. So far I wrote before I went out this morning ... I cannot add much to the gloomy picture which I have already drawn of the world, but it will interest to you know [sic] that in the last interview & the letter that followed it the P.M. acted off his own bat without waiting for any consultation with colleagues. His interview was reported to me by special messenger & I drafted a telegram as soon as I got the report which was only after de V's publication in Dakhi of the letter to which the P.M. took such exception, but before my telegram could be ciphered in London the P.M. had done what I suggested which was to stand firm & reply at once saying conference on such a basis was impossible. He has his merits – as well as a most striking personality.

---

[73] Michael Collins (1890–1922) Arrested at the Post Office, Dublin during Easter Rising. Sinn Fein MP for S. Cork December 1918 but did not take seat. Member of Northern Ireland Parliament for Armagh 1921–22. Member of Dáil for S. Cork until 1922 as a Pro-Treaty Member. Finance Minister in Provisional Government 1921–22 and Chairman from January 1922. C-in-C of Army July–August 1922. Ambushed and killed by Irish Irregulars at Bealnabla, Co. Cork 22 August 1922.

AC5/1/214

Sat night 24 September 1921
Twitt's Ghyll

My dear Ida,

... The P.M. has sent me a good final draft to de. V. which makes our position clear, notes their acceptance of it & invites them to a meeting in London on the 4th. This will, I think, produce the conference; will the conference produce peace? Nous verrons, but I think that public opinion here & abroad would not have supported us if after de V's advance we had not responded.

AC5/1/215

26 September 1921
Twitt's Ghyll

My dear Hilda,

...

I think that de Valera will come into Conference this time & I believe that his representatives will not play the fool there. They certainly want peace, but one cannot be sure of anything with them.... Unemployment is the greatest difficulty, for none of the schemes ever yet tried has been without grave defects in practice. I fear that the present Chancellor is having an awful time with falling revenue & these unexpected expenses.

AC5/1/216

7 October 1921
11 Downing Street

My dear Ida,

...

There is no further news of Ireland. Our first conference is held next week. I expect that the meetings will drag on for a long time & I look forward to them with anything but pleasure.

Unemployment is very bad. 1,750,000 still out of work & benefits & resources largely exhausted. We shall have to take special measures to alleviate the distress & the Budget prospects become gloomier than ever.

AC5/1/218   13 October 1921
                                                        11 Downing Street

My dear Hilda,

...

News I have none. The Irish Conference met twice without making progress forward or backwards ... Opposition to the Conference & to our action is growing among our own people as time passes & provocative events occur, & of course now as always it is the opponents who make their voices heard. Unemployment is the chief preoccupation. The Labour Party & organisations evidently mean to derive all the political advantage that they can from it. Parlt meets on Tuesday & may sit for 2 or 3 weeks. I hope that we shall be able to confine it to Unemployment & not have it ramble over every subject.

AC5/1/219   17 October 1921
                                                        11 Downing Street

My dear Ida,

...

But of work and worry I have enough. The Conference drags, & a section of the Party grows more restless every day. If we fail to make peace, I suppose that the party will reunite & I think that the country will be behind us. But if we succeed, we may indeed, we shall have serious trouble with a section of our own people – with how many I cannot say. But sufficient to the day! Tomorrow the House meets & Unemplt gives sufficient food for present thought – $1\frac{3}{4}$ million out of work today.

AC5/1/220   13 November 1921
                                                        11 Downing Street

My dear Hilda,

I have too much work to write. Sinn Fein & Ulster in front, the Diehards on my back & the National Union meeting on Thursday in L'pool, the stronghold of Orange Toryism – you can imagine what it all means. And I might add to my catalogue of troubles Bonar Law an Ulsterman by descent & in spirit, a very ambitious man now astonished at what he thinks his own complete recovery & itching to be back in politics where he is disposed to think that the first place might & ought to be his.

I am fighting for my political life. What L'pool has in store I don't know. The Diehards are organising fiercely & strenuously. If we are beaten there it won't be the end, but it will be very unpleasant. Thank heavens F.E. & I are absolutely at one. I believe now that we shall carry a united Cabinet & get a solution in complete accordance with our pledges. If so, we shall have done the greatest service any body of men could render to the Empire at the present time. But the strain & labour are for the time being immense.

AC5/1/221   23 December 1921
                                                 11 Downing Street

[Typescript]

My dear Ida,

All our Christmas plans have gone by the board. First of all I had to give up the idea of going to Tangier, as the Prime Minister is ordered a holiday by his doctor, and it is impossible for me to leave the country at the same time as he does without abdicating my position ...

    ...

As to public affairs, you will be as wise as I am – at any rate, as far as concerns the Irish situation ... Collins and Griffith are justifying our faith in them, and Barton and Gavan Duffy[74] have shown themselves to be the sweeps for which we took them. My impression is that there will be a majority for peace in the Dáil . My instinct tells me that the prospects are better than the writers in the press would lead one to think; but the majority may not be sufficient to be conclusive, and some sort of appeal to the people may be thought necessary by Collins and Griffith. I believe if such an appeal should take place their victory would probably be overwhelming.

This week I have been very busy with the French conversations.[75] They have ended satisfactorily, and there is a chance that they may lead to something bigger and more permanent than anything that has yet been achieved in meetings of the Supreme Council, but Briand's own position in France is very shaky – Poincaré is mustering his forces,

---

[74] George Gavan Duffy (1882–1951) Solicitor in London and later Ireland where he prepared the defence in the Casement case. Sinn Fein MP for Dublin Co. South in December 1918 but did not take seat. Member of Dáil for Dublin Co. S. to 1921, for Dublin Co. 1921–23 initially as a Pro-Treaty Member but later as an opponent of the Treaty. Minister for Foreign Affairs in Provisional Government 1922. Called to Inner Bar 1929; High Court Judge from 1936 and President of High Court of Ireland from 1946.

[75] Between 18–22 December 1921 a series of meetings were held in London with Briand at which Lloyd George proposed a general conference to consider remedying the paralysis of the European financial and commercial system, *DBFP* 1st Series vol XV, 760–804.

and Briand's Government might be overthrown at any moment. He seems more tired and depressed than we have ever seen him. I fancy that his visit to America was a great disappointment to him, for he soon found out that no practical help was to be expected from that quarter. This has one good result at any rate, in that it brings home to him the value – and, indeed, the necessity from the point of view of France – of preserving the friendship of England, and may help to prevent any more dirty tricks like the conclusion of the Angora agreement[76] behind our backs.

[76] In June 1921 the French sent Henri Franklin-Bouillon (1870–1939) to Angora without consulting the British. The mission resulted in a separate treaty between France and the Kemalists in October leaving the British isolated in support of the Greeks and the 'neutral zones'.

6

'FIGHTING ONE'S OWN FRIENDS IS HATEFUL WORK'

Coalition troubles, January – October 1922

In the aftermath of the 1918 election Law believed 'Lloyd George can be Prime Minister for life if he wants'.[1] In the event, the government survived only four turbulent years. Although 1922 was to be a critical year for the Coalition, the year began auspiciously. For all the problems during 1921, by December the fortunes and confidence of the coalition leadership were greater than for some time. A week after signing the Irish Treaty, the government claimed something of a diplomatic triumph with the four-power treaty in Washington covering Pacific and Far Eastern questions. Thereafter progress was also swiftly made with regard to naval disarmament (finally signed on 6 February 1922). Two days after the Pacific agreement, the Commons debate on the Irish Treaty provided the government with its first notable parliamentary success for some months. For the moment even Law broke the ominous silence he had maintained throughout the negotiations to declare his approval. While in the longer term the Irish Treaty was to prove both 'Lloyd George's greatest achievement, but ... also the greatest single cause of his overthrow',[2] in December 1921 it had undoubtedly restored the government's fortunes and renewed its sense of policy direction. Moreover, although relations with France had been gravely aggravated by the unilateral Angora agreement with the Turks in November 1921 and even more by French obstructionism at Washington, even Anglo-French relations provided some substance for hope. The 'conversations' with Briand in London from 18–22 December thus set in motion a process which led, via Cannes and Genoa, to an attempt to resolve Anglo-French differences over German reparations. With Ireland settled, Washington still hailed a triumph and plans already in progress for a conference offering the prospect of European peace and the restoration of prosperity, the scene was set for an attempt to engineer indirectly that which could not be achieved by direct calls for 'fusion'. Encouraged by McCurdy's grossly over-optimistic assessments of the prospects, some time before Christmas Lloyd George decided that circumstances were propitious for another coalition election. At a dinner held by Birkenhead after the Irish Treaty debate, the subject was discussed for the first time by the Coalition leaders.[3]

Although Chamberlain has been much criticized for his handling of the crisis which this decision provoked, his position was actually far clearer than his apparently

[1] M. Pugh, *Lloyd George*, 128.
[2] M. Kinnear, *The Fall of Lloyd George: The Political Crisis of 1922* (1973), 15.
[3] For these events and their background see Morgan, *Consensus and Disunity*, 264–281; M. Cowling, *The Impact of Labour*, Chapter VII–VIII.

conflicting and ambiguous utterances suggested. It was also far more complex than often conceded. As he informed Lloyd George, 'My object has been to lead the Unionist Party to accept merger in a new Party under the lead of the present Prime Minister and including the great bulk of the old Unionists and old Liberals so as to secure the widest and closest possible union of all men and women of constitutional and progressive views'. Yet he was equally convinced that this required 'time and careful preparation' and that talk of a precipitate election threatened to jeopardise this objective.[4] Chamberlain's problem was that at Birkenhead's dinner on 19 December he had been the only Coalition leader definitely to declare his opposition to the plan.[5] This opinion, even when expressed by the leader of the majority party, did not end speculation or planning for an early election. For this failure historians have been particularly critical because as Conservative leader 'his word should have carried more weight than it apparently did'.[6] In practice, however, Chamberlain did not perceive himself to be in a strong position to make effective such a supposed 'veto' – not least because he attached particular importance to the fact that ultimately the sole prerogative for calling an election rested with the Prime Minister.[7] As they disagreed over a question of timing and tactics rather than fundamental principle or objective, therefore, he probably felt it difficult to resist such pressure directly.

In such circumstances, the decision to sound Party opinion was not an abdication of responsibility or a sign of indecision. Rather it offered a more subtle and potentially more effective means of winning the argument indirectly. As Chamberlain genuinely believed the mood of the party to be hostile to such a proposal, the most likely explanation for these consultations was a desire to facilitate a party backlash to strengthen his own hand in thwarting the planned election. Certainly this was the outcome. With the exception of the West Country, party organizers vociferously opposed an early election and the prospect of fusion in the foreseeable future.[8] Malcolm Fraser, the Chief Agent, warned in similarly apocalyptic terms that 'it would split the Unionist Party from top to toe'. He also feared that it was likely to provoke the threat of independent Conservatives emerging at the polls.[9] Equally significant was Chamberlain's conduct towards Younger. Immediately after Birkenhead's dinner Chamberlain informed him of his position and his reasons for opposing an early election.[10] Younger replied privately reinforcing all of Fraser's gloomy forebodings.[11] Thus armed, Chamberlain was in a far stronger position to resist the Prime Minister and the majority view in favour of an election.[12]

[4] Chamberlain memorandum to Lloyd George, 6 January 1922, AC 32/2/27. See also to Ida, 17 January 1922, AC5/1/223.

[5] S. Salvidge, *Salvidge of Liverpool*, (1934) p225; A. Chamberlain to N. Chamberlain, AC 32/2/3.

[6] Kinnear, *The Fall of Lloyd George*, 104.

[7] A. Chamberlain to Hilda, 1 January 1922, AC5/1/222.

[8] For these warnings see AC 32/2.

[9] M. Fraser to A. Chamberlain, 31 December 1921, AC 32/4/1a.

[10] A. Chamberlain to Younger, 21 December 1921, AC 32/2/2.

[11] Younger to A. Chamberlain, 28 December 1921, AC 32/2/15a, 21.

[12] A. Chamberlain to Lloyd George, 4 January 1922, Lloyd George MSS F/7/5/1.

Unfortunately for Chamberlain, at the very moment he appeared to have regained the political initiative his strategy miscarried. Provoked by well-informed press speculation, Younger struck back in a series of press interviews on 5–6 January denouncing the 'pure opportunism and ... narrow party spirit' behind the election rumours and forcefully stating the case against such a move. He also sent a letter to all Conservative chairmen – except Chamberlain's own – reiterating the case which also appeared in the press.[13] *an attack he renewed on 22 February contending that it was no longer essential for the Coalition to continue after the next election and expressing his wish for a 'bill of divorcement' between the two wings of the Coalition.*[14] *By making the breach public in such terms, Chamberlain undoubtedly had cause to lament that Younger had 'gone rather too far' and 'overdone his protest'.*[15] *Nonetheless, the central fact remains that although Younger has usually been considered to be the chief trouble-maker, in an important sense he was 'but merely carrying out Chamberlain's wishes and loyally consolidating support behind his leader'.*[16] *Certainly in his correspondence with his sisters Chamberlain consistently acknowledged that the problem was not Younger's lack of loyalty in carrying out his leader's policy, but rather that he had gone too far in so doing. As he wrote on 4 March, 'Younger intends to be thoroughly loyal to me & to back my policy, but he has been very indiscreet, rather muddle-headed & a little vain & self-important'.*[17]

Even more unfortunate for Chamberlain was that although he prevailed tactically over Lloyd George and Birkenhead concerning an early election, at a more fundamental level his authority as leader suffered greatly from the whole affair. Although initially supportive of Younger, in the end the Party Chairman's over-zealous attacks upon Lloyd George compelled Chamberlain to come to the Prime Minister's defence. As divisions intensified, Chamberlain was thus obliged to take refuge in ambiguity. Criticisms that the repeated misunderstandings of the Conservative leader's position during this period were 'too frequent to be accidental, and result from Chamberlain's inability to state this case clearly'[18] *crucially overlooks the fact that he was playing a dangerous game. Although he agreed with Lloyd George on long-term objective and strategy, Chamberlain had unleashed the partisan passions within his own ranks opposed to the perpetuation of a Coalition in order to thwart the Prime Minister over the essentially tactical question of how this shared objective could best be realized. If Lloyd George had risked a great deal in first raising the election question, therefore, Chamberlain was guilty of dramatically increasing the stakes. Moreover, in order to achieve such a goal it was necessary for Chamberlain to attempt to reconcile two opposite positions. Hence his repeated inconsistency, ambiguity and*

---

[13] Kinnear, *The Fall of Lloyd George*, 103; Younger to Conservative Constituency Chairmen, 9 January 1922, J. Ramsden (ed) *Real Old Tory Politics*, 171–2.

[14] *The Times*, 23 February 1922, *Gleanings and Memoranda*, March 1922, 398–400. See also 'A Short Diary of a Press Campaign', AC 32/4/15.

[15] A. Chamberlain to Ida, 14 January 1922, AC5/1/224.

[16] Kinnear, *The Fall of Lloyd George*, 101.

[17] A. Chamberlain to Hilda, 4 March 1922, AC5/1/228.

[18] Kinnear, *The Fall of Lloyd George*, 104.

evasion.[19] *Ultimately, when this delicate balancing act finally became too difficult to sustain, the enduring impression of equivocation and vacillation was such as to create the appearance of chronic weakness at the top of the Unionist Party. At a time when the Party most wanted firm leadership, the logic of Chamberlain's dangerous gamble forced him to play the role of a confused ringmaster trying hopelessly to reconcile the irreconcilable. He undoubtedly recognized the dangers of siding with Lloyd George against his own party, but for compelling reasons of strategy and philosophy he could never lead his party in the direction it increasingly wanted to go. The result was disastrous for Chamberlain's reputation. As one colleague encapsulated the dilemma in late-February, 'Chamberlain looks anxious and worried, torn between loyalty to his party and loyalty to his Prime Minister'.*[20] *The problem from the outbreak of the election crisis until the Carlton Club revolt in October was that Chamberlain's remote and arrogant style of leadership left his supporters increasingly uncertain as to which way he would eventually jump. He had come a long way from March 1921 and his proud boast that Lloyd George considered him 'an awful Tory, & ... more of a Conservative than Bonar'.*[21]

Subsequent events reinforced such doubts. After a hint earlier in the month, on 27 February the Prime Minister formally offered to resign in Chamberlain's favour. Although Lloyd George's motives are open to question, in declining the offer Chamberlain displayed a curious combination of loyalty, genuine respect for Lloyd George's capacity and traces of the same self-doubt manifested in 1911.[22] *When it looked as if poor health would lead to the Prime Minister's retirement or breakdown in the following month, the strictly confidential account to his sisters also suggests more alarm than hopeful expectation at the prospect. He thus renewed his appeal as a friend, colleague and leader of a Coalition party for Lloyd George to declare his intention to continue.*[23] *Had Chamberlain been more ambitious or more confident of his abilities and seized the opportunity, the history of the next six months may have been very different. Worse still, if he privately expected to succeed as Prime Minister after another general election, he gave no public indication of such a belief to his followers. In so doing he reinforced the damaging impression that he was prepared to accept Lloyd George's leadership indefinitely.*

If these actions were the product of an excessively sensitive feeling of loyalty to

---

[19] See, for example, G. Murray, *A Man's Life*, 260–1.

[20] E. Montagu to Lord Reading, 23 February 1922, H. Montgomery Hyde, *Lord Reading: The Life of Rufus Isaacs, First Marquess of Reading*, (1967), 370–371.

[21] A. Chamberlain to Ida, 25 March 1921, AC5/1/195. By this stage Lloyd George was declaring Chamberlain and the other Conservative Leaders were 'really Liberals'. See C.P. Scott Diary, 13 October and 22 December 1922, 26 July 1923, Scott MSS 50906 fol. 191, 208; 50907 fol. 31. (British Library). Also Jones Diary, 2 August 1922, *Whitehall Diary*, I, 205.

[22] For Lloyd George's motives see Frances Stevenson Diary, 3 February 1922, Taylor (ed) *Lloyd George: A Diary*, 240–241; C.P. Scott Diary, 2 March 1922, T. Wilson (ed) *The Political Diary of C.P. Scott*, 421. For Chamberlain's motives see Dutton, *Austen Chamberlain*, 176: Petrie, *Life and Letters*, II, 174–179.

[23] A. Chamberlain memorandum to Lloyd George, 18 March 1922, AC 33/1/66.

his leader, Chamberlain's failure to deal with his own malcontents stemmed from an equally damaging sense of aloof complacency. On 14 March a meeting of over 200 Conservative MPs failed to adopt a motion defending Coalition policy and came close to repudiating Chamberlain's leadership. His response was one of anger and frustration, but this was mitigated by the sanguine belief that it had been the product of mismanagement from the chair rather than genuine opposition.[24] More important, despite continual warnings about the Diehard threat, Chamberlain consistently failed to confront this challenge because he 'was not prepared to have it recorded of him that he split the party which had been handed over to him as a united force'.[25] Ultimately this proved to be a decisively fatal error because the Diehards were handicapped by no such inhibition.[26] Indeed, his only deviation from this deliberately vague and unprovocative posture occurred on 5 April when a motion of no-confidence in the government and its 'lack of definite and coherent principle' tabled by Joynson-Hicks provoked Chamberlain to an uncharacteristically savage attack upon Hicks and his Diehard friends.[27] Although by all accounts one of his best ever speeches,[28] even here Chamberlain's assault evaded any attempt to explain his own position.

AC5/1/222

1 January 1922
Twitt's Ghyll

My dear Hilda,

. . .

Of politics I know nothing except what you may read in the papers:- that the P.M. & Lord Ch[ancellor] want a dissolution & that I am opposed to it on many ground, amongst which two stand out 1st. We have no right to go till we have carried through our Irish policy (not merely started it) & secondly I think that it will find my party in a very bad temper & a very difficult position. But dissolution, subject to the King's assent, is the special prerogative of the P.M. who need not consult his colleagues at all.

---

[24] A. Chamberlain to Hilda, 18 March 1922, AC5/1/230; to Lloyd George, 15 March 1922, Lloyd George MSS F/7/5/8.
[25] S. Salvidge, *Salvidge of Liverpool*, 233.
[26] Kinnear, *The Fall of Lloyd George*, 110.
[27] *House of Commons Debates*, 5 Series, 152 col 2373 *passim*, 5 April 1922; *Annual Register 1922*, 45.
[28] N. Chamberlain to Hilda, 8 April 1922, NC 18/1/345; Sanders Diary, 12 April 1922.

I see that Briand was saved by Bertholot's[29] resignation. What will they do at Cannes?[30] Briand has lost all hope of help from America & is talking of an alliance with us. But I think that he has missed his market & the French attitude on naval questions at Washington will make him a bad public here & in the Dominions. I advocated it more than a year ago, but then the French lent no encouragement to the idea. Now I am doubtful whether the Dominions would agree at any price; & certainly neither they nor we should be prepared for anything so extensive as they at first sketched. The matter was first broached by the French ambassador to me & I encouraged him to talk to Curzon with some cautions against asking too much & some warning of the difficulties.

AC5/1/223   7 January 1922
                                                   Twitt's Ghyll

[To Ida]

. . .

What an unsatisfactory world it is whichever way you turn. Here has Lloyd George put the fat in the fire with his talk of a dissolution, so upsetting & perhaps permanently ruining my effort to join all that is reasonably progressive in the Unionist Party with what is sound & not too tied up in old party shibboleths in the Liberal Party. Most unfortunately he was encouraged by the Lord Chancellor, & now even if he desists I do not know that the anger & excitement in the Unionist Party can be allayed. My letter bag is heavy with protests & threats never again to stand as Coalitionists. Serve him right for neglecting my advice but I am none the less vexed.

[29] Philippe Berthelot (1866–1934) French diplomat. Director of political affairs and a principal counsellor to Briand during the Great War. As Secretary-General, Foreign Ministry in 1920 he played a major role in post-treaty negotiations, particularly over Reparations and a supporter of Briand's attempted rapprochement with Germany. Resigned because of involvement with his brother in collapse of Industrial Bank of Indo-China. Returned to this post again in left-wing Coalition 1924–32.
[30] The Cannes Conference 6–13 January 1922 ended in failure and the resignation of Briand.

AC5/1/224   14 January 1922
                                              Twitt's Ghyll

My dear Ida,

Why do any of us meddle with public work? It is all worry &
disappointment & vexation whether it be District Councils or Cabinet
councils or Prime Ministers or Ministers of Health. Let us cultivate our
cabbages. At least they don't talk!

You see I am not happy. I had a week of very hard work in London
out of which I could derive but little satisfaction & I have settled to
return to London tomorrow to see Younger[31] & Derby & to give dinner
to the P.M., F.E. & Winston. Now Younger, justly outraged by the
apparent attempt to rush a decision & harrassed by the storm of protest
which arose from our Party, has gone rather too far, but I shall have
to support him even where I think he has overdone his protest, & I
shall have to confront a very angry Prime Minister. Who the deuce did
talk? Our people say the P.M.'s people & the P.M. & his people say
our people, & meanwhile the nerves of the whole Party are on edge &
I have to make a speech at Glasgow on Thursday. I'll sell my job for
6d – nay, I'll give anyone a sovereign to take it. I am very, very sick &
discouraged. I have spent a good deal of time trying to prevent more
china being broken & now I suppose that I must try to piece the broken
bits together, but – but – Oh d— ! Fighting one's own friends is hateful
work.

We were all struck by Briand's lethargy & listlessness when he was
last here – so unlike his normal self. We felt that his fall was near. I
should not have been surprised if it had come before or after Cannes,[32]
but I confess that I did not expect it in the middle of Cannes; it has a
rather ugly look. I am not impressed by the Times view that we should
have made an alliance first & tried to arrange our difficulties afterwards.
The French attitude at Angora & Washington has not made a French
Alliance more popular here & an Alliance without an understanding
seems to me almost a contradiction in terms. Well, Poincaré will have
to be more careful in office than he was in opposition & it is probably

[31] George Younger (1851–1929) Conservative MP for Ayr Burghs from 1906 until retired
in October 1922. President National Union of Conservative Associations in Scotland
1904; Chairman Unionist Party Organisation January 1917–March 1923; Treasurer
Unionist Party 1923–29. Created baronet 1911 and Viscount Younger of Leckie 1923.

[32] During Cannes Conference Lloyd George and Briand came close to agreement not
only over reparations but over the future closeness of the entente but an ill-fated golf
match during the conference (actually only a pose for the photographers) between Lloyd
George and the novice Briand was represented in France as frivolity and interpreted as
a sign that Briand was sacrificing the national interests to the wiles of the Welsh Wizard.
Briand returned to Paris next day and resigned a day later.

not a bad thing for either France or ourselves that he should have responsibility – & be used up!

AC5/1/225

21 January 1922
11 Downing Street

My dear Hilda,

. . .

And here I find the terms of the accord between Craig & Michael Collins, & tired as I am, I am at least as much excited. What a confirmation of our hopes! What a justification of our actions! I can think of nothing else. I knew that it must come but I did not dare to expect so much so soon . . .

Incidentally too I have seen enough of the P.M.'s speech to see that he has played up on the House of Lords & wiped out the foolish utterances of Freddy Guest[33] & alas! of that very able man the Attorney General.[34] So I shall go to bed tired but content &, pray heaven, not too excited to sleep.

Oliver left a letter for me: "I saw the P.M. today for quite a long time. He was really moved at your speech [at Glasgow].[35] He told me that he had not talked over what you were going to say with you before hand. He had left it to you: and he was now overcome by the extent of your loyalty —." Well, I said to Ivy 'I have given the P.M. his chance, if he will take it', & I think he has done so . . .

. . .

Sunday. Well, I went straight off to sleep as soon as I laid my head upon my pillow last night, but I woke rather earlier than I intended, for while I was away a new crisis had blown up – this time in foreign affairs, & Curzon & the Cabinet were not agreed & both Curzon & the P.M. appealed to me for assistance & I have had to try to find a way out. It is a most difficult question & I am not at ease about any solution of it, but I think my solution is better than either of the courses

---

[33] Frederick Edward Guest (1875–1937) Liberal MP for Dorset East 1910–22, Stroud 1923–24, Bristol (North) 1924–29. In 1930 became a Conservative and MP for Plymouth (Drake) 1931–37. Junior Lord of Treasury 1911–12; Treasurer of the Household 1912–15; Joint Patronage Secretary to Treasury and Chief Government Whip 1917–1921; Secretary for Air 1921–1922.

[34] Gordon Hewart (1870–1943) Liberal MP for Leicester 1913–22. Solicitor-General 1916–1919; Attorney-General 1919–1922; Lord Chief Justice 1922–40. Knighted 1916, created Baron Hewart 1922 and Viscount 1940.

[35] In an attempt to rally support for the Coalition, at Glasgow on 19 January 1922 Chamberlain praised the Coalition's achievements and paid a personal tribute to Lloyd George: a speech his brother considered 'excellent, thoughtful and statesmanlike'. N. Chamberlain to Ida 21 January 1922 NC 18/1/335.

previously proposed & that both the P.M.: who represents the general Cabinet view & Curzon, who curiously enough takes what in another one would have called the Little England view, will accept it. But I have still to see Curzon's draft & get the PM.'s assent & the Viceroy is coming at any moment. So I have not had the quiet Sunday that I wanted.

Glasgow went off well as far as I could see everyone was satisfied. I think they were glad to be steadied & felt that they had been stampeded first one way & then the other very unnecessarily. It was hard work.

AC5/1/226   29 January 1922

11 Downing Street

My dear Ida,

. . .

Egypt has given me much trouble since I came back from Glasgow & fills me now with anxiety. The Geddes Comtee[36] supplies me with much work & if I want worry I can find it anywhere in the party situation.

AC5/1/227   26 February 1922
                                                     11 Downing Street

My dear Ida,

. . .

I know what I want. My colleagues are agreed with me & Younger intends to carry out my policy; yet they all seem to conspire to prevent it. Younger humiliates the P.M. publicly, F.E. attacks Younger personally; Bonar Law tries on the crown but can't make up his mind to attempt to seize it, won't join us & share the load but watches not without pleasure the trouble of his friends, & the Die Hards, instead of responding to my advances, harden in their resistance. "Who'd be a nuss, a horrid old nuss?"

[36] Eric Campbell Geddes (1875–1937). Unionist MP for Cambridge, 1917–February 22. First Lord of Admiralty 1917–1919; Minister without Portfolio 1919; Minister of Transport 1919–1921. Knighted 1916 and created G.B.E. 1919. Chairman FBI 1923–24 and of Dunlop and Imperial Airways. Chairman of the Committee to advise the Chancellor on National Expenditure 1921. The sharp cuts proposed led it to be dubbed "the Geddes axe". Chamberlain was chairman of the Cabinet committee considering domestic policy economies on public health, unemployment insurance, Addison's housing programme and, most controversial, cuts in education and teacher's salaries.

And there I broke off my letter to go across to the Colonial Office to meet Griffith & Co. Their explanations of the proceedings of Ard Feis [sic][37] are satisfactory. They consider that they have secured a victory & that the prospects of the Treaty are much improved. They say that de V. & Co. have in effect recognised the Provisional Govt & that they have agreed not to put any obstacles in the way during the intervening period. Griffiths is very confident of success & says that they already have control of the I.R.A. everywhere except in Cork & Tipperary & that they will soon get it there also.

. . .

Fitzalan came to lunch today to talk Ireland & the political situation & when he was gone I retired to bed & slept from 4 till seven. Now I go to bed again. I am very tired. I am carrying a very heavy load & the future is obscure. On the whole I am very glad that we have lost these three elections![38]

AC5/1/228   4 March 1922
                                                      Twitt's Ghyll

My dear Hilda,

A very heavy brother sits down to write to you ... As you can imagine I have had a troublous week. Younger intends to be thoroughly loyal to me & to back my policy, but he has been very indiscreet, rather muddle-headed & a little vain & self-important, so that in a situation already sufficiently difficult, he has humiliated & offended the P.M., then 'explained' me & generally given the enemy the opportunity to blaspheme. Our local Associations are full of old prewar Tories who have learned nothing & forgotten nothing & who are I am quite convinced unrepresentative of the bulk of the electorate. They are a positive danger to us & may easily be our ruin. Just now our stock stands very low but I hope that given time we shall pick up again. Meanwhile I slave & am cursed for my pains. A weary world, my masters!

To add to the Coalition's other problems, on 9 March Edwin Montagu was

[37] Ard-fheis: Sinn Fein Convention.
[38] On 18 and 20 February 1922 respectively Labour gained Manchester (Clayton) and North Camberwell with huge swings against the government. In both, the Labour candidates vigorously attacked the proposed cuts in elementary education. The day after the Camberwell defeat the Cabinet acknowledged finally that the proposed cuts were losing them votes. On 24 February the Coalition Unionists also lost Bodmin to Isaac Foot (Liberal).

compelled to resign as Secretary of State for India. Always an irreconcilable critic of the government's anti-Turkish stance, without obtaining Cabinet approval Montagu had authorized the publication of a sensitive telegram from the Viceroy pressing the Indian desire for the evacuation of Constantinople and the restoration of the Sultan's suzerainty over the Holy Places. An acerbic exchange of letters with the Prime Minister was then followed on 12 March by a bitter speech to his Cambridge constituents notable for the defence of his own conduct with several mis-statements of fact, his vitriolic attack upon Lloyd George's dictatorial style of government and the allegation that he had been sacrificed in order to placate the Diehards. The Coalition was damaged still further by the refusal of Derby, Devonshire and Crawford to accept the office before Viscount Peel was appointed on 19 March. This rebuff from three such prominent Conservatives combined with rising Diehard unrest and the simultaneous embarrassment created by the failure of Conservative MPs to endorse the government's policy were all ominous portents for the future of the Coalition. For all this, however, by the spring of 1922 Chamberlain appeared to be in an unusually sanguine and confident mood.[39]

AC5/1/229

11 March 1922
Twitt's Ghyll

My dear Ida,

Politics are a strange uncertain pursuit. You never know when or what will happen. Was there ever anything stranger than Montagu's blunder? I am not sorry that there is to be a change in that office, but I can't help being very sorry for Montagu himself. The House cheered the news of his resignation savagely & not a single newspaper can suggest a word in his defence. It is not so that one would wish to end one's official career. And the tragedy of it is that it might have been prevented & the odd part of it is that even late on Thursday night Montagu could not see that he had done wrong. Friday's papers may have changed his view but I doubt it. I had a hectic day on Thursday. Curzon & Montagu both on the verge of tears (literally), Montagu requiring to be dismissed instead of resigning till I persuaded him five minutes before I had to answer the question; an answer about Russian famine relief to be drafted & the very indecent haste of the change of Lord Chief Justice to be explained & excused.

I said that the publication of the telegram might have been prevented. I saw it first at Cabinet on Monday when I was presiding. Curzon brought it to me & I said that of course it must not be published. I

---

[39] See, for example, A. Chamberlain to Lloyd George, 15 and 23 March 1922, Lloyd George MSS F/7/5/8, 22.

saw him take Montagu aside & as neither of them appealed to me I assumed that Montagu had agreed or yielded. Not a bit of it! He had told Curzon that he had already authorized publication. Curzon sighed & swore – & that was all. If only they had come to me I should have insisted on a 'clear the line' telegram cancelling the authorisation & it would have *arrived on time*!!

Now I am expecting Reading's[40] resignation & shall welcome it if it comes, tho' I can't think who to put in his place. A Unionist will succeed Montagu & I hope to get Eddie Winterton[41] into an Under-secretaryship.

The Coalition business is settled & our Party outlook is better. Some of the Die-hards are coming in & there is a strong & growing movement of opinion against their attitude.

...

[Postscript]
I read the old letters you sent me. They made me cry as if the tragedy had happened the day before. To think that I was that little unwanted baby that brought sorrow to everyone. Thank God that I was able to be so much to Father afterwards & never caused him sorrow or anxiety after my boyhood.

AC5/1/230   18 March 1922
                                                        Twitt's Ghyll

Yes, my dear Hilda, it has been a hectic week & at times I have felt oh! so tired. But this evening I feel quite chirpy. You ask why? Well, a lovely afternoon here may have something to do with it ... But that is not all. I have got a Sec. of State for India & I hope that tomorrow I am going to get Winterton as Under-Sec. I have telegraphed to that fidgety man the Viceroy about Montagu's speeches & my speeches & Curzon's speech until at last he has left me for 24 hours without an agitated & anxious call for more information or a fresh explanation of

[40] Rufus Daniel Isaacs (1860–1935) Liberal MP for Reading 1903–13. Solicitor-General March–October 1910; Attorney-General 1910–October 1913; Lord Chief Justice 1913–21; Ambassador to Washington 1918–19 while remaining Lord Chief Justice; Viceroy of India 1921–26; Foreign Secretary 1931. Knighted 1910, created G.C.B. 1915, Baron Reading 1914, Viscount 1916, Earl 1917 and Marquess of Reading 1926.

[41] Edward Turnour Winterton (1883–1962) Conservative MP for Horsham 1904–18, Horsham and Worthing 1918–1945 and for Horsham from 1945 until he retired in October 1951. PPS to Financial Secretary to Admiralty 1903–05; Under-Secretary for India 1922–1924 and 1924–1929; Chancellor Duchy of Lancaster 1937–1939 (member of Cabinet after March 1938); Paymaster-General 1939. Succeeded father to Irish peerage as 6th Earl Winterton 1907. Created Baron Turnour 1952.

his own position. I have made four speeches on four widely diverse
subjects – Egypt, Montagu, the Air-Force & Russian Famine relief –
on four consecutive days, & all of them went well. I have got over my
first blazing indignation & disgust at the folly & ignorance with which
that meeting of M.P.s was organised & in spite of the Harmsworth
Press I am confident that we can live it down. We have had two good
elections – L'pool [sic] & Cambridge[42] – & I am beginning to get a
number of resolutions from different parts of the country supporting
me & Coalition. [The following section annotated in margin 'Private'] -
Lastly before leaving town this morning I have fired off a strong memo
to 'the Wizard of Wales', 'the Welsh Sinccimators', in short to the P.M.
telling him that it is time that he put an end to the crisis by speaking
out; that I only made my Oxford speech[43] after consultation with him &
on the clear understanding that the 'incident' was at an end. That he
ought to have repudiated the Wee Frees instead of allowing Gladstone[44]
to repudiate him & that it is up to him to reply at once to Gladstone's
challenge.

But when I told Grigg[45] what I had done, G. replied that in fact he
is a very sick man & not fit to go on without six months rest, that Lord
Dawson[46] said that if he did not go away he would break down before
Xmas & that in fact the P.M. was much worse than he knew.

All this gives me furiously to think. I have told G. that I shall be
unfeignedly sorry if he has to resign, that such ambition as I had died
10 years ago when I gave way to Bonar Law, that I shall be well
content to go on as we are if the P.M. will put an end to the uncertainty

[42] After three disastrous by-elections in February, Sir Robert Bird held the marginal
West Wolverhampton [not Liverpool] for the Coalition on 7 March and on 16 March
Cambridge was held by an official Conservative.
[43] On 3 March 1922 at the Oxford Carlton Club Chamberlain renewed his commitment
to the Coalition and the need to fight the next election as a government.
[44] Herbert John Gladstone (1854–1930) Fourth son of W.E. Gladstone. Liberal MP for
Leeds May 1880–85 and Leeds West 1885 until he retired January 1910. Lord of the
Treasury, 1881–85; Deputy-Commissioner of Works 1885 Financial Secretary War Office
1886; Under-Secretary Home Office 1892–94; First Commissioner of Works 1894–95;
Chief Liberal Whip 1899–1905; Home Secretary 1905–1910; Governor-General of South
Africa 1910–14. Created G.C.M.G. and Viscount Gladstone 1910. Played a major role in
Liberal Party organisation 1919–24.
[45] Edward William Macleay Grigg (1879–1955) Private Secretary to Lloyd George 1921–
22. Liberal MP for Oldham 1922–25; Governor Kenya Colony 1925–30; National
Conservative MP for Altrincham 1933–1945. Parliamentary Secretary to Minister of
Information 1939–1940; Financial Secretary to War Office 1940; Joint Under-Secretary
War Office 1940–1942; Minister Resident in Middle East November 1944–1945. Created
K.C.V.O. 1920, K.C.M.G. 1928 and Baron Altrincham 1945.
[46] Bertrand Dawson (1864–1945) Physician in Extraordinary to Edward VII 1907–10;
to George V after 1907 and to Edward, Prince of Wales after 1923. Also served successive
Prime Ministers. President, Royal College of Physicians 1931. Created Baron Dawson of
Penn 1920.

which is damaging us seriously, but that I cannot consent to be a mere warming-pan, holding the place till this or that man is well enough to resume it. What will be the outcome of it all? Will it brace the P.M. up? Quite possibly. On the other hand – You & Ida can discuss possibilities. Not a word to another soul. There is a letter which makes amends for recent jejeune scraps & gives you something to gossip about.[End of section marked *'Private'*]

I don't want to think of Montagu. His 'explanation' filled me with shame & pain, but the House was so cold & he so thoroughly beaten & miserable that I had not the heart to hit him. The P.M. had been very rough with him in conversation, but even so I can't stand so swift & bitter a turn.

AC5/1/231   25 March 1922
                                              11 Downing Street

[To Ida]

. . .
I too have not been idle. Ireland, the Lock Out & its ramifications, India, the new appointments have all claimed a share of my time & often *all* at the same moment . . .

And on top of all this comes a new crisis & a very serious one . . . I am not by any means sure that next week will not see a bust-up. I am a little tired of living on a volcano!

AC5/1/232   8 April 1922
                                              11 Downing Street

My dear Ida,

. . .
I have had a great week. Monday's speech [on Genoa] which you heard about was counted a success . . . But Wednesday's attack on the Die-hards had an extraordinary success at the time & a still more extraordinary press the next day. It is a fact that I tried a style which I have not attempted before & the effort came off. I felt that I was in good form & only doubted whether the speech was not too good to be wise! But it was time that the extremists had a trouncing & they got

it, & Joynson Hicks[48] was made to look ridiculous which was the best thing for him *& for me*. Altogether I am very pleased with myself – not least because of Sir H. Warren's[49] comment that it resembled the flashing of Father's own rapier.

AC5/1/233

18 April 1922
Twitt's Ghyll

My dear Hilda,

No apology is necessary for talking to me about your garden. Gardens are the only things which interest me. Ireland makes me anxious – very anxious whenever I think about it, but only flowers interest & entertain. No! the P.M. at Genoa does both. The Press reports, the official reports & private letters all show that he is at the top of his form & handling things & people with immense skill. Private letters say that our reputation never stood higher, our influence was never greater & that the P.M. is unmistakably cock of that dunghill. So far (my news is some days old & does not yet cover the Russo-German treaty[50]) he has had a triumph won by force of conviction, acquired authority & great skill & tact. Even Barthou feels his mastery & the force of his logic & meditates asserting within limits his independence of Poincaré. Well, I would sooner spend my Easter at Twitt's Ghyll than at Genoa.

I think that I told you that the last week of the session was rather a triumphant one for me. The Genoa speech, 'the best you ever made'. The Diehard speech ditto, ditto. Everyone liked it except Joynson Hicks who told the Chief Whip that he thought I ought to know that he was very much annoyed, that he could have made quite a different speech & that next night at Twickenham he told his people all about it & that they did not take at all the same view as I did. So I said: "There's only one thing for you to say to him, Leslie, Tell him that I'm a nasty, vicious beast & that when I'm attacked, *after six months* I defend

---

[48] William Joynson-Hicks (1865–1932) Conservative MP for Manchester NW, 1908–10; Brentford 1911–1918, Twickenham 1918–1929. Parliamentary Secretary to Overseas Trade Department 1922–1923; Postmaster- and Paymaster-General 1923; Financial Secretary to Treasury (with seat in Cabinet) 1923; Minister of Health 1923–1924; Home Secretary 1924–1929. Created baronet 1919 and Viscount Brentford 1929.

[49] Alfred Haman Warren (1856–1927) Coalition Unionist MP for Edmonton 1918–1922. Knighted 1918.

[50] After the Genoa conference assembled on 10 April Lloyd George engaged in secret discussions with the Soviet delegates. At the same time Rathenau, the German foreign minister, was stampeded by the Russians into signing a Soviet-German treaty at Rapallo. Despite his efforts this was a shattering blow to Lloyd George's plans although he stayed at Genoa until 18 May.

myself" & Leslie Wilson[52] replied, That's what I told him.

AC5/1/234   22 April 1922
                                             Twitt's Ghyll

My dear Ida,

. . .

Letters from Grigg & Hankey tell of a stormy Easter at Genoa both meteorologically & politically but speak also of the P.M.'s extraordinary ascendancy. All the little Powers are very anxious for success, but the Russo-German treaty has been a bombshell. The P.M. has always foreseen this danger & more than once solemnly & emphatically warned Millerand & Briand of it. Of course the Times which I remember attacked him violently for one of these warnings given in public now says that it is his fault & repeats with gusto the utterly baseless suggestion of the Matin that he knew all about it before hand if he did not himself contrive it.

I continue very anxious about Ireland, but we must play our hand out.

AC5/1/235   28 April 1922
                                             Twitt's Ghyll

My dear Hilda,

Parliament has opened quietly enough – not to say dully . . .

Genoa has so many crises that I cannot keep pace with them or understand them. My last news received today is that the crisis is approaching – with the Russians, I think, tho' that was not made clear in the telegram. Barthou is pretty sick of Poincaré. P tries to wreck everything. The Russians are quite unreasonable & the Germans are – well, what Germans always are . . .

[52] Leslie Orme Wilson (1876–1955) Conservative MP for Reading 1913–22, Portsmouth S 1922–23. Assistant Secretary to War Cabinet 1918; Parliamentary Secretary to Minister of Shipping 1919–1921; Parliamentary Secretary to Treasury and Chief Conservative Whip 1921–1923. Governor of Bombay 1923–28 and of Queensland 1932–46.

AC5/1/237

13 May 1922
Twitt's Ghyll

My dear Hilda,

. . .

Ireland & Genoa are my chief anxieties as usual. I cannot understand Collins & I understand the P.M. only too well. When the rebels put up a fight against Collins, he negotiates. The more difficulties the P.M. encounters, the more determined he becomes. I think Collins is doing too little. I am afraid of the P.M. doing too much. I have sent the P.M. some words of caution & we have called upon Collins & Griffiths to come over to discuss the situation. As Winston says, the time has come "to put it across them straight". We shall see what the result will be.

AC5/1/238

18 May 1922
11 Downing Street

My dear Ida,

. . . Alas! I am not going to Twitt's Ghyll. The P.M. returns late on Sat night & must meet him &, if he wishes it, give up Sunday to him . . .

I expect that the P.M. will get his Hague proposals[53] through & a six months or 8 months agreement for peace & no propaganda. It will be very thankfully received by the small nations on the Russian border who have lived in a constant state of fear & unrest . . . Hankey's private letters to me from the conference & some that I have seen from Lloyd Graeme[54] are very interesting. For once I think that the Italians have played up, but the P.M. has carried the whole conference on his shoulders.

So we were beaten on Tuesday[55] – & not such a bad thing either –

[53] When the Genoa conference finally collapsed in May, it was decided to postpone the many outstanding issues to a further conference at the Hague in June.

[54] Philip Cunliffe-Lister (1884–1972) Changed his surname from Lloyd-Greame in 1924. Conservative MP for Hendon 1918–35. Parliamentary Secretary Board of Trade 1920–1921; Secretary to Overseas Trade Dept 1921–1922; President Board of Trade 1922–1924 and 1924–1929 and 1931; Colonial Secretary 1931–1935; Air Secretary 1935–1938; Minister Resident West Africa 1942–1944; Minister of Civil Aviation 1944–1945; Chancellor of Duchy of Lancaster and Minister of Materials 1951–1952; Commonwealth Secretary 1952–1955. Created K.B.E. 1920, G.B.E. 1929, Viscount Swinton 1935 and Earl of Swinton 1955.

[55] On 16 May 1922 the government proposal for a 5% levy on teachers for superannuation as part of the Geddes package of economies in education was defeated in the Commons. *House of Commons Debates*, 5 Series, vol.154 cols.263–326.

I think that our retort was neat (I was its author, I may modestly admit) & will not make the teachers or their cause more popular. 'If you won't vote, you must pay' is a strong argument & the greater fear of the taxpayer may still drive out the fear of the Teachers Union. Their agitation has been selfish & dishonest.

AC5/1/240   28 May 1922
                                                    11 Downing Street

My dear Hilda,

. . .

Your garden talk makes me homesick for my flowers. Are they being burnt up? or cut to pieces by hail-stones? or washed out of the ground by thunder storms? or beautiful as I see them in my waking dreams? Well, I suppose I shall know by Thursday next, but I had to abandon my plan of paying them a call yesterday.

Instead – Ireland, always Ireland. What a people! It is impossible to explain them or make them credible. Here have they brought over their draft constitution & for the moment every other complaint or remonstrance is laid aside, for this is a republic scarcely covered with the thinnest monarchical varnish. It is flagrantly at issue with the Treaty in half a dozen vital points. And they seem – nay, they are – genuinely surprised that we view it so gravely. They meant it to be the Treaty – of course the Treaty stretched as far as it can go in their sense – but still the Treaty. If we show them that it is not the Treaty, it shall be changed, but why, oh why, are we so meticulous & pernickety? Can't we be content to get the substance & to allow them to give us the substance in the form in which they can most easily obtain it?

We are miles asunder & they talk as if we had only to cross the street.

Well, the Genoa debate has come & gone. The P.M. owes a fine candle to the Tories & Wickham Steed,[56] for they produced a great reaction in his favour. After all he was the Prime Minister & principal representative of the British Empire. After all he was working honestly & courageously for peace & he had as uphill a task as ever man voluntarily undertook & if we don't like the man & don't altogether trust him & even think that Genoa was a mistake – well, damn it all we are

---

[56] Henry Wickham Steed (1871–1956) Journalist. Foreign Editor, *The Times* 1914–19; Editor 1919–22. Lecturer on Central European History, King's College London, 1925–38. Proprietor and editor, *Review of Reviews* 1923–30. Broadcaster on Overseas Affairs, BBC 1937–47. As editor of Northcliffe's *Times*, Steed pursued a prolonged and virulent campaign against Lloyd George from a pro-French revanchist perspective which reached a climax during Genoa.

Englishmen & we like pluck & we're rather proud of the little man & after all there's a good deal in his ideas & any way it wasn't cricket! And so, the P.M. has a great reception at the station & in the streets, a great triumph in the House & a remarkable gathering in his house at the luncheon on Friday. At which same luncheon by the way I was made to say a few words before they would disperse. As I was going out an M.P. brought up a Press-man. "I only wanted to say that in the opinion of the Press, you are making the best speeches that are made in England today." Imagine how I purred! The speech was only a few sentences round a single idea, not badly turned I think, but ordinary enough, yet compliments have rained upon me from colleagues & others & the Daily Mail (the Daily Mail, my dears!) says it was "the greatest oratorical success of the function. The brilliance of his speeches of late has astonished even his friends." Oh, la la! I suppose it was the fact that they saw that it was an impromptu which thus impressed them. Only my family know how often my speeches are made now "on my legs". Indeed I sometimes think that it is only when I am speaking that my brain will concentrate on the task in hand. It is too full of worries & anxieties at other times – but thanks to Father's early lesson, when I go to bed, I go to sleep. What a debt I owe him for insisting on that.

I spent 2 jolly hours at the Chelsea show ... on Wednesday morning ... nothing very novel but much that was beautiful. Oh, for my garden!

AC5/1/241

4 June 1922
Twitt's Ghyll

My dear Ida,

Yes, I *do* love Ireland & the Irish. I love them so much that there is no language permissible in a letter to a lady in which I can say *how* much I love them. Just when I thought that I was going to get a few days holiday in the open air & attend to my garden, they go & play the giddy goat & ___

Well thank goodness, they were so giddy that there was no difference of opinion among us & we sent them a very polite letter which said – If you don't mend your ways, the game is up! & we sat down to consider what we should do if they refused. But they did not refuse. They accepted *sans phrase* 4 out of our 6 conditions. The fifth is the Privy Council & they gently pointed out that they had some difficulty in agreeing that that was a perfectly impartial Court of Appeal between Ireland & England since Carson, Sumner & Cave (all of whom have denounced the Treaty) were members of it. One for them! & thanks to the folly of these three men our position on this point is a bad one.

The sixth point was the Crown. Here too they argued tho' they do not refuse. Everything disagreeable in Ireland, they say, has been the Crown; – Crown prosecutors, Crown proclamations, Crown this & Crown that.

But while they argue & sign pacts with de Valera & play the fool generally, they report solemnly we are going to keep the Treaty! If this or that is not the Treaty it shall be altered. Certainly if de V. or others of his party join the Govt they must sign the declaration.

Does that mean that the Collins – de Valera pact is already bust? In any other County it would but in Ireland?

I foresee great trouble about the King, for Lloyd George will wish to make it easy for them & I am not sure of some of my Unionist colleagues when the pinch comes not on a general challenge but on some detail or, as I fear, on a number of details & forms & usages.

AC5/1/242

10 June 1922
Twitt's Ghyll

My dear Hilda,

. . .

The Irish are amazing ... the only outstanding matter is the care to be taken of or rather the representation to be secured to the minority on which I am dissatisfied. But I think that Winston & I made progress with them on this point too this morning & they are to meet leading Southern Unionists on Monday under Winston's chairmanship when I hope that some tolerable arrangement will be made, but Midleton (the chief spokesman of the Southern Unionists) is one of the 'set' kind, without elasticity & difficult to do business with.

Meanwhile Belleek & Pettigo[57] will be a good lesson to Collins & a still better lesson to the rebels. But Belfast remains a scandal. The rabble, whether Catholic or Orange, is utterly out of hand, murders & burns indiscriminately & is a disgrace & a danger to the City. After Belleek, Belfast!

[57] In late May 1922 Irish Irregulars invaded the 'Pettigo triangle' and old stone fort of Belleek: a tiny piece of Ulster cut off from access to the North by Lough Erne. Although probably intended to be provocative, it was easily recaptured by British troops.

AC5/1/243

17 June 1922
Twitt's Ghyll

My dear Ida,

. . .

Politics have been quiet – except for Northcliffe's vagaries. His German visit (incognito as you doubtless remember) consisted of *two* days spent in General Godley's[58] garden at Cologne. He never budged from there . . . Rumour has it that he is off his head[59] & that Rothermere has gone out to see him.

. . .

I am to meet Poincaré at lunch at the P.M.s on Monday. I would much sooner tread on his toe or fling my wine glass in his face. Drat his impudence! Did you see that he told the Senate the other day that our troubles were due to our bad finance & unwise use of our raw material? What next I wonder! He is impossible.

On 22 June 1922 Field Marshal Sir Henry Wilson, now an Ulster MP, was assassinated in daylight by two IRA gunmen on the steps of his home in Eaton Place while dressed in full uniform. The outrage prompted a wave of indignation against the government. When Chamberlain visited Lady Wilson she greeted him with the word 'Murderer' and initially expressed the desire that no members of the government should attend the funeral.[60] These events were a bitter blow to Chamberlain and in their immediate aftermath his health again collapsed. Although he remained in the country insulated from political worries for the next three weeks, even after his return in mid-July he confessed that he remained 'pulled down & very easily tired, so that I feel my political work & worries more than I should otherwise'.[61] When the Commons rose for the Summer Recess on 4 August, few realised that when it reassembled it would be under a different Prime Minister.

---

[58] General Sir Alexander John Godley (1867–1957) Military Secretary to Secretary of State for War 1920–22: C-in-C Army of the Rhine 1922–24: GOC-in-C Southern Command 1924–28; Governor Gibraltar 1928–33.
[59] Northcliffe's nephew claims he had contracted syphilis: a condition which manifested itself in increasing signs of megalomania during the war. By 1922 his dementia had taken control and he died on 14 August 1922. C. King, *Strictly Speaking* (1969), 57.
[60] R. Blake, *The Unknown Prime Minister*, 440–1.
[61] A. Chamberlain to Ida, 22 July 1922, AC5/1/246.

AC5/1/244

25 June 1922
11 Downing Street

My dear Hilda,

I have not the heart to write to you this week about politics. Henry Wilson's murder & all the circumstances connected with it besiege my thoughts & I cannot get from them. My one chance was to get down to Twitt's Ghyll & work hard in the garden. I did actually get away on Friday night but just as I was setting to work to dig on Saturday morning I got a summons to return to town, so here we are again & I have had conferences yesterday & today ...

...
Good bye, my dear. I really cannot write a letter. It makes me think & think & think all round what I would most wish to forget.

AC5/1/245

15 July 1922
Twitt's Ghyll

My dear Ida,

Thanks for all your good wishes. I got up for the first time on Monday evening & drove down here on Tuesday. Today I have done light gardening for the first time & feel myself practically all right again though still weak & easily tired. Tomorrow afternoon I motor back to town ...

I have read no official papers since my illness ... So I have no political news for you. I *hear* that it is unlikely that Northcliffe will recover. My physician met him at some function before he went to Switzerland & told Ivy then that he saw unmistakable signs of insanity. I can express no sorrow if he is removed, for he has done an infinitude of harm & would do more as long as he could control his papers.

AC5/1/247

8 August 1922
11 Downing Street

My dear Hilda,

... I am kept prisoner in London by this abominable Conference. I was so tired & so much in need of a rest that though I knew that I ought to stop for it I had made up my mind to go away unless directly asked to stay, but when the P.M. said 'It's too big a decision for me to take alone' what could I do but return to London on Sunday night in time for a dinner with the Belgians to which he asked me. I expect that I shall not get away till Saturday.

...

I hate this Conference. I don't like the atmosphere of it. Poincaré is bent on mad courses & is so far impervious to reason. The longer a reasonable settlement is delayed, the more difficult it becomes & the less shall we ever get out of Germany, whilst if he is not careful, he will drive out Wirth[62] & hand over Germany to extreme socialists or to reactionists – possibly to both in turn. But then tho' the Balfour note[63] is reason expressed in perfect language I was (this is very secret) wholly & deeply opposed to the policy embodied in it. I think that we have permanently alienated Harding's Administration & strengthened American opinion opposed to doing anything. On the other hand we have disappointed our Allies, abandoned the beau rôle & given France the best argument she can have for her folly:- 'Since America presses you, you press us. Since you press us, we must press Germany!' And it all seems to me so futile. We have said our say &, as we feel, made an irrefutable case, & the only result is that America will be the more exacting, France the more unreasonable & of money we shall not see a sou.

You see that I am gloomy & cross at being kept in London.

AC5/1/249

24 September 1922
Westbourne
Edgbaston

My dear Ida,

...

We had a very pleasant, very busy & very useful Sunday at Chequers last week, discussing both the Turkish & the home situations. Then after three busy days in London, we came here on Thursday afternoon ...

...

Politics continue sufficiently perplexing. The P.M.'s speech to the

[62] Joseph Wirth (1879–1956) German Centrist politician. Minister of Finance 1920; Chancellor May 1921–November 1922; Minister of Interior 1930–31. Left Germany when Nazis obtained power.

[63] The Balfour Note of 1 August 1922 complained that the USA was demanding that Britain should fund her debt to the US immediately but Britain's allies must also meet their obligations to her in turn. Britain would claim from Europe no more than the USA demanded from her. Chamberlain and Horne wished to placate the USA and asked for their dissent from the Note to be recorded formally. CAB 42(22), 25 July 1922 CAB 23/30. This led to a further cooling of Anglo-American relations.

Press will tell you our policy. That of France is "Funk & Cringe". Poincaré has behaved shamefully – I had almost said treacherously. He has abandoned an Ally in the face of the enemy, & he was madder than the Mad Hatter when told so by Curzon. He raged up & down the room shrieked & roared & refused to allow C. to say a word until at last C. left the room. After reflection P. came out & apologised & C. withdrew the word 'abandon' – the sting of which was in its truth – they set to work again. C. has done very well, behaving with great self-restraint, dignity & firmness, but it was an incredible scene. And as to the facts, just consider. The positions were occupied by the Allies in common & held by a joint decision. When the Greeks threatened the Chatalja lines held by the French, Harrington [sic][64] at once warned the Greeks off & sent British troops up alongside the French. When Kemal[65] won his victory, Poincaré replied to us that he agreed that the neutral zones must be protected, & at Harrington's request, the French General sent a company of French soldiers to Chanak to show the flag alongside the British. But, *without informing us*, P. ordered them by telegraph to be withdrawn as well as any French soldiers at Ismid where the Allied Generals had planned that the French should hold about 1/3rd of the line.

Was my language too strong? I *think* we shall secure our aims with a war, but the situation is still obscure. I am sure that our only chance to avoid war was to make our position perfectly plain both to Kemal & Poincaré. P. has got himself pledged up to the neck to the Turks & is now frightened at the completeness of their success. The Turks use & despise him. They are very angry with us – & respect us.

I cannot now deal with domestic issues, but here is my calculation for the next election:

Labour	200 – 250 ⎤	against either Coalition
Wee Free	60 – 40 ⎦	or Conservative
Ulster	13 – 13	not to be counted on
	273 – 303	

out of a House of 613 or thereabouts.

Lloyd Georgians   50 – 60

[64] General Sir Charles Harington (1872–1940) Deputy Chief of Imperial General Staff 1918–20; GOC-in-C Army of the Black Sea 1920–21; Allied Occupation Forces in Turkey 1921–23; Northern Command 1923–27; Western Command, India 1927–31; Aldershot Command 1931–33. Governor and C-in-C Gibraltar, 1933–38.

[65] Kemal Atatürk (1881–1938) Member of Young Turk reform movement. In 1919 led national resistance to Greek invasion, established a provisional government in Ankara (April 1920) and led Turks to victory in War of Independence which resulted in expulsion of the Greeks, deposition of Sultan and establishment of a republic (in 1923) with himself as first President.

No Govt is possible without coalition. No Coalition on present lines & *in present conditions* is possible with Co-Libs except under a Ll.G. premiership.

And the Natl Union in Novr may declare
   (a) against coalition of any sort
   (b)   ,,   ,,   except under a Unionist P.M.
What a kettle of fish! Envy me my job!

During the summer of 1922 a strong feeling developed against the continuation of the Coalition. Three months later this culminated in the Carlton Club revolt.[66] *During these final months of the Coalition Chamberlain demonstrated his most noble personal qualities of loyalty to his Prime Minister and a granitic steadfastness of purpose towards what he perceived to be the true national rather than purely personal or party interest. Unfortunately for himself and the Coalition, however, he also displayed the very worst features of his leadership style and the political aloofness and arrogance upon which it was built – particularly at times of greatest personal stress. In such circumstances, his loyalty made him appear to be too much in Lloyd George's pocket and so mesmerized by the Welsh Wizard that he was either unable or unwilling to defend the interests of his party. As a Liberal-Unionist himself, he reinforced such suspicions with what was perceived to be an undue sensitivity to the sensibilities of the Coalition Liberals at the expense of the partisan passions within his own ranks. Personal reticence, misguided loyalty and a desire to spare the Prime Minister's feelings, thus made him play down animosity towards Lloyd George personally on 17 September when the Coalition leaders decided to hold an early election. Thereafter he perpetuated the error and its damaging effects by never explaining publicly – or even really tackling – the question of when Lloyd George would be replaced by a Conservative Prime Minister. The ability to see the bigger picture, generosity of spirit towards allies and loyalty to a leader were all noble qualities, but they were not the stuff of which Tory leaders needed to be made in such difficult circumstances. In the absence of more steel, the Conservatives looked elsewhere for a leader who would defend their interests and articulate their burgeoning partisanship.*

Such failings in his attitude toward Lloyd George and his following were compounded by Chamberlain's posture towards the discontents expressed within his own party. For all his apparent weakness in January, Chamberlain had a fixed and inflexible view of leadership. During his own extended apprenticeship he had developed a highly-tuned sense of loyalty to the Conservative Party and its leaders. Chamberlain felt justified in making the same demands of loyalty and unquestioning obedience upon his followers. Unlike Law, for Chamberlain, leadership consisted of exercising authority and giving orders rather than synthesizing opinion and explaining

---

[66] For these events see K.O. Morgan, *Consensus and Disunity*, Chapter 14; M. Cowling, *The Impact of Labour*, Chapter 11; M. Kinnear, *The Fall of Lloyd George*, Chapters 5–6.

actions. Throughout he dismissed his critics with the claim that the Conservative leaders were in agreement and it was the duty of others to follow their lead without equivocation. Those who did not, like Gideon Murray, were shunned, ostracised and crushed.[67] *Worse still, this understanding of the nature of leadership stemmed from a 'superiority complex'*[68] *borne of intellectual arrogance. As early as March 1922 Chamberlain had made it clear that if the party would not follow him, it should look elsewhere for leadership.*[69] *Still suffering from this 'hallucination of indispensability' in October, his rash insistence that the party should accept an early election or find itself a new leader was a crucial factor in uniting those who brought about his downfall.*[70]

At almost every stage in the final crisis of the Coalition Chamberlain mishandled the personal and political situation. Despite repeated and unambiguous warnings from party managers, on 13 October Chamberlain declared himself a 'convinced and unrepentant coalitionist'. He also denounced as 'criminal' folly any attempt to allow personal and party prejudice to sacrifice the national interest before a 'common foe'.[71] *During the next six days he became brutally intransigent. The decision to summon a meeting at the Carlton Club on 19 October was prompted by the desire to coerce the party and pre-empt the rebels: a strategy dictated by his high-handed belief that the greatest sanction the leadership commanded was their cohesion and near monopoly of talent.*[72] *Confronting his junior ministerial critics on 17 October he was 'definite to the point of being uncompromising' and gave the impression that 'he seemed to feel that it was not consonant with his position to seek to induce the recalcitrant group to join him. Rather it was for them to offer loyal obedience. It was not a time for cajolery – it was the occasion for the whip'.*[73] *This is a fitting epitaph to Chamberlain's own culpability for the personal disaster which followed. Even his uncompromising final speech at the Carlton Club meeting was insensitive in tone, inordinately long and ill-judged in its assertive demand to retain the Coalition without even a hint that in private he had already decided that this did not necessarily mean the perpetuation of Lloyd George's leadership.*[74] *The same combination of*

---

[67] See, for example, A. Chamberlain to J. Gretton, 21 February 1922, AC 33/1/11; G. Murray, *A Man's Life*, 259.

[68] Jones Diary, 18 September 1932, reporting Baldwin, *A Diary with Letters, 1931–50* (1954), 61; Earl Winterton, *Orders of the Day*, 115.

[69] A. Chamberlain to A. Steel-Maitland, 23 March 1923, AC35/1/49.

[70] A. Chamberlain to Birkenhead, 15 October 1922, R. Blake, *The Unknown Prime Minister*, 451. Also Bridgeman Diary, July 1922, Bridgeman MSS II fol.69–73; A. Chamberlain to L. Wilson, 12 October 1922, AC 33/2/36; Amery Diary, 10 October 1922, *The Leo Amery Diaries*, 293.

[71] Chamberlain at Birmingham, *Birmingham Daily Post*, 14 October 1922.

[72] A. Chamberlain to Birkenhead, 15 October 1922.

[73] Ernest Pollock memorandum, 'The Fall of the Coalition Government under Lloyd George in October 1922', n.d. (?1922) corrected 14 September 1931, Hanworth MSS d.432 fol.157–8 (Bodleian Library, Oxford).

[74] For Chamberlain's speech see *Gleanings and Memoranda* , LVI, November 1922, 489. For his view of future leadership see A. Chamberlain to Pike Pease, 20 October and to L. Wilson, 22 October 1922, AC 32/2/114; AC 33/2/95. For criticism of the speech and

pique, pride and a misplaced sense of authority prompted the final folie de grandeur *as Chamberlain obstinately turned the meeting into a vote of confidence in his leadership. In so doing, he compelled those present to choose between either loyalty to the Coalition and its leadership (without any indication of future change) or loyalty to their party without its current leaders. The Conservatives chose the latter by the substantial margin of 187 votes to 87. As Younger noted on the following day. 'He thoroughly deserves the defeat he had sustained'.*[75]

It was perhaps a measure of just how remote the Conservative leadership had become from party opinion about the unpopularity of the Coalition and their fears about a fundamental loss of Conservative identity that they appeared to be 'staggered' by defeat and incensed by its perceived disloyalty.[76] *For Chamberlain, Wilson's apostasy had not only 'astonished but cut to the quick' as an example of the disloyalty of the party machine to its elected leader:*[77] *a gross betrayal Chamberlain could never either forget or forgive.*[78] *Yet it says much about Chamberlain that he could never comprehend that after his repeated warnings of Coalition unpopularity were rejected with a rebuke for faithlessness, Wilson had felt compelled to speak and vote with the rebels at the Carlton Club because he was 'convinced that no other course was left open if [they] were to avoid a split which might take years to heal'.*[79] *That this obstinate and arrogant conception of leadership had forced party leaders like Younger and Wilson into a course they found personally repugnant*[80] *was a notion which simply eluded Chamberlain.*[81] *As his letters to his sisters demonstrate, in the immediate aftermath of humiliation, resignation and defeat, however, it was enough for Chamberlain to take refuge in bitterness and a sense of righteous betrayal: modest enough sources of consolation, even when spiced with a certain malicious*

its tone see Amery Diary, 19 October 1922, *The Leo Amery Diaries*, 299; Jones Diary, 19 October 1922, *Whitehall Diary*, I, 210–11; Lord Hemingford, *Backbencher and Chairman: Some Parliamentary Reminiscences*, (1946), 42.

[75] G. Younger to J. Strachey, 20 October 1922, Strachey MSS S/19/4/26b. (House of Lords Record Office). Davidson recorded the result as 185 to 88 with one abstention while Chamberlain's record shows 186 to 85 with three abstentions.

[76] Pollock memorandum 'The Fall of the Coalition ...' fol.163; Sanders Diary, 19 October 1922; Headlam Diary, 20 October 1922 reporting Baldwin, Headlam MSS D/He/19 fol.293.

[77] A. Chamberlain to L. Wilson, 22 November 1922, AC 33/2/95. For Chamberlain's special anger at Wilson's intervention at the Carlton Club see Amery Diary, 19 October 1922, *The Leo Amery Diaries*, 300.

[78] See, for example, A. Chamberlain to Hilda, 1 June 1930, AC5/1/503.

[79] L. Wilson to Lord Salisbury, 25 November 1922, Salisbury MSS 103/123 (Hatfield House). In exasperation Wilson even threatened to repudiate the leadership if the party was denied an opportunity to express its view but Chamberlain told him to await the outcome of the crisis. See Wilson to Chamberlain and reply, 11 and 12 October 1922, AC33/2/43.

[80] See, for example, G. Younger to Sanders, 25 September 1922, Bayford MSS III; Younger to H.A. Gwynne 8 October 1922, Gwynne MSS 22 (Bodleian Library, Oxford courtesy of Vice-Admiral Sir Ian Hogg); Wilson to Salisbury 25 November 1922 Salisbury MSS 103/123; Sir Alexander Leith at Newcastle, *Morning Post*, 13 November 1922.

[81] See, Pollock memorandum. fol.156.

delight at the potential discomfiture and difficulties of those who had so unceremoniously displaced him.

AC5/1/250   18 November 1922
                                                    Twitt's Ghyll

My dear Ida,

I owe countless letters to you & Hilda but I have been too busy, too tired or too *bruised* to write. Now that the fight is over I scarcely know where to begin ...

It is splendid to have all B'ham again, winning back Duddeston where Hiley[82] succeeds Hallas[83] who ratted. The one disappointment is Neville's majority. He was disquieted by its smallness but I do not yet know whether it was caused by slackness on the part of his friends from over confidence or, as I rather suppose, from the Socialists having made greater progress than was supposed. They told Harvey of the Mail before the election that they were going to win four seats – Neville's & mine for certain & probably Deritend & Kings Norton. Ladywood was where they first got a hold, but Neville & Annie had nursed it so assiduously ("There wasn't a dog-hanging" Hewins[84] told Ivy, "that they didn't attend) that I had thought that his would be one of the most decisive victories & his appointment as P[ost] M[aster] G[eneral] gave him additional prestige. It is a disappointing result of all this effort & I am really sorry & a little disturbed.

West B'ham on the other hand was a real triumph & largely, very largely a personal one for Ivy & me. She came & saw & conquered & as soon as I got to work I felt the ground solidifying under my feet. But before-hand I was very anxious. My people were thoroughly frightened. Hewins cheerfully reminded me that every leader lost his seat because he could not attend to it & I was told that my position was undermined by my absence, by concentrated street corner work of the Socialists, by industrious circulation of lies about "the Mesopotamian scandal' &c. &c. &c. & that the Socialists would turn their greatest effort onto beating me. Cheerful was it not? So much so that I told Ivy

[82] Ernest Varill Hiley (1868–1949) Town Clerk Birmingham 1908; Deputy Director of National Service 1917. Conservative MP for Birmingham (Duddeston) November 1922 until retired in November 1923.
[83] Eldred Hallas (1870–1926) Trade Union Secretary and Birmingham City Councillor 1911–1918. MP for Birmingham (Duddeston) December 1918–October 1922 elected as pro-Coalition National Democratic Party member with Conservative support but took the Labour Whip from October 1919.
[84] R.G. Hewins, Chairman of Midlands Liberal Unionist Association.

that if I was beaten I should go out of politics. But to Hewins I said: I am now free & I too will concentrate. Also I am a biggish man when I get to work & if I get a hearing I think that my speeches will tell. So I told him to find a patriotic publican with a clientele from the Ring. They need not be politicians but they must have a sportsman's love of fair play & be determined to secure it. Yes, Hewins could do that, but there would be a free fight at my first meeting & it would be broken up. "I don't mind that", said I, "if the right heads are broken too – & thoroughly!" So we took our precautions & only one meeting, the second of the last evening but one, was even disturbed ... Hewins also put all the outvoters he could to vote for me rather than in any other division & got extra workers in from Moseley. But at bottom what did it was solid argument, personality & the revival of the old West B'ham feeling. [A poster with 'You voted for Joe: Vote for Austen'] was one of my best bits of electioneering & I think & many now say that I have not only inherited but made personal to myself much of the old Chamberlain feeling. But why anyone who lives in such slums should not be a Socialist, a Communist or a Red Revolutionary I am at a loss to say. In all St. Pauls there isn't a resident elector above the smallest class of shopkeeper & All Saints tho' a little better equipped with leaders is the more socialist of the two, or was believed to be so.

Well, I am awfully pleased with that. You will not be surprised to learn that I declined the assistance of Amery[85] & more particularly of Steel-Maitland![86]

Yes, I'm glad that Leslie Wilson is out, & I chuckle every time I think of Boscawens[87] defeat. I hope that my speech in London helped to defeat him. It was meant to & I am assured that it did. He rallied at the last moment & then died. I don't mind an honest difference but I dislike men who do the dirty.

I was not surprised by Neville's decision [to join Law's government]

[85] Leopold Charles Maurice Stennett Amery (1873–1955) Conservative MP for Birmingham (South later, Sparkbrook) 1911–45. PUS for Colonies 1919–1921; Parliamentary and Financial Secretary to Admiralty 1921–1922; First Lord of Admiralty, 1922–1924; Colonial Secretary, 1924–1929 and Dominion Secretary 1925–1929; Secretary of State for India 1940–1945. A lifelong ardent tariff reformer and imperialist.

[86] Arthur Herbert Drummond Ramsay-Steel-Maitland (1876–1935) Conservative MP for Birmingham East 1910–18; Birmingham, Erdington 1918–29; Tamworth 1929–35. PUS for Colonies 1915–1917; Joint PUS for Foreign Affairs and Parliamentary Secretary to Board of Trade (Overseas Trade Dept) 1917–1919; Minister of Labour 1924–June 1929. Created baronet 1917.

[87] Arthur Sackville Trevor Griffith-Boscawen (1865–1946) Conservative MP for Tunbridge 1892–1906; Dudley 1910–21; Taunton 1921–22. Parliamentary Secretary to Ministry of Pensions 1916–1919; Parliamentary Secretary to Ministry of Agriculture 1919–1921; Minister of Agriculture 1921–1922; Minister of Health 1922–1923 but resigned after his defeat in Mitcham by-election, March 1923. Knighted 1911.

but it *hurt* awfully. But we both cared more for one another than for anything that politics could bring. When he found that I could not say that I wished him to join Bonar or that by joining he would help me, he said that he should refuse but that having thus refused to serve under both L.G. & Bonar he would feel that he had no future & would get out as soon as he could with fairness to his constituents. What more could affection offer? And equally of course I could not accept such a sacrifice, so I changed my attitude & said 'accept' & telephoned the same word next morning. So I have learned the depth of his affection & you need not fear that your brothers or their wives will quarrel.

What a tragedy it is for us two that L.G. should have done the dirty by him & Bonar by me. I am not going to quarrel with Bonar, but I won't serve with him. I am told that he & the Party wish that I should resume the Privy Seal & the Leadership of the House, but he won't offer it to me because he knows that I should refuse, & I should refuse first because I am sure that to enter the Govt now would mean for me a loss of self-respect & public credit, secondly because I could not be comfortable with him after the way he has behaved to me & thirdly (if a thirdly be needed) because 'Love me, love my dog!' I won't go back without my friends.

I saw him yesterday & had a quite friendly chat. At the end he said 'Well, one thing more, Austen, I want to say. I don't ask for an answer, but I hope that the time will come & come soon when you will feel that I have been your friend'. And all I said was: 'Don't ask me for an answer I could not say that now'. Really I believe that I feel my wings sprouting! I hear that Arthur Balfour at Whittinghame was deep in condemnation of his action as one of "those things that gentlemen don't do". Even at this interview he tried to make mischief between F.E & me, but as F.E. & I had been very frank with one another he told me nothing that I did not know & with which I was not perfectly satisfied.

AC5/1/251   20 November 1922
                                                        Twitt's Ghyll

My dear Hilda,

I believe that I promised to write more comments to you on the situation but I wrote some 20 or 25 letters yesterday & my writing zeal has passed. The fact is that there is too much to tell if I am really to summarise or explain the whole story & it is not a very pleasant one for me to ponder on.

You know, I think, that in July I called all the Unionists Cabinet Ministers together. I had previously seen the Under-Secretaries who for the most part were very restless about the continuation of the Coalition under Lloyd George & I placed their views before the Cabinet Ministers. They probably knew mine but without expressing them I invited my colleagues to speak. They *unanimously* advised that it would be madness to break up the Coalition. I agreed but we decided to meet again in October to see if there was any change in the situation. This was conveyed to the Under-Secs who then asked to meet the Cabinet Ministers.[88] They repeated their doubts & dislikes. Then F.E. scolded & browbeat them with an intellectual arrogance which nearly produced a row there & then & did infinite harm. (I remonstrated very courteously but very strongly with him next day). Balfour spoke persuasively but it is astonishing how little weight he now carries with the Party. I spoke gravely in the same sense.

On Sept 16th[89] L.G. Winston, F.E., Horne, W-Evans & I met at Checkers [sic] & discussed the whole position. I told them that I had seen Malcolm Fraser,[90] our Chief Agent. Younger & he calculated that if Natl Libs & Unionists pulled together (the most favourable assumption) the result of a careful survey of the constituencies showed that Labour would get at least 200 seats at a General Election & might get 250. Asquith would get 50; L.G. say 40 or 50. In all 300 to 350 out of a House of 615 of whom 13 would be Irish. If we split with the National Libs, Labour might get 300 or even a majority of the whole House. Therefore we must not quarrel with Lloyd George.

But here came the rub. Some 80 members or candidates of our Party were already pledged against any Coalition & more would be getting daily pledged under pressure from their Associations unless L.G. would retire & allow the Coalition to be reformed under a Unionist. They were not really against Coalition but they distrusted L.G.

Therefore, I must get rid of L.G. – induce him to retire – & keep enough of his colleagues to preserve the Liberal support that they could bring.

The whole of this I told frankly to the group at Checkers, only representing the feeling against L.G.'s premiership as the result of the natural desire of the largest section to have their own leader in the first place & slurring over, tho' not wholly omitting the purely personal

---

[88] Chamberlain met almost all the Unionist Junior and non-Cabinet ministers in his room in the Commons on 20 July. The second meeting was on 3 August in Birkenhead's room at the Lords.

[89] The meeting actually took place on Sunday 17 September, Petrie, *Life and Letters*, II, 196–8.

[90] (John) Malcolm Fraser (1878–1949) Formerly editor of the *Standard* and *Daily Express*. In the Conservative reorganisation of 1911 Fraser became head of the press bureau at Central Office before becoming Principal Agent, 1920–March 1923. Vice-Chairman, Conservative Party, 1937–8. Also Deputy Director of Airship Production at the Admiralty, 1918–19. Knighted 1919; created Baronet 1921.

aspect. I added that M.F. said that when the Natl Union met on Nov 15th it would carry a resolution against Coalition if the Die-hards were reasonable in their speeches unless Balfour & I & F.E. &c went down en masse & argued our case with them. On this statement of the case I added that delay seemed to me certain to result in a bad split, that we should not get through the Autumn Session without defeat & that I was in favour of immediate dissolution. The only question was: were we to go as a Govt as we had decided in July or not? In any case there must be reorganisation after the Election & the Unionist Party must have a larger share of the offices. If they decided to go to the Election as a Govt I was prepared to take my risks but they must clearly realise theirs. I thought F.E. & Horne too sanguine & I warned L.G. that I might fail to carry the Party & be unable to deliver the goods. And to my Unionist colleagues I said that if I tendered this advice to the Party & they rejected it, I should of course cease to be & indeed refuse to continue as 'Leader' & that might be the end of my career. They must consider what their positions would be.

L.G. at once said that he would not accept such a sacrifice from me if that were likely to be the result. Worthy was the least sanguine, but all seemed to think the contingency impossible. F.E. & Horne added that in such a case they would of course go out with me. After two long talks we decided to play out our hand & dissolve at the first moment the Turkish crisis would allow. (It was the Saturday & Sunday when Curzon went out of town without a word to any of us & informed us by telephone in response to a most urgent personal message from me that he didn't propose to return till Tuesday because his establishment at Carlton House Terrace was not monté!

If the others had felt success to be as doubtful as I did, I think that L.G. would have retired, but he is naturally sanguine & F.E. Horne & Winston were very optimistic.

On some date between this & Monday 25 we plus Curzon (who was away ill at the time of the July meeting) dined at Winston's & again discussed our problem, reaching the same conclusion. Curzon, appealed to after hearing the views of the others, said: "If that's your game, I'm in it."[91]

Balfour on his return from Geneva entirely agreed.

Meanwhile Younger & Leslie Wilson said they were dismayed at our decision. I rejoined that I had satisfied myself at Checkers that their policy – to get rid of L.G. & to retain the support of his followers was impossible. L.G. was not intending to retire then tho' I thought it

---

[91] Chamberlain's account is confused on this point. Although accounts vary, Curzon said this at Churchill's dinner on either 9 or 10 October 1922. See, Lord Ronaldshay to A. Chamberlain, 12 December 1927, AC 54/4/26.

probable that if he came back with only 50 or 60 followers he would then say that the new Parlt was not his & hand over to me. But if we turned him out now – well, think of the articles in the Northcliffe & Rothermere press & in the Morning Post. Think of the shouts of the Die-hards &c. We couldn't help its being a great humiliation & his friends must all go with him or lose every shred of reputation.

Y. & L.S. only wrung their hands & lamented – & proceeded to work against me.

On the 25th I again had all the Unionist Cabinet Ministers & again all agreed except Baldwin[92] who clearly showed his dislike but did not definitely refuse assent. He got no support.

On Oct 15 we again dined at Winston's. Curzon had a row on with L.G. about the conduct of foreign affairs & refused to come at the last moment. The wind had been getting up in the interval & he saw which way it was blowing! But Leslie Wilson was there. He had been pressing hard that I should either wait for the meeting of the Natl Union or call a special meeting. I refused saying that this would certainly split the Party in two for I & the colleagues who agreed with me would have to attend & debate the question & you couldn't debate in a gathering of 3 or 4 thousand without bringing out temper on both sides & in the end we might be nearly equally divided & at best there would be a large minority with heightened tempers, confirmed prejudices & a resolve to continue the struggle throughout the constituencies. At Winston's dinner I offered a compromise. I would summon all the M.P.s to the Carlton. I asked Leslie point blank after others had spoken: 'Now are we all agreed? Leslie do you accept that?' & he replied 'Yes, I accept that.'

Next morning I had the Unionist Cabinet again. Curzon then demurred to an immediate election (not to Coalition) on the ground of the Lausanne Conference.[93] We said that we could get it over before Lausanne & that in any case an election was inevitable, for as things were we should be tripped up over some minor matter in the autumn session & it wasn't safe to meet Parlt without a fresh mandate.

Baldwin this time definitely declared his policy to be to tell L.G. that he must go. Nobody supported him tho' Boscawen hedged somewhat on Curzon's line.

That afternoon we all saw the Under-Secs again. I explained our

[92] Stanley Baldwin (1867–1947) Conservative MP for Worcestershire Bewdley 1903–1937. Joint Financial Secretary to Treasury 1917–1921; President Board of Trade 1921–1922; Chancellor of Exchequer 1922–1923; Prime Minister 1923–24, 1924–29, 1935–37; Lord President of the Council 1931–35. Created K.G. and Earl Baldwin of Bewdley 1937.

[93] The Lausanne Conference was planned to secure a new treaty with Turkey to replace the shattered Treaty of Sèvres. In the event, it did not meet until mid-November 1922.

decision & the reasons. Led by Amery who had summoned about 20 of them to his house they were in revolt. Amery was trucculent [sic] & uncompromising. He has been discontented ever since he was not made Colonial Sec. in succession to Milner & has not hesitated to ask first for Cabinet rank & then for a Privy Councillorship before I thought his parliamentary position justified it.

The followed two hectic days of comings & goings, collogueings, deputations & interviews. Bonar could not make up his mind & actually did not make it up or did not think that he had made it up till 6 on the evening before the Carlton meeting. But I knew that he had decided to take this opportunity & his action was decisive as to the line of my speech. I was perfectly conciliatory in tone but as you saw wholly unyielding. I feared a nearly balanced decision & even more a small majority & the meeting was evidently against me, so I did not seek to obscure the difference or to find any compromise.

There, that will do for the present. You had better keep these letters. The record, imperfect as it is ... may be useful to me.

AC5/1/252   21 November 1922
                                                        Twitt's Ghyll

My dear Ida,

Here is the third & last of the sending & then I shall have made up for my long silence & told you all that can be told without sitting down with all my papers before me to write history.

What was the result of the revolution finished at the Carlton Club? It is of course nonsense to describe it as a Belgravia intrigue or a revolt in the kitchen. It was first & foremost the natural result of eight years rule by one Govt which had to bear the blame not only for their mistakes but for all that went to make the general discontents; 2*ndly* of the Irish Treaty & of the consequent Die-hard movement which became formidable when it rallied round Salisbury[94] & afforded an organisation for the discontented; 3*rdly* of the growth of party feeling & party jealousy in the machine which is far too much run by old men & paid agents; lastly of the defects of L.G.'s character.

Well, the first result was to relieve the Party of all old debts &

[94] James Edward Hubert Gascoyne-Cecil (1861–1947) Conservative MP for Darwen 1885–1892; Rochester 1893–1903. Under-Secretary for Foreign Affairs 1900–1903; Lord Privy Seal 1903–1905 and 1924–1929; President Board of Trade, 1905; Chancellor of the Duchy of Lancaster 1922–1923; Lord President of Council 1922–1924. Conservative leader in Lords 1925–31. Styled Viscount Cranborne 1868–1903, succeeded his father as 4th Marquess of Salisbury in 1903. Created G.C.V.O. 1909 and K.G. 1917.

responsibilities. A new firm started with a clear slate and much enthusiasm.

Next since I & others had stood by L.G. he determined to stand by us. Except for half a dozen reprisal cases he opposed no Conservative, steadily refused the pressure of the Manchester Guardian & others to make a bid for the leadership of a reunited Liberal Party & was, all things considered, very moderate in speech.

Third, the Labour Party played straight into B. L.'s hands by their manifesto. B.L. struck the right note when he said that the change in Govt would be rather of temperament than of policy & when he promised tranquillity – tho' as L.G. pertinently said tranquillity depends on the sea & not on the ship. By the way I have heard a curious story that Sydney [sic] Webb[95] said that the Labour Party were not yet ready for office & that he did not mean them to have it; that they must work off the capital levy some time & now was the time to be defeated on it & get rid of it & then – next time _____ !

Anyway Labour did less well than most good judges expected, but observe: in Scotland we should not have kept more than half a dozen seats without complete cooperation. There the coalition in fact continued. In all the miners & railway men's seats we fared badly. In such places even the most extreme communists & Reds were elected rather than a Liberal or Unionist. Again everywhere there was a bitter extremist element out for revolution, men & women alike. In Dundee, Winston said, they were 'spewed out of the slums – the kind of women who would spit in your wife's face!' A dangerous element, & new, I think – bitter, fanatical, ready for violence if they saw a chance. Not to be neglected those slums!

More serious. All the opposition candidates in B'ham with perhaps two exceptions were miserable creatures. Dunstan,[96] Frank Smith[97] &c were such men as we might have chosen to secure our victory. Yet look

---

[95] Sidney James Webb (1859–1947) Labour MP for Seaham 1922–29. President Board of Trade 1924; Dominion and Colonial Secretary 1929–1930; Colonial Secretary 1930–1931. Created Baron Passfield 1929.

[96] Dr R. Dunstan was Labour candidate against Neville Chamberlain in Birmingham Ladywood in 1922. Despite the confidence of both Chamberlain brothers Neville's majority fell from nearly 7000 in 1918 to less than 2500 against a more formidable candidate than his predecessor. At the 1924 election Dunstan moved to contest West Birmingham against Austen Chamberlain where he polled 7000 votes.

[97] Francis Samuel Smith (1854–1940) Unsuccessfully contested Hammersmith 1892; Attercliffe Sheffield 1894; Tradeston Glasgow 1895; Taunton 1909; Croydon 1909; Chatham 1910; Balham & Tooting 1918 before contesting unsuccessfully Austen Chamberlain's West Birmingham seat in 1922 and 1923. Unsuccessful Nuneaton 1924 but became Labour MP for that seat May 1929–October 1931. PPS to Lansbury as First Commissioner of Works October 1930.

how they polled! What would have happened if we had had a Clynes[98] or a Thomas to fight?

Lastly: Unionists polled rather over 5,000,000 votes. 'Labour' polled over 4,000,000 on a bad programme, against a new Govt a *united* press & a general reaction towards Conservatism.

Ça domise à penser. What will happen four years hence when Labour has learned wisdom & taught & organised continuously & then the Conservative Party must carry alone the whole burden of four year's disappointments & discontents?

And what will happen meanwhile? B.L.'s health is none too good. He has never before gone into action without a stronger man beside him. There is the first uncertainty. Then his young men may blossom out, but Curzon is weak & ill; Baldwin had the reputation both in business & in the Treasury of being unable to take a decision: Amery is a poor parliamentarian, very unhandy so far in spite of his brains. Peel[99] is good, Salisbury & Devonshire[100] are good too in their several ways but it is rather of the H. of C. that I am thinking. Lloy[d] Graeme is the most promising of his Cabinet & Neville outside it, but they do not look a strong team. Still I give them their four years or three at least, but I think that they will go slowly downhill.

Meanwhile I shall take things easily, attending only when interested, dining out & not sitting up when late hours rule. I do not mean to attack the Govt or to form one out of a central party, but I shall try to keep the way open for a new coalition if such becomes necessary, as I think it will, by not letting go of Lloyd George. He means to act in the same way, but will he & can he? Broad is the way of temptation above all to so restless & so sanguine a man as he is. In any case I have made my position clear to him. We dined at Sassoons[101] last Friday. L.G., F.E., Winston, Worthy, Goulding, Bull,[102] Macnamara, Guest & one or

[98] John Robert Clynes (1869–1949) Labour MP for Manchester NE (Platting after 1918) 1906–31 and 1935–45. Parliamentary Secretary to Minister of Food 1917–1918; Food Controller 1918–1919; Lord Privy Seal 1924; Home Secretary 1929–1931.

[99] William Robert Wellesley Peel (1867–1937) Conservative MP for Manchester (South) 1900–1906 and Taunton 1909–12. Joint-Parliamentary Secretary Ministry of National Service 1918; Under-Secretary for War and Air 1919–1921; Chancellor Duchy of Lancaster 1921–1922; Minister of Transport 1921–1922; Secretary of State for India 1922–1924 and 1928–1929; First Commissioner of Works 1924–1928; Lord Privy Seal 1931. Succeeded father as 2nd Viscount Peel in 1912. Created G.B.E. 1919, G.C.S.I. 1932, Earl Peel 1929.

[100] Victor Christian William Cavendish (1868–1938) Liberal Unionist MP for Derbyshire (West) 1891–1908. Financial Secretary to Treasury 1903–1905; Civil Lord of Admiralty 1915–1916; Governor-General Canada 1916–21; Colonial Secretary 1922–1924. Succeeded uncle as 9th Duke of Devonshire in 1908. Created G.C.V.O. 1912 and K.G.. 1916.

[101] Philip Albert Gustave David Sassoon (1868–1939) Conservative MP for Hythe June 1912–June 1939. PPS to Lloyd George 1920–22. Under-Secretary for Air 1924–1929 and 1931–1937; First Commissioner of Works 1937–1939.

[102] William James Bull (1863–1931) Conservative MP for Hammersmith (later South) 1900–1929. PPS to Walter Long 1903–21. Created baronet 1922.

two more to consider results & I told them all that L.G. had been hampered in the election by his alliance with us, that he had amply discharged his obligations not only to the Conservative Party but also to us & that he must now consider himself free to take any line he chose & in choosing he must understand that tho' I would not now join the Govt & could not foresee my own future or whether I had any future I was going to remain a Unionist & would not join a Centre Party & did not intend to attack or criticize the Govt unless obliged to do so.

L.G. said that that was his idea also. He did not mean to act like an ordinary chief of Opposition & to seek grounds of criticism. We each mentioned some things that would force us to oppose. They were pretty much the same, but we saw no reason to believe that Bonar would do them. We think that presently he will begin to lose elections & that time will show without our aid that we were right when we said that the parties of moderation were not strong enough to allow themselves the luxury of quarrelling over names & personalities.

All the others agreed except Worthy who wanted us or me to join the Govt at once & flung Neville in my face when I refused. I got cross & requested him to leave Neville out. I had already told him & others the true state of the case between N. & me & it shows just the strain of commonness in him that he should have used that argument. I passed a note to my neighbour that this controversy would be settled by W's not being invited to join by B.L. & so I think it has been, but I made it clear to everyone that I should not ask anyone to stand out if he wished to go in. I can't ask of others what I would not accept from Neville.

I can't see the future with any clearness at present. Am I right about the probable trend of bye-elections? Can L.G. refrain for long from full-blooded opposition? Will the Govt develop unexpected debating & parliamentary strength? Will Bonar Law's health again break down? Could I in any circumstances ever lead the Party again? Would they ever trust me? or I them? So many thoughts, so many questions, & to each two answers at least. And I can't decide among the possibilities what are the probabilities.

. . .

Yes, I give them four years. I can do a lot of reading & gardening in that time.

7

'D—— POLITICS: CULTIVONS NOTRE JARDIN'

Into the Wilderness, November 1922–December 1923

The significance of the Carlton Club revolt was that it formally destroyed the Coalition without exorcising the menacing spectre of coalitionism. When Lloyd George resigned on the afternoon of 19 October 1922 he was followed into the wilderness by some of the most experienced and talented Conservative politicians of the age. This group subsequently established their collective position in the form of a manifesto to the press reaffirming their loyalty to Lloyd George, with whom 'there had been no difference be it ... on matters of principle or policy', and portentously warning that 'other men who had given other counsels must inherit our burden and discharge its consequent responsibilities'.[1] Thereafter, when initial hopes that Law would not obtain an absolutely majority were extinguished, the Chamberlainites took refuge in pique that appeared almost inexhaustible. Under Birkenhead's effective strategic direction, the objective was to present the Chamberlainites as a coherent alternative leadership for the Conservative Party: a strategy founded upon the firm and constant conviction that incompetents and 'second class brains' could not rule empires. Given time, Birkenhead believed, the Law government would engineer its own humiliation and downfall.[2] Abstinence from office in the short-term was thus merely a prelude to permanent anti-socialist coalition. In the interim they considered it sufficient to stand aloof to avoid being tainted with the opprobrium of their successors and to pour derision upon the 'second class brains' who had succeeded them.[3]

For all the appeal of such a strategy, the year which followed the Coalition's collapse was a particularly melancholy episode in Chamberlain's career. Contrary to the repeated claims of his biographers that Chamberlain 'bore no recriminations',[4] he felt bitterly his rejection at both a political and personal level.[5] For a man who felt the obligations of personal honour and loyalty as deeply as Chamberlain, his dismissal by treacherous and ungrateful followers was a constant stinging reproach to an already keen sense of personal dignity. Moreover, isolated from the main body

---

[1] *The Times*, 20 October 1922 signed by Chamberlain and twelve other former ministers.

[2] Lord Riddell Diary, 15 January 1923 reporting Birkenhead, *Lord Riddell's Intimate Diary*, 400. Also Joan to Eddy [Balfour] n.d. (late October 1922) Whittinghame MSS 76. (National Register of Archives, Scotland).

[3] See Birkenhead at Glasgow, *The Times*, 30 October 1922 for the first use of the phrase. For Chamberlain's advice to 'go away and play', leaving the government to 'stew in its own juice' see Ruth Lee Diary, 2 February 1923, A. Clark (ed), *A Good Innings*, 236.

[4] D.R. Thorpe, *The Uncrowned Prime Ministers*, 75. Petrie also notes that Chamberlain took this reverse 'philosophically', *Life and Letters*, II, 204.

[5] C.P. Scott Diary, 6 December 1922, Scott MSS 50907 fol. 208.

of the party, he recognised that, however swiftly the government contrived its own downfall, he was 59 and his future seemed extremely doubtful. Indeed, for all their collective hubris and inexperience, he still gave them four years in office.[6] His personal torment was intensified still further by the 'feeling that B.L. behaved badly to him and that he could not serve under him' although he told Derby that 'in the event of B.L. retiring he would be perfectly ready to come back, even if not as P.M. at all events into the Cabinet'.[7] At a time when Law's retirement seemed improbable, however, the difficulties of his own position were forcefully brought home to him by his brother's acceptance of office under Law,[8] by the perceived ascendancy of the Diehards, by doubts about Lloyd George's constancy of purpose and by fears that talk of Liberal reunion would undermine his hopes for a fundamental realignment of the forces of constitutional anti-socialism.

Depressing though such concerns were, their chosen strategy offered Chamberlain considerable personal, as well as political, satisfaction. Indeed, for Chamberlain the man, as opposed to the politician, the release from office clearly soon proved to be far from distasteful – despite the circumstances in which this freedom had been conferred. Although devastated by defeat,[9] later that afternoon he affected 'a jaunty and cheerful' air.[10] Although his family letters betray something of his real mood, given the delicacy of his position he resolved to be a 'rare & inconstant visitor' to the Commons in order to avoid either attacking the government or becoming a focus for opposition to it.[11] Instead his wife ensured initially that his life was given over to the organized and enforced sociability of an interminable succession of luncheon and dinner engagements. New accommodation was obtained at Morpeth Mansions – of necessity 'cheap as such things go'[12] – and holidays were arranged. For Christmas and the New Year, the Chamberlains went to Gibraltar and then on to Morocco after spending three days with Lloyd George at Algeciras.[13] Another trip was planned for the spring to enjoy the flowers in the Dolomites. Above all, for all his political and financial frustrations, as the weeks progressed his letters to his sisters demonstrate the degree to which he came to enjoy his freedom from the Commons and from the mental and physical stress of office. In particular, there was the sheer unalloyed joy of life at Twitt's Ghyll: a life of rest, a few letters, The Times, *a little reading and his beloved garden. As he wrote revealingly to Hilda in late January, 'I am*

---

[6] A. Chamberlain to V. Cazalet, November 1922, R.R. James *Victor Cazalet: A Portrait* (1976), 89; A. Chamberlain to Ida, 21 November 1922, AC5/1/252.

[7] Derby Diary, 23 November 1922; N. Chamberlain to Ida, 18 February 1923, NC 18/1/382; Pollock memorandum, 'The Fall of the Coalition ...' Hanworth MSS d.432/163.

[8] Amery to Law, 31 October 1922 Law MSS 108/1/28 reporting N. Chamberlain; Neville Chamberlain Diary, 22 October 1922.

[9] Frances Stevenson Diary, 13 July 1935, A.J.P. Taylor (ed), *Lloyd George: A Diary*, 311.

[10] Hankey Diary 21 October 1922, Hankey MSS 1/6.

[11] A. Chamberlain to Hilda, 21 January 1923; AC5/1/257.

[12] A. Chamberlain to Ida, 3 December 1922, AC5/1/254.

[13] Lloyd George to Frances Stevenson, 14 January 1923, A.J.P. Taylor (ed) *My Darling Pussy: The Letters of Lloyd George and Frances Stevenson, 1913–41*, (1975), 56–7.

still thoroughly enjoying my liberty ... It almost seems to me as if I had never had a holiday before & when, after doing a little weeding on the terrace this morning it suddenly occurred to me that I now had all the years to finish my job I could have shouted for joy'.[14] *It would thus be wrong to portray Chamberlain in these months engulfed in nothing but gloom and black depression or to interpret his family letters as merely a brave facade — if nothing else, it was a tone and posture he was never able to sustain for long in this intimate correspondence. Perhaps a good circumstantial indicator of this new solace was the fact that, for perhaps the first time, health worries are totally absent from the correspondence for several months.*

During this period political events provided Chamberlain with ample grounds for enjoying his freedom. Above all, the obvious discomfiture of Law and the apparent weakness of his front-bench provided the Chamberlainites with malicious satisfaction. To the Commons he gave the impression of 'a man who has undertaken a distasteful task, and is prepared to carry it on a certain time and no longer':[15] a perception reinforced by widespread rumours about Law's health since his re-emergence in October 1922.[16] Moreover, Chamberlainite expectations of impending crisis were scarcely unfounded. Government failure to produce a conspicuous success in Anglo-French relations was particularly humiliating — especially when the French invaded the Ruhr in January 1923. Although Chamberlain had felt obliged to cast his first vote of the session for the government during the Ruhr debate on 19 February, this had been prompted only by the mischievous actions of Lloyd George: a fact which the Birmingham Post swiftly explained in order to dispel misapprehensions about Chamberlain's desire for a possible reunion.[17] Furthermore, the illegal handling of the rent dispute question in February and of the Irish deportees in March,[18] and the government's defeat through sheer inexperience over the employment of ex-servicemen in the following month,[19] all suggested justification for Chamberlainite expectation. In March the climax arrived when the government were 'knocked endways' by three startling ministerial by-election reverses which left Law 'more than ever like a mute at a funeral'.[20] These defeats in formerly safe Tory seats, two at the hands of Labour, appeared to vindicate Chamberlain's warning that it would be 'criminal' to sacrifice the unity of anti-socialism in the face of the 'common foe ... at a moment

---

[14] A. Chamberlain to Hilda, 21 January 1923, AC5/1/257.

[15] A. Murray to Lord Reading, 7 March 1923, Murray MSS 8808/156. Also Salvidge Diary, October 1922, *Salvidge of Liverpool*, 238.

[16] See, for example, Esher to Hankey, 21 November 1922, Hankey MSS 4/14/11; Hankey Diary, 9, 10, 26 November 1922; Headlam Diary 13 February 1923, Headlam MSS D/He/19 fol.44; Davidson to Stamfordham, 21 February 1923, Davidson MSS (House of Lords Record Office).

[17] *Birmingham Post*, 'London Letter', 20, 21 February 1923.

[18] See *Gleanings and Memoranda*, LVII, April 1923, 318–326; and memorandum in Law MSS 117/6/2.

[19] Fisher Diary, 10 April 1923 (Bodleian Library Oxford).

[20] Hankey to his wife, 5 March 1923. Also Sanders Diary 11 March 1923; Hewins Diary, 6,7, March 1923, Hewins MSS 199/44 (Sheffield University Library).

of national danger'.[21] *In the short-term Chamberlain and his followers rejoiced particularly in the electoral humiliation of Griffith-Boscawen: a ministerial rebel at the Carlton Club against whom they had nurtured a special contempt since his defection in October*[22] *and whose defeat they had done much directly to bring about.*[23] *Moreover, their satisfaction was enhanced still further when both Horne and Worthington-Evans rebuffed Law's offer of office on the night of Boscawen's Mitcham defeat.*[24] *With the political tide flowing in their direction, therefore, Chamberlain refused to countenance overtures from Beaverbrook and Rothermere who were 'trying to destroy this Government and replace it by an A.C. Govt'.*[25] *advances first communicated through the ubiquitous Locker-Lampson in February*[26] *and culminating in Beaverbrook's attempted plot in April when he was convinced that Law would resign. Having rejected such a potentially compromising and discreditable offer, Chamberlain then withdrew to Vernet-Les-Bains in the Pyrenees for a family holiday. He was still there on 20 May when Law announced his resignation.*

Although Chamberlain welcomed absence as an acquittal from the charge of being 'over eager ... to snatch at the chance [of office] if offered',[27] *by his return to London on 25 May the Cabinet had already accepted Baldwin's offer to retain their places. In reality, the prospects of Baldwin taking this opportunity to consummate a wholesale party reunion, by offers to the Chamberlainites as a group, was never more than a vague possibility.*[28] *At his meeting with Baldwin at Chequers on 26 May, Chamberlain was in no mood for conciliation or humility. Nor was Baldwin, however, and to Chamberlain's outrage and horror Baldwin's tactlessness was a painful demonstration of his own loss of political influence. Indeed, when recounting the story to his brother at the Commons a week later he was still 'evidently writhing under the humiliation he had undergone' and during the conversation 'became very emotional, shouting loudly and banging the table with the greatest violence'.*[29] *After this brutal rebuff to his pretensions to represent an alternative leadership, Chamberlain's spirits — like his political and financial fortunes — were at their nadir. During August he even considered retirement.*[30]

[21] Chamberlain at Birmingham, *Birmingham Post*, 14 October 1922.
[22] Pollock memorandum 'The Fall of the Coalition ...' Hanworth MSS d.432/173–4.
[23] See Sanders Diary, 2 March 1923. Also A. Chamberlain to the Editor, *The Times*, 2 March 1923.
[24] Neville Chamberlain Diary, 8 March 1923.
[25] A. Chamberlain to Hilda, 14 April 1923, AC5/1/270. These approaches were probably not sanctioned by Law. See A. Chamberlain to N. Chamberlain, 22 April 1923, NC 1/27/69 and Neville Chamberlain Diary, 26 April 1923.
[26] O. Locker-Lampson to A. Chamberlain 8 February 1923, AC 24/5/6.
[27] A. Chamberlain to E.M. Pollock, 21 May 1923, Hanworth MSS c.946/69. Also A. Chamberlain to L. Worthington-Evans, 24 May 1923, Worthington-Evans MSS c.894/15–16, 24–27. (Bodleian Library Oxford).
[28] See R.C. Self, 'Conservative Reunion and the General Election of 1923: A Reassessment', *Twentieth Century British History*, 3.3 (1992), 262–265.
[29] Neville Chamberlain Diary, 1 June 1923. Also A. Chamberlain to N. Chamberlain, 1 June 1923, AC35/1/37; Crawford Diary, 26 May 1923 reporting him 'white with fury', J.Vincent (ed), *The Crawford Papers*, 484.
[30] Also A. Chamberlain to N. Chamberlain, 30 August 1923, NC 1/27/74.

The situation was radically transformed by his brother's revelations on 12 October that Baldwin was about to declare for tariff reform. After the War, if not before it, there was considerable truth in Amery's charge that Joseph Chamberlain's policy had become a 'hereditary incubus' for his elder son.[31] *For Austen, 'protection was not a dogma, but an expedient'.*[32] *In the circumstances of 1923, expediency did not favour a recrudescence of the fiscal controversy. Certainly Chamberlain recognised that for the sort of party realignment against socialism that he had striven since 1918, the revival of tariff reform was undoubtedly fatal.*[33] *Nonetheless, above all other instincts, he was his father's son. While harbouring some grave and prescient apprehensions, therefore, he acknowledged that he was still 'pledged by all my traditions to throw myself wholeheartedly into the fight and give them any support I can'. As he warned, however, 'the worst thing possible' would be for Baldwin to raise expectations which he failed to fulfil.*[34] *At this juncture, he clearly believed this 'astonishingly bold policy' included food taxes.*[35] *When he learned that this was not the 'whole hog', he took no solace from his brother's strategic arguments, lamenting instead that 'the gilt was off the ginger-bread' because Baldwin's Plymouth declaration represented 'Father's policy with all that part left out for which he cared most'.*[36] *Although privately he continued to express alarm at the 'melancholy feebleness' of the campaign,*[37] *on 29 October he spoke at the Birmingham Conservative Club, accepting the policy and publicly abandoning criticism of the government, although not before confessing to be 'puzzled ... to know exactly what Baldwin's meaning was' and demanding a 'clear lead and a straight fight ... on the broadest and most direct lines'.*[38]

As the momentum for an early election gathered pace, the prospect of party reunion and the rehabilitation of the Chamberlainites returned to the agenda during November 1923. Yet contrary to Baldwin's later claims and the subsequent historical orthodoxy, this was never a significant factor in either the decision to call an election or the manner in which events subsequently unfolded.[39] *In the short-term, Baldwin's cynical manipulation of the prospect, and the treatment he handed out to Chamberlain in so doing, reinforced all the contempt and resentment against Baldwin he had*

---

[31] Amery Diary, 18 June 1924, *The Leo Amery Diaries*, 377.

[32] A. Chamberlain to B. Dugdale, 11 November 1929, B.E.C. Dugdale, *Arthur James Balfour*, (2 vols, 1936), I, 343.

[33] For this conflict see R.C. Self, *Tories and Tariffs: The Conservative Party and the Politics of Tariff Reform, 1922–32* (London and New York 1986), 178–9. See also C.P. Scott Diary, 23 October 1923, Scott MSS 50906 fol. 197.

[34] A. Chamberlain to N. Chamberlain, 15 October 1923, AC35/3/9.

[35] A. Chamberlain to Mary Carnegie, 21 October 1923, AC5/1/1233.

[36] A. Chamberlain to N. Chamberlain 24 October 1923, NC 1/27/74.

[37] Fisher Diary, 15 November 1923; A. Chamberlain to L.S. Amery 31 October 1923, AC35/3/1.

[38] A. Chamberlain at Birmingham Conservative Club, *Birmingham Daily Post*, 30 October 1923; also to Neville 29 October 1923, AC35/3/12.

[39] See R.C. Self, 'Conservative Reunion and the General Election of 1923: A Reassessment', *Twentieth Century British History*, 3.3, 249–273.

harboured since the last abortive discussion of reunion in May.[40] *For Chamberlain, however, the real significance of the 1923 election and its aftermath was that it finally convinced him that the future rested with Baldwin and that he should come to terms with this fact – painful and distasteful though it would undoubtedly prove to be.*

AC5/1/253   26 November 1922
                                                 Twitt's Ghyll

My dear Hilda,

    ... We are dining with Mary tomorrow but alas! we are engaged elsewhere on Wednesday ... I shall get out of London as soon as I can if Ivy does not fill all my evenings with dinner parties. At present by her doing or my own I seem to be dining & lunching out everyday.
        ...
    ... The first days debate in [the Commons], which is all that I have attended so far, showed a much more capable & effective Labour Party. I heard two good argumentative speeches without any rant in them. Ramsay Macdonald [sic] will be a more formidable opponent than Clynes, I think. It will be interesting to watch from my elevated perch. I have taken the corner seat on the 3rd Bench below the Gangway, Father's old seat in 92–95 & I love the sentiment of it.
    No, I really have nothing to say.

AC5/1/254   3 December 1922
                                                 Twitt's Ghyll

My dear Ida,

        ...
    You will have seen that I was entertained on Thursday by members of our group & made a speech by way of giving them a lead.[41] Indeed, it was only made a dinner in my honour to keep it from having the air of a Cave, but it drew an extraordinarily nice letter from Balfour which I hope you read. I did not go to the House on Thursday or Friday ... However I mean to take things easily. That is the only way

---

[40] 'Events of Sunday–Monday 11–12 November 1923; AC35/3/216.
[41] The dinner on 30 November held in Chamberlain's honour was attended by forty-nine MPs, AC33/2/148 – one of several such demonstrations of Chamberlainite unity. There had been a hastily arranged dinner four days after their resignation at the Victoria Hotel, *The Times*, 24 October 1922 and another ostensibly in honour of Balfour in March. For an account of this meeting and a list of those present see Law MSS 115/2.

that I shall be able to keep out of mischief! But − for there is a But −
if Curzon gives up the Straits, as I fear he is doing in fact tho' not in
name − I shall speak & vote against the Govt. He has no courage, no
backbone, & there is no one in this Govt to give him the strength that
he lacks. If the Observer is right, & I believe it is, they are going to
neutralise but not occupy a zone with occasional inspections to see that
the Turks have done nothing improper in the intervals. This is a mere
sham, quite useless. With decent roads the Turks can mount howitzers
in a day or two & make the Straits impassable. It maddens me to think
of them giving up all that we had saved.

. . .

My political work just now is chiefly to try to improve the organisation
in West B'ham.

AC5/1/255   11 December 1922
                                                         Twitt's Ghyll

My dear Hilda,

. . .

I mean to take things very easily when we come back [from Morocco]
and to go away again in Spring to Vernet or perhaps to some baths in
the Dolomites … As you say it's not my business to make a House for
the Govt & it's very difficult to sit there and say nothing …

. . .

[Postscript] I rather gather that Poincaré is proving as difficult as
ever.[42]

AC5/1/256   Sunday eve
                                                         Twitt's Ghyll

My dear Ida,

. . .

… After [the Easter holiday] I must look out for some business in
the City that will bring in a little money, but I think I am entitled to
my holiday first & indeed that I ought to take it. By the way the
Dolomites are splendid for flowers & much cheaper than France …

. . .

I keep rejoicing in my present freedom & thinking how nice it will
be to make T.G. my headquarters next year, only going to town for

---

[42] Poincaré attended the London Conference between 9–11 December 1922 where he
rejected an offer of German treasury bills to meet instalments of Reparation payments.

important debates. Shall I be able to achieve this, I wonder, or will the pressure of the younger men of our group be too great for me? In any case I must be able to see much more of my garden. Indeed I wish that I could give up the House altogether. I am out of sympathy with the present mood of my party, irritated by the sight of B.L. & his smug complacency & very doubtful whether politics hold any future for me. Mark my words: in 2 or 3 years time, unless the Labour Party plays the fool too much, the Conservative reaction will be exhausted, the position of the Govt becoming difficult & defeat confronting them whenever they go to the country, & about that time Bonar will find that his health will not allow him to remain P.M. any longer! Unless one of their younger men develops surprisingly they have no one to replace him in the H. of C. & Bonar will prove his 'friendship' by offering to make way for me. But I don't see myself taking on the job unless the Party is in a wholly different mood & I don't see the Party asking me to come back on my terms. In fact I am only fit for the House of Lords & I won't go there.

All which, you will say, shows that I too am tired & need a holiday, which is true, but if I am once rested can I keep my hands off them? Not, I think, if I am in regular attendance. So once again cultivons notre jardin!

AC5/1/257   21 January 1923
                                                          Twitt's Ghyll

My dear Hilda,

. . .

We shall hope to see you while you are in London, tho' I mean to be there as little as possible. I am still thoroughly enjoying my liberty & the sense of having time for everything. I do not propose to attend the House regularly or indeed to be anything but a rare & inconstant visitor. It almost seems to me as if I had never had a holiday before & when, after doing a little weeding on the terrace this morning it suddenly occurred to me that I now had all the years to finish my job I could have shouted for joy.

. . .

I don't observe that the world is as yet more peaceful for having got rid of Lloyd George!

AC5/1/258

28 January 1923
Twitt's Ghyll

My dear Ida,

. . .

I was up in town one night this week by request of friends for a consultation & lunched with Neville next day who had been commissioned by Peel to ask me to take the Chairmanship of the Royal Comn. on the India Civil Services, but this after reflection I have declined. It would be a very heavy piece of work & I don't want to work yet a while & it would besides tie me much more than I wish to be tied. I am still feeling as if this were the first holiday that I had ever had & I have not had nearly enough of it yet. The days are not long enough for what I find to do, & when I have read the Times & written such letter as I must write, there seems little time left for all the reading that I have promised myself. I bless my stars that I am not responsible for the Ruhr business[43] & do not admire Bonar's policy there; nor am I lost in admiration of Curzon's handling of the Lausanne Conference.[44] It seems to me that he has only stood his ground when he could not run away. And having read so far, you will agree with me that the more I can avoid the H. of C. the better it will be.

AC5/1/259

11 February 1923
Twitt's Ghyll

My dear Ida,

You will not be surprised that I have no news for you. I garden when the weather permits & I read when it does not . . .

. . .

I feel little interest & less satisfaction in politics, but the country is in no mood to listen to criticism from ex-Ministers & both L.G. & I mean to keep away from the House as much as possible as the easiest way of keeping silence.

---

[43] Despite British efforts to avert it, at French insistence the Reparations Commission declared Germany in default on deliveries of timber and coal. On 11 January 1923 French and Belgian troops occupied the Ruhr ostensibly to obtain 'productive pledges' for future delivery.

[44] The first Lausanne conference convened to reach a new peace with Turkey from 20 November 1922–4 February 1923.

AC5/1/260

20 February 1923
Twitt's Ghyll

My dear Hilda,

...

... I spent Saturday & Sunday with the Lee Warners[45] ... No doubt they were both stimulated by my visit which we all thoroughly enjoyed, talking much of old days & new ones ... Well I owe him an immense debt, for he made the happiness & the interest of my Rugby days & did more for my education in the full sense of the word than any man except Father.

I went to the House yesterday for the first time this session & voted with the Govt against L.G. I do not admire Bonar's diplomacy & think, knowing what I know of the views of the Belgian Ministers that the occupation of the Ruhr would & ought to have been prevented but I don't like 'Liberal reunion' which is either a sham or a negation of my policy; I didn't like L.G.'s speech which I though indiscreet & dangerous; I didn't like the amendment & I was not going to join in a vote of censure which by all parliamentary practice an amendment on the address is. All which will please you & disgruntles me, so I am best away.

AC5/1/261

24 February 1923
Twitt's Ghyll

My dear Ida,

...

I shall laugh if A.G[riffith] B[oscawen] is beaten again, but I fear that he will get in. In any case I don't like making a policy to fit an election.

AC5/1/26

24 February 1923
Twitt's Ghyll

My dear Ida,

...

... What a mess things are in! I think that the Govts foreign policy

---

[45] Henry Lee Warner: Chamberlain's House Master at Rugby and a great personal influence.

is nearly hopeless, but I don't see an alternative at this stage. They will be in difficulties before the Session ends.

AC5/1/267   [mis-dated] 4 March 1922
                                              Twitt's Ghyll

My dear Hilda,

What a smash at Willesden![46] And if Stanley[47] was 5000 to the bad at Willesden, I would not give much at this moment for Bosky's chances in Mitcham. I am sorry for Stanley who is a good fellow tho' not clever but I am out & out wishing for Boscawen's defeat. Certainly the Govt have not been fortunate with their bye-elections – first the fiasco at Hitchin under the eyes of Hatfield & now a big defeat. I think that I was generous when I gave them three years to find out that they had made a mistake. Well as the old tag from Horace says, it is pleasant to sit on the cliff & watch the mariner battling with the waves. Don't grudge me my unholy joy. The fact is, says Garvin today after doing his best to destroy the late Govt & to support this one, they are not strong enough for the times. Some of us said that before when he would not listen but I'll be hanged if I join them even if Lloyd George is embraced by a 'United' Liberal party. I think that he does not want reunion with the Liberals of Asquith's type but he can't afford to let it be said that he is the sole obstacle. He may be caught in the trap that he has laid, but it does not look as if he would be eagerly welcomed back, & Simon's speech must be just the sort of response that he wanted. However I am content to look on. If he falls into line with Asquith & Simon there will be an end of cooperation between us. If he does not, we may or may not cooperate again, but on the next occasion I do not at present think that it could be under his lead. If Neville had not joined this Govt I'd have had them out in six months, for with Neville out none of my people would have joined & they would be weaker still. I must say that *now* I hope that Neville will not

---

[46] At Willesden East on 3 March George Stanley, a junior Home Office Minister, transformed a 1319 majority in 1922 into a Liberal majority of 5176. On the same day Griffith-Boscawen turned a 5036 Conservative majority in 1922 into a 833 Labour majority at Mitcham. Three days later at Edgehill Major J.W. Hills transformed a majority of 4666 into a Labour majority of 1050.

[47] Lt-Col George Frederick Stanley (1872–1938) Conservative MP for Preston, January 1910–November 1922 when defeated. Unsuccessfully contested Willesden East in March and December 1923 but elected October 1924–April 1929. Comptroller of the Household 1919–21; Financial Secretary War Office 1921–22; Under-Secretary for Home Affairs 1922–1923 when resigned after by-election defeat. Parliamentary Secretary Minister of Pensions 1924–1929; Governor of Madras 1929–34.

be forced to take the M/Health & the Cabinet, for I think that in his own interest he would be better out of it.

AC5/1/268   10 March 1923
                                                       Twitt's Ghyll

My dear Ida,

...

I have spent the week in bed with lumbago, only getting up yesterday afternoon for the first time & going out today. The doctors say that trundling a wheel barrow is fatal & that I must not do it. I am growing old & it is a bore. Lawrence too has been laid up with a sore throat & swollen glands. The doctor at first suspected diptheria ... I think that we have more than our share of illness for [Ivy] is still suffering from a very stiff neck.

Well, the Govt have done badly in the bye-elections. I can remember nothing like it. Of course they badly mismanaged their housing policy. In the first place they confided decontrol & housing to two separate committees instead of treating them as they are as inseparable. Next they made bye-elections in seats where this question was vital before they had found any policy. Then they allowed the Minister to disclose their hurriedly formed & incomplete policy at an election meeting instead of stating it in the House. And then his statement was corrected by the Ministry next day & both altered by B.L. two days later who at the same time knocked the wholy [sic] policy over by destroying any vestige of fixity or certainty that it had hitherto possessed. All which shows that this Govt is like its predecessors overworked & living too much from hand to mouth. Add to your maxims of statecraft – Bye-elections make bad law. I refrained with difficulty from putting this & some other reflections into my letter to the Times[48] which I thought a model of restraint. I hope that Bonar was properly grateful to me!

But there is another point that I have constantly preached & that I have not seen noticed in the papers. The new electorate as far as the great majority of voters are concerned is not definitely – is, indeed, scarcely at all attached to any Party. The strongest body of fixed opinion is & will be Labour – at any rate until they get into power. Mark this. I am sure it is the great factor which journalists & politicians have not yet recognised or too easily forget.

[48] A. Chamberlain to the Editor, *The Times*, 2 March 1923. In the letter he was critical of government proposals for the decontrol of rents. In Labour hands, this certainly harmed Boscawen – as was intended.

I sent Neville good wishes from the bottom of my heart.[49] Congratulations I added I could not offer on his taking the post now when the pitch had been so badly queered. I gather that this responded to his own feelings tho' he was naturally pleased by the good reception given to his appointment. I felt strongly inclined to advise him to refuse, but I might have been misunderstood & in any case it was taking too great a responsibility. He will, I hope, do well but he has a most difficult task, made still more difficult by what has just happened.

As for myself the more I think (& I have thought a good deal) the less prospect do I see of any future for myself in politics. The tie between Libs. & Cons. having once been broken & party fighting revived, I am disposed to think that the forces making for Liberal reunion in the constituencies will be too strong for the obvious resistance of the leaders of both sections & meanwhile the mere talk of it tends to cut us off from L.G. & to close up the Unionist ranks & stimulate party feeling on our side in the constituencies & the House. But how do I stand with the party? Obviously the Die-hards have not forgiven me & do not meant to forgive me, nor do the new men wish to yield their places to the old men, nor Leslie Wilson & Co. desire that I should have my choice of Whips. You will have seen that as soon as the papers began to say that the Govt must be strengthened & to mention our names, the Whips reported to the Prime Minister that any attempt to bring in any of the ex-Ministers would lead to a revival of the Die-hard Party. Well, none of us, unless it be Worthington-Evans, have shown any desire to join the Govt & it was perhaps unnecessary to go through the motions of kicking us out when we were known not to be willing to enter. But it is significant that breach will only be healed by a disaster & by the time that the disaster comes I shall be too old to care to take up the burden of leadership again for four years in opposition with a possible premiership in the distance. Nor can I conceive that anything will make me join this Govt under Bonar's leadership or take over his Govt if he breaks down. I cannot join him, for I think him unfitted to be Prime Minister & I feel too deeply his conduct towards me to make it possible for me again to act under him.

I think therefore that my real political life is ended. I am sorry, since I am nevertheless still in politics, & of course I should have liked to be Prime Minister & to have tried whether I could not do some good work in that capacity. But I do not complain & except as above I have no regrets as to my own conduct last year. I knew & warned others of

---

[49] After Horne refused to accept Boscawen's vacant portfolio, Neville Chamberlain became Minister of Health on 8 March 1923 on condition that he had the freedom to reconsider the policy on rent control.

the risks that we were running & took my decision with my eyes open to the not unlikely consequences. The only thing that has & does give me pain is that Neville's course of duty lay the other way. I can no more forgive Bonar than he could forgive L.G. & therein lies the tragedy for us. Well, I have had a very interesting &, except where Bonar has twice tripped me up, a very lucky 30 years. I wish that I could go out of Parlt altogether but Ivy says "Yes, if you had been 10 years younger & could really have made for yourself other work" & I add to myself that at this stage it would be unfair to those who stood by me.

AC5/1/269

18 March 1923
36 Sloane Court West
SW3

My dear Hilda,

...
I am in no heart to write. I am away from Ivy & you know what that means. Poor little L[awrence] obtrudes on all my thoughts [ill at present]. I have 2 speeches to make in West B'ham on Monday & Tuesday & know not what to say. I cannot concentrate on them. I do not want to attack the Govt but I cannot defend their policy. Indeed I cannot see that they have a policy in any field of foreign affairs & the only home policy that they have yet declared has been a disastrous failure & has been abandoned. Poor Neville! How I wish that he were not in that galerés. Bonar is the prisoner of his Die-hard Peers, notably of Salisbury. I regard his appointment of Admiral Hall[50] to succeed Younger & Malcolm Fraser as a definite capitulation to them & a banging of the door in our faces. Hall has no political experience, sat in Parlt practically as a Brewer's agent & belongs to the narrowest sect of the Die-hards. That was his only claim or qualification for the post & it has proved sufficient. I am very miserable.

---

[50] Admiral Sir (William) Reginald Hall (1870–1943) Naval career 1883–1919. Director of Naval Intelligence 1914–19. Conservative MP for Liverpool West Derby February 1919–December 1923, Eastbourne June 1925–May 1929. 'Blinker' Hall had been a Diehard during the Coalition. Principal Agent of Unionist Party 1923–24. Created CB 1915; Rear Admiral 1917; Vice Admiral 1922; Admiral 1926.

AC5/1/265   2 April 1923
                                                            Twitt's Ghyll

My dear Hilda,

Heavenly weather at last & we are all going on well. That being so
I leave politics to slaves (i.e. the Govt) & fools (i.e. those who can't
keep quiet when they have the chance) & I cultivate my garden ...
I work all day long, for the wet summer [sic] has left my herbaceous
borders full of weeds, and one can only dig here & there & for the rest
I have to pick the weeks out from among or around the plants, & my
soil is a very heavy loam. Still it is all very delightful as long as I can
do it.

AC5/1/266   8 April 1923
                                                            Twitt's Ghyll

To Ida

   ...
Generally speaking the garden is an immense joy & I look with
horror on the prospect of some day attending the House again.
Campbell Stuart[51] came down to see me yesterday at this own request.
He is Managing Director of the Times & a nice man ... He wanted
to know "whither are we drifting" & I told him straight into a Labour
Government. This was what he thought & he was gloomy. The policy
of the Times was to support the Govt because it was the Govt but the
Govt had no policy at home or abroad. I told him that the govt would
go on for three years & that then things would be in such a mess that
Bonar would have blood pressure & retire but that I now thought it
unlikely that even then the Party would turn to me. Like me, but
without any suggestion from me, he is disturbed by the growing
predominance of the Die-hard section.

---

[51] Sir Campbell Stuart (1885–1972) Civil Servant. Served in Washington, 1917. Deputy
Director of Propaganda in Enemy Countries, 1918. Managing Editor, *Daily Mail* 1921;
Director of *The Times* 1919–60; Managing Director 1920–4. Chairman Imperial Com-
munications Advisory Committee and its successor 1933–45. Director of Propaganda in
Enemy Countries, 1939–40.

AC5/1/270   14 April 1923
                                                    Twitt's Ghyll

My dear Hilda,

Let us begin with the more important matters. The plants with which I filled up your little box were two little cuttings of Thymus Corsica ... & one of Mimulus Bartoni ...

...

The Govt are certainly not doing well ... I can only speak from what I am told & that is first that there need not have been no trouble at all but for Boyd Carpenter's[52] very unskilful speech, & secondly that the Whips evidently did not realise the state of the House or they would have kept the debate going a little longer.[53] If it is true as I was told that Baldwin was behind the Speakers Chair but sent Neville in to move the adjournment it would seem that he lost his nerve & did not show the qualities of a leader. Lastly it is obvious that they ought to have said at once next day what they refused to say until the day after & they would thus have spared themselves & the House the humiliations of Wednesday but the decision to refuse a statement the next day when it ought to have been made was I am told Bonar's & against Baldwin's advice.

I was fetched up to town on Thursday to dine with F.E. to meet – Rothermere! & if you want gossip here is some gossip for you two only. Don't mention it to Neville.

The great man was ill in bed but F.E. had seen him & gave me his message which was somewhat amplified by his son who, with Oliver L[ocker]-L[ampson] Horne & Freddie Guest completed the party.

For some reason R[othermere] hates Bonar – B. says because he refused him an earldom which allegation has not softened R.'s wrath. So he has been trying to destroy this Govt & replace it by an A.C. Govt. But he is now getting frightened. He is afraid that the Conservative Party may be destroyed also & he is in terror of the Socialists. He cares for money more than anything & feels his money-bags in peril.

On top of this comes to him Beaverbrook – "Arcades ambo: that is villains both" as Byron says. B. says that Bonar is done & will resign in a fortnight. He will advise the King to send for Curzon, Derby

---

[52] Archibald Boyd-Carpenter (1873–1937) Conservative MP for N. Bradford December 1918–December 1923; Coventry 1924–29; Chertsey October 1931–May 1937. Parliamentary Secretary Minister of Labour 1922–1923; Financial Secretary to Treasury 1923; Paymaster-General 1923–1924; Financial Secretary to Admiralty 1923–1924. Created Knight Bachelor 1926. A Diehard during the Coalition.

[53] On 9 April 1923 the government had been defeated through sheer inexperience on the employment of ex-servicemen.

or Baldwin – all three have their upholders but apparently neither Beaverbrook nor R. fancy them as bulwarks of the State. So Max Beaverbrook puts another suggestion. Will I join Bonar's Govt as Privy Seal & Leader of the House taking at the moment only Horne in with me but with Bonar's verbal understanding that he will resign on August 1st in my favour with the clear understanding that I shall then reconstruct the Govt on my own lines – a thorough reconstruction. A strange world my masters!

You will not be surprised to hear that I said, first, that I would receive no overtures from Bonar through any third person. If he had anything to say to me, he must say it himself. Secondly I said I would have nothing to do with a plan of this kind. If kept private I should have appeared to have betrayed my friends to whom I could not explain that they would be 'all right on the day' & I should be working confidentially day by day with Leslie Wilson (his Secretary) & others whom I should be intending to kick out on the 1st August. But it would certainly become public & then all who were parties to it would be equally discredited. It was the kind of bargain that public opinion most naturally & properly resented.

I added that this Govt had started so badly that nothing could save it in the long run; that to join it would only serve to tar us with its faults & that the only chance of retrieving the position was to present the country with a Govt that it would regard & treat as a *new* Govt.

Lastly I said that the Die-hards were at present in the ascendant, that if I came in I should have 40 or 50 of them always attacking from behind & that until they had played out their hand & tried & failed with Curzon or Derby or Baldwin I had no desire to take on the job.

To all this there was only one answer viz. that the Govt would somehow last till the 9 months were over during which Ministers need not seek reelection, & things had to come to such a pass that we should lose all by-elections or in other words:- It is true that this Govt can't last; but it can last long enough to make *your* position impossible. To which I could only say that may be so but I prefer that risk to the certain damnation that would follow on the acceptance of Beaverbrook's plan.

Beaverbrook told both R & F.E. in Oliver's presence (F.E. would not go to dine with him alone) that Bonar would certainly resign in a fortnight, that his throat was only a symptom & that the strain was reproducing his old trouble.

I am inclined to bet 2 to 1 that Bonar will go on to the end of the session & will then be persuaded to continue for the Recess, but he may be worse than I think. For the first time in his life he has no one to lean upon.

AC5/1/271   22 April 1923
                                             Twitt's Ghyll

My dear Ida,

. . .
  You have had a busy week & I have taken an idle one. I went up to
London for one night to dine with Ernest Pollock[54] at the Grocers
Company . . . It was a pleasant evening & I put in my third vote for
the Govt this session! I saw Neville in the lobby & begged him as a
Conservative Minister not to forget the small middle class in his housing
proposals. It is there as it seems to me that the danger lies for him.
  . . .
  I do not know whether you saw that two of last Sunday's papers
announced Bonar's retirement – only of course provoking a contradiction & a reaction, & Beaverbrook, having had his overtures
rejected by me, proceeded like the scamp he is to denounce me & my
friends as intriguers. I saw Robbins when in town. He is, as you know,
very experienced, very trustworthy & never sensational, & I told him
the whole story confidentially. He said that he *knew* that Bonar had
told some of his colleagues before the scene in the House that he was
going to retire but of course did not now intend to do so. He & all the
Gallery had thought that the handling of the House on that day very
bad. Baldwin showed levity & the House did not like it but he confirmed
that it was Bonar who refused to allow a statement to be made & he
added: "There are sure to be more scenes & blunders. This is not a
second-rate Govt. It's fourth-rate. They are without experience or tact
for the management of the House. The Minister of Labour[55] has been
pitiable in dealing with the recent disputes & Ramsay Macdonald [sic]
has enormously & even dangerously strengthened his position".

[54] Ernest Murray Pollock (1861–1936) Unsuccessfully stood as a Liberal-Unionist in
1900 and 1906. Conservative MP for Warwick and Leamington, 1910–23. Solicitor-
General 1919– 1922; Attorney-General 1922; Master of the Rolls 1923–35. Created K.B.E.
1917, baronet 1922, Baron Hanworth 1926 and Viscount Hanworth 1936. A close friend
and associate of Austen Chamberlain.
[55] (Clement) Anderson Montagu-Barlow (1868–1951) Conservative MP for Salford
(South) 1910–23. Parliamentary Secretary to Minister of Labour 1920–1922; Minister of
Labour 1922–1924. Created K.B.E. 1918 and baronet 1924. Chairman, Royal Commission
on Location of Industry, 1937–40.

AC5/1/276

13 June 1923
2 Morpeth Mansions

My dear Ida,

I will say nothing of recent events, for reflection on them only makes bad blood & is what Neville calls 'brooding', so I send you my file of papers which tells you the whole story ...

I am now a gay dog at a loose end in London & I hate it. I have been to dances two nights running & go to another tonight ... Indeed I have had only one meal at home I think. It is a detestable gay life better suited for 30 than 60 and grey hairs – & meanwhile the weeds grow at Twitt's Ghyll & I sleep off my lunches at the House. What will become of me?

...

D— politics! Cultivons notre jardin.

AC5/1/277

22 June 1923
2 Morpeth Mansions

My dear Ida,

Amery proposed my health last night in terms which, as he is not a sneak whatever defects he might have, made me doubt the report that he had actively opposed my entry into the Govt. I therefore asked him directly whether he had or had not done so & he replied that he had *not*.

Please tell Mary, I am glad that he did not. In Salisbury it was natural & I bear no grudge, but I disliked the idea that Amery was at fault.

AC5/1/278

3 July 1923
2 Morpeth Mansions

My dear Ida,

While the rest of the family is getting more & more immersed in public work I flutter about as a sort of social butterfly, immersed not in work but in 'pleasure'.

AC5/1/279   9 July 1923
                                                    Twitt's Ghyll

My dear Hilda,

. . .

Our B'ham demonstration was a great success – 20,000 people, all in good temper & good spirits. I spoke briefly but very nicely of the Govt. choosing the P.M. & Neville as my themes because it was easy to say pleasant things of them & decency demanded that I should not criticise with Neville & Amery on the platform. I could the better afford to do so because I had marked my independent position by my speech in the House earlier in the week[56] . . . On merit I was against the Govt. I fought the L.G. [land] taxes & I repealed the L.G. taxes, but I deliberately retained these returns of all actual sales. It was therefore a simple and natural thing that I should speak & vote for them out of office as I had done in office, but I meant it also to be a demonstration that I did not wish to join the Govt. & I hoped that it would prevent Baldwin from embarrassing me by an offer during the recess. I think that I succeeded in my purpose, & I have emphasised my views in a private conversation that will I trust reach the P.M.'s ears. Meanwhile I suspect that he will find himself in difficulties about McKenna's seat, for Warren Fisher tells me privately that McK. does not intend to stand as a Conservative but as a Liberal & that he won't fight a contested election. The fact is that Baldwin forgot to settle or even to raise any of the obvious difficulties when he asked McK. to join, & there is no sort of understanding between them as to how these matters are to be dealt with. Well, thank goodness McK will not be my colleague anyway.

AC5/1/282   22 July 1923
                                                    Twitt's Ghyll

My dear Hilda,

. . .

I am wondering what the Govt. will do when or if Poincaré rejects their proposals as I suppose that he will. It is a very difficult decision, but they must do something or they will make the country look very foolish & themselves too. Otherwise politics are not at the moment

---

[56] Chamberlain both spoke and paired against the government over the clause to remove the need to notify transfers of property to the Land Valuation Department in the Third Reading of the Finance Bill. His savage attack on McKenna during the Report Stage on 3 July was also intended to show that 'he was not hankering for office', AC to Birkenhead, 6 July 1923 AC35/2/22.

very interesting. I hate the Turkish peace & the manner of making it.[57]
All Europe has been made a laughing stock or at least the French &
ourselves.

AC5/1/284   1 August 1923
                                                       Twitt's Ghyll

My dear Hilda,

... I have indeed undertaken to speak in the Ruhr debate tomorrow
... but how can I make my speech or make any notes of any use until
I hear what Baldwin is going to say? ... What alarms me is that I hear
(indirectly, I need scarcely say) from MacKenna [sic] that the Govt. &
even the P.M. have gone thus far without having any idea what they
would do if France refused their proposals. Anyway, I must catch the
9 o'clock train tomorrow, hastily change into more becoming clothes
in London, & go to the House to make a speech. D— politics! They
do interfere with gardening.
       ...
    P.S. McKenna will not join the Govt. Nobody thinks of Worthy for
Chancellor except Worthy. Joynson Hicks is moving heaven & earth to
get it, but Fleet Street says the P.M. is thinking of Neville. This chimes
in with what Baldwin said to me at Chequers.
    Baldwin promised McK a City seat, but the birds in the bush won't
quit.[58]

AC5/1/287   29 August 1923
                                                       White House,
                                                       Isle of Eigg

My dear Hilda,

    So Neville is Chancellor. I have expected it for a long time. It will
not be an easy task – probably not a popular one, but it is the greatest
position a Commoner can hold next to the Premiership & Neville
enters on it with a general recognition that he has earned it & with

[57] The second Lausanne Conference, 24 April–24 July 1923, securing the demi-
litarization of the straits and restoration of Anglo-Turkish unity, was hailed generally as
a great victory for Curzon.
[58] After the early by-election reverses McKenna had made his acceptance of the
Treasury conditional on his health improving and a safe seat being found in the City of
London but the Diehard Sir Frederick Banbury (1850–1936) refused to make way for a
Liberal in a seat he had held since 1906 although he retired in January 1924 as Baron
Banbury. McKenna withdrew claiming he was not fit to take office on 13 August 1923.

general good-will. We are a remarkable family & make a record with two brothers as Chancellors. I recall only two cases of Father & *two* sons sitting in Cabinet – Chatham & Derby – only one besides myself of father & son in the same Cabinet – Derby, & only two men who were Chancellors at an earlier age than I – Pitt & Ld Henry Petty.

AC5/1/290   22 September 1923
                                                  Twitt's Ghyll

My dear Ida,

. . .

Politics are a little quieter again. On the whole I don't think the Govt. does badly in home affairs though they would do better if their ministers of agriculture[59] & labour had brains, but I dislike their foreign policy whether in the hands of Curzon or of Bob Cecil. It seems to me that we are becoming the scold of Europe. We run about shaking our fist in other people's faces, screaming that this must be altered & that must stop. We get ourselves disliked & distrusted & misunderstood & in the end we achieve nothing & relapse into humiliated silence or laboriously expln. how pleased we are. My word what a time the Govt. would have if they were faced with a single minded fighting opposition party. It makes one's mouth water to think of the possible debates & what the great men of my younger day would have made of such opportunities. And I think the Govt. needs strong criticism in this respect, for Bob Cecil is headstrong & without much judgement, the fanatic of one idea, & Curzon is convinced that all is well if he delivers an oration or pens a 'superior' despatch. But then the criticism must be on the right lines & conducted in the right spirit – not with the recklessness of utterance of Ll. George nor with the hysteria of the Daily Mail.

AC5/1/291   29 September 1923
                                                  Twitt's Ghyll

[To Hilda]

. . .

As to politics I say nothing, for I don't understand them or at least

[59] Robert Arthur Sanders (1867–1940) Conservative MP for Bridgwater 1910–23 and Somerset (Wells) 1924–29. Whip 1911–21; Deputy Conservative Chairman 1918–22. Under-Secretary for War April 1921–October 1922; Minister of Agriculture 1922–January 1924. Created baronet 1920 and Baron Bayford 1929.

I don't understand what Baldwin is at – if indeed he *is* at anything.

AC5/1/293   20 October 1923
                                                    Twitt's Ghyll

My dear Ida,

Many thanks to you both for your telegram of birthday greeting. Sixty seems to me a ripe autumnal age, & I am tempted to follow Uncle William's example & choose this moment to retire from politics. But not if _ _ _ _ _. On the contrary, I should feel bound in that case to drop all criticism & throw myself whole-heartedly into the support of the Govt.

But will they? & can they? If they do they are much bolder than I thought or much more ignorant. Certainly I think the moment much more favourable than say a year or two years ago, & the Party much more likely to support them – partly from loyalty & partly from necessity – than it would have been to support me in the same course. But what about the women-voters? They *frighten* me. The men are much more likely to be thinking of unemployment than they were in 1903 or in 1920, but the women – will they think of anything except prices? Well if the Govt. plunges, I will plunge with them, sink or swim.

Meanwhile I believe that you now take Punch ... I hope ... that you were able to appreciate the delicious humour of John Bull & the P.M. in the aeroplane.[60] It most wittily sums up all the criticisms that I have expressed or felt. Lord knows what is going to happen next & I am very anxious about the effect of whatever happens on our interests, but I cannot suppress a malicious pleasure in Poincaré's difficulties. He does so thoroughly deserve them all & I hope to live long enough to see *him* crash.

AC5/1/294   23 October 1923
                                                    Twitt's Ghyll

My dear Ida,

I don't know what Baldwin is going to do but it looks as if he might be going in for the strong & full policy, so I wrote yesterday to Neville to say that I would offer no advice but that if Baldwin came out full-blooded at Plymouth I would on Monday at B'ham publicly abandon

---

[60] 'La Haute Politique', *Punch* 17 October 1923 p363. The cartoon attracted wide attention. See for example Dawson's comments, J.E. Wrench, *Geoffrey Dawson and our Times*, 221.

all criticism of other matters & go wholeheartedly to his support. *Nous verrons.* It would be a very bold step, but it might succeed & anyway Father's sons must be both be on that side.

AC5/1/295   31 October 1923
                                                      2 Morpeth Mansions

My dear Ida,

I asked Hewins to send you the B.D.P. with a verbatim report of my speech. It is annoying that one cannot get decently reported on an important occasion in any London paper. It is a great handicap on ones usefulness.

You will see that I ranged myself definitely on Baldwin's side on conditions only that he means business: but I am very low in my own mind, for tho' I think that he *means* business, he has not gone about the right way to *do* business. He has said enough to raise the free trade base & arrière base against him but not enough to give any guidance to his friends. Neville & Amery speak with one voice, Salisbury with another, & whilst the P.M. is silent about food Joynson-Hicks with 'Ego et rex meus' binds him down. The impression left on everyone's mind is one of doubt & perplexity, reflecting only too well as it would seem the doubt [sic] perplexity of Baldwin's own mind. Ever since he returned from Paris he told Horne that Gretton[61] had been to see him with scarcely veiled threats that as the Diehards had made him so they could unmake him & had then demanded protection. Baldwin then laughed at the idea. Horne has seen him again & said to me that he felt that he was speaking to a "rattled man". "He gave me the impression that he could not see his way through any of his problems: that he was thoroughly rattled & had dropped into this in despair".

I have written to both Neville & Amery urging decision & definiteness. We have had six columns & more of speeches from the P.M. in less that a week & no-one knows what he means. You can't hunt hounds that way. Unless he takes control quickly all the hounds will be scattered after different foxes – unless indeed the bulk of them hunt a rabbit. Oh for an hour of Glasgow![62] What a contrast is this dreary, muddled opening of the new campaign.

---

[61] Col. John Gretton (1867–1947) Brewer and Chairman of Bass, Ratcliffe & Gretton, Burton-on-Trent. Conservative MP for S. Derbyshire 1895–1906; Rutland June 1907–November 1918; Burton December 1918–1943. Created CBE 1919, Baron Gretton 1944. Renounced Conservative whip in July 1921 when negotiations began with de Valera. Leader of the Diehards in the Commons.

[62] A reference to Joseph Chamberlain's speech launching tariff reform at Glasgow, 6 October 1903.

I am glad that Bonar is released from his sufferings which I fear were terrible.[63] He was a strange character. I am glad that I was able to see him after his retirement & that he liked what I said of him in the H. of C. I do not think that I could ever have worked comfortably with him again but we had no personal quarrel.

AC5/1/296

n.d. (?2 November 1923)
Twitt's Ghyll

My dear Ida,

...

We are all of us thinking a good deal of politics just now. I don't know exactly how much N. tells you, but though I know some things confidentially from him the following has all reached me from other sources by which I am not bound to secrecy.

Baldwin decided that food taxes were too dangerous tho' it is possible that he thinks that the time for them will come before long. He might put a duty on some fresh fruits but he will not touch corn or meat. He is probably saying so tonight at Manchester. He definitely authorised W. Evans to make his declaration against food taxes at Halifax.[64] Personally I am inclined to think that as things are he would have done better to go the 'whole hog – totus porcus!' as Lord Fisher said – for he would then show a much better & indeed quite definite & immediate result in orders, i.e. work. What alarms me is that neither he nor the Cabinet do at present know what their tariff is to be, & that they have prepared no statistics or material in support of their case. A Cabinet Minister came to me yesterday & asked me if I would take the presidency of a new organisation on T[ariff] R[eform] League lines to work up propaganda & said that the Board of Trade had nothing of any use. I asked what exactly is your policy? He could tell me no more than I have told you. I am alarmed both by this uncertainty & by this absence of information. It is certain that we must now have an election not later than February & nothing has been prepared for the campaign. I declined. B. is not going to fight on the old Tariff Reform lines & it would therefore be a mistake to put me conspicuously at the head of *his* organization. Moreover I don't know what his plan is & therefore I cannot expound it; & lastly tho' I am ready to support his policy, I am not ready to father it. I am prepared to tow his line but I am not prepared to say that it is my choice & to explain with conviction why no other line is possible.

[63] Law had died from throat cancer on 30 October 1923.
[64] Worthington-Evans made this speech at Huddersfield on 30 October not Halifax.

I gather from many sources that the Cabinet is tired of Curzon & that Curzon is only one degree less tired of the Cabinet & that a very little push would send him out. I have been approached indirectly by one Cabinet Minister & directly by another to know whether I would take his place or join as e.g. Minister without portfolio. Neither Minister pretended to have the P.M.'s authority tho' one of them said the P.M. had in conversation dropped a hint that he would like to have me. To all which I have replied, in one case verbally in the other in writing (1) that I will not be a party to any intrigue – or let me say organized movement – against Curzon. I have no obligation to C. & I think indeed that he failed in loyalty to my colleagues & me, but if I intended to attack him I should do it publicly & on public grounds; (2) that I will not come under any conditional understanding to join the Govt. at any time; (3) that Baldwin ought not to change his ministers now if they will accept his policy. His business now is to preserve union. The time for reorganization will come after the General Election if he wins.

. . . . I have burned my boats & shall support Baldwin, but he is not going to work the right way to win a victory. He has gone off at half cock.

AC5/1/297

14 November 1923
Twitt's Ghyll

My dear Hilda,

A line to tell you that I know no more than you what the P.M. intends to do. Baldwin would be really incredible – if he did not exist.

At our interview on Monday he hesitated & fenced with my questions as to what was really in his mind & when I said that I still did not understand exactly what he meant – the only thing that he had said that was to the point was that he had hoped that if we fought together in the election it "might be found possible" for us to join the Govt. in unspecified positions after the election – he replied that he wanted to understand what was in *our* minds. I was sick of his fencing so I accepted the challenge. Then instead of making a spontaneous & generous offer, he forced me to state terms & my terms are these:-

Assuming that when I know his policy I shall approve it & that he will accept a suggestion that I shall make for preference on wheat & meat by subsidy to freights, I & F.E. will join at once as Ministers without portfolio or salary but only on condition that after the election (if he wins!) we shall both receive offices of equal influence & importance to those we previously held i.e. Privy Seal or Secretary of State for me & the Lord Chancellorship for F.E. & that he must find room for four of our friends in suitable offices after the election. We will not join in any other capacity, nor will we give contingent promises or accept contingent assurances which he has shown himself too weak in the past & is daily showing himself too weak to make of any value. Of course all this was put very quietly & quite inoffensively e.g. I did not speak to him of weakness.

I said frankly that I would not be treated as a boy on probation, that I considered that I had been treated with great & public indignity in May & that I would not now join or advise F.E. to join except in positions that showed clearly that we were accepted on our former footing of influence & authority.

I guess that B. is in an awful mess. Bob Cecil, Ronald McNeil [sic][65] & Billy Gore[66] probably threatened resignation if we go in; Devonshire seems to be trying to get out in any case & Derby says he can't fight Lancs. without F.E. & will resign if he is not got in &c. &c,.

But imagine that Baldwin sent for us again in about an hour's time to convince Derby that an immediate election was necessary.

And since then I have not heard a word from him tho' last night he tried to get F.E. to alter his terms.

We went to see Sherlock Holmes last night & in the entre-act this old rhyme buzzed in my head.

He's not very clever, he's not very bright
But he's honest, he says so, so that is all right.
And he always comes home to his tea.
With his pigs & his pipe
With his pigs & his pipe
He *always* comes home to his tea.

AC5/1/298   17 November 1923
                                               Twitt's Ghyll

My dear Ida,

. . .

What is one to say of Baldwin? He is in my opinion a thoroughly 'rattled' man as Horne said, he would not speak openly and frankly to

[65] Ronald McNeill (1861–1934) Conservative MP for St Augustines, Kent July 1911–1918 and Canterbury December 1918–October 1927. Under-Secretary to Foreign Office 1922–1924 and 1924–1925; Financial Secretary to Treasury 1925–1927; Chancellor Duchy of Lancaster 1927–1929. Created Baron Cushenden. A Diehard.

[66] William George Arthur Ormsby-Gore (1885–1964) Conservative MP for Denbigh 1910–18 and Stafford 1918–38. Under-Secretary to Colonies 1922–1924 and 1924–1929; Postmaster-General 1931; First Commissioner of Works 1931–1936; Colonial Secretary 1936–1938. High Commissioner to South Africa 1941–44. Succeeded as 4th Baron Harlech May 1938.

Birkenhead or to me, but after our second meeting he told Derby that he should announce our accession to the Cabinet the next morning & invite us to attend. Not only so, but he had between the two interviews sought & obtained the King's approval. The first fact I know from Derby; the second from a person of absolute trustworthiness & authority who's name I do not care to write even to you.

He now explains that to include us at once would have looked like trying to bargain. What he did do was to try to buy us by contingent promises & hopes. He is not the strong, fearless man who knowingly takes his risks, but a weak, harassed creature who tumbled into his new policy in despair & without in any way seeing the consequences. Horne repeated yesterday that Baldwin had ridiculed the idea in September.

I do not know what Neville's real forecast of the result is, but I do know on good authority that the real estimate of the Central Office is a majority of 27 only including Unionist Free Traders. Neville's own secretary stands a [sic] free-trader, & several Lancashire and other Conservatives do the like, & the Central Office does not dare attempt to constrain them. Horne says that we lose 7 seats out of our 12 in Scotland; Derby says we lose 10 in Lancashire; everybody says we must lose in London, & Hewins tells me that we lose 1 at least in B'ham. And this is a policy which it would be madness to attempt without a solid working majority & which cannot be carried if there is even a marked drop in our present majority of 70!

Meanwhile tho' I deeply resent Baldwin's behaviour to F.E. & me, we shall carry out our promise to support them on the platform. I have been more anxious to take this line on F.E.'s account than on my own & he has heartily & really generously accepted it. But can you picture to yourself Baldwin sending Jackson[67] to plead with F.E. for support in Lancashire after all that has passed. Yet that is what he did yesterday & Jackson, who is a gentleman, felt the shame & humilitation[sic]. That is the answer to Neville who told me that the real difficulty was not the Undersecretaries but F.E.'s unpopularity with the party. When I left him yesterday he had 40 or more requests to speak in different places & replied to all that all his arrangements would be made through the Central Office to whom he referred the applicants.

I really cannot write calmly. Baldwin is now apparently helping on his policy. Plymouth was Protection. The H. of C. speech was Revenue. On Monday he told me that it was a general tariff. On Thursday this had become general duties whatever this may mean, & today it is

---

[67] Francis Stanley Jackson (1870–1947) Played cricket for Yorkshire 1894–1905. Conservative MP for Howdenshire, February 1915–October 1926. Financial Secretary to War Office 1922–1923. Chairman of Conservative Party 1923–1926. Governor of Bengal 1927–32. Although not a Diehard voted against Coalition on several Diehard motions in 1922.

reported that his address will speak of the whole scheme as temporary. There is not a ghost of a chance after all this bungling of carrying anything & the real fight after the election will be to save, if we can, what the coalition did.

But don't underrate Baldwin. He has united the Liberal Party & no Liberal could do that, & he has brought Beaverbrook & me together & neither Bonar nor L.G. nor F.E. had ever been able to do that. And the humour of it is that it is only by F.E. & myself that Beaverbrook has been prevented from deliberately setting out to smash Baldwin by running whole-hogger candidates in Tory seats just as he ran Liberals against L.G. last time to serve Bonar's interest.

Burn these recent letters. I am so angry & disgusted, & I must blow off steam somewhere as my feelings have to be kept out of my speeches.

8.

RETURN OF THE 'EXER EX-MINISTERS'

The Opposition front bench, December 1923–November 1924

At the Carlton Club meeting in October 1922 Balfour had reflected caustically that while 'it has never been a Conservative principle to abandon a Leader ... I concede it has sometimes been a Conservative practice'.[1] At this meeting, the Conservative Party had abandoned Austen Chamberlain. A little over a year later it appeared as if a similar fate would befall his principal successor. Amid the ruins of Law's victory for 'Tranquillity' many observers subscribed to Hankey's view that 'Baldwin, though a nice fellow is not the stuff of which British Prime Ministers are made'.[2] In the immediate aftermath of this disaster, most also assumed he would be compelled to pay the ultimate price for this inadequacy. Certainly Birkenhead was one of them. Electoral defeat was a vindication of all that he had predicted since the fall of the Coalition. Rejoicing that it had finally 'put an end to the idea that fifth rate intelligence could govern the Empire',[3] Birkenhead set in motion the final act in a strategy to which he had committed the Chamberlainites in November 1922. Between 6 and 10 December rumours abounded that the former Conservative Coalitionists were about to displace Baldwin, replace him variously with Balfour, Derby or Chamberlain and then form some sort of Liberal-Conservative combination to exclude Labour from office.[4] In the event, the plan miscarried. The apparent recrudescence of the 'old intrigue'[5] rallied the victors of the Carlton Club to defend the Party, their brand of Conservatism and, by necessity, its leader from coalitionist conspiracy. Virtually overnight, Baldwin was transformed from the wanton destroyer of Law's majority into the guarantor of Conservative principle. As Amery told Baldwin, 'you embody and personify the decision of the Party to live its own life and have its own constructive policy'.[6] Ultimately, therefore, despite much Conservative anger, frustration and despair at Baldwin's perceived folly, the impulse which brought about the coalescence of figures as diverse as the Cecils, Younger, Strachey, Gretton and the ministerial beneficiaries of the Carlton Club was the consensus that they were 'not

---

[1] This remark is quoted in Birkenhead, *Contemporary Personalities*, 20. The official report in *Gleanings and Memoranda*, LVI. November 1922, 487–495 makes no reference to it but the suspension dots on p494 may conceal the omission.

[2] Hankey Diary, 9 December 1923, Hankey MSS 1/7 fol.5.

[3] R.R. James, *Victor Cazalet: A Portrait*, 93.

[4] For the 'Birkenhead Plot' see M. Cowling, *The Impact of Labour*, Chapter XVII.

[5] J.C.C. Davidson to Wolmer, 11 December 1923, Wolmer MSS 6. (Bodleian Library, Oxford)

[6] Amery to Baldwin, 8 December 1923, Baldwin MSS 35/169–71.

prepared to cut off Baldwin's head and make Austen Chamberlain King'.[7] *They were even less inclined to install Birkenhead as Regent.*

By January 1924 Austen Chamberlain's mood was one of sullen resignation. He had been bitter and uncooperative after the failure to rehabilitate him in November. After the election, he was so appalled by the prospect of a Labour government[8] that he initially favoured an impracticable scheme for keeping Labour out involving Liberal support for a reconstituted Tory ministry under an alternative Conservative leader.[9] Yet despite such feelings, he played little part in Birkenhead's plot to oust Baldwin, although he supported it publicly.[10] By the end of December he still considered giving vent to his frustrations at the stance of both Asquith and Baldwin but eventually decided to follow everyone else and just 'wait and see'. On New Year's Day he could only lament that politics had become 'so confused and ... so disagreeable that [he] had little heart for them'.[11] During the next three weeks before Parliament reassembled Chamberlain devoted his energies to the hedging at Twitt's Ghyll. Yet despite talk of giving himself up to the 'pleasures of the country', this retirement was short-lived. Although professing to believe that if he expressed his true feelings about Baldwin he 'should become almost a hero of the Tory Party', under the guidance of his wife, Churchill, Birkenhead and Balfour, Chamberlain omitted all reference to either Baldwin or the retention of protection from his speech on the Address.[12] Although 'nought but concentrated bitterness against Asquith', his utterances on 21 January struck the right note within the Party and placed him 'once again in the odour of sanctity'.[13] a good impression reinforced five days later by an explicit declaration in favour of 'heal[ing] any differences that had existed in [party] ranks ... to lay the foundations for future success'.[14] These valuable gestures of conciliation opened the way for Neville Chamberlain's efforts finally to consummate reunion.

Having found his half-brother still determined only to return to party councils in association with Birkenhead and Horne, Neville Chamberlain raised the issue at meetings of the former House of Commons Ministers on 23 and 24 January. Although the objection to Birkenhead remained, under Neville Chamberlain's careful guidance 'there was a general feeling that if it were necessary it was better to have

[7] Derby Diary, 17 December 1923. For similar comments see Neville Chamberlain Diary, 19 December 1923; Younger to Lord Hugh Cecil, 11 December 1923, Quickswood MSS 31/146.

[8] A. Chamberlain to N. Chamberlain 8 December 1923, NC1/27/83.

[9] See Chamberlain interview, *Daily Mail*, 11 December 1923 and speech at Birmingham, *Birmingham Post*, 8 December 1923.

[10] Interview in *Daily Mail*, 11 December 1923.

[11] A. Chamberlain to E.M. Pollock, 1 January 1924, Hanworth MSS d.433/1.

[12] A. Chamberlain to Ida, 20 January 1924, AC5/1/303.

[13] A. Chamberlain to Hilda, 24 January 1924, AC5/1/304. See also Baldwin to A. Chamberlain, 21 January 1924, AC35/4/1. That this was the obvious purpose even to those on the other benches see Grigg to Abe Bailey, 24 January 1924, Altrincham MSS (Bodleian Library, Oxford). Cf. the assessment in Amery Diary, 21 January 1924, *The Leo Amery Diaries*, 364.

[14] Chamberlain at the Jeweller's Dinner, Birmingham, *Morning Post*, 28 January 1924.

F.E. in than A[usten] or Horne out'. Such a proposition was rendered more palatable by the fact that 'there was no immediate question of his taking office but simply of his being treated as an ex-member of Cabinet'.[15] *Moreover, there was the possibility, as Neville Chamberlain recognised, that once reunion had been achieved 'Austen will think that he has discharged his obligation of loyalty to F. E. and that the links which now bind them together will disappear'.*[16]

Reunion was finally arranged at a secret dinner at Neville Chamberlain's house on the evening of 5 February. During the meal the anxious host's observation that his brother 'looked a little stiff and suspicious'[17] *gravely under-estimated the real mood. Austen had recently criticised Baldwin for consulting his front bench colleagues about reunion. He had also confided to his stepmother that he would be 'rather relieved if I can still sit on the backbenches and not take responsibility for [Baldwin's] stupidity'. His acceptance of his half-brother's invitation was thus largely dictated by a sense of fraternal duty.*[18] *That the meeting proved such a success was due to two factors. First, after a 'very informal and very confidential' consultation with Balfour on the previous afternoon Baldwin had finally resolved to accept Birkenhead as the price of reunion.*[19] *Secondly, reunion was a triumph for Neville's tact and assiduous preparation over the previous two weeks, during which he had been 'working like a beaver to that end'.*[20] *Having 'carefully coached S. B. as to what to say', Neville Chamberlain was delighted when Baldwin kept to the agreed line saying 'what he had to say without any beating about the bush and after one moment's hesitation A[usten] frankly accepted the invitation. After that all went like clockwork and very soon it was My dear Stanley and My dear Austen as if they had ne'er been parted'.*[21] *Baldwin made no difficulty about Birkenhead and in return Austen Chamberlain 'left unsaid a great deal that [he] was sorely tempted to say' in the interests of harmony.*[22]

The return of the Chamberlainite ex-Ministers to the meeting of the Conservative Shadow Cabinet on 7 February in an atmosphere of 'marked affability' represented the effective dissolution of the alternative leadership which had threatened to disrupt the fragile stability of the Party for the past fifteen months. For Austen Chamberlain, as for many others in the Party during 1924, there followed a mellowing to political reality in which contempt for Baldwin's leadership was gradually accompanied by resignation to the fact that until Baldwin recognised his own inadequacy as leader, 'it was worse than useless to try and displace him'.[23] *In return Austen Chamberlain's*

---

[15] Amery Diary, 23 January 1924, *Leo Amery Diaries*, I, 365.

[16] Amery Diary, 4 February 1924 reporting Neville Chamberlain.

[17] Neville Chamberlain Diary, 6 February 1924. D. Dilks, *Neville Chamberlain*, 370 incorrectly dates the meeting as 6 February.

[18] A. Chamberlain to Mary Carnegie, 27 January 1924, AC4/1/1239.

[19] 'Memo of conversation with Mr. Baldwin' 4 February 1924, Whittinghame MSS 19 (National Register of Archives, Scotland).

[20] Neville Chamberlain Diary, 24 January 1924.

[21] N. Chamberlain to Hilda, 9 February 1924, NC18/1/425.

[22] A. Chamberlain to Hilda, 6 February 1924, AC5/1/310.

[23] A. Chamberlain to Ida, 9 February 1924, AC5/1/307. See also his letter to Chilcott in H. Montgomery Hyde, *Baldwin*, 203–4.

new influence made itself immediately apparent. Baldwin announced the purpose of the meeting and then, without even commenting on the new members or expressing an opinion himself, abdicated control of the discussion to Austen Chamberlain.[24] *Although professing to be an unrepentant 'whole-hogger', Austen Chamberlain declared the first objective should be to 'smash the Liberal Party' which he considered already predominantly Labour, and to 'repeat the history of Liberal-Unionism' by re-defining Conservatism to absorb those sympathetic Liberals who remained.*[25] *He thus advised a return to Bonar Law's 1922 position, supported by Balfour, Birkenhead and Curzon. Despite Amery and Bridgeman's efforts to struggle for a 'braver course', the Shadow Cabinet 'all tumbled over themselves to emphasise their agreement with Austen Chamberlain'.*[26]

Although the Party had been formally reunited in February 1924, fundamental differences of attitude and strategy remained. So did the residual bitterness and suspicion which had been engendered by the Coalition and its fall. This was particularly notable with regard to the overtures from Churchill and his fellow anti-socialist Liberals seeking closer relations with the Conservative Party: an issue which came to a head in February when Churchill announced his intention to stand as an Independent Anti-Socialist in the Abbey by-election against the official Conservative candidate. By championing Churchill's rehabilitation, Horne, Birkenhead and Balfour became conspicuous as the advocates of what appeared to many former opponents to be an unregenerate Coalitionism.[27] *Chamberlain's remarks at the Business Committee on 7 February suggested the same faith in anti-socialist realignment − albeit within the Conservative Party. He favoured Churchill's return, advised Baldwin to assist him at Abbey when consulted in late February and urged him to assure Churchill of a good seat if not adopted. Chamberlain's interventions also proved to be decisive on at least two occasions in assisting Churchill to obtain fair play against the opposition of protectionists like Amery, Bridgeman and his own half-brother who suspected Churchill's free trade and coalitionist inclinations. On 6 March he had become 'angry and excited' at a meeting of ex-ministers and threatened to speak for Churchill if his half-brother or Amery spoke for the official candidate.*[28] *On 15 March his intervention, again in a state of 'great excitement', forced Baldwin to reverse his veto on the publication of Balfour's letter endorsing Churchill's Conservative credentials*[29] *after* The Times *published Amery's attack upon them. This stand by the newly returned Chamberlainites clearly helped to perpetuate old suspicions and antipathies only formally buried in early February: a fact forcefully*

---

[24] Neville Chamberlain Diary and Derby Diary, both 7 February 1924.

[25] A. Chamberlain to Hoare, 28 January 1924, Templewood MSS V/I (Cambridge University Library).

[26] Amery Diary 7 February 1924. See also Neville Chamberlain Diary 7 February 1924 and Bridgeman Diary January 1924, II fol.99–101.

[27] See R.C. Self, *Tories and Tariffs*, Chapter VII.

[28] Amery Diary, 6 March 1924.

[29] Balfour to Churchill (draft) 14 March 1924, Whittinghame MSS I. For Chamberlain boasting of his role see Lady Kennet Diary, 1 April 1924, Kennet MSS D/16 (Cambridge University Library).

demonstrated in May by Baldwin's pointedly unflattering observations about his new allies and the 'Churchill plotting' in his infamous interview in the People.[30] *Although the reporters had 'a bad reputation in Downing Street' and Baldwin may have been 'indiscreet in what he said and doubly indiscreet in what he allowed to be said to him',[31] few doubted that the sentiments expressed in the* People *article were Baldwin's. Chamberlain's conspicuous efforts to pay an unnecessary compliment to Lloyd George during the Imperial preference debate in June confirmed similar suspicions.[32]*

AC5/1/299   24 December 1923
                                                          Twitt's Ghyll

My dear Ida,

. . .

I wonder & wonder about the political situation but can come to no definite determination. I incline to think that Asquith now means to keep Macdonald [sic] in if possible &, if not, out to rule with his help. I meditated a letter to the Times but have decided against it & shall just 'wait & see'.

AC5/1/300   29 December 1923
                                                          Twitt's Ghyll

My dear Hilda,

. . .

The more I think of politics the less I understand the attitude of other people. The Times writes as if they were a children's game & every child must have its turn or it won't be fair. God bless me! I want to know how the King's government is to be carried on & hold that Baldwin ought to have seen Asquith immediately after the result of the elections was known & tried to come to terms with him either for a Conservative Govt. with his support or for his Govt. with Conservative support – in either case on conditions. But he has allowed the initiative to pass to others, & I expect – or fear – ... a Liberal-Labour alliance

---

[30] The *People* 18 May 1924. For this incident see T. Driberg, *Lord Beaverbrook: A Study in Power and Frustration* (1956), 178–185.

[31] A. Chamberlain to Hilda, 25 May 1924, AC5/1/319. Also Jones Diary, 25 May 1924, *Whitehall Diary*, I, 280; A. Chamberlain memoranda on conversation with Baldwin, 21 May 1924, AC24/6/3.

[32] *House of Commons Debates*, 5 Series,vol 174 col 2260, 18 June 1924. See N. Chamberlain to Ida, 22 June 1924, NC18/1/441 for this complaint.

with an immense access of prestige to Labour & a programme which we shall not like at all.

Well, it's no good fussing & worrying when one can do nothing. But the wait-and-see attitude irks me & all my discontents turn inward & poison me. Some day I shall say publicly what I think of Baldwin as a statesman & leader & then I shall be finally done for.

AC5/1/301   4 January 1924
                                                    Twitt's Ghyll

My dear Hilda,

      ...

I was not born to waste my sweetness on the desert air of politics. Having firmly decided that I will not liberate my soul to the Times on the political situation because noone would take my advice & too many people would think that I was engaged in an 'intrigue', I have given myself up wholly to the pleasures of the country. Does anyone get such pleasure as I do out of searching my clumps of I[ris] stylosa for buds ... & filling vases variously with them & their leaves or with ... shoots of yellow Jasmine or ribes ...? Then again there is the bird table outside my window.

AC5/1/302   12 January 1924
                                                    Twitt's Ghyll

My dear Ida,

      ...

I went up to town on Thursday to swear & took the occasion to lunch with Margot,[33] Asquith being unfortunately voiceless in bed. I wanted to know what was really in A.'s mind & what he was trying or wishing to bring about. It would have been very much more interesting & instructive to have talked with A. himself for M. has of course no balance & is full of personal dislikes & without judgement; but discounting all that I came to the conclusion that if there ever was any chance of doing business with A. (which seemed doubtful) it had vanished. I should have liked us to have put him in & keep him in for a time – on certain conditions of course. But he apparently despises the Govt., hates or perhaps rather fears any taint of association with the Tory party, dreads lest half his party should join Labour & thinks

[33] Emma Alice Margaret Tennant (1864–1945). Daughter of Sir Charles Tennant. Known as Margot. Second wife of the Liberal Leader in 1894 after the death of his first wife in 1891. Published four separate volumes of memoirs.

that he can turn Labour out again when he likes without their being allowed a general election. Nous verrons!

AC5/1/303   20 January 1924
                                                Twitt's Ghyll

My dear Ida,

    ... The Times was right in saying that these debates have been on a high level & I thought Neville's speech the best that I have yet heard him deliver ... Now I am wondering whether I can screw myself up to a half-hour's speech on my own account tomorrow. Ivy wants me to speak but does not want me to make the whole speech as I see it, & Balfour's luncheon party (B & his niece Mrs Lascelles, F.E. & Lady Birkenhead & Winston & Mrs Winston) unanimously declared her to be in the right which indeed I know she is. So King Charles's head or Stanley Baldwin's is to be kept out of the beginning & any nailing of protection colours to the mast out of the end & what remains? Nought but concentrated bitterness against Asquith! I was wound up to the proper pitch by Friday but my gall & wormwood have evaporated during the weekend & I doubt now if I can do it. I wonder if a dozen oysters & a pint of champagne would put me in the right mood again tomorrow at dinner, but even then it would be too late. But if I could find expression & the right expression for all that I feel about his conduct & *for nothing else* I should become almost a hero of the Tory Party.

AC5/1/304   24 January 1924
                                                2 Morpeth Mansions

My dear Hilda,

    ...
    Well you will have seen that I got my speech off & succeeded in leaving out King Charles's head & everything else that was dangerous, so I am once again in the odour of sanctity & Stanley has got another chance of wiping out old scores & uniting the party. Will he take it? Probably not, as instead of deciding for himself he is debating with his colleagues. Neville is doing his best, but the old difficulties remain.
    Congratulations have been showered upon me for my speech, &, tho' I say it as shouldn't, it was a good one. Asquith was uncomfortable, but sent me the enclosed amusing note afterwards. I replied that I trusted that he would live long, but in any [sic] why worry about a will for he would have nothing to leave. As matter of fact, half or more of

his party is already more Labour than Liberal & of the rest not a few are more Conservative. It is I think our business now to smash that Party for it is a fraud.

AC5/1/306   4 February 1924
                                                              Twitt's Ghyll

My dear Ida,

    ...
    I go to town tomorrow for Enid's wedding & Neville has bidden me dine with him to meet S.B. I agreed, for I felt that I must, but I have nothing to say to S.B. I don't want to meet him & I grudge being kept in town. Shan't I add to the gaiety of the Party? Anyway we shall *faire les frais de la conversation* this time! Will he talk of strawberries & his digestion & whether it is unpardonable in him to pick out the biggest when lovely Mrs. B. is sitting at the other end of the table? Anyway I am not going to repeat the last performance & be bowed out of the room with a 'thank you' & no corresponding frankness on his side.

    ...
    Don't fuss yourself about the Party meeting. S.B. will get his reelection or his vote of confidence or whatever he chooses to ask for. Resignation whilst resubmitting himself is a farce.

AC5/1/310   6 February [mis-dated March] 1924
                                                         2 Morpeth Mansions

My dear Hilda,

    ...
    And I who was vexed enough to have to lose a day in the garden for Enid's wedding ... was first kept in town last night by Neville's desire that I should meet S.B. & am now detained again that I may attend S.B.'s meeting of ex-Ministers tomorrow, for the gentleman has at last taken the plunge, decided to defy the wrath of all the Cecils & at the risk of losing Bob [Cecil] & Jem [Salisbury] to invite me & F.E. to join his shadow cabinet & to sit on the front bench. Neville smiled fraternally on us both & silently administered his blessing. We were apparently all three agreed about policy & I hoped I behaved prettily. Certainly I left unsaid a great deal that I was sorely tempted to say. Well, it's the right thing for the party & therefore for us, but I should have loved to sit up aloft & keep watch on poor Jack instead of sitting beside him. Lord! what fun it would have been. My mouth waters at the thought.

AC5/1/307
9 February 1924
Twitt's Ghyll

My dear Ida,

... Still everything is just beginning to move & the garden becomes interesting just as I must hie me away to the House of Commons. We had our first shadow cabinet on Thursday, settled our policy, all but Amery being in agreement, & procedure at the Party meeting as to which I got my way. Indeed, the *exer* ex-ministers were treated with marked affability & did more than their share of the talking – I in particular as you would expect! But I am not happy, for I don't feel towards Baldwin as I like to feel towards my 'leader' & do not think him competent for his position. But unless he comes to understand that himself, it would be worse than useless to try to displace him. Balfour, whom he has been consulting said to me that he could not gage [sic] S.B.'s intelligence (I suggested that one can't gage what doesn't exist) but that he could not understand why S.B. did not retire. His thoughts, however, have gone no further, as far as I could see, than the usual company formula: retires & being eligible offers himself for re-election – a farce in this case & as such neither dignified nor honest, & I hope that I have put a stop to it. But Ned Talbot (Fitzalan) whom I suggested for mover of the resolution of continued confidence in S.B. declines, & his wife tells Ivy that he thought him so unfit for the leadership that he *could* not do it.

Well, well, why bother about these things? The wise man has said Wait & see. Let us follow his advice. I will rally forth in spite of the wind & wet.

AC5/1/308
16 February 1924
Twitt's Ghyll

My dear Hilda,

...

Ivy & I had a most amusing lunch at F.E.'s on Monday to meet Balfour & Horne. A.J.B. was at the top of his form. His description of our first shadow-cabinet sent us into convulsions of laughter & was more complimentary to his old colleagues than to his new ones. But that is now treason!

Baldwin did well on the second day but forgot Poplar & so let in Asquith. We were a little dismayed at first; but I am not sorry, for either Asquith will try to withdraw his motion or Ramsay will agree to accept the correction. If the former, Asquith will get no kudos; & if the latter he will still be kept out. I tried to indicate to him clearly that he must not expect mercy from us after his recent behaviour, I had sooner see Labour in than give him the chance of producing another (& corrected) Ll.G. budget & going to the country on that or carrying it by Labour support.

AC5/1/315   18 April 1924
                                                            Twitt's Ghyll

My dear Ida,

. . .

The London correspondent of the B.D.P. sought me out a day or two ago to ask what I thought of things. I dare say that if we were talking you would ask the same question, so I will anticipate your enquiry.

First, the Govt. has exhausted its early prestige or popularity & is on the down-grade; but observe! when that happens to an old govt., they never recover; but a young govt. may recover absolutely & rise to greater things – e.g. the Asquith govt. was beaten in March 1909, but got an entirely new lease of life out of Lloyd George's budget or our treatment of it. So this Govt. *may* recover over Snowden's budget or something else, but I do not think that it will. It is too much a one-man show. Clynes cannot lead the House; he is not supple or agile enough, Snowden's temper is too bad; & Wheatley[34] who might be the best parliamentarian is too new & also too extreme for the present H. of C. If he led, I do not think that he could afford to be moderate. There remains J.H. Thomas, one of the cleverest, one of the most experienced, but – somehow I don't think he will do or be chosen.

Next the Liberal Party is visibly bursting up. It holds constant party meetings to decide its course. Then 40 vote with the govt.; 20 vote with us, & the rest (including the leaders) walk out, or absent themselves.

Lastly, our front bench has many merits, but it is inferior to anything that I have known. It has no 'punch', no grip. It makes quite good speeches – some of them, that is; Neville Hoare,[35] Lloyd Graeme & E. Wood – but it carries no big guns; & Stanley himself never fires more

---

[34] John Wheatley (1869–1930). Labour MP for Glasgow Shettleston November 1922 until his death on 12 May 1930. Minister of Health 1924.

[35] Samuel John Gurney Hoare (1880–1959). Conservative MP for Chelsea 1910–44. Secretary for Air 1922–24, 1924–29, 1940. Secretary for India 1931–35; Foreign Secretary 1935; First Lord of Admiralty 1936–37; Home Secretary 1937–39; Lord Privy Seal 1939–40. Ambassador in Madrid 1940–44. Conservative Party Treasurer 1930–31. Succeeded as 2nd Baronet 1915. Created Viscount Templewood 1944.

than a pop gun or a peashooter at critical moments, & hasn't a ghost of an idea how to *fight*.

Nevertheless I am inclined to predict that the Govt. will be unable to last out the session without great humiliation. No party now has a man who really commands public interest & enthusiasm. If any party could find such an one, it would win.

But the exhaustion of the Labour Party is probably more felt in the House than in the country, where, I suspect that they have already gained many & are still gaining more Liberal votes. At this moment, we should not win many seats from Labour, but Labour & we should both win seats from Liberals.

AC5/1/319   25 May 1924
                                                    2 Morpeth Mansions

My dear Hilda,

...

There is no news for me to give you except that the children continue to go on well, & that Baldwin's People interview[36] has been the sensation & the scandal of the week. When I first heard of it I said like F.E., Baldwin is not the man to speak thus of his colleagues with whom he is acting; & I believe the reporter had a bad reputation in Downing St. But Baldwin told me his own story of the interview & it was enough to show that he had been indiscreet in what he said & doubly indiscreet in what he allowed to be said to him. He really is a victim of the 'manie des persecution'. I have talked & written very bluntly to him ...

AC5/1/320   14 June 1924
                                                       Twitt's Ghyll

My dear Ida,

Superior people like Neville who grow orchids & other greenhouse plants, may be able to keep the weather out of their letters, tho' even then it is a pose; but simple cottage folk like you & me know that the weather is half of our lives & all our holidays, & we may mingle our tears of sorrow & vexation at the eccentricities of our climate ... Left

---

[36] On 18 May 1924, the *People* published a long exclusive interview with Baldwin. In this 'bombshell' he denounced Rothermere, Beaverbrook and Birkenhead specifically as well as a general attack upon 'this Churchill plotting' and the desire of its instigators 'to go back to the old dirty kind of politics'.

to myself I would never spend a Sunday anywhere but here, but Mary would agree with Ivy that that would not be good for me & I should agree with Mary that it was not fair to Ivy & so & so & so I must garden as I can & when I can.

. . .

And next week I must go back to politics! Oh bother or words to that effect!

AC5/1/321   22 June 1924
                                          Government House
                                              Farnborough

My dear Ida,

. . .

I was able to tell you a fortnight ago how good a speech your brother Neville made. I may now add that I pulled off a great success in winding up the Preference Debate. Baldwin was quite good – except for one fearful *gaffe* about controlling the whole corn trade which delighted the Clyde & Snowden & disgusted our people[37] – but he is never distinguished, never one bit better than good. I really did make a speech such as the House used to hear often in old days, but has not heard for the last year or two, & I never was so loaded with congratulations from the Speaker downwards. So you need not be ashamed of your two brothers.

AC5/1/322   29 June 1924
                                              Twitt's Ghyll

My dear Ida,

. . .

I find politics very dull. Baldwin does not interest or attract me. He seems to me stupid & incommunicative, & his habit of bursting out with some inconceivable folly, like his proposal to buy up & market all Australian corn in the Preference debate without consulting his colleagues or himself knowing what he meant, is both disconcerting & exasperating. Well I am going to lunch with Balfour tomorrow & *him* I love.

Baldwin was never a good leader of Opposition and by March 1924 he was saying

---

[37] On 18 June 1924, Baldwin announced that they would buy Dominion corn for distribution at cost price: a proposal greeted by Snowden as 'the biggest Socialistic proposal' he had ever heard.

so himself.[38] *During 1924 he rarely gave an unambiguous lead. When he did, as in the case of his proposal to buy Dominion corn for distribution at cost price during the Preference debate, he did so without consulting his closest colleagues and the ensuing derision served only to confirm that his 'innocence approaches childishness'.*[39] *Austen Chamberlain's increasing frustration at Baldwin's incapacity as leader came to a head in July over his hopeless equivocation about future relations with like-minded Liberals. At a dinner at Hoare's on 3 July it had been agreed that Baldwin should 'hold out a hand' at the Lowestoft Party Conference to those Liberals supporting the Conservatives in the lobbies, but unwilling at that juncture to make the transition to the Tory benches.*[40] *In accordance with this understanding, in his speech synchronised with Baldwin's on 17 July, Austen Chamberlain announced that the Conservative Party would 'welcome in no ungrudging spirit and in no ungenerous manner recruits that may ultimately gain for our party men who ... without joining our party see eye to eye with us in this great issue'. In Baldwin's speech to the Party Conference, however, this 'ungrudging spirit' was conspicuously absent. Instead, Baldwin declared that if any Liberal was willing to 'unconditionally adopt' Conservative policy then he would be welcome if he 'came forward ... and s[aid] so like a man'.*[41]

Austen Chamberlain's reaction to Baldwin's speech was one of anger and betrayal. After giving vent to his frustration in a letter to Baldwin demanding an explanation,[42] *he retired to the country, tired and disgusted to drown his sorrows. Nor could Austen Chamberlain have been appeased by Baldwin's wounded reply, professing to believe that he had followed the spirit of the agreement, or his conclusion that 'those who agreed with us on these important questions could not be happy in their present environment ... [and] our Party offered the only home'.*[43] *Evidently, Baldwin considered that it was now up to Churchill to accept publicly his invitation or terminate negotiations. A week later Baldwin reiterated the theme of his Lowestoft speech in a slightly milder form.*[44] *Confronted by Baldwin's innocent denial of duplicity, Austen Chamberlain resolved upon 'Machiavellian' tactics to force Baldwin into at least the appearance of a more sympathetic policy. Writing in the* Evening News *on the day the Shadow Cabinet were to discuss their relations with the Liberals, Austen Chamberlain set out the full case for cooperation, innocently repeating the argument with which Baldwin had forestalled him after Lowestoft. '[A]lthough some people have* affected to discover differences *of purpose and intention between my speech and a speech delivered on the same day at Lowestoft by Mr. Baldwin', Chamberlain argued, 'to anyone who will carefully compare the two it will be apparent that they were the result of previous consultation and the*

[38] See Lady Kennet Diary, 20 March 1924, Kennet MSS D/16.
[39] N. Chamberlain to Ida, 22 June 1924, NC18/1/441.
[40] A. Chamberlain to Baldwin, 18 July 1924, Baldwin MSS 159/195.
[41] For both speeches see, *The Times*, 18 July 1924.
[42] A. Chamberlain to Baldwin, 18 July 1924, Baldwin MSS 159/195.
[43] Baldwin to A. Chamberlain, 21 July 1924, AC35/5/2a.
[44] Baldwin at Manchester, 26 July, *The Times*, 28 July 1924.

expression of a common policy still further emphasised by Mr. Baldwin at Manchester Saturday last'.[45] *Although in private he recognised that this would not be 'palatable' to all members of the Shadow Cabinet,*[46] *Austen Chamberlain's semantic subtleties had retrieved the situation.*

AC5/1/323   5 July 1924
                                                           Twitt's Ghyll

My dear Ida,

    ...

    ... Thursdays dinner was at Sam Hoare's to meet Baldwin & Winston & half a dozen others, & something may come of that if Baldwin plays his hand as arranged & as he means to do. He speaks on the 17th & 26th & W. and Horne will appear on the same platform in Edinburgh between the two occasions, & the speeches are intended to respond to one another & to advance cooperation. & which I & several others think necessary to success.

    For the rest I have been busy with my Currency & Gold Standard Comtee.[47] – a confidential Treasury affair of which I am Chairman. I always undertake these things with great misgivings &, when engaged on them, find myself more competent, & far more ready to take a decision, than I had expected. Having now heard the evidence of 6 bankers, I understand why we never choose a banker for C/E. They would be paralysed with fear at such decisions as we have to take, & would spoil any policy by niggling preconditions when only courage can carry it through. Goschen[48] proved this rule.

    ...

[45] 'Parties and Prospects', *Evening News*, 30 July 1924. Emphasis added.

[46] A. Chamberlain to Ivy, 29 July 1924, AC/6/1/544.

[47] In June 1924 a Committee on Currency and Bank of England Note Issues was appointed to consider the amalgamation of the Treasury controlled currency note issue with that of the Bank of England: an issue which inevitably led it to consider the much broader issue of the return to the Gold Standard as the Cunliffe Committee in 1918 had recommended that amalgamation should be deferred until they had a year's experience on the Gold Standard. As a former Chancellor, Chamberlain became its first Chairman and by September a full draft of the Committee's report had been prepared endorsing Cunliffe's conclusions before handing over to Bradbury in November when he became Foreign Secretary.

[48] George Joachim Goschen (1831–1907). Liberal Unionist MP for the City of London 1863–1880 and Ripon 1880–1885 when he was elected for Edinburgh East as Independent Liberal 1880–87 and St. George's Westminster 1887–1900. Paymaster-General 1865–1866; Chancellor of Duchy of Lancaster 1886; President Poor Law Board 1868–1871; First Lord of Admiralty 1871–74 and 1895–1900; Chancellor of Exchequer 1887–1892 when retired. Created Viscount Goschen 1900.

AC5/1/324

14 July 1924
2 Morpeth Mansions

My dear Ida,

...

What you say of Baldwin is very true. I am kept in a constant state of discomfort by not knowing how much of what he arranges with me is imparted by him to his colleagues ... Nobody seems to have much confidence in Baldwin except himself, but he seems to be thoroughly satisfied with all that he does. It must at least be admitted that he takes his position seriously & works very hard.

AC5/1/325

19 July 1924
Twitt's Ghyll

My dear Hilda,

...

I have retired to the country very cross & very discouraged. I told you of the dinner at Sam Hoare's at which we discussed our relations with the Winstonian Liberals & of Baldwin's promise to hold out a hand to them at Lowestoft. Winston was to carry it a step farther ... at Edinburgh & Baldwin was to clinch matters at Manchester. Almost the last words Baldwin said were that he saw his way clear to do this, & I undertook to speak on the same lines at Northampton where, through the folly of the C.O. I was billed for the same day as Baldwin at Lowestoft.

Have you read Baldwin's speech? It is throughout an attack on Liberals *as such* without one word to distinguish between Lloyd George & Winston, & the only invitation he extended to any Liberal is to leave his party & join ours "like a man". Meanwhile he had given me no hint of his change of mind & I spoke as agreed, so that our speeches are contrasted & appear to mark an obvious difference of policy.

I am "tired & disgusted". What is the use of my trying to keep in step with him if he behaves in this way, & what pleasure can there be in working with a man so unstable of purpose & so muddled of mind?

...

Saturday night. I am so "tired & disgusted" that I have drunk champagne & port. The more I think about it the more angry I feel: & now my sewage is a nuisance to my neighbour. It is the last straw! and the worst of it is that reason is on my side & I cannot find any solution of the problem.

Oh d——!

...

... But Baldwin has made me thoroughly cross & hopeless. I can find *no* pleasure in working with him. He is an ass & I think a conceited ass.

AC5/1/327

26 July 1924
2 Morpeth Mansions

My dear Ida,

...

I had my explanation with Baldwin by letter & interview on my return last Monday & what do you suppose his line was? Why that he had not changed at all, that the last three paragraphs of his speech were meant to convey exactly what I desired, & that there was no contradiction or difference between us! The Horne-Churchill meeting is to take place with his full approval in October & he will say more on the subject today at Manchester.

Sam Hoare, Horne &c. feel, as I do, that his inability to see the difference between what he said & what he thought he had said is even more difficult to deal with than would be a real change of mind. Well, we must wait & see what he will say today. Meanwhile I have written the enclosed to appear in the Evening News about next Wednesday ... I hope you will not be too shocked by my Machiavellian: "Some people have affected to discover a difference".

I long to see my garden & I hate the prospect of these lonely days. Without Ivy I feel like the domestic cat when the family has gone to the seaside.

AC5/1/332

24 September 1924
Twitt's Ghyll

My dear Hilda,

...

Ivy has gone up to see doctor today & I join her tomorrow when we hope to do the Autumn Show in the morning, & I have a Shadow Cabinet in the afternoon – Ireland, I suppose, mainly, & a disquisition of things at large. We shall return tomorrow night. But do I care about politics? No, I hate them! I gather that neither Neville nor I believe in an autumn election, but we both have many meetings, & life will be a burden. I wish that I had the courage – Yes, I think that that is the right word: – to cut the whole show & give myself up to gardening & making such money as I could.

AC5/1/333   27 September 1924
                                                  Twitt's Ghyll

My dear Hilda,

...

I take your jobation in good part. There may be something in it, but it is not as easy as you think. I have accepted Baldwin's leadership, & cannot jump his claim to first place in the House. I am often sorely tempted to spring in, half rise from my seat & then remember that it is his job, fall back & wait for him until it is too late. He chooses his own time to speak & appoints mine. I have played the game but have not found it very interesting. As to my speeches I have undertaken quite enough for anyone ... But I have had over 30 years of it & much of great interest, much close comradeship with men I liked & whose abilities I respected – & I find the present lot inferior & dull.

AC5/1/334   5 October 1924
                                                  Twitt's Ghyll

My dear Ida,

...

Are you interested in politics? My own conviction is that Ulster or at least the Ulster members, are glad to see the Boundary Bill through. They want the thing settled without a row & in their hearts believe that it will be settled by the Comn. If the Lords are wise, they won't touch the Bill, but then they are not wise enough for that! They will amend & give way when the Commons reject their amendment.

Meanwhile ... I take it that we are in for a general election. I think the Govt. will be beaten on Wednesday[49] – I only wish that they would accept that defeat – then, if they last so long, beaten again on the Russian Treaty. They must resign or dissolve on the second, if not the first, defeat, & then the deluge! I find myself absolutely unable to predict what will happen.

---

[49] After the Labour Attorney-General dropped the prosecution for sedition of J.R. Campbell, the Communist editor of *The Workers Weekly*, the Conservatives tabled a censure motion for alleged improper interference with the judiciary.

AC5/1/336   11 October 1924
                                                      Twitt's Ghyll

My dear Hilda,

  . . .

I have become more hopeful about this election. I think that our people will poll better; that we had more than our fair share of seats lost by very small majorities last election, that we shall get more Liberal votes & that 20 or 30 Liberals will vote steadily with us in every critical division in the new house, & that Squiff & Co. will not again put a Socialist Govt into office in a hurry. So I count on another Baldwin Govt with 2 Chamberlains in the Cabinet instead of one only. I am not sure that Labour will be much weaker, they will certainly win some seats from Liberals as also shall we. The Liberal calculation is, I believe, that they lose 40–50 seats pretty equally divided between the Socialists & ourselves. But a good deal depends on how far we & the Liberals can save each other by withdrawing our candidates in seats where with a three-cornered fight the Socialists will certainly win. But the local bitterness in many cases between Liberals & Conservatives is very strong. I am not sure whether the break between Socialist & Communist will help us much e.g. I expect that all Frank Smith's followers in West B'ham or nearly all will vote for Dunstan.

AC5/1/337   19 October 1924
                                                      Birmingham

My dear Ida,

I am astonishingly well & cheery for election time. I can't believe that Dunstan will do as well as Frank Smith & I *ought* to do better than last time. And I don't believe that Neville is in any danger . . .
  . . .
Shall we have a clear majority? I think so; I believe that there will be a big swing our way. The P.M. is doing very badly, & S.B. in his quiet way very well. Ramsay 'broadcasted' very badly & I hear of people who had leanings towards him being quite put off after listening-in.

AC5/1/338

30 October 1924
Midland Hotel,
Birmingham

[Typescript]

My dear Ida,

We had a rude shock here which I confess took me completely by surprise. I was justified in feeling that Dunstan's opposition was not dangerous, but even an avowed Communist is able to poll seven thousand votes in West B'ham. Ladywood is a profound disappointment, & the drop in the majorities in Aston, Deritend, & Duddeston does nothing to reassure one. As to King's Norton I can only say that Austin deserved his defeat, for he neither attended the House, nor worked his constituency, nor contributed his share of our expenditure, & I can have no sympathy with him – but I am distressed that our wonderful record shall have been broken.

. . .

The results in the country seem very satisfactory but it is curious how patchy the movement of opinion is. This new electorate is much less dependable & consistent than the old one was.

AC5/1/339

2 November 1924
Peper Harow
Godalming

My dear Ida,

. . . The future of B'ham gives me great anxiety & Neville's position in particular. I heard much this time which I had not heard before . . .

Boiled down, it all comes to this. N's manner freezes people. His workers think that he does not appreciate what they do for him. Everyone respects him & he makes no friends. I said to Hubbard[50] "Speak quite frankly about him & me. Could I have kept that seat or should I have lost it long ago?" And H. said "Oh you would have had a bigger majority – *now*. I don't know whether you realise how much you have changed in the last 15 or 20 years. N. is like when you were when I first came to B'ham. Everyone talks of the change" &c. &c. to which I replied "You see I married 18 years ago". "That may be it" he said.

Now I tell you all this because the idea that N. is not a good

---

[50] George William Hubbard (1870–1939). Journalist and editor, *Birmingham Daily Mail*, 1903–06; *Birmingham Daily Post*, 1906–33.

candidate is new to me: *2nd* because this comparison with me tells me at any rate exactly where his weakness lies (it is precisely my weakness in the House today) & lastly because I am now thinking all the time *how* can we help him? *Can* we help him? Think it over & we will talk it over.

AC5/1/340
9 November 1924
Twitt's Ghyll

My dear Hilda,

Ivy has had her way, you & Ida are gratified, I am Secretary of State for Foreign Affairs, my garden will go to ruin and you need not expect to get a letter from me for the next 4 years if I survive so long ... O how the collar galls. I feel no elation, but only a very sobering sense of great difficulties in my path.

Setting aside the exclusion of Horne, which is not only a great grief but a great loss to me, & with the one exception of Labour I think all the Ministries adequately & some of them exceptionally well filled. Health, India, Exchequer & Agriculture are the ones I class as exceptionally well filled. Hoare very good at Air, Bridgeman[51] & Worthy adequate at Admiralty & W.O. (tho' the latter appointment will not be liked in the Office for he was born a bit of a bounder & will always remain so) Jack Gilmour[52] obviously the right man for the Scottish Office & Jicks probably equal to the H.O. though Hogg[53] would have been a much stronger appointment. Only Labour is a thoroughly bad appointment ... The odds are that either S.B. will out S[teel] M[aitland]. or S.M. will out us all before long. "Besides 4 Cabinet Ministers from B'ham & not one from Lancashire! That is asking for trouble" & S.B. hasn't enough places to go round & S.M. was so comfortably on the shelf, whence noone else would have thought of taking him down. And S.B.'s way of doing things, as apart from the things done, has bitterly wounded Horne who was a real friend of his as well as of mine, & in a lesser but sensible degree hurt Derby. I have not had the

[51] William Clive Bridgeman (1864–1935). Conservative MP for Oswestry 1906–29. Secretary for Mines 1920–22; Home Secretary 1922–24; First Lord of Admiralty 1924–29. Created Viscount Bridgeman 1929.

[52] John Gilmour (1876–1940). Conservative MP for Renfrewshire East 1910–18; Glasgow Pollok 1918–40. Assistant Whip 1913–15, 1919–21; Scottish Whip 1921–22, 1923–24; Scottish Secretary 1924–29; Minister of Agriculture 1931–32; Home Secretary 1932–35; Minister of Shipping 1939–40. Succeeded as Second Baronet 1920.

[53] Douglas McGarel Hogg (1872–1950). Conservative MP for St Marylebone 1922–28. Attorney-General 1922–24, 1924–28; Lord Chancellor 1928–29, 1935–38; Secretary for War 1931–35; Lord President 1938; Conservative Leader in the Lords 1931–35. Knighted 1922, created Baron Hailsham 1928, Viscount 1929.

smallest influence on any of his appointments except the inclusion of Fred [Birkenhead] & have been left entirely in the dark about them till I heard Club gossip or read them in the Press. On the other hand he has shown the greatest consideration for me personally especially by naming me deputy leader of the House. I had no hint of this beforehand or I should have begged him not to do it lest it give rise to expectations of my playing a part is the general debates which is impossible, & can only accept it as a compliment & not as a duty to be fulfilled. But the motive is obvious, & I have thanked him in the spirit of his kindness.

. . .

Pray for me. Ramsay did well with the Dawes Report & Egypt but he has left an awful mess about Russia & an equally bad & even more delicate situation in regard to the Geneva Protocol.

Despite the very positive tone of this letter, Baldwin's exclusion of Horne was not Chamberlain's only disappointment. Chamberlain had clearly expected to be consulted about Cabinet formation and requested the opportunity to see Baldwin before he came under any commitments.[54] At this stage his plans to give places to all those who had supported him since 1922 were well advanced. Baldwin, however, proved 'a good deal changed and stiffened by his victory' and unwilling to be swayed by Chamberlain's proposals.[55] His offer of the Ministry of Labour to Horne on 'terms that made it evident that S.B. would be rather glad if he refused it'; his blatant efforts to mislead Chamberlain about the circumstances of the offer;[56] and his adamant refusal to offer anything to Oliver Locker-Lampson despite repeated pleas for such a personal favour from Chamberlain were all bitter blows suggesting that he had 'not three halfpence of influence with him'.[57] In every sense perhaps November 1924 represented a major watershed. For Baldwin it marked his final and decisive assertion of authority over the pretensions of a rival leadership still rumoured to be seeking an alliance with Lloyd George.[58] For Chamberlain, having discharged his obligations to his former supporters, it marked a release from the burden of loyalty which had blighted his career since 1922. At the age of 61, with many years of distinguished public service behind him, he was to turn his back towards domestic affairs and entered upon the most satisfying and greatest period of his ministerial career.

[54] A. Chamberlain to Baldwin, 31 October 1924, AC35/5/3.
[55] A. Chamberlain to Ivy, 3 and 5 November 1924, AC6/1/590, 592.
[56] A. Chamberlain to Ivy, midnight 5 November 1924, AC6/1/593.
[57] A. Chamberlain to Derby, 9 November 1924, Derby MSS. For same complaint see A. Chamberlain to Baldwin, 6 November 1924, Baldwin MSS 42/248.
[58] See Gretton to Baldwin, 1 November 1924, Baldwin MSS 36/22–4; Birkenhead to Dame Fanny Byron, 31 October 1924 forwarded to Baldwin by Lady Houston in early November, Baldwin MSS 159/214–5.

9·

'THE TRUE AUTHOR OF EUROPEAN PEACE'

The Foreign Office, the League and Locarno, December 1924–December 1926

Since his early student travels to France and Germany Chamberlain believed that he had been in training for the Foreign Office.[1] Although he had accepted the shadow portfolio for foreign affairs on his return to the Conservative front bench in February, however, he did not consider the Foreign Office as a possibility until Baldwin first raised the question in October 1924. At this juncture, daunted by the expense, the exacting burden of work with which he was unfamiliar and the attendant political risks, Chamberlain had been inclined to prefer a return to the India Office.[2] In the event, his wife recommended the Foreign Office and, rather uncharacteristically, he was soon confiding to his sisters that he had 'rapidly found [his] feet'.[3] Within a year he was rejoicing in a far greater sense of fulfilment from the Foreign Office than he could ever have expected from being Prime Minister.[4] To a considerable degree this satisfaction was derived from the very special nature of the position enjoyed by a British Foreign Secretary. As he noted when the offer was first made, the Foreign Office 'is the highest office in the public estimation':[5] a status reflected in the special pomp and dignity which surrounded its holder. As Eden later recalled, the Foreign Secretary's journey to Geneva was 'something of an event and took place at a measured pace. The top-hatted stationmaster and the Foreign Office representatives at Victoria, the harbourmaster at Dover bowing us on to the ship, the préfect and the mayor of Calais, then the drive across Paris and dinner at the Embassy, the night train at the Gare de Lyon, where M. Briand and some other of Sir Austen's colleagues were also embarking for Geneva. Finally, the arrival at Geneva, about 7.30 in the morning, when the whole staff was paraded to meet their chief at the station'.[6] In many respects, Chamberlain was ideally suited by character and temperament to fulfil such a role as a model British Foreign Secretary.[7]

---

[1] A. Chamberlain to Ida, 8 November 1931, AC5/1/563. This view was shared by his family see N. Chamberlain to A. Chamberlain, 7 December 1916, AC5/2/35.

[2] A. Chamberlain to Ivy, 10 October 1924, AC6/1/563. Baldwin claimed that he would have offered him the job in May 1923 had Curzon resigned, as he hoped. See Neville Chamberlain Diary, 23 May 1923; also Dawson to Milner, 23 May 1923, Milner MSS 51/76 (Bodleian Library, Oxford).

[3] A. Chamberlain to Hilda, 23 December 1924, AC5/1/342.

[4] A. Chamberlain to Amery, 21 November 1925, AC37/13.

[5] A. Chamberlain to Ivy, 10 October 1924, AC6/1/563.

[6] Avon, *Facing the Dictators*, 9.

[7] For recognition that his past 'shortcomings' may be 'positive virtues' in this office see *The Times*, 7 November 1924, Dutton, *Austen Chamberlain*, 232. For a less flattering view of

263

The special nature of his ministerial duties and work also rendered the post more congenial. Traditionally foreign policy has never been the province of the Cabinet as a whole, but rather confined to the Prime Minister and Foreign Secretary. In this case, Chamberlain was particularly fortunate in working with a Prime Minister with so notoriously little interest in foreign affairs as Baldwin.[8] As Chamberlain noted almost a year after coming to office, Baldwin was 'a queer man'.

... he leaves me to go my own way, pursue my own policy and face my own difficulties. I presume that he has some confidence in my handling of my own job and I suspect that he feels that he knows less than nothing about foreign affairs and has no opinion to offer. On the whole it works well tho' sometimes I wish that he showed me a little more interest and gave a more active support.[9]

On this basis, the policy relationship, such as it was, worked relatively well. Despite initial nervousness about the 'rigidity' of Chamberlain's mind,[10] Baldwin was soon content to delegate everything to a Foreign Secretary he trusted, supporting him where necessary with lavish compliments.[11] In return Chamberlain obtained an implicit assurance of prime ministerial support in Cabinet and the promise of non-interference from the only figure capable of becoming a real nuisance. It was perhaps a circumstantial measure of Chamberlain's satisfaction with the developing relationship that his opinion of Baldwin's skill in conducting domestic policy rose significantly during this period.[12] With Baldwin's tacit consent, therefore, Chamberlain successfully set about restoring a traditional nineteenth century pattern of diplomacy based on the influence and direction of the Foreign Office which had been so gravely undermined by Lloyd George's tenure of Downing Street.[13] He also aimed to restore the balance of power and something akin to the Concert of Europe of the mid-Victorian age.

Chamberlain arrived at the Foreign Office without any preconceived policy agenda

Chamberlain's pompous solemnity in foreign affairs debates see Sidney to Beatrice Webb, 5 March and 24 June 1925, N. MacKenzie (ed), *The Letters of Sidney and Beatrice Webb, Vol III, The Pilgrimage, 1912-47,* (Cambridge, 1978), 231, 239; F.W. Pethick-Lawrence, *Fate Has Been Kind,* 145.

[8] K. Middlemas and J. Barnes, *Baldwin,* 342-6; Vansittart, *The Mist Procession,* 347; Sir I.A. Kirkpatrick, *The Inner Circle,* (1959), 38-9.

[9] A. Chamberlain to Mary Carnegie, 20 September 1925, AC4/1/1264. See also Baldwin's comment in R.R. James, *Memoirs of a Conservative,* 174-5.

[10] Jones Diary, 8 November 1924, *Whitehall Diary,* I 303.

[11] See, for example, Baldwin to A. Chamberlain, 21 December 1926, AC53/54; Middlemas and Barnes, *Baldwin,* 344.

[12] A. Chamberlain to Hilda, 25 April and to Ida 16 May 1926, AC5/1/380, 383. The personal gulf remained. Even during this period Chamberlain went rarely to Chequers and never to Astley, unlike Tyrrell, PUS at the F.O. See also 'Character Sketches of the 1924-29 Cabinet', n.d. (1955-58?) Templewood MSS XX (A) 5, fol.15.

[13] G.A. Craig, 'The British Foreign Office from Grey to Austen Chamberlain' in G.A. Craig and F. Gilbert (eds) *The Diplomats 1919-39* (New York, 1963) vol I, 15-48. Also Avon, *Facing the Dictators,* 7; Petrie, *The Chamberlain Tradition,* 175. Cf. P. Kennedy, *The Realities Behind Diplomacy: Background Influences over British External Policy 1865-1980,* (Fontana ed. 1981), 252.

and pleaded the need for time to form 'some first impressions' of his many new problems. His first two months were then spent in a 'self-imposed isolation' with his officials mastering as much of the material as he could.[14] *From the outset, however, the crucial problem to confront the new Foreign Secretary obviously concerned the still unresolved issue of Franco-German relations and their destabilizing effects upon the rest of Europe in that uneasy period after Versailles. The issue emerged most immediately in the need to decide something about the future of the Geneva Protocol, negotiated between MacDonald and Herriot, in order to close the loopholes in the Covenant of the League of Nations. This ambitious accord sought to establish a more robust definition of aggression, to introduce compulsory arbitration for all disputes with an obligation on all signatories to enforce sanctions upon the aggressor. Chamberlain rightly feared such a protocol would create major new obligations for Britain as a peace-keeper and entail a consequent financial burden at a time when the state of the economy scarcely encouraged the desire for an expensive foreign policy. At Chamberlain's instigation, a sub-committee of the Committee of Imperial Defence examined the implications of the Protocol. It reported two weeks later totally opposed to British involvement and Hankey was appointed to lead another sub-committee to make such amendments as would render it acceptable. By this time, however, both minister and officials at the Foreign Office had resolved not to ratify this essentially open-ended Protocol. Instead a regional pact would be offered to France to cement relations with a former ally while leaving the door open to the distant prospect of extending it to include some form of reciprocal arrangement with Germany.*

In the conduct of his diplomacy, Chamberlain was frequently criticised for his excessively pro-French inclinations at a time when British opinion was often repelled by their attitudes and actions towards the vanquished Germany.[15] *Undoubtedly Chamberlain was an ardent Francophile whose pride in his fluency in the language earned him considerable scorn in some quarters.*[16] *He was also widely known to have observed that he loved France like a woman, for her defects as well as her qualities.*[17] *Moreover, his student travels had created life-long and passionate views not only about the virtues of the French, but the vices of the Germans.*[18] *Yet although*

[14] B.J.C. McKercher, *The Second Baldwin Government and the United States*, 19.

[15] See D. Johnson 'The Locarno Treaties' in N. Waites (ed), *Troubled Neighbours*, 110–111.

[16] For his pride and the belief that in French his natural coldness disappeared see A. Chamberlain to Ida, 22 January 1927, AC5/1/406; to Mary Carnegie, 2 September 1927, AC4/1/1282. For the scorn, see Jones' report that Austen's knowledge of French was considered 'a national misfortune, and Hilton Young had once remarked that he spent most of his time in Geneva with Austen trying to prevent him from making a speech in French', *Whitehall Diary* II, 161. Entry for 5 December 1928. Also Beaverbrook's snide remark that 'he knows French completely, and speaks it perfectly. His delight in showing off this accomplishment makes him keener on the side of France than the present French premier (or his predecessor)'. Beaverbrook to Borden, 29 April 1925, Beaverbrook MSS C/51.

[17] Petrie, *Life and Letters*, II, 304. Avon, *Facing the Dictators*, 7.

[18] D. Dutton, *Austen Chamberlain*, 246–7.

by his own admission 'the most pro-French member of the Government',[19] realpolitik more than admiration tended to guide his hand. Under Curzon the Entente had become less cordial than at any time since its creation and Baldwin had resolved he should not return to the Foreign Office because of the 'deplorable' effect it would have in France.[20] In contrast, Chamberlain had declared publicly that Britain 'should make the maintenance of the Entente with France the cardinal object of our policy' before returning to office.[21] Thereafter, through his personal contacts with Herriot and through the British Ambassador in Paris, he had made it known that his sympathies were with France and that he was striving to satisfy her desire for security.[22]

Initially Chamberlain thought in terms of a tripartite defensive pact with France and Belgium. Later his mind moved towards the sort of mutual security arrangement which culminated in Locarno. Throughout, however, the logic remained the same: a calculation based on the simple recognition that the French obsession with the threat from a revanchist Germany would be disastrous for the continent as a whole – particularly as France sought to obtain short-term security principally by exacerbating the grievances of the potentially most powerful state in Europe. As he told the King, 'the key to the solution is to be found in allaying French fears, and that unless we find means to do this we may be confronted with a complete breakdown of our friendly relations with France and an exacerbation of her attitude towards Germany'.[23] If French fears could be allayed, while simultaneously demonstrating to Germany that it could neither divide nor challenge the Allies, Chamberlain hoped to reduce European tension and create an environment in which it would be possible to redress legitimate German grievances. If this could not be achieved, Britain risked being 'dragged along, unwilling, impotent, protesting in the wake of France towards the new Armageddon'.[24]

In shaping Chamberlain's view of these developments, three factors were crucial. First, he believed France and Germany could not resolve their problems alone. They needed a 'moderator and a reconciler' and an 'honest broker' to bring them together.[25] This was Britain's role. As he informed Amery, 'If we withdraw from Europe I can say without hesitation that the chance of permanent peace is gone'.[26] Second, there was the recognition that, even if it wanted to, Britain could not stand aloof in a world in which scientific innovation had ensured that 'the true defence of our country ... is now no longer the Channel ... but upon the Rhine'.[27] Finally, such

---

[19] A. Chamberlain to Crewe, 20 February 1925, AC52/91.

[20] A. Chamberlain to Ivy, 10 October 1924, AC6/1/563.

[21] House of Commons Debates, 5th Series, 176 col 109–110, 14 July 1924.

[22] D. Johnson, 'The Locarno Treaties', 111.

[23] A. Chamberlain to Stamfordham, 9 February 1920, H. Nicolson, King George V, 407.

[24] Chamberlain memorandum, 4 January 1924, FO 371/11064 quoted D. Johnson, 'The Locarno Treaties', 109.

[25] A. Chamberlain to Crewe, 20 January 1925 and to D'Abernon, 19 March 1925, AC50/28, 54.

[26] A. Chamberlain to Amery, 19 June 1925, AC52/38.

[27] Chamberlain's concluding statement to 1926 Imperial Conference, C. Barnett, The

an agreement appealed because it would enable Britain to define precisely the extent of its commitments on the most prudential realpolitik *basis. By embracing a larger role, Britain would be able to contain more effectively the extent of its obligations to those issues which represented its genuine interests.*[28] *For a variety of compelling reasons, therefore, the crucial question in Chamberlain's mind was not whether Britain should become involved at all, but rather how far that commitment should go while upholding its traditional role of maintaining the European balance of power. In attitude as well as appearance, Chamberlain was 'a diplomat in the nineteenth century mould'.*[29]

Chamberlain's problem was that the policy direction dictated by such a strategic appraisal would inevitably provoke resistance from all sides. To the left, stood Cecil within the Cabinet and the League of Nations Union outside it. They believed that the Protocol needed only relatively minor amendment and campaigned tirelessly for its adoption throughout the spring and summer of 1925.[30] *To the right, the neo-isolationist position was more formidably championed in Cabinet by Birkenhead, Churchill and Amery, and outside it by Beaverbrook. In March Beaverbrook had launched a bitter press attack upon Chamberlain's proposed pact and all such schemes as 'a menace far greater than any risk they propose to remove' by threatening the military and political unity of the British Empire. Beyond Beaverbrook stood a public opinion which Chamberlain perceived to be 'intensely suspicious of any particular undertaking' and opposition parties 'ready to start on the warpath' at the first indication of a regional pact.*[31]

By the end of February 1925 Chamberlain believed he finally knew his mind. An 'awful bucketing' at two crucial Cabinet meetings on 2 and 4 March, however, disabused him of any hopes of a simple Anglo-French alliance.[32] *This rebuff compelled Chamberlain finally to turn his mind seriously towards the earlier German* démarche *of 20 January calling for a mutual security pact for the Rhineland: an essentially defensive piece of German diplomacy which had initially been received*

Collapse of British Power, 332. For the General Staff memo see H.N. Gibbs, *Grand Strategy, A History of the Second World War, United Kingdom Military Series, Vol I: Rearmament Policy*, (HMSO, 1976), 41. For a similar recognition see his speech in the Commons, 5 March 1925, Petrie, *Life and Letters*, II, 261–2; A. Chamberlain, 'Permanent Bases of British Foreign Policy', *Foreign Affairs*, July 1931, 9, 538–9.

[28] Chamberlain memo, 21 February 1925, FO 371/11064 quoted in D. Johnson, 'The Locarno Treaties', 111–12.

[29] A. E. Peters, *Anthony Eden at the Foreign Office 1931–38*, (Aldershot, 1986), 8–11.

[30] Cecil to A. Chamberlain, 17 and 21 November 1924, AC51/41, 45; Vt Cecil. *All the Way*, 186–7; D.S. Birn, *The League of Nations Union 1918–45*, (Oxford, 1981), 58–64.

[31] Lord Beaverbrook, 'Austen Chamberlain or the Empire', *Sunday Express*, 29 March 1925. Also Beaverbrook to Borden, 28 January 1925, Beaverbrook MSS C/51. For Chamberlain's perception of public opinion see A. Chamberlain to Crewe, 16 February 1925, AC52/159.

[32] N. Chamberlain to Hilda, 7 March 1925, NC18/1/475; Amery Diary, 2 and 4 March 1925, *Leo Amery Diaries*, I, 399–400. See also Vt. D'Abernon, *An Ambassador of Peace* (1930) vol III, 155.

with considerable coolness and suspicion in London.[33] *At Geneva on 12 March Chamberlain gave the first public indication of approval for the German plan while denouncing the Protocol. At the same time, however, Sir Eyre Crowe (Permanent Under-Secretary at the Foreign Office) informed him in indignant tones of the resurgence of anti-French sentiment in the Cabinet, with the likelihood that they would go back on their previous decision during Chamberlain's absence in Geneva.*[34] *Upon receiving this news, Chamberlain warned Baldwin that he would resign unless he had his way. As he told his wife:*[35]

> *If the servants get out of hand, it is Mrs Watson's [Baldwin's] business (I do not mean in her capacity as plain cook where she is admirable, but as head of the household) to keep them in order. And I yesterday sent her a wire to say that either my apartment must be run as I wished and the meals served as I ordered them or I should leave her lodgings ... I can't do my work if the other tenants are always making a racket and sticking their brooms and buckets just where I am bound to fall over them.*

On his return from Geneva on 15 March Baldwin gave Chamberlain the assurances he desired. The decisive hurdle had been crossed. On 19 March Chamberlain and de Fleuriau, the French Ambassador, established the points of agreement: German entry to the League, continued occupation of the left bank of the Rhine and that Britain should concern itself only with the Western frontiers.[36] *Next day, after prolonged discussion, the Cabinet approved his policy and Chamberlain was authorised to inform Parliament.*[37] *Chamberlain was now sole master of British foreign policy. During the next seven months he worked assiduously towards the pact of mutual guarantee which, as his biographer puts it, 'though not his in its inception, he now adopted with the devotion of a natural parent'.*[38] *Despite continued anxieties, occasional crises and a protracted 'war of Notes'*[39] *the negotiations progressed steadily. They also confirmed Chamberlain's deeply rooted prejudices in favour of the 'amazingly reasonable' French and against the 'very nearly intolerable' Germans.*[40] *The Five Power Conference held at the Palace of Justice in the small Swiss*

---

[33] For German motives and Chamberlain's response see J. Jacobson, *Locarno Diplomacy*, 4–14; F.S. Northedge, *The Troubled Giant: Britain among the Great Powers, 1916–1939* (1966), 252–4.

[34] Crowe to A. Chamberlain, 12 March 1925, AC52/240. Also S. Crowe and E. Corp, *Our Ablest Public Servant: Sir Eyre Crowe, 1864–1925*, (Braunton 1993), 472–3. For an account of the meeting see Middlemas and Barnes, *Baldwin*, 353–356.

[35] A. Chamberlain to Ivy, 15 March 1925, AC6/1/603.

[36] A. Chamberlain to Crewe, 19 March 1925, AC50/56.

[37] *House of Commons Debates*, 5th Series, 182 col 307–22; Middlemas and Barnes, *Baldwin*, 355–7.

[38] D. Dutton, *Austen Chamberlain*, 246.

[39] E. Sutton (ed) *Gustav Stresemann: His Diaries, Letters and Papers*, (2 vols. London, 1937) II, 8.

[40] For the negotiations see J. Jacobson, *Locarno Diplomacy*, 12–26. For Chamberlain's attitudes to the French and Germans see pp58–59 and 125–6. Also D'Abernon, *An Ambassador of Peace*, III, 194–5 for his astonishment and frustration at such prejudice.

lakeside resort of Locarno between 5–16 October 1925 was to be hailed as the greatest triumph of Chamberlain's career. Amid emotional scenes it was fitting that the pact should be initialed on 16 October, Chamberlain's sixty-second birthday. Although actually consisting of several agreements, the core was the Treaty of Mutual Guarantee imposing equal obligations to guarantee Germany's western frontier and the demilitarization of the Rhineland. It also embodied an undertaking of France, Germany and Belgium not to make war on each other, the promise to accept arbitration or conciliation of border disputes and to render military assistance to any signatory who fell victim to a 'flagrant' act of 'unprovoked aggression'.[41] *At the time, no one doubted that* The Times *was correct in proclaiming 'Peace at last' or that Chamberlain had fulfilled his ambition to 'close the war chapter and start Europe afresh as a society in which Germany could take her place as an equal with the great nations'.*[42]

With greater distance, opinions of Locarno cover an extremely wide spectrum. Even now, some would contend it represented 'the greatest achievement of British diplomacy between the two wars' and a conclusive proof of Chamberlain's 'diplomatic genius'.[43] *Others, however, have dismissed Locarno as a 'collective act of escapism' of significance only on paper.*[44] *The most fundamental criticism is that the absence of corresponding guarantees to states on Germany's eastern border not only divided Europe but almost invited Germany to expand eastwards.*[45] *Others have argued that Locarno damaged the League and its Covenant, while still more have contended that the terms of the guarantee to respond to 'flagrant' acts of aggression were 'no more than a hollow gesture to soothe the French; a bogus commitment, a fraudulent IOU that was given only because the English Government never thought for a moment that they would ever have to make it good'.*[46] *Inasmuch as it was a distinctively British conception of the agreements which prevailed, such criticisms reflect directly upon the nature of Chamberlain's supposed triumph. In some respects they also fail to appreciate what Chamberlain hoped to achieve from Locarno.*

The over-riding objective throughout had been to resolve the principal destabilising problem of post-war diplomacy while at the same time limiting British commitments in accordance with the General Staff objectives as outlined in February 1925. With the full benefit of hindsight such a goal may have been ill-conceived, but this was

---

[41] For the conference and the agreements see Jacobson, *Locarno Diplomacy*, 60–68. For a description of the ceremony see A. Chamberlain to Tyrrell, 18 October 1925, AC52/769.

[42] A. Chamberlain to D'Abernon, 19 March, 4 November 1925, AC50/54, 37/98. Also Balfour to Chamberlain, 16 October 1925, AC37/24; D. Richardson, *The Evolution of British Disarmament Policy in the 1920s*, (1989), 42–3.

[43] R. Lamb, *The Drift to War, 1922–1939* (1989), 20; B.J.C. McKercher, *The Second Baldwin Government and the United States*, 9.

[44] C. Barnett, *The Collapse of British Power*, 331; A.J.P. Taylor, *English History, 1914–45* (Oxford, 1965), 221–2; H. Dalton, *Call Back Yesterday, Memoirs 1887–1931*, (1953), 170.

[45] D. Dutton, *Austen Chamberlain*, 332–3.

[46] Barnett, *Collapse of British Power*, 332–3; A.J.P. Taylor, *The Origins of the Second World War*, 54. For a contemporary recognition of this see Amery to A. Chamberlain, 15 June 1925, AC52/37.

Chamberlain's objective and he achieved it. As he told the House of Commons during the Locarno debate, 'I do not think that the obligations of this country could be more narrowly circumscribed to the vital national interest than they are in the Treaty of Locarno'.[47] *D'Abernon may have been correct in saying that Locarno ensured that the Polish Corridor became 'the danger-spot in Europe'.*[48] *Yet the reality both then and for some time afterwards, as Chamberlain put it, paraphrasing Bismarck, was that the Polish Corridor was something 'for which no British Government ever will or ever can risk the bones of a British Grenadier'.*[49] *In making such an agreement Chamberlain did not believe either that he had done anything contrary to the spirit of the Covenant or the League. Nor, in truth, did Cecil or the LNU at the time.*[50] *From the outset, in his speech to the League Council on 12 March, Chamberlain had made it clear that the objective was 'to supplement the Covenant by making special arrangements in order to meet special needs'.*[51] *Moreover, this was not simply a convenient rationalisation. First, German entry to the League was crucial to Chamberlain's scheme and he expected that there would be recourse to the League where conflict arose. He believed that this, combined with the arbitration treaties with Poland and Czechoslovakia, offered sufficient reassurance to states on the eastern frontier.*[52] *Secondly, his preference for regional agreements rather than international settlement conformed with his general view of the League as well as with the British desire for limited commitments.*

> *I am firmly convinced that the true line of progress is to proceed from the particular to the general and not as hitherto embodied in Covenant and Protocol, to reverse the process and attempt to eliminate the particular by the general. A form of guarantee which is so general that we undertake exactly the same obligations in defence shall I say, of the Polish Corridor (for which no British Government ever will or ever can risk the bones of a British Grenadier) as we extend to these international arrangements or conditions on which, as our history shows, our national existence depends, is a guarantee so wide and general that it carries no conviction whatever and gives no sense of security to those who are concerned in our action.*[53]

Whatever its defects, Locarno represented an honest attempt to resolve the impossible dilemma confronting British policy makers since 1919. If it is true that the 'real British gains from Locarno were of a negative character', they also appeared undeniably to be substantial. It had detached Germany from Russia and brought

[47] *House of Commons Debates*, 5 Series, 188 col 429, 18 November 1925.

[48] D'Abernon, *An Ambassador of Peace*, III, 221.

[49] A. Chamberlain to Crewe, 16 February 1925, AC52/189.

[50] Vt. Cecil, *All the Way*, 189; D.S. Birn, *The League of Nations Union*, 61–2.

[51] Chamberlain to League Council, 12 March 1925, W.N. Medlicott, *British Foreign Policy Since Versailles, 1919–63* (1968), 334.

[52] A. Chamberlain to D'Abernon, 18 March 1925, AC52/264; CAB 35(25), 7 July 1925, CAB 23/50. Also Chamberlain in *House of Commons Debates*, 5 Series, 185 col. 1555–70, 24 March 1925.

[53] A. Chamberlain to Crewe, 16 February 1925, AC52/189.

about her rehabilitation; it had permitted a British guarantee of French security without alienating Germany; it removed general uncertainty. Moreover, it achieved all this at the lowest conceivable price in terms of British commitment and it was a price which all agreed that it was unlikely ever to be called upon to honour.[54]

This was also undoubtedly Chamberlain's triumph. Despite Chamberlain's ceaseless claims to the contrary, it has been objected that the concept of such a pact had originated with Stresemann and thus 'in a very real sense Locarno should be viewed as an achievement of German foreign policy'.[55] Yet the literal truth of such a proposition does not detract from the fact that when Chamberlain's initial preference for an uncomplicated Anglo-French security pact was thwarted, he recognised that a Rhineland pact offered the only basis upon which the Cabinet would accept such a British assurance and only his tenacity kept the proposal on the agenda in March and left it there at a time when few were prepared to go as far or as fast. As he later recalled, 'it was not my policy but it was a policy which I believed could be worked, and I was prepared to attempt to work it'.[56]

For his efforts Chamberlain was showered with telegrams, letters, poems and songs of congratulation from those overjoyed by the opening of a new era of European peace. He received the Nobel Peace Prize and was offered the Grand Cross of the Legion of Honour which he reluctantly declined.[57] Refusing a peerage, the King then did him the signal honour of granting him the Garter without waiting for a vacancy in accordance with the precedent set in 1878 when Beaconsfield returned from Berlin bearing 'Peace with Honour'. Although 'frightened by the completeness of my success', anxious about the inevitable reaction and sufficiently realistic to see Locarno 'not as an end of appeasement and reconciliation, but as its beginning', Chamberlain shared fully in the euphoric national mood.[58] Locarno left him in heroic spirits. In circumstances analogous to those which had followed the ending of the Napoleonic War a century earlier, he saw himself in Castlereagh's image, found he had 'been talking Castlereagh (adapted to the XXth century) without knowing it' and insisted that a portrait of Castlereagh should look down upon the signing of Locarno in London in December 1925. It was his finest hour and he knew that he would 'never have such a chance or make such use of it again'.[59] Sadly he was right. As his brother noted, it was 'a great moment for him, the greatest in his life up till now, perhaps in the future'.[60]

[54] F.S. Northedge, *The Troubled Giant*, 269–272; Jacobson, *Locarno Diplomacy*, 35–7.

[55] D. Dutton, *Austen Chamberlain*, 249–50.

[56] A. Chamberlain to D'Abernon, 11 September 1930, AC39/2/35.

[57] A. Chamberlain to Hilda, 26 December 1925, AC5/1/372. For these congratulations see AC37/1/1–478.

[58] A. Chamberlain to Ida, 28 November 1925, AC5/1/370; *House of Commons Debates*, 5th Series, 188 col. 420, 18 November 1925.

[59] A. Chamberlain to Hilda, 26 December 1925, AC5/1/372; to Tyrrell, 18 October 1925, AC52/769. See also Chamberlain's remarks while presiding at the inaugural lecture of Dr C.K. Webster at the LSE, *The Times*, 9 March 1933.

[60] Neville Chamberlain Diary, 22 October 1925.

AC5/1/342   23 December 1924
                                             2 Morpeth Mansions

My dear Hilda,

. . .

I have become a pure slave of my Department & can give little attention to what my colleagues are doing. I notice however a general feeling that housing must be alright because Neville is at the M/H[Ministry of Health] & he knows all about it if nobody else does. And it does give me great satisfaction to sit in Cabinet with him. Indeed I think my tombstone shall bear the simple inscription

Fortunate in his family life
Thrice fortunate in his marriage
He spent many years in the Public Service
And sat in Cabinet
First with his Father
And afterwards
With his brother

But, goodness! it was time that I had some rest. From the outbreak of the Egyptian crisis[61] I think that I never got more than a 7 hour night & more usually it was 6 hours or at most $6\frac{1}{2}$. But work is slackening off now for the Xmas season ... I did not know how tired I was till I had time to rest. Abroad [at Geneva] I was never alone from 10 a.m. till past midnight & then I had always some papers to read or some writing to do. For the first time in 18 years I failed to send a daily letter to Ivy & left her to gather news of me from the papers. But it was all extraordinarily interesting; I was able to do what I wanted to do with complete & signal success (my ambition was a more modest one than some of 'our correspondents' supposed) & there cannot be a doubt that I was well advised to go ...

What does interest me is to find that I seem to fall naturally into the business, & tho' I entered on this new chapter as indeed on each fresh episode of my life, with great diffidence & some misgiving, I rapidly found my feet & began to acquire confidence with the first important telegram that I redrafted & with the effect of my redraft on my advisers. And it is an immense pleasure to me to think that the opportunities Father gave me in my young days are my qualifications for my present post. I shall make my mistakes (have, indeed, made some) but I hope not more nor worse than another man.

---

[61] Sir Lee Stack, Sirdar of the Egyptian Army had been assassinated on 19 November 1924.

There is a very egotistical letter for you, but I suppose you like it, & it is like a Highbury family talk.

AC5/1/343

28 December 1924
Twitt's Ghyll

My dear Ida,

. . .

I get two boxes of papers about 8.30 every night – one 'urgent' to be done before I go to bed ... Still it is the daily drip, drip, drip, the never being carefree that wears one out in the long run & makes one glad when the opposition becomes the government ...

The Germans have played the fool as usual about Cologne,[62] demanding to know why which is just what the French were anxious to tell them; so they will be told, & the case will pile up against them whilst I was playing for time for myself – & them.

AC5/1/346

15 February 1925
Twitt's Ghyll

My dear Ida,

. . .

As to me I move among crises – Albania, Egypt, the Oecumanical Patriarch, the Dantzic pillar boxes & the eternal question of Security which would be better described as the question of Insecurity. It is profoundly interesting & I know what *I* am working for; but when you deal with the ponci follies of the French, the incurable Oumnifeit of the Germans, the susceptibilities of the Italians, & the various & unsettled views of my colleagues, & the public opinion of each country which is sometimes the excuse & more often the reason for their conduct, taking one consideration with another the politicians lot is not a happy one. And the work is terrific! ... Yes the work is congenial & I feel I know what I am doing & wanting to do & that a bit of it is done, but the exertion & the labour are constant & terrifying.

---

[62] The Treaty of Versailles provided for the evacuation of Cologne on 10 January 1925 but the French argued there was a good legal justification for a prolongation of the occupation as Germany was not fulfilling the Treaty.

AC5/1/347   1 March 1925
                                                   Foreign Office

My dear Ida,

. . .

I have now got my policy clear & definite in my own mind; but can I carry the Cabinet? It is an awful fight & adds tremendously to my labours & anxieties. The policy is not an easy one, may meet with much opposition inside & outside the Govt, deals with fundamentals & tremendous issues – and time is of the essence of its success. I know not what the result will be, but at this moment I am banking on the Prime Minister to weigh in with authority at the critical moment. He astonished me, & several others I think, by the power that he showed in a Cabinet discussion on Friday on the political levy. Watch for his speech on the bill next Friday. I have bet Sam Hoare £5 that he will bring it off *triumphantly* – the Attorney General to decide whether the adverb is justified![63]

Meanwhile I get some consolations. The Office is very happy. *We* have a policy for Egypt & the Sudan, approved by Cabinet after a stiff tussle, for Italy & for Albania where I have been left alone, & for France, Germany & Security. They say that the Foreign Office view gets presented to the Cabinet & defended in Cabinet as it has not been for years, & that they are astonished by my 'grasp'. Indeed I have found them very constantly accept [sic] as improvements the major alterations that I have suggested in policy or despatches & telegrams.

And the Diplomatic Corps sing the praises of their new 'Chief' . . . "They like your frankness" says Crowe . . .[64]

AC5/1/350   19 April 1925
                                                   Twitt's Ghyll

My dear Ida,

. . .

I am glad that Briand is Foreign Minister. Painlevé[65] I scarcely

---

[63] F.A. Macquisten proposed a Private Members Bill to compel trade unionists to 'contract in' rather than 'contract out' of the political levy. Baldwin opposed it on grounds of timing and tactics to preserve the government's role as defender of industrial peace. His speech to the Commons with the plea 'Give peace in our time. O Lord', was a triumph.

[64] Sir Eyre Alexander Crowe (1864–1925) Assistant Under-Secretary at FO 1912–19; plenipotentiary to Paris Peace Conference 1919; Permanent Under-Sec FO 1920–25.

[65] Paul Painlevé (1863–1933) French Minister of War 1917, 1925–6; Prime Minister 1917, 1925; Minister of Air 1930–31, 1932–33.

know & Caillaux[66] not at all except by his rather unsavoury reputation. I sent a note to Herriot[67] & got back a very nice reply. He had been stuck by my loyauté & determined to reciprocate. Certainly he was always straight to me. I suppose that business will begin again now that there is again a Govt in Paris, but what about Germany?

AC5/1/351

25 April 1925
Twitt's Ghyll

My dear Hilda

. . .

I am in great distress. Sir Eyre Crowe, the head of my office, is dying if he be not at this moment already dead. He was a great public servant, devoted to duty, delightful to work with, of immense knowledge & experience & proved judgement. He has been ill for a long time, yet would not leave his work. At last I had got him to take 3 months leave of absence – too late alas! It ought to have been done 2 years ago. I did not think that I could have felt so much for a man whom I have only known intimately for a few months.

AC5/1/352

3 May 1925
Twitt's Ghyll

My dear Ida,

. . .

Hindenburg's[68] election was a surprise to me & a disagreeable one, but except for the adverse effect it has on French opinion I don't think that it is a bad thing. And I am glad to say that the French Govt do not appear to be going to alter their policy in any way on account of it.

But what do these things matter when half your cottage tulips have been eaten off by slugs . . .

[66] Joseph Caillaux (1863–1944) Socialist Radical Deputy, 1898–1919 when convicted of treason. Amnesty 1924 and Senator 1925–44. Minister of Finance 1899–1902, 1906–9, 1911, 1913–14, 1925, 1926, 1935; Prime Minister 1911–12. Chairman of Commission of Finances 1937–40.

[67] Edouard Herriot (1872–1957) Mayor of Lyon 1905–47; French Prime Minister 1924–25, 1926, 1932. Foreign Minister 1926–36; Pres. Chamber of Deputies 1936–40; Pres. National Assembly 1947–54; President Radical Party 1919–40 and Socialist-Radical Party 1945–57.

[68] Field Marshal Paul von Hindenburg (1847–1934). German C-in-C 1916–19; elected President of German Reich April 1925–34 after death of Ebert in February.

AC5/1/354

17 May 1925
Twitt's Ghyll

My dear Ida,

...

... But take it for all in all there is no pleasure like gardening & d—
politics. All the same you need not believe the Daily Chronicle which
says that I am so pro-French that my colleagues can't stand me & that
I am going to resign. Not just yet, anyway.

We jog along slowly but steadily. Our relations with France are
better than at any time since the War, & our relations with Italy
astonish Sir W. Tyrrell,[69] et je suis pour quel que chose as he very
readily admits.

M. de Fleuriau[70] told me a delightful bon mot of Briand's that was
new to me. At the famous game of golf at Cannes Briand, says Fleuriau,
did not really play golf: he hit at the ball & missed it. Then Lord
Riddell[71] (owner of a none too respectable Sunday paper & press
manager for Ll.G. at all conferences[)], made a successful drive. Tiens!
exclaimed Briand, il lance sa balle comme une fausse nouvelle![72] Good,
isn't it!

Your loving brother
DON'T take too many committees

AC5/1/355

31 May 1925
Twitt's Ghyll

My dear Ida,

...

... I am well content. Things are at last moving. The Disarmament
note has gone off to Germany. It will create a howl, but I think that

---

[69] William George Tyrrell (1866–1947) Entered Diplomatic Service 1889; Principal
Private Sec. to Foreign Secretary 1907–15; Ass. Under-Sec 1918–25; Permanent Under-
Sec 1925–28; Ambassador in Paris 1928–34; Pres. Board of Film Censors 1935–47;
Knighted 1913, created Baron Tyrrell 1929.

[70] Aimé Joseph de Fleuriau (1870–1938) Entered French Diplomatic Service 1892;
Counsellor of London Embassy 1913–20; Minister to Peking 1921–4; Ambassador to
London 1924–33.

[71] George Riddell (1865–1934). Chairman *News of the World* 1903–34 and one-time
Chairman Newspaper Proprietors Association. Created Baron 1920.

[72] Translated as 'He sets his ball flying like a bit of false news'. An example, supposedly,
of Briand's famous wit, *Down the Years*, 180–1.

they will comply. And our reply has gone to Briand (about the Pact)[73] & been not ill received as far as my present information goes, & he wants to get on & so do I, so perhaps together we shall achieve some progress. The Cabinet left the consideration of the reply to a strong Comtee which took my drafts without alteration & almost without criticism. They only asked a question or two & were satisfied with the answers which I gave. Marvellous! It was not necessary for "Mrs Watson" to say a word to the other "lodgers".

AC5/1/357

27 June 1925
2 Morpeth Mansions

My dear Ida,

It is a very tired but a happy brother who sits down to write to you this weekend. Winston said to me yesterday: "you ought to be happy, for your fence lies behind you – & all Beaverbrook's campaign has gone for nothing". I think that it is true that I have won the battle here, & it is equally the case that my speech has had an excellent reception in France where, I will admit, I was afraid that they might not like to see the i's dotted & the t's crossed as I dotted & crossed them. There remains only Germany where the Press is bad but all reports of the attitude of the Govt including Hindenburg, are good ... It is rather a triumph, is it not? & though it is true that I could not have done it without my colleagues Neville would confirm that it would never have been done but for me. Except for my insistence, we should have had no policy but 'wait & see', the German initiative would have been still-born, & even after the Cabinet had decided on a policy, they would have gone back upon it. The constructive sentences of the Geneva declaration were put in by Balfour expressly to cover my policy, & it was my speeches in the House in March which gave them a definite meaning both for France & Germany & bound the Cabinet to them, so that if the policy succeeds I shall feel some title to the reputation which Houghton[74] assures me will be mine as the true author of European peace, & in that case my long but somewhat broken public career will not have ended without one solid & complete achievement.

---

[73] The Note to France, 28 May 1925 reported that any new British obligation should be confined to the western frontier (and could not guarantee arbitration treaties between Germany and non-signatories). It also enshrined the principle that force would only be used after the defaulting nation had been allowed to refer the dispute to conciliation by the League thus compelling France to have a clean record on arbitration.

[74] Alanson B. Houghton (1863–1941) American businessman and diplomat. US Ambassador to Germany 1922–25 and to London 1925–29.

All which though it sounds rather boastful is in fact written with great humility but also with considerable thankfulness.

AC5/1/358

11 July 1925
2 Morpeth Mansions

[To Ida]

. . .

No, I don't want to break off relations with Russia. It's easily done & I have ample justification, but it does no good & some harm. Above all it would force the moderates of the Labour Party, now fighting their extremists to the death, to unite in condemnation of the Govt. Most, if not all, of the Liberals would do the same, but that is of less consequence. Secondly it would confirm the Bolshies in the estimation of the Chinese in their part of protectors of Chinese nationalism. Thirdly, the more indifference we show, the more frightened the Soviet Govt are of us. The more we talk to them the better they are pleased. When we court them, they think that they are indispensable: when we denounce them, they feel that they are dangerous, but when we ignore them, they begin to ask themselves what is to become of them.

AC5/1/362

16 August 1925
Twitt's Ghyll

My dear Hilda,

. . .

I left London on the whole very happy. China is full of vexation & anxiety, but the talks with Briand were A1. & after seeing him off at 10.50 I was able to despatch a telegram by 5 o'clock to tell him that the Cabinet had approved all we had done. He is a good man to deal with, *courageous*, liberal-minded, supple & anxious to agree. His chef de cabinet said to Selby:[75] – M. Briand had two possible policies before him when he came into office: one was to confirm & extend the system of alliances with the East European states; the other was to make a security pact with England. Mr C. has made the second policy possible for him & he infinitely prefers it.

And on the only point of substance & difficulty that we had to settle, he accepted my proposal. I said: I believe we can guarantee your

[75] Sir Walford Harmood Montague Selby (1881–1965). Ass. Private Secretary to Foreign Secretary 1911–15; First Secretary Cairo 1919–22; Principal Private Secretary to Foreign Secretary 1924–32; Ambassador to Vienna 1933–37 and to Lisbon 1937–40.

security in the only case in which it can be seriously menaced, but if you ask to keep your right to make war for trifles as given you by the Treaty of Versailles, my public opinion here will not allow of any guarantee.

"Il ne faut pas lâches la praie pour l'oubre" said B. "I'm ready to fight on that", & he silenced his experts.

Moucheur the Belgian Ambassador, said to me: "Its wonderful, Mr Chamberlain. Its your doing. Curzon could never have done it."

Now for the German! I believe that we shall bring it off. Here I put great faith in Briand's reasonableness & persuasiveness. If we do, well then I recall Mr Houghton's: "Mr C. if you bring this off, you will be the founder of European peace".

My dear Hilda all of this sounds very boastful. But it is my work. Without me the policy would never have had a dog's chance & I do believe that I am doing good work & I think how Father & Beatrice would have felt about it.

AC5/1/365

22 September 1925
2 Morpeth Mansions

My dear Hilda,

...

Ivy & I spent a fortnight [in Geneva] & only had one meal alone, ... Briand was charming as ever & I was well satisfied with my conversations with him ... Do you realise that except for Bank holidays & some Sundays I have had only three days away from my work since I took office? We are now talking of Egypt at Xmas, for I must have a real let up before long ... I felt obliged to revolt & have now much reduced the work, for I felt that my temper was getting threadbare & that questions were dwelling too much on my mind, & that if this continued my work would suffer & I should not be ready for the meeting with the Germans on Oct 5th "somewhere in Switzerland["]. I wish I knew exactly what they were at & that I could measure more closely the influence & power of certain sections of opinion. They & the Poles are the restless elements in Europe north of the Balkans. Poland, which as Briand said, is the rheumatism of Europe & catches you in the back when you try to move. Except for the Poles everyone in Geneva was now taking the pact nicely & seriously – even more amiably behind the scenes than in public.

AC5/1/366   2 October 1925
                                                   2 Morpeth Mansions

[Typescript]
My dear Ida,

. . .

... I am much rested by my fortnight at Twitt's Ghyll; still, work reaches me there daily even though owing to my arrangement with the Foreign Office I have had much less than usual; and, (even so) it prevents one from getting one's mind free from the daily worries and anxieties, for it is naturally the most troublesome questions that have to be brought to my notice.

You will have gathered from the papers that the German Government played the fool at the last moment by handing to the various Allies a very contentious declaration.[76] Briand, however, showed his usual good-sense and moderation and refused to allow himself to be deflected from the path which he had marked out. I gave the German Ambassador a piece of my mind. His Government and he himself were obviously uncomfortable. They knew that they had done a foolish and provocative thing for the sake of conciliating Nationalist opinion in Germany, and they implored us to take no notice of what they had said; and Sthamer[77] even went so far as to suggest that any reply, unless it were of the most conciliatory kind, might destroy the whole negotiation. However, each time he returned to the Foreign Office I caused him to be addressed in sterner language, and finally sent a reply which I carefully made a little stiffer than the French answer, for I wanted to show him that we resented the German action quite as strongly as the French, and to put in writing – what I had said in conversation – that the German Government was a most difficult Government to help and that had the French shown as little wisdom and generosity as the Berlin Cabinet there would have been no prospect of a pact at all. I am rather pleased with the result, for all the German parties except the Nationalists are blaming the Nationalists for having drawn upon Germany a new rebuff and prejudiced the position of her negotiators at Locarno, while the Nationalists themselves feel that the effect of their declaration has been destroyed by the simultaneous publication of the replies of the allied

[76] Under pressure from Hindenburg and right-wing Nationalists on 26 September 1925 the Germans insisted that the 'War Guilt' issue should be resolved and Cologne evacuated before any further progress could be made. This infuriated Chamberlain and eventually the Germans gave way.

[77] Dr Friedrich Sthamer (1856–1931) German lawyer and diplomat. Senator for Hamburg 1904; Chargé d'Affaires for German Republic in London February-August 1920 and then Ambassador until 1930.

Governments, and one or two of their papers have noticed that my reply was, as they expressed it, some degrees less friendly than Briand's. I hope that it will be a lesson to them and help them to show wisdom at Locarno.

Mussolini has not yet said whether he will come or not – but I do not expect him. To tell the truth, I think that he is afraid – though this sounds a queer statement; but I was struck by an observation of Painlevé's that for the purpose of maintaining his position and prestige he could not afford to appear too much in public, and Painlevé gave me a curious instance of his reluctance to take a first hand in a negotiation in connection with a visit Benes[78] paid to Rome where he had to do his whole negotiating with the Secretary-General of the Ministry of Foreign Affairs and other experts whilst Mussolini, with whom he was supposed to be personally negotiating, sent one excuse after another to explain his inability to be present at the different meetings.

I hate having to go away again, but at any rate it marks progress that the time for a personal meeting has come, and though I see considerable difficulties in the path, especially in connection with Poland, I hope that we shall really make progress, but I scarcely expect to finish the negotiations in a single meeting.

AC5/1/367

31 October 1925
Twitt's Ghyll

Yes, my dear Ida, what a life! I got back at 11 o'clock last night after a busy morning & the long journey to find 4 boxes marked urgent & one file where every minute began 'this question is very urgent & of the very highest political importance' & so forth. Incidentally I may add that it was a problem quite unconnected with any of the matters with which I have been dealing & of whose urgency or even existence I had had till then no hint – a warning from Esme Howard[79] that the U.S.A. are about to present a claim for many millions for damage done to their nationals by our blockade of Germany before they entered the war. Incredible, is it not?

Well, I got down here (not without difficulty) by lunch time & have

---

[78] Eduard Beneš (1884–1948). Czechoslovak Foreign Minister; President League of Nations Assembly 1935; President of Czechoslovakia 1935–38 and 1945–48. President in exile in London 1942–45.

[79] Sir Esme William Howard (1863–1939) Consul-General Hungary 1908–11; Minister to Switzerland 1911–13 to Sweden 1913–19; Ambassador to Spain 1919–24 and to USA 1924–30. Created Baron Howard of Penrith.

slept for three hours this afternoon, so I feel a little better & hope to enjoy a fine day in the garden tomorrow. It was sad to leave Ivy alone & in bed, but she was insistent that I should come, & apparently she ought to have a rest-cure ...

...

Sunday night ... I am astonished & a little frightened by the completeness of my success & by its immediate recognition everywhere. What pleased me first was to do the work, next to do it with the good will of all the foreign representatives & with the very able and delightful support of my own office. Then came the telegrams from the King & Prime Minister both recognising in such generous terms that it was *my* policy. That is true; it was mine in conception & still more mine in execution, but I did not think that they would feel this. Still less did I suppose that all the world, beginning with the little community of Locarno & spreading to the U.S.A. would hail it as Great Britain's triumph. "We are simply *it*!" as Lampson proudly exclaimed one day at Locarno when he had seen the effect produced in the Conference by my definition of Great Britain's attitudes to the east-European situation, & one could not but be proud for one's country & for oneself when one saw how everybody hung on the British Secretary's words last week in Paris. They begin to understand British policy & to understand me & they are mightily impressed. Paul Boncour,[80] protagonist of the Protocol & my very friendly & most eloquent adversary at the Assembly, said to me: "I begin to see. You are doing just what you said you would. You are building up a jurisprudence for the League – & you are always a little better than your word".

It is *pro*digious, as the Dominie said. Of course I have had my luck & much luck, but I say for myself that I have known how to use every bit of luck that came my way, that I am myself the author of some of my luck & that noone else (except perhaps Tyrrell) inside or outside the office would have seen the importance of the early moves or made them, & that not another member of the Cabinets since the Peace had understood the conditions of such a policy or could have carried it out.

So you see I do not *under*rate my own part, but I am frightened by my success & by the thought of the reaction & disappointments that are bound to come.

Germany troubles me, but I am not troubling myself much about Germany. This Treaty is going through – no nation can afford to reject it – but why can't other nations keep foreign affairs outside of & above domestic party politics?

[80] Joseph Paul-Boncour (1873–1973) Chef de Cabinet to French Prime Minister 1899–1902, 1906–09. Republican Socialist Deputy 1909; Minister of Labour 1911; President of Foreign Affairs Commission, Chamber of Deputies, 1927–31; Minister of War 1932; Prime Minister 1932–3; Foreign Minister 1932–4, 1938; Minister for League Affairs 1936.

What I most pride myself upon is that I secured the Eastern settlement & that I have taught Germany or at least her wisest statesmen that her security lies in our friendship with France not in dividing France & us.

The League secured a great & legitimate success in the Greeko-Bulgarian incident.[81] The Greeks behaved very badly, but were quickly brought to book, & the League & that alone prevented a war.

Well, well, I must stop. Much love to you both.

By the way as you will be curious; nothing has reached me officially about an honour, but as Tyrrell had been sounding Ivy I have privately stated that I cannot (a fact & more polite than will not) take a peerage suggested to relieve me of H. of C. & constituency work. I should take the Order of Merit, which involves no change of style, if offered; but I am led to think that it will be the Garter, & if that is offered I have decided to take it. I hope that you will not be too distressed. I confess that that peculiar distinction attracts me, & I think it would be good business from the point of view of my standing with foreign countries.

AC5/1/368   7 November 1925
                                                Twitt's Ghyll

My dear Ida,

...

German parties & French crises don't make our path easier, but I have faith or fatalism enough to hold that the Locarno treaties cannot go wrong. It *must* work out right. The world would be too bad a place if it did not. As to the possible honour you feel about it much as I expected. Of course you will not say a word about it to anyone. I have told *noone* but you, for it is all enrapt in great obscurity & doubt, & though Ivy was asked about my feelings I am not sure with what authority that was done. In any case there is at present no vacancy & by the time that there is one the gilt may be off the gingerbread & my stock at discount again.

---

[81] A border clash between Bulgarian and Greek troops on 19 October 1925 escalated and three days later Bulgaria called on the League to intervene. After League Council on 23 October its President, Briand, sent a telegram to both sides urging a cessation of hostilities and withdrawal of troops and then an observer party to report back to the Council: a well-established League technique to reduce tension which proved very effective in this case.

AC5/1/370
28 November 1925
2 Morpeth Mansions
My dear Ida,

...

Our holiday plans are changed ... Egypt is out of the question. It looks as if trouble were brewing there & it would certainly be assumed by everyone that I went out on business & that the 'holiday' was only a transparent subterfuge. So I should get no rest & should only be in Lloyd's[82] way. He has begun well & inspires us with confidence but he has got trouble on his hands sooner than I had hoped. I knew it must come some time – the King being what he unfortunately is, sly, scheming, corrupt & autocratic.

...

Meanwhile H.M. has *volunteered* that he will not wait for a vacancy but will confer the G[arter] on me on Tuesday immediately before receiving the Delegates. If you knew all that this means to me you would appreciate the immensity of the favour. I am not sure that it has ever been done before for anyone but royalties ...

Neville like you is a little shocked by the Sir & would have preferred to add a peerage, but I don't think that I should have liked that even if I had had the means to support it for myself & my successor. To tell you the truth my feelings are strangely mixed. Two or three months ago Winston was speaking of these things & I said I would never take an honour. Then he said 'But if it were the garter! that stands so apart.' & I replied that my father was a bigger man than I should ever be & I did not think that I could bring myself to accept an honour which he had not worn. 'Besides I should hate to be Sir Austen & I could not take a peerage'. Even now I feel that in no other position except that of F.S. would I have accepted, but in my present world such things have a value. It will be understood everywhere. In foreign eyes the garter stands alone among our orders & almost, perhaps quite, alone among orders British or foreign in these days. It sets, in the eyes of all foreigners, the seal upon my work; it endows it with additional importance & me with additional authority; & though I regret the plain "Mr. C" which Father wore & tho' I can 'step outside & look at myself' with a smile half ironic & half pathetic, I have not the same affection for the "Mr *A*.C." to which Neville's success condemns me & I can reconcile myself to the 'Sir' with the garter where it would have been abhorrent to me in any other connection.

[82] George Ambrose Lloyd (1879–1941). Conservative MP for Staffordshire (West) 1910–18; Eastbourne 1924–25. Governor of Bombay 1918–23; High Commissioner for Egypt and Sudan 1925–29; Colonial Secretary and Leader of House of Lords 1940–41. Created Kt 1918 and Baron 1925.

And so I ramble on to myself & you, a little perplexed & troubled, yet feeling that in this last year I have done a big thing which not only would not but *could* not have been done without me, which required for its full success both Stresemann[83] & Briand, above all Briand but would not have succeeded at all but for the British Govt. & that in the critical moment the British Govt. policy was found by me, imposed upon the Cabinet by me in face of Curzon's & even Balfour's opposition before I went to Paris & Geneva in March, re-imposed by my telegram from Geneva to the P.M. (when Crowe reported to me that the Cabinet Comtee. was going back on me) that I should carry on at Geneva & on my way home in Paris on these lines but I should resign at once on my return if I were not supported; & that it depended for its success on my personal handling of each situation as it arose & on the confidence which French & Germans felt not so much in the British Govt. as in *this* British Govt. because I was its foreign secretary.

It is curious, but it is true, that before the Conference, at the Conference & since the Conference I have sought rather to minimise our part; that, nevertheless, all the world regards it as a British policy & a British success; & that, in spite of this, no sign of jealousy has appeared, so far as I know, in any of the other countries which were represented at Locarno nor above all among my colleagues at the Conference, who in their own countries, no less than in their relations with me personally, have been generous in their acknowledgements of the part played by me.

I was called to face a situation comparable to that which faced Castlereagh after the fall of Napoleon. I had to face it without having been, as he was, the representative of my country in the years which won victory for the Allies & without any of his acquired prestige & little, very little, of his personal knowledge of & intercourse with foreign rulers. I came into office with clear ideas of what must be done & with confidence that I knew how & how only it could be done. A little later Webster's "Castlereagh's foreign policy" was published & I found that I had been talking Castlereagh (adapted to the XXth century) without knowing it. And I like to think that there is a continuity of British foreign policy; I am grateful that I can feel that I have justified my father's belief in me & repaid the care he gave to my training, & I am proud to feel that as the foreign minister of a great nation I have restored confidence in our word & won back our old influence.

And now I could – as far as all public affairs are concerned – willingly sing my *Nunc dimittis* & retire. Never again will it be possible to win a like success. Very probably day by day, under the stress &

[83] Gustav Stresemann (1878–1929) German Chancellor 1923; Minister of Foreign Affairs 1924–29.

strain of the passing hour & its worries & difficulties, the glamour of the achievement of yesterday will disappear & the fruit will seem all ashes in the mouth. "Whom the gods love, die young" or, at least, opportunely. Locarno will never again find its due place till long after I am dead. There is bound before long to be a reaction from the present exaggerated expectations. My moment came. I seized it & knew how to use it (that is my real contribution). At any rate what the King proposed to do will show how contemporaries regarded it & will help its present success. It *does* please me, it means much to Ivy &, when it is known, I believe the whole F.O. will rejoice as if they had at last after weary & difficult years come into their own.

You see that all my instincts are so opposed to 'honours' (as distinct from honour) to a Chamberlain that I carry on a troubled debate with my own inner self.

I cannot remember whether I told you that the P.M. asked if I should like the G.B.E. for Ivy as a recognition for her part in Locarno. I accepted gratefully & it will be announced, & I hope conferred, at the same time.

AC5/1/371   19 December 1925
                                                    Hotel Bristol
                                                    Rapallo

My dear Ida,

. . .

Geneva was vile – snow, bise, mist, fog ... I found the Council atmosphere equally trying this time, for Mosul befogged it & gave to it all a touch of discomfort & intrigue that I have not felt before. It would shock some of our League of Union freinds [sic] if they saw it as we saw it this time ...

AC5/1/372   26 December 1925
                                                    Hotel Bristol
                                                    Rapallo

My dear Hilda,

. . .

I am doing absolutely no work & not troubling my head about politics, but I think over the past year – an annus incrabilis indeed for me – & the more I think the more do I come back to the reflection how simple it was when once one had got the right idea & how extraordinary & unforeseen even up to the last by me was the extraordinary wave of approbation which greeted Locarno & my share in it. I knew that we were doing a big thing but I was doubtful till the end whether at home or elsewhere its importance would be recognised & I certainly did not expect that so large a share in the success would be attributed to me. Well I have long been wont to say of others that, if you could trace their history, the "lucky man" would be found to be the man who had seized & used his opportunities. I shall never have such a chance or make such use of it again.

AC5/1/375

5 March 1926
2 Morpeth Mansions

[Typescript]
My dear Ida,

... I start to-morrow for Geneva to play as difficult a hand as ever fell to a man's lot. Not a trump has been dealt me, *and*, the worst of it is, the discussion here has clearly shown the poverty of the land. I do not like the job and am anxious about it.

I got down to Twitt's Ghyll last Sunday – a lovely day – and thoroughly enjoyed my rock-garden. I counted over forty different species of flower ... It is a shame to think that I have only seen the garden twice since the middle of November and that I shall not see it again for another three weeks. But such is the life of a Foreign Minister!

My love to you both, and if you are attached to any particular Saint, burn a candle on my behalf.

AC5/1/379

18 April 1926
Twitt's Ghyll

My dear Ida,

...

I remain a little anxious about the Russo-German [Treaty?] tho' if Stresemann has correctly described it to D'Abernon[84] there is nothing intrinsically wrong in it. It has fluttered the dovecotes of Poland & the Little Entente a good deal & has annoyed Briand tho' he has kept his head. The funny thing is that Berlin seems almost as frightened of Warsaw as Warsaw is of Berlin & is as much perturbed by the Polish-

---

[84] Edgar Vincent (1857–1941). Conservative MP for Exeter 1899–1906; contested Colchester for Liberals December 1910. Ambassador to Germany 1920–26; Head British Economic Mission to Argentine and Brazil 1929. Kt 1887. Created Baron D'Abernon 1914, Viscount 1926.

Roumanian treaty as Warsaw is by the Russo-German one. What a world to deal with! I was born to be a gardener, not a foreign minister. Have I made that observation before?

As the General Strike loomed, Chamberlain's detachment from domestic politics became even more evident – much to his half-brother's disgust when he failed to attend Cabinet during the crisis.[85] As his letters demonstrate, however, Chamberlain simply felt that he had little to contribute in such matters. Just as he wished the Cabinet to leave foreign affairs to the experts, so he was content to leave the problems of coal to those who knew more than he did. Anyway, the proposed German admission to the League as a condition of Locarno had provoked another crisis both at home and in Geneva. Anxious to redress the failure of Locarno to provide corresponding guarantees to the states on Germany's eastern borders and to placate anti-German feeling at home, Briand pressed the claims of Poland for a permanent seat on the Council. At the end of January 1926 he even persuaded Chamberlain to put the idea before the Cabinet. Such a proposal, in defiance of the initial idea that these seats should be reserved for Great Powers, prompted similar claims from Brazil and Spain who threatened to obstruct Assembly business if they did not get their way: a demand which in turn encouraged similar claims from Belgium and China. Confronted by conflicting claims for permanent seats and potential deadlock, a formula was finally agreed to give Germany a permanent seat with a temporary seat to Poland. Excluded from all this secret diplomacy, the Brazilian and Spanish delegates refused to accept the rebuff and gave notice to withdraw from the League. The crisis was finally resolved in September when Poland became one of the new 'semi-permanent' members of the Council and Spain and Brazil resigned.[86]

There is some controversy about Chamberlain's motives in accepting Briand's proposal.[87] Whatever the impulse, however, his support for the French plan provoked an upsurge of opposition. It revived the indictment that the Foreign Secretary was too easily led by Briand into a blindly pro-French position. The resort to secret diplomacy with Briand at Geneva to find a way out of the crisis also served only further to frustrate those nations excluded from such talks, and to outrage opinion at the League of Nations Union and on the backbenches.[88] Despite Baldwin's defence

---

[85] N. Chamberlain to his wife, 7 May 1926, NC1/26/364.

[86] For the crisis see D. Carlton, 'Great Britain and the League Council Crisis of 1926', *Historical Journal*, XI. 2.(1968); J. Jacobson, *Locarno Diplomacy* , 68–76; F.S. Northedge, *The League of Nations: its Life and Times, 1920–1946*, (Leicester, 1988), 101–103.

[87] D. Carlton considers Chamberlain's logic to be 'quite plausible' and 'cogent', *Anthony Eden*, 21. Dutton, however, describes it as 'somewhat unconvincing'. *Austen Chamberlain*, 267. For Chamberlain's own account see A. Chamberlain to Baldwin, 18 March 1926, Petrie, *Life and Letters*, II, 297–303.

[88] D.S. Birn, *The League of Nations Union*, 62–3. Also Beatrice Webb Diary, 15 March 1926, N. and J. MacKenzie (eds), *The Diary of Beatrice Webb*, (1985), IV, 70. For other countries resentment at the 'Locarno cabal' see W.M. Jordan, *Great Britain, France and the German Problem, 1918–39* (1943), 98–100.

of Chamberlain, the government's majority was more than halved by a backbench revolt on 4 March. Although he survived another motion of censure in the Commons on 23 March his reputation had been seriously damaged both in public and in Cabinet where it had been agreed that Cecil should be sole British representative to the League Committee charged with finding a solution after the Special Assembly crisis in March.

AC5/1/380

25 April 1926
Twitt's Ghyll

My dear Hilda,

. . .

As to public affairs I suppose that they will always be difficult as long as I live, & it will be long before the world can settle down again to the comfortable satisfaction of the Mid-Victorians. Happily for me, coal is other men's business & I am forced to trust to them. When I *can't* go to the root of a thing, my motto is: Trust the man in charge . . . Baldwin has the right character for the job since all men trust him & rightly but I wonder whether he is quick enough to see & to seize an opportunity when it presents itself, or himself to create it. All I can say is that he has developed amazingly since he became Prime Minister a second time.

I shall have a difficult & anxious year in my own sphere, for all the world is nervy & easily gets an attack of the jumps, & the Germans are prodigiously difficult to guide or keep in the path of their own real interests. But I shall "bear right onwards" losing neither heart nor hope, for that is the first essential of success, &, although I am troubled & a little − rather *much* − perplexed to descry the issue, I am sure that it is there & that somehow I shall find it. But d— Brazil or its President especially, & may the Yellow River blot China off the map & King Fuad[89] die of any of the plagues which afflicted his ancestors.

AC5/1/381

3 May 1926
Twitt's Ghyll

My dear Ida,

. . . I have got up today, but I am very stiff & "brittle" − if you know that feeling in lumbago − and quite unable to get back to London . . .

[89] Ahmed Fuad (1868–1936) Youngest son of Ismail Pasha, succeeded as Khedive of Egypt 1917 and assumed title of King when British protectorate ended in 1922.

I wonder what is happening today about coal. It looks as if we were really in for the big fight with all the principal unions this time. They seem to have been dragged along reluctantly but impotently by the miners, for those who were negotiating for the Govt. certainly got the impression that they themselves wanted peace. Cook[90] too is said to have tried for peace in private but had his own wild words cast up against him & Herbert Smith appears to have been stolidly obstructive & unhelpful. I fear that it must mean terrible loss to the country & a great setback in the trade revival which was just beginning to show up, but there is to be said that the wider the strike the shorter it is likely to be. A coal strike is a long one. Noone but a miner can get coal, but a good many people drive engines, lorries & so forth ...

AC5/1/382

8 May 1926
Twitt's Ghyll

My dear Hilda,

I feel a terrible shirker for I have stayed down here the whole week. My attack of lumbago has not been severe, but it has been very persistent ... I had planned to go up in time for Wednesday's Cabinet but when the morning came I did not dare ... I don't think that I have been really needed in town ... As to the strike it has been better dealt with by my colleagues. I could only have stood by & said ditto to them. What a portent it is! It makes me think furiously. I cannot doubt that the Govt will win any more than I could doubt during the War that the Allies would win, but the struggle is as serious & almost as ruinous though it cannot be as long continued ... But govt & social order as well as liberty would go under if we did not beat it – & we shall. In one way at least [the? sic] problem is made easier by the wide extension given to it. There will be more *reluctant* strikers looking only to the chance of getting back, a heavier drain on Union funds & therefore less money for the miners, & last but not least it is easier to find strike-breakers for the railways than for the mines. Noone but a trained miner can get coal, but many a volunteer can drive a lorry or even an engine with a little training.

---

90 Arthur James Cook (1883–1931) General Secretary MFGB 1924–31.

AC5/1/383

16 May 1926
Twitt's Ghyll

My dear Ida,

. . .

So the strike is over, & I as an outsider say Well done British public & well done the Govt which organised them. I am struck by the great confidence which the P.M. has inspired. I am not sure he was as good as others I have known in the negotiation but he was without a rival in inspiring confidence when once the strike had come that he would not 'let down' the men who stood by their work or carried on the work of others & at the same time giving the assurance to the moderate elements that he would not use victory to serve reaction – altogether a very striking personal position. I am led to reflect that what saves England is her immense reserve in personal strength. You can never tell how much an Englishman can do until he is called upon to do it.

By the way Nelson made very much the same remark.

AC5/1/385

28 May 1926
Twitt's Ghyll

My dear Hilda,

. . .

Political weather is uncertain at home & abroad & "visibility" bad. The coal strike looks like a long affair. There is apparently no sort of rapprochement at present & masters & men vie with each other in obstinate unreason. Nor is the political outlook on the continent any better. Briand's govt. is reported to be very insecure: Poland may settle down again but it will be on the top of a revolutionary movement which does not make for stability or financial recovery, the Little Entente is again in a ferment about the Hungarian note forgeries & trouble is brewing in Egypt. Of such is the life of a foreign secretary.

AC5/1/386

19 June 1926
Twitt's Ghyll

My dear Ida

. . . China is a constant source of anxiety to me. I see no way through its troubles or the troubles that it causes us. Egypt threatens trouble. I do not suppose that it can be long avoided though we have won the first round. The U.S.A. are as difficult to deal with as they always have been because the Administration chops & changes its policy to catch a favouring breeze or avoid a squall in the Senate. And then comes "Red gold" & the scare in Suburbia because of the Daily Mail's clamour. I don't want to break off relations for it will do no good abroad, confuse the issue at home & lead, as I know by experience, in a few weeks or months to an agitation from traders here to take them up again somehow & anyhow & to a general cry among the Labour people that our breach with the Soviet is the *cause* of unemployment. So far the Prime Minister & the Cabinet are with me, but Soviet provocation is continuous & may easily become intolerable. I do not know whether it will be possible to forebear indefinitely ...

We had an unexpectedly brief Council session at Geneva, did some good work, avoiding any serious quarrels & upon the whole may congratulate ourselves upon the outlook. But I doubt whether we can snatch the Spanish brand from the burning, & am very sorry for it. They injure themselves by the line they are taking but it is a question of amour propre, personal & national, & you can't argue with amour propre.

AC5/1/387

27 June 1926
Cumberland Lodge
Windsor

My dear Hilda,

...

The Russian debate was rather interesting. Oliver Locker Lampson spoke in perfect form & taste – I wish I could get him to take a larger part in the work of the House, but he has too many irons in the fire – & Hilton Young made one of his admirable speeches, as wise as it was well-expressed. I think that our people were fairly well satisfied when they saw that we were not duped by Soviet pretences & understood that it was not because we were blind to their doings or tender to their feelings that we refrained from action.

What is going to happen in France? Tell me that – & in Canada & in Egypt & in S. Africa & in China & in half a dozen places! what a troubled world it still is. Here's the King of Spain coming over & I propose to entertain him at lunch at the Foreign Office. He is a clever, ambitious man. Can I make him see sense & the true interest of Spain? I don't suppose so, & I expect that my various conversations will be of a difficult & delicate kind. Well, we must do our best.

AC5/1/395

8 October 1926
Twitt's Ghyll

My dear Hilda,

. . .

So you have not settled the coal strike in my absence. I am disappointed though not altogether surprised but this long stoppage must mean terrible embarrassment to our finances next year & will place the Govt. in great difficulties. I have the lowest opinion of the leadership on the part of the owners as well as the men . . .

. . . My meeting with Mussolini was most pleasant & successful & my visit to Briand on my way through Paris silenced the mischief-makers there & at home. Briand & Stresemann at Thoiry[91] dreamed dreams & saw visions that will not easily be realised, letting their imaginations run away with them, but what an outcome since Locarno & what a justification of my policy! Well, well the world moves tho' it has to travel a rough road.

It was a remarkable thing that Mussolini should come up to Leghorn especially to see me. He was most satisfactory politically & most cordial personally, making me inspect the Destroyer Tigre so that it might salute me with 19 guns! Tyrrell is lost in wonder & admiration at the change which I have produced in Italy's treatment of questions in which we are interested.

AC5/1/396

17 October 1926
Shiplake Court
Henley

My dear Ida,

. . .

I worked all morning, took a stroll with [Wargrave] & Ivy after lunch, & have since been at work again drafting for the Imperial Conference the second half of a paper on Locarno, Part I "Before & at Locarno" was admirably done by the Office, but they could not grasp or execute my idea of Part II "The Harvest of Locarno", so "if you want a thing done." Well, I have done it myself. It is something

---

[91] On 17 September Briand and Stresemann met in secret at Thoiry near Geneva and came to a far-reaching agreement to remove German war guilt, grant mandates, return the Saar without a plebiscite and evacuate the Rhine within a year. In return, France would obtain substantial and much-needed payments to bolster the Franc. The stabilisation of the Franc and financial objections in Britain and France led to the collapse of the plan.

of a cock a doodle but justified by the facts. It is to be handed to the Prime Ministers to supplement what I say on the same subject in my address on foreign affairs...

...

... Tyrrell wrote me a pleasant little note in which he repeats what he said to me the other day: "In my 30 years experience I have never known such a quick return as you have reaped in your foreign policy" & he adds "If I may say so, nobody deserved it more than you did". He recalled how after I had wrung approval from the Cabinet, Curzon dragging Balfour with him came to my room only two days before I was leaving for Paris & Geneva to protest, forced me to a new Cabinet & tried to upset the whole policy. Well, well, I look at Europe & feel I have not lived & worked in vain.

AC5/1/397

25 October 1926
2 Morpeth Mansions

My dear Hilda,

...

Chatting with F.E. last week at Paddy Gouldings I said "After all, F.E. it is you & I in India & foreign affairs who have so far achieved the successes of the present Govt". "Yes & Neville in Housing. Neville's is a marvellous success" was F.E.'s reply.

I spoke or read for 3 hours to the [Imperial] Conference. Mackenzie King[92] to me & Herzog[sic][93] to Ivy & Amery have both expressed great admiration & relief. M.K. said: "Curzon seemed always dominating & menacing as if determined to impose our will on others. You seem to get underneath them somehow & give them an uplift" & another time he added "Curzon made me shudder. It seemed as if we were going into a new war with France. My French-speaking colleague was happy this time".

[92] William Lyon Mackenzie King (1874–1950) Canadian economist and politician. Deputy Minister of Labour, 1900–8; Liberal MP 1908–11, 1921–49; Minister of Labour 1909–11; Liberal Leader 1919–48; Prime Minister 1921–30, 1935–48.
[93] Dr General James Barry Munnik Hertzog (1866–1942) South African soldier and politician. Cabinet Minister 1910–12 when resigned to establish National Party; Prime Minister 1924–1939; Minister of Native Affairs 1924–29; Minister of External Affairs 1929–39.

AC5/1/398

31 October 1926
2 Morpeth Mansions

My dear Hilda,

. . .

. . . The Imp. Conf. is going well as far as I can judge. Neither Hertzog nor O'Higgins[94] mean mischief & I do not think that there are any great differences between us – certainly not on principle – tho' some details or applications are in dispute & may give us trouble before we find the right solution.

AC5/1/399

7 November 1926
2 Morpeth Mansions

My dear Ida,

. . .

I am kept very busy but am well pleased by the attitude of the Conference to all that concerns my special business. It is, however, anxious to see how Amery with all his ability & intense zeal fails completely for lack of any sense of preparation or judgement. Balfour said to me after our last meeting: I could hardly keep from screaming & I had earlier passed a note to another colleague: "I shall scream. He has jumped with both feet into the thorniest bush in the Conference thicket, & only last night I begged him to avoid it!" Amery sat on Balfour's left, & I on his right, & A.J.B. was about as quiet as a parched pea in a frying pan & Amery was utterly unaware that anything was wrong & when I afterwards tried to suggest that, as Balfour was presiding, we must allow him to conduct the business & not take it out of his hands, Amery naively explained that Balfour did not know what to do so he had gone to his rescue! And he irritates the Dominion Prime Ministers as much as he worries his colleagues. Result, Mackenzie King is all out to get rid of the Dominion Office & some of the other Prime Ministers are not far behind him on the same road.

For the moment he & China are the flies in my ointment, but if it comes to the worst I *can* kick *his* shins as I understand one colleague was already obliged to do at a Conference by way of conveying to him that he was saying the wrong thing & that in another moment one of the Dominions was going to explode!

Funny, isn't it!

[94] Kevin O'Higgins (1892–1927) Sinn Fein MP 1918–22. Minister of Home Affairs of Irish Free State 1922–3; Vice-Pres and Minister of Justice 1923–27.

AC5/1/400   21 November 1926
                                             2 Morpeth Mansions

My dear Hilda,

. . .

You will read in tomorrow's Times the report of Balfour's Committee[95] which embodies all the principal political work of the Imperial Conference, & I hope you will feel that we have good reason to be satisfied. What it cannot give you is the personal impressions which we who sat on it have formed. Hertzog goes back with an entirely new conception of the British Empire & declares that we should have a closer cooperation than ever. Mackenzie King, now master in his own house, has been a different man & most helpful. Even the Irish, with all the sensitiveness & rawness of their public opinion, have worked harmoniously & with a real desire to cooperate, & I am confirmed in my belief that only time is needed to bring them heartily on our side.

In spite of this positive tone, Chamberlain's hopes of enlisting Dominion adherence to Locarno were dashed at the Imperial Conference. Given the Dominion mood and the increasing loosening of the diplomatic unity of the Empire, however, criticism that Chamberlain's presentation of the British case 'displayed all the diffidence of an English gentleman touching a friend for a fiver' would appear to be a little too scathing.[96] In the event, the Dominions merely expressed 'satisfaction' at the Treaty and congratulated the British on its successful negotiation.[97]

AC5/1/402   2 December 1926
                                             2 Morpeth Mansions

My dear Ida,

. . . I expect to have a good deal of business to do [at Geneva], some of it perhaps troublesome but none of it I hope presenting any grave difficulties. And I leave in a happier frame of mind because after huge labour I have worked out the basis of a policy for China, got Cabinet approval for it & sent the necessary instructions to our new Minister,

[95] The Balfour Report of the Inter-Imperial Relations Committee declared the equality of the Dominions with each other and with Britain, in free and voluntary association under the Crown.
[96] C. Barnett, *The Collapse of British Power*, 201.
[97] Cmd. 2768, *Imperial Conference 1926: Summary of Proceedings* (1926), 28–9.

Lampson[98] who is already at Shanghai on his way north & is a Man. The Office says that our Chinese policy has always been made [in?] Peking & that that our recent experience of getting no guidance from our Minister there is a deplorable novelty, but it seems to me that they have become so dependent on this help that they themselves are paralysed without it. I cannot help continually feeling the contrast between the grip & force of our Central Dept & the uncertainties, lamentations, regrets & contradictions of the Far Eastern Dept who are excellently equipped technically but don't rise to any large constructive view. But Lampson was the head of the Central Dept & already I see a new spirit stirring in his first telegrams. Now he will know what we think best to be done, he will tell us clearly how it looks to him & I shall feel confidence in his judgement.

AC5/1/403
20 December 1926
Twitt's Ghyll

My dear Hilda,

. . .

. . . The Foreign Office really is terrific work if you do it. Not only is there so much of it, but the issues are so big & the consequences may be so serious if you decide wrongly. But it is fascinatingly interesting & it is really rewarding to find for how much we count & how high our influence now stands. I was well satisfied with Geneva where we accomplished all that I thought it wise to try for, & very nearly all that I had hoped to do. The Saar was the exception & there I thought Stresemann unreasonably sticky & troublesome, so I shoved it over to another meeting. Altogether it was a singularly pleasant meeting, everyone in a good temper & some very interesting discussions. The new members of Council are pleasant people & promise well . . . they all treat me exceedingly nicely & are very apt to look to me for a lead. They begin, I think, to understand my line & to see that I have served the League well if less noisily than some others & have made it a bigger force than it was when I took my seat on the Council. Besides, they know now that we only have one policy, the same in London as at Geneva — which was not always the case.

I do not yet know the amount of my share of the Nobel Prize in

[98] Sir Miles Wedderburn Lampson (1880–1964) Diplomat and Pro-Consul. Entered F.O. 1903. Second Secretary Tokyo 1908–10; High Commissioner to Siberia 1920; Minister to China, 1926–33; Ambassador to Egypt and High Commissioner to Sudan 1934–46; Special Commissioner to South-East Asia 1946–48. Created Baron Killearn 1943.

English money ... but there are a diploma & a gold medal on their way to me ...

The Home Office requires countless signatures but will not at this time of year give me much work. Birkenhead reviewed all the strike cases before he left: I warned Jix that I would sanction no floggings & the worst I shall have to do is deciding whether murderers are to be hung or reprieved ... Curiously enough I have no scruple about hanging in a proper case. I would indeed far sooner hang than flog, for say what you will, flogging is torture, & I couldn't bring myself to apply it even to that cad Moseley[99] [sic] who I suppose is in for Smethwick by this time but thank goodness! out of B'ham.

...

Oh I must tell you. Out at Geneva one of the Germans was complaining of the French attitude & of Poincaré in particular. "I know you don't like him I said". You think him stiff, unconciliatory, insensible to the feelings of others, brutal even. I was once saying something of the kind to a Frenchman who replied: "Poincaré est Lorrain, et qui dit Lorraine dit moche Allemand." Now do you want to know how you Germans look to the rest of the world? You seem to all of us a *nation of Poincarés.*

Ho ho! Ha ha! I can't tell you what satisfaction it gives me to have said it. It gave Briand almost as much when I told him.

---

[99] Oswald Ernald Mosley (1896–1980) Conservative MP for Harrow 1918–20 then Independent 1920–24 and later Labour May–October 1924. Unsuccessful Labour candidate against Neville Chamberlain in Birmingham Ladywood October 1924; Labour MP Smethwick December 1926–February 1931 then New Party February–October 1931. Chancellor Duchy of Lancaster 1929–30; Leader New Party 1931–32, of British Union of Fascists 1932–40, of Union Movement 1948–66. Interned 1940–44. Succeeded 6th Bart. 1928.

10.

'WHAT A TROUBLED WORLD IT STILL IS'

The Foreign Office after Locarno, January 1927 – June 1929

Success at Locarno massively enhanced Chamberlain's authority in the management of foreign affairs to the extent that it appeared he would remain unshakeably in control for the duration of Baldwin's second administration. Yet perhaps the greatest tragedy of this period in Chamberlain's career was that his most glorious triumph should have come near the beginning of his term in office rather than as a natural culmination and fitting climax at its end. Although Chamberlain had always acknowledged that Locarno was but a beginning and 'there are still difficulties to be faced and still a long road to travel',[1] critics have argued that after the plaudits and glories of Locarno Chamberlain demonstrated too little appetite for the wider issues of collective security and arms limitation. Under the spell of his personal triumph perhaps he too easily allowed a note of complacency to creep into the conduct of foreign affairs.[2] Apparently not sure what to do next, he is thus often depicted as 'a spent force after his efforts at Locarno ... satisfied with his semi-detached relationship with Europe, qualified only by a tendency to lean towards France and to grumble over German ingratitude and demands for further revision of the Versailles treaty'.[3] Yet, while some of this criticism may be valid, it also needs to be seen in its proper context. Certainly, as Chamberlain later described it himself, Britain came to occupy a 'semi-detached position' in relation to Europe after Locarno.[4] Yet even before it, he had always contended that the security of the eastern European states was not only a problem for the future, but also one that it was not for Britain to solve. While his apparent indifference to events east of the Rhine may have been demoralising in central Europe,[5] therefore, British reluctance to take a lead in extending the Locarno system outside the sphere of vital national interest was the almost inevitable corollary of Chamberlain's policy motivation for pursuing a Rhineland Pact in the first place. The 'spirit of Locarno' was not to be a model for future British action but rather a beacon to guide others in assuming the initiative elsewhere.

After Locarno the ambivalent, but always essentially limited, nature of Chamberlain's expectations of the League also became more apparent. Although he continued

---

[1] A. Chamberlain to F.S. Oliver, 3 November 1925, AC37/323.

[2] See M. Gilbert, *The Roots of Appeasement* (1966), 117–25; C. Petrie, *Life and Letters*, II, 294; F.S. Northedge, *The Troubled Giant*, 270–1; Gibbs, *Grand Strategy*, I, 44; Johnson, 'The Locarno Treaties', 120; J. Connell, *The 'Office'*, 87.

[3] C.J. Bartlett, *British Foreign Policy in the Twentieth Century* (1989), 37.

[4] A. Chamberlain, 'Great Britain as a European Power', *International Affairs*, 9, (1930), 188 in Jacobson, *Locarno Diplomacy*, 378.

[5] Professor Zimmern to Jones, 3 February 1928, *Whitehall Diary*, II, 129.

to attend the League Council, with time his sense of detachment also grew. His vague tone of condescension and the occasional lapses in which he spoke of 'your League' sometimes bewildered and irritated other members.[6] *'Austen always treated the League as if it were certain to be up to some kind of mischief and he administers a rather pompous lecture at short intervals' was Cecil's view of the underlying attitude.*[7] *Moreover, if he was 'always sensitive and rather intolerant to criticism' in Cabinet,*[8] *he was far less receptive to criticism from other League members. As one contemporary observer caricatured both his tone and the message: 'We are perfect. We are British. And yet you, you dagoes, dare to come here and criticise US!'*[9] *Always believing that the League should be allowed to develop slowly into its long-term role, after Locarno he also tended to suggest that the pact and the continued cooperation of the four great European powers had somehow reduced the need for such a body.*[10] *Little wonder that Cecil later lamented that Chamberlain 'thought of it as just one cog in the diplomatic machine, to be used or not at the discretion of the Cabinet'.*[11] *Nor did Chamberlain's increasing reliance upon the close personal relationships forged at Locarno and private 'tea parties' at Geneva to resolve all problems do much for League prestige or his own reputation.*[12] *Yet, to the end of his ministry, Chamberlain continued to believe that England was still 'the key to the situation' and that, as the architect of that position, he remained indispensable.*[13] *After December 1926, however, the German question receded from the Cabinet agenda almost completely to be replaced by a myriad of crises in other parts of the world which were less receptive to the Foreign Secretary's much-vaunted 'bed-side manner'.*

In Egypt, one of the most insistent of these problems flared up almost as soon as Chamberlain took office. Amid a renewal of violence in Egypt, on 19 November 1924 Sir Lee Stack, Pasha, Sirdar of the Egyptian Army and Governor-General of the Sudan was assassinated while driving through Cairo. The reaction of the High Commissioner, Lord Allenby, was immediate and severe. Without waiting to decipher the long Foreign Office cable for fear that Zaghlul might forestall him and resign as Prime Minister, Allenby drove with a cavalry escort to the Egyptian parliament to deliver a harsh ultimatum demanding an apology, a £500,000 fine, an end to all political agitation, withdrawal of the Egyptian Army from the Sudan (in which British control would henceforth be exclusive) and acceptance of further areas of

[6] G. Craig and F. Gilbert, *The Diplomats*, 43. For favourable comments about the spirit at Geneva see A. Chamberlain to F.S. Oliver, 17 January 1927, AC54/408.

[7] Cecil to Irwin, 29 September 1927, Cecil MSS 51084/58–9.

[8] Bridgeman Diary, November 1929, Bridgeman MSS II fol. 189.

[9] W. Steed, *The Real Stanley Baldwin*, (1930), 129.

[10] D. Dutton, *Austen Chamberlain*, 270.

[11] Cecil, *All the Way*, 190. Also Hilda Memoir, BC5/10/1.

[12] For a contemporary defence of these methods by the head of the F.O. Press Department see Sir Arthur Willert, *Aspects of British Foreign Policy*, (1928), 55.

[13] See A. Chamberlain to Hilda, 14 March and 15 October 1927, AC5/1/412, 434 and to Ida 22 January, 3 April and 12 December 1927, AC5/1/406, 414, 440.

cotton irrigation in the Sudan.[14] *When Zaghlul, the Wafd leader, declined some of these demands, the British Army occupied the Alexandria Customs House. The crisis finally passed with Zaghlul's resignation on 23 November, to be replaced by Ahmed Ziwar Pasha who acceded unconditionally to all British demands.*[15] *Although the British government did not disavow Allenby's actions, the new Foreign Secretary's confidence was shaken – particularly as the Foreign Office specifically warned against both the demand of an indemnity and the risks of inflaming Egyptian fears about the extension of the cotton irrigation scheme. When Chamberlain despatched Nevile Henderson to Cairo as Minister Plenipotentiary, Allenby rightly took this as a sign of no confidence and tendered his resignation.*[16]

Allenby's successor, Lord Lloyd, was an able, tough-minded Imperialist whose obstinate refusal to believe that the Empire was in decline provided living proof of the proposition 'that Imperialism could touch a man's soul as deeply as religion'.[17] *From the outset, Lloyd was determined to adhere to the advice MacDonald had allegedly given him before departure: 'Be as liberal as you may be ... but be firm, eternally firm'.*[18] *Yet increasingly Lloyd felt frustrated at the drift in British policy and the almost impossible constraints imposed upon him. 'We cannot carry on much longer as we are', he lamented to a friend:*[19]

> We have magnitude without position; power without authority; responsibility without control. I must ensure that no foreign power intervenes ... (where all seek to do so), and I must achieve this without upsetting the Parliamentary regime which we forced upon the country in face of the King's wishes; without weakening the power or alienating the loyalty of the Monarchy which we set up, and without displaying the military power which is in fact our sole remaining argument. I must maintain and respect Egyptian independence, and yet justify our army of occupation ...

In Lloyd's mind, at the heart of this ambiguity in Imperial policy was the unilateral British declaration of March 1922, which had ended the protectorate and recognised Egypt as an independent state, while 'reserving' four crucial questions relating to security, defence and the Sudan to be settled by a future treaty. Convinced that the 'qualities of steadiness and firmness' were lacking in Egyptian factions and parties, Lloyd believed it was incumbent upon the British to provide that lead if there was to be any hope of permanent accommodation. Throughout, therefore, he pursued 'a policy of maintaining the status quo *with the strictest firmness', making no attempt at progress with negotiations upon the reserved subjects until the Egyptians saw*

---

[14] P. Mansfield, *The British in Egypt*, (1971), 251–2.
[15] P.J. Vatikiotis, *The History of Modern Egypt : From Muhammed Ali to Mubarak* (1991), 283.
[16] For Allenby's role and reactions see B. Gardner, *Allenby, 1st Viscount 1861–1931*, (1965), 239 *passim*.
[17] Compton Mackenzie's remark quoted in C. Forbes Adams, *Life of Lord Lloyd*, (1948), 94.
[18] Lord Lloyd, *Egypt Since Cromer* (1934) vol II, 143.
[19] C.F. Adams, *Life of Lord Lloyd*, 197–9.

sense, recognised the special interests of Britain in Egypt and negotiated on that basis.[20]

By the summer of *1927* the differences between the High Commissioner and the Foreign Office had become painfully evident. Despite his firm but successful handling of a crisis over the control of the Egyptian Army earlier in the year, on his visit to London in July Lloyd appeared 'still terribly upset over what he considered the readiness of the FO to let him down during the last crisis and not yet recovered from the nervous strain of practically disobeying instructions'.[21] Tensions were intensified by Lloyd's unorthodox methods. Although a personal friend for whose judgement Chamberlain initially had some regard, Lloyd's attempts to go over his head and circumvent official channels through direct appeals to the Cabinet or personal letters to Baldwin offended the Foreign Secretary's deep sense of propriety.[22] Lloyd's firmness also conflicted with Chamberlain's personal view that Britain should 'be content to work the *1922* declaration loyally and to give the Egyptians in the largest measure possible the independence which we promised them'.[23] The Foreign Office took an even more hostile line towards Lloyd's 'reactionary' posture, his status as 'an outsider', his independent methods and his pretensions to be 'something between a Secretary of State and an ambassador or Viceroy' rather than a 'common or garden ambassador'.[24] Also suspecting that Lloyd's provocative firmness was intended to create a crisis in Egypt in order to provide the pretext for the vigorous imposition of British will, officials placed considerable pressure upon Chamberlain to dismiss him.[25]

In the event Lloyd remained, but Chamberlain used the occasion of an Egyptian state visit to London by the King and Sarwat in August *1927* to begin negotiations for a new treaty, despite Lloyd's opposition and expressed doubts about the ability of any non-Wafd government to carry it through parliament. In so doing Chamberlain hoped to resolve the perennial problem which had defeated British governments in *1920* and *1921*; namely, to find a means to hand over power to an independent Egyptian government while retaining an effective military presence sufficient to defend the Suez Canal and control the Sudan.[26] The Sarwat-Chamberlain negotiations

---

[20] Lord Lloyd, *Egypt Since Cromer*, II, 143; C.F. Adams, *Life of Lord Lloyd*, 196.

[21] Amery Diary, 16 July 1927, *Leo Amery Diaries*, 516. For the Army crisis see Mansfield, *The British in Egypt*, 255–6 and Lloyd, *Egypt Since Cromer*, II Chapter XII-XIII.

[22] Amery Diary 16 July 1927; Neville Chamberlain Diary 15, 21 July 1927; Lloyd to Baldwin, 10 November 1927, *Whitehall Diary*, II, 114.

[23] A. Chamberlain to Salisbury, 1 November 1927, AC54/444.

[24] Tyrrell to A. Chamberlain, 13 September 1927, Baldwin MSS 129/22–3 cited in D. Dutton, *Austen Chamberlain*, 245. For Foreign Office dislike see Lord Vansittart, *The Mist Procession*, 372. For criticism of Lloyd's methods and style from the First Secretary in Cairo see M. Peterson, *Both Sides of the Curtain: An Autobiography*, (1950), 66–7.

[25] Tyrrell to A. Chamberlain, 15 June 1927, AC54/476; A. Chamberlain to Hilda, 22 October 1927, AC5/1/435. For these problems see Petrie, *Life and Letters*, II, 351–60.

[26] M. Beloff, *Dream of Commonwealth 1921–42*, Vol 2 of *Imperial Sunset*, (1989), 44–5; J. Charmley, *Lord Lloyd and the Decline of the British Empire*, (1987), 141–149. See also Jones Diary, 11 November 1927, *Whitehall Diary*, II, 114–15.

produced a British proposal for a treaty of alliance which the Cabinet approved and Chamberlain hailed as 'the new Locarno'.[27] *Settlement, however, was also to elude Chamberlain. The death of Zaghlul on 23 August doomed any hope of ratification as his younger, and less influential successor as head of the Wafd, Mustafa al-Nahas, sought to show that he was an equally fervent champion of unfettered Egyptian independence.*[28] *Although these events turned out as Lloyd had predicted, this did nothing to restore his standing with London. Nor did they reduce the Foreign Office's hope that British security needs could be met by a treaty with a friendly Egypt without a considerable measure of control over its internal affairs.*[29]

The other problem to confront the new Foreign Secretary on taking office was China. In some respects, Chamberlain's problems were not entirely dissimilar to those he confronted in Egypt. Thus, at one and the same time he sought to protect British interests and nationals while negotiating a revision of the status of foreigners in China in such a way as to not leave those national interests vulnerable to the extension of Soviet influence. Hopes that the nine power treaty on China at the Washington Conference of 1921 would bring about a peaceful China that was well disposed towards Britain soon proved to be facile. A wave of nationalist revolt rapidly seized the country effectively dividing it between a Koumintang-controlled south based in Canton and the north in the grip of warlord rivalries. As the nation with the greatest economic and commercial interest in China, Britain naturally became the principal target for the nationalist campaign against western imperialism. After British police fired on striking Chinese in Shanghai on 30 May 1925, unrest rapidly spread to other British extra-territorial settlements in Hankow, Kiukiang and Canton. The result was a long and bitter anti-British boycott that did not end until October: a 'source of constant anxiety' to the Foreign Secretary and a foretaste of what was to come in 1927.[30] *After May 1926 the British position was rendered more difficult by the KMT decision to launch an offensive under Chiang Kai-Shek towards the north which inevitably threatened the dense mass of British settlements and interests in the Yangtse basin.*

By the end of 1926, Chamberlain was beginning to feel a new sense of confidence in British policy towards the region. First, after a 'huge labour' he had decided upon a radical change in British policy towards China, for which he had obtained Cabinet approval based on a liberal and conciliatory revision of the international settlement laid out at Washington in 1921: a policy embodied in the so-called 'December memorandum'.[31] *At the same time, Chamberlain was evidently relieved to have a Minister in China in whom he had complete trust for the first time. Before the*

[27] A. Chamberlain to Ida, 12 November 1927, AC5/1/437.

[28] See J.J. Terry, *The Wafd, 1919–52*, (1988), Chapter 8.

[29] In July 1928 Chamberlain again raised the issue of a military agreement in Cabinet, Amery Diary, 11 July 1928, *Leo Amery Diaries*, 555–6. See also J. Marlowe, *Anglo-Egyptian Relations 1800–1953* (1954), 280–4.

[30] F.S. Northedge, *The Troubled Giant*, 287–8, 292–3; A. Chamberlain to Hilda, 18 July and 16 August 1925, AC5/1/359, 362.

[31] F.S. Northedge, *The Troubled Giant*, 297–8.

appointment of Sir Miles Lampson late in 1926, Chamberlain had complained that he had no confidence in the advice received from the Far Eastern Department of the Foreign Office, not least because it had become utterly dependent on the Minister in Peking for a policy lead. When this was not forthcoming, these officials became so 'paralysed' they were capable only of a stream of 'uncertainties, lamentations, regrets and contradictions'. In contrast, Lampson had been head of the respected Central Department and had accompanied Chamberlain to Locarno. He was also 'a Man', and from his first telegrams in November 1926 Chamberlain began to detect 'a new spirit stirring' in the management of British diplomacy in China.[32]

Yet for all this optimism, the situation was extremely grave. In October 1926 Hankow had fallen to the nationalists. By early January 1927 the threat from anti-British rioters compelled the Cabinet to authorise the abandonment of the British concession. Although reluctant to act unilaterally, much to Chamberlain's disgust, no joint action was forthcoming from either Japan or the United States despite repeated pleas. On the advice of the Chiefs of Staff, in mid-January the Cabinet also agreed to reinforce Shanghai with a Defence Force of 20,000 troops complete with tanks, aircraft and artillery to prevent a repetition of the withdrawal from Hankow. In the absence of effective international cooperation, the British pursued what Northedge has described as a 'dual policy': a combination of 'reserving force for the really critical occasions, the definition of which had to be left largely to the authorities on the spot, while taking the lead among Washington powers in a forward looking attitude towards the Chinese problem'.[33] Yet in practice, it appears that these two elements were less part of a single coherent strategy than an essentially reactive and, at times, uncomfortable compromise between the position of the Foreign Office view and that of the majority of the Cabinet led by Amery, Birkenhead and Churchill who believed 'the only way to preserve peace is to take a high and drastic line' with the Chinese.[34]

In private, Chamberlain undoubtedly espoused the merits of such a dual policy.[35] In Cabinet, however, he was often almost totally isolated when advocating a policy which appeared to the unsympathetic to be perilously close to one of 'scuttle and surrender'.[36] In part, his desire for a conciliatory and unprovocative stance was based on a genuinely enlightened belief that he was 'thinking of our relations with

[32] See A. Chamberlain to Hilda, 18 July 1925 and to Ida, 2 December 1926, AC5/1/359, 402. In fairness, the proposal for a bolder policy of treaty revision enshrined in the December memorandum had emanated in August 1926 from Sir Victor Wellesley, head of the Far East Department of the F.O., W.R. Louis, *British Strategy in the Far East*, (Oxford, 1971), 152–3.

[33] F.S. Northedge, *The Troubled Giant*, 294.

[34] Amery Diary, 26 January 1927, *Leo Amery Diaries*, 494.

[35] See A. Chamberlain to Ida, 22 January 1927, AC5/1/406.

[36] Amery Diary, 4 February 1927, *Leo Amery Diaries*, 495. Cf. Petrie's misleading claim that there were 'no differences among his colleagues in the Cabinet with regard either to the despatch of the troops or of the conciliatory attitude to be adopted towards the Chinese if they refrained from violence', *Life and Letters*, II, 366–7.

China for the next hundred years'.[37] *It also reflected the Foreign Office expectation that there would soon be a breach between the Communists (urged on by Moscow) and the nationalist right within the KMT. It was hoped that Lampson's nine days of talks with Chen, the Canton Foreign Minister, and the subsequent publication of the December memorandum on 18 December would assist the split.*[38] *For the same reason Chamberlain deprecated all hostile action pending the delicate negotiations with Chen over Hankow and Kiukiang. Thus, when the despatch of the Shanghai Defence Force was used as a pretext to repudiate the agreement, Chamberlain alarmed the 'hawks' by proposing to divert the force in return for Chen's pledge to sign the Hankow agreement. Although such 'wobbling' was over-ruled by the combined voices of Lampson, the naval commander on the spot and Amery and Churchill,*[39] *Chamberlain remained 'sticky' over the Governor of Hong Kong's proposal to threaten serious action against Canton if they began an assassination campaign in the Colony and he successfully opposed the service chiefs' plan for active sanctions, including the complete control of the Yangtse.*[40]

The expected rift in the KMT ranks finally occurred in mid-April when Chiang Kai-Shek took action against the communists in Shanghai and established a rival KMT government at Nanking two days later. By early May the government decided on a 'do-nothing course'[41] *in order to await developments. Thereafter Chiang's success and Britain's decision to return to a policy of strict neutrality between the Chinese factions on 19 May witnessed a gradual reduction in tension. In retrospect, it is undoubtedly true that more success was achieved in British policy towards China than in any other non-European country except Kemalist Turkey and that Chamberlain deserved much of the credit for this outcome.*[42] *At the time, however, the course which he pursued did little to build confidence in his diplomacy or to provide him with a conclusive victory over his increasingly vociferous detractors in Cabinet.*[43]

In the very same month, Chamberlain suffered another significant defeat over relations with Russia. Again, it was a policy reverse inflicted by the same right-wing Cabinet critics of his conciliatory China policy. Since coming to office Chamberlain's policy towards Russia had been consistently moderate and cautious despite growing evidence of hostile and provocative acts: a policy he upheld with increasing difficulty after the General Strike, despite deteriorating relations on both sides.[44] *In February and March 1927 he succeeded in averting an immediate breach*

---

[37] A. Chamberlain at Birmingham, *The Times*, 30 January 1927.

[38] P.A. Reynolds, *British Foreign Policy in the Inter-War Years*, (Westport 1954), 75.

[39] See Amery Diary, 1, 4 and 7 February 1927, *Leo Amery Diaries*, 494–6.

[40] Amery Diary, 28 March 1927, *Leo Amery Diaries*, 502.

[41] Amery Diary, 2 May 1927, *Leo Amery Diaries*, 505.

[42] F.S. Northedge, *The Troubled Giant*, 292; P.A. Reynolds, *British Foreign Policy in the Inter-War Years*, 74; P. Lowe, *Britain in the Far East: A Survey from 1819 to the Present*, (1981), 132.

[43] See Amery Diary, 28 March 1927 for criticism and ridicule of Chamberlain's 'triumphs'. Also N. Chamberlain to Hilda, 5 February 1927, NC18/1/561.

[44] See A. Chamberlain to Ida, 11 July 1925 and 19 June 1926; to Hilda 27 June 1926; F.S. Northedge and A. Wells, *Britain and Soviet Communism : The Impact of a Revolution* (1982), 43.

despite strong pleas from Birkenhead, Churchill and Amery,[45] *but the Cabinet agreed that 'given the state of public opinion ... if the present policy of the ... Soviet Government was continued, a breach of relations within the next few months was almost inevitable'.*[46] *Eventually in May, Chamberlain was forced to give way after Joynson-Hicks had authorised a raid on the Soviet Trade Delegation and the All-Russian Cooperative Society (ARCOS). Although the material obtained proved disappointing, the Cabinet decided to break off diplomatic relations anyway on the vague grounds of 'anti-British espionage and propaganda'.*[47] *Despite his staunch rearguard action for almost eighteen months, Chamberlain had suffered another major defeat.*

Alongside reverses over the Egyptian treaty, criticism about 'scuttle' in China and the inability to avert the breach with Russia, 1927 also plunged Chamberlain into the morass of disarmament: an issue which brought him into conflict with two of his greatest bêtes noires in the form of Lord Robert Cecil and the Americans. Chamberlain had devoted little time, and even less effort, to the subject before the middle of 1927 when the Three Power Naval Disarmament Conference met at Geneva to consider Coolidge's proposal to extend the Washington agreements on capital ships to cruisers, destroyers and submarines.[48] *Although the Conference collapsed amid Anglo-American recrimination, for Chamberlain it was important in two respects. First, conflict within Cabinet over the issue finally precipitated Cecil's long-desired resignation from a government in which he had become an increasingly awkward and isolated figure.*[49] *As acting Prime Minister in Baldwin's absence, Chamberlain was more than a little responsible for the crisis by allowing Churchill to re-open discussion of the British position immediately after Baldwin's departure for Canada.*[50] *Although he had little but contempt for Cecil as a colleague or as an influence on foreign policy,*[51] *as acting Prime Minister Chamberlain was placed in the invidious position of trying to placate Cecil in order to contain the damage.*[52] *In the event, when Cecil did resign on 30 August his letter of resignation had been through five drafts and much of the sting had been drawn.*[53]

[45] Amery Diary 16 and 18 February, 16 March 1927, *Leo Amery Diaries*, 496–7, 500.

[46] CAB 3(27) 18 February 1927, CAB 23/54.

[47] C. Andrew, *Secret Service: The Making of the British Intelligence Community* (1987), 469–471.

[48] A. Chamberlain to Baldwin, 12 September 1927, Baldwin MSS 129/13–16. For the Conference see D. Carlton, 'Great Britain and the Coolidge Naval Disarmament Conference of 1927', *Political Science Quarterly*, LXXXIII (1968), 573–98; D. Richardson, *The Evolution of British Disarmament Policy in the 1920s*, Chapter 9.

[49] Cecil to Irwin, 7 June 1927, Cecil MSS 51084/43–5.

[50] Davidson to Baldwin, 27 July 1927, Baldwin MSS. For the background see Hankey Memorandum, 30 August 1927, Hankey MSS 8/5/1–11; Cecil, *A Great Experiment: An Autobiography*, (1941), 358–63.

[51] A. Chamberlain to Mary Carnegie, 2 September 1927, AC4/1/1282. For early displays of contempt see Jones Diary, 13 April 1921, *Whitehall Diaries*, I, 148; A. Chamberlain to Ida, 22 September 1923, AC5/1/290; to Ivy, 5 November 1924, AC6/1/592.

[52] For Chamberlain's efforts see A. Chamberlain to Cecil, 8 and 14 August 1927, Cecil MSS 51079/165–6, 169–172.

[53] Cecil did outline a catalogue of earlier differences with the Government in

The more enduring significance of the failure of the Naval Conference was that it had reawakened Chamberlain's deep disgust for the self-interested cynicism of the United States at a time when he was about to begin a long period of dealing with Anglo-American relations. In truth, such feelings had never been far beneath the surface since Chamberlain's involvement with the USA during the War. Despite the fact that he had an American step-mother whose father had been Secretary of War during Grover Cleveland's first administration, to accuse Chamberlain of being an early believer in the romantic illusion of 'pan Anglo-Saxonism' or a subscriber to the naive 'myth of cousinhood and common interest' with the United States is grossly misleading.[54] Indeed, alongside his love for France, perhaps the most abiding theme in his political diary letters is his profound loathing and abiding contempt for American politicians, their political process and the smug, self-interested isolationism and obstructionism of US foreign policy, cravenly drifting in response to every new breeze of public opinion.

Until the breakdown of the Coolidge Naval Conference, Anglo-American relations had remained firmly in the background for Chamberlain, largely because of the skilful diplomacy and social charm of Sir Esmé Howard. As British Ambassador in Washington, Howard had done much to maintain a satisfactory balance between London and Washington and in so doing earned himself the respect of foreign policy-makers on both sides of the Atlantic.[55] From mid-1927 onwards, however, Chamberlain took a far more central role in Anglo-American relations and not always with happy results. Early in 1928 American Secretary of State Kellogg had proposed a pact to outlaw war as an instrument of policy. Although Chamberlain reserved a special contempt for its author[56] and suspected this was one more example of naive American diplomacy dictated by a cynical desire to appease domestic opinion, under Howard's calming influence Britain signed the Kellogg-Briand Pact on 27 August 1928, although not before offending American sensibilities.[57] Unfortunately a month earlier, without consulting any other power and without Cabinet authorisation, Chamberlain had prematurely revealed the existence of secret negotiations on the so-called Anglo-French Compromise on the Limitation of Armaments.[58] The content of this agreement was an almost calculated affront to both Germany and Italy. Worse still, it plunged Anglo-American relations arguably to their lowest point this century.[59]

Parliament, *House of Lords Debates,* LXIX, col 84–94, 16 November 1927. See also Cecil to Irwin, 29 September 1927, Cecil MSS 51086/54–9.

[54] C. Barnett, *The Collapse of British Power,* 261–2.

[55] B.J.C. McKercher, *The Second Baldwin Government and the United States,* 29–32. See also by the same author, *Esmé Howard: A Diplomatic Biography,* (Cambridge, 1989)

[56] The F.O. shared Chamberlain's dislike, calling him 'Nervous Nellie', Vansittart, *The Mist Procession,* 344.

[57] Jones Diary, 14 May 1928, *Whitehall Diary,* II, 136–7, reporting the US Ambassador.

[58] *House of Commons Debates,* 5 Series, 220 col 1837, 30 July 1928. For the compromise see D. Carlton, 'The Anglo-French Compromise on Arms Limitation, 1928'; *Journal of British Studies,* VIII (1968–9).

[59] This is the view of McKercher, *The Second Baldwin Government,* 1. For a contrary view that the lowest point was in 1915–16 see D.C. Watt, 'America and the British Foreign

At home, in Italy and at Geneva the disclosure also revived all the old charges of 'secret diplomacy' and conspiracy with France. The result was an unmitigated disaster and marked the undoubted low point in Chamberlain's diplomacy.[60]

AC5/1/405   8 January [mis-dated December] 1927
                                          Twitt's Ghyll

My dear Ida,

      . . .
      China is so critical that I must be in London all next week . . .
      . . . The whole situation is perplexing in the last degree & the evacuation of Hankow settlement has come as a great shock. It *may* have been necessary – would in certain circumstances have been unavoidable – but neither Lampson nor we were prepared for it in the actual conditions. If I were with you, I might talk about it, but I am not in the mood to renew my grief by writing about it.

AC5/1/406   22 January 1927
                                        2 Morpeth Mansions

My dear Ida,

      Your letter found me here this morning, for again I decided that I must not leave London. All decisions were finally taken as regards military reinforcements on Friday & the orders went out for the troops to embark as soon as the shipping, which was engaged last week, is ready for their reception. Thus the big decision is taken; we are actively seeking a settlement of differences on a most liberal basis by negotiation but we won't be hustled or driven out of Shanghai as we were out of Hankow. I am disappointed in my first efforts to secure co-operation with & common action by Japan, but events may yet bring them along. But the decisive factor for us is that our reinforcements take much longer to arrive, & we can not wait as they can afford to do. So we have taken, as I say, the great decisions, but much may yet be in the hands of diplomacy, & I must remain at my post. I have not been working long hours, as my hours go, but the tension has been great. It

Policy-Making Elite, from Joseph Chamberlain to Anthony Eden, 1895–1956', in D.C. Watt, *Personalities and Policies, Studies in the Formulation of British Foreign Policy in the Twentieth Century*, (1965), 30–36.
      [60] Even Petrie echoes this view, *Life and Letters*, II, 324–5. Also D. Carlton, 'The Anglo French Compromise', 151; D. Dutton, *Austen Chamberlain*, 280.

is a great satisfaction that for all the crucial decisions, we have had absolute unanimity among us.

Sunday . . .

Here is a pleasant little episode. While at Twitt's I wrote in my best French (two mistakes corrected by Tyrrell!) a longish letter to Mussolini, enclosing my Rectorial Address.[61] I meant it in part as a friendly gesture to him to maintain our pleasant personal relations, but I also meant it as an appeal not to underrate the League or to allow Italian policy to be governed by the anti-League views of the extreme Fascisti. I sent it to our Ambassador to read & deliver, which he did but with a warning to me not to be too sanguine of any result. My letter was despatched on the 10th after my return to town. On the 19th Paulacci, Mussolini's Chef de Cabinet called on the Ambassador to say that Attolico, the 2nd Assistant Secretary of the League & principal Italian on the staff, was appointed Ambassador to Rio & that Mussolini had proposed to Eric Drummond[62] the appointment of Paulacci himself to succeed him. "In suggesting this appointment Signor Mussolini had desired to emphasize the interest & importance he attached to the League & Marquis Paulacci said that I might consider (so the ambassador telegraphed) His Excellency's action as the first fruits of the recent private communication you had made to him on the subject". And a cordial personal letter from M. follows.

Yesterday I had a minute from one of the Asst. Secretaries of the F.O.: – "Germany, Poland & Lithuania are all as irritable & irritating to one another as possible at this moment. The only person who can calm them is the S/S if he will speak to them at Geneva." My bedside manner again! But there is a basis of truth for it, & I may have to try. After all it is the fact that personality counts for so much that makes this work so attractive.

AC5/1/409
                                        16 February 1927
                                        17 Dean's Yard

My dear Hilda,

. . .

I have not dared to leave town on account of China, first because I did not feel that I could rest or even be comfortable unless in immediate touch with the F.O. etc & secondly because even if there were nothing

---

[61] Rector of Glasgow University, 1925–8.

[62] (James) Eric Drummond (1876–1951). British diplomat. Private Secretary to Asquith, Grey and Balfour, 1913–19; First Secretary-General League of Nations 1919–33; British Ambassador to Italy 1933–9. Succeeded as 16th Earl of Perth 1937.

for me to do, the public would think that there must be something & that I was neglecting it. I have had a most anxious week & a worrying one as I could [not?] see a way through in any direction, having regard to the military situation as defined by our Chiefs of Staff: but the political situation has begun to change; international cooperation is now more likely. If Japan will at length play up, the military & political problems are simplified & at any rate I now see a clear line of policy to propose to the Cabinet tomorrow. I am more hopeful.

AC5/1/410   20 February 1927
                                                 Twitt's Ghyll

My dear Ida,

      . . .
    I have had rather too much work & anxiety – and contention, & it is the last which makes the strain. The Cabinets have been very tiring & contentious, & I have been disappointed at receiving so little support from some of my colleagues & having my informed & considered opinions swept aside so lightly by them under pressure from the Daily Mail & the backbenchers who don't know what I know of the *state* of Europe & how thin the crust is on which I have to tread.
    Neville for reasons of his own is nearly as disgruntled as I am & both your brothers, plagued by inadequate incomes & so money worries, begin to ask themselves why they ever tried to serve their country.
    Well, well, the rock garden begins to be of interest . . . So down here I have something to console me & I try to forget my troubles for a little . . .

AC5/1/411   27 February 1927
                                                 Twitt's Ghyll

My dear Hilda,

      . . .
    I have had a lighter week, China has troubled *me* less, & for the time being we have not broken with Russia – a breach which I dread not for the sake of Russia but for its reactions on Europe & especially on Germany & the Baltic States. I fear that it will come nevertheless before long, though some few of them, Stalin now their biggest force among them, are beginning to realise that world revolution does not pay them. But I doubt if they can keep off it, & the toes of my colleagues are itching to kick them even tho' it be but a useless gesture. I took the

idea of a Note[63] as a compromise, for it gives me a little time & others a warning, but I wish rather than hope that it might not be necessary to go further.

AC5/1/412

14 March 1927
2 Morpeth Mansions

[Typescript]
My dear Hilda,

We got back last night and I found your letter this morning. As far as weather went, Geneva was perfectly odious. It rained most days and the mountains were always shrouded in cloud. However, I did not go there for pleasure and our business was satisfactorily accomplished. The final sittings on Saturday were extremely interesting and the discussion between Stresemann and Briand reminded one of similar combats at Locarno. But it was all the more interesting because on this occasion, though there had been a great number of crossing conversations à deux, we had never met à trois or à quatre, and France and Germany left to themselves were unable to come together. We were all agreed that this time we must avoid the meetings in my room of which the French and German public were getting a little jealous. But England is still the key of the situation and her help is needed to bring the parties together. Our last day, therefore, was very dramatic. Everybody had had their attention fixed upon this question of the Saar during the whole week. It was known that the conversations between Briand and Stresemann had not led to an agreement and it was generally anticipated that the Council would have to take a vote and decide their differences by a majority.

Saturday's proceedings opened with a first-class statement on behalf of the Governing Commission of the Saar by the Canadian chairman, Mr. Stevens.[64] Nothing could have been better done and he produced a great effect. Then, however, came Stresemann's long argument in opposition to the Commission's recommendations. It was conducted in an admirable temper and, though he obviously wished to find a solution by agreement, he made proposals which it was known the French could not accept. As he spoke in German, a double translation was necessary and it was lunch time by the time these translations were finished.

[63] Chamberlain's stiff note warning the Russians to mend their ways or risk a rupture in relations was delivered on 23 February. CP25(27) CAB 24/184.
[64] Henry Herbert Stevens (1873–1973) Canadian accountant, broker and politician. Conservative MP 1911–34 and then for Reconstruction Party 1934–40. Minister of Customs & Excise 1926; Minister of Trade & Commerce 1921 and 1930–31. First leader of Reconstruction Party 1934–38.

After lunch Briand took up the tale and was equally friendly and equally resolute. Then came a rejoinder by Stresemann, followed by some further explanations by Stevens. All this time, I and others were watching the situation carefully, but it is simple truth to say that everyone was looking to me to find the solution and anxiously hoping that they might not have to choose between two Great Powers. At lunch time I was still quite unable to see my way, but while Briand was speaking I made up my mind and I intervened as soon as the translation of his speech was finished.

My intervention was decisive. Scialoja[65] added a few words to my appeal and Vandervelde[66] made his usual *gaffe*. But my speech had settled the matter. Stresemann responded to my appeal. Briand accepted the interpretation I had placed upon his words, and it only remained to draw up an agreed report.

It is disappointing that the English papers do so little to make clear the decisive rôle which England played or even hint at the fact (which was obvious to every soul in the room) that if there was to be an agreed solution, it must be found by us; for we alone could speak with sufficient authority and were sufficiently possessed of the confidence of both parties. The other members of the Council showered congratulations on me and we came out with added prestige in which the Council shared.

I must report to you Viscount Ishii's[67] *bon mot*, though I am not quite sure that it is fitted for ears polite. "The others made the baby, but you were the *sage femme*!" Briand's comment was equally good. "I quite understand," he said, "that Dr. Stresemann desires to carry a branch of laurel back to Berlin, but it is not necessary that he should always choose *my* garden in which to pick it."

[65] Vittorio Scialoja (1856–1933). Italian lawyer and politician. Senator 1904; Minister of Justice 1909–10; Foreign Minister 1919–20; delegate at Peace Conference 1919 and to League of Nations 1921–32.

[66] Emile Vandervelde (1866–1938) Professor, University of Brussels. Belgian Social Democrat MP. Minister of Justice 1918–21; Minister Foreign Affairs 1925–27; Minister without Portfolio 1935–36; Minister Public Health 1936–37.

[67] Viscount Kikujiro Ishii (1866–?) Japanese diplomat. Attache, Paris 1890–96; Consul in Korea 1896–1900; Ambassador to France 1912–15, 1920–27; Foreign Minister 1915–16. Negotiated Lansing-Ishii agreement, November 1917 recognising that Japan had a special interest in China. President of the Council and Assembly of League of Nations. 1923, 1926. Retired 1927. Created Viscount 1916.

AC5/1/414

3 April 1927
Twitt's Ghyll

My dear Ida,

... The Chinese situation grows worse, & though we are doing all we can to secure united action at least by the U.S.A., Japan & ourselves & though our Ministers are agreed in recommending a policy & our representatives at Shanghai are cooperating as well as their institutions permit, Tokyo & Washington are doubtful factors. Kellogg[68] is an old woman without a policy & trembling at every breeze which blows from the Senate & Japan will save her bacon at our expense or at least try to ... So I am anxious & worried ... & was beginning even to dream China, & so I thought a couple of days change was needed.

AC5/1/416

1 May [1927]
Twitt's Ghyll

[Not addressed]

China remains as big a worry as ever. Shanghai & Hongkong are for any & every violent measure, Peking for hitting someone on the head & that quickly, & my office for doing nothing. The Cabinet & I incline to a middle course. We shall have to take a final decision tomorrow, but I should be happier if there were less to be said for the do-nothing course – or more. The arguments are sufficient to raise doubts & make one hesitate but not conclusive.

AC5/1/418

15 May 1927
Twitt's Ghyll

My dear Ida,

...

But I expect you would sooner hear about Arcos than about the garden. The warrant was to search Arcos for a stolen Govt. document – a military manual, I think – which the police had good reason to know was or had been in their hands. When I last heard they had not found it, but at that time they had not opened the safes, some of which were

[68] Frank Billings Kellogg (1856–1937). US Senator 1917–23; US Ambassador in London 1924–25; US Secretary of State 1925–29. Awarded Nobel Peace Prize 1929 for his part in the Briand-Kellogg Pact 1928.

concealed behind panelling & some bedded in deep concrete in the basement. I can only trust that they will find something worth all the fuss. They & we will look foolish if they don't but to tell you the truth I have no great faith in Sir Wyndham Childs[69] or in some of his people.

...

China is troubling me rather less for the moment, though I suppose it is only a brief interlude, & it looks as if the new Japanese P.M. who is also M.F.A. were more forthcoming & friendly than the last from whom I could never strike a responsive spark. But Mussolini is troublesome. I wish he would not read the papers or were less sensitive to what they say. Any rag in Serbia, Germany or above all France can upset his temper & distort his policy.

AC5/1/420   16 June 1927
                                          2 Morpeth Mansions

My dear Hilda,

...

I have had a long & not unsatisfactory talk with Sarwat[70] but it is too soon to say whether anything will come of it & I have been harassed beyond endurance by the outrageous behaviour of the American delegation & press correspondents at Geneva & the stupidity & ignorance of old woman Kellog [sic] at Washington. Goodness knows what will be the ultimate result, but I am very anxious. Save me from countries whose politics are run by Steel Trusts & which for two years out of every four are thinking of the next Presidential election!

AC5/1/425   11 July 1927
                                          2 Morpeth Mansions

[Typescript]
My dear Ida,

...

... Troubles succeed one another with unceasing regularity. The Chinese situation remains as confused & fluctuating as ever. I still have

---

[69] (Borlase Edward) Wyndham Childs (1876–1946) Entered Army 1900; War Office 1910–14; Ass. Adjutant-Gen GHQ France 1914–16 and then War Office 1916; Director, Personal Services War Office 1916–19; Ass. Commissioner Metropolitan Police and head of Special Branch from 1921–28. Knighted 1919.
[70] Abd al Khalek Sarwat Pasha (1873–1928) Govenor Assiat Province 1907; Minister of Justice 1915; Minister of Interior 1921; Foreign Minister 1922, 1926–27; Prime Minister of Egypt 1922, 1927–8. Resigned after failure to negotiate Anglo-Egyptian Treaty.

before me in September the very difficult problem of how to decide the quarrel between Hungary and Roumania upon which I have to report to the Council, and meanwhile the Franco-Spanish Conversations on Tangier have all but broken down and to prevent a complete breach I shall have to intervene there, and on top of all this comes the serious divergence of opinion between ourselves and the American Delegation at Geneva and the risk that Coolidge's conference may start a new and most poisonous race of armaments instead of as we all hoped leading to a further limitation. You will see that I have enough to do both in quality and quantity. But even that does not exhaust the list, for to-morrow I must have my first business conversation with Sarwat – not an easy conversation to conduct, for Sarwat is very clever, quite untrustworthy and has his own game to play which may loom larger in his mind than the interests of Egypt. The fact is that Fuad, Sarwat and Zaghloul[71] are all clever men, but they hate each other like poison and none of them are straight and none of them like us. It is not exactly a tempting or hopeful job, but being of an optimistic nature and having a great faith in the power of straight dealing and sympathy combined, I am not altogether without hope that some good may result. I do not intend to conduct any negotiations here. The problem I have to determine is whether there is any chance of such negotiations being successfully entered upon by Lloyd and Sarwat when they are back in Cairo.

Today there is to be a Foreign Office debate in the House of Commons which all the papers speak of as a debate on disarmament; but Ponsonby,[72] who opens it on Macdonald's [sic] behalf, has sent me word that he does not propose to deal either with the Disarmament Conference or the three Powers conversations and I suppose that I shall have to listen to an hour's dreary and probably mischevious pessimism on the general outlook in Europe in which he will do whatever he can to irritate both France and Italy. Such is the nature of the man. In private life an amiable and cultivated gentleman, but in politics extreme and mischevious as for some queer reason appears to be the case with every gentleman by birth who joins the Labour Party. I had much sooner deal with Macdonald himself, with Thomas,

[71] Sa'ad Zaghlul (1860–1927). Egyptian politician and leader of nationalist Wafd party. Deported 1919, returned 1921, deported again 1921–3. Prime Minister 1924 but forced to resign after murder of Lee Stack. President Chamber of Deputies 1925–27.

[72] Arthur Augustus William Harry Ponsonby (1871–1946). Liberal MP for Stirling Burghs 1908–18; Labour MP Sheffield Brightside 1922–30. Private Secretary to Prime Minister 1905–8; Under-Sec Foreign Office 1924; Under-Sec Dominions 1929; Parliamentary Secretary Transport 1929–31; Chancellor Duchy of Lancaster 1931; Labour Leader in the Lords 1931–35. A founder of Union of Democratic Control. Created Baron Ponsonby of Shulbrede 1930.

or Snowden than with the Ponsonbys, Trevelyans[73] and Mosleys of the Labour Party.

AC5/1/426   1 August 1927
                                                    Twitt's Ghyll

My dear Hilda,

    . . .
    Indeed I have had a terrific time for the last month – ever since I came back from Geneva that is. The hours have been long but the quality has been even more exhausting than the quantity of the work . . . Every day for a fortnight I have had the equivalent of two Cabinet meetings, sometimes actually two, at others a Cabinet & a Cab. Comtee. or a negotiation which raised equally big issues & required equally close attention; & all the time in the background of such work as is known to my colleagues, other great & crucial questions of foreign policy – China, the Occupied Territory, Tangiers . . . I ought to be a wreck & yet I am wonderfully well considering the strain & am astonished at my own powers of endurance . . . So you see I am pretty hale & hearty as I approach my 64th birthday. But – I should like to let up.
    . . .
    My conversations with Sarwat Pasha were extraordinarily interesting & important. What if anything will eventually come of them is on the lap of the Gods – very probably nothing but even so they are most useful, for they have enabled me to win his confidence & he has shown a more serious desire for agreement & in private a clearer understanding of the facts of the situation than any Egyptian Minister has yet done. As a result of what I said at our first conversation he produced a draft of a treaty of perpetual friendship & alliance. At our second I handed him a counter-draft to which I had obtained Cabinet sanction. He says he cannot accept it as it stands, but he is taking it to Egypt & means to return in October with authority to negotiate. It may well be that with Zaghul [sic] & even more extreme forces at work in Egypt, no agreement will be possible, but in any case I have put us on firmer grounds & my Office is very happy.
    Tyrrell says: "You put your European policy on the right footing by Locarno. You did the same for China with your December declaration; now you have done the same for Egypt. You are on firm ground in all

---

[73] Charles Philips Trevelyan (1870–1958). Liberal MP Elland 1899–1918; Labour MP Newcastle Central 1922–31; Parliamentary Secretary, Education 1908–14; President Board of Education 1924, 1929–31. Succeeded as 3rd Bart. 1928.

three." And Selby says: "Do you remember saying some time ago that you had won your niche in the temple of foreign affairs by your work in Europe & ought to get out before you lost it in China or Egypt? Well, you won't lose it now in Egypt. I can't tell you how delighted I am, for I have been anxious about Egypt".

AC5/1/427

7 August 1927
Twitt's Ghyll

My dear Ida,

...

Well, I have had a hectic time. The P.M. may find the Cabinet still complete when he returns or he may find it minus the Chancellor of the Duchy – at present I cannot tell which – but at one moment last week I had four resignations threatened, three of them actually in my hands. I told the P.M. it was not safe for him to leave until the Geneva Conference was over, & he will never go so far afield again if I can prevent him ...

AC5/1/434

15 October 1927
2 Morpeth Mansions

My dear Hilda,

...

I myself have returned [from holiday] very well & rested, but I too have not the reserves with which I entered office. However I have told the P.M. in answer to his question ... that I would go on for another Parliament!

...

My international position continues what you know it to be & is steadily strengthened. England will never be popular on the continent. For that you must belong to & identify yourself with one of the contending groups, but we are respected & trusted, our sympathy is courted, our advice & our help continuously sought ...

AC5/1/435

22 October 1927
Twitt's Ghyll

My dear Hilda,

I have had enough to do since I came home but so far have not been over-tasked. It is a "quiet time" i.e. there is no great crisis but China continues troubled as ever ... I have very big problems confronting me in the near future in Egypt or in connection with Egypt, for Lord Lloyd does not heartily accept my policy & my principal advisers would wish me to get rid of him, which would make a first class row inside & outside the Cabinet in this country. I have got to give a good deal of thought to the matter while I am here.

AC5/1/436

6 November 27
2 Morpeth Mansions

My dear Ida,

. . .
I have had a very heavy week. Breakfast each morning at 8.30 & twice to bed at 2.30 a.m. And the character of the work – noone not engaged on it can get an idea of its daily responsibilities & anxieties ...

. . .
Well, if I have toiled it has not been in vain. I have on my desk the draft of a Treaty of perpetual friendship & alliance between Egypt & this country which I believe that Sarwat would accept & which seems to me a prodigious achievement – yes Pro-digious as the Dominie said – but I have before me a very stiff fight with a section of the Cabinet & I shall not begin to be comfortable or at ease till that is over successfully. If I can't carry them or if they can't support me in such a question, the P.M. must find another foreign secretary. Yes, that is how I feel. I lay in bed most of yesterday, only getting up at 6 p.m. to do the day's work & dine quietly with Ivy, & then with my mind rested & fresh I read the draft over to Ivy ...

. . .
Now what do you think of that bearing in mind that our Law Officers past & present have more than once stated that if the Egyptian Govt. could in present circumstances find a way to bring the presence of our troops in Egypt before the Hague Court the decision would probably go against us?
Look at the passage on foreign affairs in the P.M.'s Guildhall speech on the 9th. I think you will like it. I wrote it – & it's very generous of me to give such good stuff away to another speaker.

AC5/1/437

12 November 1927
2 Morpeth Mansions

My dear Ida,

...

For the [Egyptian] treaty has passed the Cabinet & subject only to Dominion concurrence which is being sought I am authorized to sign whenever Sarwat is ready. And that is the nicest possible way with the Cabinet overwhelmingly in my favour – in fact only three dissenting & they expressing their views very quietly & in an excellent spirit & I carefully refraining from saying to any of them that I should resign if the Cabinet did not support me until the decision had been given when I told the P.M. and C/E that I was so convinced that it would be suicidal for us to reject such a treaty that I could not have remained responsible. I think the P.M., at least, knew it, but he whole-heartedly agreed with me & I was able to avoid any threat.

My dears, I am very, very pleased & ten years younger than on Monday last. I regard it as a great triumph for British diplomacy & it will be so regarded abroad – whenever we are able to publish it. The King has again sworn to support Sarwat in carrying it & Adly[74] whom Sarwat has taken fully into his confidence has told Sarwat that if such a treaty were offered to him he would be justified in going to all lengths to carry it. Sarwat himself seemed very confident. He told Selby that I had put 'des atouts' into his hands i.e. the window dressing words which would enable him to win, so we will hope for the best. In any case our case will be much stronger in future even if the Egyptian Parliament refuses its assent.

AC5/1/438

26 November 1927
2 Morpeth Mansions

My dear Ida,

How one small island can endure so many Chamberlains & all so active passes my comprehension. I suspect that this is what some people mean who say we are over-governed. The baleful influence spreads itself all over the island & even beyond its shores, but the real centre of the virus is evidently Hampshire. I am really rather horrified at the number of Comtees & meetings that you two attend especially as like Neville's work (as *he* conceives it) they involve so many *déplacements*! Don't overdo it is the advice of all the little devils to the other sinners.

[74] Adly Pasha Yeghen. Egyptian Liberal statesman.

For my part I don't know why Neville is alive or why I keep so well. Neville confesses to being tired & so am I physically though, unless I get the extra strain of a speech, it not does now seem to affect my powers of mind. But the work is tremendous & I doubt whether any of my colleagues even fully appreciate the immense load of responsibility which I carry daily as apart from the long hours which I work.

Speeches are chancey things. As you say I had a little triumph on Thursday ... The only thing for which I had prepared notes was the comparison between the Covenant & Protocol.

To tell you the truth I am greatly comforted by the success of the speech for my H. of C. speeches as Foreign Minister have not been good & I had come to feel that I had lost my power & that working under such a strain I had not the physical reserve required for the additional brain effort for which making a speech calls. There is, however, something in what Tyrrell says with reference to Grey's speeches & my own – that a Foreign Secretary speaks with one hand tied behind his back & can hardly ever make his full case but that on this occasion R.M[acDonald] untied me by his opening of the discussion.

AC5/1/440   12 December 1927
                                                              Geneva

My dear Ida,

... We are leaving for home tonight ... Once again we are well satisfied with the results. France, England & Germany have pulled well together. (If anyone tells you that Locarno is dead, tell them that they are talking nonsense) & while these three are united I am not greatly afraid of a breach of the peace by anyone else. The Lithuanian-Polish question was more dangerous than it looked &, if the Council had not obtained a clear statement that "the state of war" was at an end, would have become really critical. Marshall Pilsudski[75] believed that we could not do it & was meditating recourse to force, but we did it for there are few things that France, Germany & Great Britain cannot do when united.

...

I have never found time to read more than a few pages of the first two volumes of our Pre-War Despatches ... Our diplomacy may not

[75] Jozef Pilsudski (1867–1935). Polish soldier and nationalist politician. Founded Polish Socialist Party 1892. Head of State and C-in-C of Army with dictatorial powers 1919–22. Refused presidency 1922 but resumed power in coup d'état 1926 and, as head of government and War Minister, was effective head of state until his death.

always have been the best possible but it has always been very simple, direct & honest. I doubt, however, whether it has ever been quite as frank & confidential as in these days when your brother knows & talks with almost every foreign minister in Europe.

AC5/1/441

17 December 1927
2 Morpeth Mansions

My dear Hilda,

. . .

The defeat of the Prayer Book was a surprise to me at any rate. Neville & I both voted for it on the grounds that the Church must be allowed to govern itself tho' neither of us liked it, but all the honours of the debate were with the opponents & almost from the opening votes were being won or won over against it. I feel confident that enough votes were changed or decided by the debate to make the difference between success & failure & I very much doubt whether if all Nonconformist votes had been eliminated there was a majority of Churchmen for the measure. I think my chief feeling is one of profound sympathy with the Archbishop of Canterbury. He was a tragically pathetic figure as he left the gallery after the result was declared.

Ivy & I found great enjoyment in Geneva. Everyone was very pleasant & we worked extremely well together & scored a real success in the Polono-Lithuanian affair. I now think that I am going to get Primo[76] to withdraw Spain's resignation & to resume Spain's full & active cooperation. If I can do that, it will be another real coup.

But what do you say to Prest. Coolidge & his 25 "light" cruisers of 10,000 tons each? What a difficult people they are to live with! It is a really heartbreaking task to try to improve our relations. We were told that the settlement of the Irish question & the payment of the debt had produced such a greatly improved feeling & now it seems to be as good business as ever to twist the lion's tail. Ah me! Ah me!

AC5/1/442

23 December 1927
2 Morpeth Mansions

My dear Sisters,

. . .

. . . Scratch me & you find the Nonconformist. I may not be a very

[76] Miguel Primo de Rivera y Orbaneia (1870–1930). Spanish dictator from military coup in 1923 until 1930 when retired to Paris. Spain rejoined the League in 1928.

orthodox Unitarian if there is such a thing as orthodoxy in that very heterodox body, but in every fibre of my being I am Protestant with the biggest 'P' that you can put to it.

AC5/1/445   16 January 1928
                                                    Twitt's Ghyll

My dear Ida,

   ...

   Egypt is going badly. Sarwat seems frightened & shuffling.

AC5/1/449   31 March 1928
                                                  2 Morpeth Mansions

My dear Hilda,

   ...

   ... As far as work is concerned, it has been a rather harrassing time, but I hope to clear up my difficulties before I go down to Twitt's for Easter. I am much in need of a little rest – blood pressure always low now lower than usual, cause or result ... digestion out of order & consequently much discomfort & rather a despondent feeling about everything. So I have arranged ten days holiday beginning on the 12th.

AC5/1/452   30 April 1928
                                                    Twitt's Ghyll

My dear Ida,

   ...

   Our short holiday was very pleasant to the end tho' a dinner & luncheon party of diplomats & royalties every day is too much for my simple tastes. Still it was rest compared to being at home. Problems crowd upon me & the most difficult are those raised by Kellogg's proposals – & methods. I am fairly puzzled how best to deal with them. And the Lord Chancellor[77] was unable to help me to a decision which, if you knew him, would alone be sufficient to show you how extremely difficult of solution these problems are & what very delicate questions they raise. I have devoted my morning to their consideration ...

---

[77] Viscount Hailsham had succeeded Cave as Lord Chancellor on 28 March 1928.

AC5/1/453

9 May 1928
2 Morpeth Mansions

[Typescript]
My dear Hilda,

Many thanks for the short letter you sent me with your congratulations on the successful conclusion of the immediate Egyptian trouble. My final note was very well taken by our press & Tyrrell says that I achieved a miracle in that I was praised on the same day & for the same thing by both the "Morning Post " and the "Manchester Guardian". Neither of them is accustomed to lavish praise upon me ...

We are to have a discussion on Foreign Affairs in the House tomorrow when Egypt and the American proposal will, I suppose, form the staples of debate. I do not think that the leaders of opposition either wish to attack me or could make a successful attack, and if some of the Labour extremists denounce the Egyptian policy it will not do me any harm, more particularly as Nahas[78] has closed the correspondence by expressing his thanks for the moderation of my reply and his earnest desire to keep on good terms. Of course, I cannot trust him for a moment, but as he thanked me for my moderation he has rather spiked the guns of any who would wish to attack me for bullying.

I think I am beginning to see my way in the matter of how to treat the American Note and that I shall be able to bring France and the United States into line.

AC5/1/453

20 May 1928
2 Morpeth Mansions

My dear Ida,

...

My American note is published today. The first comment here from the Observer & Sunday Times is rather more favourable than I expected. What will be the American reaction? After all I mean what Kellogg & Coolidge mean but they would have preferred the exchange of a wink among the augurs to an honest statement of their mental reservations. I hope, however, for the best. Much depends on Kellogg.

[78] Mustafa Nahas Pasha (1876–1965). Egyptian lawyer and politician. Succeeded Zaghlul as leader of Wafd in 1927. Many times Prime Minister of Egypt; led delegation which negotiated treaty of perpetual alliance with Britain in 1936. Dismissed by Farouk December 1936 but recalled at British insistence 1942–1944. Recalled to power 1950 but displaced by Neguib 1952.

Incidentally in protecting ourselves against misrepresentation I have built a bridge for the French.

AC5/1/455   30 May 1928
                                                          Twitt's Ghyll

My dear Ida,

      ...
      Primo de Riviera [sic] is giving me trouble over Tangier & Mussolini causes me some anxiety. China is troublesome as ever & what will Mr Kellogg do next? Such is life but I begin to feel my age. I cannot sit all the week in my office & then turn to & garden as I used to on Saturday & Sunday.

AC5/1/458   2 July 1928
                                                       2 Morpeth Mansions

My dear Hilda,

      ...
      ... I am now deep in the second volume of [Curzon's] Life, admirably done by Lord Ronaldshay who has met & overcome with great skill the not inconsiderable difficulties of his task ... The middle period is his time of greatness though it ended in bitter quarrels & rather squalid tragedy & left upon him an indelible mark which made his Foreign Secretaryship a weak, hesitating performance & as I think spoiled his whole later career.
      ...
      I am better. I have cut my work down to an absolute minimum, go nowhere except to what I may call 'commands' & betake myself to bed at 11.00. I feel justified in allowing myself this holiday momentarily but I should really not be happy to remain Foreign Secretary for long if I could not soon keep a closer watch upon the work. As it is I see none but the few most important papers such as big lines of Chinese & Egyptian policy & the Pact of Kellogg whom Allah rewards according to his deserts.

AC5/1/459

9 July 1928
2 Morpeth Mansions

My dear Ida,

...

After cursing Kellogg night & morning for a fortnight past (& he deserves it!) I begin to see my way or think I do, & therefore less troubled in mind. I think that we can guard the Government & Locarno in spite of him – but I hope that he will have an indigestion for the rest of his life!

Egypt is very interesting but not at present worrying & George Lloyd seems almost to have got into a habit of tendering the advice I want. Tyrrell, when I observe that Lloyd now apparently understands my policy & is applying it, says that L. doesn't understand but as he never thought out any policy is by this time convinced that this is the policy that he was always pursuing.

...

Two engagements to meet King Alfonso[79] were all my outings last week. He was very friendly, pleasant & talkative as usual. He remarked that I was the League & when I modestly deprecated this exaggerated view no, its not the League. Its you – you! You first talk to a man for five minutes and then he turns right round & does what you want. Well, its a useful reputation to have.

On 31 July 1928, the day after his disastrous disclosure to Parliament of the Anglo-French Compromise, Chamberlain suffered a total collapse from over-work and a chill soon developed into pneumonia. After the physical exertion and nervous strain of the previous two years, by the spring of 1928 Chamberlain confessed himself 'tired, tired, tired!'.[80] Although a brief trip to Holland and Belgium offering 'a "wild loose life" – all luncheons and dinners, caviare, plovers eggs and Rhine salmon' did something to revive him, he was soon complaining that he felt his age.[81] When the collapse came it was, as Neville realised, 'the result of prolonged overwork by a man who hasn't got a great reserve of strength'.[82]

The departmental burden Chamberlain carried at the Foreign Office in these years was undoubtedly prodigious. It was also seriously exacerbated by the demands of deputising for Baldwin in the autumn of 1927 and the physical infirmity of his

[79] King Alfonso XIII (1886–1941). King of Spain from birth until deposed with fall of Primo de Rivera in 1930.
[80] A. Chamberlain to Hilda, 8 April 1928, AC5/1/450.
[81] A. Chamberlain to Ida, 18 April and 30 May 1928. AC5/1/451,455.
[82] N. Chamberlain to Hilda, 5 August 1928, NC18/1/622.

ministerial team.[83] *Although there was little he could do to regulate the emergence of new crises, the scale of the work-load was at least partially something of his own making. From the outset, he was determined not to tolerate any repetition of the ambiguous position that had existed under Curzon.*[84] *Suspicious of Cecil's previous role as Lord Privy Seal with special responsibility for the League, Chamberlain had initially opposed Cecil's appointment and then done everything in his power to circumscribe his freedom of independent action by refusing to send him Foreign Office papers and warning him that he should make no statements on foreign affairs until authorised by Cabinet. 'I must make it clear', he warned, 'that there is only one foreign policy and only one authorised exponent of it'.*[85] *Chamberlain's decision to represent Britain at the League Council was prompted by the same desire to exclude Cecil and to ensure that Britain spoke with only one voice at Geneva and in London – a degree of harmony conspicuously absent when Cecil represented the government.*[86] *It has been argued that the decision was not a wise one, adding gravely to an already crushing burden of work, necessitating frequent absence from London and leaving too little time to supervise the administration of his department and none to much needed reforms within the Foreign Office.*[87] *Although such essentially personal contracts represented the very cornerstone of Chamberlain's diplomacy, there can be no doubt that they must have sapped his strength and arguably contributed to some of the policy failures in 1927–28.*[88]

Chamberlain did not return to London until mid-November 1928 after a long cruise and three weeks rest with friends in California. Even then, he clearly could not shoulder the burden he had borne before and at times became seriously over-wrought.[89] *Doubts were also increasingly expressed about his judgement and his resilience.*[90] *For all that, however, his officials found that although the life and energy*

[83] Neville Chamberlain Diary 1 July 1927 says Cushenden was 'a broken man' and Locker Lampson 'too much of an invalid to get more responsibility'.

[84] For Chamberlain's contempt at Curzon's position under Lloyd George see Derby Diary, 15 March and 23 November 1922.

[85] Chamberlain to Cecil, 11 November 1924, Cecil MSS 51078/25; to Salisbury, 2 January 1925, AC52/704; to Baldwin 9 November 1924, Baldwin MSS 42/270-1. For similar complaints of exclusion from the policy process by Godfrey Locker-Lampson (Under-Secretary at F.O.) see Amery Diary, 18 February 1927, *Leo Amery Diaries*, 497-8.

[86] Vt Cecil, *All the Way*, 166, 185. For satisfaction at the consistent voice see A. Chamberlain to Hilda, 20 December 1926, AC5/1/403.

[87] G.Craig and F. Gilbert, *The Diplomats*, 44. For such criticisms from his Permanent Under-Secretary see Crawford Diary, July 1928, 3 January and 13 April 1929, J. Vincent (ed) *The Crawford Papers*, 522.

[88] Vt Cecil, *A Great Experiment*, 194 concedes this point.

[89] See Amery Diary, 27 March 1929, noting 'I left Austen almost in tears', *Leo Amery Diaries*, 593.

[90] For Baldwin's uncertainty on whether Austen would 'crack up' see Jones Diary, 24 October 1928 and 25 February 1929, *Whitehall Diary*, I, 154, 172. For doubts on his judgement see Hankey to Balfour, 18 December 1928, S. Roskill, *Hankey*, II, 454; Bridgeman Diary, July 1929 Bridgeman MSS II fol. 173; Bridgeman to Baldwin, 29 August 1928, Baldwin MSS 175/42-5.

had gone out of him, Chamberlain did not relax his control of affairs.[91] Moreover, despite problems with France over the evacuation of the Rhineland, and with Cabinet and the US over belligerent rights,[92] Baldwin continued to have faith. Despite an approach to Grey to neutralise the electoral impact of the League issue in January 1929,[93] Baldwin continued to talk of Chamberlain as 'irreplaceable' at the Foreign Office.[94]

AC5/1/461

7 October 1928
Burlinghame
California

My dear Ida,

. . .

I am wonderfully better but I am still inconceivably weak. I weighed on arrival just 9 stone (normal 10.2 to 10.5 – lowest record 9.6 in the war) & I am still very lame with sciatica, but I must be putting on weight in this wonderful house & with such excellent food ... But any exertion tires me & my hand still trembles so that shaving is a perilous job ...

AC5/1/462

8 December 1928
2 Morpeth Mansions

[Typescript]
My dear Ida,

There is no peace in this world & Ivy & I are off to Lugano[95] this afternoon. If I am to believe the Berlin press, I shall find the Germans in a very bad temper, but I think a good deal of their indignation is artificial and it may be useful to point out to them quietly & nicely that if they will insist on asking for trouble they will get it.

I have so far kept to my resolution that I would not do office work after dinner, but as I have had to make one speech at a public meeting and two at public banquets within seven days, this has not given me

---

[91] Crawford Diary, 3 January 1929, J. Vincent (ed) *The Crawford Papers*, 522.
[92] See J. Jacobson, 'Locarno Diplomacy', 232–5, 277; Johnson, 'The Locarno Treaties', 118–9.
[93] K. Robbins, *Sir Edward Grey: A Biography of Lord Grey of Falloden*, (1971), 360.
[94] Jones Diary, 5 March 1929, *Whitehall Diary*, II, 174. Also Baldwin at Great Yarmouth, *The Times*, 28 September 1928.
[95] Lugano Conference, 9–14 December 1928.

quite the relaxation which I intended to provide. However, I have been none the worse for my exertions ...

Ivy is pleased with my performances as she says I have got back the old tones of my voice and vigour of utterance. Certainly, the speaking itself was done with singularly little effort and I might almost say the same of the matter of the speeches, though the one on American relations was a delicate task.

It is these same relations which have been the principal subject of my thoughts since I turned my face homeward and they must continue to be my principal preoccupation for some time to come. The United States is never an easy country with which to deal, for at any moment an international question may become an instrument of party warfare regardless of the international consequences. That seems to be very much the situation at the present time and upon the whole I think that for the moment our safest course is to watch and wait.

AC5/1/463

17 December 1928
2 Morpeth Mansions

[Typescript]
My dear Hilda,

...

As to our time [at Lugano], I am well content. We were able to clear up a good many misapprehensions and to restore the proper atmosphere. We did not attempt to take any new decisions and indeed there was no need for it. But the spirit was good and if Stresemann, Briand & I were left alone to find the solution, I think we should manage to secure the evacuation of the Rhineland within a reasonable time. But then we are not being left alone and shall not be left alone, and once again I found myself telling Schubert[96] that the Germans were the most difficult people to help in this world. They are always rolling back down the mountain the stone which I have laborious rolled up it.

The Chancellor's speech during the meeting and the whole attitude of the German press create difficulties which it may be impossible to overcome. Stresemann himself was at first in a mood of pessimism which exaggerated the ordinary gloom of the German delegation and it was to be attributed in part to his ill health. As one of the French delegation said, "Briand has to undertake a psychological cure every

[96] Carl von Schubert (1882–1947). German diplomat. Counsellor in London before Great War and then head of British section at Wilhelmstrasse; Under-Secretary of State for Foreign Affairs 1925–30; Ambassador to Italy 1930–32.

time he meets him". Still when all is said and done I am encouraged by the way in which we have overcome past difficulties to hope that we shall somehow find our way through present ones.

AC5/1/464

26 December 1928
Polesden Lacey
Dorking

My dear Ida,

. . .

For the moment my F.O. sky is fairly clear of clouds except in the West tho' Persia gives some trouble. But my real anxiety concerns relations with the U.S. They are so terribly difficult to deal with & we have a mass of thorny questions to handle. I am glad to say that the P.M. & I see eye to eye as far as we see at all, but some of my colleagues frighten me & there is no help in Houghton & no backbone or courage – only a weak man's obstinacy in Kellogg.

I need not tell you that I am not going to take a peerage. Some idiotic pressman appears to be starting that rumour again.

AC5/1/465

20 January 1929
2 Morpeth Mansions

My dear Ida,

. . .

Twitt's Ghyll is not yet sold but a purchaser is nibbling. I think it will go off in early spring & I am very sad at having to part with it, but the truth is that I cannot afford it, & I fear that we shall just have to do without.

AC5/1/467

5 February 1929
2 Morpeth Mansions

[Typescript]
[Not addressed]

I am getting along very well with my work which has been reduced very much in volume, but I find I tire more easily than I used to do and am glad of whatever extra rest I can get on Saturday or Sunday . . .

. . .

I found D'Abernon's first volume very interesting . . . it fills in gaps in my knowledge and illustrates the perverse working of the German mind and the difficulties of doing business with them and still more of helping them. Apart from this, there are some very shrewd pictures of some of the actors of the scene and a better appreciation of Lloyd George's qualities, and still more his peculiarities than I have seen elsewhere. D'Abernon very truly says that Lloyd George's instability was in method rather than in purpose and that no man ever more obstinately persisted in an idea when once it had definitely formed in his mind ...

...

We have made some progress this week in the committee which is dealing with all the questions outstanding between the United States and ourselves. At last I see light and at any rate now know what I want to do, and find myself in agreement with the Lord Chancellor whose judgement on all questions I think as good as that of any member of the Cabinet and, on the particular points at issue, better, since he is more familiar with them. It is a great comfort to me that he has come to the same conclusion as I have done, for it is a surprise to both of us to find what that conclusion is. Certainly if anyone had said at the beginning of the enquiry that we were likely to favour the solution which now commends itself to us as the least bad of the many that we have examined, we should, I think, have laughed at the suggestion.

AC5/1/474

May 12 1929
Twitt's Ghyll

My dear Ida,

I have not been able to face this place since we decided that we could not afford to keep it, but I miss it physically as well as morally & decided that I must have some fresh air before starting out on the elections, so I came down here after lunch yesterday ...

II.

'B.M.G.... "BALDWIN (THIS TIME) MUST GO!"'

The frustrations of Opposition, June 1929 – July 1931

Although electoral defeat and loss of office can never be a welcome experience, in June 1929 the pain of Austen Chamberlain's transition to the Opposition benches was temporarily alleviated by a sense of personal relief at his continued presence in the House of Commons at all. After the 1924 election he had confessed that the position in his West Birmingham constituency made him 'very anxious'. Predicting that 'it will be a stiffer fight next time' he had thus resolved to 'try somehow to see more of them'.[1] Four and a half years at the Foreign Office did nothing to help him redeem that pledge. By 1929 Chamberlain confronted not only an increasingly difficult situation in West Birmingham where the slums and poverty had given him cause to wonder at a Conservative victory in the past, but also the general electoral disillusion with the Baldwin's government's promise of 'Safety First' and their failure to revive the economy. Although never an active or particularly diligent constituency MP,[2] in 1929 Chamberlain almost fell victim to a more general decline in Conservative support within the West Midlands. Since 1886 the Conservatives had never lost more than one Birmingham seat. In 1929 Labour were in confident mood and took no less than six of the twelve seats.[3] After the canvass returns, Chamberlain had warned his family to expect defeat and during the two counts he confessed himself to be 'in a very philosophic mood'.[4] In the event, he scraped in by just 43 votes in a seat held continuously by a Chamberlain for almost half a century.[5]

To his half-brother's astonishment, Austen Chamberlain initially remained in a philosophical mood at the prospect of a Labour Foreign Secretary reaping where he had sown, albeit that he would have preferred Thomas to Henderson as a successor.[6] As the implications of defeat sank in, however, this soon gave way to depression, in what he called 'a natural reaction to disappointed hopes'.[7] Defeat also coincided

---

[1] A. Chamberlain to Ivy, 31 October 1924, AC6/1/587

[2] N. Chamberlain to Hilda, 27 January 1917 and 20 September 1924, NC18/1/99, 452.

[3] M. Kinnear, *The British Voter: An Atlas and Survey Since 1885*, (1968). For an analysis of the trend and the explanation that this was largely because the younger generation 'who knew not Joseph' defected while older voters remained loyal to Conservatism see K.W.D. Rolf, 'Tories, Tariffs and Elections. The West Midlands in English Politics 1918–1935'. (Cambridge D. Phil. 1974), 213–8.

[4] A. Chamberlain to Mary Carnegie, 13 May 1929, AC4/1/1297; to Ida, 6 June 1929, AC5/1/475.

[5] Joseph Chamberlain sat for Birmingham from 1876 and for West Birmingham from 1885 until his death on 2 July 1914.

[6] N. Chamberlain to Ida, 2 June (mis-dated May) 1929, NC18/1/656.

[7] A. Chamberlain to Ida, 25 June 1929, AC5/1/476.

with a number of other personal disappointments, not least, the final and extremely painful parting with Twitt's Ghyll after so many years of blissful happiness. Believing that this time Labour was likely to remain 'in for a long spell' Chamberlain also reconciled himself to the fact that his official career had come to an end: a sense of resignation reinforced by the pressing financial need to devote himself to earning some money after a long and expensive period in office.[8]

The political difficulties of returning to Opposition were no less trying. Released from the constraints imposed by office, almost immediately there was an outbreak of intense intra-party conflict over personalities and fundamental issues of policy on the front-bench which disgusted those on the benches behind them.[9] *This was to be but a foretaste of things to come. For almost the next two years British politics witnessed what one veteran observer described as 'a display of the worst qualities of the Conservative Party under the effects of defeat'.*[10] *Never a good – or even competent – leader of Opposition, between 1929–31 Baldwin showed himself at his undoubted worst.*[11] *Although in his later years at the Foreign Office Chamberlain had become 'something of an elder statesman before his time, removed from the day-to-day run of party politics'*[12] *during this period in Opposition he returned to far greater prominence within the parliamentary party. The experience was to reinforce in him an abiding contempt for Baldwin personally and left him almost in despair at the lack of leadership. This irritation began almost at once when Baldwin again refused to grant the 'personal favour' of some form of honour for Oliver Locker-Lampson.*[13] *His 'profound disappointment' and asperity over this trivial incident, however, was as nothing to his feelings about Baldwin's handling of either India or the challenge from Beaverbrook's Empire Crusade.*

During the summer recess Chamberlain went off for a two week cruise to the North Cape. When he returned the Conservatives were already embroiled in Imperial problems of a different sort from those raised by Beaverbrook's campaign for Empire Free Trade. The first involved the dismissal of Lord Lloyd. Against a background of rising tension between Lloyd and Chamberlain, Arthur Henderson soon came under vigorous pressure from Sir Ronald Lindsay, Permanent Under-Secretary at the Foreign Office, to dismiss the increasingly wayward High Commissioner. As his 'ideas were so ingrained in his character', Lindsay had argued Lloyd's inflexibly repressive attitude precluded the possibility of acquiescence in a more liberal policy.[14] *Despite Henderson's initial reluctance, Lloyd was summoned home for 'discussions'.*

[8] His brother shared this belief. See N. Chamberlain to Hilda, 13 October 1929, NC18/1/672.

[9] N. Chamberlain to Ida, 13 July 1929, NC18/1/661; Gretton to Linlithgow, 10 July 1929, Hopetoun MSS 1002; L.S. Amery, *My Political Life*, II, 508–9.

[10] Bridgeman Diary, July 1930, Bridgeman MSS II fol.219.

[11] For Baldwin's own recognition of this fact see MacDonald Diary, 7 May 1929, fol. 260 reporting Baldwin; Baldwin to Balfour, 11 November 1929, Whittingehame MSS 19; "The Second Labour Government", n.d. Templewood MSS VI.2.

[12] D. Dutton. *Austen Chamberlain*, 266.

[13] A. Chamberlain to Baldwin, 25 June 1929, Baldwin MSS 164/28.

[14] R. Lindsay to A. Chamberlain, 17 June 1929, AC55/315.

Indeed, at one point it appeared as if he would be dismissed en route before Vansittart intervened to warn MacDonald that while 'Prime Ministers are always entitled to be served as they please, ... they can't kill pro-consuls with croquet mallets'.[15] After some further indignities at the hands of the Foreign Office, Lloyd resigned on 24 July 1929.

The debate in the Commons two days later caused a parliamentary sensation. In his speech, Henderson made great play of the 'stream of dissatisfaction' in the relations between his predecessor and a High Commissioner who had shown a 'marked determination to misinterpret, or ungenerously to misapply' policy from London: a proposition substantiated by citing five outstanding instances where Cabinet adjudication had been needed.[16] In so doing Henderson had skilfully exploited undeniable differences between Chamberlain and Lloyd to open divisions in the Conservative ranks and to justify his own actions. Chamberlain would undoubtedly have been embarrassed by these revelations. Under pressure from his officials he was doubtful whether he would have extended Lloyd's posting at the end of his five year term.[17] Furthermore, only two days before the poll in 1929 Chamberlain had felt it necessary to despatch a long memorandum to the High Commissioner restating at length the principles upon which British policy in Egypt was based:[18] a lecture to which Lloyd replied on the day of Chamberlain's departure from the Foreign Office in terms which suggested that he remained diametrically opposed to those underlying principles or further concessions 'except as part of a general settlement involving Egypt's acceptance of our minimum requirements'.[19] Although Chamberlain believed Henderson had 'showed somewhat ... indecent haste' in disposing of Lloyd, therefore, he was also convinced him that Lloyd was 'incapable of understanding [his] policy and was certainly unfitted by temperament to execute it'.[20] Yet the claim of Lloyd's biographer that Chamberlain almost conspired in his dismissal, both by making it apparent that he favoured such a course and in his refusal to defend Lloyd, would appear to be without foundation.[21] Nor was Chamberlain guilty of 'pointedly

---

[15] Vansittart, *The Mist Procession*, 372–3. For Lindsay's studied discourtesy to Lloyd when in England see C.F. Adams, *Life of Lord Lloyd*, 221–2; J. Charmley, *Lord Lloyd and the Decline of the British Empire*, 158–162.

[16] For Henderson's speech see *House of Commons Debates*, 5 Series, 230 cols. 1637–46, 26 July 1929. For his discussion of the differences see CP 181(29), 13 June 1929, CAB 24/204.

[17] A. Chamberlain to Lindsay, 17 June 1929, AC55/314; to Ida, 1 August 1929, AC5/1/479. Chamberlain told his brother on 9 August 1929 he thought of moving Lloyd to East Africa where his organisational talents could be used to create an East African federation, NC 1/27/98.

[18] Chamberlain's despatch of 28 May 1929 (AC39/6/1) is quoted at length in Lord Lloyd, *Egypt Since Cromer*, II, 293–6.

[19] Lloyd to Chamberlain, 17 June 1929, AC39/6/1; Henderson to A. Chamberlain, 24 June 1929, AC38/3/87. Lloyd remained unrepentant to the end. See Lloyd to Loraine, 29 July 1929, G. Waterfield, *Professional Diplomat: Sir Percy Loraine of Kirkharle 1880–1961*, (1973), 149.

[20] A. Chamberlain to N. Chamberlain, 9 August 1929, NC1/27/98.

[21] C. F. Adams, *Life of Lord Lloyd*, 219–20, 222.

absenting himself from the Commons'.[22] *In fact, he was still returning from his cruise – a trip he had planned in late June, well before the crisis broke.*

Of far longer-term concern to Chamberlain were developments in Indian policy precipitated by the Irwin Declaration of 31 October 1929 reaffirming that the ultimate goal of British policy was for India to achieve Dominion status.[23] *Although in a sense Irwin was merely giving new expression to an established truism, Chamberlain strongly opposed the use of the term 'Dominion Status' on the grounds that it would arouse unrealistic hopes when inevitably interpreted in very different ways in Britain and India. He was thus vigorous in condemning Irwin's use of language. He also blamed Baldwin for becoming embroiled in the affair: an involvement which Chamberlain attributed to Baldwin's friendship for the Viceroy.*[24] *Despite, or perhaps because of, his role in attacking the Irwin Declaration in November, Baldwin invited Chamberlain to attend the discussions with the other parties about the future of India after the publication of the Simon Report. As Chamberlain himself acknowledged, in many respects this was a curious and surprising decision given both his lack of recent experience with India and the fact that he was markedly less progressive on the subject than either Baldwin or Peel, the former Secretary of State for India and the otherwise obvious candidate for the job.*[25] *Certainly Baldwin's decision did not please Irwin: 'It really makes me weep to think that in a matter of this kind Stanley Baldwin should submit his judgement to Austen, whose contact with India is distant and whose mind is always that of a log of wood'.*[26] *During these discussions Baldwin did nothing to endear himself to Chamberlain or to build his confidence in the leadership by permitting him to do most of the talking (and work), while simultaneously undermining his efforts by leaving the vague impression that the two were not in complete agreement.*[27] *Despite confessing that he had 'not been so anxious about anything since the war',*[28] *and eager to continue, his involvement was cut short in the autumn when Salisbury*

[22] D. Carlton, *MacDonald versus Henderson : The Foreign Policy of the Second Labour Government*, (1970), 287. Also H. Dalton, *Call Back Yesterday*, 226; J. Charmley, *Lord Lloyd and the Fall of the British Empire*, 167; C. Wrigley, *Arthur Henderson*, 171. Curiously, Dutton also notes him 'conspicuous by his absence', *Austen Chamberlain*, 168. For his prior plans see A. Chamberlain to Ida, 25 June 1929, AC5/1/476.

[23] For the declaration and Irwin's motives see S. Gopal, *The Viceroyalty of Lord Irwin*, (Oxford, 1957): G. R. Peele, 'A Note on the Irwin Declaration', *Journal of Imperial & Commonwealth History*, May 1973.

[24] A. Chamberlain to Hilda and Ida, 6 and 11 November 1929, AC5/1/485-6. In some quarters this revived old suspicions of resurgent coalitionist sympathies. See Hoare to Irwin, 13 November 1929, M. Gilbert, *Winston S. Churchill*, V. Companion 2, 111; Davidson to Irwin, 9 November 1929, R.R. James, *Memoirs of a Conservative*, 308.

[25] A. Chamberlain to Hilda, 14 June 1930, AC5/1/504. Dutton does not consider it surprising, *Austen Chamberlain*, 287.

[26] Earl of Birkenhead, *Halifax: The Life of Lord Halifax*, (1965), 288. For other criticism as 'very wooden and stupid' on India see George Lane-Fox to Irwin, 21 August 1930, M. Gilbert, *Winston S. Churchill*, V. Companion 2, 180.

[27] A. Chamberlain to Hoare, 9 September 1930, AC22/3/22.

[28] A. Chamberlain to Ida, 7 July 1930, AC5/1/508.

exercised a firm but polite veto on Chamberlain's inclusion in the four person Conservative delegation to the forthcoming Round Table Conference because of his part in the Irish settlement of 1921.[29]

If the party had slumped into a mood of 'depression, distrust and despair' by October 1929,[30] *the growing threat from Beaverbrook's Empire Crusade was even more devastating to morale, particularly after his decision to form the United Empire Party in February 1930 in order to carry the fight to the constituencies. By the beginning of 1930 even veterans of the Balfourian party conceded they had 'not known so much grousing for more than 20 years'.*[31] *Among them, Chamberlain claimed he had 'never felt as hopeless as now' and turned his mind increasingly to the problem of ensuring that his half-brother's succession would not be jeopardised by Baldwin's inertia, incompetence and blundering. This was particularly so after June 1930 when Neville Chamberlain succeeded Davidson as Party Chairman. While Neville had been active in leading attempts to remove Davidson because he was 'a fool and a danger in his post',*[32] *Austen was extremely alarmed that his acceptance of the Chairmanship would so inextricably associate Neville's reputation and future with Baldwin's that he would undermine his own chance of the leadership.*

When Parliament went into recess in August 1930, Chamberlain was deeply despondent and blamed Baldwin's 'blind self-complacency' for all their troubles.[33] *After a holiday marred by bad weather he returned in October even more pessimistic. Claiming to have 'never known such a complete collapse of a reputation' and lamenting that Baldwin appeared to be 'living in a fool's paradise' oblivious to the problems around him, he rapidly concluded Baldwin was finished.*[34] *With this in mind he proposed to broach the subject of a new Party Chairman with Baldwin until his half-brother dissuaded him. Yet at almost exactly the same time Neville also appears to have entertained similar thoughts himself. At the Business Committee meeting on 7 October Baldwin had led in accepting Neville Chamberlain's 'unauthorized programme' of drastic economy, an emergency tariff, a wheat quota and a free hand on other imports to improve Imperial trade relations.*[35] *Immediately after the meeting Neville Chamberlain consulted Hoare and Austen about his plan to call another front bench meeting in Baldwin's absence to discuss the leadership*

[29] Salisbury to Baldwin, 4 August 1930 and Chamberlain to Baldwin 11 August 1930, Baldwin MSS 104/23–26, 30.

[30] N. Chamberlain to Ida, 22 October 1929, NC18/1/673.

[31] Bayford Diary, 7 February 1930. Also Steel-Maitland to Baldwin, 28 January 1930, Steel-Maitland MSS GD 193/120/3(3); Gwynne to Northumberland, 18 December 1929, Gwynne MSS 21.

[32] Elibank 'Notes re. Empire Free Trade' entry for 29 March 1930, Elibank MSS GD 32/25/69 fol. 43.

[33] A. Chamberlain to Ida, 4 August 1930, AC5/1/510.

[34] A. Chamberlain to Mary Carnegie, 9 October 1930, AC4/1/1302; to N. Chamberlain, 9 October 1930, AC39/2/40.

[35] N. Chamberlain to a sister, 21 September 1930, NC18/1/742. For the policy see Neville Chamberlain at Crystal Palace, *The Times*, 22 September and to Amery 30 September 1930, NC7/2/46.

and presumably to change it in his favour. Yet after meeting Baldwin later the same evening, at which it appeared he had given no thought to resignation, Neville Chamberlain concluded that there was nothing his colleagues could usefully do at that juncture and that 'if any move is made, it should really come from the House of Commons – the body which makes, and can presumably unmake, leaders'. Austen endorsed this view and the whole plan was dropped in favour of a public exchange of letters in which Baldwin formally endorsed the 'unauthorised programme'.[36] As both Chamberlains recognised, however, such an expedient was designed merely to 'save S.B.'s bacon long enough to enable him to go later without a triumph for R[othermere] or B[eaverbrook]'. In the interim they were prepared to 'await events'.[37]

The moment for action soon arrived. By February 1931 Baldwin's prestige had reached its nadir amid widespread reports of the collapse of Conservative support in the regions.[38] The brutally uncompromising memorandum from Sir Robert Topping to this effect, with its conclusion that 'in the interests of the Party ... the Leader should reconsider his position' was forwarded to Baldwin by Neville Chamberlain on 1 March. Initially Baldwin's inclination was to resign until Bridgeman, and later Dawson and Camrose, urged him to make a fight of it against the press Lords.[39] With the emergence of Duff Cooper as a pro-Baldwin candidate for the St George's by-election two days later the matter was settled and Baldwin said nothing more about resignation.

Austen Chamberlain had worked more closely with his half-brother during the crisis of 1930–31 than at any time since they had been in the House together.[40] During the first week of March 1931 he had figured prominently in the confidential discussions with his brother, Amery and Hoare designed to find a way to force Baldwin to recognise the hopelessness of his position and resign.[41] When Baldwin appeared to be 'thoroughly bucked' by the success of the Irwin-Gandhi pact on 5 March, Austen Chamberlain decided he could no longer defer his challenge. At the Business Committee on 11 February, he bluntly asked Baldwin when he was going to relieve his brother of the Party Chairmanship, as his debating talents were desperately needed on the front bench since Churchill's resignation and the death of Worthington-Evans; a challenge not revealed to Neville in advance for fear he would repeat his earlier veto because of the closeness of the family connection. To all those present, however, it was 'pretty plain what he had in mind'. As Amery noted 'even S.B. could hardly miss the underlying implication that it was to free Neville for the successorship'.[42]

[36] N. Chamberlain to A. Chamberlain, 8 and 10 October 1930 and Austen's reply, 9 October 1930 AC39/2/39, 40 and AC58/75.

[37] N. Chamberlain to Ida, 11 October 1930, NC18/1/712.

[38] Amery Diary, 26 February 1931; Neville Chamberlain Diary, 23 February 1931; Derby to N. Chamberlain, 25 February 1931, NC8/10/21; Bridgeman Diary, 20 February 1931, Bridgeman MSS II, fol.229.

[39] Bridgeman Diary, 1 March 1931, Bridgeman MSS II, fol.229.

[40] N. Chamberlain to Hilda, 25 May 1931, NC18/1/739.

[41] Amery Diary, 5, 6, 7 March 1931, J. Barnes and D. Nicholson, *The Empire at Bay*, 152.

[42] Neville Chamberlain Diary, 11 March 1931; Amery Diary, 7 and 11 March 1931, *The Empire at Bay*, 152–3.

For all its blunt brutality, the manoeuvre succeeded in its objective. After an icy conversation with Baldwin, Neville Chamberlain resigned as Chairman. During the next two weeks Baldwin's fate was fought out in the safest Conservative seat in Britain. From the outset, as Beaverbrook explained, his candidate was standing in St. George's 'to make an attack upon Baldwin and the primary issue ... will be the leadership of the Conservative party ... If [Petter] wins Baldwin must go, and Empire Free Trade must become the accepted policy of the Conservative Party'.[43] *Cooper's victory on 19 March with a majority of almost 6,000 signalled the effective end of the Beaverbrook Crusade. Despite Austen Chamberlain's efforts, it would be another six years before his brother would succeed Baldwin as Conservative leader and become Prime Minister and he would not live to see it.*

AC5/1/475   6 June 1929
                                                        2 Morpeth Mansions

My dear Ida,

... I thought so ill of my chances when the canvass returns began to come in that I warned Ivy & the elder children not to be surprised if I were defeated & during the two counts I found myself in a very philosophic mood with a pulse as steady as at any moment. Still I am glad that the 43 were on the right side! At first I was disposed to put it all down to the housing conditions which are terrible, but as the same wave swept all the industrial districts I think on reflection that a wider explanation is necessary, & I am disposed to say that Baldwin's 'safety first' was a good cry in '24 & a bad cry in '29, & that our salesmanship was bad & our programme insufficiently precise. But most of all I suspect that since '26 or rather '27 when they had recovered from the first shock of depression the working classes have been nourishing a silent resentment more like continental class hatred than anything we have experienced in my life time. The old people still supported us but the young were sullen & resentful & voted socialist almost solidly. The few Conservatives who have escaped in similar constituencies appear to have literally danced themselves into safety with the Flappers.[44] Funny, is it not?

Neville is saddened by the fear that much of his good administration may now be undone by his successor. I do not fear this at the Foreign

[43] Beaverbrook to Brisbane, 3 March 1931, Beaverbrook MSS C/64. For the by-election see C. Cook and J. Ramsden, *By-elections in British Politics*, (1973) Chapter 4.

[44] In 1918 women over 30 were given the vote. In 1928 with the Representation of the People (Equal Franchise) Act the government extended the franchise to women over 21 – popularly known as the 'Flapper vote'.

Office where I feel rather that the other side will now gather fruits that I have carefully cultivated & watched till now they are just ripe such as evacuation of the Rhineland & an agreement with the U.S.A. But this is no more than the normal sequence of events & if the right things are done I have no right to complain. I am only sorry that J.H. Thomas is not apparently to be my successor but that Henderson is to follow me. I hear that there has been a battle royal between them for the post. I should have preferred Thomas because he is by far the abler man & is sound in essentials. Henderson I have always thought very stupid & rather afraid of responsibility.

AC5/1/476   25 June 1929
                                          2 Morpeth Mansions

[Typescript]
My dear Ida,

I am subject to the lassitude – called by plain people idleness – which is apt to descend upon one when one is suddenly set free from hard and continuous work ... The fact is that whilst I took the first news of our defeat very philosophically, I am now feeling the depression which is the natural reaction to disappointed hopes. It is annoying to have ones work interrupted and not wholly consoling to feel that others will reap where one has so laboriously sown.

However, this feeling will presently pass away and I shall be happier if I get, as I think I soon may, some other work which if not of equal importance will at any rate give me something to live upon. I have had to leave my private affairs to look after themselves while I have been absorbed in public work and the result has been disastrous and causes me much anxiety.

Twitt's Ghyll was looking lovely on Sunday ... I shall not go there again, for though the purchase is not completed, we have sold the place and I am so sad at parting from it that I think a visit does me more harm than good.

AC5/1/476   1 July 1929
                                          2 Morpeth Mansions

[Typescript]
My dear Hilda,

...

I am as cross as two sticks with Stanley Baldwin, for he has again refused my request for some recognition for Oliver Locker-Lampson.

When I first asked it on the formation of the Government, he refused on grounds which were not disclosed to me till a year or two later. The moment they were disclosed I was able to disprove the malicious stories which he had heard and he himself admitted the perfect propriety of Oliver's conduct. I asked again, this time as a personal favour to myself and I thought that having regard to the fact that Oliver had suffered through his loyalty to me at the time of the fall of the Coalition and to my own services to the Party and my relations to Baldwin that I had a right to expect compliance with my request. However, Baldwin thought otherwise and though he wrote me a very nice letter, I am not mollified. I shall not allow the episode to affect my conduct or my relations with him in any way, but I am hurt that he should again have refused a request preferred in such terms.

AC5/1/478

13 July 1929
2 Morpeth Mansions

[Typescript]
My dear Hilda,

. . .

Our party was much disturbed by Neville's speech which they not unnaturally interpreted in the light of Beaverbrook's pronouncement in his papers in favour of free trade within the Empire and a tariff against everyone else.[45] This is pure mischief-making on his part as he himself knows as well as anyone that no single Dominion would throw down its tariff walls against us. When Neville made his speech he had not read Beaverbrook's article, and though he at once corrected the misinterpretations to which his speech gave rise it made our people a little uneasy. On top of this came Amery's outburst on Tuesday with his direct repudiation of Winston and what was held to be a clear indication that he was out for the 'whole hog'. This very nearly produced a revolt in the party, not to speak of the indignation caused among his colleagues. The members of the late Cabinet met to consider the position on Thursday when we had happily a very quiet and friendly discussion which .... showed a quite satisfactory measure of agreement amongst us for the present at least, with the possible exception of Amery. What he will do, I do not know, but he must either conform or leave the front bench as the party will not stand an

---

[45] Neville Chamberlain spoke to the Empire Industries Association early in July in favour of protection, denying the manifesto limitations any longer applied. On 9 July Amery launched a long-suppressed tirade against Churchill's obstruction of Safeguarding. Beaverbrook launched his Empire Crusade with 'Who is for the Empire?' *Sunday Express*, 30 June 1929.

independent policy from one of the front bench leaders.

We are to have a further discussion next week when we may set up a committee to consider imperial and industrial policy, but I am myself a little doubtful whether much can be achieved until we see more of the development of the Government's policy, for apart from their threatened onslaught on Preference – which after all may not mature – they seem to be moving on the same lines as we should wish to take. The end of the first week of the new Parliament found our party very happy and pleased with the way things had gone up to that time. This week's events upset everything and put them in a bad temper, but I do not think any permanent harm has been done and I hope that we shall avoid such mistakes in future. The more I think over things the more likely it seems to me that Labour is in for a long spell. In any case, as far as I myself am concerned, if I succeed in getting permanent work with a permanent salary, I have pretty well made up my mind that I ought not again to sacrifice it for the hazards of office ...

AC5/1/479   1 August 1929
                                                        2 Morpeth Mansions

My dear Ida,

...

Well, I am not sorry or at least not altogether sorry to have missed the discussions on Lloyds recall. I had not decided what I should have done myself but the office was pressing strongly that Lloyd's appointment should not be renewed at the end of its five years & I was hoping that a place might be found for him as High Comr. in East Africa under the new arrangements. He has courage, energy & ability, but his qualities are more suited to an administrative post or a time of crisis rather than to the more diplomatic duties which he was called upon to discharge in Egypt. I had advised Henderson not to recall him whatever I might have done myself, on the ground that for a new Govt. to change the High Comr. as soon as they came in would be to needlessly arouse suspicion & fear in certain quarters here & to excite hopes, which must be disappointed, in Egypt & would add to his difficulties there. As to the manner of his dismissal & its announcement I think Henderson & his colleagues blundered as much as it was possible for men to do, but I should have been a good deal handicapped in the discussion by the last exchange of despatches. I had felt it necessary to restate our policy & Lloyd, replying on the very day we resigned, said that if he 'might be permitted a criticism' of my interesting despatch he entirely disagreed with me!

AC5/1/481   16 August 1929
Allensmore, Hereford

My dear Hilda,

. . .

I am not very happy about the Egyptian treaty[46] where it goes beyond my own with Sarwat – Heaven knows mine was liberal enough – but I cannot stir myself up to the Morning Post pitch of frenzy. Nor am I very happy about proceedings at the Hague[47] tho' in that case everything depends on what is going on behind the scenes. If Henderson & Snowden bring off a settlement all is well & methods & manners don't matter, but if there were a breakdown it would be serious for everyone.

AC5/1/485   6 November 1929
2 Morpeth Mansions

[Typescript]
My dear Hilda,

. . .

I have had a rather busy ten days – mainly owing to the part that was imposed upon me, rather against my will, in endeavouring to clear up the situation in respect of the Government's communications with Baldwin in regard to the Viceroy's declaration[48] ... I am gravely alarmed by the use of the words "Dominion *Status*". It may purchase present peace and cooperation, but it is already understood in one sense by the Government and in a different sense by what is called 'moderate' Indian opinion, and is certain to lead to charges of breach of faith in the future. It is curious to see how the "Times", which in other circumstances would have been certain to criticise and even denounce the use of this dangerous expression, is entirely governed by Dawson's friendship for Irwin.

---

[46] On 6 August the draft agreement was published. Only slightly more generous to Egypt than Chamberlain's, it ended the occupation of Cairo and Alexandria, withdrew British troops to the Canal and liquidated Capitulations. Rejected by new Wafd government in December 1929.

[47] The First Hague Conference, 6–28 August 1929 finally reduced German reparation payments in accordance with the Young Report, June 1929. The Rhineland would also be evacuated five years ahead of the date fixed at Versailles.

[48] On 31 October 1929 the Viceroy, Lord Irwin (formerly Edward Wood) had declared that it was 'implicit in the Declaration of 1917, that the natural issue of India's constitutional progress is the attainment of Dominion status'.

AC5/1/486   11 November 1929
                                                      2 Morpeth Mansions

[Typescript]
My dear Ida,

...

I am not at all happy about the impotent conclusion of the Indian debate. Baldwin attained an unusually high level in his speech, but he has not the knack of driving home a particular point. Lloyd George's opening was powerful and showed him at his best, but later he got into an unfortunate altercation with Benn[49] which altered the tone and character of the debate, and Benn himself after a rather skillful opening allowed his temper to get the better of him and refused to repeat in the House of Commons the answer which Parmoor[50] had already given in the Lords and which was all that Baldwin required of him. The result is ... a dangerous *équivoque* and indeed I believe that Benn deliberately fostered the uncertainty. This may avert immediate trouble, but is dangerous to our future peace. Personally I am, of course, strongly opposed to the use of the new term "Dominion Status". It has been the policy of the India Office carefully to avoid it because it connotes not merely the eventual partnership of India on equal terms in the British Commonwealth but because it implies and is understood in India to mean a similarity of institutions of which Indian conditions do not admit. There is the further objection that whatever Dominion status may have meant in Montagu's day, it means something different now and is indeed a constantly changing relationship. I cannot think how Irwin came to favour the use of such a dangerous term and I regret that Baldwin should have been so much under the influence of his friendship and admiration for Irwin as to give it even a tentative and conditional acceptance.

[49] William Wedgwood Benn (1877–1960). Liberal MP for Tower Hamlets (St. George's) 1906–18 and Leith 1918–27; Labour MP for Aberdeen (North) 1928–31; Manchester (Gorton) 1937–41. Whip 1910–15; Secretary of State for India 1929–31; Secretary for Air 1945–46. Created Viscount Stansgate 1942.

[50] Charles Alfred Cripps (1852–1941). Conservative MP for Stroud 1895–1900; S.E. Lancs (Stretford) 1901–6 and Wycombe 1910–14. Lord President 1924 and June–August 1931. British representative at League of Nations Council 1924. Created Kt. 1908 and Baron Parmoor 1914.

AC5/1/487

18 November 1929
House of Commons

My dear Ida,

...

We had a gay weekend including ... a drive down to Leatherhead on Sunday to lunch with Beaverbrook where we met Tim Healy[51] & Reading amongst others, & I continued the conversations begun by Neville & pursued by N & Baldwin jointly. Beaverbrook was friendly & even cordial to me (though his papers are not). I think it may be possible to do something in that quarter tho' it is by no means certain. It is, I think, clear that his heart is in the business & that it is not mere mischief or spite against S.B.

AC5/1/490

7 December 1929
2 Morpeth Mansions

My dear Ida,

...

Govt. are in a mess over the Insurance Bill & at their wits end on unemployment ...

Mrs Churchill : 'I must go & sort out Winston, he's been brooding quite long enough!'

Mrs Baldwin (archly): 'I *never* disturb Mr Baldwin when *he's* brooding. He sometimes lays a *golden* egg, you know!"

Oh Lord! I had to tell *somebody* and you are safe.

AC5/1/493

19 January 1930
2 Morpeth Mansions

My dear Hilda,

...

As to politics ... I find the outlook very gloomy. I have had my ups & downs, my pleasures & disappointments; have fought desperately against heavy odds & been beaten or again floated on a favouring tide, but I have never felt as hopeless as now. Hubbard of the B'ham Post came to see me on Friday & spent nearly three hours with me. For the

---

[51] Timothy Michael Healy (1855–1931) Irish Nationalist MP for Wexford 1880–83; Monaghan 1883–5; S. Derry 1885–6; N. Longford 1887–92; Louth N. 1892–December 1910; N.E. Cork July 1911–18. Governor-General of Irish Free State 1922–28.

first time he impressed me: – he was seriously considering starting a campaign – B.M.G. – if these initials mean anything to you. "Baldwin (this time) must go!"[52] He found him hopelessly inadequate & in my heart I agreed with him; but I discouraged him from dotting his i's & crossing his t's. Instead of leading up to "B.M.G." I urged that his conclusion should be 'This is what we expect of our leader; this is what B. must do & be'. Time enough to say the personal things if B. failed to respond or to wake up. I wish Neville were back;[53] I see noone but him in our ranks capable of developing a constructive policy & winning confidence. He has trained on wonderfully & I hope that it may come to him before it is too late & in conditions which are tolerable & have not created a state of feeling which condemns any man's efforts to futility.

AC5/1/495   24 March 1930
                                                17 Deans Yard, SW1

My dear Hilda,

. . .

I am made very sad by Balfour's death. It is the snapping of the last link with the older generation, the parting of the last man to whom I looked up in the political world. He was always extraordinarily kind & affectionate to me & I returned the affection in full measure. You think of him chiefly, I expect, as the man who failed to come along as we had hoped on the question of Tariff Reform, & whatever view one takes of it that was certainly the least successful part of his career; but the work he did then & later in other respects was immense. Even in the unsuccessful years of his Prime Ministership he made the Entente with France & the Alliance with Japan; he created the Comtee. of Imperial Defence & marked out its line of work, & he settled the Education question & Licensing for a generation – & all this was constructive work & the three last entirely his own work.

---

[52] The phrase 'B.M.G., Balfour Must Go' began to circulate after the publication of an article critical of his leadership by Leo Maxse in the *National Review* in September 1911.

[53] Neville Chamberlain was absent on a visit to Kenya from 11 December 1929 until 8 March 1930.

AC5/1/496

30 March 1930
58 Rutland Gate

My dear Ida,

. . .

Politics are looking up a little but S.B. is amazingly hard to move. At last we have forced him to have a Council of leaders under the name of Comtee. of Business & to fix a regular weekly meeting. Policy will now, I hope, get proper consideration. Salisbury's letter was irritating;[54] the Cecil temperament & Cecil conscience are queer things, but whilst S.B. held no meetings & indeed seemed bent on keeping us all aloof from him & apart from one another how could anything go right or we keep step with one-another. His Hotel Cecil speech,[55] however, really 'went' with his audience; he abandoned reading & spoke up & out. I can only hope that he will follow it up vigorously at Manchester next week. From all parts of the country we get better reports.

AC5/1/502

26 May 1930
58 Rutland Gate

My dear Ida,

. . .

I had two good meetings in B'ham where my people are in much better fettle, & the Socialists rather piano, but I don't want an election yet – and I don't think we are going to have one. Mosley's resignation[56] & the rift in the Liberal-Labour lute are amazing & all to the good, but it would be a mistake to treat them too seriously. Master Mosley is thoroughly disliked & distrusted in all parts of the House & will have no following. I must say that I have never forgotten or forgiven his conduct at the counting of the votes in 1924 & rejoice to see him in the wilderness.

[54] Salisbury's letter to the Editor, *The Times*, 25 March 1930 was strongly free trade in tone and dismissive of Beaverbrook's campaign. It briefly upset attempts to restore relations with Beaverbrook.
[55] At Hotel Cecil on 4 March 1930 Baldwin's speech publicly announced the referendum on food taxes agreed with Beaverbrook the day before and was widely welcomed for restoring Conservative unity.
[56] Mosley resigned from the government on 20 May after Cabinet rejection of his memorandum advocating public works to relieve unemployment. His attempts to rally support in the PLP on 22 May received only 29 votes.

AC5/1/503

1 June 1930
58 Rutland Gate

My dear Hilda,

. . .

Snowden's temper is abominable & Winston acts on him like a red flag on a bull. I think the Budget will have a rough passage unless S. learns patience & to control his temper. We are likely to have two more late sittings this week. I can't say that I like them & I am much more upset the next day than I used to be, but my staying all night & taking part mightily pleased our young men, so it was worth doing.

. . .

Yes, Davidson[57] has resigned at last. It would have been far better for everyone, himself included, if he had gone at least a month ago. All sorts of rumours are about as to possible successors. Of course the new man's name ought to have been announced simultaneously with D's resignation & thus stopped further rumours. The last name I heard mentioned was Leslie Wilson's! I have told Neville that I couldn't & wouldn't stand that first because he has no brains & secondly because he was absolutely & grossly disloyal at the time of the fall of the Coalition. If S.B. appoints him I shall go on to the Back Benches.

AC5/1/504

14 June 1930
House of Commons Library

My dear Hilda,

. . .

India has continued to be my chief preoccupation during the week ... I have been at two more conferences with Baldwin where he has been as useless as before, but at least he has not allowed the impression to continue that he differed from me – so that is something gained. He is an odd creature; the natural person for him to have chosen for such a conference as his companion was his Secretary of State for India, but he preferred to take me. He seems to me to distrust or actively dislike most of his colleagues & to be afraid of all of his opponents & of himself. I go on defending him when necessary, but there is little pleasure in working with such a man.

[57] John Colin Campbell Davidson (1889–1970) Conservative MP for Hemel Hempstead, 1920–23, 1924–37. PPS to Bonar Law 1920–21; 1922–23; to Baldwin 1921–22. Chancellor Duchy of Lancaster 1923–4. 1931–7; Financial Secretary to Admiralty 1924–6; Conservative Party Chairman 1926–30. Created Kt. 1935 and Viscount Davidson 1937.

. . .

We did well last week in the House & shook the Govt. well up which was a good thing, without beating them which was perhaps just as well. As to N. Norfolk[58] I draw a different moral from most people. If we could come within 200 of winning *in spite of* food taxes, it shows that the cry is not as frightening as it used to be & confirms my opinion that with a united party & hard continuous argument the sting could be drawn *before* a general election, but the party is not united on that issue & many members are far too frightened to face it.

AC5/1/505

14 June 1930
58 Rutland Gate

My dear Hilda,

. . .

I have to open a debate on unemployment on Wednesday, I have an impression that we are not far from a landslide on protection. I had a very interesting conversation with Graham[59] just before the House rose. "It sometimes seems", he said, "as if there were a conspiracy against our trade", & again: "If you consent to join the suggested Three Party Conference on agriculture, I don't conceal that we shall have difficulty with Snowden, but you will find some men with very open minds", whilst George Lambert[60] said to me the same afternoon that he had told Lloyd George & the Liberal Party meeting that nothing could save agriculture except protection. "I'm a free trader & I'm sorry for it, but there it is["]. It seems to me that the whole side of the mountain is beginning to move & when a crack once appears, who shall say where it will stop.

. . .

[*Postscript*] The Simon report[61] is full of wisdom & facts, but it's not going to conciliate the malcontents!

[58] North Norfolk by-election 9 July 1930. Lady Noel-Buxton, the wife of the former candidate retained the seat for Labour but on a reduced majority of only 179. The Conservative candidate renounced the official party policy on food taxes and increased his vote by 2,000.

[59] William Graham (1887–1932). Labour MP for Edinburgh Central 1918–31; Financial Secretary to Treasury, 1924; President Board of Trade 1929–31.

[60] George Lambert (1866–1958) Liberal MP for S. Molton 1891–24, 1929–45 – a National Liberal from 1931. Civil Lord of Admiralty, 1905–15; Liberal Party Chairman 1919–21. Created Viscount Lambert, 1945.

[61] Cmd. 3568–9 *Report of the Indian Statutory Commission,* (2 vols) *Parliamentary Papers,* (1929–30) xi, 1, 443. Published in May – June 1930 said a federation, including the princely states, must be set up before responsible government could be granted. Seen by many to suggest indefinite postponement.

AC5/1/506

22 June 1930
58 Rutland Gate

My dear Ida,

...

I don't wonder that Hilda found Neville depressed. I have been through a comparable situation before & I have not now the possibilities before me which Neville has & ought to consider; but I find the situation trying enough. Never have I known so *blunt* a spearhead as S.B. or a man who left so large a gap between the recognition that he must act & action. Whenever you have settled something with him one day, you must seek him out the next to ask if he has yet done it or even put it in train. If at N's suggestion I had not done this the Party Meeting would have been fixed for Tuesday week instead of Tuesday & the letter to Ramsay MacDonald would not yet have been written. 'Too late & in the wrong way' sums up my criticism of his leadership. I have told N. & S.B. that N. ought not to take the Central Office on any terms even temporarily. I think N. was relieved that I volunteered my opinion so clearly & decisively.

Yes, I liked my speech on Unemployment, made without a note (tho' not without thought). I gave the discussion a new turn ... I think that incidentally I laid a good foundation for our refusal to enter a conference where all radical cures would be taboo & only palliatives or aggravations of the present evils be considered.

I am now deep in the second volume of the Simon Report – secret advance copy sent by Simon himself after I had felt moved to express to him my appreciation of his first vol. Would you believe that at least up to a couple of days ago Wedgwood Benn had not sent him a word of thanks or appreciation!

Well, well! this is an odd government & an unsatisfactory world – but it is a very interesting one all the same.

AC5/1/507

26 June 1930
58 Rutland Gate

My dear Hilda,

We have got to that point in the London season when one passes without a pause from one engagement to another & has no quiet time to rest or think, but ever since the conference on India to which I went at Baldwin's request my mind is beset with the Indian problem & all else seems trifling beside it. I derived the very worst impression from the P.M. & still more from Benn who is obviously quite unequal to his responsibilities & has completely lost his nerve. Baldwin kept as silent as he could but unfortunately gave the impression to MacDonald that he did not agree with me – the real fact being that he has not read the Report, has had no time to spare for India, admittedly is quite at a loss on that field &, not trusting himself, is afraid even to say ditto to me. Lloyd George & Reading, I need not say, showed a far greater grasp of the matter & backed me strongly on the fundamentals though not on the immediate procedure. I have insisted that Baldwin should call a council on India at once & we are to meet on Monday before we see MacDonald again. Meanwhile the views expressed by Ll. G., Reading & me will be telegraphed to the Viceroy for his consideration & remarks. It is terrible in such a critical situation to have a leader who is afraid to say even Bo to a goose. Men, says Ll.G., ought to be labelled like railway wagons – load not to exceed so much. Benn is a two-ton lorry under a 10 ton load ... Unless the Govt. pull themselves together & get rid of Benn, they will lose India. Meanwhile the P.M.'s one idea is to save it by soft words which we interpret in one sense & Indians in another. As I feared, it is not carelessness or accident that they had said no word of thanks or appreciation to Simon. The situation is such that they & the Governor General dare not & they seem to think only of how they can secure some present relaxation of the tension by misty phrases like Dominion Status which seek to glaze over the hard facts.

AC5/1/508

30 June 1930
58 Rutland Gate

[Typescript]
My dear Hilda,

...

As to home affairs, you will have heard from Neville more than I can put in a letter. His acceptance of the chairmanship has given immense satisfaction in the party, but I remain very sorry that he should have had to undertake it. The fact, however, is that no-one was very clearly indicated for the position and most of the people whose names were mentioned were unfitted for it. I hope that Neville will stick to his determination to hand it over before very long. He would sacrifice far too much by devoting himself to that particular task. His own unselfishness in taking it even temporarily is recognised on all hands and I hope gratitude may last as long as he holds the position.

I think we all had the feeling that though the party meeting[62] was a necessary and useful gathering, it really settled nothing. I have had no opportunity of discussing the situation with Neville since the meeting, but I am inclined to think that if we can hold on for a few months events will resolve our difficulties about the Referendum. Thomas, who as Dominions Secretary will play a leading part in the Imperial Conference, said to a friend of mine that if we thought that they would leave anything over for us we were much mistaken; they would lick that platter clean and there would be nothing left for us to feed on and nothing for which the Dominion Governments would come to London again if summoned by us. I am inclined to think that this is true, for there is a very considerable Protectionist and Imperial movement going on in the Labour Party. It seems to me therefore probable that one of two things will happen at the Conference – either a good scheme of inter-Imperial trade involving food duties will be worked out and accepted by the Labour Government or it will be shown that even for protective duties on their food the Dominions are not ready to make adequate return. In either of these cases the Referendum would disappear from our programme and the same will be true in the third – but as I think less probable – case of the Dominions making a good offer and the Government rejecting it because it involved duties on food.

There are no doubt other possibilities but I think that these are the most probable and whichever of them occurs we shall be in possession of all the information which we should not otherwise have had at a general election and the obtaining of which would have been a reason or excuse for the Referendum.

Baldwin's speech was not what I had hoped, but his mind does not work in the same way as mine and apart from deliberate rejection of my suggestions I do not think that he ever really understood them. I thought the balance of the speech was wrong and that there should have been more insistence on and development of his policy and less though equally incisive talk about the press. I think too that he makes a mistake in trying to put Beaverbrook in the same class with Rothermere. The difference between the two men is illustrated by their replies this morning to his Saturday's speech. Beaverbrook is dignified, avoids personalities and goes to the root of the matter. Rothermere scolds like an angry fishwife. Another man than Baldwin would, I think, have kept Beaverbrook and might yet get him on our side. Altogether I am not very happy though I think things are rather better than they

---

[62] Caxton Hall meeting of Conservative MPs and candidates, 24 June 1930. Baldwin launched a scathing attack on the press Lords – particularly Rothermere.

were, but my mind at every moment goes back to India where things seem to be as bad as bad can be.

AC5/1/508

7 July 1930
House of Commons Library

My dear Ida,

. . .

... On Saturday, having gone to B'ham in the morning, lunched at the Conservative Club with a pleasant party of business men, & attended the annual Unionist garden party ... all in good spirits & particularly pleased with the Banker's manifesto.[63] Did I write to Hilda last week that I thought that there would soon be a landslide? ... The movement of opinion is very marked. Beaverbrook in spite of all the mischief he has made has certainly helped it forward. Now come the Bankers & the Trade Unions. Where is it going to stop? I had begun to think that I should not see it any more than Father. How it would have delighted him.

You will have seen this morning the resolution drafted by Neville which S.B. is to move & N. to support. Provided that we do not bungle again the tide is flowing our way strongly, but shall we escape fresh blunders? Both N. & I are driven nearly to despair by S.B.'s ways, but between us we are getting some order into our affairs by degrees, greatly to the satisfaction of our colleagues. N. does the heavy work & I do the trimmings.

That however is not true of India where I have pulled the labouring oar, keeping in close touch with Reading, Lloyd George & Simon, leading our policy & taking on my shoulders practically the whole of our side of the discussions which the four of us have had with Lloyd George & Benn.

Wednesday ... The Prime Minister is I think at his wits end about India – the Viceroy is certainly contemplating the abandonment of the scheme of Central Government on which this Commission lays such stress: when it is known that the Viceroy is giving way everyone in India will be on the run. The P.M. I think sees the dangers but does not know how to meet them. His Party is far more extreme than he is & he is in terror of being supposed to be less liberal than the Viceroy.

I have not been so anxious about anything since the war & cannot yet see any way through the difficulties.

[63] The Bankers' manifesto of 4 July 1930 advocated sweeping extensions of Safeguarding legislation. The TUC Economic Committee also issued a report on 26 June calling for the development of Imperial economic relations but was divided on tariffs.

AC5/1/510   4 August 1930
                                                        Little Paddocks,
                                                        Sunninghill, Berks

My dear Ida,

The session is over & I bid it goodbye with no regrets. The Government has indeed lost its bloom; the only Minister who comes out of it with an enhanced reputation is Morrison[64] (Transport); the Prime Minister's authority in his part is gravely impaired; so is Snowden; Thomas's has gone altogether; Clynes has none. Only Henderson, party manager & wirepuller in the background, Foreign Secretary officially, retains his power & there are many rumours that he intrigues against MacDonald as earlier against Thomas & seeks to supersede him. With a Government thus shaken, we ought to be on the high road to success, but our Party is divided, disgruntled & confused. I have just read a few lines of a speech delivered at Worcester on Saturday which also disgusts me with their dull egoism & vanity.[65] What is to be done in face of such blind self-complacency? Besides I am furious with him for his attitude throughout our Indian discussion. He has given both the Prime Minister & the Times to understand – perhaps I ought rather to say, allowed them to infer that he did not agree with me & beyond this has contributed nothing. I insisted on consultation with our colleagues at every stage & had the whole of them with me. If he had not allowed it to be seen that he differed, we should have had Simon in the Conference as well as the party representatives. Altogether, as you have perceived, I am so cross that I can only splutter. I should be ill if I had not relieved myself by telling him plainly that it was not pleasant for a colleague to find himself thus let down. Well, its time we all had a holiday.

---

[64] Herbert Stanley Morrison (1888–1965) Labour MP for Hackney South 1923–4, 1929–31, 1935–45; Lewisham East 1945–50; Lewisham South 1950–59. Minister of Transport 1929–31; Minister of Supply 1940; Home Secretary 1940–45; Lord President 1945–51; Foreign Secretary 1951. Deputy Labour Leader 1945–55; member of L.C.C. 1922–45 and Leader 1934–40. Created Baron Morrison of Lambeth 1959.

[65] To his Worcester Constituency Association on 2 August Baldwin defended the referendum at a time when virtually everyone else wished to abandon it in favour of the 'free hand'.

AC5/1/511

11 August 1930
58 Rutland Gate

My dear Hilda,

...

... I have one bit of news for you. Something that Salisbury said one day when we were discussing India led me to feel that he had not forgiven me my part in the Irish settlement. I accordingly suggested to S.B. that it would be just as well to make Salisbury a member of our delegation, for he would have a greater sense of realities & more responsibility inside than outside. S.B. however replied that he would not have Salisbury in that job for anything & repeated his decision emphatically when I again broached the subject. When, therefore, S.B. formally asked me to be one of the four representatives of our Party I made it a condition of my acceptance that he should first consult Salisbury & ask him plainly whether I should have his confidence & support, to which S. replied quite nicely but firmly in the negative. S.B. reports this with surprise & regret & still offers me the place with an assurance that he will back me in everything; but, as you will not be surprised to hear, I declined to take on so difficult & thankless a job with the knowledge that the Leader in the Lords mistrusts my judgement if not my principles. I was ready to take on the task as a public duty in the hope that I might do some good or at least avert some evil, but so handicapped I feel that I should be in an impossible position & could not hope to succeed in such conditions. I feel no obligation to undertake the labour & responsibility though I should not be human if I did not feel some irritation with Salisbury & some regret at the loss of an opportunity of service where I think my knowledge & my qualities would have been useful.

As to firm [?] of R[othermere] & B[eaverbrook], I cannot say that I think worse than before of R., for he has behaved as I should have expected him to do, but I can only explain B's conduct by supposing that R. has a hold upon him of a kind which I had not earlier suspected. Neville is doing extraordinarily well.

AC5/1/515

20 September 1930
58 Rutland Gate

My dear Ida,

...

I think I told you that the Crockers, our Californian hosts, are over here ... Yesterday the D'Abernon's came to meet them ... D'A. was very gloomy about Hitler – not dangerous, he thought, if there were a *man* to fight him, but since Stresemann's death Germany had no man. What a troubled world it is! I hear from Fleuriau that Briand's position is much shaken in France by Hitler's success ...

Talking of Stresemann, I had read D'Abernon's third volume, 'Locarno' – I need not say with much interest. How far I wonder did Stresemann really mean to go when he launched that suggestion. I am sure that he did not mean or foresee what it became in our hands but it is his imperishable title that he not only made the first move but that as it developed he saw all the opportunities that it offered & grasped them with courage & amazing skill.

AC5/1/516   4 October 1930
                                              58 Rutland Gate

My dear Ida,

You will have heard of us from Neville ... & what is more you will have heard from him how his active mind has been at work devising a policy for the party.[66] Thank goodness, we have one man with a clear constructive mind, but I am more than ever vexed that S.B. should have prevailed upon him to take the Central Office. It requires too much time & what is worse it involves him in difficulties & enmities which ought not to be his affair. So much do I feel this that I even sounded him as to my undertaking to bell the cat & gently indicating to S.B., that is was time for him to go, but Neville thought that I should do more harm than good & asked me not to try it. So there we are – none of us happy except S.B. & his cronies & Neville's future chances being seriously jeopardised by his new office & his old leader.

We drove down to lunch with Lady Hudson today & met Havenga[67] of S. Africa, Forbes[68] of N. Zealand & Ferguson,[69] Prime Minister of

---

[66] In a speech at Crystal Palace on 21 September Neville Chamberlain had launched his own 'unauthorised programme' of drastic economy – particularly on unemployment insurance – an emergency tariff, a wheat quota and a free hand on other imports to improve Imperial trade relations. This was accepted by all but Churchill at the Business Committee on 7 October 1930.

[67] Nicolaas Christian Havenga (1882–1957) South African attorney and politician. (Nationalist, then Afrikaner then Nationalist again). MP from 1915. Minister of Finance 1924–39, 1948–53. Leader of Afrikaner Party 1939–48 before rejoining Nationalists.

[68] George William Forbes (1869–1947) New Zealand farmer and politician. Leader of Nationalist Party then United Party after 1928. Various offices 1928–31. Prime Minister 1930–31, 1931–35.

[69] George Howard Ferguson (1870–1946) Canadian barrister and Conservative politician. MP Ontario 1905–30. Premier of Ontario 1923–30. Resigned to become Canadian High Commissioner in London 1930–35.

Ontario with their wives. None of them sounded happy about the way the Conference[70] had opened; they thought Ramsay McD[sic] looking very old & tired & perplexed as indeed I did when I saw him at the farewell luncheon to Sthamer.

...

But the week has been saddened for me by Birkenhead's death. I can well understand anyone who had no more than a passing acquaintance with him detesting him cordially, but if you once got really to know him it was impossible not to like & even to love him. It is striking to see how everything written of him by those who were ever his friends – no matter how great their differences of outlook, character & faith – it is the loyalty & generosity of his friendship that is uppermost in their thoughts. I can well believe that if I had not known him intimately, I should have detested him. As it was I had a great affection for him & shall never find a truer or more affectionate friend.

And now to close the week comes this horrible disaster of the great airship.[71] The times are very difficult & disaster follows hard upon disaster.

AC5/1/517

11 October 1930
58 Rutland Gate

My dear Hilda,

Frankly I am puzzled by the situation. I approved S.B.'s statement in which & above all in the rapidity with which it was issued I saw Neville's hand; but I don't know enough of Bennett's[72] mind to make any guess as to how he will receive Neville's plan.[73] If we were the Government at this moment I believe that we could bring off a good arrangement, but will Bennett look at it – still more take it up & work it in face of a hostile English government & in the absence of anyone who will expound its merits & defend it. Bennett's own proposal, if I understand it, asks too much of us & offers too little in return. It sounds

---

[70] The Imperial Conference met in London from 1 October to 14 November 1930.

[71] The R.101 airship crashed near Beauvais at the beginning of a trial flight to India on 5 October 1930 with 48 fatalities including Lord Thomson the Air Minister.

[72] Richard Bedford Bennett (1870–1947) Canadian barrister, businessman and Conservative politician. MP Federal Parliament 1911–17, 1925–38. Minister of Justice 1921, 1926. Leader Conservative Party 1927–38; Prime Minister 1930–35. Created Viscount Bennett 1941.

[73] On 8 October 1930 Bennett made his famous offer to all Empire countries of a preference in the Canadian market in exchange for a like preference in theirs. Snowden prevented the government from responding but Chamberlain drafted a statement endorsing Bennett's proposal thus disposing of the referendum and giving the Conservatives a 'free hand' when returned to office.

well but applied in practice would by itself do little for us, I fear, but I do not feel sure that I understand it fully & I do not know in the least how far he will be able to modify it. At any rate as Neville writes me this morning the discussion & S.B.'s statement have completely changed the situation & given S.B. a new chance. What I have chiefly feared is that S.B. would drag down all his colleagues & particularly Neville with him. I shall perhaps see my way more clearly after our adjourned meeting on Tuesday. I can't bear that Neville should be included in "the Old Gang".

D'Abernon's book sent me back to my papers. Reading my letters to D'A. & Crewe it is clear to me that I quickly seized the importance of Stresemann's offer but that I was wholly unable to take it up because I could get no decision from the Comtee. of the C.I.D. (or Cabinet) to which the Protocol had been referred & had no idea whether the Cabinet would follow me or not. Curzon, who presided over that Comtee. wanted to do nothing; Bob Cecil wanted an amended Protocol; noone else wanted anything. I had started on the idea of turning the Protocol into an option of giving a particular & effective guarantee of the Franco-Belgian frontier instead of a general & ineffective guarantee of every frontier. Examination by a small sub-committee of officials proved this to involve such prodigious changes in the Protocol as to make the plan impossible & I fell back on the idea of a bi-lateral treaty with France & had a memo prepared in the F.O. on these lines. I believe that it was the fear that I might carry out this policy which was the decisive factor in Stresemann's mind when he put forward the mutual guarantee & I certainly should never have got assent to this latter plan except by saying that I would not carry on with no positive policy at all but would accept Stresemann's offer as an alternative to or rather substitute for my original idea of a bilateral alliance. How I got the assent of the Cabinet I do not know to this moment. Even after I got it Curzon, dragging Balfour with him, came to protest & the whole question was reopened as I was on the point of leaving for Paris & Geneva, & even at Geneva I got a letter from Crowe saying that the Cabinet had gone back on their decision which caused me to telegraph my resignation to Baldwin. What actually happened I have never understood, whether Crowe misunderstood the Cabinet Comtee. or whether they again changed their minds, but after my return from Geneva in March '25 I had no further difficulties with them. Its a very odd story if its ever told fully. D'A. says he had no idea of my difficulties with the Cabinet – which shows how loyal I was to them, but it's certain there would have been no Locarno policy but for me. I will add but for D'Abernon himself. We were a very happy combination, I would add that it was a god-send that Briand's courage replaced Herriot's timidity at that moment.

AC5/1/518

27 October 1930
58 Rutland Gate

My dear Hilda,

...

I have seen no politicians since Ida lunched here & know little or nothing of the inwardness of things. My Chairman in West B'ham, an admirable man, is very nervous about food taxes, but I am heartily glad we have got back to the free hand & d— the consequences. I believe that S.B. thinks he has been quite consistent & eminently sagacious. At any rate he has got a new lease of life & I am not sorry for I think that his succession at this moment would have been a *damnosa hereditas*. I expect that Winston will face up presently tho' I have done my best to calm him, but he cuts no ice with the Party & I really don't see how he can change sides again though Ll.G. would no doubt be glad enough to get him.

I am looking forward to this session with more than usual interest, for it is only when the House is sitting that one can really judge the trend of events or make any forecast of their issue. That the Govt. is at its wits end, disunited & unstable is clear, but from that point to a dissolution is often a long step. I don't expect any sensational happenings on the Address or at any early date, but I think that we shall pull together & that they will continue to disintegrate & some day – probably in the New Year – there will be an accident & "the thing will come to pieces in my 'and Mum!"

Your loving brother

How alike all Cecils are – be they brothers or sisters!

AC5/1/519

2 November 1930
58 Rutland Gate

Dear Ida,

...

If the effect of reading S.B.'s speech[74] is as you say, then for once he sounded better than he read. He had a great ovation when he entered &, though it is true that his argument was weak, his manner was strong & his final words impressive. The only other really good speech

---

[74] At another meeting at Caxton Hall on 30 October 1930, Baldwin faced his Conservative critics on the day of the South Paddington by-election. Although the by-election was lost by 914 votes, Gretton's hostile resolution was defeated by 462 to 116 votes.

was Hailsham's. Kindersley,[75] Marjoribanks[76] & Mildmay[77] were all wretchedly bad, but the most noticable feature was the dislike of – the violent animus against, 'the Old Gang'. My foreign policy in Egypt & China were specifically attacked; so was Winston's finance. Jix loomed in the background. Noone was given any praise or excluded from the censure. Not pleasant! ... I believe myself modestly to be still fitted to do good work in the sphere of foreign policy & I don't believe anyone in sight on our side to be at present as well fitted for that work as I, but I begin to see that youth is getting not unnaturally impatient & to suspect that it would prefer my room to my company. The temptation to chuck in my hand is great.

The minority was larger than I expected. It included of course the so-called Diehards of the Gretton type who would pursue a reactionary policy that the country would not stand. It included the group habitually described as the Forty Thieves,[78] hangers on of business, not of the best type & I suspect a good many old & disgruntled Peers, but I should like very much to know how many young men of a decent type were numbered in its ranks. The Beaverbrook-Rothermere campaign is evidently strongest in the safest seats of the Home Counties, it has scarcely touched the North tho' of course there is much dissatisfaction there too. Any way the issues are getting clearer & one thing is evident – that the Party has now got to fight on the issue of food taxes or be forever damned. So far so good.

AC5/1/520   9 November 1930
                                                 58 Rutland Gate

My dear Hilda,

        ...
    St George's Chapel is beautiful but the ceremony was really spoiled by the Sovereign & Knights being in ordinary morning dress. It is the King's fault. He is incorrigible about such things & has no appreciation of the value of ceremonial ... I sat under my banner & crest & noticed that the plate with my arms is now in place in one of the stalls. It is

---

[75] Guy Molesworth Kindersley (1877–1956) Conservative MP for Hitchin 1923–31.

[76] Edward Marjoribanks (1900–32) Conservative MP for Eastbourne 1929 until his suicide in April 1932. Stepson of Hailsham and co-author of life of Carson.

[77] Francis Bingham Mildmay (1861–1947) Liberal MP for Totnes 1885–86, then Liberal Unionist 1886–1911 then Conservative 1911–22. Lord Lieut of Devon 1928–36. Created Baron Mildmay of Flete 1922.

[78] An informal group of Conservative backbenchers with banking and industrial interests. Poorly regarded and generally very right-wing. Also known as the 'Industrial Group'.

absurd the pleasure I take in my Gartership. I laugh at myself but kindly & admit that I am as pleased as a child with a toy which seemed absolutely beyond its reach.

...

Shipley[79] was an agreeable surprise but I wish our man had not put out a no Food-tax poster. It is clear that he would have won on the whole ticket & this will only make trouble for him in the future.

And talking of the future, we may speculate about it but it seems to me that all prophesy is at present futile. I have not the least idea whether S.B. would ask me to take the F.O. again if he had to form a Govt. nor whether I should accept if he did. There is no such dramatic stroke now as was Locarno. In this last 12 months or so, Great Britain seems to have lost all influence on the Continent & at Geneva. Just think of being left in a minority of two with China as our sole supporter! Look where I will, I see a terrible recrudescence of trouble & unrest & it is easier to see the perils that beset peace than to find a remedy. Mussolini's attitude has changed & not for the better; Germany lacks the strong guiding hand of Stresemann & France, frightened by Hitler's success & Mussolini's flirtations with Hungary & Bulgaria has reacted violently against the policy of appeasement. There is good work to be done at the F.O. but there is no easy success & perhaps no success at all to be reaped.

Incidentally it is a great satisfaction to me that the lines I laid down for our policy in China have stood the test of time & experience. The seed at first seemed to have fallen on stony ground indeed, but it has sprouted & I think my X'mas declaration is now recognised by Chinese & Europeans in China alike as having been a wise & farsighted act. At least I have received many testimonies to that effect & I am naturally the more pleased because it was essentially my own policy & the head of the far-eastern Dept of the F.O. yielded only to my persistence & insistence.

Can S.B. *fight?* That is now the question. I don't know the answer, but I still cherish some little hope.

AC5/1/520(b)

16 November 1930
58 Rutland Gate

My dear Ida,

...

... Undoubtedly [Neville] has been of immense service to S.B. &

---

[79] In their first ever victory in the seat, on 6 November 1930 the Conservatives won Shipley from Labour.

through him to the Party, but I am not sure how far S.B. realizes it & certainly the position is a disadvantage to N. himself. N. is, I think, best thought of by those who are brought into closest touch with his work & who therefore see its special quality, but I am rather unhappy about his standing with the Party at large. He somewhat fails to impress many people with his real gifts of leadership – he seems somewhat to miss that personal influence which everyone felt who came into touch with Father. I fear that we should find a very divided Party if we had to choose a new 'Leader'.

. . .

So the Imperial Conference is over & the Indian [Round Table] Conference has begun. Absit omen! As far as I can see nothing constructive has issued from the former & an unequalled opportunity has been allowed to pass unused. I cannot observe a single constructive & centripetal suggestion to balance the free play given to centrifugal forces, & the Govt which deliberately sets out to raise the price of coal to maintain miners wages just as deliberately sets out to trade upon the Free Food cry. Ramsay looks very ill & is certainly very overworked; the air is full of rumours of ministerial differences & of the possibility or probability of R.'s resignation; but though I should not be surprised if he broke down, I cannot bring myself to believe in his resignation. He really enjoys his position too much.

AC5/1/521

22 November 1930
58 Rutland Gate

[Typescript]
My dear Hilda,

. . .

It is too soon as yet to forecast the result of the Indian Conference, but such news as I get is not reassuring. The conservative elements of the Conference seem to have been carried away on the flood tide of the popular movement. The Princes, instead of affording a solid conservative groundwork, are obviously anxious not to place themselves in opposition to it and appear also to be very discontented by what I believe to be the well-founded and proper claim of the British Crown to 'paramountcy'. The Princes contend that the power of the Crown over them is confined strictly to the points covered by their treaties or agreements and that if a dispute arises between them and the Crown it should be decided by some arbitral court. The Government, on the other hand, following the Butler Commission, hold that the right to interpret treaties rests with the paramount Power and that its decision is final and conclusive.

I have had no opportunity of discussing this situation with Reading, but I can see that he is much disturbed about it and, to use his own words in an aside to me at luncheon the other day, 'the whole situation is altered'. The fact is that it was a mistake ever to convoke a conference of this kind and at this moment. We were so preoccupied by the greater mistake of proclaiming 'Dominion Status' as the goal that we allowed the idea of the Conference, already accepted by the Simon Commission, to pass without comment. This omission is, however, not of much consequence as the Viceroy and home Government were already committed up to the hilt and our protest would have been as useless as was the protest we made against the use of the phrase "Dominion Status."

I entirely agree with your views on the Education Bill. I am in any case opposed to raising the school age at the present time. But the payment of maintenance grants is not a question of opportunity but of principle ... We seem to be drifting into the notion that parents may bring children into the world without having any responsibility for them thereafter. I do not want to see a nation of foundlings.

[Handwritten] The European situation is steadily deteriorating. Franco-Italian relations & Franco-German relations are certainly worse than they were when we left office. In neither case, of course, were they any too good then, but I think that I did something to moderate the expression of differences which now clash directly without any buffer to absorb or divert the shock. As far as I can learn Henderson has failed to secure any position for himself & carries no weight in any quarter, & the loss of British influence & initiative is felt by all the nations. I have been carefully considering the desirability of initiating a general debate on the foreign situation & our foreign policy, but I am afraid to do so lest Henderson should make matters worse by his reply. I have no confidence that H. would give the right answer to my questions or even that he would understand what was involved in them.

AC5/1/522

30 November 1930
58 Rutland Gate

My dear Ida,

...

Baldwin who had made, as I thought, a very good speech to the Council of the National Union a week ago made one of his most futile speeches on the Vote of Censure. He sawed at his tough material with a blunt knife until I would have cried with weariness and vexation. I really had hoped that he was learning to fight but this speech was flabby & pointless throughout. It really is enough to break one's heart.

AC5/1/525   9 January 1931
                                          Little Compton Manor
                                   Moreton in Marsh, Gloucestershire

My dear Hilda,

    . . .
    I have had a quiet week ... disturbed only by Reading's volte-face &
complete surrender in the Indian Conference. Goodness knows what
will be the end of it all. It argues to me that, say what they may, Lloyd
George & the Liberal Party have been bought by the offer of the
alternative vote & are determined to throw all else overboard to keep
the Govt. in office & tho' Baldwin talks confidently of an early general
election I don't see how it is to be brought about ...

AC5/1/527   17 January 1931
                                              58 Rutland Gate

My dear Ida,

    . . .
    I have done nothing ... except dine at P. Sassoons with Horne &
Simon. We wished to put fire in the belly of the latter & my text was:
you are a great figure. I want you to be a great force. To be that, you
must do as my father did in '86: organise as well as speak. Horne
thinks, perhaps rightly, that he has the key to dissolution in his hands
if he will work.[80]

AC5/1/528   2 February 1931
                                              58 Rutland Gate

[Typescript]
My dear Ida,

    . . .
    I do not see much chance of getting the Government out whilst the
Liberals remain in their present mood. Unless their supporters in the
country put pressure on them it is pretty clear that they will do nothing
to risk a general election, although the longer they continue to support
the Socialist Government the more they will be tarred with that brush
and the less chance they will have of recovering their position.

[80] Part of a broader Conservative strategy to encourage the formation of a Liberal
National group to oust the Labour Government.

I thought that Ramsay's speech on Saturday showed signs of worry and strain, but his intention of staying in as long as he can is clear. He, too, is hoping that something may turn up to his advantage.

AC5/1/530

16 February 1931
Dalingridge Place

My dear Ida,

...

I am shocked by Worthington-Evan's sudden death. He had not been well for some time & had seemed very poorly the last few days, but I was completely taken by surprise when the news of the sudden end was telephoned yesterday. He was a very useful member of our counsels & personally a very good fellow tho' a bit of a bounder in manner. How my contemporaries & juniors are falling off!

I give up Lloyd George. His last speech was I think the most mischievious that he has ever made. He has of course always been heretical in matters of finance & currency, never having got below the surface of certain obvious difficulties & perhaps having a mind that is not capable of really grasping financial problems, but even that won't excuse the passion & prejudice he imported into Thursday's debate.[81] He has made the position of Snowden & Ramsay infinitely more difficult & become for the moment the hero but the untrusted hero of their discontented Back-Benchers. How a man like MacLean,[sic] who has always disliked & distrusted him, can bring himself now to support him passes my understanding. Misfortune makes strange bedfellows indeed.

AC5/1/532

28 February 1931
58 Rutland Gate

My dear Ida,

...

And so I run on any subject to avoid the most disagreeable theme of all, namely our own party's position. Here is the Government twice defeated in one afternoon, not by a snap vote but on important issues:

[81] On 11 February 1931 Snowden agreed to appoint a committee to recommend cuts in national expenditure (May Committee). Next day MacDonald apparently agreed to a scheme of national development while blurring the question of financing them Lloyd George welcomed the declaration and launched into a radical attack on the 'money barons' of the City to the satisfaction of the Labour left. *House of Commons Debates*, 5 Series, 248 cols. 725–33, 12 February 1931.

here are the discontents & divisions in their Party being steadily accentuated: here are the Liberals, themselves divided & sinking lower & lower in public estimation: and here are we unable to profit by all these favourable circumstances because S.B. is not a leader & nothing will ever make him one. I don't know how much Neville will care to write or feel able to say to you at this moment, but I think that a crisis is rapidly approaching & it would be a mistake now to do anything to defer it. S.B.'s leadership was always the 'accident of an accident'. Considering his total lack of many of the qualities which are ordinarily needed to bring a man even into the front rank, the largeness of his personal following in independent quarters & the considerable success which for a time he achieved were remarkable; but even more remarkable is the total slump which has followed. Noone so poor to do him reverence! Men who have most loyally supported him through thick & thin now declare him impossible. Agents say his name has ceased to be an asset & become a drawback. Lancashire has left him; Scotland no longer trusts him; in London his name stinks. Old contributors to the Party funds refuse to subscribe; officials are in despair. He has got to be told squarely what the situation is & invited to consider it & poor Neville has got to do the job. Never has any Party been more patient with incapacity; never has a man been given so many chances or pulled out of the water so many times; but I think that at last the end has come & that the Party will be forced to get rid of its own [sic] man of the sea if it is not prepared to be drowned by him. Neville has spoken to half a dozen colleagues – no to four, I think, myself included – and we all agree as to the facts. I have urged Neville to act at once. St George's is one degree worse than East Islington,[82] for the candidate comes out directly on the question of leadership & I believe it to be not unlikely that he will be successful. How sick it all makes me! And I am the more sick because I fear that Neville's immolation of himself on the Party altar has diminished his chances of the succession by withdrawing him from our debates & by identifying him with S.B. so much as to obscure his own personality.

---

[82] The Conservatives hoped to win East Islington on 19 February 1931 but the late intervention of a Crusade candidate pushed the Conservative into third place allowing Labour to win.

AC5/1/533

7 March 1931
Rowfant

My dear Hilda,

...

As to the general situation I feel as gloomy as you do. As far as I can gather S.B. is thoroughly bucked by the outcome of the Irwin-Gandhi negotiations[83] which he feels is a personal triumph for himself & he has reverted to his earlier idea that he will lead the Party to victory at the next election, skim the first two years cream off the new Parlt. & then hand over to a successor – a plan which to me seems to combine almost every possible vice if it could be carried through, but which I do not believe to be practicable. For granted that the turn in Indian affairs has dimmed Winston's glory or rather blunted his weapons & that S.B.'s position is better for the moment, I am certain that he cannot now regain his old authority & that before long there will be another slump in his stock. He may not sink for a time, but he is heavily waterlogged & he is pulling down all who stand around him. If he were competent to lead in the Commons or even knew how to work his team, there would be less talk about the Old Gang & inefficiency. I see no chance of an early election as things are going now; I don't know what would happen if there were one, and in any case I don't believe that S.B. can stay the course. Why, then, don't I speak out. You may well ask and the answer – a most unsatisfactory one – is because I don't see my way clear.

(i) As things now are, I can't tell what would happen if we had to choose a new leader. The Party has become so much divided that, although I believe that they would in present circumstances choose Hailsham, I am not sure they would really rally to him, or that his deputy in the House of C could hold the fort.

(ii) I am afraid of still further injuring Neville's position & indeed of definitely making his succession impossible;

(iii) I am told by some of those who know him best that nothing I might say at this moment would have any effect on S.B. who would be assured by Davidson & Willie Bridgeman that I had been got at by 'traitors' & represented nothing but the usual gang of backbiters, press gangsters and all that is selfish & corrupt in politics. S.B. really thinks that he is the standard bearer of 'Pure Politics' (his own phrase) & that his surrender would be the end of decency in public life.

---

[83] On 4 March the Viceroy and Gandhi signed an agreement in which the latter accepted the constitutional principles laid out at the Round Table Conference and agreed to attend when the sessions resumed. Civil disobedience was abandoned.

A pretty kettle of fish! I want to get N. out of the Central Office & don't see how to do even that just now.

"There is nothing to do but go into a corner & say d— d— Damn!" to quote the great Sir William.

AC5/1/534   13 March 1931
                                                      58 Rutland Gate

My dear Ida,

...

... After ascertaining from Neville that as far as he knew S.B. meant to stay on till he was forced out, I enquired of S.B. at our Wednesday business meeting when Neville who, as I understood, had now done the special work he went to the Central Office to do, was going to be released for his natural duties on the Front Bench, remarking that we had lost Winston & Worthington-Evans & were deprived of N.'s help, with some further observations which I fear S.B. did not like! S.B. replied that he had not thought about this & I retorted that he ought to have done. S.B. said he & Neville must discuss it.

N. said afterwards that he was not sure that I had helped him. Well I don't know; at least I brought things to a head & spoke only after carefully weighing up the pro's & cons largely influenced by Ivy's strong feeling, which I shared, that S.B. would take all he could get with little or no gratitude & complete egotism. He is so made.

Anyway S.B. did open the matter with N. today. N. told me that he had perceived that an East wind had been blowing every since he had sent S.B. Topping's memo[84] & that he was considering sending in his resignation to S.B. before I spoke. Today S.B. asked him if he wished to resign; he replied yes. S.B. expressed no word of regret or of thanks for work done & merely asked if N. had thought about what was to be done then, & who could be his successor. N. was prepared for that & suggested names. He told S.B. that he had written a letter for him & will send that letter tomorrow. I believe that he has already told you of the conversation which Davidson had with one of N.'s people at the CO & which D. specially desired to have repeated to N. Its gist was that S.B. felt that he had not been properly supported by Hailsham in particular & his other colleagues in general! It is difficult to be patient. I have definitely come to the conclusion that, unless there is a very

---

[84] Sir Robert Topping, Conservative Principal Agent, produced a brutally uncompromising memorandum on 26 February 1931 reporting that support for Baldwin's leadership had declined so dramatically since October that even his most loyal personal followers now shared the widespread view that 'in the interests of the party ... the Leader should reconsider his position'.

early election, S.B. cannot stay the course & that the sooner he goes the better. If he consults or challenges me, I shall tell him so. Only Beaverbrook & Rothermere prevent me from volunteering it. Indeed N. warned me off – he says S.B. is in no mood to listen to me & that I should merely anger him without any chance of persuading him. So that is how things stand at the moment.

S.B. made the best speech he has ever made in the Indian debate. If he had ever put a fraction of the power & passion which he shows when rebuking his own followers into his attacks on the government, we should not be in the difficulties we now are. He had a success but a success which will rankle, I fear, in too many hearts. He is incurably clumsy.

AC5/1/535

21 March 1931
58 Rutland Gate

My dear Hilda,

Well, as Rosebery once began a speech, & what do you think of it all? I don't find it very satisfactory. S.B.'s stock is up again, but I don't believe he can keep it up. His speech at the Queen's Hall[85] has pleased people, as far as I can judge, because for once he showed fight, but the figures in St Georges don't show any enthusiasm among Conservatives & do show that there are a lot of people who will vote for anything for a change. I still feel that Messrs R & B would leave him alone, he would fall of himself, & even with their help I doubt his being able to stand up for long. The truth is that he has no House of Commons gifts, can't debate or think or act quickly & always addresses the Prime Minister as if he were a Lower School boy who had undertaken to voice the discontent of his comrades & knew that he would be swished before he got out of the room. And with it all, he is so terribly complacent & talks more than ever of 'my' government, 'my' young men & what I I I will do till he makes me sick.

. . .

You will have heard from Neville all about his letter to & conversations with S.B. Nothing could have been less gracious than the latter's attitude; though I think this is more inability than purpose, it does spring in part from his being so self-centred & self-satisfied that he receives all we give him as a matter of course & takes offence at the

---

[85] At the Queen's Hall, Westminster on 17 March 1931, two days before the St George's poll Baldwin turned on the Press Lords and their 'engines of propaganda' declaring 'what the proprietorship of these papers is aiming at is power, and power without responsibility – the prerogative of the harlot throughout the ages'.

least sign that we are not completely at his service for whatever use he likes to make of us. To tell the truth I am 'fed up' with him & his ways. There I've said it, & I feel better now!

Although the St George's by-election effectively brought to an end eighteen months of leadership crisis, Chamberlain still remained gloomy about the prospects of a return to office. At the end of 1930 he was vaguely consoled by the rumours of dissension, intrigue and crisis in the government ranks but he was prepared to go no further than to say that there was 'plenty of ground for speculation, but none for prophesy'.[86] By the end of June 1931 he still believed the government would remain in office for another two years. Even in late July he still refused to place any faith in the now insistent rumours of an autumn dissolution and appears to have been completely unaware of the discussion about a National Government.[87] Within ten days he would be consulted by his half-brother about the Party's response if a coalition were proposed by a desperate Labour Government.

In the interim, Chamberlain became involved once more in the disarmament issue. On 4 February 1931 the Cabinet established an important committee under Henderson to recommend policy on disarmament with an eye to the forthcoming Geneva conference. Two days later, MacDonald approached Lloyd George about the possibility of framing all-party proposals and the latter suggested a C.I.D. sub-committee to consider the question. A month later Baldwin had nominated Austen Chamberlain, Hoare and Eden to represent the Conservatives.[88] In its ten meetings between 18 March and 15 July Chamberlain played a prominent role in the Three-Party Sub-Committee's work.[89]

AC5/1/537   25 April 1931
                                                  58 Rutland Gate

My dear Ida,

          . . .

Are you wondering what the Budget will disclose? Beyond taxes on land values I feel that nothing is certain & none of us can conceive what the alternative of the usual form of notice or the extra day allowed for discussion portend. Neville has asked me to 'stand by' for Thursday & I have of course promised to do so, though with no enthusiasm for the

---

[86] A. Chamberlain to Mary Carnegie, 18 November 1930, AC4/1/1304.

[87] Neville Chamberlain Diary, 24 July 1931. Also A. Chamberlain to Hilda, 11 July 1931, AC5/1/547.

[88] Baldwin to MacDonald, 12 March 1931, Baldwin MSS 129/47. Hailsham was later added to balance the numbers.

[89] For the Sub-Committee's work S. Roskill, *Hankey*, II, 538–40.

task. I intended never to have anything more to do with Treasury business. To have made five Budget statements & criticised ten glutted my appetite for that kind of business.

Foreign affairs look very bad again. I fear that the Franco-Italian naval agreement has gone west. The Austro-German Customs Union & the manner & moment of its announcement have set France's nerves jangling again, shaken Briand's position badly & left Europe more uneasy than at any moment since Locarno. Henderson hurried back from Rome too soon. A couple more days work on drafting then might have saved him much subsequent disappointment & ill-success, but the Govt. use him so much for Party & Home politics that he has not time for foreign affairs. 'I don't see how he can do his work' I said to Craigie[90] who answered: 'He doesn't do it!'. They would be glad to have a minister again who would give himself to his office.

I don't believe in a dissolution this year though I think Neville still does.

AC5/1/538

2 May 1931
58 Rutland Gate

My dear Hilda,

...

Neville did well both in his few remarks of the first Budget day & his considered criticism of the second day. His speeches are always full of meat, well dressed & cleanly served & both Annie & I are agreed that this session he is using his voice better than ever before. I no longer detect the slight whine in it which used to weaken the effect & tended to make his serious criticism sound querelous.

AC5/1/541

n.d. [early June?] 1931
Hartsholme Hall
Lincoln

My dear Ida,

...

I entirely agree with you about the Insurance Report[91] but what shall

---

[90] Sir Robert Leslie Craigie (1883–1959). Diplomat. Counsellor at F.O. 1928–34: Assistant Under-Secretary of State 1934–37; Ambassador to Japan 1937–41; UK representative on United Nations War Crimes Commission 1945–48.

[91] On 4 June 1931 the Interim Report of the Royal Commission on Unemployment Insurance (Cmd. 3872) recommended increased contributions and reduced benefits.

we do I know not. S.B.'s one firm conviction is that we should wait & see. He really gets upon my nerves. He is useless in council & useless in the House. Whether he is doing any good with his meetings I don't know. He shows no signs of bearing malice for what I said to him, but what his feelings about us really are neither I nor any of his colleagues know.

AC5/1/542

12 June 1931
58 Rutland Gate

My dear Hilda,

I seem to have spent a busy week & yet not to have accomplished anything. I have had a lot of stuff to read on the subject of disarmament for the subcommittee of the Comtee of Imperial Defence on which the Three Parties are represented, & the more I read & hear the less do I see any way through the difficulties. I am promising myself some fun from the conflict between the quite impracticable views of Lloyd George & the more sober appreciation of possibilities on the part of the Govt. I also think that I detect some difference of opinion between Henderson & the Service Ministers but hitherto we have only gathered information ... It's an awful tangle.

As to the Budget, I have really taken no part, for there was in fact no room for me as well as Neville in the very brief periods allowed for discussion, but I did intervene for a few moments late on Thursday to do what S.B. ought to have done but is, I fear, incapable of doing. It is so terribly true, as Balfour once said to me that a man who can't debate is 'no use' in the H. of C. & Stanley can't debate & what is more won't try. A debater is made not born & for all the effort he makes might just as well be in Kamschatka. Why, Annie is reported to have asked, does our dear leader always lick the Order paper when his colleagues are speaking? Why indeed? The moment is ill-chosen & it is a nasty habit in any case.

I agree with you that an advertised crisis never becomes a crisis. Sooner or later the formula will be found & the compromise patched up & having asserted their 'independence' the Liberals will troop into the Govt. lobby. So I see the events of Tuesday next, but the Dole report might tempt the Govt. to a dissolution if the Liberals were too exigent in the hope that they could saddle on us the odium of the Comtees recommendations. Of course we are not yet provided with a policy thanks to S.B.'s invincible inertia & reluctance to take decisions or allow others to do so. However, there is now a committee at work on the subject. In short we behave like the Govt. – postpone all action as long as possible & then refer to a committee!

AC5/1/543

21 June 1931
58 Rutland Gate

My dear Ida,

...

N & I & some other people are excessively nervous as to what S.B. will say tomorrow on the Insurance question. We have done our best to prime him, but we don't know whether he has understood what was said to him whilst, even if he has understood & tries to do the right thing, there is no certainty that he will succeed. He is so unhandy where any delicacy is needed in treating a situation. I think the Govt. are in for another two years.

I was rung up at 1.30 a.m. to say something about Hoover's assent to postpone debt payments for a year ... I am not going to gush over the 'generosity' of a belated act of common sense dictated by self-interest & nothing short of admiring gush would meet the American appetite.

...

I am not pleased with the way the C.I.D. Sub Comtee. is going. The P.M. swung suddenly round to Ll. G.'s point of view last Friday. We decided nothing & don't meet again for a fortnight by which time Ll. G. is to have put something into writing. I may see my way more clearly then. At present I am bothered. The P.M. & Ll. G. seem more concerned to make a splash than to do business; if they do just what they appear to wish, Europe will be more disturbed than ever instead of being pacified. They seem bent on pulling the lynch-pin out of the coach.

AC5/1/544

26 June 1931
58 Rutland Gate

My dear Hilda,

...

The week has been a bad one both for the Govt. & the Liberals. Snowden was over-ruled by the Cabinet & took it out of the Liberals whose measure he has taken & whose noses he rubbed in the dirt. They had to swallow the peck of dirt he administered to them but it has given them indigestion though not courage. They are now going to 'stand firm' on an amendment which the Govt. would not treat as vital even if they were defeated upon it. Neville has done very well. S.B. has actually taken the trouble to say to him & has urged him to take a week's holiday as soon as the Budget is over. I wish he would, but he only replies that he has so many engagements.

AC5/1/545   3 July 1931
                                                         58 Rutland Gate

My dear Ida,

...

Yes, a lot of people are talking of an autumn dissolution. Don't believe them! The P.M. doesn't mean to go out, Henderson wants to stick in; & the majority of the Liberals dare not let go of the plank to which they cling. It may not be two years but it won't be this year.

AC5/1/547   11 July 1931
                                                         58 Rutland Gate

My dear Hilda,

...

... You will have seen that I was moved to address a letter to the Times, published this morning, on [foreign affairs]. The Times had a first rate leader two days ago & I thought it would not be a bad thing to drive home their point. The Germans are unchanged; they give the world every reason to distrust them & we in this country are far too prone to forget what they were & overlook what they remain. I fear that my letter will be read with some anger in Berlin & some pleasure in Paris, but the things I said needed saying & will do no harm. My hope is that they may do some good.

People go on talking about an election in the autumn, but I don't see why there should be one & don't believe in it.... .

The Belgian Ambassador has just rung up to thank me for my letter in most complimentary terms & the French Ambassador has sent a note round by hand for the same purpose. I have *not* heard from the German!

AC5/1/548   18 July 1931
                                                         58 Rutland Gate

My dear Ida,

...

We have finished our Disarmament Committee, at any rate for the present, & agreed upon a statement of principles which has received the approval of our Conservative colleagues. The curious thing about it is that from first to last the Govt. members of the Comtee. have not contributed a single word – literally not a single word – to the statement. How do they do their work when they are alone? We were impressed by Alexander's[92] good sense & grasp. Henderson was all blether & mush & very angry when the P.M. sided with me on a very important point against him. Lloyd George became more & more reasonable as we proceeded & preferred my drafts on several points to Bob Cecil's. Shaw[93] joined the 'mushy' group; Amulree[94] seldom broke his silence & the P.M. hovered over the discussions occasionally criticising, vague but sensible, but never constructive. At one point I suggested that he should draft a proposal for our consideration as the words I & others had produced had led to a good deal of criticism by himself & others, but he only replied that he had tried & it wasn't easy!

...

Parliament has been uninteresting except for the revolt of the Left Wing on the Anomalies Bill.[95] It contains some good speakers & granted their premisses [sic] – which were those of the whole Labour Party at the General Election – their case was unanswerable. The speeches were bitter & feeling runs high.

AC5/1/549

25 July 1931
58 Rutland Gate

My dear Hilda,

My blessed constituents have decided that this year for the first time in their politically associated lives that they will make an excursion to London when their member will show them the Houses of Parliament, they will visit the Tower, feed with the lions at the Zoo & in short make a day of it. Needless to say they forgot to tell me ... till all their

---

[92] Albert Victor Alexander (1885–1965) Labour MP for Sheffield Hillsborough 1922–31, 1935–50. Parliamentary Secretary to Board of Trade 1924; First Lord of Admiralty 1929–31, 1940–45, 1945–6; Minister without Portfolio 1946; Minister of Defence 1946–50; Chancellor Duchy of Lancaster 1950–51; Labour Leader in Lords 1955–64. Created Viscount Alexander of Hillsborough 1950, Earl 1963, K.G. 1964.

[93] Thomas Shaw (1872–1938) Labour MP for Preston 1918–31. Minister of Labour 1924; Secretary for War 1929–31.

[94] William Warrender MacKenzie (1860–1942) Secretary for Air 1930–31. Created Kt 1926, Baron Amulree 1929.

[95] The need for applicants for uncovenanted benefit to prove they were 'genuinely seeking work' was abolished on 13 March 1930. Rapid growth in the number of claimants after the repeal of the test – particularly among married women – led to the Anomalies Act of July 1931 empowering the Minister to draft regulations governing claims from married women, seasonal, casual and short-time workers. Although bitterly contested by the ILP in Parliament it had a dramatic effect on these groups – particularly the former.

arrangements & mine were made. They can't change theirs, so I must change mine. Bang goes our passage in the Empress of Britain to Quebec, bang goes our hoped for week at the farm with William & Louise! We shall sail instead in the Sesargovia on Sept 26th direct for New York & I shall plunge into my work as soon as I arrive. It is exasperating is it not? but I can't afford to offend them.

... The London Conference[96] has come & gone; a respite has been secured but no problem has been resolved & none seems nearer solution. Two gleams of light I see – first the growing perception in America that her problems are locked with ours & the growing courage of leading Americans in saying so & secondly the rapprochment between the French & German ministers. Something may come of both these factors &, if it does, I think it must be for the better.

I did not see Briand, but I hear that he is very aged & broken & his influence terribly diminished. He does not sleep at night & kept dropping off at the Conference table. It makes me very sad to think of him.

Neville confided to me yesterday the news which he has gathered as to conditions in the City, Budget prospects & political possibilities. It is all as gloomy as possible. The times are indeed out of joint & I do not see the man to set them right.

AC5/1/550   2 August 1931
                                                  58 Rutland Gate

My dear Ida,

...

The dinner at Neville's was very interesting – Hailsham, Sam Hoare, Cunliffe Lister & our two selves – to hear Neville's story of what had been passing behind the scenes & to consider what we should do if a coalition were proposed. Of course, no definite decision was or could be taken, but we 'explored the avenues' – what a detestable phrase! – & exchanged ideas. Nobody liked the idea, nobody thought it probable, but Sam & I were convinced that the Govt. *could* not do what is necessary even with our support if that support were given from outside; & the more I think about it, the more I doubt whether we could fight the battle successfully against the whole Labour Party – electorally I mean. But I would far rather see us shut out from office

---

[96] London Seven-Power Conference, 20–23 July 1931. After the failure of discussions in Paris on 18 July to provide a collective loan to Germany, Henderson hoped a full-scale international conference would produce a plan for financial relief for Germany. The Conference broke down because of French attempts to impose unacceptable political terms in return for financial aid.

than winning office by pledges that would be the ruin of both the country and ourselves.

Well, the next move is with the Govt. I don't envy them their task or their thoughts.

12

'I AM GOING THROUGH A MENTAL HELL'

Political crisis and the Admiralty, August – December 1931

Austen Chamberlain did not play a significant role in the events leading up to the political crisis or the decision to form a National Government on 24 August 1931. The eventual outcome of those developments, however, delivered a bitter blow to his self-esteem and marked a major watershed in his career. Had the Conservatives won the 1929 election, Chamberlain believed Baldwin would have returned him to the Foreign Office as he had promised.[1] He continued to nurture this expectation throughout the period in Opposition. Even after being struck forcibly by the 'violent animus against the "Old Gang"' and the very specific attacks upon his foreign policy in Egypt and China at the Caxton Hall meeting in October 1930, he still consoled himself with the thought that none of his colleagues were excluded from criticism; that the critics consisted mainly of reactionary, disreputable or disgruntled groups (often all three) without 'many young men of a decent type'; and that such grousing was symptomatic of the frustration engendered by Baldwin's lack of leadership and a natural impatience for youth to have its chance. As a result, he remained content to believe that not only did he still have much to contribute in foreign affairs but that there was no one else with a comparable claim to the portfolio.[2]

Chamberlain appears genuinely to have been unaware of the substantial hostility towards his return to the Foreign Office which had existed in 1929 and had grown substantially thereafter. According to Tom Jones, 'Austen's announcement in Birmingham that S.B. had promised him the Foreign Secretaryship again if returned to office had sent a wave of depression, not only through the ranks of Labour, but of moderate Liberals, and many Conservatives'.[3] At the same time, Bridgeman's election travels left him 'quite surprised at the universal dislike amongst our party of our foreign policy and of Austen',[4] while in October Neville informed his sisters how 'unpleasantly surprised' he had been to find 'how quickly his [brother's] popularity in the party has been dissipated'.[5] A year later Bridgeman's loyalty to Baldwin

---

[1] Jones Diary, 5 March 1929, *Whitehall Diary*, II, 174; Neville Chamberlain Diary, 11 March 1929. Bridgeman was sceptical about Baldwin's intentions, but there is no other confirmation. Bridgeman Diary, July 1929, Bridgeman MSS II fol.173.

[2] A. Chamberlain to Ida, 2 November 1930, AC5/1/519.

[3] Jones Diary, 20 June 1929, *Whitehall Diary*, II, 191. See also W. Steed, *The Real Stanley Baldwin*, 108.

[4] Bridgeman Diary, July 1929, II fol.173. Also Amery to Baldwin, 11 March 1929, Lady Asquith to Baldwin, 2 June 1929, Baldwin MSS 36/90, 221; 'Character Sketches of the 1924–29 Cabinet', n.d. (1955–58) Templewood MSS XX(A)5, 17.

[5] N. Chamberlain to Hilda, 13 October 1929, NC18/1/672.

undoubtedly encouraged him to exaggerate when he claimed that almost all of the criticism at the Caxton Hall was directed at Austen and that he was 'the greatest factor in making S.B. and our party unpopular'.[6] *Nonetheless, even Neville Chamberlain was convinced that after Joynson-Hicks and Churchill, his half-brother was one of the central causes of discontent about 'Old Gang' domination.*[7] *Such feelings represented a major obstacle to his return to the Foreign Office after 1929 in even the best of circumstances. Chamberlain's scarcely veiled contempt for Baldwin's leadership culminating in his efforts to extricate Neville from Central Office in mid-March could not have helped his claims either.*[8]

In the event, the constraints imposed by the decision to form a National Cabinet with only ten members, drawn from across the parliamentary spectrum, precluded any realistic hope of a return to the Foreign Office. At first, Austen acknowledged that it was simply impossible to 'have two Chamberlains out of four' Conservatives in Cabinet. He was also determined not to accept office for only a few weeks if Baldwin had already resolved to drop him after the election – not least because of the disastrous implications this would have on his personal finances. At this stage Baldwin told Neville Chamberlain that 'he would like to have a younger man at the F.O. (I suppose Irwin) but that, without binding himself, what he would like would be to have [Austen] as Lord President with a Peerage leading the Lords'. At 6.30pm on 24 August Austen Chamberlain was prepared to consider the offer, but only in the Commons. It was, after all, 'a post of high dignity (Balfour's last) with interesting and important duties attaching to it'. He adamantly refused, however, to countenance one of the 'minor administrative offices which would be much better bestowed on a younger man'.[9] *After much flattery from Baldwin and the assurance that ministers would not have to give up their directorships, by the middle of the next day he had accepted precisely such a post as First Lord of the Admiralty: an ironic choice less because it had been his first government office in 1895 than because at the Foreign Office 'anything which an Admiral said always irritated him, & the expression of any strong opinion by the Sea Lords was a red rag to him'.*[10]

At this stage Chamberlain appeared to be resigned to his duty. He was aware that his refusal would be construed as 'sulking'. His half-brother had also urged him strongly to accept on the grounds that he had much to contribute in council and his 'name alone, especially abroad, was worth much'. Moreover, the government might last longer than anticipated and once out, he would be out for good and soon forgotten. Even Baldwin had done his bit to reconcile Chamberlain by putting the offer 'as nicely as it could be put' and later offering him the Privy Seal as an office

---

[6] Bridgeman to Davidson, 2 November 1930, R.R. James, *Memoirs of a Conservative*, 352.

[7] N. Chamberlain to Bridgeman, 18 November 1930, NC8/10/16b. Also Amery Diary, 6, 9 November 1930, *The Empire at Bay*, 87, 89.

[8] For Chamberlain's recognition of this factor see A. Chamberlain to Ida, 11 October 1931, AC5/1/560. Given Baldwin's treatment of Hailsham against whom he felt particularly bitterly in March this seems more than plausible.

[9] A. Chamberlain to Ivy, 24 August 1931, AC6/1/801.

[10] Bridgeman Diary, November 1929, Bridgeman MSS II fol.189.

of higher dignity when Hailsham refused it.[11] *Unfortunately, by the following day this mood of resigned acceptance had been transformed into one of indignant affront at his invidious position and having been used. This stinging sense of resentment, and the deep personal 'humiliation' which accompanied it, continued to seethe for several days and increasingly came to find expression in the old animus and contempt towards Baldwin. In an angry letter to Hilton Young, written almost a week after accepting the Admiralty, Chamberlain still confessed that 'I can't keep my own bitterness & sense of having made a* useless *sacrifice out of my letter': a worthless gesture made at financial cost to his family which had left him nothing more than a 'cypher.'*[13] *Perhaps the most moving demonstration of this distress came during a 'rather painful' and depressing family dinner with Neville and his step-mother. In an already 'very emotional condition' Austen had 'burst out that he was humiliated and treated as a back number'. As Neville later informed his wife, as he did so Austen's 'lips trembled and tears came into his eyes and altogether he made us all very unhappy and uncomfortable'.*[14]

The intensity of such a response was the product of a combination of factors beyond simply disappointment at not having obtained an office for which he still believed he was uniquely qualified. First, a rational recognition of the constraints imposed by the National nature of the Cabinet did not preclude the deeper conviction that Baldwin could have striven harder to obtain the post had he really wished. His fury at Baldwin's failure to do anything on behalf of Peel, Hilton Young, Eden and others was thus a manifestation of the deeper belief that 'if S.B. had been different I should have been there as Foreign Secretary'. Second, the disappointment was rendered doubly unpalatable by the fact that his claim had been sacrificed not for one of MacDonald's supporters but for a Liberal.[15] *The concession of the Foreign Office was particularly galling when it was announced that the Liberal in question was none other than Lord Reading. Having been led to believe that he was being passed over to enable a younger Conservative like Irwin to go to the Foreign Office, the appointment of a Liberal who was both older and far less experienced than himself undoubtedly rankled bitterly.*[16] *At another level Chamberlain must also have been oppressed by the realisation that such an offer represented a final token gesture to an 'old party hack' at the end of his ministerial career. Moreover, given the unpopularity of the government's economy programme and the narrowness of his majority in 1929, Chamberlain also recognised that involvement might well signal the end of his parliamentary career as well.*[17]

Beyond all of these factors, the most likely explanation for the sheer intensity of his emotional state was the sense of personal, rather than purely political, humiliation

---

[11] A. Chamberlain to Ivy, 25, 26 August 1931, AC6/1/802–3.

[13] A. Chamberlain to Hilton Young, 31 August 1931, Kennet MSS 15/2/a.

[14] N. Chamberlain to Annie, 29 August 1931, NC1/26/452.

[15] A. Chamberlain to Ivy, 27 August 1931, AC6/1/802.

[16] For his low initial opinion of Reading see A. Chamberlain to Ivy, 3–4 September 1931, AC6/1/809,810.

[17] A. Chamberlain to Ida, 31 August 1931, AC5/1/551.

he experienced. As in the past, Chamberlain had prepared a secret code to keep his wife informed of developments. In the event, the code did not reach her and his telegram to Aberdeenshire informing her 'I am returning to my first love' she wrongly interpreted to mean not the Admiralty (his first government position) but rather in a more literal sense, the Foreign Office. She thus wrote congratulating him, noting that she knew Baldwin would not let him down.[18] As Neville later noted, ultimately it was this misunderstanding which led his half-brother to feel so deeply humiliated. 'I am sure it is because he feels himself lowered in her eyes that he has made himself so miserable', Neville wrote to his wife. 'Of course he does absurdly exaggerate the position but there is enough truth in his idea to make it very galling and I hate his being so unhappy about it'.[19]

Unfortunately Chamberlain's ten week tenure of the Admiralty was to prove a rather turbulent end to his ministerial career. Although when offered a choice he believed 'the Admiralty with some duties was preferable to the Privy Seal with none',[20] he soon found the department effectively ran itself, leaving the minister with a life of idleness and less than an hour's work each day.[21] Yet at precisely the same time as Chamberlain was enjoying the fruits of this official leisure by watching the Schneider Cup from the flight deck of HMS Courageous at Portsmouth, 'an extraordinary succession of administrative blunders' in the handling of the pay cuts for naval personnel proposed by the May Committee provoked the Atlantic fleet to 'mutiny' at Invergordon.[22]

On 15 September news of the cuts prompted the majority of crews on the larger ships to refuse to sail for exercises. Next day, support spread and the acting-Commander of the Atlantic fleet warned that the situation might get 'entirely out of control'. Chamberlain presented the situation to Cabinet on 16 September, at which the First Sea Lord's face-saving formula was adopted and all ships were instructed to return to their home ports to permit cases of hardship to be investigated.[23] Although this defused the situation, information subsequently reached the Cabinet on 21 September that the returning crews intended to repeat the Invergordon action at their home ports, with the likelihood that 'very serious rioting would ultimately result and the revolt might induce other classes of the community to join in'.[24] In the absence of any effective means of enforcing discipline, the Cabinet resolved to pre-empt the action by reducing the cuts to 'not more than 10 per cent' for the Navy as part of

[18] A. Chamberlain to Ivy, 24, 25 August 1931, AC6/1/801–2.

[19] N. Chamberlain to Annie, 29 August 1931, NC1/26/452. Also A. Chamberlain to Ivy, 24 and 25 August 1931, AC6/1/801–2.

[20] A. Chamberlain to Ivy, 26 August 1931, AC6/1/803.

[21] A. Chamberlain to Ivy, 4 and 27 September 1931, AC6/1/810, 813.

[22] S. Roskill, Hankey, II, 555. For the mutiny see S. Roskill, Naval Policy Between the Wars (2 vols, London 1968–1976), II, Chapter 4; D. Divine Mutiny at Invergordon (1970); A. Ereira, The Invergordon Mutiny (1981). The latter is extremely hostile to Chamberlain and the Admiralty generally.

[23] CAB 56(31)3, 16 September 1931, CAB 23/68.

[24] Admiralty summary quoted in D. Divine, Mutiny at Invergordon, 16–17.

another face-saving formula to include all three Services, teachers and the police.[25] Chamberlain was essentially correct in asserting that this was essentially 'a "down tools" movement by men who were really frightened for their wives & homes & who were swept off their feet by the suddenness & severity of the cuts ... On the whole good men gone wrong'.[26] In his eagerness to play down the whole affair, however, he concealed even from his family the more ominous facts of the case. As Hankey noted after it was all over, 'it's no use blinkering the fact that the Cabinet yielded to force and that it was a mutiny'.[27]

Chamberlain's responsibility for these events has been the subject of dispute. Petrie has been content to relieve Chamberlain of all blame, depicting the mutiny as 'his misfortune, not his fault': the 'logical sequel to a series of blunders on the part of various people at the Admiralty, and of these blunders the disruptive element took advantage'.[28] Conversely, Dutton follows Roskill in placing some of the blame firmly on the Minister's shoulders both for the crisis and its unfortunate personal consequences for many of those involved.[29] In mitigation it is fair to note that Chamberlain was poorly briefed by the Board of Admiralty on the implications of these decisions on pay. By an unfortunate series of misfortunes, he also confronted the crisis with little experienced or competent support. The Permanent Secretary had been at the Admiralty since 1897 but was absent throughout the entire crisis and the colourless First Sea Lord was in hospital with pleurisy during the main crisis. For the rest, Lord Stanhope the experienced Junior Minister considered the Board 'far the worst I have ever served with'.[30] The Board can also be rightly arraigned on a number of other counts − not least, the failure to acquaint itself with the effect of such cuts or to take note of warnings about feeling on the lower deck.[31]

Yet it would also be fair to observe that given Chamberlain's resentful state of mind and his frequent references to the lack of work at an office he considered a political backwater, there must be something in the allegation that the minister probably did not devote to the Admiralty all the political skill, leadership or attention of which he was capable. Indeed, quite the reverse. His whole attitude towards the summoning of the Board was extremely relaxed and until the crisis actually broke he does not appear to have made any effort to become aware of the seriousness of the decisions already taken.[32] Chamberlain's admission that the Board was not free from blame but that it is 'so easy to be wise afterwards' would thus not appear to be

[25] For details of these deliberations see Hankey Diary, 20 and 26 September 1931, Hankey MSS 1/7 fol.27-8.

[26] A. Chamberlain to Mary Carnegie, 27 September 1931, AC4/1/1312. His official account in the Admiralty record also excised any reference to the perceived threat of further trouble.

[27] Hankey Diary, 26 September 1931, Hankey MSS 1/7, fol.27.

[28] C. Petrie, The Chamberlain Tradition, 198; Life and Letters, II, 382.

[29] S. Roskill, Naval Policy Between the Wars I, 38; II, 92-3.

[30] Stanhope to Admiral Sir John Kelly, 3 September 1931, D. Divine Mutiny at Invergordon, 86-7. Stanhope had also been Civil Lord 1924-29.

[31] For the full indictment see D. Divine Mutiny at Invergordon, 204-13.

[32] Ibid, 85, 88.

entirely satisfactory. The Board may have been misled by the absence of existing discontent about pay rates. They may also have lacked sample budgets to quantify the magnitude of the effects upon ratings and their families. Yet the handling and timing of the May Committee's cuts and the decision to remove a further £2M from the 1932–33 Estimate also demonstrated more than a little insensitivity on the part of the minister, as well as his officials and the Board – particularly when what was proposed amounted to not only a breach of contract but also (by the Admiralty's own estimate) in some cases to a reduction of 25 per cent in basic pay.[33] Chamberlain has also been criticised for the pledge in the Commons on 17 September that there would be no looking back and 'no penalisation': a decision which ensured that a great many officers and men were subsequently dismissed from the service denied even the ordinary Common Law right to explain and defend their actions.[34]

The crisis soon passed, but not before the Gold Standard was hastily suspended on 21 September. With the fleet 'quickly ... back into apple pie order',[35] Chamberlain was returned to relative obscurity, leaving him a frustrated observer on the edges of the action. In his verdicts upon subsequent events, Chamberlain expresses what were to become the commonplaces of Conservative asperity. MacDonald was 'a poor shivering mannikin' incapable of decisive action to resolve Cabinet differences for fear of being portrayed as a 'mere puppet of the Tories'.[36] True to type, Baldwin initially proved that his 'incapacity and uselessness are beyond belief' but then uncharacteristically went on to impress.[37] Samuel was always a 'slippery twisting eel' to be despised and mistrusted.[38] As the prospects of an election loomed, Chamberlain looked forward to the possibility of destroying not only socialism but also Samuel and his section of the Liberal Party. In the event, he was not to be disappointed. Having modestly hoped to regain three or four of the six seats lost in Birmingham in 1929, Chamberlain was delighted when they made a clean sweep of all twelve in a landslide which also swept every Labour candidate and all but two Liberals from the Chamberlainite West Midland fiefdom.[39]

Yet this victory also marked the end of the ministerial phase in Chamberlain's long career. Never able to come to terms with his position as 'a glorified Under-Secretary' and what this implied for the future, Chamberlain affected to believe that having done his duty he could 'walk out with dignity and contentment'.[40] Confident that neither Baldwin nor MacDonald would have him at the Foreign Office, and assuming that Reading would inevitably retain it, well before the election Chamberlain had already virtually decided not to take office again. In so doing he expected to

[33] *Ibid,* 17, 89–90, 99–100. For his defence see A. Chamberlain to Ida, 26 September 1931, AC5/1/555.

[34] S. Roskill, *Hankey,* II, 557–8.

[35] A. Chamberlain to Mary Carnegie, 27 September 1931, AC4/1/1312.

[36] A. Chamberlain to Ivy, 5 October 1931, AC6/1/824.

[37] A. Chamberlain to Ivy, 28 August and 7 October 1931, AC6/1/806, 825.

[38] A. Chamberlain to Ivy, 14 October 1931, AC6/1/835.

[39] K.W.D. Rolf, 'Tories, Tariffs and Elections'.

[40] A. Chamberlain to Ivy, 2 October 1931, AC6/1/820.

relieve his increasingly parlous financial circumstances while avoiding the indignity of remaining in an invidious position of declining influence.[41] *On the day after the poll he wrote to Baldwin from Birmingham waiving any claim to office in favour of younger men.*[42] *When he learned that Reading had been replaced by Simon at the Foreign Office, he was obviously shaken and clearly wished he had still been available, but it was too late.*[43] *When news of his withdrawal became public there was some consolation in the flood of tributes both to a great career and an action which, in the King's words, was 'in harmony with the public spirit and self-sacrifice which have always characterised [his] career'.*[44] *In reality this selflessness was also accompanied by the belief that his self-denial would make Neville's claim to the Treasury irresistible. When this proved to be so, the older brother's response was genuinely heart-felt: 'That you should be C/E at this moment of all others', he wrote on 5 November, 'gives me the deepest satisfaction'.*[45]

I was the first Chancellor to introduce in a very humble way Imperial Preference into a Budget. You will be the Chancellor to complete the building of which I laid the first brick in 1919. Father's great work will be completed in his children. Then I shall be ready to sing my Nunc Dimittis whenever my time comes.

Don't think me absurd or pretentious if I say that I feel something for your success of what Father thought of mine. It is something more than a brotherly interest, it is an immense love and a possessive pride.

Almost thirty years since Joseph Chamberlain had first raised the banner of tariff reform, his successors were within three months of the fulfilment of an ever-present vision.

AC5/1/551

31 August 1931
United University Club

My dear Ida,

... I am going through a mental hell & must work my way out somehow for myself, but it is not easy. I have never yet refused my help when it was needed & asked, & I did not like to do so – felt I could not, must not – on this occasion. But I am put where a dozen or so men could do my disagreeable work equally well & where I am

---

[41] A. Chamberlain to Ida, 11 October 1931, AC5/1/560; to Ivy, 2–3 October 1931, AC6/1/820–1.

[42] A. Chamberlain to Baldwin, 28 October 1931, Baldwin MSS 45/188.

[43] Avon, *Facing the Dictators*, 22.

[44] King George V to A. Chamberlain, 6 November 1931, H. Nicolson, *King George V*, 495. See also *The Times* (leader), 4 November 1931.

[45] A. Chamberlain to N. Chamberlain, 5 November 1931, NC1/27/99.

disabled from making the special contribution which I know it was in my power to make to this Govt. I was asked to accept a sacrifice & to help by example. How was I to refuse. But the net result is that I am a cypher & worse than that; except to a few people I appear not as someone who gives all he can to help in a crisis but as an old party hack who might be dangerous outside & so must have his mouth stopped with office. I doubt if I even bring the value which the inclusion of my name was intended to have. I have allowed myself to be deeply humiliated &, as I see it, with no advantage to the Govt. or to the country. It is all very bitter to me – not rendered less so by the fact that, as what we had had to do, will probably lose us such a seat as mine, I have to think of this as the last act of my political life. That is something which I have not yet dared to speak to Ivy. It has been a bitter disappointment to her, but she has been splendid throughout – as always ...

I don't know whether the real history of this crisis ... will ever be known. If it is, Neville will, I believe, stand out as the dominant figure in the solution which is being attempted. S.B. has been by the accounts of all who saw & heard him worse than useless and – is more than ever satisfied with his heroic self! But for Neville, Ramsay would not have carried on. S.B.'s contribution to his persuasion was to tell him that he would be hissed on the floor of the House if he joined with us!

AC5/1/552   6 September 1931
                                                    Dalingridge

My dear Hilda,

Yours was a comforting letter to receive & I thank you for it. No doubt I have been all the gloomier because I was alone, tied to London & yet with only half an hours work to help me pass the day. Time has hung dreadfully heavy on my hands & I have been eating my heart out. However, the House meets on Tuesday & what is more important Ivy returns the same day so I shall be neither so lonely nor feel so completely 'out of it' this week as I did last.

AC5/1/553   15 September 1931
                                                    Admiralty

My dear Ida,

          ...
Rather disturbing news this morning from the Atlantic fleet – I hope not serious but disquieting.

In the House all has gone well. Yesterday like the earlier days went badly for the ex-Ministers – who from being the accusers have become the accused. Henderson funked & did not appear until the discussion. He is not having a happy time.

AC5/1/554

20 September 1931
58 Rutland Gate

My dear Hilda,

. . .

My own trouble with my foot in Scotland is now diagnosed as gout! Me with gout! Very slight it is true – no pain to speak of but now a horrid sort of gouty eczema on the palm of both hands. Neville merely observes "You've earned it, I haven't" . . .

Well, when I wrote to you last I did not think that my 'caretakers' job was going suddenly to become a centre of danger & interest. I have had some anxious days & my anxieties are not yet over, but in spite of a rather disquieting bit of news this morning I am soberly hopeful. The trouble at Invergordon was lamentable; the only bright features were that there was not a single act of disrespect to officers; that the men, tho' refusing duty, stood to attention unordered when the flag was hoisted each morning or when the Admiral's barge passed a ship, & that certainly the general spirit was not revolutionary or Bolshevist. On the Admiral's ship the men in charge of the switchroom picketed it themselves, without orders, when a rumour of sabotage reached them, & no doubt many men joined unwillingly in the refusal of duty, but they did join. They were afraid for their families. I hope that what we shall be able to do will satisfy the mass & if there is any further trouble enable us to separate the sheep from the goats. I suspect Glasgow reservists as being the nucleus of the trouble.

AC5/1/555

26 September 1931
58 Rutland Gate

My dear Ida,

. . .

. . . I wish I felt I quite understood how we got into this awful mess. I can see some things quite clearly, but did not some blame attach to the City & our financiers? Had we not more money than was prudent or necessary placed in Germany or Austria? Was the Bank wise to help Austria in conditions in which France refused to participate? I wish I knew.

At last S.B. has had a meeting of all his colleagues & takes us into his confidence. He spoke to us unusually well, & we found ourselves completely agreed as to what to strive for: – An early election, a national appeal, no whittling down of our tariff policy but entire readiness to serve under Ramsay for the restoration of the balance of trade as we had done for the restoration of the balance of the Budget. As little change as possible in the Govt. before the elections & for the Liberals whatever their conduct may deserve in & after it. It is curious how universal is the dislike & distrust of Samuel, in some quarters, particularly with those dealing with India, of Reading too. Simon would be welcome but 'the Portuguese' are not liked anywhere. Hailsham is back now but he has lost much by going abroad at this time. That is felt even more than his refusal to serve except as Lord Chancellor.

I shall have a very anxious time for the next few days taking our final decisions about the Fleet. All is going smoothly at present & I am soberly hopeful but I dare not prophecy. The situation for a time was very grave. There is no use shirking facts; the confidence both of the Navy & the public in the Board of Admiralty has been very much shaken. I am not sure myself that the Board could not have foreseen the effect of the cuts more clearly than they did tho' it would have been very difficult without having before us sample domestic budgets such as we now possess. We were misled by the fact that men were already serving happily & contentedly on the new rates & did not foresee how great would be the commitments of men who had felt assured of the higher pay. Our fears concentrated on the probable charge that we had broken faith – not on the individual hardships – & the urgency of the situation & the established practice caused us to announce far too abruptly the changes which were made. It is so easy to be wise afterwards.

AC5/1/556

3 October 1931
58 Rutland Gate

[Typescript]
My dear Hilda,

. . .

It has indeed been one of the most hectic weeks politically that I ever remember. Ramsay Macdonald – whether he is worn out by the strain he has undergone or because such is at all times his nature – seems incapable of taking a decision. More than once he has had the ball at his feet. If the Samuels & MacLeans would not play the game, he had only to bow them out and call to his aid Reading, Simon and Runciman – all better men who were ready to go through with it. But each time at the critical moment his heart fails him and when Samuel says "I won't" he replies then in that case he can't. As we all agree that it is important that he should lead the national appeal, he has become the *clou* of the piece, and with the idea of finding something that he could accept and that would bind him, Neville devised his formula last Tuesday and took it to Ramsay on Wednesday morning. Ramsay at once accepted it for himself and we thought it would be smooth sailing. It was then confidentially communicated to the Cabinet but Samuel said that he could not accept it on any consideration. Here was the moment for Ramsay to get rid of Samuel and call in the others, for Reading took a different view and would have stayed in the Government, whilst Runciman as well as Simon was willing to join. But Ramsay could not decide. Samuel and MacLean were allowed to go to Churt, where Lloyd George fulminated against any such arrangement. Reading visited Churt next day but neither persuaded Lloyd George to alter his mind nor changed his own. Then Samuel, swearing he would ne'er consent, consented and suddenly swallowed the formula!

I have never seen such gloom, turned rapidly to fierce resentment, as swept over our party when this became known in the lobbies, and our men were naturally not soothed when Archie Sinclair[46] bragged that the Liberals had conceded nothing and that their position was unchanged. However, when Samuel consulted the Liberal Ministers they threw him over and he reverted to his old position. A sigh of relief went up from our party who detest him, and from his colleagues in the Cabinet (except the Prime Minister) who have found him insupportable – but even then Ramsay would not act. He went to Seaham on Friday and the other Ministers met at 2.30 to try again whether any accommodation was possible and above all to secure that if there was a break it should come in such a way that Ramsay would not throw up the sponge.

They sat for more than two hours but could reach no agreement. Ramsay got back to town this morning. Baldwin is going to try and see him after his breakfast with the King and to put some backbone into him.

It really is hard lines that after being led for these two years by a man so unhelpful and inert as S.B., Neville should now be driven in the bitterness of his heart to exclaim to me that Ramsay is 'infinitely worse'. Nevertheless I hope that Ramsay's doubts and hesitations will now come to an end and that by Monday the rubicon will definitely be crossed.

---

[46] Archibald Henry MacDonald Sinclair (1890–1970) Liberal MP for Caithness & Sutherland, 1922–45. Scottish Secretary 1931–32; Secretary for Air 1940–45; Liberal Party Leader 1935–45. Succeeded as 4th Baronet 1912, created Viscount Thurso 1952, K.T. 1941.

You can imagine that I have found my position almost intolerable. For thirty years or more I have been at the very centre of events. After such an experience it is not easy to adjust oneself to the position of the fly on the wheel.

My troubles in the Navy are, I hope, at an end ... I have got from the Cabinet (who, I may say, treated my very generously) the decisions which I thought necessary, and the Sea Lords are grateful and enormously relieved. I have completely won their confidence and I think that they feel that I have done for them what no Minister of less experience and authority could have accomplished. I was in fact prepared to tell the Cabinet that I could not remain First Lord unless they agreed our requests: but I never use language of this kind till it has become absolutely necessary and on this occasion they accepted my view even before I had finished the exposition of my case.

AC5/1/558
7 October 1931
58 Rutland Gate

[Typescript]
To Miss Ida Chamberlain

...

Samuel, confronted with the Prime Minister's decision, remains a member of the Government and so, I suppose, will all the Liberal Ministers with the probable exception of Lloyd George's son.

The nett result of the last fortnight's choppings and changes is therefore that we have lost a good deal of impetus not all of which we shall be able to make up, and that Samuel stands out as quite the most unpopular figure in our political life. I have known other men like father himself, or Mr Gladstone or even Lloyd George who have roused equal hatred, but they have evoked equal passionate loyalty from friends. Samuel's position is unique in that he is passionately disliked in every quarter of the House and cannot count on a friend anywhere.

The election will, I am afraid, result in a regular cat and dog fight in which in many cases Liberals and Conservatives will oppose each one another; but I think it will secure a clear mandate for the work that lies before it including the imposition of a tariff and the regulation of imports. But what Samuel will do, except make a nuisance of himself after the election, no-one can say. Probably fate will remove him by the loss of his seat. I do not think anyone will induce the Conservatives of Darwen to support him.

As to myself ... It will be a disagreeable election, but our people in Birmingham are hopeful and think they may win back three if not four seats whilst keeping the 6 we already hold.

AC5/1/560
11 October 1931
Westbourne,
Edgbaston

My dear Ida,

Thank you both once again for your generous help with my election expenses. It is an immense relief to me, how great a relief I can hardly say. You are really the nicest sisters in the world & I thank God that alike in our own homes & in our wider family circle we have such enduring love & sympathy.

"Well, & what do you think of it all". I have just presented Neville with that celebrated utterance of Rosebery's for the opening of his first speech. Of course he won't use it, but it is singularly appropriate to the times. Never have I known a party in such utter confusion as the Liberal party at this moment. Never has there been such a confused & confusing electoral situation. Ramsay Muir[47] has finally cooked Samuel's goose & made hash, I should think, of the prospects of a good many more of his followers if indeed anybody can be described by that word.[48] I have never known anyone so unanimously disliked & distrusted. Other men have been as much hated by some people, but then they have been passionately loved by others. Gladstone & Father are instances. And even when their battle was at its fiercest, still more when it was over, they were respected by all. But Samuel hasn't a friend in the world.

I foresee immense difficulties when it comes to Cabinet reconstruction after the election – if we win as I suppose we certainly shall. Ramsay is so frightened of being called a puppet in Tory hands that he will do all he can to keep or put key positions in Liberal hands where he has not Labour men to fill them. Nor, apart from the fact that for some reason or another he *hates* Simon, will he count him & his immediate band in the late Parlt. as Liberals for this purpose. He will of course keep Reading as Foreign Secretary & indeed could not do otherwise. I felt this in my bones when Reading was first appointed, not because he wanted to go to that post but because S.B. did not want him to go to the India Office as he himself desired. I don't think Ramsay would

---

[47] (John) Ramsay Bryce Muir (1872–1941) Professor of Modern History Liverpool and Manchester Universities, 1906–21. Liberal MP for Rochdale 1923–24, unsuccessfully stood elsewhere 1926, 1929, 1931, 1935. Chairman, Organising Committee of Liberal Party 1930–31; Chairman of National Liberal Federation 1931–33; President 1933–36.

[48] As N.L.F. Chairman, on 10 October Muir wrote to all Liberal Associations declaring they should 'support the National Government as free traders or not at all' and urged constituencies to 'not abstain from fighting Protectionist sitting members merely because they support the Government'.

wish me to be at the F.O. in any case (he always seemed a little jealous of me there & tho' I certainly gave him a generous share of credit both publicly & privately for the good work he had done at the F.O. he seemed always to feel that I had got the laurels which were rightfully his) & for some time past I have been conscious that for a reason which I don't know (tho' I can make guesses at his motives) S.B. did not intend to offer me that post again. Probably if he had not been obliged to reserve the Lord Presidency for himself, he would have offered me that place.

I of course fully recognise that in existing circumstances they *could* not, if they would, make me Foreign Secretary, but the knowledge that they would not wish to even if they could & the fact that neither of them thought it worth an effort to bring me into their counsels in these critical days is a sign I cannot disregard. I do not wish to outstay my welcome or to sit on as a survival with lessening influence. I have, therefore, practically made up my mind that, unless something quite unforeseen happens, I shall not again take office after this election. I did not intend in any case to stand again for Parlt. after the close of this next one, when in the normal course of parliaments I shall have passed the age of 70.

My private circumstances come to reinforce both these decisions.

I did not mean to tell you this at present. The only people who know it are Ivy who heartily approves & Neville who I think genuinely regrets but does not, I think in his heart disapprove my decision.

There will therefore be no difficulty for me or about me, but I am concerned for Neville though I hope that in his case things must come right. But Ramsay will certainly wish & perhaps try to make Runciman C/E. lest he should be thought to be too much in Tory hands if he has so stout a Tariff Reformer as Neville in this key position. And S.B. has fallen down so often that I don't trust him to meet any such suggestion at the outset as it should be met. But I think the appointment of anyone but Neville to succeed Snowden would raise such a revolt in our ranks that it will be seen to be impossible. N. has twice renounced the place to facilitate the formation of a govt.; he has unparalleled claims not only because of this double sacrifice but by reason of the part he took last session & throughout the August crisis & since. I don't think that S.B. can let him down or that Ramsay can pass him by. But these are times of hateful confusion & uncertainty for everyone.

The news from the Far East is very bad. The Japanese Army seems completely out of hand.[49] I am anxious for the League's reputation. It

---

[49] After occupying Mukden on 18 September 1931, the Japanese Army rapidly invaded the whole of Manchuria. China's appeal to the League was debated inconclusively in Council on 22 September.

is a situation requiring firmness, unity & great tact. Briand is a broken man, Cecil is headstrong & Reading tho' certainly not rash, is weak; & all Europe & America are deeply immersed in their own critical affairs. What will come out of it?

Two lovely days. I move tomorrow to the gloom & noise of the Midland Hotel. Lord, how I have come to hate elections!

AC5/1/561

24 October 1931
Midland Hotel
Birmingham

[Typescript]
My dear Ida,

. . .

There is a complete change of atmosphere since the last election, and Moonie and Diane, who have been out at all hours up to 7 o'clock, have not met with a rude word.

. . . I don't like to be too sanguine, but I do not see how I can have a majority of less than two thousand.

I agree with your comments on the broadcasts, judging of them as I have had to do by the newspaper reports. Lloyd George's attitude is deplorable. I think something must be attributed to the fact that he is still a sick man and that his illness affects his judgement.[50] Of course, he has never been able to get over the fact that the election was not postponed until he was ready to take the platform. It has been sad to see a man who rendered such great service to the country doing all he could to destroy his reputation.

AC5/1/562

1 November 1931
58 Rutland Gate

My dear sisters,

Thank you for your congratulations. The size of my majority eclipsed all my expectations. On the canvass I made it 6000, Basely & Canning[51] reckoned it at 4000. I only wrote 2000 to you because I was seized with superstitious dread of counting my chickens before they were hatched, & although I thought last times canvass was a losing one on

[50] Lloyd George had an emergency operation on his prostate gland on 29 July which kept him convalescing at Churt throughout the crisis.
[51] Respectively Conservative Agent and Constituency Association Chairman for West Birmingham. Chamberlain's majority increased from 43 in 1929 to 11,941 in 1931.

the face of it, it had seemed to show that with our vast modern electorate a canvass was far less trustworthy than of old. It is an immense satisfaction to me that my parliamentary contests finish so satisfactorily & above all that once more "We are twelve". I had not hoped to see that again.

I wrote to S.B. from B'ham the day after the poll waiving all claim to office & placing the one I hold at his disposal for a younger man. I made my sacrifice when I consented to take the Ad[mira]lty. & serve for the crisis without a seat in the Cabinet. I felt then, as you know, that I had signed my own fate. Whatever of bitterness there was in the renunciation I felt then; now I feel only relief that an impossible situation is brought to an end. Only for Ivy's sake do I really care.

I hope that my elimination will make Neville's accession to the Chancellorship easier to secure. I regard that as his due & vital to the Party & the cause. Obviously Ramsay would like to magnify his personal triumph & the 'national' character of the victory by doing as little as possible for the Conservatives & especially for the men of most marked position & views; & the Times aids & abets him. I am furious with Geoffrey Dawson. They have hectored & lectured & scolded the Conservatives for opposing Samuel; they have not had one word of rebuke to Samuel for writing in support of Liberal candidates brought out to oppose sitting Conservatives or for his ill-tempered attack on Simon. But I don't think they can keep Neville out of the Exchequer & at any rate I have got his promise this time not to accept any other post without first consulting his friends.

I keep speculating about what the ultimate result of all this is to be, but I can form no clear idea even in my own mind. But ' 'twas a famous victory' & for the moment let us be content with that.

AC5/1/563

8 November 1931
58 Rutland Gate

My dear Ida,

Ivy got back on Friday, decidedly better, I think, but not as much as I should have hoped would be the case. She has an indomitable spirit but I wish her heart were stronger. She had found it very trying to watch all that was passing from so far away & to feel that my fate was being decided when she could not be at my side, & though I pressed her to stay away longer I think now that she was right to return & will find it easier to bear disappointment here than anywhere else.

I am very glad not only that I took my decision but that I made it known to Baldwin when I did. I have had an extraordinary number of extraordinarily nice letters from the King downwards to unknown correspondents, so nothing could be better than the manner of my going. I *know* (tho' noone else seems to in this country) that I could have done service in the F.O. which noone else can do; but from the moment that was seen to be out of the question there was no other place that could not be as well or better filled by a younger man, & it is not good for the party or for the country that opportunity should be lacking for them to gain experience.

Simon is an experiment [at the Foreign Office] as every new appointee must be. Of his great ability there can be no question & I see no reason why he should not succeed nor, I think, is there anyone who was more qualified than he for the post. I don't think any of the younger men have trained for that particular post as I did first by my student days abroad & then by a long study & watchfulness in that field. So I must heartily wish success to Simon. He has a gigantic task – nothing less than to put England on the map again. I can't forgive the late govt. the way they have muddled away our influence & lowered our prestige.

Neville wrote me a delightful letter; he must have felt much to write so warmly, for you know how tongue-tied in matters of sentiment he usually is. He has a no less prodigious task than Simon's but I have a great confidence that he will be equal to it. The Tariff will be the least of his problems but it is a profound satisfaction to me that as it was my good fortune to be the C/E who first put Imperial Preference into a Budget so it will be Neville who builds the complete structure. This would have given Father deep pleasure & satisfaction, & so his sons pay something of the debt we owe to him.

Well, I am determined to keep my interest in life alive. I think I may play sometimes a useful part in debate but I suspect that the first lesson I shall have to learn will be to keep my hands off the wheel when the navigation of the ship is the business of a junior. I have been told that on first promotion Captains find it very difficult to refrain from interference with the Commander when he is doing very well but not exactly as they would have done.

Until the House rises I want to stay in London. After that, we have as yet no plans. We must make new & more modest arrangements. I suppose that must be our first concern.

AC5/1/564   15 November 1931
                                               58 Rutland Gate

My dear Hilda,

Well, what do you think of the debut of the new Ministry of All the Talents? I can tell you what the House thought – I believe without exception: that the P.M.'s opening speech was one of the worst he ever made, as full of words as a dictionary but with no meaning attached to any of them. I don't suppose that he could have said very much for our comfort at that moment, but he gave me the impression of a man who was for the time being physically worn out & whose heart could not pump blood to his brain so that the brain itself was not working. The speech dismayed & angered our men & was the worst possible opening for the new Parliament. Happily S.B. on Friday was at his best &, though necessarily indefinite, restored confidence & gave a lead. Meanwhile we have been given to understand that an anti-dumping bill[52] will be introduced at once & I hope that when passed it will be used.

You will have seen that I felt moved to say a few kind words to Samuel. He is a dirty dog & I think I must devote a little of my Sunday leisure to a rejoinder to his reply from Darwen. He actually claimed one of the larger ministerial rooms at the H. of C. on the ground that he must have somewhere for the Liberal Shadow Cabinet to meet, but I cannot call the Conservative colleague to whom he said it as a witness against him. I do not like to say he is a dishonest man, but I have watched him for two years & I think he has the most dishonest mind of any politician with whom I am acquainted.

I heard from Hailsham a warm tribute to the cogency & tact with which Neville had argued the anti-dumping case in Cabinet. What a load of responsibility he has to carry.

AC5/1/565   22 November 1931
                                               58 Rutland Gate

My dear Ida,

    . . .

I am assuming that Runciman's list [of manufactures subject to duty] is only the first of several. It is a good beginning but 'such a little

---

[52] Cabinet agreed to introduce an emergency duty of up to 100% to forestall 'dumping' on 12 November. This was passed as the Abnormal Importations Act, CAB 76(31)1, CAB 23/69.

one' & as all the world begins to talk of retaliation because we give them a homeopathic dose of their own medicine, we may as well at once increase the dose to respectable proportions.

This is not going to be an easy House to guide. It is uneasy about agriculture on which I suppose some satisfaction will be given before we separate, uneasy about India & very uneasy about the effect of the Statute of Westminster[53] on the Irish Treaty. This last anxiety I share. Of course when the Bill came on last Friday both Ramsay & S.B. were away & Thomas & the Solicitor General carry little weight with the House & failed to allay its doubts. I thought the situation so serious that I got busy behind the scenes with the result that Thomas promised further consideration of the point at issue & so saved a division which might have been a defeat. What will happen on Tuesday when the subject is resumed I don't know but I have suggested a course which I think would be satisfactory & Winston has said would satisfy him.

The Permanent Secretary of the Admiralty[54] was on sick leave when I made my farewell so I could not see him. He has now written that he thinks my tenure of the office was the shortest on record "it is therefore all the more remarkable that it should be the universal opinion that we have lost the greatest First Lord that anyone now here can remember". It's a fine epitaph for my official tombstone!

AC5/1/566

28 November 1931
58 Rutland Gate

My dear Hilda,

I begin to feel that I should like to have a weekly letter from Neville to tell me the news. One wonders a good deal what the inside of the Cabinet is like & what they are doing with some of the big problems that confront them. In the House they are getting on satisfactorily ... So long as they keep moving in the right direction I don't think there will be any serious grumbling. Winston is inclined to make mischief but he is winning no influence with the younger men ... They begin to ask what his game is & I am told that they contrast my speeches which they see as helpful with his to his disadvantage. Certainly I did the Govt. a good turn with my appeal to & criticism of Samuel &

---

[53] The Statute of Westminster of November 1931, guaranteed the equality of status of Dominion Parliaments with Westminster by stipulating that henceforth the UK Parliament should not legislate for a Dominion except with its consent (already the conventional position) and that no law made by a Dominion Parliament should be invalidated because repugnant to English law.

[54] Sir Oswyn Alexander Ruthven Murray (1873–1936). Entered Admiralty 1897; Permanent Secretary, Admiralty 1917–36.

equally though more behind the scenes in the matter of the Statute of Westminster, for it was I who warned them of the uneasy feeling in the House & suggested that a formal declaration by Cosgrave[55] that the Treaty was binding & could only be altered by consent of both parties would satisfy the great majority of their supporters. S.B. made one of his very good speeches in the debate.

. . .

. . . I can't help being anxious when I think of the variety & complexity of the problems with which [Neville] has to deal – problems which are in many cases entirely new to him & which will be made easier or the reverse according as Simon can or cannot gain the confidence of the French. Laval's[56] speech was menacing & up to a point France appears to hold the whip hand. But I rather think that we could call her bluff safely & that strength if shown *with* a real desire for friendship & cooperation as the alternative ought to produce a great improvement in the situation.[57] The deposits of the Bank of France in sterling in London are so large that if France forces the £ down the Bank may well lose a sum equal & more than equal to its whole capital – which is a comforting reflection.

AC5/1/567	19 December 1931
58 Rutland Gate

My dear Ida.

. . .

. . . I am now up & about again. I thought it necessary to get up because I was so happy spending all day in bed with a minimum of food & a maximum of books & sleep that I felt that in a short time I should not have the courage ever to confront the world again. I still feel my bruise a little . . . but I am practically all right again. Fortunately I fell before lunch & not after dinner, so there is no room for scandal but it was a silly & unnecessary performance.

. . .

We lunched with Neville & Annie yesterday & I sat & talked with Neville till 4 o'clock & heard all his news. On the whole I found it very

---

[55] William Cosgrave (1880–1965) Chairman, Irish Provisional Government 1922; first Taoiseach, Irish Free State 1922–32.

[56] Pierre Laval (1883–1945) French Deputy 1914–19, 1924–7; Senator 1927–44. Minister 1925, 1926, 1930; Foreign Minister 1932, 1934–6, 1940; Prime Minister 1931–2, 1935–6.

[57] On 12 November the French imposed a 15% surtax on British imports. Britain retaliated with the preparation of a Customs Duties (Foreign Discrimination) Bill. The threat was sufficient to force the French to withdraw. See CAB 86(31)3, with Appendix, CAB 87(31)8, 9–10 December 1931, CAB 23/69.

reassuring. Tho' I am perhaps not quite as well satisfied as Neville – for I of course see only the result & not all the perils of the route – I am a good deal easier in my mind than I was. Like Neville I want the Govt. to last & I think there seems a good prospect of its going on successfully. But I wonder what would happen to it if Neville were laid up! I think he gets a good backing from some of his colleagues but I don't see a capacity for leadership among them & as to our reputed leader I find it difficult to understand how a man so nul in council can make on occasion such good speeches as he does or anyone who can make those speeches can be such a fool in council. He seems to fall into every trap that is digged for him whether by accident or design. In Cabinet he says nothing; out of Cabinet he is ready to accept any suggestion which Ramsay puts to him.

D— Garvin! Why can't he get on?

13

'THESE ARE NOT REALLY MY PROPER JOBS'

Searching for a role, January 1932 – April 1933

Participation in the first brief National Government had disabused Chamberlain of many of his fondest illusions. Before the crisis he believed he still had a uniquely valuable role to play in foreign affairs and that others recognised such a claim to the Foreign Office. He also believed his voice carried considerable weight in party councils. The crisis and its aftermath appeared to suggest that this was not so. Or at least, it showed him that Baldwin and MacDonald had other ideas. While not entirely the same thing, such a realisation hurt him more rather than less.[1] By the time the initial crisis had passed, Chamberlain had come to recognise that his ministerial career was at an end. Secure in a seat he intended to hold for only one more Parliament, he felt he could now 'sing [his] Nunc Dimittis politically'.[2] Many felt that this spelt the end of Chamberlain's political influence as well as his ministerial career. Even before the 1929 election, critics like Amery had believed that his proper role was as 'the obvious successor to Balfour as principal Elder Statesman in a non-administrative office'.[3] Certainly Chamberlain gave every outward appearance of being more rooted firmly in the parliaments of the late nineteenth than in the twentieth century. In his dress, manner and parliamentary conduct he seemed to many observers to be a charming anachronism. Yet such appearances were deceptive. For the next eighteen months Chamberlain was plunged into the depths of depression as he sought to accommodate himself to these new circumstances and to find a new role for himself – or even to discover whether there still remained a useful role for him to fulfil.

Initially Chamberlain's spirits were lifted by the astonishing speed with which the citadel of free trade had finally fallen to permit the triumph of his Father's policy. Introducing the Import Duties Bill on 4 February 1932, Neville Chamberlain had carried the House with a sense of historic fulfilment. In contrast to the main body of his speech, his peroration was charged with emotion. In a moving 'personal note' the Chancellor concluded with a tribute to his father's frustrated vision, claiming that 'he would have found consolation for the bitterness of his disappointment if he could have foreseen that these proposals, which are the direct and legitimate descendants of his own conception, would be laid before the House of Commons ... in the presence of one and by the lips of the other of the two immediate successors

---

[1] See A. Chamberlain to Ida, 11 October 1931, AC5/1/560.
[2] A. Chamberlain to Ivy, 28 October 1931, AC6/1/847.
[3] Amery to Baldwin, 11 March 1929, Baldwin MSS 36/90.

to his name and blood'.[4] *Although Neville Chamberlain would have 'preferred to keep my feelings to myself', he relented when he 'realised that this would have been misunderstood when everyone else was full of the historic completeness of it all'. As he later conceded, the House was moved as it was not often moved.*[5] *For the Chamberlain family who packed the Commons that day the occasion was one of particular poignancy. As the first British Chancellor to introduce Imperial preference, Austen had for some time looked forward to the day when 'Father's great work will be completed in his children'.*[6] *Having listened from the Speaker's Gallery to Neville introduce the Bill, his step-mother had rejoiced. 'How proud your father would have been and how happy that at long last the cause for which he sacrificed his all of strength and health should be brought to fulfilment by his son'. 'I think he was very near us', she wrote to Austen later, and her 'heart was very full as I listened to Neville and looked at you sitting in your father's seat'.*[7] *Yet while immensely gratifying, such emotions were not likely to sustain his optimism for long. Anyway, the triumph of his brother at the very centre of events only served to heighten his own sense of exclusion from the pivotal position to which he had grown accustomed over the past thirty years. Indeed, this feeling of increasing remoteness was intensified still further by the burdens of office upon his half-brother. That new closeness between the two brothers which had developed for the first time in opposition after 1929 swiftly came to an end. Despite Neville's fraternal assurances that he would continue to need his older brother's political help and advice because he was 'still a child in comparison with [Austen's] vast experience of responsibility',*[8] *even their meetings at the Commons became infrequent. By the middle of the following year they had scarcely met socially in over six months.*[9]

Having waived his chance of office, Chamberlain had optimistically reassured his wife and sisters that he was still fit enough to 'find plenty of useful work to do & life will be full of interest'.[10] *He also recognised that 'the first lesson I shall have to learn will be to keep my hands off the wheel when the navigation of the ship is the business of a junior'.*[11] *This proved to be an extremely difficult rule by which to live. Within a few weeks he was already conscious that he risked becoming 'a bore or an unhelpful critic' through an over-zealous inability to leave others to steer the ship.*[12] *He then lapsed into a state of depression, lethargy and despair. In February, he confessed that he was 'bored stiff & the time I spend at the House hangs very heavy on my hands'. Approaching the fortieth anniversary of his election to the Commons, his only perverse consolation lay in the conviction that this would be his*

[4] *House of Commons Debates*, 5 Series, 261 col.296. For his full speech see cols. 279–296.
[5] N. Chamberlain to Mary Carnegie, 6 February 1932, NC1/20/1/156; to Ida, 6 February 1932, NC18/1/769.
[6] A. Chamberlain to N. Chamberlain, 5 November 1931, NC1/27/99.
[7] Mary Carnegie to A. Chamberlain, 5 February 1932, AC4/2/277.
[8] N. Chamberlain to A. Chamberlain, 28 December 1931, AC39/3/53.
[9] A. Chamberlain to Ida, 22 July 1933, AC5/1/626.
[10] A. Chamberlain to Ivy, 4 November 1931, AC6/1/856.
[11] A. Chamberlain to Ida, 8 November 1931, AC5/1/563.
[12] A. Chamberlain to N. Chamberlain, 27 December 1931, NC1/27/103.

last parliament.[13] By September he was resigned to 'eat my heart out in idleness & see my work undone & feel myself unwanted & unregretted'.[14] Even efforts to involve him in a meeting between Herriot and Mussolini only brought home to him the decline in his influence and position.

Yet as his diary letters show, life was far from one of complete idleness. Free from the burdens of high office, and under the anxious coaxing of his wife and half-brother, Chamberlain accepted a variety of positions during this period as Deputy Governor of Rugby School, as a member of the Board of the Post-Graduate Medical School and Chairman of the General Committee of the School of Hygiene & Tropical Medicine. At this time he also became rather more active in cultivating his own constituency. Perhaps because of these visits to the poorer parts of a constituency that had become 'one vast slum', in his later years Chamberlain also became a campaigner for better housing for the first time.[15] Yet for all this activity, even into the spring of 1933 he remained deeply depressed by his predicament. As he frequently lamented, he involved himself in such matters simply for occupation rather than because he made any unique contribution to the work. As he put it after listing an extensive range of engagements in February 1932, such activity merely 'illustrated the old proverb that Satan finds some worthless job for idle hands to do!'.[16] As so often in the past, depression and anxiety tended swiftly to make themselves apparent in the state of his health and his sensitivity to his own symptoms.

A key factor in engendering this depressed state was a resurgence of the perennial concern about his own financial security. His chief regret at the prospect of waiving office had been for the 'straitness and uncertainty of our means'.[17] This foreboding increased markedly as the slump deepened. 'I am in urgent need of every penny' he confessed in June 1932, 'for my capital has dwindled to next to nothing & my income from investments has fallen in proportion'. By the end of the year this 'constant gnawing anxiety' for his wife and children had become even more insistent and lay 'really at the root of all [his] pains – physical & moral'.[18] One response to these needs was writing and lecturing. During the first half of 1932 Chamberlain decided to follow Churchill's example and planned a lecture tour to America for the coming winter on the ground that there was 'no easier method of earning money'.[19] He also devoted much of his unwanted leisure time to writing a book of 'memories and portraits' (later published as Down the Years*) along with a string of articles for all manner of periodicals from a personal reminiscence of Briand for the* Sunday Times *to mark his death – 'better than anything I have seen about the man as*

[13] A. Chamberlain to Ida 28 February 1932, AC5/1/576.

[14] A. Chamberlain to Hilda, 11 September 1932, AC5/1/596.

[15] A. Chamberlain to Mary Carnegie, 31 May 1929, AC4/1/1297; to Hilda, 18 December 1932, AC5/1/604. 'New Homes for this New Britain', *Sunday Chronicle*, 4 November 1934, 10; Hilda Memoir, BC5/10/1 fol.11.

[16] A. Chamberlain to Ida, 28 February 1932, AC5/1/576.

[17] A. Chamberlain to Ivy, 2–3 October 1931, AC6/1/820–1.

[18] A. Chamberlain to Hilda, 5 June and 5 November 1932, AC5/1/584, 599.

[19] A. Chamberlain to Ida, 15 April 1932, AC5/1/580. The trip was cancelled when the Agency organising the tour experienced financial problems.

distinct from ... his life & work' – to a series of articles about his garden for The Countryman *for the princely fee of 15 guineas per 1000 words.*[20] *A more significant source of financial relief was provided by the League Loans Committee, of which he assumed the chairmanship in June 1932: an appointment proposed by the Bank of England in the hope of recovering some outstanding money at a time when virtually all the debtor nations were on the brink of defaulting. Although he began the work believing it a 'fearful task' and always pessimistic about its outcome,*[21] *these protracted negotiations provided both income and diversion at a time when Chamberlain desperately needed both of these things. One unexpected consequence of this role was that Chamberlain visited the League at Geneva in his official capacity in October 1932: an experience which left him 'profoundly disturbed' and deeply saddened by the institution's decline under very different circumstances from those which had prevailed during his last visit little more than three years before.*[22]

Yet even with this modest relief from boredom and financial anxiety, Chamberlain's problems were by no means resolved. When MacDonald offered him the Lord Wardenship of the Cinque Ports, with Dover Castle as the official residence, in October 1933 Chamberlain was reluctantly compelled to decline. Although offered 'in the nicest terms & ... with genuine feeling' and deeply attracted by the historic setting, the large gardens and the traditions, the fact remained that the garden alone required four gardeners and the Office of Works would provide only one: a situation which necessitated an expenditure of £1500–2000 per annum. As he lamented to his sister, 'The honour & the castle remain but all its fees & emoluments have been abolished. It's a pity I was born when the era of sinecures & pensions was drawing to a close. I feel I was intended for a pluralist'.[23] *By this time, however, Chamberlain's spirits had markedly recovered as he began to forge a new role for himself within the House of Commons and British politics. Within a few months this revitalised sense of purpose had persuaded him to change his mind about retiring at the next election.*[24] *In many ways, what followed is rightly considered to be one of the greatest and most distinctive periods in his career. It was also one wholly consonant with his lifelong love and devotion to the House of Commons.*

[20] A. Chamberlain to Ida, 10 March 1932 and to Hilda, 23 May 1932, AC5/1/578, 582.

[21] A. Chamberlain to Ida, 25 June 1932, AC5/1/587.

[22] A. Chamberlain to Ida, 9 October 1932, AC5/1/597.

[23] A. Chamberlain to Ida, 7 October 1933, AC5/1/634.

[24] A. Chamberlain to Ivy, 21 February 1934, AC6/1/1027.

AC5/1/569   2 January 1932
                                             Polesden Lacey

My dear Ida,

The Cartiers have arrived & the Simons. Maggie Greville remembers
Madame Cartier as a lovely woman with white hair. She is now an old
hag with a yellow wig. He is the Belgian Ambassador & pleasant
enough. She is American & one of the biggest bores I know. But I fly
to her for comfort as soon as Lady Simon appears! Lord, how I pity
poor Annie if she has to make friends of the wives of N's colleagues.
For really desperate, noisy boreing [sic] vulgarity, commend me to
Lady S. She was the first Lady S's nurse. I should think the noise she
made killed her patient & when Maggie after long hesitation finally
decided that she would not marry Sir John, he went off in a huff &
married this woman forthwith. If I had done the same, I should end
on the gallows.

I hope I shall feel better now! But she really is *awful*.

AC5/1/570   17 January 1932
                                            58 Rutland Gate

My dear Ida,

No, I have no excuse for not having written last week except the
one which you rejected in advance – that I had nothing to write about.
Of course every literary critic will tell you, & truly, that is just people
so situated who write the only letters worth reading by posterity, but
then what has posterity done for me that I should write letters for it?
Besides I felt lax & indulged myself & that is in fact all there is to say
about it ...

I have no news of the great world or of politics. I am glad for his
own sake that Briand has at length resigned. Indeed I wish that he had
retired earlier: it would have been better for him & his reputation.
Fleuriau said to me the other day in explanation of the lessened
influence of the League "in your day the Foreign Ministers made
the policy." With the disappearance of Stresemann & the advent of
Brüning[25] & Ramsay MacDonald, the Foreign Ministers have ceased
to count & that is at any rate part of the trouble. I don't like the
outlook for either of the forthcoming conferences. All one can say is
that their failure would be such a misfortune, if not actual disaster, that

[25] Heinrich Brüning (1885–1970). Member of Reichstag 1924–33; Reich Chancellor
1930–2; Professor of Government, Harvard, 1937–52 and Cologne 1952–5.

they may be forced to some sort of agreement. I should like them to be able to say to the U.S.A.: – There, you told us to settle European affairs ourselves. Well we have done so & here is our solution, but it all depends on you doing your part. Now what about it? I am not sure that America could resist & I am inclined to think that that is just what Hoover wants.

AC5/1/571

24 January 1932
58 Rutland Gate

My dear Hilda,

. . .

You may have seen that I spoke at B'ham on Friday after Hailsham & gave my blessing to the Govts. solution of their crisis[26] ... Well, I am glad that [Neville] is pleased & in good spirits, but I confess to you that the more I think about it the less I like it. It seems to me to be fraught with endless difficulty for the future; it gives excuse & precedent to all the frondeurs present or to come in our own party & I don't trust Samuel & Co to use the liberty allowed to them with any moderation or discretion. Let us hope that I wrong them. Certainly if we had only to consider domestic issues, I would sooner they had left the Govt. now while Runciman was staying on. Tariff issues must continue to arise & he & Neville may not always agree. The only thing that reconciles me at all to the solution is the state of foreign & Indian affairs. The former seems to me to be worse than at any time since the Ruhr. Indian affairs go better under Willingdon[27] & Hoare & I am glad to see H. emphasised that the Cabinet is united on Indian policy, on disarmament & on reparations, debts & all the vast field of present day exchange & currency problems. Anyway, determined to do the best I can for the Govt., I have, as I said before, given them my blessing & made another of what Winston calls my 'boyscout speeches' – a daily good deed. I think Ll. G. must be licking his chops at the thought of what he will be able to say about Samuel & I should rather enjoy being in opposition myself.

I gathered from Hailsham that S.B. was as mad as usual in this affair & that the solution was actually proposed by H. himself. That it

---

[26] The 'agreement to differ' suspending collective Cabinet responsibility over the tariff question was accepted at Cabinet on 22 January 1932.

[27] Freeman Freeman-Thomas (1866–1941) Liberal MP for Hastings 1900–1905; Bodmin 1906–10. Lord-in-Waiting 1911–13; Governor of Bombay 1913–18 and of Madras 1919–24; Governor-General of Canada 1926–31; Viceroy of India 1931–36; Lord Warden of Cinque Ports 1936–41. Created Baron Willingdon 1910, Viscount 1924, Earl 1931, Marquis 1936.

should originate with him must, I should think, have surprised all his colleagues as it certainly surprised me.

AC5/1/572   30 January 1932
                                                      58 Rutland Gate

My dear Ida,

. . .
. . . the most interesting . . . feature of my week [was] . . . my dinner with Neville last night. I thought he looked well & he was in excellent spirits. He gave me no details but it was clear that the Govt's. policy has much more in it than the mere 10% proclaimed to the public. N. indeed says that it does in fact give us all we should have done if the Govt. had been formed from our Party only . . . He added that so far all the indications were that Snowden, Samuel & Co. did not intend to abuse the liberty accorded to them.

AC5/1/573   6 February 1932
                                                      58 Rutland Gate

My dear Hilda,

If they are not already echoing in your thoughts look at the end of the second volume of Boyd's edition of Father's speeches & read the last words he spoke to a public meeting.[28]
I am glad that you were present to share personally in Neville's triumph & in the emotions of that historic scene. I thought Neville's speech perfect in tone, arrangement & lucidity & was deeply moved by his concluding passage for which I anxiously waited. I had no knowledge of what he intended to say but I felt that he must & would say just that. I can say my nunc dimittis now with a full & grateful heart. How proud father would have been of Neville & how it would have moved him that Neville should complete his work. Have you noticed Griffith Boscowen's letter in today's (Saturday's) Times. It is kindly of him to recall that it fell to me to place Imperial Preference on the Statute Book for the first time.
Thank Ida for her letter. Yes, we were all thinking of Beatrice as well as of Father.

[28] At Bingley Hall, Joseph Chamberlain's final words to a public meeting contained the 'hope I may be able to live to congratulate you upon our common triumph, but in any case I have faith in the people . . . I look forward to the future with hope and confidence, and "Others I doubt not, if not me, the issue of our toil shall see".' C.W Boyd, *Mr Chamberlain's Speeches*, (1914).

Samuel's speech was an outrage on good taste & political morality. He is a bounder. He not only does not play the game but he is incapable of understanding what the phrase means. Both Horne & I were so angry that we refrained with difficulty from jumping up at once to follow him and give him what he deserved. I have told S.B. that loyally as I have supported the Govt. & strongly as I have defended in public the agreement to differ (whatever doubts I have felt about it in private) I will myself move a motion calling for Samuel's resignation if he continues on that line ...

Between the deep emotions stirred by Neville's speech & the passionate anger roused by Samuel I came home to dinner literally trembling in every fibre ...

AC5/1/574   14 February 1932
                                                        58 Rutland Gate

My dear Ida,

    ...

What a warring world it is – disarmament at Geneva, war in the Far East,[29] a League which seems to have lost its grip, a Germany which has forgotten Stresemann & a France which rejects Briand. Chaos seems to have come again & I will not attempt to prophecy [sic] the result. It is not without significance that that shrewd American observer, Frank H. Simmonds, in his newly published "Can Europe keep the peace?" has for chapter heading for his conclusion "Back to Locarno" & ends with the words: "The task is not to adjust life to a dogma but a dogma to life; not to make the world safe for democracy but Democracy safe for the world . .. . For isolation is not merely one, but perhaps also the last of the illusions of Democracy." Pretty shrewd! I am sure of one thing – that the key to many of our present difficulties is Fulfilment. Leave to the future the changes which the future may make necessary & render possible. Keep your hopes but meanwhile renounce force as a method of realising them; accept the map of Europe & its public law as it is, fulfil your obligations to the measure of your ability & you will secure relief where relief is urgent, create confidence & earn good-will & find that much becomes possible which is now unobtainable. Fulfilment by Germany, honestly & consistently of her political obligations would soon result in the settlement of our economic difficulties & in a sensible reduction in other nation's armaments.

[29] The World Disarmament Conference opened in Geneva on 2 February 1932 under Henderson just after the Japanese attack on China itself.

All very badly expressed but you may perhaps be able to discover my meaning.

AC5/1/575   19 February 1932
                                                            58 Rutland Gate

My dear Hilda,

... Neville has continued to speak well. Sinclair did not give the same offence as Samuel but in essence his speech was just as menacing for the future. I don't believe that the agreement to differ can continue much longer. The trouble will begin again on the Budget if their words mean anything & my fear is that they are now only waiting to go out till they find a 'popular' cry & they see it in opposing any remission of income tax & the slogan (that I should write that word) don't tax the People's food to relieve the rich of income tax. I am getting mildly abused for having supported the experiment.

AC5/1/576   28 February 1932
                                                            58 Rutland Gate

My dear Ida,

Neville goes from strength to strength. The [Import Duties] Bill as he remarked, had an easy passage for the inefficiency of the Front Opposition Bench is beyond belief & makes my fingers itch. It tempts me to go into Opposition myself just to show how an opposition should be conducted. As Leo Amery said to me the other day: – "Just think what a chance for Samuel if he had gone out & what a position he would now have!" Nevertheless part of the credit for the Bill's smooth passage must go to Neville, for his handling of it has been at once firm & conciliatory. He is, I think, very happy, & has every reason to be so. As to me I am bored stiff & the time I spend at the House hangs very heavy on my hands. Well, this will be my last Parliament. After all in three weeks time I shall have had forty years of it.

I have consented under pressure to join the Executive Committee of the League of Nations Union! What will come of it I don't know, for in the past I have more frequently than not differed from its expressions of opinion. However, opponents as well as friends welcome my accept- ance & I shall try gradually to persuade it to confine itself to its proper work & refrain from assuming to itself the duties of the League Council & the British Govt. Anyway I felt bound to try for except Jack

Hills[30] we have scarcely a representative left upon the Comtee. & the Union & our Party were becoming increasingly estranged.

AC5/1/577   5 March 1932
                                                         58 Rutland Gate

My dear Hilda,

...

I had a most pleasant dinner as [Hamar] Greenwood's guest at the H. of C. last Monday. He had collected a distinguished gathering in honour of Sir John Anderson & I found myself seated between Lord Camrose[31] & the Governor of the Bank, both very interesting & pleasant. But my chief contribution was made after most of the guests had left when Ferguson, the High Comr. for Canada & J.H. Thomas who had each had a glass more [than? sic] was good for him & who had previously got completely across one another frightened me seriously for the success of the Ottawa Conference. So I did the Elder Statesman, rebuked Ferguson for threatening to report private conversations, told J.H. that if that was his mood he had better not go to Ottawa at all & generally told them off & knocked their heads together to the great satisfaction of the half-dozen others who were present. I think it was a good thing I was there. It is a calamity that Thomas should be S/S for the Dominions at this moment. He has not the mind for such a task & is without discretion.

Londonderry,[32] who has for some time been representing the Govt. at Geneva was home last weekend & saw Ivy in the H. of L. on Monday. He told her he wanted to see me particularly; for he said nothing had struck him so much at Geneva as the enormous influence I had evidently possessed there not only as concerned myself personally

---

[30] John Waller Hills (1867–1938). Conservative MP for Durham 1906–22; Ripon 1925–38. Financial Secretary to Treasury, 1922– March 23 when defeated at Edge Hill by-election.

[31] William Ewart Berry (1879–1954). With his brother, James Gomer Berry, Lord Kemsley, purchased a number of newspapers and periodicals after 1924 including *Daily Sketch* and *Daily Telegraph* (1927) Founded *Advertising World* 1901. Editor-in-Chief, *Sunday Times* 1915–36 and *Daily Telegraph* from 1928 until his death. Chairman of Financial Times Ltd and Associated Press. Advisor to Ministry of Information 1939. Created Baronet 1921, Baron Camrose 1929; Viscount 1941.

[32] Charles Stewart Henry Vane-Tempest-Stewart (1878–1949) Conservative MP for Maidstone 1906–15. Under-Secretary for Air 1920–21; Leader of the N. Ireland Senate and Minister of Education 1921–26; First Commissioner of Works 1928–9, 1931; Secretary for Air 1931–35; Lord Privy Seal and Conservative Leader of Lords 1935. Styled Vt. Castlereagh 1884–1915. Succeeded as 7th Marquess of Londonderry 1915. Created K.G. 1919.

but in raising the prestige of England. It is pleasant that he should receive this impression three years after I was there for the last time.

AC5/1/578   10 March 1932
                                                           58 Rutland Gate

My dear Ida,

... Briand's death is a great personal blow to me for ours was a very true & real friendship. I cross tomorrow for the funeral which I attend as a personal friend ...

AC5/1/579   10 April 1932
                                                           58 Rutland Gate

My dear Ida,

...

As I think you know I composed a chapter on Berlin in the Eighties while I was with you & I am now trying to do another on Paris in '85, but the letters which have survived from that date are poor & meagre. I wish now that I had been a better correspondent! My idea is to do enough of these articles to make a book of "Portraits & Memoires".[33] It is a great fag, but it keeps my busy & excited besides destroying whatever of good there was in my handwriting.

AC5/1/580   15 April 1932
                                                           58 Rutland Gate

My dear Ida,

... I attended a sub-committee of the L/N Union as the Private Manufacture of Arms; only three people turned up, including myself, & we found ourselves of four different opinions. This I consider rather a triumph for the chances were that the other two – a Col. Carnegie & Miss Courtney would have combined against me. Neither of them agreed with me but they equally disagreed with each other & Col. Carnegie, if I understand him (he is terribly prosey & not very intelligible) disagreed also with himself.

I think I am going to do a really heavy tour this winter – say 20 lectures before Xmas & as many after with a fortnight for recreation in the middle, but we are not yet agreed about the fee. It will be an

[33] Published as *Down the Years*, (Cassell, 1935)

appalling grind but as Winston says I know no easier method of earning money.

And I am very busy writing: Memories & Portraits

...

AC5/1/581   15 May 1932
                                                        Cumberland Lodge
                                                                Windsor

My dear Ida,

...

We had an interesting discussion on disarmament on Friday. I have no fault to find with Simon's line as far as it was disclosed. Indeed I agreed with most of what both he & Winston said, contradictory as this may appear at first sight, but I must confess I don't see the channel through which we may sail to any solution. I agree with Winston that it would be disastrous to allow Germany's claims to equality & I think it equally impossible to accept the French proposals for 'security'.

I fancy that Neville sees almost equal difficulties in the path of the Lausanne Conference.[34] Only Ottawa offers hope, tho' there seems to be *some* favourable movement of opinion in the U.S.A.

AC5/1/582   23 May 1932
                                                 House of Commons Library

My dear Hilda,

... am now bracing myself for a fierce battle at the Executive of the L. of N. Union to prevent them from passing a resolution in favour of creating an International Bombing Force under the orders of the League.

Oh! these peace lovers. They are far worse than the men of war.

[34] Lausanne Conference June–July 1932. Agreed three year moratorium and then reduced German reparations to a nominal final payment in return for US waiving war debts. The US refused and France defaulted in December 1932 followed by Britain in 1933.

AC5/1/583

29 May 1932
58 Rutland Gate

My dear Ida,

. . .

I think I am doing some good at the L.N.U.. I could not get them to condemn *on principle* the idea of an International Police Force, tho' I was rather unexpectedly supported by Lord Dickinson[35] & Lady Parmoor,[36] & I was obliged to compromise on a resolution which urged it was most inexpedient that the subject should be discussed at the Cheltenham meeting of the Council. But they had to listen to a serious examination of the proposal & its consequences such as, in my short experience, this Executive Comtee. has not given to any question yet, & I believe I made a considerable impression on them. The B. Post correspondent came up to me in the Lobby on Friday & said 'I hear you had a great Triumph at the L.N.U. yesterday'.

'For heaven's sake, don't say so!' I replied.

'No, but I hear it was a great triumph all the same. Two people whose names you would not guess have already spoken to me about it. They were very much impressed.'

The afternoon Comtee. on the Far East was equally satisfactory. We extinguished our mischievous secretary, Dr Maxwell Garnett,[37] & agreed unanimously on a bald statement of undisputed fact without his mischievous comments. And then I spent $\frac{3}{4}$ hour expounding to them my view of how the League should develop. Not thrown away I think. They are all very nice to me personally & very anxious to retain me.

The Governors [of the Bank of England] came to ask me to take the chair of a small but strong committee to press on the Govt. & the world the importance of maintaining the sanctity & special position of what may be called the League Loans, every recipient of which is now threatening to default. London is in to the tune of £40,000,000. Paris, I think, to the tune of five or less, & wants priority for pre-war loans &c.

I most heartily agreed with the Governor's view & as he volunteered

[35] Willoughby Hyett Dickinson (1859–1943) Liberal MP for St Pancras N. 1906–18. Joined Labour Party, 1930 and National Labour 1931. Member, Speaker's Conference on Electoral Reform 1916–17. Vice-President League of Nations Union 1924; British Delegate (Substitute) to League Assembly 1923. Created Baron Dickinson 1930.

[36] Marian Emily Ellis. From 1919 second wife of Charles Alfred Cripps, first Baron Parmoor (1852–1941). Active Christian, pacifist, supporter of the League. International Committee of the World Alliance for Promoting International Friendship; Executive, British Council and LNU; World President, YMCA 1924–8. British Representative at the League 1924.

[37] (James Clerk) Maxwell Garnett (1880–1958) Mathematician; Fellow of Trinity and Principal, Manchester College of Technology. Secretary, LNU 1920–38.

that 'they' attached such importance to it that 'they' were prepared to pay an honorarian to the Chairman & Vice-Chairman on the scale of a director's fee, I accepted.

AC5/1/584   5 June 1932
                                              58 Rutland Gate

My dear Hilda,

... You will see I have 'commenced author' [sic] seriously ...

... The question is whether that will suffice [for a volume of memoirs]. If it does & succeeds I shall be tempted to try a second volume.

In addition I have agreed ... to deliver 25 lectures at $700 dollars (£140 *at par*) apiece, all expenses paid from door to door for Ivy & self & one other in America in January & Feb of next year. I am in urgent need of every penny of the money for my capital has dwindled to next to nothing & my income from investments has fallen in proportion.

The proposal of the Governor of the Bank has not yet matured – he has met with some unexpected difficulties but I think they are in course of resolution. I did not draft the letter to the Times on disarmaments – it is not my style – but you are right in seeing me in it, for they felt it essential to secure my signature & drafted it with an eye to acquiring my consent. Unless you put that in, Buffy (Balfour) Dugdale[38] [said,? sic] I don't think he will sign. She is a sensible & clever woman.

We had another long meeting this week & I *think* I have got my way, with the necessary compromise on my part, about a representation to the Govt. on the Minority Treaties. I am trying incidentally to improve the manners & the grammar of the Executive's communications. The snake in the grass is Maxwell Garnet [sic], the secretary, but he is beginning to find that he must watch his steps. I would have had the skin off his back if I had learned a few weeks ago what I only heard on Friday – that he had been sending from the Head Office resolutions of Branches denunciatory of Japan direct to the Japanese Embassy. This was stopped by Simon before I heard of it – but the rod is still in a pickle!

What is one to say of events in Paris & Berlin. I &, incidentally the

---

[38] Blanche Elizabeth Campbell ("Buffy") Dugdale (1880–1948) Balfour's niece and biographer. Naval intelligence 1915–17; Permanent staff of LNU 1920–28; member of British delegation to World Disarmament Conference at Geneva 1932. Lifelong Zionist.

German Ambassador would have preferred Tardieu[39] to Herriot & Paul Boncour. Herriot is weak & P.B., though he makes socialist & pacifist speeches takes his policy on disarmament from the Council Superieur de Guerre or whatever it's called, the nearest French equivalent to our Comtee. of Imperial Defence, & blocks every reform by attaching to its acceptance impossible conditions – another snake in the grass.

And Germany! It is too soon to say what the new Govt. portends, but its composition & declaration have not added to the general sense of security or to the prospects of a successful issue from Lausanne or Geneva.

I am gloomy & it's not my wont.

AC5/1/585   10 June 1932
                                                         58 Rutland Gate

My dear Ida,

...

Last night I dined [at the House] with the Prime Minister & four or five Under-Secretaries with Neville coming in for such time as he could be spared from the front bench. I found the conversation extraordinarily interesting & was much struck with the young men. On foreign policy it was curious to see the coincidence of judgement between the P.M. & myself on men & policy. All were struck by it ... I rose from the table (at midnight) more hopeful than I had sat down at 8.0.

AC5/1/586   18 June 1932
                                                      School House, Rugby

My dear Hilda,

...

D. MacLean was a man whom everyone respected & liked but he did not bring any great strength to the Govt. I hope there won't be a row over his replacement. I don't see any Liberal fit for it in the Samuel group which is not a strong one.

Lloyd George made a quite first class speech on the Irish treaty. He felt keenly on the matter & was at the top of this best form. He swept

---

[39] André Pierre Gabriel Amédée Tardieu (1876–1945) Journalist and French politician. Founder and leader of Republican Centre party almost continuously in office 1926–32. Prime Minister 1929, 1930, 1932.

Cripps[40] into the limbo where he belongs. Nothing could have been worse than *his* performance.

Lausanne seems to me not to have begun badly.

AC5/1/587   25 June 1932
                                                    58 Rutland Gate

My dear Ida,

...

Then on Thursday ... I lunched with two Rothschilds & a representative of Barings ... to discuss the Hungarian Loans position ... & on to my League Loans Comtee. A fearful problem this is; how much good can we do it is hard to say but at present every country which had a League Loan has defaulted or seems on the point of doing so.

AC5/1/588   2 July 1932
                                                    58 Rutland Gate

[Typescript]
My dear Hilda,

...

I had to spend the greater part of Thursday in the train getting down to Lord Kilbracken's funeral at a small place in Kent not far from Deal; but I went down to the House of Commons in the evening to hear Neville's statement. I saw him for a few moments before hand and was very pleased with his appearance. He was wearing his gout-boot for which I was thankful. But what is more important he was in excellent spirits and his voice was particularly strong. The effect of his speech in the House[41] was most favourable and, as you see, it has been not less so in the country. It is a prodigious operation such as has never been presented before, but for this very reason it gives an unexampled proof of our strength and is a triumphant result of the Government's policy.

[40] (Richard) Stafford Cripps (1889–1952) Labour MP for Bristol East 1931–50; Bristol SE 1950. Expelled from Labour Party 1939–45. Solicitor-General 1930–31; Ambassador to Russia 1940–42; Lord Privy Seal and Leader of House 1942; Minister of Aircraft Production 1942–5; President Board of Trade 1945–7; Minister of Economic Affairs 1947; Chancellor of Exchequer 1947–50. Knighted 1930.

[41] On 30 June 1932 Neville Chamberlain announced the conversion of the War Loan. The operation was a great success with 92 per cent of the £2,084 millions of outstanding 5 per cent War Loan 1929–47 converted to a $3\frac{1}{2}$ per cent War Loan 1952 and after. Bank Rate was also reduced to 2 per cent on the same day and it remained there until August 1939, *House of Commons Debates*, 5 Series, cols. 2121–6, 30 June 1932.

I gather that Neville has found his Lausanne experience very interesting and he and the Government are very hopeful as to the issue, though difficulties keep cropping up just as everything seems settled ...

AC5/1/589   17 July 1932
                                                      Warsash

My dear Hilda,

...

I have had a busy week & as usual not much to show for it – another L/N Comtee., the usual row ending in a compromise not wholly satisfactory to anyone. In addition to including a first-class collection of cranks, the Comtee contains some of the most churlish & ill-mannered people I have ever had to work with.

AC5/1/590   22 July 1932
                                                   58 Rutland Gate

My dear Ida,

...

I was very busy with the Bulgarians about League Loans in the early part of the week & used my spare moments in writing begging letters for the School of Hygiene & T.M. So far I have got about £1650 a year for seven years & one donation of £100, but it is desperately hard work in these bad times ... I have finished with the L/N Union till Sept 23rd (if I attend then) & last time got through without a row with anyone & without feeling utterly exhausted & disgusted by the struggle to make them see sense ...

I am very glad that Grandi[42] is coming here & he will like it for it has always been his wish, but it will be, I fear, a great loss for all who have to deal with the Italian F.O. He has done extraordinarily well as Foreign Minister & has got the sack, I expect, merely because he was not assertive enough to please Mussolini.

As to Germany I cannot read the signs, but there seems to be much thunder in the air.

[42] Dino Grandi (1895–1988) Italian Count and diplomat. Member of Fascist Grand Council; Foreign Minister 1929–32; Ambassador to London 1932–39; Minister of Justice and President of Fascist Chamber 1939–43. Brought about Mussolini's fall in 1943 and condemned to death by Verona rump in 1944.

AC5/1/592   10 August 1932
                                                   Houlgate
                                                   Calvados

My dear Hilda,

Your news of Neville [at the Ottawa Imperial Economic Conference]
was very interesting. I am afraid that I distrust Bennett; I do not think
that he is really a strong man & I doubt if he has the courage really to
fight his manufacturers. But let us hope for the best ...

AC5/1/595   3 September 1932
                                              58 Rutland Gate

My dear Ida,

... My last hours in France were spent on M. Pierre Dupuy's Yacht.
We went aboard at Deauville early on Wednesday & crossed to
Cherbourg. Here we were joined a little before dinner by Herriot ...
Herriot was in capital form at dinner & entertained us with many witty
stories, but before & after dinner in more serious talk he was very
gloomy & depressed. All his entourage & I think he himself want me
to join Dupuy's yacht in the Mediterranean & to be present at a
meeting with H. & Mussolini when they are sure that my influence
would somehow bring about an agreement. Indeed they have a most
flattering but highly exaggerated idea of my influence which is *nil* at
home & I suspect not much greater abroad now that I am out of the
ranks of Ministers. I shall have a talk about it at the F.O. but my own
instinct is against it. It would be different if I were still a Minister.

AC5/1/596   11 September 1932
                                              58 Rutland Gate

My dear Hilda,

    ...
Nor is there anything in public affairs to console me. If I felt older &
less able to work, it would be easier to reconcile myself to the place on
the shelf to which I have been relegated. As it is I am bitter at heart
tho' not even Ivy knows that & still thinks me a marvel of charity &
forgiveness, but I eat my heart out in idleness & uselessness & see my
work undone & feel myself unwanted & unregretted.
    All this is very bitter – forgive me & destroy this screed. I shall
recover my equanimity one of these days, but just now I am in despair.

I do what work comes to me – I wish there were more – but I find little pleasure in it. After giving up everything to public life, it is hard to feel that you are in your coffin before you are dead. Bah! Enough of that.

I am pursued by this project of a meeting with Herriot & Mussolini, & an Under-Secretary of State is to descend on me on my way through Paris. Meanwhile the whole European situation is as bad as can be ... Without a policy or influence, I would make a fool of myself & be blamed for making a fool of others. I must keep out of [it? sic] somehow but I wish these French friends would take no for an answer. They won't believe that I have not my old authority or shall not again tomorrow.

There! I think I feel a little better after thus railing at fate & all concerned. It's better to spit the poison out than nurse it in one's inside. But it's disagreeable for the by-standers. Forgive me.

AC5/1/597   9 October 1932
                                                  58 Rutland Gate

My dear Ida,

... I was met at Cannes by a telegram from John Simon asking me to go to Geneva about our League Loans memorial & leaving Chillie [Chilcott][43] to bring the girls back to London I went direct to Geneva ...

It was interesting but sad to be at the League again in such altered circumstances. Everything was unrest & uncertainty, no grip, no direction, no leadership. I have returned profoundly disturbed. There is, I believe, even yet a great role for England to play, tho' the sands are running out: but we are [not?] playing it. Simon & MacDonald are not on good terms; I doubt if either of them has a policy – they are content with patchwork, when a very bold strong lead is needed & action at Paris, Rome, Washington as well as in Berlin. Eric Drummond is in despair; he sees what might be done but is himself powerless. We are drifting back upon the rocks. I have always been an optimist, but now I am very anxious.

It was delightful to be received with such genuine pleasure & cordiality by all old friends but sad to find them all so defeated, the assembly a dead thing, the Council without confidence in itself or authority elsewhere & people as little given to hysterics or high fallutin

[43] (Harry) Warden Stanley Chilcott (1871–1942) Businessman. Conservative MP for Liverpool Walton 1918–1929. Special foreign missions for Government 1917–22; Foreign Political Secretary, Law Officers 1918–22. Kt 1922.

as Beneš saying: 'I tell them they are too frightened. We are not going to have war now. We have five years before us, perhaps six. We must make the most of them'.

AC5/1/598   16 October 1932
                                                     58 Rutland Gate

My dear Ida,

Many thanks for your letter & good wishes, but you will get no letter from me this week. For why? Because I am busy, because I have my birthday presents, because, because **Because** at lunch-time yesterday I received in volume form the final proofs of Vol. 1 of the Life.

I read till 2 a.m., began again at 9 this morning & am just finishing & break off only to write this note to you before the post goes out at 11.0.

I can be no critic of such a biography of Father. 600 odd pages to the fall of Gladstone's Govt. in 1886.

Will the public stand it? Will they read a work on this scale. I don't know, but there is no padding in it & no intrusion of Garvin's personality. I could strike out a few sentences ... & I do not accept every judgement, still less every criticism in the form in which it is expressed. But I repeat I detect no padding &, with these slight exceptions, I feel that any omission would be loss of something that counts & is worth while.

But the size! I find Queen Victoria's Letters more fascinating than any novel. Most biographies of men who are worth while leave me wishing for more, but what others think & what they will say I cannot judge. But I think it is *well* done.

AC5/1/599   5 November 1932
                                                     58 Rutland Gate

My dear Hilda,

It is a rather tired brother who takes up his pen to write to you. I am particularly well, "looking ten years younger" &c &c & I feel like it – *only* I have a recurrence of indigestion, have been sleeping badly & am full of aches & pains for which I am undergoing treatment with hope but with lessening confidence! It's an odd combination. I don't feel my age – except perhaps for an increasing tendency to be a laudator tempous acti & a certain temptation to say of this or that problem; "I don't know. Younger men must settle that" – but I suppose these signs have some meaning. Well, when the time comes I shall be able to say like Beatrice 'Content either way' as far as I myself am concerned, but I feel a constant gnawing anxiety about Ivy & the children when I can no longer earn what little I can still make. I dare say that that is really at the root of all my pains – physical & moral.

...

Then on Tuesday I attended, by special request, the Political Comtee. of the League of Nations Union as the result of some observations made by me on the dangers menacing us from Germany at the Executive Comtee meeting. You are right in seeing the result of my work in Cecil's broadcast speech ... Cecil sent me the Ms next day saying look at the marked passage. It is the result of what you said: I have followed this up & Murray[44] & Cecil have drafted a warning for the next issue of Speakers Notes on the subject which I have approved, & 'Headway' will I hope have a signed article by Patrick M.P.[45] on the subject in the next issue. Eppur se murve. They confess to having had a shock when the facts were laid before them.

AC5/1/600   12 November 1932
                                             58 Rutland Gate

My dear Ida,

...

... I am encouraged to find that somewhere you have unearthed a tribute to my contribution to the Disarmament Debate. It really was an important one & I have been profoundly discouraged that so little attention was paid to it. Two or three M.P.s spoke to me about it & Geoffrey Lloyd told me that some of the young Liberals, who had never heard me, were much impressed by what they called its 'high parliamentary style', but the Times Lobbyist ignored it, their report omitted what was vital to it & a perfunctory reference at the fag-end of their article was little compensation. À quoi bon? What's the use of anything? Oh d—!

I don't understand today; that, I suppose, is the trouble. I read that

---

[44] (George) Gilbert Aimé Murray (1866–1957) Professor of Greek, Glasgow University 1889–1899 and Regius Professor Oxford 1908–36. Delegate to League of Nations for South Africa 1921–3 and member of League Committee on Intellectual Cooperation from 1922. Chairman LNU Executive 1923–38 and President 1938–40. President United Nations Association 1945–9.

[45] Colin Mark Patrick (1893–1942) Diplomat 1919–30. Conservative MP for Tavistock 1931–42. P.P.S. to Hoare at India Office and F.O. 1933–December 1935 and to Lord Cranborne when Under Secretary for Foreign Affairs 1935–38.

Baldwin's speech[46] was the greatest he has made since his plea for industrial peace [in 1925]. All I can say is that around me noone could understand what he was at. He explained that the air-menace was the worst, that all treaties & prohibitions would be broken & disregarded in war as they always had been, that it was hopeless to attempt to control it & then he enquired of the young men What are you going to do about it? To me it was the utter bankruptcy of ideas & policy & would have justified a vote of no confidence – Apparently I am wrong.

I have had another pottering week – two pleasantish lunches, two or three committees each resulting in more chores but not affording much matter for satisfaction, & several hours of electric treatments, destroying my morning's work. Next week promises to be much the same.

I'm 'tired & disgusted'. I wish I were merely drunk.

AC5/1/602   7 December 1932
                                               58 Rutland Gate

My dear Hilda,

I went out today for a short walk for the first time since I took to my bed, & then drove to Goadby's to have an injection of iron & quinine which I can take better through my blood than through my stomach. The result of the air & exercise was that I got two hours *refreshing* sleep this afternoon. I am still feeling very depressed & of course I am very run down, but it is something to be able to do a little work again & to feel that I have really got a move on. My figure is almost as elegant as Joe's!

I have just finished the page proofs of Garvin's Vol II. What a titanic struggle! I feel like Neville who writes of Vol I 'G ... has produced a most vivid & impressive picture. While reading it, I have experienced the same sort of feeling that I do in reading a book on astronomy: I have felt myself growing smaller & smaller until I became insignificance itself.' I am going to suggest to Garvin a little shortening of Vol II & press for the alteration of one passage.

---

[46] On 10 November 1932 in a short but sensational speech Baldwin warned 'the bomber will always get through. The only defence is in offence, which means you have to kill more women and children more quickly than the enemy if you want to save yourselves'.

AC5/1/604

18 December 1932
58 Rutland Gate

My dear Hilda,

. . .

You may have seen that I irrupted [sic] into the Housing debate. I spoke in restrained language but could not & did not try to conceal my deep emotion, & the speech produced a great impression in the House & appears to have been widely read, judging by the flood of letters it has brought me from all over the country. I am now trying to follow it up; my trouble is that I know so little, but what I have seen I have seen & I don't believe we are dealing with the problem on right lines. I am trying to get help ... I won't let the matter rest where Shakespeare[47] left it in his reply.

I am busy again at collecting for the School of Hygiene & Tropical Medicine — there is much work to be done there & I have had myself put on the Board of Management ... And now comes the Minister of Health begging me in the name of the University, the County Council, the Lord Dawsons & Moynahans [sic][48] at *hoc genus omne* to take the Chairmanship of the London Post-Graduate School of Medicine for which Neville is finding £300,000, & just as I had made up my mind to refuse comes an S.O.S. from Neville himself saying that he worked at this for years & that he believed "it is going to be one of the most valuable pieces of work" which he undertook during his term of office at the Ministry.

And Ivy has got me roped in to take the Presidency of a Comtee, yet to be formed to try to promote a better understanding between France & England, & in both cases of course I am the one indispensable person & it may take a little time at first but I shall have every help &c. &c. &c. And I know what all that means & that if I undertake them I must give time to get sufficient knowledge & to see that the things are done in what I think the right way, & so I fritter my time away doing the work of which I have no experience. Oh d—!

. . .

[Postscript] I had a most pleasant lunch at Philip Sassoon's on

[47] Geoffrey Hithersay Shakespeare (1893–1980) Liberal MP for Wellingborough 1922–3; Norwich 1929–45 (National Liberal from 1931), Private Secretary to Lloyd George 1921–3; Liberal National Chief Whip 1931–2; Parliamentary Secretary to Health 1932–6 and to Education 1936–7; Financial Secretary, Admiralty 1937–40; Secretary, Board of Overseas Trade 1940; Under Secretary, Dominions 1940–2; Director and later Deputy Chairman Abbey National 1943–77. Created Bart 1942.

[48] Berkeley George Andrew Moynihan (1865–1936) Surgeon. Kt 1912. Created Baron Moynihan 1922.

Thursday – Philip himself, Hailsham, Derby, Cunliffe-Lister, Marg-esson, who kept silent till he & I were alone & myself. The talk turned first on the amazingly disloyal action of Amery at Ottawa & then on the incredible ineptitude, egotism & idleness of mind of S.B. That subject kept the floor till we parted. Not a soul had a good word to say for him except myself & my praise was strictly confined to his Peace in our Time speech & to the support (though not the help) which he gave me as Foreign Minister. His reputation in the country is inexplicable to anyone who has worked with or under him in Cabinet & council.

AC5/1/606   21 January 1933
                                               58 Rutland Gate

My dear Ida,

... I have agreed to take on the Post Graduate Medical School which Neville is keen about – but these are not really my proper jobs though there is some good work to be done at them. League Loans & League of Nations Union continue to afford a good deal of occupation.

AC5/1/611   12 March 1933
                                               58 Rutland Gate

My dear Hilda,

I had made up my mind to ask if you could have me without Diane for this weekend ... when on Thursday I felt an ominous tickling in my throat which by Friday had become a streaming cold ... Today I am ... much better & am going out to lunch, but I feel depressed rather than unwell. I have had more colds this winter than for a long time past, & I have not had my normal innoculations which may or may not be the reason; but I think it is due in part also to the fact that there has been a good deal to worry me & that such work as I have now is done for occupation rather than because I have any particular qualification for it or special interest in it. It's no use pretending to you that I don't feel out of it & I have not the stimulus of being in opposition which one generally gets in those cases ...

I had a very interesting morning in B'ham looking at a [slum] clearance area, an improvement area ...

The rest of my week has been mainly occupied by interviews between the League Loans Comtee. & the Prime Minister of Bulgaria about their debt. I find it very exhausting to argue in French what it is difficult enough to understand & to express in any language, & most of the talking on our side is left to me. The position in Bulgaria is deplorable, but they are not doing even what they could to put their house in order & we have no real means of putting any pressure upon them, whilst just now the League is torn with strife & afraid to do what it could.

. . .

The world is hollow & my doll is stuffed with straw. In fact I am at this moment horribly depressed. Perhaps I shall feel better after lunch. If not, I shall feel tempted to take to bed again & drink.

14.

'I CONTINUE VERY LOQUACIOUS!'

Leading from the backbenches, April 1933 – June 1935

During the spring of 1933 there was a sudden and dramatic improvement in Chamberlain's spirits as the clouds of gloom which had hung over him since leaving office began to disperse. At last, Garvin's efforts were beginning to bear fruit as the first two volumes of the long-awaited Life of Joseph Chamberlain appeared to a favourable reception from both the family and the general public. Chamberlain was also beginning to earn some money to at least alleviate his financial worries. The principal reason for this renaissance, however, was a growing confidence that his stock was rapidly rising both in the Commons and outside it. No longer physically and mentally exhausted by the constant demands of office, his speeches became the subject of 'pleasant observations' and genuine praise from lobby correspondents and fellow Members. Moreover, as new problems and threats emerged to confront the Empire, Chamberlain also became convinced that he still had a valuable contribution to make and a voice capable of carrying that message with authority. A significant barometer of this recovery in his morale is to be found in the greater length and detail of his diary letters during this period.

The growth in Chamberlain's stature in Parliament after the spring of 1933 was truly remarkable. It was the more so, given the position from which such a revival had begun. At the Foreign Office, he had become so detached from domestic politics and the Commons that he was rarely to be seen on the front bench except for foreign affairs debates and was wholly unknown to most of the younger members on his own side.[1] Less than a year after Locarno, even his half-brother lamented that he had 'been almost out of sight ... gradually becoming more hazy and legendary as he is less familiar'.[2] As a result, by the time the party moved into Opposition in 1929 there was much in Bridgeman's charge that while he could still make a good speech on most subjects 'he has little or no hold on the present H. of Commons'.[3] Moreover, this decline in influence was exacerbated during the next two years as he became one of the central targets of the vociferous agitation against the 'Old Gang' and their influence upon the leadership. Against this background, widespread agreement that after 1933 Chamberlain enjoyed perhaps the greatest period of his career would appear to be all the more astonishing. As his half-brother summed up the view of many contemporaries soon after Austen's death, 'although only a private Member, in his last years his influence in the House of Commons was such as no other Member possessed, and indeed was greater than when he himself had held

[1] H. Macmillan, Winds of Change, 174.
[2] N. Chamberlain to Hilda, 10 August 1926, NC18/1/539.
[3] Bridgeman Diary, November 1929, Bridgeman MSS II fol.189.

high office'.[4] *It was a position of influence similar to that his father had held from the same seat below the Gangway in the Parliaments of 1886 to 1892 and he revelled in the historic completeness of it all. In part this new authority rested upon his perception of the influence he exerted over the front bench both formally and in informal gatherings such as Philip Sassoon's weekly luncheons for ministers to which he obtained a standing invitation in late 1933. He was also consulted regularly by Simon and Eden about foreign affairs. More important, however, Chamberlain revelled in his rising stature among the younger Conservatives in the Commons for whom he provided a focus and a spokesman for their discontents. As Vansittart described the transformation, 'From a joke after Locarno he became an oracle in Westminster. "Let us hear what Austen has to say" became a refrain from younger men'.*[5] *This was to be an accolade upon which Chamberlain came to place enormous value.*

In many respects Chamberlain was an ostensibly unlikely candidate for such a position in the affections of his younger backbench colleagues. In 1933 he was 70 years old. More than just his age, he also gave every outward appearance in dress, manner and parliamentary conduct of having become a quaint reminder of a by-gone age. As one parliamentary journalist observed of these years:[6]

> *In Sir Austen we saw the ideal Parliamentarian of a generation that was fast passing away. He was fastidious in his get up, with frock coat, and the inevitable monocle. By the wearing of the silk hat, and by raising it whenever he was mentioned, whether in praise or criticism, he maintained old tradition. Not only was he ceremonious in habit but he also gave a lesson in studied courtesy to a new generation.*

In his parliamentary utterances he also increasingly sounded like the Elder Statesman to younger ears. As a devoted lover of the institution and its customs he placed enormous significance upon the skills of oratory and the cut and thrust of debate. As a result, he deplored Baldwin's lack of such skill and lamented the general decline in the speeches of his contemporaries when compared with the halcyon days of Gladstone and his Father. For him it was a great compliment to be described as 'the last survivor of an older style of speaking'.[7]

Undoubtedly such an image appeared strange to many of the younger intake to the Conservative benches. As Harold Macmillan recalled, 'in appearance, costume, method of speech, he seemed almost a survival. His top-hat, his eyeglass, his exquisite

[4] C. Petrie, *The Chamberlain Tradition*, 280–1. See also Lord Lee's comment at the same time in A. Clark (ed), *A Good Innings*, 339; E. Percy, 'Austen Chamberlain', *Public Administration*, XV.2 (April 1937), 126; Baldwin, *Service of the Day*, 86–7; D.R. Thorpe, *The Uncrowned Prime Ministers*, 83; J.R. Clynes, *Memoirs*, II, 254–5.

[5] R. Vansittart, *The Mist Procession*, 549.

[6] Sir Alexander Mackintosh, *Echoes of Big Ben*, 122.

[7] A. Chamberlain to Ida, 14 and 28 May 1933, AC5/1/616, 618. For Chamberlain's views on the decline in interest in parliamentary debates when compared with his first parliament of 1886–92, as a witness before the Select Committee on Procedure in 1931, see R. Butt, *The Power of Parliament*, (1969), 141–2.

courtesy and his rotund oratory marked him out from his colleagues'.[8] *Contrary to the legend which subsequently developed, not all backbenchers responded positively to this public persona. T.B. Martin, one of the new Conservative entrants in the 1931 landslide later contended that 'Austen was not taken seriously by the younger MPs. His clothes and manner were Edwardian, and he talked the language of the past'.*[9] *At the same time 'Chips' Channon found his views 'ossified, tedious and hopelessly out of date'. Even some of those younger Conservatives who shared many of Chamberlain's views on the German menace were inclined to dismiss him as 'a kindly creature, but his vision in terribly limited and created for him by other persons'.*[10] *Yet despite such testimony, there would still appear to be much evidence to confirm the verdict that from his father's old seat on the corner below the gangway on the government side Chamberlain was listened to with genuine respect and exerted considerable influence in these years. 'He is the Elder Statesman', a more sympathetic young observer wrote in 1936, 'the back benches have given him what the Front Bench never did – disciples'.*[11]

Chamberlain's claim to authority rested upon two central pillars encompassing both substance and style. First, he had great direct personal experience with two of the key problems to haunt policy-makers during this period – those of India and the rapidly emerging threat from Germany. His utterances on these subjects thus naturally carried some weight at a time when many backbenchers were becoming increasingly restive about the policy stance of the front bench. Secondly, although progressively more alarmist in his anti-German statements,[12] *Chamberlain's general tone in addressing the great questions of the day – and the government's deficiencies in dealing with them – was one of constructive moderation. By design, he conspicuously avoided that nearly hysterical lack of balance which so often undermined the credibility of Churchill's opposition during the same period. As his most recent biographer has characterised it, Chamberlain tended to assume the role as 'the conscience of the MacDonald and Baldwin governments rather than their scourge'.*[13] *For this reason, Chamberlain rather than Churchill became the most influential and most respected backbench critic of the National Government until his death in 1937.*

This tone of studied and constructive criticism was not purely fortuitous. From the outset, Chamberlain had been determined to avoid drifting into that 'carping and critical attitude' towards former colleagues which so often became 'the pit into which so many retired Ministers fall'. Although harbouring grave doubts about the wisdom and practicability of the 'agreement to differ' in January 1932, in public he dutifully supported it. 'My desire to keep the Government together is great', he wrote to an

---

[8] H. Macmillan, *Winds of Change*, 174–5.

[9] R. Lamb, *The Drift to War*, 122.

[10] Channon Diary, 27 July 1936, *Chips*, 73; Headlam Diary, 13 May 1935, S. Ball (ed) *Parliament and Politics*, 333.

[11] R. Cartland to his sister 1936, B. Cartland, *Ronald Cartland*, (1941), 70. See also A. Chamberlain to Ida, 12 November 1932, AC5/1/600.

[12] See Headlam Diary, 2 and 9 May 1935, S. Ball (ed) *Parliament and Politics*, 331–332.

[13] D. Dutton, *Austen Chamberlain*, 306.

old friend, 'greater still perhaps my reluctance to appear as a critic of men whose colleagues I have been for so long & so recently'.[14] *He also conspicuously refused to intrigue and cabal against Simon or his policy towards Germany. Indeed, perhaps the only significant departure from this loyalty occurred over the terms of the German Commercial Treaty in May 1933 when to everyone's surprise, and the evident discomfiture of Baldwin and the Chief Whip, Chamberlain made a very effective speech against the agreement, challenged a division and voted against the government in what some observers perceived to be a direct personal vote of no-confidence.*[15]

On the German question, Chamberlain's attitude was well known and even more deeply-rooted. Even in the heyday of Locarno, his cordial personal relations with Stresemann had not diluted an otherwise scarcely concealed loathing for the German temperament or its malign influence upon state policy. As the European liquidity crisis deepened during the summer of 1931 he lamented that 'the Germans are unchanged; they give the world every reason to distrust them & we in this country are far too prone to forget what they were & overlook what they remain'.[16] *Six weeks after Hitler became German Chancellor, he felt the international situation was 'worse ... than at any time since 1914'. In a world which had forgotten or turned away from Briand, Stresemann and Locarno he feared 'the powder magazine may blow up at any moment'.*[17] *Soon repelled and disgusted by 'the domestic brutality of the [Nazi] regime & with deepening anxiety about its external consequences' Chamberlain saw the recrudescence of German militarism as evidence of the old and ineradicable flaw in their national character. 'The spirit which inspires this campaign against the Jews inside Germany is the spirit which inspired the attempt of Germany to dominate the world before the Great War'.*[18] *In his first major speech on the subject in the Commons on 13 April 1933 he presciently gave full vent to these feelings and became one of the earliest voices calling for resistance.*[19]

For Chamberlain, German hectoring and bullying in 1933 required the same determination to resist threats with iron determination as it had demanded in 1925 and 1914. When the Germans understood this, he hoped that Hitler may follow Mussolini's example and 'settle down into something more reasonable & states-manlike'.[20] *If not, nothing would be lost. 'The only hope of peace is to make it plain to the Germans that whilst we would do our best to meet the legitimate claims of a peaceful Germany', he wrote in 1933, 'we will do nothing for a Germany*

[14] A. Chamberlain to F.S. Oliver, 26 January 1932, AC39/5/12.

[15] Amery Diary, 1 May 1933, *The Empire at Bay*, 293; Headlam Diary, 1 May 1933, S. Ball (ed) *Parliament and Politics*, 267–8.

[16] A. Chamberlain to Hilda, 11 July 1931, AC5/1/547.

[17] See A. Chamberlain to Ivy, 17 March and 24 May 1933, AC6/1/978, 1018.

[18] A. Chamberlain to Hilda, 23 August 1933, AC5/1/629; to E. Canning, 25 April 1933, AC40/4/14.

[19] *House of Commons Debates*, 5 Series, 276 col. 2759, 13 April 1933.

[20] A. Chamberlain to Hilda, 11 November 1933, AC5/1/639. For similar sentiments see his letter to Sir Horace Rumbold, 13 November 1933, M. Gilbert, *Sir Horace Rumbold: Portrait of a Diplomat 1869–1941* (1973), 388.

which outrages humanity at home and menaces her neighbour's peace'.[21] *Two years later he was repeating the same strategy with ever increasing insistence: 'To a people who believe in nothing but force, force is the only answer'.*[22]

Whilst the Germans behaved in what Chamberlain perceived to be an entirely predictable and characteristic manner, the real problem lay in the lack of clarity and firmness of the British response. For this he swiftly came to blame Sir John Simon, the Foreign Secretary. Although the increasingly strident tone of his anti-German harangues did not attract widespread support, Chamberlain's lamentations about Simon certainly did. Although initially prepared to be charitable, after Chamberlain's visit to Geneva in October 1932 the prevailing sense of despair alarmed him at the lack of a strong British lead.[23] Thereafter complaints about drift, indecision, weakness and vacillation in face of German threats became the recurrent leitmotif of his correspondence. By February 1934 he was thoroughly convinced that 'Simon is a very bad Foreign Secretary. He has no policy, is very pleased with himself & wholly unconscious of the effect he produces on others'.[24] The more complaints which reached Chamberlain from ministers, officials and anxious foreign observers, the deeper became his conviction that Simon must be replaced to restore confidence in British policy among her allies and correct the disastrous impression in Germany that Britain was on the run. To this end, at the end of 1934 he had pleaded with Neville to work for Simon's removal from the Foreign Office.[25] In the event, he would have to wait another seven months for this wish to be fulfilled.

If Chamberlain found Simon's weakness frustrating, then he was maddened by the antics of the League of Nations Union whose Executive he had joined rather reluctantly in February 1932. The LNU had been established as a non-party organisation with the intention of pursuing an almost Fabian-like strategy of 'permeation' to influence the policy process through friends in office, irrespective of the party in power. To this end membership had been actively solicited in all the major parties, but prominent Conservatives were always in a notable minority.[26] One of Chamberlain's main reasons for accepting a position on the Executive had been to redress this imbalance and to reduce the danger of the Conservative Party becoming estranged from the Union. As a former Foreign Secretary, but a backbencher, such a choice enabled the links to be maintained at a comfortable distance from the front bench.[27] Chamberlain was also anxious to ensure that the large proportion of the electorate supposedly enthusiastic about the League were not alienated from the Conservatives because they believed them uninterested or unfavourable to that

[21] A. Chamberlain to H. Armstrong, 17 July 1933, AC40/5/72.

[22] A. Chamberlain to Hilda, 5 May 1935, AC5/1/698.

[23] A. Chamberlain to Ida, 9 October 1932, AC5/1/597.

[24] A. Chamberlain to Ida, 3 February 1934, AC5/1/650. For Simon's policy see M. Cowling, *The Impact of Hitler: British Politics and British Policy 1933–1940* (Cambridge, 1975), 74–77.

[25] A. Chamberlain to N. Chamberlain, 11 November 1934, NC1/27/119.

[26] D.S. Birn, *The League of Nations Union*, 28–9.

[27] See Baldwin to A. Chamberlain, 17 February 1933, AC40/5/9.

institution.[28] *Yet for all its political and electoral advantages, this was never likely to be a congenial position for a former Foreign Secretary who confessed that in the past he had more frequently than not differed from the Union's expressions of opinion and policy.*[29] *Indeed, the LNU's continued campaign on behalf of the Geneva Protocol after Chamberlain formally proclaimed it dead had prompted him to threaten to resign from the organisation altogether in June 1925, while its vigorous attacks upon his role in the League Council crisis of March 1926 left him bitter in his denunciations against the 'consistent wrongheadedness' of an Executive he had now been called upon to join.*[30] *His only consolation was that he expected to be in a position 'gradually to persuade it to confine itself to its proper work & to refrain from assuming to itself the duties of the League Council & the British Govt.'.*[31]

From the inside, Chamberlain found the LNU Executive infinitely more objectionable than from the outside. As he never tired of complaining, 'In addition to including a first-class collection of cranks, the Comtee, contains some of the most churlish & ill-mannered people I have ever had to work with'.[32] *During his first two years on the Executive, Chamberlain was involved in an unremitting battle with such people against LNU support for an 'International Bombing Force' under League auspices; against its stance on the private manufacture of armaments in October–November 1933; and against their desire to impose sanctions upon Japan for its aggression in Manchuria at a time when the situation was beyond repair and could only distract attention from the European menace where something useful could be accomplished.*[33] *During this period, Chamberlain's skill and continued threats to resign enabled him to emerge as the only figure capable of containing Cecil's domination of the Union. Frustration reached such a peak over the Peace Ballot that Chamberlain again came very close to resigning in 1934–35. Alarmed by the ease with which the ballot could be rigged through biassed instruction, Chamberlain and his Conservative allies had drafted a blue paper pointing out the shortcomings of the ballot to counter a green paper which they believed had already been circulated by polling agents on behalf of the Union of Democratic Control. In the end neither was distributed but Chamberlain refused to be mollified. When Cecil published another information leaflet, allegedly without clearing it with the Conservatives on the LNU Executive, Chamberlain wrote 'the hottest letter' he had ever written to* The Times *on 12 November protesting about the whole affair. 'It will bring a hornets nest about my ears', he confessed to his half-brother, 'but I should have had apoplexy if I hadn't found a vent for my feelings'.*[34] *Although the dispute eventually*

---

[28] A. Chamberlain to F.S. Oliver, 3 August 1933, AC40/5/84.

[29] A. Chamberlain to Ida, 28 February 1932, AC5/1/576.

[30] Chamberlain annotation on a Selby memorandum, 4 February 1926, D. Birn, *The League of Nations Union*, 61–4.

[31] A. Chamberlain to Ida, 28 February 1932, AC5/1/576; to Tyrrell, 13 February 1933, AC40/5/12; to Cecil, 11 January 1932, Cecil MSS 51079/194.

[32] A. Chamberlain to Hilda, 17 July 1932, AC5/1/589.

[33] D.S. Birn, *The League of Nations Union*, 104–6, 115–118. C. Thorne, *The Limits of Foreign Policy: The West, the League and the Far Eastern Crisis of 1931–1933*, (1972), 339–341.

[34] A. Chamberlain to N. Chamberlain, 11 November 1934, NC1/2/118.

fizzled out, this was not before Cecil informed Chamberlain that if he thought the Union leaders were 'all dishonest liars' he should resign.[35] *At this juncture Chamberlain was not ready for resignation, but the breach could not be long deferred.*

Perhaps the greatest demand upon Chamberlain's time during 1933–34 was provided by the Joint Select Committee on India established to consider the proposals to emerge from the Round Table Conference, published on 18 March 1933. The purpose of the Committee was to find a new constitutional settlement which would offer a greater measure of Indian self-government while still binding it firmly into the Imperial structure. As his letters to his sisters testify, the labour was prodigious. The task of taking evidence and considering all the issues was a mammoth one in itself when confronting an issue of exquisite complexity. From the outset Chamberlain was also gravely concerned about the unwieldy structure, size and procedures of the Committee which were to necessitate it sitting formally for eighteen hours a week after October 1933. Yet for all his genuine doubts and anxieties, Chamberlain was to enjoy significantly more success in this sphere of policy than over Germany, at the LNU or at the League Loans Committee.

The Joint Committee clearly imposed a substantial additional physical and mental burden on an already busy man in his seventieth year. His sense of burden – but also satisfaction – was intensified at an early stage by the belief that he was destined to play a pivotal role both in the deliberations of the Committee and in determining its eventual outcome.[36] *Nor was this simply vanity. Sam Hoare, the Secretary of State for India, also believed that the support of politicians like Chamberlain in the Commons and Derby in the Lords would be critical in order to overcome the determined opposition from Churchill and the Diehard right-wing of the party.*[37] *During the Committee's proceedings Salisbury and the Diehards made much of the running and lengthened proceedings enormously by their detailed examination of witnesses. To counter this influence, six months after the Joint Committee commenced, Chamberlain mobilised a nucleus of 'moderate or middle opinion in the Comtee.'. The self-styled 'Derby House luncheon group'*[38] *consisted inter alia of Derby, Zetland, Hardinge, Percy and Cadogan, and sought to obtain the support of like-minded moderates such as Peel, Reading and Attlee. Its purpose was 'to act together on all main issues & so afford at least a nucleus of moderation on the basis of the acceptance of the main postulates of the White Paper whilst insisting on considerable modifications within those limits'.*[39]

From the outset Chamberlain was convinced that Indian constitutional reform was 'a fearfully dangerous experiment' and equally confident that he wouldn't like the result of the Joint Committee's work, whatever it was. He was also certain,

[35] D.S. Birn, *The League of Nations Union*, 146–8 for the so-called 'Rainbow' controversy.

[36] A. Chamberlain to Hilda, 3 July 1933, AC5/1/624.

[37] Hoare to Willingdon, 17 March 1933, J.A. Cross, *Sir Samuel Hoare: A Political Biography* (1977), 166, 168; Hoare to Sir George Stanley, 22 May 1934, M. Gilbert, *Winston S. Churchill*, V. Companion 2, 794.

[38] A. Chamberlain to Ida 7 October 1933; to Hilda, 16 March 1934, AC5/1/634, 656.

[39] A. Chamberlain to Ida, 18 November 1933, AC5/1/640.

however, that it was not possible to 'go back on the past' and that there were no alternatives but to go forward.[40] *When appointed he had thus warned Hoare that 'you must not count upon me as an unqualified supporter ... though you may be sure that it will be my wish to be helpful'.*[41] *By adopting the strategy he did, Chamberlain performed precisely the role for which Hoare had prayed. Inevitably there were differences between the Derby House luncheon group and the Secretary of State — particularly over the form of representation in the Indian federal lower house. Yet what Chamberlain never fully realised was that Hoare also recognised that Conservative doubters outside the Joint Committee were more likely to accept its report if it could be shown that its deliberations had significantly modified the White Paper with which they had begun. For this reason, Hoare was always prepared to make concessions to Chamberlain and his supporters — as, for example, over the granting of additional power to governors in connection with terrorism. Even over the far more fundamental amendment concerning the method of election to the lower house of the federal Central Assembly, Hoare was prepared to be flexible in the belief that it was necessary in order to secure the commitment of moderate Conservative opinion for a scheme offering responsible government at the Indian federal level.*[42]

Before the Joint Committee had completed its work, Chamberlain was also involved in the related and equally delicate problem engendered by his membership of the Commons Committee of Privileges. On 16 April 1934 Churchill had raised as a matter of privilege in the Commons the role of Hoare and Derby in an attempt to alter the evidence submitted to the Joint Committee by the Manchester Chamber of Commerce the year before.[43] *Although a member of the Privileges Committee since leaving office in 1931, Chamberlain considered himself to be in an invidious position both because he had sought to dissuade Churchill from pressing the matter and because he was a member of the Joint Committee. His potential embarrassment was no doubt intensified by his belief that it was 'a borderline case' in which his allies had perhaps 'unwittingly overstepped the mark'.*[44] *In the event, despite his concern about its effects, Chamberlain did serve on the Committee which completely exonerated both Derby and Hoare on 8 June 1934.*

After more than 170 sittings, the Joint Committee concluded its deliberations in mid-October 1934. The report appeared in November. A process which in four years had encompassed three Round Table Conferences, a White Paper, a Joint Select Committee and culminated in Parliamentary debates containing nearly 2000 speeches and totalling $15\frac{1}{2}$ million words had come to an end. The final report of the Joint

[40] A. Chamberlain to Hilda, 26 March 1933, AC5/1/612.

[41] A. Chamberlain to Hoare, 23 March 1933, AC40/1/2.

[42] J. Cross, *Sir Samuel Hoare*, 168–9; Hoare to Willingdon, 13 April 1934, M. Gilbert, *Winston S. Churchill*, V. Companion 2, 754. See also G. Peele, 'Revolt over India', G. Peele and C. Cook, *The Politics of Reappraisal 1918–1939*, (1975), 140–1.

[43] For these events see M. Gilbert, *Winston S. Churchill* V, 511–548; J. Cross, *Sir Samuel Hoare*, 170–3; S.C. Ghosh, 'Pressure and Privilege: the Manchester Chamber of Commerce and the Indian Problem 1930–1934', *Parliamentary Affairs*, XVIII, No.2 (Spring 1965), 201–15.

[44] A. Chamberlain to Ida, 22 April 1934, AC5/1/660.

Committee laid the foundations for the Government of India Act of 1935 whose 478 clauses and 16 schedules made it the longest Act on the British statute book.[45] As the effective leader of that group of open-minded moderate Conservatives on the Joint Committee, Chamberlain was right to feel satisfaction at the outcome and for having played a crucial role in securing the support of the great mass of the Conservative Party for the National Government's India policy. 'Certainly the Govt. ought to be grateful to me', he wrote with justifiable satisfaction when victory was in sight, 'for if I had gone against them, there isn't a doubt but that they would have been beaten & indeed, unless I had exerted myself, I doubt they could have obtained a working majority'.[46]

AC5/1/612

26 March 1933
58 Rutland Gate

My dear Hilda,

...

I have agreed to serve on the Joint Committee on India.[47] Why? A sense of duty, I think, I could find no good reason for refusing but it will mean an awful lot of work & I am sure that I shall not like the result whatever it is. It is a fearfully dangerous experiment, but one can't go back on the past & what one has to ask oneself at every moment as faces [sic] a step one doesn't like is well & what is the alternative. It will only be contemplation of the alternative that will get me over the fences.

I laugh at myself. I could not help wondering whether the Govt. would ask me to serve; I should have felt it rather a grievance if they had not, or let me say a slight, & the moment they do ask in a very nicely worded letter from Sam Hoare I begin cursing and swearing at having the thankless task shoved on me. Such is disgruntled human nature. Hit high or hit low, there's no pleasing it.

Upon which confession there follows naturally my comment on the P.M.'s recent performances. Briefly I did not like his speech at Geneva – it made me uncomfortable as one is made uncomfortable by someone

[45] D. Judd and P. Slinn, *The Evolution of the Modern Commonwealth, 1902–1980*, (1982), 58.
[46] A. Chamberlain to Ida, 15 December 1934, AC5/1/680. Uncharacteristically Petrie plays down Chamberlain's role on the Committee, *Life and Letters*, II, 391.
[47] A Joint Select Committee of both Houses of Parliament considered the proposals to emerge from the Round Table Conference published as a White Paper on 18 March 1933. It sat from April 1933 to October 1934.

who strikes just the wrong note in any Society[48] – but I think he was absolutely right to go & right to propose a convention, & that for all that part of the Govt. policy Eden made a really admirable & conclusive defence, but Rome —? What did he do at Rome?[49] what is the policy he has brought back with him? Where does he stand? & where do we stand? Does he know what he wants or what he means? If he does, noone else does. His speech, tho' not quite as verbose as usual, was as empty & deserved all Winston's gibes. I have not a ghost of an idea what he is at. He seems to have gone to Rome with one policy, to have been handed another by Mussolini as he stepped out of his aeroplane & thenceforward to have become M's creature – & after Locarno he served the King with notice that he could not meet Mussolini even at a State Banquet at the Palace.

. . .

I have seen nothing of Neville. I don't envy him his job & fear that he is going to have a very difficult time with his Budget. Keynes is extraordinarily clever & marvellously lucid; he has it to his credit that he was the one man who at the moment of the peace negotiations made a true estimate of Germany's capacity to pay; but he is not, I am convinced, a safe guide in business or politics. He excels in theory but his theories are too fine-spun to stand the wear & tear of work-a-day practice.[50]

[48] Anxious that adjournment would lead to unlimited German rearmament, on 16 March 1933 MacDonald proposed a stop-gap plan in order to prop up the disintegrating Disarmament Conference. The speech was a painful demonstration of MacDonald's failing strength and powers during which he even momentarily lost consciousness.

[49] At Mussolini's invitation, MacDonald visited Rome on 18 March 1933 on his way home from the World Disarmament Conference at Geneva. The Italians proposed a four-power pact (with Britain, France and Germany) promising Germany equality of rights even if the disarmament conference failed. Although initially enthusiastic, French opposition convinced him otherwise. The four-power pact signed in June was purely consultative and bore no resemblance to Mussolini's initial proposal.

[50] In four articles in *The Times*, 13–16 March 1933 Keynes returned to his earlier advocacy of public works but this time employing the 'multiplier' concept and more radical than the past in arguing that depressed business expectations required the Chancellor to pump in additional purchasing power, not only by loan-financed public works but also by remitting taxation without reducing current expenditure. This is almost 'deficit finance' in the full sense. These proposals were reprinted in expanded form as *The Means to Prosperity* (1933).

AC5/1/613

1 April 1933
58 Rutland Gate

My dear Ida,

...

My week has been occupied chiefly by two interests – the Indian debate & the League of Nations Union. The former passed off as expected without the much foretold crisis coming to a head but a storm has boiled up within the latter which may lead to the resignation of Jack Hills, who has been one of its pillars, & myself.

The Indian debate was of more sustained interest & kept on a higher level than any I recall of recent date. Simon was very adroit; indeed that is his weakness as a speaker. He would carry more conviction if one did not feel his adroitness so clearly that one is tempted all the time to ask oneself how he could put the opposite case if briefed to argue it. S.B.'s speech I thought really disclosed his state of mind & method of approach to every question. I believed it made me feel again that he is lazy even in thought & that he has not the equipment for the position he occupies. But the most curious episode of the debate was Winston's sudden loss of temper followed by his total inability to recover his stride or regain the interest of the House. I can recall no parallel. He had begun well & was being listened to with attention & interest by all & with sympathy by many. Then came his rash & rashly worded charge of subserviency in the Civil Service amounting to sycophancy & of proscription of independence by the Govt. & Viceroy. Of course some discount must be made for the natural & proper desire of Govt. Servants not to act or speak against the declared policy of Govt. to entrust the highest & most important positions to men who, being wholly out of sympathy with that policy, are not likely to make a success of it; but if it was necessary to say this, it required to be stated with great care & reserve whilst Winston's language was gross & unqualified. Even so, he might have recovered, but Winston of all men calling a quiet & able fellow member – one who moreover was [has? sic] given much time & study to Indian problems – a bully because he asked a fair question in fair & moderate language was too much for friends & foes alike. The House rocked with laughter; Winston stammered & blundered & for the rest of a very long speech had a steadily dwindling interest & an offended audience. The fact of the matter is that on this subject he has become hysterical. It is impossible to discuss it with him even privately. I tried a joke with him the day before & was sorry I had spoken! He can see only one side of the question & listen to only one view.

I had two Comtees. of the L.N. Union during the week – one of the

Disarmament Comtee. or Sub. Comtee. where it did my heart good to hear Cecil denouncing the Germans as *"impossible* people" & urging that we should do what we thought just but *"never* try to satisfy a German!" Here we agreed with some compromise on both sides on a resolution dealing with disarmament & the injection into its discussion of the Rome Pact, which by the way I don't like any better on seeing the account of it which appears in the Times this morning from their Paris correspondent. On Thursday we had the almost weekly (3 out of 4) meeting of the Executive Comtee. & at this there was before us a report from a sub-comtee. presided over by Cecil recommending the creation of an International Air Force to be under the control of the League. Cecil naturally argued in favour of it. Nothing less would induce France to disarm, therefore nothing less would save [?] the Disarmament Conference. Jack Hills argued seriously & well against it. It would entirely change the whole character of the League & stultify all that he had ever said in support of it. Two or three other members supported Cecil. Then I spoke strongly against the proposal. Lady Parmoor as a Pacifist agreed with me; Norman Angel [sic][51] as ditto agreed with Bob; so to my surprise did Baffy [sic] Dugdale (A.J.B.'s niece & biographer). I was right, she said on the long view but Cecil on the short view & the latter must prevail, & so the discussion went on. I pleaded that we must agree to differ – everyone free to advocate his individual view but the Union not to embody this vital change in its programme. This suggestion was repelled by Cecil – the majority could not bind the minority but the majority view must be the official policy of the Union. We divided: 16 for the report 10 against. One at least of our men had left, & I think one or two members of the Comtee. did not vote.

Cecil made an urgent appeal that nothing should be said about our discussion or vote till the subject comes before the Council (= the 1000) of the Union at their meeting in June. There for the present the matter rests. But if this vote is maintained & supported by the Council both Jack Hills & I shall resign our membership of the Union – or so we think at present.

[51] (Ralph) Norman Angell Lane (1874–1967) As Norman Angell published *The Great Illusion*, 1910. General Manager, *Paris Daily Mail*, 1905–14; Editor *Foreign Affairs* 1928–31; Labour MP for Bradford North 1929–31. Knighted 1931; Nobel Peace Prize 1933.

AC5/1/614

18 April 1933
Salterns, Warsash

My dear Ida,

...

I am glad to see from the newspapers that Neville is having good sport. I hope it will put him in good heart & health for the work ahead of him. I do not envy him *his* job.

You will have seen that I used the last hours of the session to say what I thought of the Germans.[52] It was in truth a very good debate. Attlee[53] spoke really well for Labour, Ramsay better than usual of late though he added nothing to our knowledge of the Rome conversations about which I have not had an intelligible word from him either in public or private though I have been shown the actual Italian text by a foreigner & given what purported to be the British amendments. Winston was more restrained than usual & therefore better; though not very effective he supported the case usefully & the House seemed quite unanimous in feeling & sentiment. I am sure that the debate has done good & I hope that Simon will follow it up privately now that Ramsay is off to America. He told me that he agreed with every word that I had said & added that all the trouble arose from Ramsay's habit of loose talk. The Germans, as Ronald Lindsay[54] once wrote to me, can't stand corn [sic] & it was high time that someone spoke plainly to them.

AC5/1/614(b)

24 April 1933
58 Rutland Gate

My dear Hilda,

...

[Postscript]
Secret Mussolini has sent his ambassador to me to explain his ideas.

---

[52] On 13 April 1933 Chamberlain launched his first uncompromising attack upon the 'new spirit of German nationalism' and warned it was not a country to which 'we can afford to make concessions'.

[53] Clement Richard Attlee (1883–1967) Labour MP for Limehouse 1922–50; Walthamstow W. 1950–55. Under Secretary War Office 1924; member of Simon Commission 1928–30; Chancellor Duchy of Lancaster 1930–31; Postmaster-General 1931; Lord Privy Seal 1940–42; Dominion Secretary 1942–3; Lord President 1943–45; Deputy Prime Minister 1942–45; Prime Minister 1945–51. Deputy Labour Leader 1931–35 and Leader 1935–55. Created Earl Attlee 1955; KG 1956.

[54] Ronald Charles Lindsay (1877–1945) Entered Diplomatic Service 1898; Assistant Under-Secretary Foreign Office responsible for Near East 1921–24; Ambassador to Turkey 1925–6 and Berlin 1926–8; Permanent Under-Secretary Foreign Office 1928–30; Ambassador in Washington 1930–9. Knighted 1925.

He thought he was carrying out the Locarno policy – so he says, & I must say the idea as put by him is much more sensible than Ramsay's speeches would have led one to suppose, but all the stage-management was bad. I had a heart-to-heart with Grandi. It may do some good.

AC5/1/615
30 April 1933
58 Rutland Gate

My dear Ida,

...

Neville's budget has not excited anyone but I think it is generally approved. Certainly in the City they would have been aghast if he had taken Keynes' advice & gone in for the three year gamble. In theory the idea is attractive & had attracted me before Keynes wrote, but the more I thought about it, the more evident it became that it would be a pure gamble which might well end in disaster.

So far so good, but I am [sic] good deal perturbed about the Commercial treaties. It seems to me that Runciman has given away too much & my jewellers are all up in arms about the German treaty. I must go to the House tomorrow & see what R. has to say; I don't think that I can vote for it & I may have to vote against it.[55] I mind this less with the *German* treaty than with any other; still it would be a vote against the Govt & on an important issue.

I expect you will have noticed Benes' reference to my speech & his own sensible remarks & you will have seen that Grey expressed agreement with me & that the Times article on Saturday reduced 'Revision' to its proper terms & warned the Germans not to ask or to expect the impossible. Perhaps these results were not wholly unconnected with a dinner at Selby's two nights before, where I had much talk with Grey & Kennedy[56] & some argument with the latter. He writes the Times articles on foreign affairs. I am more than ever glad that I spoke when & *as* I did & am satisfied that it has done good.

I have had five hours more Indian Comtee. this week. It is interesting, but how we are ever to get to the end of our work I don't know. There are 30 members of the Comtee. & in a weeks time 30 Indians will arrive to 'assist' us.

For the rest I have had a meeting of my League Loans Comtee ...

These, however, are trifles. The real events of the week are that I

[55] The Birmingham Jewellers' & Silversmiths' Association opposed the Anglo-Gernam Trade Agreement. Chamberlain made a very effective speech, forced a division and led fifty-four other Conservative MPs into voting against the Government on 1 May 1933.

[56] Aubrey Leo Kennedy (1885–1965) Journalist. Correspondent of *The Times* 1910–42; BBC 1942–5.

had plovers eggs at Cartiers & that Sir Malcolm Hailey[57] has sent me a dozen Bombay mangos in excellent condition. Nothing else matters.

It has been a lovely day & I had a long walk in Hyde Park this morning.

...

AC5/1/616

14 May 1933
58 Rutland Gate

My dear Ida,

...

I have had nothing very interesting ... On the whole the India Comtee. was the most interesting but nine hours a week of it is exacting toil. I said a few words, hardly to be called a speech, in the F.O. debate on Tuesday. It gave me a chance which I was seeking to defend the Govt. & praise Ramsay & to chaff Samuel mildly, & though I did not think much of it, I received more of the compliments which recent speeches have brought me. The fact is, as S.B. said to me that I am the last survivor of an older style of speaking & it rather interests the House & especially the younger members.

...

I am looking forward with much curiosity to Hitler's speech to the Reichstag on Tuesday. Will he say anything really reassuring? I doubt it. I hope our people will not be duped by mere words. At present it is amazing how he has roused British opinion & united it against him. The Times, Telegraph, Observer, Sunday Times & Manchester Guardian, all ring with the same tune. Herr Rosenberg[58] with his swastika on the Cenotaph has aroused even Garvin to fury & they all unite to proclaim; To a Germany much, to *this* Germany nothing! And a very good thing too.

---

[57] William Malcolm Hailey (1872–1969) Entered Indian Civil Service 1895. Chief Commissioner Delhi 1912–8; Member, Viceroy's Executive Council 1919–24; Governor of Punjab 1924–8 and United Provinces 1928–30 and 1931–4. Member, League of Nations Permanent Mandates Commission 1935–9; Director, African Research Survey 1935–8; Chairman, Air Defence Committee 1937–8 and Colonial Research Committee 1943–8; BBC Advisory Council 1953–6. Knighted 1922; created Baron 1936; P.C. 1949; O.M. 1956.

[58] Alfred Rosenberg (1893–1946) Editor of Nazi Party newspaper 1921–38; Member of Reichstag 1930; Director of Nazi Party Foreign Bureau; Supervisor of Youth Education 1940–41; Minister for Occupied Eastern Territory 1941–5. Tried at Nuremberg and hanged October 1946.

AC5/1/617   20 May 1933
                                               58 Rutland Gate

My dear Hilda,

...

No, I will not write an article for Le Temps on how peace can be secured in Europe. No, I will not take the Chairmanship of a Govt. Comtee. on how to attract foreign engineering & technical students to English Universities, so that on returning to hold posts in their own countries they may naturally be led to recommence the placing of orders in the country; nor will I open bazaars in my constituency, nor attend *all* the Embassy & Legation celebrations of the national fête days of their respective countries, nor be the honoured guest of engineers of every imaginable description at their annual banquets no – in short I will henceforth harden my heart & do only what pleases me or has money in it for myself or for something in which I am interested ...

India keeps me very busy. It has really filled up four mornings this week & four from seven leaves three, Sundays included, for all other business. When will there be an eight hours day for brain-workers? Not in my time or Neville's, I fear. I get really anxious about the strain on him. He is incorrigible. He is lecturing this weekend at the Bonar Law College. Why can't he leave that to S.B.? It's just what he is fit for.

...

Yes, I did a tidy bit of work on Mander's silly bill. Simon left the House & left the matter to chance. Mander[59] is *not* popular; he is a Liberal member of the L. of Nations Union, very anxious to advertise it & more so to advertise himself & generally doing or saying something foolish. I was afraid that either the House would let it slip through contemptuously, making us all ridiculous & creating an embarrassing position for the Govt., or that it would be opposed by some equally foolish right wing man who would only encourage the Germans. So I opposed in a three minutes speech & the walls of Jericho fell, as Neville was pleased to say. 'You must be careful what you do' red-headed but attractive Buchanan[60] of the Clyde said to me afterwards; 'We're all afraid of you. The *Govt.* are afraid of you & the Opposition are afraid of you & when you point your finger at any of my little party of three we are afraid of you. Oh, you'll have to be careful'.

[59] Geoffrey Le Mesurier Mander (1882–1962) Liberal MP for Wolverhampton E. 1929–45. Joined Labour in 1948. PPS to Sinclair at Air Ministry 1942–4. Knighted 1945. A League zealot and persistent speaker on foreign affairs.

[60] George Buchanan (1890–1955) ILP MP for Glasgow Gorbals 1922–39, then Labour MP until 1948. Under Secretary for Scotland 1945–7; Minister of Pensions 1947–8; Chairman National Assistance Board 1948–53.

AC5/1/618

28 May 1933
58 Rutland Gate

My dear Ida,

Yes, I continue very loquacious! Three speeches this week ... They all had the kind of success they get now, the audiences were interested in the matter & find in the manner something which is old fashioned enough to be novel. I suppose S.B. was right when he said that I was now the sole survivor of an earlier age, & at any rate, I do *debate* & too many speakers now-a-days either dribble like Lansbury[61] or deliver an essay. Anyway I got my full share of compliments ... Everybody says that I am speaking better than I have done for some years which praise I attribute partly to the fact that they are less inclined to criticize a backbencher than a Minister & largely to the fact that I am not over-worked & do not come to the debate with a tired mind & body.

...

The World Economic Conference[62] fills me with anxiety rather than hope. I fear that it may prove not only a most arduous but also a very thankless task for Neville. I feel that Roosevelt desires to be helpful, but does he know enough &, dictatorial though his powers are for the moment, is his power sufficient & will it last long enough to enable him to do what is needed?

AC5/1/619

6 June 1933
58 Rutland Gate

My dear Hilda,

...

The news from America looks very bad for the Economic Conference, I fear. Roosevelt is already in conflict with Congress &, according to the Times, foreign policy will be sacrificed to the necessities of the home front. And the Conference opens in a few days & the King will be made to broadcast & the P.M. will gush & then – Neville will have to face the difficulties.

---

[61] George Lansbury (1859–1940) Labour MP for Bow & Bromley 1910–12, Poplar 1922–40. First Commissioner of Works 1929–31; Labour Leader 1931–5. Editor, *Daily Herald* 1913–22. Member Poplar Council 1903–40 and Mayor 1919–20, 1936–7.
[62] The World Economic Conference was opened by the King in London, 12 June 1933. The last of the great international conferences between the wars.

AC5/1/620   12 June 1938
                                                          58 Rutland Gate

My dear Ida,

. . .

We dined last night at the Belgian Embassy where we met Coligin [sic],[63] Prime Minister of the Netherlands, Jaspar[64] & Hymans[65] of Belgium, Ishii of Japan, all old friends of Geneva days & the Austrian Chancellor, Dr Dollfuss;[66] & today I lunched with Walford Selby to meet Dollfuss again. I had much talk with him last night & today, a little man, standing about five foot nothing, self made & self educated but full of courage & determination, but speaking alas! no other language but German & something of a patois at that. I found great difficulty in understanding him & more in answering, but we were pleased with one-another. He sought my advice on several points & I gave him all the help & comfort I could. He is confident that he can hold Austria *if* the Germans are restrained & all the Austrians were certain that a few plain words from England, with which Mussolini would be only too glad to associate himself, would suffice to restrain Hitler & Co. I urged him to put his whole case before Simon as strongly as he could, but will Simon understand & act? Alas! none of them seems to turn to Simon or to trust him. It is a terrible misfortune.

The conversation with Hymans was also very interesting. I was delighted to find that like me he thought the most striking thing about [the Four Power Pact?] was Mussolini's explanation of it to the Senate – the revival of the policy of Locarno (Did you see the Times report of his speech in last Thursday's issue?) & the approach to France. My dear Ida, it is odd to see Mussolini understanding & believing in my policy more than my own Govt.

Noone seems to cherish much hope of the Conference. I am deeply

[63] Hendrikus Colijn (1869–1944) Soldier and administrator, Dutch East Indies until 1909 when elected to Dutch Parliament. Minister of War 1911–13; Minister of Finance 1923–26; Prime Minister 1925–26, 1933–39; Minister of War 1935–37; Foreign Minister 1937. Vigorous opponent of Nazis. Arrested 1941; interned in Germany 1942 where he died.

[64] Henri Jaspar (1870–1939) Belgian politician. Minister of Economic Affairs 1918; Minister of Foreign Affairs 1920–4, 1934; Prime Minister 1926–31; Finance Minister 1932–4.

[65] Paul Hymans (1865–1941) Belgian Liberal politician and diplomat. Ambassador in London 1915–17; delegate to Paris Peace Conference 1919; President of first League of Nations session 1920; Foreign Minister 1918–20, 1924–5, 1927–34.

[66] Englebert Dollfuss (1892–1934) Austrian Christian Social politician. Chancellor of Austria 1932 until murdered by Nazis during attempted coup d'état in July 1934.

concerned for Neville on whom the burden must rest. It seems to me not only a thankless but an almost hopeless job with Roosevelt's eyes turned inwards & his hands & feet in chains.

AC5/1/621

16 June 1933
58 Rutland Gate

My dear Ida,

This has been a week, I imagine, of intense strain & worry for Neville but also a great success. I thought his conference address was *masterly* & I am told that his reading of it was perfect & that it produced a great impression. What the ultimate result may be, I am in no position to judge; I can only wish & hope. At the moment when I thought Roosevelt beaten, he appears to have triumphed – at what ultimate cost I know not, but it allows one to continue to hope.

For myself I am sunk deep in India & can see no outlet & no end. The Comtee. is ill-constructed; I doubt whether any Comtee. would be unanimous, but what worries me is that there are not enough independent members who might be convinced on this Comtee. & therefore the majority will not carry the weight it might have done. I don't see a single member who represents the mass of the younger Conservatives – men who might be persuaded to accept the scheme, perhaps with some modifications but who are full of honest doubt & anxiety. And if the Comtee. is ill-chosen, the procedure is impossible. For to the 30 or so committee men are added as many or more delegates from India, not merely for the purpose of conference but also for the examination of witnesses. Sixty men to put questions to each witness! For the last 2 days (six hours) we have had Sir M. O'Dyer[67] [sic] in the Chair & only 20 members of the Comtee. have yet had an opportunity of putting any question to him. At this rate it would be 4 sittings of 3 hours each for each witness & we may have 100 witnesses!

June 17. I have been enjoying & publishing to all the world a gaffe of the Germans. I think I told you that Ian Hamilton,[68] who on

[67] Michael Francis O'Dwyer (1864–1940) Entered Indian Civil Service 1885; Revenue Commissioner NW Frontier 1901–8; Acting President Hyderabad 1908–9; Viceroy's Agent, Central India 1910–12; Lieut-Governor of Punjab 1913–9. Knighted 1913. Author of *India as I knew it* (1925)

[68] Ian Stanish Montieth Hamilton (1853–1947) Chief of Staff to Kitchener 1901–2; General 1914; Commander Home Defence Force 1914–15 and Mediterranean Expeditionary Force at Gallipoli, March–October 1915 after which received no further command. Knighted 1900. Scottish President of British Legion. Enthusiast of understanding with Germany and apologist for Nazi regime in 1930s.

Reading's resignation was elected President of the Anglo-German Assn., telegraphed to me that the Germans were dining *privately* with him on Tuesday & asking if I would come to meet them. I accepted, thinking I might get a chance of a quiet & useful talk with Neurath,[69] whom I know & whom I was among the first to welcome at my house when he came here as Ambassador. On Tuesday, however, Ian Hamilton arrived in a state of great indignation & excitement, saying that an abominable thing has happened that he felt grossly insulted, that he was furious &c. &c. & scarcely knew how to tell me. 'Don't worry', said I, 'I know exactly what's happened, the Germans have refused to meet me!' 'Yes', said I.H. 'I'm furious. And it isn't the Embassy. Hoesch[70] & Bernstorff[71] know & were delighted that you were coming & I'm certain that Neurath also knew & was pleased. They've had instructions from Berlin.' Hamilton was evidently afraid that I should visit my wrath on him. I reassured him on this point & added 'But if you want to please me, will you tell them what damned fools they are & say that it is just because they are such fools that they never succeed?' 'I *will*' he replied with fervour. I have taken great pains to spread the story. It has gone all over the Conference & Ivy says it was over Ascot. Dollfuss has returned to Vienna much bucked up by the sympathy he found everywhere here & by his reception in the Conference which amounted to a demonstration.

AC5/1/623

24 June 1933
58 Rutland Gate

My dear Ida,

. . .

Tuesday morning I spent at the League of Nations [Union?] Council meeting where the cranks, pacifists & hoc genus omne were all well represented.

. . . It is time that I made another speech on Germany. I should like to make yet another on 'how not to do things' & all my illustrations would be drawn from the United States, but this speech will not be

---

[69] Baron Constantin von Neurath (1873–1956) Ambassador to Italy 1921 and to Britain 1930. German Foreign Minister 1932–8; Gauleiter for conquered Czech territory of Bohemia and Moravia 1939. Jailed at Nuremberg and released 1954.

[70] Leopold von Hoesch (1881–1936) Entered German diplomatic service 1907; Third Secretary London 1912–14. Served Sofia 1915, Constantinople 1916, Oslo 1918; Counsellor in Paris 1921–24; Ambassador to Paris 1924–32; Ambassador to London 1932–36.

[71] Albrecht Graf von Bernstorff (1890–1945) Secretary to German Embassy in London 1923; Counsellor 1925–30; Senior Counsellor 1930–3; left Civil Service in 1933 because an uncompromising opponent of Nazi regime. Imprisoned Dachau Concentration Camp 1940. Murdered by Gestapo in Berlin, April 1945.

made by me though an exasperated Neville might some day blurt it out – when he too has retired to the back benches & becomes an "elderly moralist".

AC5/1/624

3 July 1933
58 Rutland Gate

My dear Hilda,

Oh! These Americans! I had a few words with Neville at the Speaker's dinner & reception on Friday evening. I gather that he had not abandoned hope of some good coming out of the Conference then, but he could not have foreseen Roosevelt's latest.[72] I wonder whether any business can be done with *anyone now*, ... But I confess that it makes me mad when I see Roosevelt declaring from the other side of the Atlantic that he won't have the Conference "diverted" from real business to the question which only a short time ago he insisted must be their first task. I sometimes wonder whether, if we could survive the first explosion of American wrath, it would not in the long run be good for Anglo-American relations if for once Englishmen would unite to tell them exactly how they appear to everyone who has tried to do business with them! By the way at the Speaker's I sought an introduction to Mr Cordell Hull.[73] He showered flattery upon me – & left me with the impression of a very amiable, gentlemanly & ineffective personality. But even the much-heralded Professor seems unable to follow the workings of the President's mind from the moment that he left his side. I think we must look elsewhere for our salvation.

I have had another full week .. On Monday ... I presided at a luncheon which we [School of Hygiene] gave to the Chancellor [of University of London] & other big-wigs ... Over a cup of tea at the School afterwards Baldwin told me that two years at the F.O. had knocked up Simon completely & that he was now unable to take a decision. Bad news indeed! His colleagues are I believe trying to get him to take a long sea voyage. I wish he were a better man for the job. It was the wrong place to put him. I swear Anthony Eden[74] would do better.

---

[72] On 3 July Roosevelt rejected the idea of an agreement for the international stabilization of currencies because it would hamper national policies designed to raise the purchasing power of the people at home through currency regulations. This effectively torpedoed the World Economic Conference.

[73] Cordell Hull (1871–1955) US Secretary of State 1933–44. Nobel Peace Prize 1945.

[74] (Robert) Anthony Eden (1897–1977) Conservative MP for Warwick & Leamington 1923–57. PPS at Foreign Office to G. Locker-Lampson 1924–6 and to A. Chamberlain 1926–9; Under Secretary for Foreign Affairs 1931–4; Lord Privy Seal 1934–5; Minister for League of Nations 1935; Foreign Secretary 1935–8, 1940–5, 1951–5; Dominion

...

... Incidentally [Sir Malcolm] Hailey ... is only a looker-on at the Indian Comtee but that he & the other lookers-on have come to the conclusion that everything depends upon what I do, & Lady Willingdon who has been seeing a lot of the Indians said to me today that they feel much the same – very flattering no doubt but in so far as it is true it does not lessen my responsibility. It is more & more brought home to me how very unwise the Govt. has been in the choice of men to form the Comtee. Salisbury, Nall,[75] Craddock[76] are, I should judge impervious to any impressions other than those with which they entered the Comtee. Simon does not attend; the Lord Chancellor may & I believe will be useful, but so far has done little or nothing. Hoare is first-rate but what use is his Under Secretary[77] for purposes of persuasion? or Davidson? or Miss Pickford?[78] or ——. In short where are the members of the House who would represent the great bulk of the Party – men who know there must be great changes, who want to support the Govt. but are yet full of doubt & anxiety? The Archbishop, Hardinge, Derby – all in the other House & neither H. nor D. carry great weight outside. Oh d–n!

AC5/1/626   22 July 1933
                                                      Lytchett Heath
                                                      Poole

My dear Ida,

    ... I hope to get Neville & Annie to dine one evening before they go north for I have scarcely spoken to them this year! I want a holiday

Secretary 1939–40; Secretary for War 1940; Prime Minster and Conservative Leader 1955–7. K.C. 1954. Created Earl of Avon 1961.

[75] Joseph Nall (1887–1958) Conservative MP for Hulme, Manchester 1918–29, 1931–45. President, Institute of Transport 1925–6. Knighted 1924; created Baronet 1954.

[76] Reginald Craddock (1864–1937) Entered Indian Civil Service 1884; Chief Commissioner Central Provinces 1907–12; Member, Viceroy's Executive Council 1912–7; Lieut-Governor of Burma 1917–22; First Chancellor, Rangoon University; Member, Royal Commission on India Civil Service 1923–4; Member of Council of Indian Empire Society 1931. Knighted 1911.

[77] Richard Austen Butler (1902–82) Conservative MP for Saffron Walden 1929–65. Under Secretary for India 1932–7; Parliamentary Secretary, Labour 1937–8; Under Secretary Foreign Office 1938–41; President, Board of Education 1941–5; Minister of Labour 1945; Chancellor of Exchequer, 1951–5; Lord Privy Seal 1955–9; Home Secretary 1957–62; Deputy Prime Minister 1962–3; Foreign Secretary 1963–4; Conservative Party Chairman 1959–61; Chairman, Conservative Research Dept 1945–64; Master of Trinity College, Cambridge 1965–78. Created Baron Butler of Saffron Walden 1965; K.G. 1971.

[78] Mary Ada Pickford (1884–1934) Conservative MP for Hammersmith N., 1931 until her death.

myself, for India worries me awfully. I never worry once I see my way & have taken a decision, but in this case I don't see my way nor where I can look for help. I think the Govt. have loaded the dice against themselves & fear that there will be much trouble in the party before we have done. Meanwhile we are to sit into the first days of August & I have to sacrifice my Cowes week. I am very cross!

AC5/1/629

13 August 1933
Salterns, Warsash

My dear Hilda,

...

... Events in Germany fill me with disgust at the domestic brutality of the regime & with deepening anxiety about its external consequences. What is our Govt. doing? Is it going to swallow the insolence of the official announcements about our representations & the continued broadcasts against the Austrian Govt. & recurring frontier incidents? Is Germany to be allowed to rearm & are we to continue to press others to disarm? Have we in fact a policy & is the Cabinet behind it, & do our representatives abroad know what it is if it indeed exists? I hear from a sure source that since Simon took office if not earlier, no Ambassador has received a private letter from the Sec. of State or even seen his signature?!

Another thing troubles me. I wonder what Neville thinks about it or has had time to think of it. If Roosevelt's policy fails, I suppose that there will be a worse crash than ever in the U.S.A. with unhappy reactions for us & everyone else. But if he succeeds? Shall we not be confronted with an enormously difficult & dangerous demand to follow the same policy in spite of our wholly different circumstances? I think I dread his success even more than his failure in its consequences to us.

AC5/1/631

3 September 1933
Hotel Royal, Rome

My dear Hilda,

...

I had an hours' very friendly & interesting conversation with Mussolini yesterday evening. I was extremely glad to have the opportunity of renewing our relations & found him in excellent health & spirits.

... Mussolini's improvements here are really magnificent & will make Rome an extraordinarily fine city.

AC5/1/634
7 October 1933
58 Rutland Gate

My dear Ida,

Diane & I got home [from Corsica] an hour late last Sunday & I found myself at once knee-deep in business. The India Comtee is now sitting 18 hours a week in an endeavour to get to the end of the evidence & finish all that has to be done with the assistance (?) of the Indian Delegates. I shall be glad to be rid of them. Two or three of them occupy an interminable time in examining witnesses & generally do as much harm as possible to their own cause in that process. They are inconceivably stupid & unteachable in this respect. Instead of setting themselves to convince the Comtee. that the reforms are safe, they think only of the Indian gallery & say & do everything they can to make the Comtee. suspicious of their intentions & to convince us not only that all the safeguards are necessary but that we must supplement them by further precautions. I begin, however, to see my way of gathering together a nucleous [sic] of moderate or middle opinion in the Comtee. which may prove decisive in the long run. Harding[e], Derby, Zetland,[79] Cadogan[80] & I to being with. We ought to have help from the Archbishop & Reading, Peel & perhaps Attlee. The last named has impressed me & his help would be very useful as he is the principle [sic] or at least most distinguished Labour member.

AC5/1/635
14 October 1933
58 Rutland Gate

My dear Hilda,

Many thanks for your birthday congratulations. One cannot pretend that one is any longer young at 70, but I don't feel old & I suppose that that is what really matters. I hated being fifty, but since that point was definitely past, more or less doesn't seem to matter so long as I am not an invalid & a trouble to myself & others ...

---

[79] Lawrence John Lumley Dundas (1876–1961) Conservative MP for Hornsey 1907–16. Governor of Bengal 1917–22; Secretary of State for India 1935–40 and for Burma 1937–40. Known as Lord Dundas 1876–92. Earl of Ronaldshay 1892 until succeeded as 2nd Marquess of Zetland 1929.
[80] Edward Cecil George Cadogan (1880–1962) Secretary to the Speaker 1911–2; Conservative MP for Reading, 1922–3, Finchley 1924–35, Bolton 1940–5. Member, Indian Statutory Commission 1927–32 and Joint Select Committee on the Indian Constitution 1933–5. Knighted 1939.

And now, what do you think of the latest German move?[81] I want time to digest its meaning & think out its consequences. I suspect, as the French do, that their real objection to a probationary period of inspection without 'samples' is that the inspection would reveal that they had already manufactured & possessed some at least of the forbidden weapons. Davis[82] supported Simon at Geneva … & I shall read anxiously his exact words & those of the Italian representative if the Times will give them to me on Monday. Much will depend upon the degree of unanimity & cooperation which can be obtained among the Four Powers where the U.S.A. ought to take the place of Germany in this inner council of the League – I don't mean by formal entry into it but by close cooperation with it. But has Roosevelt any time or power to make a contribution to world peace?

I have, as you know, always thought the courting of Germany at the time of her first secession from the Conference a mistake & have disliked the assurances then given her as an inducement to return. I believe that firmer handling then would have prevented this last development. But, as I used to say at the F.O., it is no use jobbing backwards; that merely shirks the actual problem, which is not whether we were right or wrong six months or a year ago but what ought we to do now.

"I must fink, Auntie; I must fink."

Would it not be possible to bring them before the Council of the League – they remain members for 2 years after giving notice of withdrawal – & to secure a judgement against them? I'm not sure, but I think it might be worked &, if so, with some very interesting & useful consequences.

But I need time & knowledge of what is passing in Geneva & the great capitals to digest the news & perceive its consequences, for I confess that I have not really believed that Germany would take this step though I have been alarmed at what has seemed to me encouragement from certain quarters to 'try it on.'

---

[81] Germany had rejected the French proposal for a disarmament convention on the basis of a four year trial period during which there would be no new weapons building, all round reduction in armed strength and automatic, regular inspection. On 14 October Hitler announced Germany's withdrawal not only from the Disarmament Conference but also from the League of Nations.

[82] Norman Davis (1878–1944) American banker and diplomat. Financial adviser to Wilson at Paris Peace Conference 1919; Assistant Secretary to Treasury 1919–20; Under-Secretary of State 1920–1; US delegate to Geneva Economic Conference 1927; to Disarmament Conference 1932–3; to London Naval Conference 1935; to Nine Power Brussels Conference 1937. Vansittart described him as 'the most wearisome' of the 'American Amateurs'.

AC5/1/636

22 October 1933
Chartwell
Westerham, Kent

My dear Ida,

Here I am in the lion's den & alone, for Ivy has a very bad cold & is still confined to her room ...

... Anthony Eden asked me to lunch yesterday saying that he wanted my advice. Walter Elliot[83] & Philip Sassoon were the other guests & I got from Anthony & W.E. some further light on the attitude of the other Powers & that bit of knowledge, where before I was guessing helped me on & conversation & argument cleared my mind, so that presently I was fairly confident in submitting suggestions. These were briefly to get the conference adjourned indefinitely to negotiate a definite disarmament text with France, Italy & the U.S.A. & when this was privately agreed, to reassemble the Conference, carry it through, initial it *ne varietus* i.e. not to be further amended but to be taken or left in that form, offer it to Germany & ratify subject to the accession of all the Great Powers & a sufficiency of lesser States so that our own ratification would only take effect when the rest ratified.

If Germany denounces the Treaty of Versailles or of Locarno or rearms meanwhile, bring her before the League Council under Article 10, 11 or 15 of the Covenant (I cite the numbers from memory). The point is to choose the Article which enables the Council to give a binding decision by unanimity *excluding* the parties to the dispute, but this needs more examination & consideration.

I think that Eden's mind had been working on the same lines tho' he had come to no decision & that W.E. was convinced by my arguments & answers to the difficulties to which he sought a reply.

It will be interesting to see the results. I was careful to insist that such issues could be decided finally only by those who were in possession of all the threads: there might be factors of which I was unaware but they had asked ...

Above all, no running after Germany & no payment of blackmail this time. Don't let us repeat the mistake the Powers made when Germany withdrew last year. Paying blackmail was always bad policy; it was an even worse policy with Germany than with anyone else.

I gather that they had had a most unsatisfactory & inconclusive

---

[83] Walter Elliot Elliot (1888–1958) Conservative MP for Lanark 1918–23. Glasgow Kelvingrove 1924–45, 1950–8, Scottish Universities 1946–50. Parliamentary Secretary of Health for Scotland 1923–4, 1924–6; Under Secretary for Scotland 1926–9; Financial Secretary to Treasury 1931–2; Minister of Agriculture 1932–6; Scottish Secretary 1936–8; Minister of Health 1938–40.

Cabinet ending with a decision that Simon should draw up a memo showing the various courses open to them which he only consented to do on one condition – that he was not asked to advise them which of those courses they should adopt!!![84]

This confirms what the Lord Chancellor said to me the other day: "I wish we had you in Cabinet. We want advice terribly!"

...

... Yesterday there was Eden's lunch & now I am spending the week-end with the W. Churchills. I discuss Marlborough as much & India as little as I can. Only the family here, with a guest or at most two at meals – very pleasant but on the tiring side, for both Winston & Randolph[85] roar [?] when excited in argument.

AC5/1/637

28 October 1933
58 Rutland Gate

My dear Hilda,

...

My week-end at the Churchill's was very pleasant. We differed about India without quarrelling, agreed about Marlborough, felt equally free from any obligation to S.B. or R.M. & viewed the future with equal anxiety but with opposite hopes. He anticipates that he & his Indian Die-Hards will continue to hold about 1/3rd of the Party, that the India Bill will be carried but that the fight will leave such bitter memories that the Govt. will have to be reconstructed. Only Ramsay, S.B., Sam Hoare, Irwin & perhaps the Lord Chancellor are so committed that they would have to go. Simon could stay & it would still be a National Government, but who is to lead it? Obviously, I am this man! & so he led me up into a high place & showed me the kingdoms of the world. I was not greatly tempted. I told him that I saw the situation developing differently; that I recognised, as he urged me to do, that I must not view the Indian problem in vacuo but must have regard also to wider issues, but so must he & his friends, & all of us must remember the greater danger of a Socialist dictatorship of the

---

[84] On 23 October 1933 the Cabinet endorsed Simon's view that as there was little point in continuing while Germany was absent, Britain should press for an adjournment in the hope of finding a compromise. CAB 54(33)1, CAB 23/77.

[85] Randolph Frederick Edward Spencer Churchill (1911–68) Churchill's only son. After leaving Oxford without a degree 1932, he worked for many newspapers. Unsuccessful parliamentary candidate 1935 (twice), 1936, 1945, 1950, 1951. Conservative MP for Preston 1940–5.

Cripps[86] pattern. We must fight out our Indian battle as friends & bury the hatchett [sic] as soon as it was over. I did not see any reason for resignations, I was not anxious, indeed was wholly averse to becoming P.M. at 70 or 71 & saw no reason why I should submit to such a burden. At the same time, as long as I was in politics, I was not going to say that I would not serve again in any capacity, if the necessity arose, or wipe my name finally off the slate. Sufficient unto the day were the decisions thereof, & I wasn't going to give definitive answers to purely hypothetical questions or write myself down a dotard before I felt any signs of mental decay.

Rather ticklish grounds! I don't want what he wants, but if I had replied bluntly I am too old & won't in any case look at it, I should have lost influence all along the line. This is the second approach made to me on the same lines, & I get from all quarters more flattering testimonials than I have ever enjoyed in my life. I need scarcely add that Ivy is more ambitious for me than I am or ever have been for myself & is even more convinced than I am that I can do some things better than any of the present men & that they made a mistake in not making use of me & she does not like me to talk of being too old at 70, so I have to have regard for her feelings as well as my own. But Heaven save me from a call to be the saviour of my country or even my party.

East Fulham[87] is a nasty knock whatever the true explanation. I hope it is not the beginning of a landslide.

AC5/1/639

11 November 1933
58 Rutland Gate

My dear Hilda,

. . .

I see my end clearly before me. I shall be found one day done to death by cruel Indian uncles & buried among masses of hecto-graphed leaves. The thing is becoming a nightmare & the moment I have a

---

[86] (Richard) Stafford Cripps (1889–1952) Labour MP for Bristol East 1931–50; Bristol SE 1950. Expelled from Labour Party 1939–45. Solicitor-General 1930–1; Ambassador to Russia 1940–42; Lord Privy Seal and Leader of House 1942; Minister of Aircraft Production 1942–5; President Board of Trade 1945–7; Minister of Economic Affairs 1947; Chancellor of Exchequer 1947–50. Knighted 1930.

[87] On 25 October 1933 Labour won East Fulham, sensationally transforming a Conservative majority of 14521 into a Labour majority of 4840. Although the result reflected electoral discontent with local housing and domestic issues, the fact that Labour fought on an explicitly disarmament platform was widely interpreted at the time as a vote against rearmament and it supposedly had a major impact on Baldwin's attitude.

little extra work or pressure of engagements it gets upon my nerves & makes me fretful as the porcupine ...

I send you the reprint of my German speeches with a foreword by me & will in due course send you an article I have written for Chilcott's paper, the National, which will appear in about a week ... I send you also a very interesting note from Rumbold[88] on Hitlerism ... Upon the whole, I find grounds for hope in it. I would sooner deal with Hitler himself than with von Papen[89] on the one hand or Goebbells[90] [sic] & Goehring[91] [sic] on the other. The bigger man Hitler is, the more chance there seems to me to be that he will settle down into something more reasonable & statesmanlike than his first manifestation.

You do me too much honour in supposing that I had anything to do with Eden's admirable exposition of the case for Locarno. That was entirely his own work. The questions Simon put to me had reference only to how Germany's withdrawal from the League affected the Treaty: (1) did it render the treaty void, or (2) did it release us from our obligations to Germany alone whilst leaving us bound to France & Belgium; or (3) was the treaty unaffected by the withdrawal? I thought the first position untenable, the second arguable, but the third in all the circumstances the best policy. That was certainly Eden's view also & I *think* Simon's. But has Simon a clear view on policy. No man can state a case more lucidly, but is he capable of taking & sticking to a decision.

[88] Horace Rumbold (1869–1941) Entered Diplomatic Service 1891. Chargé d'Affaires, Berlin July 1914; Minister in Berne 1916–9 and Warsaw 1919–20; High Commissioner Constantinople 1920–24; Ambassador to Madrid 1924–8; in Berlin 1928–33. Vice-Chairman Royal Commission on Palestine 1936–7. Succeeded as 9th Baronet 1913.

[89] Franz von Papen (1879–1969) Military Attaché Washington 1914–6 but expelled for sabotage. Chancellor June–November 1932; member of Hitler's Cabinet 1933–4; Ambassador to Vienna 1934–8. Tried at Nuremberg and acquitted 1946.

[90] Joseph Goebbels (1897–1945) Appointed by Hitler Gauleiter of Berlin 1926; Founder of Berlin Nazi newspaper *Der Angriff* (The Attack) 1927; elected to Reichstag 1929; Propaganda Leader of Nazi Party 1929; Minister of Enlightenment & Propaganda 1933–45. Committed suicide Berlin May 1945.

[91] Hermann Goering (1893–1946) Follower of Hitler from 1923. Elected to Reichstag 1928 and its President 1932–3; Prime Minister of Prussia 1933; C-in-C German Air Force 1933–45; Commissioner of Four Year Plan 1936; President, General Council for War Economy 1940. Committed suicide before death sentence carried out October 1946.

AC5/1/640

18 November 1933
58 Rutland Gate

My dear Ida,

...

Philip Sassoon has now given me a standing invitation to his Thursday luncheons to Cabinet & other Ministers. I enjoy them, for they keep me in touch to some extent with the circle in which I used to live & enable me sometimes to get & sometimes to give information. On this occasion the party comprised Hailsham, self, Simon, Hankey, Cunliffe-Lister, Runciman, Neville & Philip himself in that order.... . At Derby's luncheon [with half a dozen members of Indian Committee], we made good progress. He, Hardinge, E. Percy,[92] Hutchinson,[93] E. Cadogan, Zetland & I will certainly be able to act together on all main issues & so afford at least a nucleus of moderation on the basis of the acceptance of the main postulates of the White Paper whilst insisting on considerable modifications within those limits.

...

I am very uneasy in my mind about the public outlook generally. Public opinion seems to me very unstable, very easily stampeded & apparently incapable of pursuing a steady course on any subject for any length of time. I don't know what members of the Govt think about the matter, but the third year is apt to be the critical one in a government's life & things don't seem to me to be going well at present. They have failed to strike the imagination. In spite of all the good work which they have done there is nothing dramatic about them & least of all about the two leaders whose failings, I suppose, reach to an ever widening audience & damp such enthusiasm as there might otherwise be. As to foreign affairs, sympathy seems to have swung back to Germany & the attack on the Govt is led by the Times. I am furious with that paper. Even the Express is steadfast compared to its wobbling. It doesn't seem to know where it stands or what it wants. I think our prospects are bad, at present.

---

[92] Eustace Sutherland Campbell Percy (1887–1958) Conservative MP for Hastings 1921–37. Parliamentary Secretary to Education 1923 and Health 1923–4; President, Board of Education 1924–9; member of Joint Select Committee on India 1933–4; Minister without Portfolio 1935–6. Known as Lord Eustace Percy from 1899. Created Baron Percy of Newcastle 1953.

[93] Robert Hutchinson (1873–1950) Liberal MP for Kirkcaldy Burghs 1922–23, Montrose Burghs 1924–32 – from 1931 as Liberal National. Chief Whip 1926–30; Paymaster-General 1935–38; Chairman, National Liberal Organisation 1936–40. Kt 1919. Created Baron Hutchinson of Montrose 1932.

AC5/1/641

26 November 1933
Farnham Chase
Bucks

My dear Hilda,

...

You may have seen I also delivered a speech at the Constitutional Club. They turned up to hear me in greater numbers than had ever attended before & I think I may say that I had a success, but it was delicate going. My text was 'Hang together lest you hang separately' or in other words support the Natl. Govt. & fight on 'National' as opposed to mere party lines & I knew that in that strong party club it was a theme which they were not too well prepared to accept & that I must watch my steps. Think then how much I was aided & cheered when Paddy Hannon,[94] Chairman of the Political Comtee. in proposing my health ended his speech with the sentiment Let us stick to the old Conservative name & have no more of this nonsense about a National Party. You may imagine that in such an atmosphere I had to walk warily, but said all that I wanted to say &, I think really impressed them, but it was hard work, for at any moment a rash phrase or an ill-chosen word would have destroyed all the effect which I was gradually building up.

AC5/1/643

17 December 1933
58 Rutland Gate

My dear Hilda,

...

... I am depressed about public affairs. Two things particularly interest me – housing & foreign affairs. I am uncomfortable about both. I have an uneasy feeling that Hilton Young whom I like very much, is dealing quite inadequately with the former & that he regards it all as a great bore. He gives the impression that his heart is not in it & that is fatal.

As to foreign affairs I have this week seen the French Ambassador,

---

[94] Patrick Joseph Henry Hannon (1874–1963) Conservative MP for Birmingham Moseley 1921–50; Vice-President, Tariff Reform League 1910–4; General Secretary, Navy League 1911–8; Director, British Commonwealth Union 1918–28; Secretary Empire Industries Association 1925–50; President, Industrial Transport Association 1927–37. Knighted 1936.

Tyrrel [sic], Avenol[95] the new Secretary-General of the League & a very competent junior in the F.O. All are very disturbed & very hopeless about our shifts of policy. We go on talking about our influence & we *ought* to exercise great influence, but to me it seems ... we are losing influence all the time. France has lost confidence in us, Italy goes its own way & Germany snaps her fingers at us all. 'Whom would you make Foreign Secretary?' I asked Tyrrell. 'You, of course'. 'But I'm out of it'. 'Then Neville. He's the only one who understands'. Pity there aren't half a dozen Nevilles. And to think that in times like these we have no better men to lead the three parties than Ramsay, S.B. & Lansbury. Oh for a *man*!

. . .

Asquith's letters are twaddle. They should never have been published. Foreigners, puzzled as usual by our eccentricities, enquire why does Lady Oxford publish her husband's letters to his mistress.[96]

AC5/1/644   26 December 1933
                                           Polesden Lacey

My dear Ida,

. . .

You will have seen that I said a few words on foreign affairs on the motion for the adjournment, I was not very pleased with my own performance but I did say one or two things which I thought needed saying, including a protest against the mock Reichstag trial in London & an appeal to Simon to give the country more guidance. My friends thought that the signs were a little more hopeful & as if after much shilly shallying the Govt. were settling down again on sound lines. But try as I may, I can't feel any confidence in Simon or shall I say any more confidence than do his colleagues. After my speech the debate switched over to the Beef import order, so I went to lunch! A moment later S.B. followed & sat down at my table. 'I liked your speech', he said & then went on 'It was a great comfort to have you as foreign secretary during those five years. I always felt very happy & comfortable with you there' – which belated compliment I think I cannot be wrong

---

[95] Joseph Avenol (1879–1952) Deputy Secretary-General, League of Nations and later Secretary-General 1933–40.

[96] Among the many women to whom Asquith wrote was Mrs Hilda Harrison. These letters were edited by Desmond MacCarthy as *H.H.A. : Letters of the Earl of Oxford and Asquith to a Friend* (2 vols. 1933–4). Asquith's daughter lamented 'The editing of these letters has been of course a great blow to us and I fear to many others', Lady Violet Bonham Carter to A.G. Gardiner, 4 December 1933.

in considering as a reflection on my successor rather than a tribute to myself.

AC5/1/646   7 January 1934
                                                            58 Rutland Gate

My dear Ida,

. . .

I have found Spender's[97] 'Fifty Years' very interesting ... but I can't help feeling between the lines the strong Liberal partisan ... I feel about him as I felt about Asquith in the first Coalition – that he was inwardly & always a party man, patriotic of course & not the least self-seeking but quite unable in his approach to any problem to divest himself of party-feeling which probably quite unconsciously tinged all his thoughts & decisions.

AC5/1/650   3 February 1934
                                                            58 Rutland Gate

My dear Ida,

. . .

My weeks doing include the resumption of attendance at the India Comtee which is now beginning to feel its way towards a report, some attendance at the House & some pleasant social occasions ... on Wednesday I had ... luncheon with Derby & our Indian friends by which I mean our group of members of the India Comtee – half a dozen men who now say that they will follow where I lead ... What we shall make of it I don't know. I have to dine next week with Reading one day & Sam Hoare another to expound our views & hear theirs.

. . .

What, you ask, do I think of the new British White Paper?[98] Well, the answer, I think must be that given the premises which in fact were

---

[97] John Alfred Spender (1862–1942) Journalist and author. Editor, *Westminster Gazette* 1896–1922; Member, Royal Commission on Divorce and Matrimonial Causes and Private Manufacture of Armaments; Member, Special Mission to Egypt 1919–20. Published 18 books including a memoir, *Life, Journalism and Politics* (1927), *Fifty Years of Europe* (1933)... Staunch friend and ally of Asquith and co-author of *The Life of Lord Oxford and Asquith* (1932).

[98] The British note on 29 January 1934 was less harsh than the MacDonald plan of the previous year, allowing Germany still only 200,000 troops but permitted tanks up to 6 tons and the right to build military aircraft to parity with her neighbours after ten years if no world agreement on their abolition was reached in two years.

given away as the price of Germany's interim return to Geneva, it is a sensible & good proposal; but I am gravely disquieted by the way in which Germany is "getting away with it" & the encouragement which she thus receives to raise her demands again & again. The fact is (& its no use my pretending anything else to you) that Simon is a very bad Foreign Secretary. He has no policy, is very pleased with himself & wholly unconscious of the effect he produces on others. He has been telling me & others of the great success he had in Rome. An emissary, who came to me from Mussolini last Sunday gave me a different picture practically summed up in the phrase: − I want to talk to a statesman & I find nothing but a lawyer! & the impression left on M.'s mind was that the British Empire *could* not have a policy & Great Britain *had* not got one. All of which reminds me that on Thursday I lunched by request (urgently repeated after first refused) with P. Sassoon to meet Billy [Ormsby] Gore, Eden, Walter Elliot & Hankey to discuss the foreign situation. They are all alarmed & in despair at Simon's attitude.

AC5/1/651   10 February 1934
                                             58 Rutland Gate

My dear Hilda,

      . . .

On Thursday I lunched with Philip Sassoon − Hailsham, Simon, Maurice Hankey, Clive Wigram[99] (the King's Secretary) Londonderry & Billy Gore the other guests. Imagine my surprise when Simon began: 'Austen I want you to hold forth about Austria. I want your advice!' I gave it to the best of my ability but its about as useful as telling me what to do when I try to play billiards. No doubt the advice I receive is good but the result is disastrous because I bungle the shot. I fear I told him some disagreeable truths but I tried to present them as unobjectionably as possible. But the truth is that he has no policy & is content to live from day to day. Hardinge tells me what indeed everyone else confirms, that neither the officials at the F.O. nor our representatives abroad know what he is at or what they should try for. Everyone is without direction. Henderson, they say, could not write a dispatch but he did know & say in a muddled sort of way what he wanted & they could put it into words for him, but noone can express a policy which is non-existent. He has allowed the Germans to think that they have

---

[99] Clive Wigram (1873–1960) Indian Army 1897–9; Aide-de-Camp to Curzon as Viceroy, 1899–1904; Assistant Private Secretary to King George V 1910–31; Private Secretary 1931–5. Knighted 1928. Created Baron 1935.

got us on the run — indeed I fear they have — and nothing could be more dangerous ...

AC5/1/656

16 March 1934
58 Rutland Gate

My dear Hilda,

...

... Today India at which I again presided in Linlithgow's[100] absence ...

India has reached a very interesting stage. The 'brain wave' was really Attlee's. I saw from quite early days that his experience on the Statutory Comtee had suggested some idea to him different from the White Paper ... but I could not get a clear exposition of it from him. This week he has given it & I am very much attracted. So are Zetland (to whose opinion I attach much weight) & others of my friends. From the first I have wished to substitute indirect for direct election to the legislative chamber at the Centre; & to reduce, if possible, the numbers of the two Houses. Attlee agrees & adds a plan for remodelling government at the centre in a conservative sense — something that I was looking for & could not find. We (the Derby House luncheon group) must examine it more closely but I hope that we shall be able to adopt it with modifications. Sam Hoare is respectful but I think at heart hostile. What will be the outcome of it all. I may know next weekend.

AC5/1/658

4 April 1934
Salterns, Warsash

My dear Hilda,

...

I am haunted by the riddle of the Indian problem to which I cannot find a solution. I have with others help evolved three changes each of which would in my opinion be an improvement & the three taken together not only a very great improvement but a sufficiently striking change to present a different issue to public opinion at home & allow us to reassure many of those who are now very uneasy. They are

[100] (Victor) Alexander John Hope (1887–1952) Civil Lord of Admiralty 1922–4; Deputy Chairman, Conservative Party 1924–6; Chairman, India Joint Select Committee 1933–4; Viceroy of India 1936–43. Known as Earl of Hopetoun 1887–1908 when succeeded as 2nd Marquess of Linlithgow. K.G. 1943.

indirect election to the Lower House at the Centre, smaller Houses at the Centre & irremovability of the Govt except by a 2/3 rds majority to give it greater strength & stability. But I fear that Sam Hoare is only prepared to accept the last named, our party in the Comtee is hopelessly broken up & I fear a disastrous split in the House & country. I have a feeling that things are not going well with us just now in spite of a Budget surplus & improving trade. Altogether my Easter thoughts are gloomy.

AC5/1/660   22 April 1934
                                                        58 Rutland Gate

My dear Ida,

Yes, I think N's Budget a very good one & that he has solved that most difficult problem of how to dispose of an inadequate surplus most successfully. It has had too a very good reception & has given the Govt. a much needed 'reviver'.

The Committee of Privileges ... comprises the leaders of the Parties & some of the more experienced Parliamentarians from the Back Benches & I have been on it since I left office. I had at first decided not to sit during the consideration of Winston's complaint[101] as he had consulted me as a friend of long parliamentary experience about raising the matter & I had tried to dissuade him from doing so, & had indeed replied that I thought that he had got hold of a mares nest as far as my knowledge went before he spoke of Privilege at all. Of course I had not seen his papers & it was not a decision or an opinion on the question of Privilege & what I did say referred much more to Derby than to Hoare, still it seemed to me to place me in rather an invidious position & I didn't see why I should expose myself to the possibility of criticism. But the Comtee after hearing my opinion were unanimously of the opinion that there was nothing in what had passed between W. & me which ought to debar me from sitting & added that my not serving would rather embarrass them, so I have yielded. To tell the truth it is certainly a borderline case & I am by no means sure that our friends have not unwittingly overstepped the mark. I hoped the matter would not be raised; now that it has been I shall have to examine the evidence & find a verdict. I am not prejudiced but am still a little afraid that I may be thought so.

[101] In the Commons on 16 April 1934 Churchill raised an allegation of Breach of Privilege against Hoare and Derby for having improperly exerted pressure on the Manchester Chamber of Commerce to alter their evidence to the Joint Select Committee on India in the previous June. The inquiry unanimously dismissed the complaint and in the debate on 13 June Churchill was isolated and humiliated.

AC5/1/661

28 April 1934
58 Rutland Gate

My dear Hilda,

...

Yes, wireless is a marvellous invention & makes one feel more than anything else that nothing is incredible ... I suppose we are not very far off practical television ... Whether we are really the better for all this progress is another question. There are moments when I wish we had neither telephones nor motor cars and that life ran less rapidly. Obviously I am getting old.

I have had a very busy week with my two Committees & am much puzzled & concerned about the problems of both – particularly the Indian one. Sam Hoare's attempt to meet me & my friends is a compromise so hedged with conditions that I think it would give him the worst of both worlds. The Chairman has another compromise in mind which is better & I think more defensible, but I doubt whether it is good enough or would stand the racket of attack here & in India. Mine was a definite, coherent scheme & had the merits of such but Sam declares that taken as a whole (& it was its merit to be a whole) it would leave him without a supporter in India. I see the point of danger on which he lays stress & could meet him on that if he would take the rest as it stands but I can't see my way at all through the maze of his objections. I fear that both his & the Chairman's proposals are so open to criticism that they would altogether fail to win the increased support in the House & the country without which I fear we shall meet with disaster.

I foresee equal difficulties though less danger in the Comtee of Privileges, for as far as indications go at present we are much divided in temper & the problem is one of great difficulty & perplexity. Oh! cursed spite!

AC5/1/662

5 May 1934
58 Rutland Gate

My dear Ida,

... Indeed I have had another hard week ... [mostly Privileges Committee]

...

Derby would not hold his weekly luncheon of our Indian circle so I asked them here [on Tuesday] as the position is critical & found them resolute not to accept Hoare's amended scheme for the election &

composition of the Federal legislature or Linlithgow's suggested alternative. It was agreed that I should see Hoare & Halifax[102] & put the position to them. For this purpose I fixed that they should lunch with me on Thursday when we had a most serious talk. This afternoon I received from Hoare another plan which *may* perhaps be made to do.

AC5/1/663   n.d. May 1934
                                                        58 Rutland Gate

My dear Hilda,

. . .

There has been a lull in the Joint Comtee on India (in which I am still working for an agreed change in the scheme for the election & composition of the Central Legislature) but the time thus set free has been swallowed up by the Committee of Privileges. We shall not get that finished until after Whitsuntide but in fact we have already agreed upon all the issues & only the drafting remains to be done.

There was a dickens of a row at the Executive Comtee of the L/N Union last Thursday morning when an adjourned discussion took place on the statement of policy issued by Cecil, Murray & myself. Unfortunately it clashed with Privileges & I could not be present, but I had written a letter which was read in which I recited how I had been asked to sign such a statement in order to reassure people who were repelled because they confused us with certain Pacifist Asstns, how I had refused unless Cecil & Murray signed also, how my principal contribution was the preamble & the citation from the Charter & how it was then further amended by Cecil & Murray until we were all in agreement. I concluded by saying that in my view it would be incompatible with our duty as holders of a Royal Charter to oppose the forces of the Crown & also inconsistent with the Covenant − & a little more.

Of course the attack came from the Pacifists led by Miss Courtney[103] who, however, was a little troubled when it appeared that Cadbury[104] had volunteered that he thought it an admirable statement; but I am told that Cecil & Murray completely went back on me, not denying

---

[102] Edward Wood, Lord Irwin and the former Viceroy, had succeeded his father as 3rd Viscount Halifax in 1934.

[103] Dame Kathleen D'Olier Courtney (1878–1974) Philanthropist. Hon. Sec. National Union of Women's Suffrage Societies 1911–4; a founder, Women's International League; Member, Executive Committee League of Nations Union after 1928 and Vice-Chairman 1939; Chairman United Nations Association 1949.

[104] Edward Cadbury (1873–1948) Director, British Cocoa & Chocolate Company; Life Governor, Birmingham University; Owner, *Daily News*.

what I had written of its genesis or compilation but saying that they could not think how they had passed the peccant words referring to O.T.C. & Cadet Corps ... I am told there was an unholy row, but it was finally pointed out to them that they could not alter a document signed by other people & it was agreed that C & M should see me & report to me the various changes which had been suggested.

I am rather looking forward to that interview! If they are not careful, there will be not merely a row but a bust up. I should not have put the Cadet Corp in if it had not been that they were in the original draft sent to me, but I won't consent to take them out.

AC5/1/666   9 June 1934
                                                          58 Rutland Gate

My dear Hilda,

. . .
We three are going to Arundel for the weekend – my first outing since the accident[105] & tonight I shall sit up for dinner for the first time
. . .
My rib & knee are nearly mended ... but my powers of work & concentration are poor and Sir Kenneth [Goadby, his doctor], ... insisted that I must take a fortnight's cruise under penalty, if I refused, of a breakdown later in the year ... It does look like throwing away 15 months work on the India Comtee & I had hoped to see the session through, but when one is spoken to like that, there is no answer if one has others as well as oneself to think of.

AC5/1/670   15 July 1934
                                                          58 Rutland Gate

My dear Ida,

. . .
... I wrote Garnett of the L. of N. Union two snorters to protest against his (or Bob Cecil's) iniquities ... To be even a sleeping partner in the L/N Union is my hair-shirt. It will I hope save me some years of purgatory. I also enclose a copy of the revised statement on the policy of the Union in which I have marked the new or altered phrases. It was submitted to the Executive Comtee & passed by them as a proper statement to be issued by us i.e. they wash their hands, neither

---

[105] In May 1934 Chamberlain fell from a taxi and spent some time recuperating from injuries to his knee and ribs.

approving nor disapproving, but since it is signed by both President & Chairman & the third most influential member I think it is pretty authoritative.

Ivy & I did a most rapid change on Monday night & arrived at Corbin's[106] dinner table with the soup ... & after dinner Barthou made a bee-line for me & set to work to reassure me about French policy in general & his own attitude in particular. He is a sprightly young man of 73 or 4 I believe with a flow of words that at times submerged even my loquacious self. Corbin had evidently reported to him pretty fully a conversation which the Ambassador had with me a little time ago in which I spoke pretty freely about his Genevan outburst[107] & said that the impression produced on my mind by this & other speeches was that, having picked up a new friend, he no longer cared much for what an old friend thought or did. He did not directly refer to my conversation with Corbin but he set himself to answer it point by point. He excused himself for the exuberance of his Balkan utterances by admitting his excesses but asking indulgence for a man drunk with flattery & honours!

Anyway his visit here has been a great success & I am happier about the position than I have been for a long time. Cordiality & community of purpose have been restored between France & England: Mussolini has rallied at once & a sensible change in the foreign policy of Russia has begun under the fear of a German-Japanese combination. For the first time I give Simon great credit for his part which was, I think, though Barthou indirectly denied it, sensibly to modify the French plan by making it a real Locarno, i.e. a reciprocal insurance & not an anti-German alliance. I thank Hitler for having definitely separated Russia from Germany. The House was very thin on Friday but representative & unanimous.

But here comes in my second 'fret' of yesterday. I was told at luncheon at the Brazilian Embassy that Simon had already got cold feet in consequence of the German attitude to the new proposals. What else did he expect? Will he never learn what Germans are? I envy him the hand he has now to play, but if he waivers or hesitates he will lose the rubber. He ought to keep on hammering at them with all his might & drive home in no uncertain tones the consequences of a

---

[106] André Charles Corbin (1881–1970) French Attaché 1906; Chief of French Foreign Office Press Service 1920; French Ambassador to Madrid 1929–31; to Brussels 1931–3, to London 1933–40. Honorary knighthood 1938.

[107] At the final session of the Disarmament Conference at Geneva on 30 May 1934 Barthou made it clear that further discussion was useless while his bitter attack upon Germany was combined with criticism of Simon. He then attempted to revitalise French alliances with visits to Poland, Czechoslovakia, Romania and Yugoslavia and to create an entente with Italy by evolving a grandiose eastern European pact known as the 'Eastern Locarno'.

refusal: I pointed that path to him in my speech – it was a badly constructed, clumsily expressed speech but it had some good points in it – but has he – forgive my Saxon brutality – has he the guts for his task? I fear not.

. . .

P.S. I think it is now becoming clear that the Reichswehr will henceforth be the master in Germany & that before long the Junkers will direct her policy. She will not be less threatening for that but there will less chance of the powder going off spontaneously or at least of its being fired by little boys playing with matches.

AC5/1/671

21 July 1934
58 Rutland Gate

My dear Hilda,

It is easier to set a stone rolling than to say where its course will end. The 'Declaration'[108] pot has not yet boiled over, but the brew is getting pretty hot as you will see from the enclosed letters which bring the story up to date ... I am going to discuss the matter with Cranborne[109] & Eustace Percy on Monday. My present inclination is to publish a disavowal & to offer my resignation. I clearly ought to have insisted on resigning when I could no longer attend personally & regularly. Garnett is not to be trusted out of your sight & Bob Cecil is a fanatic who in the slang of the day is constantly 'going off the deep end' & whose actions are always on the verge of hysteria. Of course Bob has a grievance & a real one because the dangers of the course he was steering were not pointed out & objection taken earlier, but he dominates & intimidates the Comtee. & so prevents a free expression of opinion from people who do not feel themselves & he will not treat as his equals, & it has been quite impossible for me to find time to read the masses of papers, important, unimportant & indifferent, which I have received from the League (& Cecil's own letter I have not received) whilst attempting to digest the even larger mass of material circulated to the India Comtee.

. . .

[108] 'The National Declaration on the League of Nations and Armaments', otherwise known as the Peace Ballot. Results declared 27 June 1935.

[109] Robert Arthur James Gasgoyne-Cecil (1893–1972) Conservative MP for Dorset South 1929–41. Under Secretary for Foreign Affairs 1935–8; Paymaster-General 1940; Dominion Secretary 1940–42, 1943–5; Lord Privy Seal 1942–3, 1951–2; Commonwealth Secretary 1952; Lord President 1952–7; Conservative Leader of Lords 1942–57. Styled Viscount Cranborne 1903–47 and summoned to the Lords as Baron Cecil of Essendon 1941. Succeeded as 5th Marquess of Salisbury 1947. K.G. 1946.

I think Simon did really good work in his talks with Barthou, quite his best achievement since he took office, but he will require all the strength he can muster & all the skill he undoubtedly possesses to carry the project to a successful conclusion.

AC5/1/672   27 July 1934
                                      League Loans Comtee
                                      Bank Buildings

My dear Ida,

. . .

There has been a devil of a commotion in the League of Nations Union. They got really scared when they heard my letter & saw themselves faced with the possible resignation of half a dozen members of the Comtee, but the Declaration had already gone too far when, thanks to you, I first heard what was being done, for any really satisfactory solution to be found. They offered, however, to circulate an additional paper to be prepared by us. I am not wholly content with what we have proposed, but the offer did not leave me good ground for a breach. Our representatives are very much to blame for not having fought the case earlier, but the result will, I think, be that a complete breach will be postponed – I fear it is not more than a postponement – & when it comes will take place on another issue. I have today written another letter (1) protesting against any resolution condemning the Govt's decision on the Air-force or demanding delay in its execution & (2) recalling my protest two years ago against any proposal for an International Air-force under the League & saying that the Comtee will remember the strength of the convictions then expressed by me & others, which remain unaltered. A resolution on the lines of (1) is to be proposed to the Executive on Monday & a resolution for (2) was carried by the Council a few weeks ago. What will happen next?

I feel almost physically sick when I think of the murder of Dollfuss & I cannot get it out of my thoughts. Cold-blooded murder of a defenceless man is always revolting, but to leave him to linger on in agony, refusing to allow him either a doctor or a priest seems to me to reach the limit of callous brutality. I have never met a man who captured my sympathy more quickly; he was so transparently honest, so simple & so brave & withal had a personal charm which is so rare.

Saturday You may well wonder, as we all do, what will be the result of his death. He *was* the Government; & in Austria men of force &

character are rare. Staremberg[110] [sic] inspires no confidence; Schaussenig[111] [sic] I know nothing about. But the first results seem to be that Germany is frightened at her handiwork & that the Austrians are more determined to keep their independence than before this outrage, but that Austria is likely to be more Fascist though not more German. It is curious that Austria produced two such leaders as Hitler & Dollfuss, both men of the people of very humble origin. It was a country where the people had not much chance of rising to the top in the old days. I wish that Upper Austria was not the stronghold of Fascism, for I think it is in the mountains that the best stock is to be found.

AC5/1/675   18 October 1934
                                                 58 Rutland Gate

My dear Ida,

. . .

Yes, what a horrible & senseless tragedy that was at Marseilles[112] & alas! how badly the French police authorities show up. A man ready not only to risk his life but to accept certain death can perhaps not be prevented from accomplishing his murderous purpose, but in this case the police arrangements were obviously inadequate & Barthou a victim of complete disorganisation & incompetence. He simply bled to death for lack of the simplest attention . . .

And Poincaré is dead too – a great but not an endearing figure. I have written, with some difficulty, a short appreciation of him for the Paris 'Journal'. I am not quite sure how it will be received in France at this moment, though I said the least I could in criticism with any regard to honesty.

Buxton[113] is dead too. When with him one could not realise that he was 80 & I had not heard that he was ill, so it gave me a shock. Your memories of him will I expect be of the years when he made dull &

[110] Prince Ernst Rüdiger von Starhemberg (1899–1956) Austrian Christian Socialist politician and head of its para-military Heimwehr. Aristocratic landowner. Right-wing and monarchist but abhorred Nazism and Hitler, playing major role in crushing the Nazi rising after the assassination of Dollfuss, Vice-Chancellor 1934–6.

[111] Kurt von Schuschnigg (1897–1986) Elected Austrian Parliament 1927. Minister of Justice 1932–4. Austrian Chancellor 1934–8. Imprisoned at Dachau until 1945. Professor of Government at St Louis 1948.

[112] On 9 October 1934, Barthou, the French Foreign Minister was assassinated at Marseilles along with King Alexander of Yugoslavia by a Croatian terrorist.

[113] Sydney Charles Buxton (1853–1934) Liberal MP for Peterborough 1883–5, Tower Hamlets 1886–1914. Under Secretary, Colonial Office 1892–5; Postmaster-General 1905–10; President, Board of Trade 1910–4; Governor-General, Union of South Africa 1914–20. Created Viscount Buxton 1914 and Earl 1920.

irritating speeches on colonial questions, but as the Times said thereafter he steadily grew in stature & was a very good Governor General in S. Africa, which when I came to know him well in later years I found him far from the dull, wizzened, bloodless creature I thought him in those days. He owed much, I think, to his second wife who sweetened his life with happiness & a pleasant sense of humour.

. . .

The India Comtee has at last ended its labours after more than 170 sittings. Ouf! For this relief, much thanks. Our report won't soften the Lloyds, Winstons & the like but the changes we have made in the White Paper do improve it & will, I hope, reassure doubters. But any policy now possible in India is an experiment open to grave objections. The only thing I am sure of is that the India Defence League's policy is the worst of all.

AC5/1/677   11 November 1934
                                                  58 Rutland Gate

My dear Hilda,

I am not less indignant than you about the Declaration Comtee. who appears entirely unscrupulous in their determination to steal a verdict. Indeed, as I looked further into the matter, by blood rose to fever heat & I penned a letter to the Times which you will have read tomorrow. I feel a little better since doing so, but I don't think that I have ever seen such dirty work covered by respectable names.

AC5/1/678   17 November 1934
                                                  58 Rutland Gate

My dear Ida,

. . .

On Thursday morning I fought with beasts at Ephesus, in other words, faced the League of N. Union Executive where five of us out of nearly 30 I think refused to vote confidence in our representatives on the Declaration Comtee. or give any kind of approval to the Ballot – again a tiring business & a disagreeable one. I wanted to resign at once but the other four thought this a bad issue to break on, so I am still a member. I wonder how you would endure a County Council composed of such people. The annoying thing is that quite a lot of them, now too deeply committed to turn back appear to have expressed grave doubts when the thing was first mooted but to have been overborne by Cecil. I believe that if I had been there then I could have stopped it.

. . .

Tyrrell also came today, very gloomy about the general situation. He is in despair about Simon, he echos [sic] Smut's declaration: "You will never do anything with that man. Geneva is like the House of C. It soon sums a man up. It has seen through Simon". He told me that he had twice on verbal instructions from Simon come to an agreement with Tardieu at Geneva. The third time he had said to Simon: "You will put that in writing"[.] "Why"? asked Simon, & Tyrrell told him bluntly. Simon only laughed! He said he did the same thing at Berlin & Neurath told Rumbold that he never wished to have anything to do with him again.

AC5/1/679   24 November 1934
                                          58 Rutland Gate

My dear Hilda,

. . .

You see that there will not be much rest for me this side of Christmas & I have to admit to myself that I cannot work as long hours as formerly.

Even a conversation takes more out of me than it used to. I have just been expounding my views for a long hour to Dr. Maxwell Garnett. I believe that if I were his Boss I could work with him, though noone seems to trust him, least of all Bob Cecil, whom I should have thought he served very favourably. I could certainly get on with Gilbert Murray but between Bob's view of how the League ought to be run & what the Union's proper task is, there is an impassable gulf. I wonder what will happen at the Council Meeting in December & shall I then be set free? Nous verrons.

Yes, the reception of the India Report is very much what I expected & that is none too good either here or in India. But I think that it will carry great weight, probably increasing weight as it filters down into men's minds. At any rate the Govt. can now take up a defensible position & even sally out to the attack of their opponents entrenchments. Their 'wait for the Report' attitude of the last two years was, to say the least, a selfdenial [sic] ordinance from which they have suffered severely, but it is not too late to convince & rally waverers & it is with them that I hope that the Report will have influence. What will happen in the Lords I don't know, for there Salisbury's influence is very formidable. He carries more weight in that Assembly than any other peer & Hailsham has somehow failed to gain the influence that a Lord Chancellor usually wins there.

With the publication of the Joint Select Committee's report in November 1934, both sides recognised that they had a 'very stern fight' before them.[114] At the Conservative Party's National Union Council meeting at the Queen's Hall on 4 December, Baldwin made an effective speech in defence of the report. Salisbury then moved an amendment accepting provincial self-government but opposing the principle of responsible central government and Churchill supported him. Chamberlain also intervened with a good speech supporting the report and the Diehard amendment was defeated by 1,102 votes to 390. Eight days later, on the last night of the Commons debate on the report, Chamberlain again 'excelled' in his speech replying to Churchill's equally excellent attack.[115] This time the anti-Government amendment was defeated by 410 votes to 127. On 15 December Salisbury's attempt to move another anti-Government amendment in the Lords was defeated by 239 votes to 62. A crucial hurdle had been cleared and Chamberlain had every justification for satisfaction with his own decisive part in carrying the policy through the Joint Committee and on the road to the Statue Book. At any rate, he believed, it was 'enough to make [him] feel that it was worth while to remain a member of Parliament & to keep [his] public position' for one more election.[116]

Yet in spite of its success over India, by January 1935 the National Government's fortunes were showing unmistakable signs of decline. Of the forty contested by-elections since the 1931 general election, the Coalition had lost no less than eight to Labour. The outcry over the Unemployment Assistance Board's new relief scales in January 1935 suggested no prospect of a rapid return to popularity at a time when there were still over two million workers unemployed. For some time, the Government had also been under attack from its own right-wing. In January 1935 this took on a new form when Churchill's son Randolph stood as an independent Conservative at Liverpool Wavertree on a platform of more defence expenditure and opposition to the Government's India policy. In the event, he polled 10,575 of the total Conservative poll of 24,346 and in so doing allowed Labour to win the seat on a narrow minority vote. Although the indignation created by this 'success' had the unintended effect of rallying many critics back to the Government for fear that such a trend would permit Labour to triumph at the next election, Chamberlain was not alone in perceiving the result as a vote against the Government and a demand for reconstruction. MacDonald also interpreted the official Conservative position during the contest to mean that he was being 'left to the wolves': a perception Baldwin apparently did nothing to deny. By the end of March, MacDonald finally decided to withdraw as Prime Minister,

[114] Churchill to Ian Colvin, 3 November 1934, M. Gilbert, *Winston S. Churchill* V, 585.
[115] Headlam Diary, 4, 12 December 1934, S. Ball (ed) *Parliament and Politics*, 316–17.
[116] A. Chamberlain to Hilda, 22 December 1934, AC5/1/681.

although the arrangements for Baldwin's succession were not completed until well into May.[117]

Although Chamberlain had remained throughout a convinced believer in the value of the 'National' label as a bastion against resurgent socialism, he had been disturbed by the Government's weakness and evident failure to 'strike the imagination' of the electorate for over a year before Wavertree. Among the principal causes of the problem he diagnosed a lack of direction and weakness in the management of foreign policy. Anxious about unemployment and its electoral implications, and true to his coalitionist past, he was also curiously attracted by increasing talk of Lloyd George's return to office to champion his 'New Deal' proposals: a scheme which predictably aroused little enthusiasm with any of his other siblings.[118]

AC5/1/680

15 December 1934
58 Rutland Gate

My dear Ida,

...

I have certainly done my full share of work to secure the acceptance of the India Report. I am convinced that it is better than any thing else now open to us, but I feel my responsibility all the more because so much is uncertain & so many dangers lurk round every corner. Certainly the Govt. ought to be grateful to me, for if I had gone against them, there isn't a doubt but that they would have been beaten & indeed, unless I had exerted myself, I don't think they could have obtained a working majority. If I had been a little differently made, it was a glorious opportunity to follow Palmerston's example & "give Johnny Russell a tit for his tat." And what fun it would have been if only it were not all so damnably serious.

There is no doubt that my meeting with members in the Comtee. room & my speech to them produced a very great effect & my short speech to the [National Union] Council seems to have been as effective in its way though I myself thought poorly of it until the opinions of others obliged me to change my own. As to my speech in the House itself, members enjoyed my retort to Winston & the speech itself had the merit of producing at least one new argument on the third day of the debate. Winston's speech was the best that he has made for some time & contained no such gaffes as have ruined one or two of his recent efforts but the best speeches made in a debate which kept a

[117] D. Marquand, *Ramsay MacDonald*, (1977), 767–9.
[118] Neville Chamberlain Diary, 11 December 1934, 30 January 1935.

pretty high level throughout were Wolmer's[119] on the one side & Eustace
Percy's brilliant bit of debating on the second day. I was disappointed
by the division.

. . .

AC5/1/684   12 January 1935
                                             58 Rutland Gate

My dear Ida,

. . .

The only other matter of interest that I have to record this week is
that as a result of a conversation some time ago with Professor
Lindemann[120] of Oxford, I drafted a letter to the Prime Minister
protesting that in the light of a number of insoluble problems that were
in fact solved under the pressure of war, it was premature to declare
that there was no defence to night-bombing except counterbombing &
that the search for one ought not to be left to the Air Ministry. I
suggested a sub-committee of the C.I.D. with a man like Lord Weir[121]
as chairman, a soldier, an airman, two or three scientists & means to
carry out any experiments they thought useful & directions to find a
defence. Most of these details were put in a letter from Lindemann to
Londonderry which I drafted for him & in the letter to the P.M. I
referred to that correspondence. I got Winston to sign with me &
yesterday received a most friendly & satisfactory interim reply from the
P.M. I think this is a good bit of work & I hope that the enquiry which
may take two or three years will be productive of results.[122] I feel sure

[119] Roundell Cecil Palmer (1887–1971) Conservative MP for Newton 1910–18, Aldershot
1918–40. Parliamentary Secretary, Board of Trade 1922–4; Assistant Postmaster-General
1924–9; Minister of Economic Warfare 1942–5. Styled Viscount Wolmer 1895–1942 when
summoned to the Lords as Baron Selborne 1941. Succeeded as 3rd Earl of Selborne
1942. Grandson to 3rd Marquess of Salisbury and married to Churchill's cousin.
[120] Frederick Alexander Lindemann (1886–1957) Worked at Physical Laboratory RAF
1915–18; Professor of Experimental Philosophy (physics) Oxford 1919–56; Member,
Expert Committee on Air Defence Research of C.I.D 1935–39. Unsuccessful by-election
candidate, Oxford 1937. Personal assistant to Churchill 1940–41; Paymaster-General
1942–45, 1951–53. Created Baron Cherwell 1941 and Viscount 1956.
[121] William Douglas Weir (1877–1959) Shipping contractor and pioneer motor car
manufacturer. Scottish Director of Munitions 1915–7; Member of Air Board 1917;
Director-General of Aircraft Production 1917–9; Secretary for Air 1918; Air Ministry
Advisor 1935–9; Director-General of Explosives 1939; Chairman, Tank Board 1942.
Knighted 1917, created Baron Weir 1918, Viscount 1938.
[122] M. Gilbert, *Winston S. Churchill*, V, 623, claims Lindemann had drafted a letter
signed by Chamberlain and Churchill urging a full C.I.D. inquiry into defence against
air attack. MacDonald agreed but subsequently found there was already such a committee
under Henry Tizard. On 14 February 1935 Chamberlain and Lindemann visited

that the Air Ministry are so set in their opinion that nothing can be done that left to themselves they will do nothing.

AC5/1/686

19 January 1935
58 Rutland Gate

My dear Hilda,

. . .

I have not studied Ll. G. yet.[123] I am very anxious that he should not be driven into bitter opposition as he might easily be dangerous, but he is a man for a crisis when heroic remedies must be tried, not the physician for a patient who has had a great shock but is slowly convalescing & regaining his health. I distrust his slap-dash methods when he has noone to control him & by temperament I am not formed for rash adventure, but we move today at such speed that all youth is impatient & attracted by the novel & dramatic & we have large numbers in desperate plight to whom the plea for patience may well appear a hollow mockery & who are the natural prey of quacks. Therein lies the danger. Ll. G.'s dish is such a curious composition alike in what it includes & what it excludes that it is not easy to say what support he will receive, but at present he is not irreconcilable & it is not our interest to make him so. I think Neville handled him pretty well for first thoughts, but those two are oil & vinegar & can't mix – more's the pity, for together if they were together they might do a great deal.

You are quite right that the Govt. can't 'get their stuff across'. Hilton Young is a conspicuous example; Kingsley Wood[124] the brilliant exception. I am not sure that Walter Elliot is a stayer & Hoare-Belisha[125] [sic] is a young man in a hurry who may easily involve *his* motor-coach in a bad smash if he is not more careful. K.W. is the first Postmaster-General I have known who ever succeeded in doing anything worth

MacDonald and again pressed the need for a special sub-committee which he finally conceded on 19 March 1935.

[123] At Bangor on 17 January 1935 (his seventy-second birthday) Lloyd George launched his 'New Deal' policy to end unemployment.

[124] (Howard) Kingsley Wood (1881–1943) Conservative MP for Woolwich West 1918–43. Parliamentary Secretary for Health 1924–9 and for Education 1931 Postmaster-General 1931–5; Minister of Health 1935–8; Secretary for Air 1938–40; Lord Privy Seal 1940; Chancellor of the Exchequer 1940–3. Knighted 1918.

[125] (Isaac) Leslie Hore-Belisha (1893–1957) Liberal MP for Plymouth Devonport 1923–45 – Liberal until 1931 then Liberal-National 1931–42 then National Independent 1942–5. Parliamentary Secretary Board of Trade 1931–2; Financial Secretary to Treasury 1932–4; Minister of Transport 1934–7; War Secretary 1937–40; Minister of National Insurance 1945. Created Baron Hore-Belisha 1954.

while at the Post Office & it is the first time in my experience that P.O. administration has been well spoken of & the P.O. become an asset to the Govt.

AC5/1/688   2 February 1935
                                             58 Rutland Gate

My dear Hilda,

. . .

I am trying to make a book of newspaper articles with a good deal hitherto unpublished & have yet to write one or perhaps two additional chapters to satisfy the publishers now & he wants something gossipy i.e. about people rather than events & I am finding it exceedingly hard to do. If the volume ever appears it will be a frightful hotchpotch. Of course the desire to make some money supplies the driving force . . .

Our chief interest in London is the Wavertree election[126] & the Anglo-French conversations. Of the former I hear the most conflicting reports. Our people seem anxious lest the socialists should slip in; Winston & his crowd are very sanguine not indeed of Randolph's success but of his having a good vote but Lloyd George's special observer staked his reputation that R. would forfeit his deposit. I only hope that he will.

As to the Anglo-French conversations[127] I gather that their tone & temper are all that one could wish but up to noon today I don't think that they had reached any agreement on any of the really difficult points & I should doubt if much will come of them though the fact of their being held is all to the good. Lothian seems to have succumbed entirely to Hitler's wiles. He is not the first; the man must have a way with him, as the saying goes.

---

[126] On 6 February 1935 Labour won Liverpool Wavertree after the intervention of Churchill's son, as an Independent Conservative. The result rallied support for the National Government among those critics who were more afraid of a socialist victory at the next general election.

[127] In London from 1–3 February 1935 MacDonald, Simon and Eden met Flandin and Laval. Although wide-ranging, the talks proved abortive because the French refused to accept German rearmament without a British guarantee of military aid in the event of German attack.

AC5/1/689

9 February 1935
58 Rutland Gate

My dear Ida,

...

Wavertree is very bad. I don't myself believe that it indicates widespread dissatisfaction with the India Bill though that disturbs many minds. I think it is a grave sign. I believe that it indicates a very wide spread dislike of the Prime Minister & dissatisfaction with the Government, & I am inclined to believe that nothing but the reconstruction of the Government will stem this adverse tide & that reconstruction must include an attempt to bring Lloyd George in – a proposal against which Neville is obstinately set. For myself I have never thought that personal proscriptions could form the basis for a wise policy.

Of course Randolph's charm & oratorical powers counted for a great deal but he took advantage of the desire for change, the seeking after the same new thing, the love of a stunt which is one of the chief elements in the life of the mass of electors today, of whom so few are definitely attached to any party or any political creed. A film star could win almost any seat in the country, and Randolph would make an excellent film star. Frankly I am alarmed. I think the situation is graver than the Government recognise.

...

But on Wednesday I dined at Grillons & thereby hangs a tale. I shared a taxi from the House with Ormsby Gore & on our way remarked that, whilst I could not pretend to be an unqualified admirer of Simon as a Foreign Minister, I must say that every step he had taken from the time of the Saar initiative[128] appeared to me to have been well conceived, skillfully prepared & admirably executed. 'Yes,' replied Billy Gore 'and into everyone of those steps he has been kicked by Anthony Eden & the Office from behind & driven in spite of his own resistance by the insistence of the Cabinet.'
Comment would spoil it.

[128] On 5 December 1934 Eden informed the League that Britain would contribute troops to an international force to supervise during the Saar plebiscite scheduled for 13 January 1935. Simon had opposed Eden's plan which was only accepted after Baldwin's intervention.

AC5/1/690   16 February 1935
                                             58 Rutland Gate

My dear Hilda,

...

I think that my hastily written sentences in my last letter have given you a wrong impression of what I had in mind. Of course there is a personal antipathy between Neville & Lloyd George, but I certainly never meant to convey that Neville subordinated public interests to personal feelings. What I do feel is that his judgement of Lloyd George was formed primarily on his personal experiences of him & that these have implanted in N.'s mind an unconquerable distrust of him. I think that Ll.G. behaved shamefully to Neville & showed in his relations with him all the worst traits in his character. If I had had the same experiences, & those only, I should have felt as Neville feels; if I feel differently, it is because my experience was different & I have seen another side of Ll.G. & a better one. I believe that he & Neville, if they could work together, would make a very strong combination & I also believe that if Ll.G. is simply repulsed, he can do & will inevitably do a great deal of mischief.

I agree with you that R. MacDonald has become an incubus for the Govt. & though Baldwin improves his position in the House & perhaps in the public at large, his idleness & lack of all initiative make him a bad though inevitable successor. But when MacDonald goes, & go he must before long I think, there is no-one to take his place – Thomas is worse than useless – & the basis on which the Govt. stands is inevitably narrowed. I wish that I could see the way to broaden it, for I think the return of Lansbury, Cripps & Co. to power at this time would be a national & Imperial disaster of the first magnitude &, as things stand, I do not feel at all sure that this is not what is going to happen. This fear haunts me & lies at the root of all my speculations. Can we strengthen the National Govt, – that seems to me the most urgent of our problems. I have no idea of accepting Ll.G. as dictator, but I at least shall regret it if he is rejected *ab initio* as a possible collaborator.

AC5/1/692   9 March 1935
                                             Bognor

My dear Hilda,

...

I am rapidly becoming a maid of all work for the Government. I am used whenever India gets difficult & on Wednesday Margesson[129] asked me to move an amendment to the Labour Vote of Censure on the White Paper[130] which had been drafted by Simon, but it began with a piece of Simonian smugness that I did not like & there was nothing in it to rally the doubtful or to draw attention to the real case for the Govt. so I drew an amendment of my own which you may read in the Times of today. I think it is rather a skillful one but you may say that that is mere vanité d'auteur. Anyway it is better than Simon's draft.

Although the following letter is clearly dated 'January', all the internal evidence suggests that it was actually written on 16 March 1935. Certainly Chamberlain's reference to the 'S.O.S. from Sam Hoare' over the India Princes corresponds with the fact that in mid-March Hoare was extremely anxious about the future of the India Bill and desperately rallying support for the Princes' Resolution to be debated on Wednesday, 20 March.[131] Equally clearly Chamberlain made an extremely effective speech on the 11 March in the debate as the Government's Defence White Paper published the pervious week. In response to Attlee's censure resolution concerning the proposed £10 Million in additional defence spending, Chamberlain launched a devastating attack upon the Deputy Labour leader. 'If war breaks out' he asked, 'do you think he will hold the language he held today? If he does, he will be one of the first victims of the war, for he will be strung up by an angry, and justifiably angry, populace to the nearest lamp-post'.[132] He then sat down to an ovation from his own side of the House.[133] During the remainder of the spring of 1935 Chamberlain continued to reiterate these now familiar themes while despairing increasingly of Simon, whom he considered 'a positive danger' at the Foreign Office. Although urged to lead a revolt to displace him, however, Chamberlain declined to do so.[134] Not until the ministerial reshuffle following MacDonald's withdrawal from the Premiership in June 1935 was Simon finally moved to the Home Office.

[129] (Henry) David Reginald Margesson (1890–1965) Conservative MP for Upton 1922–3, Rugby 1924–42. Assistant Whip 1924–6; Whip 1926–9, 1931; Chief Whip 1931–40; Secretary for War 1940–2. Created Viscount Margesson 1942.

[130] On 4 March 1935 Cmd.4827 *Statement Relating to Defence* was published. Although only nine pages long, it was of major significance by drawing attention to the threat posed by German rearmament and announcing that additional British expenditure on defence can 'no longer be safely postponed'.

[131] Hoare to Willingdon, 15 March 1935, M. Gilbert, *Winston S. Churchill*, V. Companion 2, 1109–1110.

[132] Avon, *Facing the Dictators*, 128. For the speech see *House of Commons Debates*, 5 Series, 299 cols. 71–8.

[133] N. Chamberlain to Annie, 12 March 1935, NC1/26/506.

[134] A. Chamberlain to Hilda, 5 May 1935 AC5/1/698.

AC5/1/685   16 March [mis-dated January] 1935
Salterns, Warsash

My dear Hilda,

. . .

I was quite astonished by the success of my speech on the White Paper. I know I had something to say & felt as I spoke that the House was interested, but I had no idea that I was doing anything out of the common & was amazed at the 'ovation' which followed its close. It certainly was the speech of the day for Baldwin was very far from his best & Simon was positively bad. I was cross with him, for Cripps, to use a cricketing metaphor, had patted a ball from my bowling right into his hands & he not merely muffed it but funked it. However for two days bouquets were flung at me by everyone I met & I had some charming letters, especially one from Hankey who was under the gallery & declared it the best speech on defence that he had ever listened to. Of course it was not that, for he must have heard some of Balfour's, but it shows that it stood out as remarkable in the eyes of a most competent listener . . .

. . .

Last night Pathé gave a Trade Show of the Jubilee film, 'Twenty-five Years a King' with the Trade in the stalls & a distinguished company in the dress-circle. There were other features & the band of the Grenadier Guards, so it was quite an evening's entertainment, but of course my film was what most concerned me. It was a great success, much to my surprise; the pictures on a big screen came out so much better than on a small one. As to myself, I thought that I was more narrow chested & uglier than I had supposed & my voice sounded as if I had a cold, but I gathered that this was not the general verdict. Indeed Diana Duff-Cooper[135] was overheard exclaiming that he's a Garbo & Margot Oxford rang me up this morning & lavished praise upon the film, the voice, my appearance [,] manner, choice of words & in short on everything. I am thinking of trying my fortune as a film star.

But I am called back to earth by an S.O.S. from Sam Hoare asking for my help in Wednesday's debate on another White Paper – this time the Indian Princes, a nasty snag that, half funk & half blackmail & largely, I think, misunderstanding sedulously fostered by Winston & Rothermere.

---

[135] Lady Diana Olivia Winifred Maud Manners (1896–1986) Daughter of 8th Duke of Rutland, wife of Sir (Alfred) Duff Cooper. Famous beauty and socialite.

AC5/1/693

24 March 1935
58 Rutland Gate

My dear Ida,

...

I gave up on the idea of speaking on the India Bill on Tuesday for two reasons; first, I was very unhappy about the foreign situation as it developed over the week end & felt that I must speak in the F.O. debate on Thursday, &, secondly, I found that Eustace Percy wanted to speak on India & I thought that he would deal with the position of the Princes on just the same lines as I should have done. His speech, tho' not as good as some which I have heard him make, quite satisfied me. The House in fact is beginning to get bored with Winston's alarums & excursions.

But, after all, I did not speak in the F.O. debate. I felt that what I had intended to say would have struck a discordant note after Lansbury's & Samuel's speeches which on this occasion were unexceptionable & would be better reserved for my speech at B'ham on Friday night. As I had told Simon that this time I was going to be critical, I think he was relieved by my silence. He did in fact blunder badly & though he has since done all he could to retrieve the blunder, it will be long before its effects pass away. Indeed they won't pass while he reigns.

I don't say he was wrong or the Cabinet to decide that the Berlin visit [on 25–26 March] should be paid but it was a capital error not to explain our intentions & our reasons in Paris & Rome before instead of after they were communicated to Germany & publicised to the world. Germany's action was not merely a grave breach of international law & good faith; it was an act of defiance & a slap in the face for this country, coming at the moment when it did;[136] & Simon by his blunder made it worse for it appeared to divide France & England in face of German provocation instead of at once bringing them & Italy together as it should have done in the eyes of all the world. The French will never trust Simon & I can't blame them. I should not like to go tiger shooting with him myself. In the course of two days he gave me three different reasons for his action & at least one of them was untrue, for it contradicted the others.

---

[136] On 16 March Hitler decreed conscription of a 500,000 man army in violation of Versailles. Italy and France wanted Simon's planned visit to Berlin cancelled but without consulting them Simon merely issued a formal protest.

AC5/1/694   31 March 1935
                                                            Terling Place
                                                            Chelmsford

My dear Hilda,

    . . .

    On Monday we lunched with the Vansittarts[137] & he poured out to
me the story of his woes. He is, I think, fed up with Simon & I should
imagine very near breaking point with him. Apart from mistakes of
policy, total inability to understand the Latins & other faults he alleges
against Simon, he complains that he is not straight, tells him one
thing & then does another, goes behind his back, keeps him in the
dark & on occasion lies to him. A pleasant portrait of a Chief by one
who is ex officio his right-hand man.

    . . .

AC5/1/695   6 April 1935
                                                           58 Rutland Gate

My dear Ida,

    . . .

    I had a very interesting talk with Baldwin on foreign affairs [on
Tuesday] . . . & later with Neville. S.B. was the more unguarded of the
two. He did not conceal from me that the Cabinet had no confidence
in Simon & meant to send the P.M. as well as Eden to Stresa.[138] I have
no great confidence in the P.M. in his present state of health but he
has the root of the matter in him whereas Simon is basically wrong.
Grandi told me yesterday that he did not dare to transmit what Simon
had said to him to Mussolini as it would produce a deplorable effect – &
the Times chooses its moment to assure the world that Simon has the
people of this country behind him as never before. The Times is
apparently entirely under Lothian's influence at present; it's articles
might have been written in Berlin. I am very, very anxious about the
future. The possibility of a war is *nearer* than at any time since 1914. A

---

[137] Robert Gilbert Vansittart (1881–1957) Entered Diplomatic Service 1902. Assistant
Clerk at Foreign Office 1914; First Secretary 1918; Counsellor 1920; Secretary to Curzon
1920–4; Assistant Under-Secretary and Principal Private Secretary to Foreign Secretary
1928–30; Permanent Under-Secretary at Foreign Office 1930–8; Chief Diplomatic Adviser
to Foreign Secretary 1938–41. Knighted 1929; P.C. 1940. Created Baron Vansittart 1941.
[138] A three-power Conference was convened at Stresa, 11–14 April 1935 for Italy, Britain
and France to present a united 'front' to Germany and to show that it could not do to
Locarno what it had done to Versailles.

meeting of 70 Conservative M.P.s during the week was in revolt against Simon & I believe that every member of the Govt. would like to get him out of that post. Will the P.M. & S.B. have the courage to do it?

AC5/1/696

12 April 1935
58 Rutland Gate

My dear Hilda,

. . .

I began my week with three speeches on Monday . . .

On Tuesday I had three hours with the Bulgarians & on Wednesday six hours. They were as difficult as I had feared & we only just avoided a complete rupture . . . Ouf! Six hours of Free Exchange, Blocked Exchange, pledged revenues &c. &c. &c all in French. Then I went to Grillons & called for champagne before I could swallow so much as an oyster.

In the intervals I have written my letter to the Times & also one on Defence to the B'ham Branch of the Women's Union of Teachers which pleased my colleague so much that they asked to be allowed to sign it. It began by expressing 'surprise that so responsible a body should pass so irresponsible a resolution' & after a statement of the facts, ended with the words that 'the only maintainable criticism of the Govt, is not that they have gone too far & too fast but that they have done too little & too late' – a 'snorter' in fact!

AC5/1/698

5 May 1935
Killerton, Exeter

My dear Hilda,

. . .

All the interest in the H. of C. this week centred in the Foreign Affairs debate. The P.M. read his statement but it was good. After him the chief interest was in the speeches of Winston & myself & in Simon's winding-up, but the last produced a very bad impression. He did not answer any of my questions & the fact is that he could not, for he never got to the bottom of Hitler's mind when he went to Berlin. But I was pleased with the general tone of the debate; it revealed a very considerable measure of agreement in the House, has acted as an antidote to the very mischievious article in the Times which could only serve to encourage Germany & has given the Germans to think. I feel strongly that our only chance of preserving peace lies in the plainest warnings to them & in close cooperation with the peace-loving nations.

To a people who believe in nothing but force, force is the only answer. As to Simon, he has become a positive danger & if I would take the lead – which I won't though asked to do so – the govt majority would drive him out of office. Nobody in my quarter has any faith in him – least of all the Cabinet & the F.O.! But Sinbad has let the Old Man of the Sea mount his back & does not know how to shake him off.

AC5/1/699   11 May 1935
                                                    58 Rutland Gate

My dear Ida,

. . .

I attended & addressed the Foreign Affairs Comtee of the Party last Thursday. When I first joined it on leaving office only a dozen or 15 people attended. This time there must have been over a hundred (well over, I should think) all anxious & on the verge of revolt against Simon by name. I expressed their dissatisfaction with policy whilst avoiding any mention of Simon's name. But I wish I knew what the P.M. & S.B. really wished – no, not wished but *meant* to do & *when*. In politics a deathbed repentance does more harm than good.

AC5/1/700   18 May 1935
                                                    58 Rutland Gate

My dear Hilda,

. . .

The air is now full of rumours of reconstruction of the Govt. I don't think it can be much delayed & I hope that it will not be. The last story that reached me from a parliamentary gossip is that S.B. is to become Prime Minister, Ramsay Macdonald [sic] to take the F.O. till the General Election & Simon to be Lord President & Deputy Leader of the House – Londonderry to go & possibly Hilton Young & Gilmour or Cunliffe Lister or both. I believe both the last named would like peerages. But all this is pure gossip unless the P.M. to the F.O. was put to me as a feeler. I don't like the idea, for I don't think the P.M. is physically or mentally equal to the strain of that office, however lightly he takes it, but I should prefer almost anyone to Simon. I wish Mussolini had not chosen this moment to run amock[sic]. His determination to have a quarrel with Abyssinia & to fight it out as soon as the rains are over – for that I fear is what it comes to – is calamitous for Europe. At Vansittart's request I spoke very earnestly about it to Grandi & wrote him a letter which he could pass on to Mussolini, but I came away with the impression that though Grandi saw clearly the disastrous reaction it would have on Anglo-Italian relations & the European situation, he had no hope that Mussolini could now be deflected from his purpose.

AC5/1/701   25 May 1935
                                                     58 Rutland Gate

My dear Ida,

...

What do I think of Hitler's latest?[139] Well, it is like the curate's egg, good in parts, but it needs very careful examination & very diplomatic treatment. I thought Baldwin's handling of it just right – he said enough but not too much. But oh! how I wish we had another Foreign Secretary to conduct the negotiations. It is vital to preserve the confidence of Paris & Rome & Simon is completely distrusted in both places. Where indeed is he not distrusted? If he thinks he is ever going to be made Prime Minister by any party he deceives himself or I will 'eat my hat'. By the way there is going to be an early reconstruction. That is decided, but I have carefully refrained from asking what form it was likely to take.

I was interrupted for an hour in the middle of the last paragraph by Princess Antoine Bibesco[140] who called by appointment ... Incidentally, she told me that Lady Oxford is reconciled to Ramsay MacDonald by their common dislike of Simon.

To go back to Hitler for a moment, you have of course put your finger on one of the worst features of his 13 points – the incredible number of his army. If that is final, there will be no disarmament & I should think no limitation of weapons, quantitative or qualitative. I wish I knew what our government was doing or means to do. A phrase dropped by Simon in an interrupted conversation the other day makes me anxious lest he should allow himself to be trapped.

Eden seems to have had another success at Geneva. Time is gained & that is something but I fear that trouble will begin when the rains cease which is the end of August or early September.

[139] On 21 May 1935 Hitler assured the world that Germany's rearmament was not a threat to peace and denied any intention of breaking its foreign obligations. He also declared Germany's willingness to accept parity in the air and a fleet of 35 per cent the strength of Britain's.

[140] Elizabeth Charlotte Lucy Asquith (1897–1945) Seventh and youngest child of H.H. Asquith. In 1919 married Prince Antoine Bibesco, a Rumanian diplomat.

AC5/1/702   1 June 1935
                                                       58 Rutland Gate

My dear Hilda,

     . . .
     . . . We shall probably spend the . . . weekend [after next] at Warsash;
by that time I suppose we shall know what S.B.'s reconstruction of the
Govt. amounts to. I have not even a guess at what he intends so far.
He told me yesterday that he did not like the job of turning out old
colleagues. I can well believe that it is about as hateful a task as a man
can have to undertake – especially when it is complicated by the fact
that it is a coalition government & you have got to balance among
parties as well as among men.

AC5/1/703   11 June 1935
                                                       58 Rutland Gate

My dear Ida,

     We got back from Huirley today where we had quite a pleasant visit.
S.B. seemed in excellent spirits & was quite talkative . . . I did not hear
anything about Under-Secretaries except that Cranborne goes to the
Foreign Office, but I strongly pressed Geoffrey's claim.[141] Thomas will
not stay at the Dominion Office after the elections (he is as much a
danger there as Simon was at the F.O.) & Simon is *not* to have the
Garter nor is he to be given No. 11 which will go to Neville. That is
all the gossip I could pick up except that Sankey[142] when told by S.B.
that he must go, showed the yellow streak in him, turned on Macdonald
[sic] & made it a personal quarrel.

---

[141] Geoffrey Lloyd. He remained PPS to Baldwin until 28 November 1935 when
appointed Under Secretary at the Home Office.
[142] John Sankey (1886–1948) Lawyer. Lord Chancellor, 1929–1935. Knighted 1914.
Created Baron Sankey 1929 and Viscount 1932.

15.

'SLY, SIR, DEVILISH SLY!'

The torments of Baldwin, July 1935 – March 1937

Chamberlain had little to say about the Cabinet reshuffle in June 1935 'except to thank heaven that Simon has left the F.O.' Although initially satisfied with the performance of Sam Hoare, Simon's successor, Chamberlain's mood throughout the summer of 1935 was one of gloom whenever he considered 'what a mess the whole world is in'.[1] He remained very depressed about tensions with the other two 'Stresa front' powers when Parliament was dissolved for the General Election on 25 October 1935. Although still opposed by his old Labour adversary who had haunted the doorsteps of West Birmingham so assiduously since 1929, from the outset Chamberlain was remarkably confident about the result; 'my people don't seem afraid of him . . . B'ham trade is good and people look happier than they did a few years ago'.[2] Moreover, during the campaign he was particularly heartened to find that the old Chamberlain spirit kindled by his father continued to be an active force in what was a 'regular "slum" constituency'.[3] In the event, his confidence was well founded. In West Birmingham he was returned with a majority of over 7,000, the Conservatives again took all twelve seats in the city and the National Government returned with a majority of 255 to exceed even Chamberlain's wildest expectations.

In spite of such satisfaction, the autumn of 1935 brought a number of unwelcome changes to Chamberlain's personal life. In September he had effectively broken with the flamboyant Warden Chilcott after many years of close friendship. The now customary extended holiday at Chilcott's home in Corsica in September was marred by appalling weather, the 'odour of whale' emanating from a forty foot corpse on their favourite beach and a host who was 'in a very difficult mood' from the outset.[4] A more painful separation concerned the need to move from Rutland Gate, their home since February 1930, under a now ineluctable financial pressure. When leaving office in October 1931 the Chamberlains had discussed the depth of their financial problems and the need for more modest accommodation, but the decision had been deferred.[5] Despite his best endeavours to generate a steady income thereafter, on the eve of his daughter's wedding early in 1935 Chamberlain was finally forced to confront the unavoidable reality. As he wrote to his half-brother in January:[6]

. . . I must tell you in confidence . . . that my position is desperate. Nearly all

[1] A. Chamberlain to Hilda, 16 June 1935, AC5/1/704.
[2] A. Chamberlain to Ida, 13 October 1935, AC5/1/709.
[3] A. Chamberlain to Hilda, 17 November 1935, AC5/1/714.
[4] A. Chamberlain to Ida, 22 September 1935, AC5/1/708.
[5] A. Chamberlain to Ivy, 2 October 1931, AC6/1/820.
[6] A. Chamberlain to N. Chamberlain, 15 January 1935, NC1/27/120.

my capital has gone & I have little besides the income which I am earning. As soon as Diane is married we shall have to change our whole way of life, let or dispose of this house & move into something – flat or house – much smaller. If it were possible I should apply for a Cabinet Minister's pension, but I don't see how I can do that …

It is a sorry story & I am much to blame for not having faced the facts earlier. There are some excuses & I have had misfortunes for which I do not think I can blame myself, but the fact remains that I ought to have acted long ago.

Yet although the decision to move was taken in November, given their shortage of funds for a deposit, the task of finding a smaller property proved far from easy. For the next ten months Ivy searched for suitable accommodation before eventually finding a house in Egerton Terrace. In the interim, the Chamberlains were forced to move into the Goring Hotel in Belgravia. Although he put a brave face on it, this was not a happy period in his life, separated from his books and belongings. It was probably of this period that Vansittart wrote when he recalled that Chamberlain 'retired into straits and a small flat' to emerge for public engagements and private dinners 'immaculate in frayed white shirt and shiny tail-coat'.[7]

In politics too, the period immediately after the election was one of brief tantalising opportunity followed by bitter and humiliating disappointment. Throughout Hoare's tenure of the Foreign Office, the central policy problem had been posed by Italian ambitions in Abyssinia. As a lifelong friend of Italy, enjoying a relationship of mutual admiration with Mussolini and strong contacts with his Ambassador, the Foreign Office hoped to use this influential unofficial channel to warn Italy against the use of force to obtain their objectives in Africa. Yet as with Japanese aggression in Manchuria, it is apparent that Chamberlain's main concern in so doing was based less upon international political morality, than a realpolitik *conviction that illegal Italian action would distract attention away from the German threat to Europe. On the other hand, however, he also recognised that failure to do anything in face of Italian aggression would fatally compromise the League and the cause of collective security.[8] As the crisis developed Chamberlain's attempt to balance this belief in the importance of Anglo-Italian cooperation as a bulwark against Nazism with public support for the League led him into an increasingly ambivalent and problematical position. In the longer-term, it prompted his resignation from a now intolerable position on the LNU Executive in May 1936.[9] In the short-term, the effect was to prevent both Chamberlain and Churchill from establishing a consistent line of policy which others could follow. It was perhaps indicative of this inner confusion that Chamberlain did not speak at all on the subject in the Commons*

---

[7] Lord Vansittart, *The Mist Procession*, 549.

[8] N. Thompson, *The Anti-Appeasers: Conservative Opposition to Appeasement in the 1930s*, (Oxford 1971), 79–81.

[9] D.S. Birn, *The League of Nations Union*, 162.

debate in October 1935.[10] *When consulted by Hoare and Eden in August 1935, Chamberlain had been 'most clear and insistent' that provided the French were agreeable, collective action in the form of economic sanctions was 'inevitable'. Should they attempt to evade such a course, 'a great wave of public opinion would sweep the Government out of power'.*[11] *By December, however, he had come round to the view that the victim of aggression would have to make some concessions in order to reach a solution acceptable to the aggressor.*[12]

Although the Hoare-Laval Pact essentially embodied just such a solution, its premature revelation by the French press in mid-December placed Chamberlain in a peculiarly delicate position. As a member of the four-man LNU delegation to the Prime Minister about the matter, Chamberlain had given some support to Baldwin's attempted defence of the Pact.[13] *Yet in private he believed the whole affair was a 'tragedy' in which Hoare had 'blundered badly'. The more he learned from Baldwin and Vansittart, the more depressed and uneasy he became. As a result, at this stage, he was uncertain how he would speak − or even how he would vote. With dismayed Conservative MPs looking for a lead, however, it was a measure of Chamberlain's perceived influence on the backbenches that Baldwin came to believe that the action of this Elder Statesman might well prove decisive in determining the fate of the entire Government.*

Before Chamberlain could make his scheduled speech to the Conservative Foreign Affairs Committee on 17 December 1935, Baldwin had sent for him and hinted tantalisingly that 'when Sam has gone, I shall want to talk to you about the Foreign Office'.[14] *With this in mind, Chamberlain had gone to the Foreign Affairs Committee intending to be critical, but nonetheless still to secure support for the agreement on the grounds that it was 'the least bad of several bad alternatives'.*[15] *In the event, the hostile mood of the meeting induced him to make another speech forcefully condemning the Pact as a 'betrayal of the League'. He declined, however, to say which way he would speak in the forthcoming debate.*[16] *Reports from the Whips about the mood among Conservative backbenchers at this meeting was a crucial factor in the Cabinet decision to sacrifice the Foreign Secretary in order to save the Government.*[17]

The crisis came to a head in the full-scale debate on 19 December. By all accounts Hoare spoke well: 'He was a Cato defending himself; for 40 minutes he held the House breathless, and at last sat down, but not before he had wished his

---

[10] Chamberlain's explanation was that he had a head cold and Hoare, Eden and Churchill had said all he wished to be said. A. Chamberlain to Ida, 26 October 1935, AC5/1/711.

[11] F. Hardie, *The Abyssinian Crisis*, (1974), 55.

[12] D. Dutton, *Austen Chamberlain*, 315.

[13] D.S. Birn, *The League of Nations Union*, 162.

[14] I. Colvin, *Vansittart in Office* (1965), 83.

[15] Viscount Templewood, *Nine Troubled Years*, (1954), 187.

[16] Jones Diary, 14 January 1936, *A Diary with Letters*, 161. L.S. Amery, *My Political Life*, III, 184; Channon Diary, 17 December 1935, *Chips*, 48.

[17] Middlemas and Barnes, *Baldwin*, 890.

successor better luck, and burst into tears'.[18] *Baldwin followed Attlee with an extraordinarily poor speech. Recognising Chamberlain's pivotal position in determining the outcome of the debate, the Speaker called him immediately after the Prime Minister's statement. As Chamberlain was aware, he had the Government's fate in his hands. Yet if he was really 'torn between his own misgivings about the Government's behaviour and his intense desire to return to the Cabinet',*[19] *it was a dilemma he swiftly resolved. Turning on the Labour leader's earlier claim that the issue involved a 'question of the honour of this country, and ... of the Prime Minister', Chamberlain suddenly diverted the entire thrust of the debate towards Attlee's apparent attack upon Baldwin's integrity. In so doing, he deflected attention from the central issue and, as so often in the past, this served to rally disaffected Conservative backbenchers to Baldwin's defence.*[20] *The Government carried the vote by 397 to 165 and the crisis was effectively over.*

What happened next reinforced everything that Chamberlain most despised about Baldwin. Amid widespread support for Chamberlain's interim return to the Foreign Office,[21] *Baldwin sent for his saviour on the day after the debate. As Austen recalled the conversation for his half-brother, Baldwin then announced that 'he would have "loved" to offer the post to me but felt that at my age I could not last out a Parlt. & that noone would consider my appointment as more than a stop-gap'. To make matters worse, Baldwin elaborated 'on the "iron nerves" required for the post & said that such often failed to recognise when their powers failed, illustrating the danger by the example of Ramsay MacDonald whom he had to "carry" for two years'. Having then asked Chamberlain's opinion in a manner which precluded disagreement, Baldwin enquired as to his view of Eden as a likely successor.*[22]

This interview was a true lineal descendent of those equally disastrous occasions in May and November 1923 when Chamberlain had entered the room expecting office and left it humiliated and with his hopes dashed. It was with such occasions in mind, perhaps, that Chamberlain told his half-brother that he found the opening part of the interview 'very characteristic!'. As in the past, too, the reference to his age as a disqualification was galling from a man only four years his junior. This time, however, the comparison with MacDonald added particular insult to the offence. 'He told me I was ga-ga' was how he later related the tale.[23] *In retrospect, it is extremely difficult to accept the view that Chamberlain 'read more into a casual conversation than Baldwin intended' when he first hinted at the possible reversion of the Foreign Office.*[24] *Yet whatever the truth of Baldwin's intention, Chamberlain's*

---

[18] Channon Diary, 19 December 1935, *Chips*, 48–9.

[19] D. Dutton, *Austen Chamberlain*, 316.

[20] F. Hardie, *The Abyssinian Crisis*, 190.

[21] N. Chamberlain to Baldwin, 22 December 1935, Baldwin MSS 47/181–2; Channon Diary, 20 December 1935; *Chips*, 49; Avon, *Facing the Dictators*, 315–16; W. Selby, *Diplomatic Twilight 1930–1940*, (1953), 54–5.

[22] A. Chamberlain to N. Chamberlain, 20 December 1935, NC1/27/124.

[23] 'Invitation to join Mr Baldwin's Government, December 1935', AC41/1/68; Avon, *Facing the Dictators*, 316.

[24] J. Barnes and D. Nicholson, *The Empire at Bay*, 337.

embittered belief that he had been used by a sly and cynical leader played a major role in shaping his increasingly critical stance towards the Government throughout the rest of his life. Moreover, the offer of a non-departmental Cabinet post with a salary of £5000 on the following day did nothing to assuage the bitterness, not least because Chamberlain rightly inferred from these events that 'what he really wanted was not my experience or my advice but the use of my name to patch up the damaged reputation of the Govt.'.[25]

Chamberlain did not have to wait long to give vent to his resentment. In the Commons on 14 February 1936, he 'caused a minor sensation'[26] by launching a stinging attack upon Baldwin's personal and policy deficiencies: an attack all the more devastating because he had conspicuously gone 'out of his way to attack S.B.' Turning to the central theme of the debate, Chamberlain made 'a very weighty speech' supporting the call for the appointment of a Minister of Defence to coordinate the work of the three Service Ministries and to chair the CID.[27] As Chamberlain told his sisters, his purpose in making the attack had been partly to shake Baldwin out of this lethargic complacency and partly an attempt to coerce him into making an adequate appointment at a time when he feared either that the Prime Minister would do nothing or would appoint the now broken MacDonald or the ineffectual Eustace Percy to the post. In Chamberlain's mind only Churchill, his increasingly close ally, was uniquely qualified for the post.[28] Although Amery was given the same story, he suspected that there was 'a little more to it'. For Amery the tone suggested the speech was intended as a 'definite reminder of [Chamberlain's] existence as a potential leader if S.B. failed to wake up', spiced with revenge for the manner in which he had been treated when Hoare resigned.[29]

Baldwin was evidently much surprised by the attack.[30] He was also utterly adamant that under no circumstances would he appoint Churchill.[31] At one stage he even proposed to Neville Chamberlain that he should take the new office himself with his half-brother replacing him at the Treasury.[32] Baldwin probably did not expect him to agree. Anyway, Austen advised against acceptance and Neville never mentioned the suggestion of the Treasury to Austen. In the end, to widespread disappointment and Chamberlain's disgust, a rather different post of Minister for the Coordination

[25] A. Chamberlain to Hilda, 22 December 1935, AC5/1/718.
[26] Thomas Jones to Lady Grigg, 17 February 1936, *A Diary with Letters*, 174.
[27] Amery Diary, 14 February 1936, *The Empire at Bay*, 408.
[28] See also A. Chamberlain to Duncan Sandys, 17 February 1936, M. Gilbert, *Winston S. Churchill*, V. Companion 3, 48–9; to Midleton, 18 February 1936, AC41/3/18; Winterton Diary, 16 February 1936, *Orders of the Day*, 214.
[29] Amery Diary, 14 February 1936, *The Empire at Bay*, 408. Also Crozier interview with Hore-Belisha, 15 July 1936, A.J.P. Taylor (ed) *W.P. Crozier, Off the Record: Political Interviews 1933–1943*, (1973), 64.
[30] N. Chamberlain to Ida, 16 February 1936, NC18/1/949.
[31] Hoare to N. Chamberlain, 23 February 1936, M. Gilbert, *Winston S. Churchill* V. Companion 3, 55.
[32] Neville Chamberlain Diary, 19 February 1936.

of Defence was filled by Sir Thomas Inskip, the Attorney-General.[33] *an appointment perhaps not unfairly described by Lindemann as 'the most cynical thing that has been done since Caligula appointed his horse as consul'.*[34] *Such a move was scarcely calculated to restore Baldwin's reputation for leadership. Nor did it do anything to impress his most effective critic on the backbenches who now found himself increasingly 'being driven into opposition or nearly so' alongside Churchill, Croft, Grigg and Winterton.*[35] *Moreover, his criticism was not confined solely to Baldwin. In early-April Chamberlain had demanded a clear statement on colonial appeasement which forced his own half-brother into an 'evasive and embarrassed' reply which left Austen rightly suspicious that he was 'anything but sound' on the subject.*[36]

During this final stage of his career Chamberlain worked more closely with Churchill than at any time in their nearly forty years of personal and political association.[37] *Despite profound differences of temperament and politics, by the end of the 1920s a certain warmth had developed between them.*[38] *Although prominent on opposing sides during the battle over India, both had attempted 'to conduct the controversy so that friendship [wa]s never disturbed even by a crumpled roseleaf'.*[39] *In practice, the harmony of the relationship was also sustained by their increasingly close cooperation in warning of the German menace. In conjunction with Churchill's tirades against the government's policy deficiencies, Chamberlain's attack on Baldwin in February 1936 immediately provoked press speculation about a concerted campaign against Baldwin.*[40] *In May, the exposure in the press of an 'Anti-Baldwin Shadow Cabinet' caused mild embarrassment to the participants and aroused suspicions that the 'naughty boys' in 'The House Party' were engaged in 'dark schemes to torpedo the government'.*[41] *Combined with his increasingly aggressive anti-German speeches and his close links with the Churchill group, Chamberlain's general drift into a position of greater opposition than at any time since leaving office undoubtedly damaged his influence and authority on the backbenches.*[42] *As the European situation*

[33] See, for example, Winterton Diary, 15 December [sic] 1936, Earl Winterton, *Orders of the Day*, 214.

[34] Reported in Lord Lloyd to his son, 25 March 1936, M. Gilbert, *Winston S. Churchill*, V, 716.

[35] A. Chamberlain to Hilda, 15 March 1936, AC5/1/729.

[36] Amery Diary, 6,7 April 1936, *The Empire at Bay*, 413; N. Chamberlain to Ida, 13 April 1936, NC18/1/956.

[37] Churchill to Ivy Chamberlain, 18 March 1937, M. Gilbert, *Winston S. Churchill* V. Companion 3, 626.

[38] A. Chamberlain to Churchill, 20 October 1930, *Ibid*, V. Companion 2, 200–201.

[39] A. Chamberlain to Churchill, 25 October 1930, *Ibid*, 893.

[40] Amery Diary, 14 February 1936, *The Empire at Bay*, II, 408; Winterton Diary, 16 February 1937, Earl Winterton, *Orders of the Day*, 214.

[41] A. Chamberlain to Ida, 29 May 1936, AC5/1/735; Channon Diary, 26 May 1936, *Chips*, 61. Also Lord Winterton *Orders of the Day*, 216–7; R.R. James, *Churchill: A Study in Failure 1900–1939* (1970), 264–5; A. Boyle, *Poor Dear Brendan : The Quest for Brendan Bracken* (1974), 207; Lord Croft, *My Life of Strife*, (London n.d. 1948), 285–6.

[42] N. Chamberlain to Ida, 4 July 1936, NC18/1/968. See also his warning to Baldwin in Jones Diary, 22 May 1936, *A Diary with Letters*, 204. Chamberlain was also a prominent

deteriorated, however, Chamberlain persisted with his course in the belief that it was his duty to attempt to educate both an electorate and a government reluctant to face distasteful realities. 'I know that I do not represent our public opinion at present', he confided to his sister, 'but what I say needs saying & can be better said by one like me who will never again hold office with a freedom & plainness that Ministers & potential Ministers would be unwise to use'.[43]

AC5/1/710   20 October 1935
                                                58 Rutland Gate

My dear Hilda,

. . .

I am miserable about public affairs. I see no ray of light anywhere & grave dangers at every turn. We have to bear the whole brunt of Italian hostility & partly owing to Laval's shuffling & duplicity & partly to their own fierce internal factions a large section of French opinion is equally bitter & unrestrained. I am on tenterhooks about the immediate results & profoundly depressed by the effect which I think all this will have on future British foreign policy. I dislike intensely having to hold an election in the midst of these commotions & feel that it makes their issue much less certain than it was before. Altogether I am, as you see, very depressed at the moment & could almost wish that I were out of it & could turn my thoughts to other things & other times. It doesn't make things better that a nasty roughness in my throat makes me fear that I am in for a cold just as work begins in earnest.

AC5/1/711   26 October 1935
                                                58 Rutland Gate

My dear Ida,

The debate in the House [on foreign affairs] went very well & I am perhaps a little less gloomy than last week, but it is not possible to be cheerful about the international situation & I loathe the idea of electioneering once again. It is my thirteenth or fourteenth election & all but three of them have been contested. I am to have my old opponent, Willey,[44] a violent left-wing socialist indistinguishable except

member of the secret but well connected Focus for the Defence of Freedom and Peace, Thompson, *The Anti-Appeasers*, 128–129.
    [43] A. Chamberlain to Hilda, 28 March 1936, AC5/1/730.
    [44] O.G. Willey. Lecturer in economic history. Former member, National Executive of Workers' Educational Association; member National Union of General & Municipal Workers.

by his label from a communist. I suppose that he will poll a good many more votes than last time but Canning does not think that he has made any headway or that the voters are showing any interest in him ...

My cold continues troublesome & my head has felt very woolly all the week which was one of the reasons I did not speak in the debate [on Abyssinia] – the others being that Hoare's & Eden's speeches both put the case very well while Winston in his admirable speech on the last day said the only things which I desired to add.

. . .

I lunched with Philip Sassoon on Thursday & met Hoare, Eden, Vansittart, Hankey, Runciman & Neville. I like these lunches as they keep [me? sic] in touch with Ministers. I took the opportunity to ask when S.B.'s election address would be out & what would be in it & learned that Neville had been engaged in writing it that morning. Sic nos non nobis! Does S.B. ever do anything for himself except talk about I—I—I. No. I will not write about him in my new book or he would not like it as much as he does the 'spirit' of the present one.

AC5/1/713   3 [mis-dated 17] November 1935
                                                58 Rutland Gate

My dear Hilda,

. . .

I can't tell you how distasteful it was for me to take a leading part in the Albert Hall meeting [of LNU] & I am glad that that at least is over. The presence of the Archbishop [of Canterbury] & myself did, I think, exercise a restraining influence on the other speakers, with the possible exception of Bob Cecil, & was therefore useful & nothing was said to worsen the situation. My own speech was laboured at the beginning but ended pretty well & on reading it I did not find that I had said anything which I would wish unsaid.

. . .

My guess for the National majority in the next Parlt, is 145 which allows Labour to win 150 seats & expects Samuel to lose 10 or 12. I believe that London, L'pool & Manchester will all be bad for us. Our L'pool organisation is rotten – the mot juste – & Manchester not much better.

I agree with you about the Manifesto, but raising the school leaving age is *not* popular in my constituency. The 'blackcoated' insurance is very good.

AC5/1/712

10 November 1935
Midland Hotel
Birmingham

My dear Ida,

I don't think there can be any doubt about my election this time. The only question seems to be what majority I shall have, & that depends upon whether we can get people who think that there is no danger of a Socialist victory to take the trouble to vote. The canvass, as far as it has gone, is 3 to 1 in my favour ...

AC5/1/714

17 November 1935
58 Rutland Gate

My dear Hilda,

Ouf!
Yes, that is how I feel & Ivy is, I fear, quite worn out ...
But to go back to the election. Of course the women & the men too where they were at home loved Ivy's visits & she only met two cases of rudeness the whole time. It is wonderful how Father's memory is still cherished − I saw your dad. I carried a torch in the procession. We've always voted Chamberlain. My dad thought everything of Joe & so on & so on in every variety of expression. And yet it's a regular 'slum' constituency, good wide streets but courts & back to back houses, many still to be condemned, over 3000 voters fewer than 4 years ago. Really one's heart is warmed by their kindness & one's admiration roused by their courage, but thank God there were none of those idle youths leaning against doorposts & railings of whom I saw so many last time. They are all now in work. The out-of-work now are the men of 50 upwards, particularly if they have any physical weakness. It is very difficult for them to get back.
...
Thanks to Canning I have probably the best organisation in B'ham. & we in West B'ham. take up the old cry: "we are Seven" − six City councillors & the M.P.
...
And to keep all twelve seats with good majorities! Bravo B'ham! There's not another city like it.
As to the country at large, it is astonishing. I guessed our majority three weeks ago would be 145 & was told by two newspaper editors that I should have an ugly surprise. For other comments, I echo your own. I was glad to see Samuel beaten, for I think that he has often

played a shabby part in Parlt. I rejoice that Lloyd George's ramp fizzled out so completely; I am really sorry for Macdonald [sic][45] & I am glad to see Herbert Morrison back as he is I think the ablest of the Labour leaders.

I have not said so publicly but I mean this to be my last election.

AC5/1/715   24 November 1935
                                                        58 Rutland Gate

My dear Ida,

Many thanks for your kind congratulations. Yes, Father was first elected for B'ham in 1876 for the West Division in 1885. I don't know of any parallel case & the record is, I hope, equally creditable to electors & elected ... – 21 elections in all, Bye & General, 12 for Father ... 9 for me ...

I don't think I could face another four or five years hence, when I shall be about seventy five, in what will probably be much more difficult circumstances ... Besides I don't want to outstay my usefulness in the House of Commons or to lose my influence there.

AC5/1/717   15 December 1935
                                                        Farnham Park.
                                                        Bucks

My dear Ida,

    ...
    ... Laval has behaved treacherously but I fear that Sam Hoare has blundered badly. I don't know what part I shall take in the debate nor even how I shall vote. Much will depend on the speeches of Hoare & S.B., but they will have an extraordinarily difficult task. I have never known the political sky cloud over so suddenly nor have I seen blacker clouds on the horizon. Dismay is not too strong a word to use for the feeling among their supporters when the news leaked out & nothing that has happened since has reassured them. Baldwin spoke very frankly to the four of us who went as a League of Nations Union deputation & Vansittart gave me even more details, but there was nothing to comfort one in what they had to say. I am left with the feeling that when all is

---

[45] Samuel was defeated by a Conservative in Darwen and MacDonald by Labour in Seaham. The latter returned to Parliament in January 1936 but the former did not. During the summer and autumn of 1935 Lloyd George spent nearly £400,000 on Council of Action business and £100,000 supporting candidates pledged to the campaign.

said & done ... it is still impossible to regard Hoare's actions in allowing himself to be associated with the French proposals & to recommend them as other than a bad blunder. If the election were just about to begin instead of being just over, the Govt. would not get half their present majority. It is certain that the Cabinet themselves were wholly unprepared for such developments, & I can only explain Hoare's action by the fact that he was absolutely worn out & that his mind did not take in their effect or consequences. It is a tragedy.... At present I am miserable & can think of nothing else.

AC5/1/718   22 December 1935
                                                              Goring Hotel

My dear Hilda,

Neville will show you the hurried letter I wrote to him after seeing Baldwin on Friday. You should read it before reading this one which concludes the story.[46]

B. asked me to see him again on Saturday & I went to Downing Street at 3 o'clock. He had by then done another '24 hours hard thinking' which must be an unusual task for him. He had by then decided to make Eden Secretary of State for F.A. & to abolish the post of League of Nations Minister which he created so short a time ago, but he said that he wanted my help & asked me to 'render another great public service' by joining the Cabinet as Minister of State i.e. without a department. My experience would be useful in foreign affairs & in the great & urgent questions of defence which must be decided in January. I could do as much or as little as I liked; if at any time I felt tired I could go away for a fortnight & he thought that on these conditions & without a department there was no reason why I "should not last out this Parliament" (textual).

He again spoke of the uselessness of Ramsay MacDonald, of his inability to make up his mind on any subject, of the tragic spectacle offered by a man whose faculties it was evident to everyone except himself had failed, & of the lack of experience in the Cabinet & the failure of the younger men to develop. He had told me the day before that Oliver Stanley[47] had failed because he had 'no guts'. He now

---

[46] Baldwin told Chamberlain that his age precluded the Foreign Office, but asked his opinion of Eden as a possible successor to Hoare.

[47] Oliver Frederick George Stanley (1896–1950) Conservative MP for Westmorland 1924–45, Bristol West 1945–50. P.P.S. to Percy 1924–9; Under Secretary, Home Office 1931–3; Minister of Transport 1933–4; Minister of Labour 1934–5; President, Board of Education 1935–7; President, Board of Trade 1937–40; War Secretary 1940; Colonial Secretary 1942–5. Younger son of 17th Earl of Derby.

hinted that another unnamed colleague was no use & he added, rather naively considering the nature of his offer to me, that Percy's appointment had been a mistake & that P. himself was unhappy & restless because there was not enough for him to do.

I see that I have omitted to say that he had observed that if Ramsay could not find a seat in the course of the next six months & was obliged therefore to retire, I could then have the Lord Presidency if I cared about it. He concluded by again saying that he thought I could do this work without breaking down & asked me if I could not accept at once to think it over before deciding.

I told him that I certainly would not answer at once for I had promised Ivy that if he did ask me to join the Govt. I would neither accept nor refuse till I had consulted her.

I then said that I was sorry to have to raise the question of money but what salary would attach to the post?

He suggested £3000. I replied that I was now earning my living, that if I gave up the positions I held I could not hope to make a new career four years hence & that if I accepted I should be obliged to ask for £5000. Would that cause him any trouble or affect his offer? He said that it would not; he thought that considering my experience & the offices I had held it was quite reasonable.

I told him I would think it over & let him know my decision today.

I already knew my own mind, but I put the proposal to Ivy without any expression of my feelings & views & as objectively as I could, & she at once said she thought I should refuse. As we were thus agreed, I sent my refusal by hand last evening. In my letter I said that after carefully considering his proposal & discussing it with my wife "I have decided that it is not one that I can accept".

As we had both reached this conclusion without hesitation, I thought I ought to let him have it at once, so that he might complete his arrangements without delay.

I went on:-

"You laid so much emphasis on my age & health both when I saw you yesterday morning & again this afternoon that I am compelled to add that anxiety about my health has played no part in my decision.

If you should feel at any time that I could be of use in the C.I.D. as a Privy Councillor without ministerial position or salary I am at your service".

You may observe a certain coolness in this letter. I certainly feel under no obligation to him for his offer. After he had taken such pains to explain & emphasise that he thought me physically unfit for hard work & that he feared I may become as much of an incubus as MacDonald, I could only infer that what he really wanted was not my experience or my advice but the use of my name to patch up the damaged reputation of the Govt. He could scarcely have put it more plainly ...

P.S. I saw & see no prospect of real usefulness in the position he offered to me but his manner of offering it made acceptance in any case impossible for a man with any self-respect.

AC5/1/719   28 December 1935
         Polesden Lacey

My dear Ida,

...

Yes, I should like to write about the real S.B. but it is wiser not to do so, for the S.B. whom we know does not fit in at any point with the picture which the public have made of him for themselves. They think him a simple, hardworking, unambitious man, not a 'politician' in the abusive sense in which they so often use the word, whom nothing but a stern sense of duty keeps at his ungrateful task, a man too of wide & liberal mind who has educated his party.

And we know him as self-centred, selfish & idle, yet one of the shrewdest not to say slyest of politicians but without a constructive idea in his head & with an amazing ignorance of Indian & foreign affairs and of the real values of political life. "Sly, Sir, devilish sly!" would be my chapter heading & egoism & idleness the principle[sic] characteristics that I should assign to him.

Well, Laval has escaped by the skin of his teeth this time. How long will he last, I wonder & who will be his successor & what will happen now. I am glad that Eden is at the F.O. but he is young to bear so great a load. Nevertheless I have great confidence in him & I should have felt afraid of Halifax's mysticism in that office.

AC5/1/721   12 January 1936 [mis-dated 1935]
         Goring Hotel

My dear Ida,

...

The days seem to pass quickly, though what I have done with them it would be hard to say, for there is nothing to show for it. A luncheon here, a visit there, an occasional committee, a book or two read, a chapter of a new volume begun but making no progress & enough letters to keep Miss Johnson busy in the mornings & that is all ...

AC5/1/722   19 January 1936 [mis-dated 1935]
                                                              Goring Hotel

My dear Hilda,

I can think of nothing but the King. I suppose that we may hear at
any moment of his passing ... Well, I have seen two changes of the
Sovereign & I had hoped that the King who is younger than I would
outlive my time. How well has he played his part & what a place he
has made for himself in the hearts of his people. I think that his
broadcasts have made him more intimately known to his peoples
overseas than any of his predecessors, and have strengthened the
attachment of distant peoples to the throne ...

What will the Prince make of his task? I am hopeful but he has been
going downhill of late & must pull himself together if he is to carry on
the great tradition to which he is heir.

AC5/1/723   25 January 1936
                                                          Goring Hotel

My dear Ida,

   ...
I did not find quite what I was looking for in King Edward's
declaration. He quoted the admirable words of his father but he added
no personal touch of his own ... What pleased me was that he seemed
to have won a new reassurance. As he read his declaration his hands
were steady, he stood firm on his feet & there was none of that fidgetting
with his tie, his belt or whatever it might be that has always been
noticeable when he had to address an audience.

The whole ceremony was simple & dignified & conjured up before
one's eyes past centuries of our history.

AC5/1/725   15 February 1936
                                                                Goring Hotel

My dear Hilda,

. . .

Well, I am wondering what Neville will say to you of my yesterday's speech.[48] I did rather flutter the journalistic dovecotes & I think rather surprised S.B. To tell the truth I thought that the time was overdue for trying to shake him out of his self-complacency. Of course it is true that no man can do all the work which in these days the Prime Minister is supposed to do, but what angers me is that the present Prime Minister does none of it & this, mustering all my self-restraint I refrained from saying. But S.B. had better show himself more alive to his duties or he will get into serious trouble, for discontent is spreading & becoming more serious. It is discontent bred of anxiety as to the results of his slackness & having done much to save him in December when an adverse vote would have been a direct vote of censure & necessitated his resignation, I decided to use this non-party debate when no vote would be taken to tell him what not only the older but many of the younger members are privately saying. If there is any truth in the rumour – I don't believe there is – that he proposes to hand over Defence to Ramsay MacDonald there will be a howl of indignation & a vote of no confidence, nor is Eustace Percy the man for that job. In my view there is only one man who by his studies & his special abilities & aptitudes is marked out for it, & that man is Winston Churchill. I don't suppose that S.B. will offer it to him & I don't think that Neville would wish to have him back, but they are both wrong. He is the right man for that post & in such dangerous times that consideration ought to be decisive.

AC5/1/726   23 February 1936
                                                                  Chartwell,
                                                            Westerham, Kent

My dear Ida,

. . .

Well, I am glad that Neville has decided to stick to the Exchequer. I suppose that the new man is to be Lord Weir or Sam Hoare. Of the two I think I should prefer Weir, tho' he is lacking in political

[48] Chamberlain bitterly attacked Baldwin's policy errors and inertia and called for the creation of a Minister of Defence.

experience which is needed as well as drive & business ability & knowledge. My own choice would be Winston Churchill whom I consider marked out by study, genius, power of drive & imagination for this particular post, & here I am staying with him for the weekend. It is a man's party – Robert Horne, Edward Grigg, Page Croft,[49] Guy [sic] Boothby[50] & 'the Prof' otherwise Professor Lindermann [sic] of Oxford.

Is it a Cave? Well some would like to make it so, but I am not a cave man. I chose Friday for my speech just because the bill was not a party measure & the occasion could not be turned into a vote of censure & I acted independently & without consultation with anyone. I think I achieved the purpose with which I spoke & now I mean to lie low for a time & give the Govt a fair chance to do what urgently needs doing. If Baldwin had a mind above electioneering, they would have begun long ago. I believe that next year will be a dangerous one for Europe & it will not be easy to do half what needs to be done in that time. Committees grind & grind but their wheels move very slowly. I got busy about air defence otherwise than by guns & counterbombing a year ago, but though we secured the appointment of a strong Comtee no experiment has yet been tried out. S.B. does not follow things up. When I write a book of Characters like Bulwer Lytton,[51] one chapter will be devoted to "Baldwin – the Idle Man".

We were a merry party last night & the talk was good. There were almost as many opinions as men, but on one thing we were all agreed – that Germany was a danger, the one danger that might be fatal to us, & that that danger had been too long neglected.

Incidentally surprise was expressed that Baldwin should have attempted no answer to my speech. Imagine Balfour or Father thus arraigned! They would have given me a Roland for my Oliver.

[49] Henry Page Croft (1881–1947) Conservative MP for Christchurch 1910–18, Bournemouth 1918–40. Under Secretary, War Office 1940–45. Rabid protectionist and leading member of 'The Confederacy'. Chairman, Tariff Reform League Organisation Committee 1913–7; Chairman, Empire Industries Association Executive 1928–45; leading Diehard and Principal Organiser of the National Party 1917–22. Created Bart 1924, Baron Croft 1940.

[50] Robert John Graham Boothby (1900–1986) Conservative MP for Aberdeenshire East 1924–58. P.P.S. to Churchill 1926–29; Parliamentary Secretary, Ministry of Food 1940–1; British delegate to Consultative Assembly, Council of Europe 1949–57. Knighted 1953. Created Baron Boothby 1958.

[51] Edward Bulwer Lytton (1803–73) Liberal MP for St Ives 1831–2, Lincoln 1832–41, Conservative MP for Hertfordshire 1852–66; Colonial Secretary 1858–9. Created Bart 1838, 1st Baron Lytton 1866.

AC5/1/727

29 February 1936
Goring Hotel

My dear Hilda,

...
... I am very satisfied with the Govt's reorganisation of the Defence duties, but the new man will have a terrific task & I do not believe that anyone now in the Govt is fit for it except Neville, who I am glad to know has definitely refused it, & I am dreadfully afraid that Baldwin will appoint some incompetent. The position is complicated by the fact that already two out of the three Service Ministers are in the Upper House & the Govt is very weakly placed for defending its plans & estimates in the Commons. They can scarcely leave that task, the most important of the Session entirely to Under Secretaries.

AC5/1/728

7 March 1936
Goring Hotel

My dear Ida,

Here is grave news indeed [of the German remilitarisation of the Rhineland]. So far I have only a summary over the telephone, but I fear it is a true account of what Hitler has proposed & done. Eden came to see me this morning at his own request & I found that his mind was moving very much on the same lines as my own, but at that time neither of us knew for certain what Hitler was going to do & still hoped that at least there would be no immediate & irreparable action. That hope appears to have been rudely dashed to the ground. "I must fink, Auntie. I must fink" – & think devilish hard.

10pm. I have just been listening to this evening's broadcast. The only reassuring thing about it is that everyone is keeping his head – the French Govt as well as everyone else. Perhaps I shall see my way more clearly tomorrow morning. For the present I have refused to make any comment. It is an occasion which affords an excellent opportunity for keeping silence. I write to you tonight because I want to be free for anything I may wish to do – if I do wish to do anything – tomorrow.

AC5/1/729   15 March 1936
                                                    Goring Hotel

My dear Hilda,

Public affairs & public opinion make me very unhappy. That has happened against which we guaranteed France & Press & public seek excuses for evading our pledge. The Govt which asked (& received) promises of support from France when it thought us in danger now hesitates to keep its solemn engagement. Hitler against the advice of the more moderate elements in his Govt – Schacht[52] & the Chiefs of the Army – has marched into the Rhineland to escape from an internal crisis urged on by Goering & Goebels. The economic crisis will recur, but when it does his army will be much stronger, the Army chiefs will not again seek to hold him back, every country in Europe will feel that England is a broken reed & the end can only be the complete triumph of Germany & I fear our own ultimate ruin. And our Govt has no policy. As far as I can make out it is as much divided as Asquith's Cabinet on the eve of the Great War. My confidence is rudely shaken.

On top of all this Baldwin chooses Inskipp[53] [sic] – a man with no experience in administration who has never given a thought to problems of defence, as the new Minister. Record said to me at B'ham last night: 'You know why? He mistook the War Book for the Prayer Book". He is a very astute politician but he is the worst Prime Minister since that other great & good man, Aberdeen.

I agree with what you say of Neville's speech [in the debate on the new Defence White Paper]. He needed another ten minutes, but it was the only speech worth listening to from the Govt front Bench ... but I thought that Winston's for knowledge, force of logic & delivery one of the best, if not the very best, that I have heard for many a year. He was not as carefully prepared & he was not as good at the Jewellers last night but the audience rose spontaneously when he sat down & stood cheering for a minute. And the country may not have his services in a post for which noone has equal qualifications for fear lest Hitler takes his appointment ill & because the Prime Minister has a little mind & is both jealous & unforgiving.

---

[52] Hjalmar Schacht (1877–1970) Economist and banker. Managing Partner, National Bank of Germany 1915–22; Senior Partner, Schacht & Co Bankers; Reich Currency Commissioner 1923; President, Reichsbank 1924–30 and reappointed by Hitler March 1933; Minister of Economics 1934–7. Tried at Nuremberg but acquitted 1946.

[53] Thomas Walker Hobart Inskip (1876–1947) Conservative MP for Bristol Central 1918–29, Fareham 1931–9. Solicitor-General 1922–4, 1924–8, 1931–2; Attorney-General 1928–9, 1932–6; Minister for Coordination of Defence 1936–9; Dominion Secretary 1939, 1940; Lord Chancellor 1939–40; Lord Chief Justice 1940–6. Knighted 1922. Created Viscount Caldecote 1939.

You will see that I am being driven into opposition or nearly so.

AC5/1/730   28 March 1936
                                                        Goring Hotel

My dear Hilda,

The event of the week is Eden's speech.[54] It was a first-class parliamentary performance such as we rarely get now-a-days. He used notes only – none of that dreary reading that is so common on the Front Benches in these times. His delivery was admirable & he spoke as one having authority, with courage & decipión, like a man who knows what he is about & at what he is aiming. I think & hope that it will enhance his position both at home & abroad.

The whole debate was on a high level ...

On the whole I was well satisfied with it. I hope that thoughtful people will see that there is more to the question than e.g. the Times leading articles have led them to suppose. I know that I do not represent our public opinion at present, but what I say needs saying & can be better said by one like me who will never again hold office with a freedom & plainness that Ministers & potential ministers would be unwise to use.

Neville did well & comes more & more into the light as the dominating mind of the government & the only possible successor to Baldwin, but his speech raised more questions than he or I or anyone else have yet found solution for. It is curious that the net result of recent events is to throw us more & more back on the essence of the Locarno policy – a definite guarantee of peace in the area where we are vitally interested & the restriction of our obligations elsewhere; but it is in what exactly we propose to do "elsewhere" that the real difficulties arise. Is it to be in what we did in regard to Manchuquo [sic] or what we are doing in regard to Abyssinia?

[54] On 26 March 1936 Eden declared that although seeking 'a peaceful and agreed solution', as a guarantor of Locarno Britain would support France and Belgium if attacked. 'I am not prepared to be the first British Foreign Secretary to go back on a British signature'. *House of Commons Debates*, 5 Series, 310 cols. 1439–53.

AC5/1/731   4 April 1936
                                               Goring Hotel

[Typescript]
My dear Ida,

   ...

At last I have done all my speeches unless indeed I take part in
Monday's Debate. I have delivered thirteen since the beginning of
March, which is a great deal too many for an old gentleman my age
who has no ministerial responsibilities.

AC5/1/732   2 May 1936
                                               Goring Hotel

[Typescript]
My dear Ida,

I have returned on Thursday evening from my Easter holiday, if the
word holiday can be applied to it, for in fact I had scarcely a moment
to myself, and seem to have been talking or listening to others the
whole time I was abroad ... I saw everyone of consequence in the
Governments and representatives of the great families of Austria and
Hungary ...

   ...

Speaking broadly, the trip confirmed impressions I had already
formed and gave them increased precision and life, but did not sensibly
modify my opinions. The Danube Basin is a regular Witches' Cauldron.
Every country in it has a discontented minority. Austria and Hungary
are essentially monarchical in spirit, and the fears, jealousies and
rivalries between the various countries make it difficult to mark out
any sensible line of policy. Hitler appears, from a telegram which was
shown to me, to have got into a perfect stew about the purpose of my
visit and to have attributed to me a semi-official mission to try to effect
the restoration of the Hapsburgs! This perhaps is as good an illustration
as one could have of the sensitiveness of the body politic and of the
capacity of people to swallow any alarmist rumour, however improbable
or unfounded.

*For Chamberlain the German renunciation of Locarno and the remilitarisation of
the Rhineland on 7 March 1936 transformed the entire situation. He strongly
deprecated the widespread view that Germany had simply 'marched into her own*

back yard'.[55] *During the next month the central theme of his many speeches was to explain that the real issue had been 'whether in future the law of force shall prevail or whether there shall be substituted for it the force of law'. In the Commons on 26 March he had chided MPs that they needed more than reassuring words from Hitler.*[56] *Six days later he returned to the theme in a speech elucidating the probability that Anschluss would provoke a Central European domino-effect. 'The independence of Austria is a key position', he warned the Commons on 1 April, 'If Austria perishes, Czechoslovakia becomes indefensible. Then the whole of the Balkans will be submitted to a gigantic new influence. Then the old German dream of a Central Europe ruled by and subject to Berlin will become a reality from the Baltic to the Mediterranean and the Black Sea with incalculable consequences not only for our country, but for the whole Empire'.*[57] *It was a prescient, if unheeded, prediction and he would be dead before it became a reality. During the remainder of April 1936 Chamberlain and his wife visited Austria, Hungary and Czechoslovakia where they met most leading politicians including their old friend Beneš: an experience which confirmed all Chamberlain's worst apprehensions about the instability in the region and the magnitude of the German menace.*

Chamberlain's warnings had equally fundamental implications for Anglo-Italian relations and the conflict then concluding in Abyssinia. With Germany on the march, Britain and France could not afford to alienate their Stresa front ally. Although always strongly supportive of Italy, but perhaps prompted by his Central European trip, on 6 May Chamberlain again spoke out in the Commons against the continuation of sanctions against Italy now that Abyssinia had been conquered. To go further and expel Italy from the League, he declared, was both foolish and dangerous, serving only to weaken the anti-German Stresa front without forcing Mussolini to disgorge his new spoils.[58] *At the same time he finally resigned from an increasingly uncongenial position on the LNU Executive on the grounds that he could no longer support its policy of sanctions when the danger in Europe made the risk of conflict with Italy in the Mediterranean unthinkable.*[59] *In private, Chamberlain's attempts to moderate Mussolini's behaviour drew a flattering response from Grandi who held out the hope of closer relations with Italy but little of substance.*[60] *Although the speech brought him 'a sheaf of abusive & reproachful letters', this action was simply one more manifestation of Chamberlain's belief that Germany was the principal threat; that nothing should be permitted to distract attention from it (whether Manchuria or Abyssinia); that safety lay only in restoring the Stresa*

[55] E. Spier, *Focus : A Footnote on the History of the Thirties* (1936), 26. For British response to the Rhineland crisis see R. Griffiths, *Fellow Travellers of the Right: British Enthusiasts for Nazi Germany, 1933–39*, (Oxford 1983), 201–10.

[56] *House of Commons Debates*, 5 Series, 310 cols, 1482–7, 26 March 1936.

[57] R. Lamb, *The Drift to War*, 197. Also Chamberlain to *The Times*, 2 April 1936.

[58] *House of Commons Debates*, 5 Series, 311 cols. 1769–71, 6 May 1936.

[59] D.S. Birn, *The League of Nations Unions*, 162–3. He was persuaded by Murray to defer the announcement until 23 June 1936.

[60] See N. Thompson, *The Anti-Appeasers*, 97–8; C. Petrie, *Life and Letters*, II, 413.

front to uphold the guarantees given at Locarno; and that the electorate needed to be confronted with these unpalatable truths whether they wanted to or not.

At the same time, Chamberlain asked his brother for a secret session of the House of Commons to discuss divisions about foreign policy. When discussed in Cabinet on 6 July few were enthusiastic about the prospect. Instead the Cabinet accepted Baldwin's proposal that he should receive a deputation for confidential discussions. On 28–29 July 1936 Baldwin and Inskip met the deputation led by Chamberlain for the Commons and Salisbury for the Lords. In many ways Baldwin was astonishingly candid about the electoral constraints upon rearmament; the over-riding desire to win an election and obtain a free hand; about his lack of faith in League sanctions; about the difficulties in assessing Hitler's intentions.[61] Privately, among fellow Conservatives, Baldwin was being as honest as he could and the deputation went away temporarily satisfied.

Although these meetings defused the situation in the short-term, Chamberlain continued to campaign for urgent preparations against the threat from Germany. He also lamented that Baldwin was 'becoming a public danger' and that new challenges demanded new qualities from leadership. As in 1930, he feared that Baldwin would leave a disastrous legacy to his successor.[62] Unfortunately, these twin themes tended increasingly to ensure that Chamberlain appeared to be 'more and more tied up with Winston's crowd'. This perception undoubtedly damaged his influence in the Commons as the voice of constructive criticism free from the hysteria associated with Churchill's chilling Jeremiahs.[63] After a foreign affairs debate in July 1936, 'Chips' Channon had noted that 'old Austen Chamberlain, the doyen of the House of Commons donkeys, made a really stupid speech in which he attacked Germany with unreasoning violence. He is ossified, tedious, and hopelessly out of date'. Such criticism from one of the most pitifully credulous Conservatives to fall under the 'champagne-like influence' of Ribbentrop and the German regime at this time is perhaps predictable.[64] Even among those who shared Chamberlain's concern about the German menace, however, there is evidence of increasing concern at his tendency to lapse into the 'regular anti-German harangue'.[65] Yet by the summer of 1936 Chamberlain was right to be alarmed. Baldwin's health had collapsed and he stood on the verge of a nervous breakdown.[66] Anxious not to compromise his half-brother's chances of obtaining the succession, however, Chamberlain could not bring himself to launch the final attack upon Baldwin's failures that he so desired.

---

[61] For a record of the discussion see M. Gilbert, *Winston S. Churchill* V. Companion 3, 425–36.

[62] A. Chamberlain to Hilda, 4 July 1936, AC 5/1/739.

[63] N. Chamberlain to Ida, 4 July 1936, NC18/1/968.

[64] Channon Diary, 27 July 1936, *Chips*, 73.

[65] Headlam Diary, 2 and 9 May 1935, S. Ball (ed) *Parliament and Politics*, 331–2.

[66] Middlemas & Barnes, *Baldwin*, 962–3.

AC5/1/733

10 May 1936
Hever Castle, Kent

My dear Hilda,

...

My speech[67] has brought me a sheaf of abusive & reproachful letters. I really did not want to make it, but I felt it would be cowardly to shirk saying what I thought & that it might help Eden & the government if I belled the cat. They are in an extraordinarily difficult position with a public opinion that is all sentiment & passion & will not face realities. I wish that I could see any issue from our troubles, but I don't see my way at all clearly. That is not because I don't know my own mind, but because I don't believe public opinion will at present allow us to pursue the only wise policy which is to call off sanctions, to restore what is called the Stresa front & then to sit down seriously to try to come to terms with Germany if possible & to fortify peace against her if it is not. But how is this to be done when the country is so irritated with France & so determined to have no dealings with Italy? I am in fact very gloomy & unhappy. Ivy says it is the reaction from the excitement & strain of our holiday where I was all the time giving out, & she may be partly right.

AC5/1/734

16 May 1936
Goring Hotel

My dear Ida,

...

As to Foreign policy what a mess it all is and how dangerous. I was quite taken by surprise by Schussing's [sic] coup. I thought that he & Starhemburg had agreed that they must work together & settled how to do it ... If you ask my opinion on it, I should be inclined to say that it is not a bad thing if Schussing [sic] is strong enough to keep him in order, but that is a very big if like all other ifs in present day politics.

S.B. has put his foot in it again with his Albert Hall statement that no small country has done anything for its own defence. Belgium, Switzerland & Czecho-Slovakia are furious & have approached me to correct it – which I shan't do. I expect that other minor powers are almost equally angry.

[67] In the Commons on 6 May 1936 Chamberlain called for an end to sanctions on Italy. On 17 June the Cabinet announced the end of sanctions.

What a nasty business this Budget leakage is! I don't think J.H. Thomas would deliberately sell a secret but I think he must have leaked – he is a notoriously leaky vessel – & he certainly had a most undesirable set of friends. At heart I am sorry for him, but I don't see how he can save himself.

AC5/1/735   29 May 1936
                                                            Goring Hotel

My dear Ida,

We spent last Sunday at the Winterton's in Sussex ... The other members of the party were the Winston Churchills, Edward Griggs, Page Croft & Robert Horne – we discussed some serious questions of defence & foreign policy laughed & amused ourselves a great deal. If you were a reader of the News Chronicle, you would have learned that 'the Anti-Baldwin Shadow Cabinet' met at Shillingtree Park & discussed who was to be the new Colonial Minister & what the village pub thought of it. I am bound to say their young man gave a most amusing account of it & I hope that he got a rise of salary in consequence. I wish that I could spin as light & amusing tale out of nothing.

AC5/1/736   4 June 1936
                                                            Goring Hotel

My dear Hilda,

I am sorry for Thomas. I don't believe that he would knowingly betray a Budget secret but I can imagine that if Butt[68] said to him "I am having a gamble on the Budget, I have insured a lot of people against a rise in income tax or tea" that Thomas might blurt out "Oh I wouldn't do that" or something of the sort. Anyway he must have leaked & it is a sad close to a remarkable career. I am glad the son is acquitted. That will be some comfort to the father."

---

[68] Alfred Butt (1878–1962) Conservative MP for Balham 1922 until his resignation over the Budget leak in 1936.

AC5/1/737

14 June 1936
Exbury House
Southampton

My dear Ida,

. . .

I agree with all you write about Thomas. His speech was dignified & moving. It is one of three – no, four – very painful scenes I have witnessed in my 40 odd years in the House & I don't want to see such another. For Butt there was little sympathy.

AC5/1/738

20 June 1936
Goring Hotel

My dear Ida,

. . .

Yes, Simon made a very powerful speech ... The P.M. recovered a little ground but he is in danger of going out like a tallow candle & leaving a very embarrassing estate to his successor. Some people say that he is now getting jealous of Neville & hopes that Inskip will train on to succeed himself, but apart from these personal issues he is really becoming a public danger. I have never known so rapid a descent of any man in public estimation. His moral reputation, which was his strength, seems gone. There is no man now to praise him. The need for a leader, a man of courage & initiative, is more [&] more widely felt & the language I hear about S.B. whether in the H. of C. smoking-room or at luncheons or dinners is angry & contemptuous in turns. Yet the party still rallies to him when attacked. Now he has Duff Cooper[69] & Londonderry on his hands. He will not spend a happy weekend I fear.

AC5/1/739

4 July 1936
Goring Hotel

My dear Hilda,

I really think that Baldwin is becoming a public danger. The arrogant assertion of his City speech that he & he alone is to be judge of when

[69] (Alfred) Duff Copper (1890–1954) Conservative MP for Oldham 1924–29, St George's 1931–45. Financial Secretary, War Office 1928–9, 1931–4; Financial Secretary Treasury, 1934–5; War Secretary 1935–7; First Lord of Admiralty 1937–8; Minister of Information 1940–1; Chancellor Duchy of Lancaster 1941–3; British representative with Free French 1943–4; Ambassador in Paris 1944–7. Created Viscount Norwich 1952.

he will retire is such a claim as I cannot recall in the mouths of any other leader & more suited to a Mussolini or a Hitler than to the Prime Minister of a great democracy. I believe that I should openly attack him but for the fact that by so doing I should damn Neville's chances as the kindly gossips would never believe that I was not doing it in his interest. The fact is that every Prime Minister has something to contribute & becomes Prime Minister because he is the right man at the conjuncture; but autre temps, autres moeurs. The conditions of today require other qualities & the problems of today are just those to which Baldwin has given least study & for which he has least aptitude. I can never forget how when Ramsay MacDonald called the leaders of other parties into conference about the future of India (in 1930, I think) he sat silent & left me to fight the whole battle, As we left the room he said:- I was so grateful to you, Austen, I know nothing about India, I really must begin to read something about it! And the Simon Report was already out & he had been Prime Minister twice. He is a shrewd domestic politician, very self-centred, very idle, very inert mentally but with qualities or a cleverness of apprehension which have given him a great hold over that great mass of left-centre opinion which decides our fate today, but he hasn't the elements even of the qualities which are needed to make a statesman or to give a lead in facing & solving the problems & dangers of today.

I should not wonder if he had started or encouraged the Inskip idea. To have done so would have been completely in character & there was at least some evidence that it originated in sources near him. In any case he will leave a damnosa hereditas to his successor.

AC5/1/740   12 July 1936
                                                    The Hill
                                            Stratford-on-Avon

My dear Ida,

. . .

I am a little stunned by the German-Austrian agreement[70] & find it difficult to measure its consequences. Everything depends on the loyalty with which it is observed & on the purpose which lies behind it in Hitler's mind, but as far as it goes it relieves present tension & that is

---

[70] On 11 July 1936 Germany and Austria signed an agreement to re-establish 'normal and friendly relations' which involved Hitler's pledge to recognise his neighbour's sovereignty in return for the promise that Austrian policy would be 'based always on the principle that Austria acknowledges herself to be a German state'. Both agreed not to interfere in each other's domestic politics.

to the good, if it is not merely the prelude to an attack on Czechoslovakia. But one needs more time to judge it.

AC5/1/745   4 October 1936
                                                        Goring Hotel

My dear Ida,

...

Did you read with pleasure Neville's Tribute to S.B. at Margate or did you feel with me that he had said to himself, well, as I must in any case say more than I think, I may as well make it a whopper at once? I am glad that Neville himself was so well received, tho' I did not doubt that he would be, & I am glad that in spite of Sam Hoare the [Annual] conference spoke out firmly on the mandated colonies. Is it not curious to see how Walter Elliot's fame has faded? I confess I always thought him over-rated.

Did I tell you that the copy of the D.T. with my second article was banned in Germany? So Camrose told me. Is the action of the German censorship more silly or dangerous? At first I inclined to the former opinion, but I think that I was wrong. If you can ride ... a people in blinkers, they will be your tools for any purpose for which you need them.

AC5/1/746   10 October 1936
                                                        Goring Hotel

My dear Hilda,

...

Yes, I think S.B. or his Missus must have been getting a little disturbed to find that he was not quite so indispensable as he thought. What you tell me of him is so characteristic of his sense of his own importance & of his lack of any consideration for others. My fingers itch to be at him, but it would be very unwise for me to give way to this impulse. I have to be doubly careful lest I should injure Neville but if only I might play – *longó intervallo* – Dizzy to his Peel, what fun I should have & how I should enjoy laying about me with a nice cane!

AC5/1/747   31 October 1936
                                                        Goring Hotel

My dear Ida,

Everyone seems to lead a busier life than I do at the present time. You & Hilda & Ivy seem always to be at Comtees or meetings of one kind or another meanwhile I sit at home & read, occasionally receive visits from Frenchmen, Italians, Americans & Japanese who seem to think that I have some influence on affairs or at least am in a position to predict their course, & wonder what is happening & still more what will happen, & try to compose another article for the D.T which won't take shape. I have lunched out most days, dined out three times & generally taken a short walk in the course of the day. And there is a picture of my life. News I have none & you must find Neville's letters now-adays much more nourishing than mine.

. . .

By the way how helpful Ribbentrop[71] must feel that Goering & Goebbels speeches are to his mission of peace & freedom! There is I suspect no love lost among these gentry. Ivy says that the two G's were never present at the same party while she was in Berlin.

. . .

Anthony Eden has asked to see me this afternoon. What for I wonder? I am curious.

AC5/1/749   14 November 1936
                                                    Goring Hotel

My dear Ida,

. . .

. . . I send you some of the reviews [of *Politics from Inside*] culled from the Press. They give it a good send-off & I am really glad to see that they do realise what our home-life was like & what Father was to his family. I was awfully nervous about that & very shy about publishing the few intimate letters but I feel now that my decision was right & that they have given the atmosphere of home as nothing else could have done.

. . .

Now here's a rum go. You may remember that about a fortnight ago I told you that Eden had asked to see me. Well that was only about the coming foreign affairs debate in the H. of C. which I missed on account of my visit to Lyon ... But at Monday at his luncheon he spoke to Ivy about our relations with Italy & the difficulty of getting into touch with Mussolini whom our Ambassador never sees & asked her whether she thought that I would make some excuse for going out & then have a heart to heart talk with him. He has since explained

---

[71] Joachim von Ribbentrop (1893–1946) Aide-de-Camp to German peace delegation in Paris 1919; head of wine import-export business in Berlin 1920–33; National Socialist Deputy, Reichstag 1933; Ambassador to London 1936–38; SS-Gruppenführer 1936; Foreign Minister 1938–45. Found guilty at Nuremberg and hanged.

a little more fully what he thinks that I could do & I am considering it & shall probably decide next week after seeing him again & talking with Grandi. It is all very vague & very difficult – a mission without a mission, an excuse or pretext which will deceive noone & so on – & I scarcely know what to do. But if I think there is a chance of being useful I suppose that I ought to go, however risky the job is. At present this is I believe known only to Eden, Vansittart & us, but he may have spoken to the P.M. since my talk with him.

Talking of the P.M. his passage about the Fulham election in his speech on Thursday[72] made me shiver. Briefly summarized it comes to this: I knew the country was in danger but I was afraid to tell them so, lest I should lose more by-elections. My God! & he thinks that is leadership.

AC5/1/750   22 November 1936
                                         Yattendon Court

My dear Hilda,

...

The Italian project is held up for the present as Grandi before leaving for Rome last week spontaneously enquired of Eden whether he would see any objection to my being asked to address the Foreign Affairs Association in Rome. Of course it would be much better if the initiative comes from that end, so we will 'wait & see'.

AC5/1/751   29[?] November 1936
                                         no address

My dear Ida,

On Monday[73] ... with half a dozen old stagers like myself, interviewed the Prime Minister about the future of a certain lady[74] which fills us all with the gravest anxiety, but I can't write about it even to you. Everyone

[72] On 12 November 1936 Baldwin told the Commons that after the Fulham by-election 'supposing I had gone to the country and said that Germany was rearming and that we must rearm, does anybody think that this pacific democracy would have rallied to that cry at that moment? I cannot think of anything that would have made the loss of the election ... more certain'.

[73] A deputation of Salisbury, Selborne, Derby, Crewe, Fitzalan, Samuel and Austen Chamberlain met Baldwin in his room at the Commons at 5.30 on Monday, 16 November 1936, Viscount Samuel, *Memoirs*, (1945), 265–6. This letter must, therefore, be dated earlier than 29 November.

[74] Wallis Simpson (1896–1986) Soon after divorcing second husband married Edward, Duke of Windsor, 3 June 1937.

is talking about it, though the newspapers have preserved silence about it so far – perhaps unwisely ...

...

Merry del Val,[75] the formerly Spanish Ambassador, [now representing the Burgos Government] called upon me [Tuesday] morning & we met him & his wife again at lunch at the Netherlands Ministers on Wednesday. They were full of tragic stories of the fate of friends & relations in Spain. I wish that Franco could make a quick end of it for the longer the civil war lasts the greater the international complications & dangers.

...

Much more important than any of these are Eden's two speeches at the end of last week & yesterday. They give a very necessary precision to British policy & have I think, done much good. But what are we to say of German-Japanese doings & where exactly does Mussolini stand? The world is full of conundrums to which I have no answer.

AC5/1/752

6 December 1936
Goring Hotel

My dear Hilda,

Yes, a catastrophe indeed, as you say. I feel that I don't want to meet anybody, for there is only one subject of conversation & I do not want to discuss it with anybody. It has been bad enough for months past, but until a few weeks ago I thought the King had so strong a sense of public duty that there could be no question that he would subordinate his personal feelings to the needs of the State & to the dignity & usefulness of the Crown. I still hoped this even after the Aberdeen escapade[76] & perhaps it would be better for him & for us if criticism had come earlier & he had been less sheltered. His grandfather as Prince heard some very plain speaking & learned his lesson. He at least knew what could & could not be permitted to the wearer of the Crown. Ah me! what a tragedy it is! He seemed so pre-eminently fitted by temperament & training to be the King of the new age – if only he

---

[75] Alfonso de Merry del Val (1864–1943) Entered Spanish Diplomatic Service 1882. Tutor in English to King Alfonso XIII 1892–1902; Minister in Brussels 1911–13; Ambassador to London 1913–31; subsequently representing Burgos Government. Awarded Grand Cross of Royal Victorian Order 1918, Created Marquis 1925.

[76] In September 1936 the new King had put off opening a hospital wing in Aberdeen to meet Mrs Simpson at the railway station on the implausible excuse of deep mourning. It sent a wave of resentment through Scotland and prompted press speculation everywhere else.

had known how to be King ... He would have been judged specially fitted to rule if he had not come to the throne.

It looks now as if he was so much in the toils of this woman that he would abdicate rather than leave her ...

Well, I suppose that we shall know something definitely tomorrow, but whatever happens it will take long to repair the damage done here & throughout the Empire.

In September 1936 Ivy finally found a suitable house with a small garden which they could afford. The prospect of moving out of the Goring Hotel which had been his home for the past year was tantalising. 'It will be a blessing to have one's books about one again', he told his sister, 'the table at the Goring is excellent & not too rich, but what is it that makes all hotel food, however good, pall after a few weeks?'.[77] In the event, the need to re-wire the house delayed them from taking up residence. Not until the first week of January 1937 did they begin 'camping' at their new house in Egerton Terrace, SW3. Within ten days, however, the books were sorted and Chamberlain had planned the position of his single flower bed. He then departed for a 'most pleasant visit' to Paris where he and his speeches – in English and French – were given a cordial reception. As he recalled, 'What I enjoyed ... was my visit after more than 50 years to the Ecole des Sciences Politiques & the delightful reception which the students gave me'.[78] For the next two months the small garden provided him with a renewed source of pleasure, occupation and detail for his diary letters.

AC5/1/759   31 January 1937
                                                            24 Egerton Terrace

My dear Ida,

Yes, it is very pleasant to be in one's own house again, to have one's things about one & in short to be at home. I think that we shall be very comfortable here ...

And Acland[79] has begun sending me flowers again. Last week I received cyclamen cousu, witch-hazel, snowdrops, sprays of cherry

[77] A. Chamberlain to Ida, 18 September and to Hilda, 27 September 1936, AC5/1/743–4.

[78] A. Chamberlain to Hilda, 17 and 24 January 1937, AC5/1/757–8.

[79] Francis Dyke Acland (1874–1939) Liberal MP for Richmond, Yorks 1906–10, Cranborne 1910–22, Tiverton 1923–4, North Cornwall 1932–9. PPS to Haldane 1906–8; Financial Secretary, War Office 1908–10; Under Secretary, Foreign Office 1911–15; Financial Secretary, Treasury 1915; Parliamentary Secretary Agriculture 1915–16. Succeeded 14th Baronet 1926.

plum & actually a spray of 'lobster-claws' grown in the open. I could only reply that if I had a Devonshire garden, nothing would induce me to leave it for Parliament.

AC5/1/760

13 February 1937
24 Egerton Terrace

My dear Ida,

... I finished my article on Grey's Life & have sold it to the D.T.... It will appear on March 1st when Trevelyan's book will be published. Don't forget to read the book. Its a lesson in German ways. I hope that the younger generation will read it, for they could learn much from it.

...

I exhausted myself this morning clearing away part of the rubbish, bits of flagstone & the like, which the workmen had thrown at random on the rockery at the end of our garden. I have revealed two or three clumps of crocuses & other bulbs & a fern or two. Except the trees, one of which is certainly dangerous & must come down, a laburnum & some privet which must come out, they are the only living things in it, if I do not count wood-lice & I suppose slugs which will reveal themselves as soon as there is anything for them to feed on. But I have begun making enquiry for a few plants & Sir G. Hill of Kew has given me a Magnolia Soulangeana over 5 feet high in a pot so that I can put it in without disturbing its roots & Mr Hay of the Royal Parks is to send me Primula dentala ... & some Gentiana Sino-ornata ... I feel already quite excited about it, but I can't now work all day long as I used to do at Twitts Ghyll. I soon tire.

AC5/1/761

20 February 1937
24 Egerton Terrace

My dear Hilda,

We shall be delighted to have you both to lunch on March 2nd ...

Yes, I think this has been our worst week as well as yours − not a single day without rain & generally heavy rain & sometimes sleet. Never-the-less I got the privet & the young lime trees cleared away from the front of the house & have filled the borders with P. denticulata, seven dozen of them, I think, good clumps just coming into blooms. Almonds are out just up the street & I am going to put in a cherry & a crab for variety.

I have had a busy week. On Tuesday I lunched with John Bailey, Abe's[80] son ...

On Wednesday I addressed the Union of the Students of the London School of Economics ... I had a lot of heckling afterwards. They are a queer crowd, socialists & communists prevailing, of English, Indians, Chinese, Japs & Arabs. If there were any Germans present except refugees they won't have liked what I said ...

And now guess what I did with the rest of the week! Well, I don't think you are likely to have guessed right. I spent two long mornings being filmed (a Talkie) for a film John Drinkwater[81] is making on 100 years of English History for Coronation Year! If it had been a stage performance my part would have lasted I suppose 3 minutes – five at the most, I merely appear as myself & converse those few moments with J.D. but for the film it took $4\frac{1}{2}$ working hours without 'walking time'. I wouldn't be a film artist & I have come to the conclusion that they are not over-paid. It's maddeningly irritating. First they are never ready at the appointed time. Then there is a blow-out i.e. something fuses, or the camera makes too much noise or a lamp crackles. And finally this morning there were moments of brilliant sunshine between the storms & then we had to stop because the light was quite different from what it had been on the first day. This for the mere mechanical slips & troubles. Add the human mistakes ... & you will understand that it requires the patience of Job. And why do I do it & what do I get out of it? Well they present me with my garden with widened border, rockery remade, rubbish removed & new soil put in, done to a specification which I have approved & that will cost them £50. So my labours are not wasted, but I think that in future my fee will be £100 down & a refresher. I should not have got away before 2 o'clock today if the workmen had not insisted that their dinner hour was well past & that it was against Trade Union rules to work longer.

[80] Abe Bailey (1863–1940) Major mine-owner in Transvaal. Created Baronet 1919 for services in promoting South African Union. His son John Milner Bailey (1900–46) married Churchill's eldest daughter Diana in 1932 but divorced 1935 – the first of three wives.

[81] John Drinkwater (1882–1937) English poet and dramatist. Close associations with Birmingham where he was born. Birmingham Repertory Theatre first produced his most famous play *Abraham Lincoln* in 1918.

AC5/1/762   7 March 1937
                                              24 Egerton Terrace

My dear Hilda,

When I went to bed last night, it was raining; when I woke this
morning it was snowing & now it is all slush! When will my garden be
ready & shall I be able to plant the flowering trees & bushes that I
want to see there? I had hoped to be planting this weekend but the
work takes longer than I had expected.

I had hardly expected a letter from you this week. It was good of
you to keep up the custom in spite of our recent meeting. On
Wednesday & Thursday we attended banquets which were like the old
times. All the ladies wore tiaras & their best gowns & the men
decorations. The first was at the Granards[82] for Queen Mary & it is
characteristic of them that we were the only commoners invited. I'll
bet it was Queen Mary who put us on their list. The second banquet
was at the French Embassy which has become very smart under
Corbin. One meets the right people there now. Finally on Friday we
dined with Mary & then went on to Mrs Fitzroy's[83] party where we
found a good many friends apart from members of the House. I was
glad to dine quietly at home yesterday evening & am thankful that we
shall do the same tonight though we have to go out to lunch with Lady
Cunard[84] today who is taking Ivy to a concert.

Yesterday Arthur Preston, a year or two younger than I who was at
Miss Smith's at Brighton with me, came to lunch to show me some family
silhouettes & left with me another drawing of my great grandfather & one
of Sarah June Chamberlain Grandpapa's half sister, who married Edward
Sutton Nettlefold, grandfather of Ted & Hugh & that big family. I took
the opportunity of asking Mabel & her husband (Robin, is he not?) as she
wanted to see the portraits & relics. She seemed very well & was as bright
as usual but my word! isn't he a dull dog? He scarcely uttered.

Your loving brother,
Austen
Neville spoke well this week.

[82] Bernard Arthur William Forbes, 8th Earl of Granard (1874–1948). Military career.
Lord-in-Waiting to King Edward VII 1905–07; Master of Horse, 1907–15, 1924–36;
Assistant Postmaster-General 1906–9. Member, Irish Senate, 1921–34; Member Irish
Convention.
[83] Wife of Edward Algernon Fitzroy (1869–1943) Deputy Chairman of Committees,
House of Commons 1922–8; Speaker of the House of Commons 1928–43. She was
created Viscountess Daventry on his death.
[84] Maud (called herself Emerald) Cunard (1872–1948) Wife of Sir Bache Cunard.
Society hostess; according to Boothby, one of the great five with Mrs Ronnie Greville,
Lady Astor, Colefax and Londonderry.

It seems particularly appropriate that this last letter to his sisters should have dwelt upon the twin themes which had occupied so much attention in the past – his plans for the garden and the havoc the weather brought to the gardener's dreams. Five days after writing this letter Chamberlain suffered a mild heart attack which confined him to his home. On the 16 March he felt a little better, got up for lunch and in the evening he took a bath. As Neville recalled in his diary:[85]

A moment later he called Ivy: she ran upstairs and found that he had dried himself and put on his vest and drawers and sat down in a chair. He had then fallen over striking his head against the basin. She got some brandy as he was still breathing and he just gulped it down but died immediately. The doctor who was called in said that he had not suffered at all. It was a merciful end far preferable to Father's 8 years of martyrdom. But it was a great shock and I feel stunned.

'Austen happy in sudden death' was Tom Jones' epitaph.[86]

The following afternoon, in a 'real House of Commons day',[87] Baldwin paid tribute to Austen Chamberlain in a speech which all who heard it believed to be his very finest style. He praised the man who had been his sponsor to the House twenty-nine years before, as a 'very great Parliamentarian' whose loss diminished the place and broke its link with the 'great days of Parliamentary tradition'; as a courageous, honorable and formidable politician in office; as an Elder Statesman whose transition to the backbenches had brought an even greater glory and respect than he ever achieved during a distinguished career in office. Above all, he eulogised him as as an honest and supremely loyal colleague. 'One remembers, and always will remember those two things', Baldwin told an emotional House, 'the loyalty not only in action in big things, but loyalty of thought and word where so many of us go wrong'. In his peroration Baldwin turned to the evocative phrase of his rural home and echoed in the traditions of the Commons itself: 'When our long days of work are over here there is nothing in our oldest customs which so stirs the imagination of the young Member as the cry which goes down the Lobbies, "Who goes home?" Sometimes when I hear it I think of the language of my own country-side and my feeling that for those who have borne the almost insupportable burden of public life there may well be a day when they will be glad to go home. So Austen Chamberlain has gone home. The sympathy of this House from the heart of everyone one of us will go out to those who are left'.[88]

The speech was Baldwin at his supremely sentimental best. As Tom Jones noted,

[85] Neville Chamberlain Diary, 16 March 1937. Petrie claims Austen died suddenly while taking a book from a shelf, *Life and Letters*, II, 415: an error reproduced in a vast number of subsequent works.

[86] T. Jones to Lady Grigg, 18 March 1937, *Diary with Letters*, 325.

[87] Channon Diary 17 March 1937, *Chips*, 117.

[88] Baldwin to the House of Commons, 17 March 1931, reprinted in *Service of our Lives: Last Speeches as Prime Minister*, 84–93.

'whatever S.B. cannot do, he can speak a funeral oration'.[89] Neville Chamberlain listened to this 'beautiful tribute' and 'rejoiced profoundly that it had fallen to [Baldwin] to express what the House felt'.[90] It was a speech which 'reduced many Members to actual tears'. Even the ever-critical 'Chips' Channon found Baldwin so eloquent and moving that he briefly wondered whether he had got Austen wrong. At the very least he was forced to concede that 'there must be rejoicing in Germany tonight that this desiccated patriarch ... is no more'.[91] On 19 March 1937 Chamberlain's urn was deposited in a grave at St Marylebone Cemetery in north London. 'The flowers were marvellously beautiful and the spot chosen looks over a wide view', Neville wrote in his diary later, 'The birds were singing in the trees and I felt it was a good place'.[92] In a little over ten weeks the event that Austen had dreamed of, prayed for and worked towards for so long finally occurred when Baldwin retired as Prime Minister to be succeeded by Neville Chamberlain. Unwittingly perhaps, that self-centred, idle but most cunning of politicians appears to have cheated him even to the end. Yet Austen went to his grave confident in the knowledge that his half-brother's succession could not long be delayed.[93] As for the rest, Churchill was undoubtedly correct in his reassurance to Lady Chamberlain that 'when one surveys the scene of our brief lives from an impersonal standpoint, I must confess that my strongest impression is one of his wonderful good fortune'.[94]

> To preserve up to the vy last a complete mental & physical efficiency, & to die at 73 in a peaceful flash is surely the reward which should attend a lifetime of fidelity & honour. The tributes the like of which I have never heard surpassed in the H of C are only one measure of the esteem & love which A. commanded on all sides. His life added lustre to the famous name he bore. We shall never see his like again – a great gentleman, a true friend of England, an example & an inspiration to all.

[89] Tom Jones to Lady Grigg, 18 March 1937.
[90] N. Chamberlain to Baldwin, 17 March 1937, Baldwin MSS 173/32.
[91] Channon Diary 16–17 March 1937, *Chips*, 117.
[92] Neville Chamberlain Diary, 19 March 1937.
[93] N. Chamberlain to Hilda, 30 May 1937, NC 18/1/1005.
[94] Churchill to Ivy Chamberlain, 18 March 1937, M. Gilbert, *Winston S. Churchill* V. Companion 3, 626.

BIBLIOGRAPHY

1. *PRIMARY COLLECTIONS*

Altrincham MSS — Papers of Sir Edward Grigg, 1st Baron Altrincham, microfilm at the Bodleian Library, Oxford

Baldwin MSS — Papers of Stanley Baldwin, 1st Earl Baldwin of Bewdley, Cambridge University Library

Bayford MSS — Papers and diaries of Sir Robert Arthur Sanders, Baron Bayford, in the care of the Conservative Research Department.

Beaverbrook MSS — Papers of Sir William Maxwell Aitken, 1st Baron Beaverbrook, House of Lords Record Office.

Bridgeman MSS — The Political Diaries of William Clive Bridgeman, 1st Viscount Bridgeman, courtesy of Mrs A Stacey and the Trustees of the Bridgeman family archive.

Cecil MSS — Papers of Robert Gascoyne-Cecil, Viscount Cecil of Chelwood, British Library, Add.MSS.

Austen Chamberlain MSS — Papers of Sir Joseph Austen Chamberlain, Birmingham University Library.

Neville Chamberlain MSS — Papers and diaries of Arthur Neville Chamberlain, Birmingham University Library.

Chelwood MSS — Papers of Robert Gascoyne-Cecil, Viscount Cecil of Chelwood, Hatfield House.

D'Abernon MSS — Papers and diaries of Edgar Vincent, 1st Baron D'Abernon of Esher, British Library, Add.MSS.

Davidson MSS — Papers of Sir John Colin Campbell Davidson, 1st Viscount Davidson, House of Lords Record Office.

Derby MSS — Papers and diaries of Edward George Villiers Stanley, 17th Earl of Derby, Liverpool City Central Library.

Elibank MSS — Papers of Gideon Murray, 2nd Viscount Elibank, Scottish Record Office, Edinburgh.

Fisher MSS — Papers and diaries of Herbert Albert Laurens Fisher, Bodleian Library, Oxford.

Lloyd George MSS	Papers of David Lloyd George, 1st Earl Lloyd-George of Dwyfor, House of Lords Record Office.
Griffith-Boscawen MSS	Papers of Sir Arthur Sackville Trevor Griffith-Boscawen, Bodleian Library, Oxford.
Gwynne MSS	Papers of Howell Arthur Gwynne, Bodleian Library, Oxford, courtesy of Vice-Admiral Sir Ian Hogg.
Hankey MSS	Papers and diaries of Sir Maurice Pascal Alers Hankey, 1st Baron Hankey, Churchill College, Cambridge.
Hanworth MSS	Papers of Sir Edward Murray Pollock, 1st Viscount Hanworth, Bodleian Library, Oxford.
Headlam MSS	Papers and diaries of Sir Cuthbert Headlam, Durham Record Office.
Hewins MSS	Papers and diaries of William Albert Samuel Hewins, Sheffield University Library.
Hopetoun MSS	Papers of the Marquess of Linlithgow, National Register of Archives (Scotland), Edinburgh.
Kennet MSS	Papers of Sir Edward Hilton Young, 1st Baron Kennet and the diary of Lady Kennet, Cambridge University Library.
Law MSS	Papers of Andrew Bonar Law, House of Lords Record Office.
MacDonald MSS	Papers and diaries of James Ramsay MacDonald, including the papers of Miss Rose Rosenberg on Loan to the P.R.O., Public Record Office.
Maclean MSS	Papers of Sir Donald Maclean, Bodleian Library, Oxford.
Milner MSS	Papers and diaries of Sir Alfred Milner, 1st Viscount Milner, Bodleian Library, Oxford.
Murray MSS	Papers of Lt. Col. Arthur Murray, 3rd Viscount Elibank, National Library of Scotland, Edinburgh.
Quickswood MSS	Papers of Hugh Cecil, 1st Baron Quickswood, by courtesy of the 6th Marquess of Salisbury, Hatfield House.
Reading MSS	Papers of Sir Rufus Daniel Isaacs, 1st

	Marquess of Reading, India Office Library.
Salisbury MSS	Papers of James Edward Hubert Gascoyne-Cecil, 4th Marquess of Salisbury, by courtesy of the 6th Marquess of Salisbury, Hatfield House.
Scott MSS	Papers and diaries of Charles Prestwich Scott, British Library, Add.MSS.
Steel-Maitland MSS	Papers of Sir Arthur Herbert Drummond Ramsay Steel-Maitland, Scottish Record Office, Edinburgh.
Strachey MSS	Papers of John St. Loe Strachey, House of Lords Record Office.
Templewood MSS	Papers of Samuel Gurney Hoare, 1st Viscount Templewood, Cambridge University Library.
Whittinghame MSS	Papers of Arthur James Balfour, 1st Earl of Balfour and Gerald William Balfour, 2nd Earl of Balfour, National Register of Archives (Scotland), Edinburgh.
Wolmer MSS	Papers of Roundell Cecil Palmer, Viscount Wolmer, 3rd Earl Selborne, Bodleian Library, Oxford.
Worthington-Evans MSS	Papers of Sir Laming Worthington-Evans, Bodleian Library, Oxford.

2. PARLIAMENTARY PAPERS

Hansard, *Parliamentary Debates*, Fifth Series.
Cd.8610. Report of the Commission appointed by Act of Parliament to Enquire into the Operations of War in Mesopotamia, May 1917.
Cd.9038. Conference on the Reform of the Second Chamber: Letter from Viscount Bryce to the Prime Minister, April 1918.
Cmd.2768. Imperial Conference 1926: Summary of the Proceedings.
Cmd.3568–9. Report of the Indian Statutory Commission (1929–30), May–June 1930.
Cmd.4827. Statement Relating to Defence, March 1935.

3. BIOGRAPHIES AND MEMOIRS

The following have been cited in the text. Place of publication London unless otherwise stated.

Adams, C. Forbes,	*Life of Lord Lloyd* (1948)
Amery, Leopold S.,	*My Political Life* (3 vols, 1953–1955)

Attlee, Clement R.,	*As it Happened* (1954)
Avon, Earl of,	*The Eden Memoirs: Vol 1: Facing the Dictators* (1962)
Baldwin, A.W.,	*My Father: The True Story* (1955)
Baldwin, Stanley,	*Service of our Lives: Last Speeches as Prime Minister* (1937)
Ball, Stuart, ed	*Parliament and Politics in the Age of Baldwin and MacDonald: The Headlam Diaries 1923–1935* (1992)
Barnes, J. & Nicholson, D.,ed	*The Leo Amery Diaries, Vol 1 1896–1929* (1980)
Barnes, J. & Nicholson, D.,ed	*The Empire at Bay: The Leo Amery Diaries, 1929–1945* (1988)
Beaverbrook, Lord,	*Men and Power 1917–18* (1956)
Beaverbrook, Lord,	*The Decline and Fall of Lloyd George and Great was the Fall Thereof* (1963)
Birkenhead, Lord,	*Contemporary Personalities* (1924)
Birkenhead, Lord,	*America Revisited* (1924)
Birkenhead, Earl of,	*Halifax: The Life of Lord Halifax* (1965)
Boyle, Andrew,	*Montagu Norman: A Biography* (1967)
Boyle, Andrew,	*Poor Dear Brendan: The Quest for Brendan Bracken* (1974)
Blake, Robert,	*The Unknown Prime Minister: The Life and Times of Andrew Bonar Law 1858–1923* (1955)
Boscawen, A. Griffith-,	*Memories* (1925)
Busch, Brian Cooper,	*Hardinge of Penshurst: A Study in Old Diplomacy* (1980)
Carlton, David,	*Anthony Eden: A Biography* (1981)
Cartland, Barbara,	*Ronald Cartland* (1941)
Cecil, Viscount,	*A Great Experiment: An Autobiography* (1941)
Cecil, Viscount,	*All the Way* (1949)
Chamberlain, Austen,	*Down the Years* (1935)
Chamberlain, Austen,	*Politics from Inside: An Epistolary Chronicle, 1906–1914* (1936)
Charmley, John,	*Lord Lloyd and the Decline of the British Empire* (1987)
Chilcott, Warden,	*Political Salvation 1930–32* (1932)
Churchill, Randolph,	*Winston S. Churchill,* (2 vols, 1966–67)
Churchill, Randolph,	*Winston S. Churchill,* Companion volumes (5 vols, 1967–1969)
Churchill, Winston S.,	*The World Crisis: The Aftermath* (New York, 1929)
Clark, Alan, ed,	*A Good Innings: The Private Papers of Viscount Lee of Fareham* (1974)

Clynes, J.R.,	*Memoirs* (2 vols, 1937)
Colvin, Ian,	*Vansittart in Office* (1965)
Croft, Lord,	*My Life of Strife* (n.d. 1948)
Cross, J.A.,	*Sir Samuel Hoare: A Political Biography* (1977)
Crowe, S & Corp, E.,	*Our Ablest Public Servant: Sir Eyre Crowe 1864–1925* (Braunton, 1993)
Cullen, Tom,	*Maundy Gregory: Purveyor of Honours* (1974)
Curzon, Marchioness,	*Reminiscences* (1955)
D'Abernon, Viscount,	*An Ambassador of Peace* (3 vols, 1929–1930)
Dalton, Hugh,	*Call Back Yesterday: Memoirs 1887–1931* (1953)
David, Edward, ed	*Inside Asquith's Cabinet: From the Diaries of Charles Hobhouse* (1977)
Dilks, David,	*Neville Chamberlain, vol 1, 1869–1929* (Cambridge, 1984)
Driberg, Tom,	*Lord Beaverbrook: A Study in Power and Frustration* (1956)
Dugdale, Blanche,	*Arthur James Balfour* (2 vols, 1936)
Dutton, David,	*Austen Chamberlain: Gentleman in Politics* (1985)
Elletson, D.H.,	*The Chamberlains* (1966)
Ellis, E.L,	*T.J.: The Life of Dr Thomas Jones, CH* (Cardiff, 1992)
Feiling, Keith,	*The Life of Neville Chamberlain* (1947)
Fitzroy, Sir Almeric,	*Memoirs* (2 vols, n.d.)
Gardner, B.,	*Allenby: Edmund Henry Hynman Allenby 1st Viscount, 1861–1931,* (1965)
Garvin, J.L & Amery, J.,	*Life of Joseph Chamberlain* (6 vols, 1932–1969)
George, David Lloyd,	*War Memoirs of David Lloyd George* (6 vols, 1933–1936)
George, Frances Lloyd,	*The Years that are Past* (1967)
Gilbert, Martin,	*Winston S. Churchill* (vol III-V, 1971–1976)
Gilbert, Martin,	*Winston S. Churchill Companions to vol III-V,* (8 vols, 1972–1982)
Gilbert, Martin,	*Sir Horace Rumbold: Portrait of a Diplomat, 1869–1941* (1973)
Gopal, S.,	*The Viceroyalty of Lord Irwin* (Oxford, 1957)
Graham, Thomas N.,	*Willie Graham: The Life of the Rt. Hon. W. Graham* (n.d.)
Grigg, John,	*Lloyd George: The People's Champion, 1902–1911* (1978)
Grigg, John,	*Lloyd George: From Peace to War, 1912–1916* (1985)
Hancock, W.H.,	*Smuts: The Fields of Force, 1919–50* (2 vols, Cambridge, 1962–68)

Hardinge, Lord,   *Old Diplomacy: The Reminiscences of Lord Har-
                                dinge of Penshurst* (1947)
Harrod, R. F.,   *The Life of John Maynard Keynes* (Pelican ed.
                                Harmondsworth, 1972)
Hemingford, Lord,   *Backbencher and Chairman: Some Parliamentary
                                Reminiscences* (1946)
Hyde, H. Montgomery,   *Lord Reading: The Life of Rufus Isaacs, First
                                Marquess of Reading* (1967)
Hyde, H. Montgomery,   *Baldwin: The Unexpected Prime Minister* (1973)
James, Robert Rhodes, ed,   *Chips: The Diaries of Sir Henry Channon* (1967)
James, Robert Rhodes,   *Memoirs of a Conservative: J.C.C. Davidson's
                                Memoirs and Papers, 1910–1936* (1969)
James, Robert Rhodes,   *Churchill: A Study in Failure, 1900–1939* (1970)
James, Robert Rhodes,   *Victor Cazalet: A Portrait* (1976)
Jenkins, Roy,   *Baldwin* (1987)
Jones, Thomas,   *A Diary with Letters 1931–1950* (1954)
Kirkpatrick, Sir I.A.,   *The Inner Circle* (1959)
Lawrence, F.W. Pethick-,   *Fate Has Been Kind* (n.d. 1943)
MacKenzie, Norman, ed,   *The Letters of Sidney and Beatrice Webb, vol
                                III, Pilgrimage, 1912–47* (Cambridge, 1978)
MacKenzie, N. & J., eds,   *The Diary of Beatrice Webb, vol 4 1924–1943*
                                (1985)
Mackintosh,   Sir   Alex-   *Echoes of Big Ben, A Journalist's Parliamentary
ander,   Diary 1881–1940* (1945)
Macmillan, Harold,   *Winds of Change 1914–1939* (1966)
Macmillan, Harold,   *The Past Masters: Politics and Politicians,
                                1906–1936* (1975)
Marquand, David,   *Ramsay MacDonald* (1977)
Massey, V.,   *What's Past is Prologue* (1963)
Masterman, Lucy,   *C.F.G. Masterman: A Biography* (1939)
McFadyean, Sir Andrew,   *Recollected in Tranquillity* (1964)
McKercher, B.J.C.,   *Esmé Howard: A Diplomatic Biography*
                                (Cambridge, 1989)
Middlemas, Keith, ed,   *Thomas Jones: Whitehall Diary* (3 vols, 1969–
                                71)
Middlemas, K & Barnes, J.,   *Baldwin: A Biography* (1969)
Morgan, K.O, ed,   *Lloyd George Family Letters 1885–1936*
                                (Cardiff, 1973)
Morgan, K.O, & Jane,   *Portrait of a Progressive: The Political Career of
                                Christopher, Viscount Addison* (Oxford, 1980)
Murray, Gideon,   *A Man's Life* (1934)
Newton, Lord,   *Retrospection* (1941)
Nicholson, A.P.,   *The Real Men in Public Life. Forces and Factors
                                in the State* (1928)

Nicolson, Harold,	*King George V: His Life and Reign* (1952)
Nicolson, Nigel, ed,	*Harold Nicolson: Diaries and Letters 1930–1939* (1966)
Peters, A.R.,	*Anthony Eden at the Foreign Office 1931–1938* (Aldershot, 1986)
Peterson, M.,	*Both Sides of the Curtain: An Autobiography* (1950)
Petrie, Sir Charles,	*The Chamberlain Tradition* (1938)
Petrie, Sir Charles,	*The Life and Letters of the Rt. Honourable Sir Austen Chamberlain* (2 vols, 1939–1940)
Pimlott, Ben, ed,	*The Political Diary of Hugh Dalton, 1918–40, 1945–60* (1986)
Pound, R & Harmsworth, G.,	*Northcliffe* (1959)
Pugh, Martin,	*Lloyd George* (1988)
Ramsden, John, ed,	*Real Old Tory Politics: The Political Diaries of Robert Sanders, Lord Bayford, 1910–1935* (1984)
Riddell, Lord,	*Lord Riddell's War Diary, 1914–1918* (1933)
Riddell, Lord,	*Lord Riddell's Intimate Diary of the Peace Conference and After, 1918–1923* (1933)
Robbins, Keith,	*Sir Edward Grey: A Biography of Lord Grey of Falloden* (1971)
Roskill, Stephen,	*Hankey: Man of Secrets* (3 vols, 1970–74)
Rowland, Peter,	*Lloyd George* (1975)
Salter, Lord Arthur,	*Memoirs of a Public Servant* (1961)
Salter, Lord Arthur,	*Slave of the Lamp: A Public Servant's Notebook* (1967)
Salvidge, Stanley,	*Salvidge of Liverpool* (1934)
Samuel, Viscount,	*Memoirs* (1945)
Selby, Walford,	*Diplomatic Twilight 1930–1940* (1953)
Snell, Lord,	*Men, Movements and Myself* (1936)
Steed, Wickham,	*The Real Stanley Baldwin* (1930)
Sutton, Eric, ed,	*Gustav Stresemann: His Diaries, Letters and Papers* (2 vols, 1937)
Sykes, Major-Gen. Sir Frederick,	*From Many Angles: An Autobiography* (1942)
Taylor, A.J.P., ed,	*Lloyd George: A Diary by Frances Stevenson* (1971)
Taylor, A.J.P., ed,	*W.P. Crozier, Off the Record: Political Interviews, 1933–1943* (1973)
Taylor, A.J.P., ed,	*My Darling Pussy: The Letters of Lloyd George and Frances Stevenson 1913–41* (1975)
Taylor, H.A.,	*The Strange Case of Andrew Bonar Law* (n.d.)

Templewood, Viscount,	*Nine Troubled Years* (1954)
Thorpe, D.R.,	*The Uncrowned Prime Ministers* (1980)
Vansittart, Lord,	*The Mist Procession* (1958)
Vincent, John, ed,	*The Crawford Papers. The Journals of David Lindsay, twenty-seventh Earl of Crawford and tenth Earl of Balcarres 1871–1940 during the Years 1892 to 1940* (Manchester, 1984)
Waterhouse, Norah,	*Private and Official* (1942)
Wedgwood, Joseph,	*Memoirs of a Fighting Life* (1940)
Williams, Francis,	*A Pattern of Rulers* (1965)
Williamson, Philip, ed,	*The Modernisation of Conservative Politics. The Diaries and Letters of William Bridgeman 1904–35* (1988)
Wilson, Trevor, ed,	*The Political Diaries of C.P. Scott 1911–1928* (New York, 1970)
Winterton, Earl,	*Orders of the Day* (1953)
Wrench, J.E.,	*Geoffrey Dawson and our Times* (1955)
Wrigley, C.,	*Arthur Henderson* (Cardiff, 1990)

4. *OTHER PUBLISHED WORKS*

The following have been cited in the text. Place of publication London unless otherwise stated.

Adams, R.J.Q.,	*Arms and the Wizard: Lloyd George and the Ministry of Munitions 1915–1916* (1978)
Aldcroft, D.H.,	*The British Economy, vol 1. The Years of Turmoil 1920–1951* (Brighton, 1986)
Andrew, Christopher,	*Secret Service: The Making of the British Intelligence Community* (1987)
Barker, A.J.,	*The Neglected War: Mesopotamia 1914–1918* (1967)
Barnett, Correlli,	*The Collapse of British Power* (Gloucester, 1984)
Bartlett, C.J.,	*British Foreign Policy in the Twentieth Century* (1989)
Beloff, Max,	*Imperial Sunset, vol 1, Britain's Liberal Empire, 1897–1921* (1969)
Beloff, Max,	*Dream of Commonwealth 1921–42, vol 2 of Imperial Sunset* (1989)
Birn, Donald S.,	*The League of Nations Union 1918–1945* (Oxford, 1981)
Bourne, J.M.,	*Britain and the Great War, 1914–1918* (1989)
Boyce, D.G.,	*Englishmen and the Irish Troubles 1918–22* (Cambridge Mass., 1972)

Boyd, C.W.,   *Mr Chamberlain's Speeches* (2 vols, 1914)

Burk, Kathleen, ed,   *War and the State: The Transformation of British Government 1914–1919* (1982)

Burk, Kathleen,   *Britain, America and the Sinews of War, 1914–1918* (1985)

Butt, Ronald,   *The Power of Parliament* (1969)

Carlton, David,   *MacDonald versus Henderson: The Foreign Policy of the Second Labour Government* (1970)

Cassels, A.,   *Mussolini's Early Diplomacy* (Princeton, 1970)

Connell, J.,   *The 'Office': A Study in British Foreign Policy and its Makers, 1919–1951* (1958)

Cook, C. & Ramsden, J.,   *By-Elections in British Politics*, (1973)

Cowling, Maurice,   *The Impact of Labour 1920–1924: The Beginning of Modern British Politics* (Cambridge, 1971)

Cowling, Maurice,   *The Impact of Hitler: British Politics and British Policy, 1933–1940* (Cambridge, 1975)

Craig, G.A. & Gilbert, F.,   *The Diplomats 1919–1939 vol 1: the Twenties* (New York, 1968)

Cronin, James, E.,   *The Politics of State Expansion: War, State and Society in Twentieth Century Britain* (1991)

Dangerfield, George,   *The Damnable Question: A Study in Anglo-Irish Relations* (Quartet ed. 1979)

Dewey, C. & Hopkins A.G., eds,   *The Imperial Impact: Studies in the Economic History of India and Africa* (1978)

Divine, David,   *Mutiny at Invergordon* (1970)

Eriera, Alan,   *The Invergordon Mutiny* (1981)

Fair, John, D.,   *British Interparty Conferences: A Study of the Procedure of Conciliation in British Politics, 1867–1921* (Oxford, 1980)

Ferro, Marc,   *The Great War 1914–1918* (1987)

Gibbs, H.N.,   *Grand Strategy. A History of the Second World War, United Kingdom Military Series, vol 1. Rearmament Policy* (HMSO, 1976)

Gilbert, Martin,   *The Roots of Appeasement* (1966)

Grieves, Keith,   *The Politics of Manpower 1914–1918* (Manchester, 1988)

Griffiths, R.,   *Fellow Travellers of the Right: British Enthusiasts for Nazi Germany 1933–1939* (Oxford, 1983)

Hardie, Frank,   *The Abyssinian Crisis* (1974)

Hazelhurst, Cameron,   *Politicians at War: July 1914 to May 1915* (1971)

Howson, Susan,   *Domestic Monetary Management in Britain 1919–1938* (Cambridge, 1975)

Jacobson, Jon,   *Locarno Diplomacy: Germany and the West 1925–29* (Princeton, 1972)

Jordon, W.M.,   *Great Britain, France and the German Problem, 1918–1939* (1943)

Judd, D & Slinn, P.,   *The Evolution of the Modern Commonwealth 1902–1980* (1982)

Kennedy, Paul,   *The Realities Behind Diplomacy: Background Influences on British External Policy 1865–1980* (Fontana ed. 1980)

Kinnear, Michael,   *The British Voter: An Atlas and Survey since 1885* (1968)

Kinnear, Michael,   *The Fall of Lloyd George: The Political Crisis of 1922* (1973)

Lamb, Richard,   *The Drift to War, 1922–1939* (1989)

Lenman, B.P.,   *The Eclipse of Parliament: Appearance and Reality in British Politics since 1914* (1992)

Liddle, P.H., ed,   *Home Fires and Foreign Fields: British Social and Military Experience in the Great War* (1985)

Lloyd, Lord,   *Egypt Since Cromer* (2 vols, 1934)

Louis, W.R.,   *British Strategy in the Far East* (Oxford, 1971)

Lowe, Peter,   *Britain in the Far East: A Survey from 1819 to the Present* (1981)

Macardle, D.,   *The Irish Republic* (1968)

Mallet, Sir B. & George, C.O.,   *British Budgets, Second Series, 1913–14 to 1920–21* (1929)

Mansergh, Nicholas,   *The Commonwealth Experience, vol 1. The Durham Report to the Anglo-Irish Treaty* (1982)

Mansfield, Peter,   *The British in Egypt* (1971)

Marlowe, John,   *Anglo-Egyptian Relations, 1800–1953* (1954)

McKercher, B.J.C.,   *The Second Baldwin Government and the United States, 1924–29: Attitudes and Diplomacy* (Cambridge, 1984)

Medlicott, W.N.,   *British Foreign Policy since Versailles 1919–63* (1968)

Moggridge, Donald,   *British Monetary Policy 1924–1931: The Norman Conquest of $4.86* (Cambridge, 1972)

Morgan, E.V.,   *Studies in British Financial Policy, 1914–25* (1952)

Morgan, K.O.,   *Consensus and Disunity: The Lloyd George Coalition Government, 1918–22* (Oxford, 1979)

Northedge, F.S.,	*The Troubled Giant: Britain and the Great Powers, 1916–1939* (1966)
Northedge, F.S.,	*The League of Nations: Its Life and Times 1920–46* (Leicester, 1988)
Northedge, F.S. & Wells, A.,	*Britain and Soviet Communism: The Impact of a Revolution* (1982)
Peele, G. & Cook, C.,	*The Politics of Reappraisal 1918–1939* (1975)
Pigou, A.C.,	*Aspects of British Economic History 1918–25* (1947)
Pugh, J.D.,	*Electoral Reform in War and Peace 1906–1918* (1978)
Ramsden, John,	*The Age of Balfour and Baldwin 1902–1940* (1978)
Reynolds, P.A.,	*British Foreign Policy in the Inter-War Years* (Westport, 1954)
Richardson, Dick,	*The Evolution of British Disarmament Policy in the 1920s* (1989)
Roskill, Stephen,	*Naval Policy between the Wars* (2 vols, 1968–1976)
Rowland, Peter,	*The Last Liberal Governments: The Promised Land 1905–1910* (1968)
Self, Robert C.,	*Tories and Tariffs: The Conservative Party and the Politics of Tariff Reform 1922–1932* (New York and London, 1986)
Spier, E.,	*Focus: A Footnote on the History of the Thirties* (1936)
Taylor, A.J.P.,	*The Origins of the Second World War* (1961)
Taylor, A.J.P.,	*English History 1914–1945* (Oxford, 1965)
Terry, Janice J.,	*The Wafd, 1919–52* (1982)
Thompson, Neville,	*The Anti-Appeasers: Conservative Opposition to Appeasement in the 1930s* (Oxford, 1971)
Thorne, Christopher,	*The Limits of Foreign Policy: The West, the League and the Far Eastern Crisis of 1931–1933* (1972)
Townshend, C.,	*The British Campaign in Ireland 1919–21* (Oxford, 1975)
Turner, John,	*Lloyd George's Secretariat* (Cambridge, 1980)
Turner, John,	*British Politics and the Great War: Coalition and Conflict 1915–1918* (New Haven and London, 1992)
Vatikiotis, P.J.,	*The History of Modern Egypt: From Muhammed Ali to Mubarak* (1991)
Waites, Neville, ed,	*Troubled Neighbours: Franco-British Relations in the Twentieth Century* (1971)

Waller, P.J., — *Democracy and Sectarianism: A Political and Social History of Liverpool 1868–1939* (Liverpool, 1981)

Watt, Donald Cameron, — *Personalities and Politics: Studies in the Formulation of British Foreign Policy in the Twentieth Century* (1965)

Willert, Sir Arthur, — *Aspects of British Foreign Policy* (1928)

Williamson, Philip, — *National Crisis and National Government: British Politics, the Economy and Empire 1926–32* (Cambridge, 1992)

Wilson, Trevor, — *The Myriad Faces of War: Britain and the Great War, 1914–1918* (Oxford, 1986)

Wrigley, Chris, — *Lloyd George and the Challenge of Labour: The Post-War Coalition 1918–1922* (1990)

5. *ARTICLES*

Carlton, David, — 'Great Britain and the Coolidge Naval Disarmament Conference of 1927', *Political Science Quarterly*, LXXXIII (1968).

Carlton, David, — 'Great Britain and the League Council Crisis of 1926', *Historical Journal*, XI.2. (1968)

Carlton, David, — 'The Anglo-French Compromise on Arms Limitation, 1928', *Journal of British Studies*, VIII. (1968–9)

Chamberlain, Austen, — 'Permanent Bases of British Foreign Policy', *Foreign Affairs*, 9. (July 1931)

Close, D.H., — 'The Collapse of Resistance to Democracy: Conservatives, Adult Suffrage and Second Chamber Reform, 1911–1928', *Historical Journal*, 20.4 (1977)

Craig, Gordon A., — 'The British Foreign Office from Grey to Austen Chamberlain', in G.A. Craig & F. Gilbert, *The Diplomats 1919–39 vol 1: The Twenties* (New York, 1968)

Dewey, C., — 'The End of the Imperialism of Free Trade: The Eclipse of the Lancashire Lobby and the Concession of Fiscal Autonomy to India', C. Dewey & A.G. Hopkins (eds) *The Imperial Impact* (1978)

Edwards, P., — 'The Austen Chamberlain – Mussolini meetings', *Historical Journal*, XIV.1. (1971)

Ghosh, S.C.,   'Pressure and Privilege: the Manchester Chamber of Commerce and the Indian Problem, 1930–1934', *Parliamentary Affairs*, XVIII.2. (Spring 1965)

Goold, Douglas,   'Lord Hardinge and the Mesopotamia Expedition and Inquiry 1914–1917', *Historical Journal*, 19.4 (1976)

Johnson, Douglas,   'The Locarno Treaties', N. Waites (ed) *Troubled Neighbours: Franco-British Relations in the Twentieth Century* (1971)

McCrillis, N.R.,   'Taming Democracy? The Conservative Party and House of Lords Reform, 1916–1929', *Parliamentary History*, 12.3 (1993)

Nelson, K.,   'The "Black Horror on the Rhine": Race as a Factor in Post-World War I Diplomacy', *Journal of Modern History*, 42.4 (December 1970)

Porter, B.,   'Britain and the Middle East in the Great War', P.H. Liddle (ed), *Home Fires and Foreign Fields* (1985)

Peele, Gillian,   'Revolt over India', G. Peele and C. Cook, *The Politics of Reappraisal 1918–1939*, (1975)

Percy, Lord Eustace,   'Austen Chamberlain', *Public Administration*, XV. (April 1937)

Self, Robert C.,   'Conservative Reunion and the General Election of 1923: A Reassessment', *Twentieth Century British History*, 3.3 (1992)

6. *UNPUBLISHED THESES*

Rolf, K.W.D.,   Tories, Tariffs and Elections. The West Midlands in English Politics 1918–1935 (Cambridge University, D.Phil. 1974)

INDEX

Where a note reference is given in brackets, this signifies that there is a short biographical or explanatory note on the person or event concerned.